The Larousse
ENCYCLOPEDIA
of
PRECIOUS GEMS

Pierre Bariand
Curator of Minerals, Faculty of Sciences, Université Pierre et Marie Curie

Jean-Paul Poirot
Service Public du contrôle des diamants, perles et pierres précieuses,
Paris Chamber of Commerce and Industry

In collaboration with Michel Duchamp
for seals, cylinders, intaglios, and cameos

Photographs by Nelly Bariand

Translated by Emmanuel Fritsch, Ph.D.
Research scientist, Gemological Institute of America

VNR Van Nostrand Reinhold
New York

Copyright © 1985 by Librairie Larousse

Originally published in France under the title *Larousse des pierres précieuses: fines, ornementales, organiques*

Published in the English language in 1992 by Van Nostrand Reinhold

Library of Congress Catalog Card Number 91-9256
ISBN 0-442-30289-4

Printed in Hong Kong by Excel Printing Company.

Design:
Maxence Scharf

Drawings:
Mustapha Altintas
Gilbert Macé
Lucien Mathieu

Corrections and Revisions:
Bernard Dauphin
Claire Dumont
Marie-Pierre Gachet
Alexis Witt

Iconography:
Christiane Champougny

Van Nostrand Reinhold
115 Fifth Avenue
New York, New York 10003

Chapman and Hall
2-6 Boundary Row
London, SE1 8HN, England

Thomas Nelson Australia
102 Dodds Street
South Melbourne 3205
Victoria, Australia

Nelson Canada
1120 Birchmount Road
Scarborough, Ontario MIK 5G4, Canada

16   15   14   13   12   11   10   9   8   7   6   5   4   3   2   1

Library of Congress Cataloging-in-Publication Data

Bariand, Pierre.
    [Larousse des pierres précieuses. English]
    The encyclopedia of precious gems / Pierre Bariand, Jean-Paul Poirot, in collaboration with Michel Duchamp for seals, cylinders, intaglios, and cameos; photographs by Nelly Bariand, unless otherwise indicated; translated by Emmanuel Fritsch.
        p.   cm.
    Translation of: Larousse des pierres précieuses.
    Includes bibliographical references.
    ISBN 0-442-30289-4
    1. Precious stones—Dictionaries.   I. Poirot, Jean-Paul.
II. Duchamp, Michel.   III. Title.
TS722.B3713   1992
553.8'03—dc20   91-9256
                                                                           CIP

Contents

Foreword   v

Preface   vi

Acknowledgments   vii

Part 1 Introduction   1

The Symbolism of Gems   1
The Origins of Gems   5
The Physical Properties of
    Gems   13
Synthetics and Simulants   43
Gem Identification   52
Classification   52
Nomenclature   53

Part 2 The Gems   55

Actinolite   55
Agate   55
Alabaster   58
Alexandrite   58
Almandite   59
Alunite   60
Amazonite (Microcline)   60
Amber (Succinite)   60
Amblygonite   67
Amethyst   67
Ametrine   70
Andalusite   70
Andradite   70
Apatite   70
Aquamarine   71
Aventurine   73
Axinite   73
Azurite   74
Benitoite   74
Beryl   75
Beryllonite   76
Bezoar   76
Blende   76

Bonamite   77
Bone   77
Brazilianite   77
Bronzite   77
Cacholong   77
Cairngorm   77
Calcite   77
Cameo   78
Carbuncle   78
Carnelian   78
Cat's-Eye   79
Ceylonite   80
Chalcedony   80
Charoite   80
Chiastolite   81
Chloromelanite   81
Chrysoberyl (Cymophane)   81
Chrysocolla   81
Chrysolite   82
Chrysoprase   82
Citrine   83
Collophane   84
Coral   84
Cordierite (Iolite)   88
Corundum   88
Cupid's Darts   90
Cymophane   90
Danburite   90
Demantoid   91
Diamond   91
Diaspore   113
Diopside   114
Dioptase   114
Dumortierite   115
Elephant Hair   115
Emerald   115
Enstatite   125
Epidote and Clinozoisite   125
Euclase   126
Feldspar   126

Fibrolite   126
Fluorite   126
Gahnite   127
Garnet   127
Goshenite   128
Grossular   128
Halbanite   130
Hawk's-Eye   130
Heliodor   130
Heliotrope   130
Hematite   131
Hessonite   131
Hiddenite   131
Horn   131
Hyacinth   132
Hydrophane   133
Hypersthene   133
Idocrase   133
Intaglio   133
Iolite   133
Ivory   133
Jade   137
Jadeite   142
Jasper   142
Jeremejevite   142
Jet   143
Kornerupine   144
Kunzite   144
Kyanite   145
Labradosite   145
Lapis Lazuli   145
Lazulite   150
Lydian Stone   150
Magnetite   151
Malachite   151
Marble   152
Marcasite   153
Meerschaum   153
Melanite   153
Microcline   153

Moldavite   153
Moonstone   153
Morganite   153
Morion   154
Nacre   154
Nephrite   156
Obsidian   157
Odontolite   158
Olivine   158
Onicolo   158
Onyx   158
Opal   159
Orthoclase   164
Padparadscha   164
Pearl   164
Pectolite   174
Peridot   174
Perovskite   177
Petalite   177
Petrified Wood   177
Phenakite   178
Plasma   178
Pleonaste   178
Prase   178
Prasiolite   178
Prehnite   179
Pyrite   179
Pyrope   179
Quartz   180
Rhodizite   186
Rhodochrosite   186
Rhodolite   187

Rhodonite   187
Rock Crystal   187
Rubace   190
Rubellite   190
Rubicelle   190
Ruby   190
Rutile   195
Sapphire   196
Sapphirine   201
Sard   201
Sardonyx   202
Scapolite   202
Sepiolite (Meerschaum)   202
Serpentine   203
Siberite   204
Sillimanite (Fibrolite)   204
Sinhalite   204
Smithsonite (Bonamite)   204
Sodalite   205
Spectrolite (Labradorite)   205
Spessartite   205
Sphalerite (Blende)   206
Sphene   207
Spinel   207
Spodumene   210
Staurolite   210
Steatite   211
Succinite   211
Sugilite   212
Sunstone   212
Taaffeite   212
Tanzanite   212

Thetis Hair Stone   213
Thulite   213
Tiger's-Eye   213
Titanite (Sphene)   213
Topaz   214
Topazolite   218
Tortoise Shell   218
Tourmaline   219
Tsavorite   224
Tugtupite   224
Turquoise   224
Uvarovite   231
Variscite   231
Venus Hair Stone   231
Verdelite   232
Verdite   232
Vermeil   232
Vesuvianite (Idocrase)   232
Werherite   232
Xanthite   233
Zircon   233
Ziconia   234
Zirkelite   235
Zoisite   235

Appendix 1 Average Physical Constants and Chemical Composition of Gems   236

Appendix 2 Museums   240

Glossary   244

Bibliography   245

Foreword

This book was published first in French in 1985 by Librairie Larousse, a major French publisher. It encompasses a section on the properties of gemstones followed by a relatively brief encyclopedia of gemstones. A somewhat similar book that comes to mind is Joel Arem's *Color Encyclopedia of Gemstones,* but the authors of this volume, Pierre Bariand and Jean-Paul Poirot, approach the subject in a slightly different, more exciting manner. One example is their treatment of toughness. Although it is similar in many respects to the American concept, the authors divide this property into resistance to mechanical, thermal, and chemical shocks. Also, instead of stressing, as most American texts do, that a stone must be rare to be valuable, they point out that while a gem can be too abundant to be valuable, it can also be *too* rare. They cite tanzanite and brazilianite as gems reserved for collectors because of their scarcity. Perhaps they might better have cited benitoite and the medium to slightly dark red beryl, but their point is well taken.

It is interesting to read books translated into English from another language, because they inevitably contain new words and new ideas. These differences are not necessarily better or worse, but the fact that they are different adds a new dimension for the reader. Occasionally the reader may be brought up short by an unexpected word or thought. For example, one hardly expects to encounter the word *pulverulent* in a description of a gem mineral. A word not often seen in an English text, it is used by the authors to describe a powdery American turquoise. It means "crumbly." The authors state that turquoise varies in hardness: Persian material has a hardness of 6.25, whereas some semipowdery turquoises from the United States have a hardness of only 1.5 and therefore cannot be considered gem material.

This book is particularly valuable to people behind the counter in a jewelry store, because it is rich in both lore and etymology. It is interesting reading for the curious customer as well as the jeweler/gemologist. It might extend the interest of the customer from the more familiar species, such as diamond, ruby, emerald, and sapphire, into the realm of lesser-known but equally beautiful gems. In France those gemstones not in the so-called precious family are called "fine stones," in the sense of the medieval meaning of "noble." This is similar to *Edelstein* in German, which also translates as "noble stone."

Pierre Bariand is very well known to fellow mineralogists in this country and elsewhere for his expertise in minerals and his interest in gem minerals. He is the curator of minerals for the Pierre and Marie Curie University in Paris, France. Jean-Paul Poirot is head of the Laboratory for Diamonds, Natural Pearls, and Precious Stones at the Paris Chamber of Commerce. In that capacity for many years, after training under the renowned George Gobel, Poirot has had an exceptional opportunity to study a wide variety of very fine gemstones. Their collaborator in the area of engraved gems was Michel Duchamp; the French text was translated into English by Emmanuel Fritsch, Ph.D., of the Gemological Institute of America's research staff. The two authors each bring exceptionally fine credentials to a work such as this. Their qualifications are disparate but well balanced, in that Poirot is working with gem identification and grading problems every day, whereas Bariand brings his geology and museum background to the task. Adding to the balance of experience and good writing skills is the excellent photography of Madame Bariand and nicely reproduced color plates. *The Larousse Encyclopedia of Precious Gems* makes an excellent addition to any gemologist's library. It is an attractive publication, written at a level that should make it appealing to the layperson as well as the gemologist.

RICHARD T. LIDDICOAT

Preface

Lustrous pearls, brightly colored stones, and glistening gems have always been associated with the concept of treasure. In the past they represented the wealth of a state, which its rulers would display on special occasions. The Egyptian king Ramses impressed Assyrian ambassadors with his lapis lazuli and turquoises; Louis XIV of France dazzled the shah of Persia's representatives with his diamonds. The advent of the Industrial Revolution brought with it an emphasis on technological achievements: just as Renaissance rulers sent their galleons to the New World in search of gold and precious stones, so great modern nations now launch their spacecrafts in quest of precious technology.

Gems—admired, desired, and so often counterfeited, of which people have dreamed for thousands of years—are introduced in this book. Included herein are some collector's stones, whose nature prevents them from ever superseding better-recognized gems. Although it covers a wide range of gems and ornamental materials, this book will enable you to identify gems and cannot be considered a gemology field guide or handbook.

Previously unpublished photographs of precious objects, loaned by private collectors, illustrate the permanent attraction and power of gems. For example, two glyptic masterpieces from the first century are pictured:

- In the opening of part 1, the amethyst seal of the Roman emperor Titus, who, imitating Augustus, marked the prestige of the new Flavian dynasty by creating the seal.
- The Burmese ruby cameo, shown in the discussion of rubies in part 2. Not mentioned by Pliny the Elder in his *Natural History,* it does not feature the emperor Vespasian but his son (and double), the same Titus. This seemingly useless prestigious object made Rome's emperor the gods' equal. Domitian, Titus's brother and successor, would be crowned *Deus et Dominus* (god and master) in A.D. 86.

A remarkable counterfeit from the same period illustrates the forger's astonishing abilities: a glass mold of the famous intaglio engraved by Evodos in aquamarine. Supposed to represent the Virgin Mary, the original was set in Carolingian times in a jewel in such a way that taking a casting was impossible. The mold also displays one of the characteristics of glasses mentioned by Pliny—the presence of bubbles.

This volume will also introduce the reader to the treasure hunters who, in today's El Dorados, dream of and search for the stone that will make them rich.

In addition, the art of faceting is examined, along with photos of jewelry of various periods, ranging from the extraordinary to the more modest. Such gems are a tribute to the skills of the diamond cutter or lapidary who carved, cut, and polished them and to the jeweler who displays them, craftspeople who, by the thousands, work to serve a dream.

Note from the Translator

This translation was undertaken as a tribute to the work of two friends, Pierre Bariand and Jean-Paul Poirot, one a mineralogist and the other a gemologist, whose collaboration has produced a remarkable book. The present work is unique because its goal is to encourage the public's fascination for natural gems by telling a bit of both science and lore; it is not intended to be one more academic gemology handbook. The slight revisions and updates we have brought to the original text respect this spirit.

The English translation was prepared as an international version for gemstone enthusiasts the world around (even in France, since the original French version has long been out of print). To achieve this, some of the chapters and reference sections have been modified. The text refers to international units, although many times English units have also been provided for the convenience of some of our Anglo-Saxon readers. We hope the present translation will pass on some of the fascination the authors and translator of this work feel for precious gems.

Acknowledgments

We greatly appreciate the warm reception we were given by the great Parisian jewelry houses. Managers as well as staff were always helpful and cooperative as we photographed their treasures.

We would first like to thank the members of the Haute Joaillerie de France (Designer Jewelry of France): J. Arpels (of the Van Cleef & Arpels Company), A. Boucheron, J. and P. Chaumet, A. and P. Mauboussin, and H. and F. Mellerio.

We are also very indebted to: S. Fred, L. Gérard. A. Reza, and J. Vendôme, who entrusted us with their creations; the Cartier Company, which made their workshop designs available; the De Beers Company of London, which kindly loaned pieces from their photographic archives to illustrate the discussion of diamonds; and Ms. Alberico of the Japan International Trade Organization, who provided material illustrating the discussion of pearls.

Museums, collectors, antiques and diamond dealers, and gem cutters were indispensable to the realization of this book. We would like to express our gratitude to: P. Amiet, Chief Curator of Oriental Antiques, and M. Bernus-Taylor, Curator of Oriental Antiques (Muslim arts section) at the Musée du Louvre; the curator of minerals at the Paris School of Mines; the administration of the Paris Private Technical School of Jewelry and Goldsmithing; B. Messager of the Société Garland, J. Amster of the Compagnie Générale de Madagascar, J. Sirakian of the Taillerie de Royat, and S. Pinson of the Boutique Argana; H. Benami, J. Cassedanne, Cl. Charensol, M. De Bry, M. Duchamp. J.-F. Sirakian, S. Ratzel-Billard, E. Ruskoné; the curator of the German Gemstone Museum and Mr. G. Becker of Idar-Oberstein, Germany; John White, curator at the Smithsonian Institution in Washington, D.C., Susan Hendrickson of Miami, and A. Caplan of New York.

We also acknowledge all those whose advice and encouragement guided us during their work.

Part One: Introduction

Thirteenth-century reliquary crown of Saint Louis, Louis IX of France, who donated the relics to the Dominicans of Liège. Musée du Louvre. Photo: Lauros.

The Symbolism of Gems

The excavation of all prehistoric tombs has yielded bone and shell parures. The mining of and common uses for ornamental stones have been recorded in some of the earliest writings and drawings. Apparently the attraction of gems and jewelry is as old as humanity itself. But, beyond their beauty, did they have a more profound significance? We can never know for certain, but judging by their use throughout history, gems and jewelry have been employed for a variety of purposes: as talismans, medicines, insignia, and symbols of power, as well as simple adornment establishing the individuality of the wearer.

Basic Symbolism

It was color, of course, that first attracted our ancestors' attention to ornamental stones and gems, and color also imparted symbolic meaning. Because their colors are reminiscent of new plant growth and future crops, emerald and green jasper became symbols of hope and revival and therefore eternity. Rubies and red garnets, which suggest blood and fire, were taken as symbols of strength and life and therefore ardor. Sapphires and lapis lazuli, which recall the blue of the sky from which rain, wind, and thunderstorms originate, represented the divine powers and thereby also become symbols of mediation with the gods. Gold and amber, evoking the sun, source of beneficent warmth, were chosen as symbols of divine protection.

Divine Attributes of Gems

Because of the symbolism connected with them, gems were first considered to be divine fragments, used to pay homage to the gods to appease their anger and gain their favors. For example, the so-called Son of the Sky, the emperor of China, used the *pi* (a symbol of the sky) to intercede in favor

The Seal of the Roman emperor Titus, who reigned from A.D. 79–81. Amethyst intaglio. Height: 1.37 cm. M. De Bry collection.

1

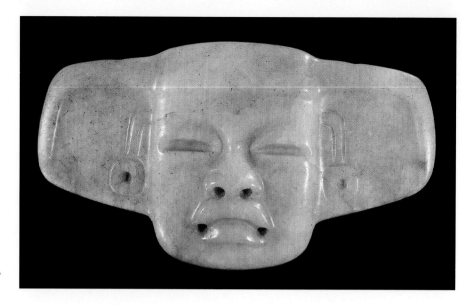

Olmec mask in jade from Mexico Width: 9 cm. Private collection.

Intaglio quartz scarab with the cartouche of the Egyptian king Thutmose III, who reigned from around 1504–1450 B.C. Height: 6.76 cm. Private collection.

of his people (see JADE). The Aegean tyrant Polycrates threw his ring into the sea in an effort to soothe the goddess Fortune. The Chibcha of South America offered gold and emeralds to Lake Titicaca (see EMERALD). Tribal chiefs, priests, and monarchs, who interceded with the gods in the name of their peoples, naturally had to display the emblems of the divine power they represented. Royal and imperial crowns of the Middle Ages were thus ornate with sapphires, symbolizing the union of the monarch and the sky, and rubies, symbolizing the monarch's fierceness in combat.

Gems as Social Insignia

Throughout history, gems have indicated social status, not only of rulers, but also of subordinates and enemies. To display his power and impress his adversaries, a monarch would cover himself with stones and jewelry, as Charles the Bold, duke of Burgundy, did for his entire life (1433–77), and as both Francis I of France and Henry VIII of England did when they met on the Field of Cloth of Gold in 1520 in the hope of political gains.

In a highly hierarchic society, such as the Roman republic, such insignia marked social ranks, such as the knights' signet ring, still called *chevalière* in France, from the French word for knight, *chevalier*. Similarly, during the Renaissance, the jeweled crest worn on the hat indicated to some extent its owner's rank.

Gems as Trademarks and Tokens

In ancient times gems were also carved to become seals, which were used to vali-

date a wish or mark property. The Sumerian trader was buried with his seal, tangible proof of his individuality. The monarch's seal became an emblem of power, and the keeper of the seals was an important state figure. To entrust an ambassador with the signet ring amounted to giving him full power: a seal had the same significance a signature does today. A specially engraved gemstone could also indicate the membership of an individual in a particular group. It could be given as a reward or worn as a sign of submission. On a private level, it could symbolize an exchange of vows, as in an engagement ring.

Gems as Amulets and Talismans

Established as symbols of faithfulness and divine emblems, gems were only a step away from being transformed into talismans, ensuring divine protection for its wearer, in that the stone showed a representation of a god or simply a cabalistic sign. The scarab or dung beetle, one of the personifications of the sun and a symbol of eternity in ancient Egypt, was very popular and often carved from a green stone. In the Middle Ages, many people wore a gem engraved with the famous "abrasax," the exact meaning of which remains obscure. To thank God, especially for recovery from an illness, a small votive gem carving representing the affected part of the body was offered in a temple; soon the gem itself was considered to be the true protecting agent. Gems were supposed to protect their wearers from both physical harm and moral misfortune. These kinds of superstitions were encouraged by numerous charlatans attempting to charm the masses, but they were vigorously discredited by their contemporaries. For example, Pliny the Elder (A.D. 23–79) wrote, ''I will demonstrate the odious lies of sorcerers who spread the most shameless statements about gems,'' though he also described in detail the most fantastic virtues attributed to gems of his time.

Gems as Medicine

Ancient physicians believed that the curative action of a gem was efficient only if the stone was ingested. Various potions were therefore based on powdered gems. Such practices gave rise to true abuses during the Middle Ages, which led to quaint traditions, some of which still survive. (Some of these beliefs are described in part 2.) With regard to the healing properties of gems, consider the words of A. Boèce de Boot (1609): ''[We see] the meanness of men who, often against the poignant remorse of the conscience, guided only by a disgusting greed, attribute divine qualities to precious stones, to sell them at an excessive price!''

The Christian Symbolism of Gems

At the same time that these gem-related superstitions were developing, they were illustrated in Marbodus's volume on lapidary. Marbodus, future bishop of Rennes (he was nominated in 1096) would bitterly regret his literary work of youth, too often cited and interpreted. Concurrently, the ecclesiastic leaders were doing their best to take advantage of these beliefs about stones; they modified them by producing an interpretation of the twelve stones of the ''great priest pectoral'' (Exodus 28:17–20) and of the twelve stones of Jerusalem's guardian in Saint John's Apocalypse (21:19–20). The new symbolism was completed with that of the twelve stones of the Virgin Mary's crown, attributed to Saint Hildefonse; it is well illustrated in the thirteenth-century *Lapidary in Verse*, commissioned by Louis IX of France (Saint Louis; 1214–70).

Modern Superstition Associated with Gems

In the middle of the eighteenth century, the Jewish community in Poland undertook a new interpretation of the Bible, which led it to assign a stone to each of the twelve zodiac signs and consequently to each of the twelve months. The practice quickly spread throughout Europe, and

Ninth-century French ivory depicting a majestic Christ. Photo: Michel Desjardins-Réalités.

Portrait of Elizabeth of Austria by François Clouet. Musée Condé, Chantilly. Photo: Lauros-Giraudon.

Eighteenth-century Turkoman silver, gold, and carnelian bracelet from central Asia. Diameter: 8 cm. Private collection.

many believed that wearing birthstones would bring luck. This belief grew strong enough to attract the attention of various trade associations, which devised their own lists of birthstones, based, however, on different sources—perhaps stemming from commercial motives.

Gems as Currency

Every group that recognizes the importance of a gem, for whatever reason, assigns it value by this mere fact, and thus the gem can be regarded as a kind of investment or currency. This is presently the case with diamonds, but not with jade; although the latter is highly regarded by Oriental society, it is little valued in the West. It is possible that the nacre necklaces of our ancestors might have been used as money, enabling the exchange of goods, much as American Indians used wampum. The gem is then simply a symbol of financial power.

Gems as Beautiful Ornaments

A piece of jewelry represents a bit of all this symbolism. The natural, and therefore unique, gem enhances the personality of the wearer by signifying his or her uniqueness. But by its similarity with gems of a similar nature, it is also proof that one belongs to a given sociocultural group. By its size and rarity, the gem indicates the social rank its owner has achieved. The gem must also be in harmony with a person's physical qualities (a blond does not wear the same gems as a brunette) and character (a quiet person feels uneasy wearing a gem of too "aggressive" a color). A gem should complement the person it adorns, vibrant and "living" in unison with her or him.

The Origins of Gems

Gathering Gems

Gems and minerals have often been discovered quite by chance; since ancient times their unique characteristics have evoked a fascination that soon made them essential to adornment.

The weathering of rocks through the combined action of climate and erosion liberated from their matrixes certain minerals, such as gold and precious stones, which, while moving slowly down slopes toward riverbeds, were quickly noticed because of their color. In an arid climate, the absence of vegetation made it that much easier to spot the colorful outcrops of metal veins; it is not entirely by chance that copper metallurgy and the use of turquoise began in the arid Middle East.

The quest for gems and ornamental materials was first directed toward alluvial deposits, where minerals were densely concentrated. This type of mine was very attractive, since it avoided the need for costly excavation of hard rock; only simple, inexpensive processes that separated materials using gravity were necessary. Underground mining techniques had little relevance to the gathering of precious stones in contrast with their extensive use for extracting metals. Only at the beginning of this century, when the diamond became a strategic material, did sophisticated prospecting techniques and heavily mechanized mining methods come into use—and even then, only for the extraction of industrial diamonds.

Even today, gems are mined in rather primitive ways, adapted to fit the nature of the deposit.

The Etymology of Gem

According to the French scholar Claude de Saumaise (1588–1653), the Greek word *eima*, which poetically described an ornamental garment, was transformed into *gemma* by the Aeolians. Adopted into Latin, *gemma* means adornment in a broader sense: a bud on a plant, a crystal in a metal vein, a precious stone worn by someone. The word *gem*, when translated as an ornamental garment, thus accounts well, for the sensation of nakedness felt by some when they take off their jewelry. And, when translated as a "stone bud," it connotes the belief in the regeneration of mineral deposits. Indeed, miners exploiting metal veins to collect gold, silver, copper, tin, and the like who come across geodes covered with well-formed transparent crys-

Quartz crystals from Corinto, Minas Gerais, Brazil. Height: 15 cm. Sorbonne collection.

Washing diamond-bearing gravel in Minas Gerais, Brazil. Photo: J. Cassedanne.

tals of such minerals as quartz, fluorite, and calcite considered these crystals to be buds that enabled the vein's further growth. Crusts of malachite or sulfates that formed on wood used in the mines also contributed to the myth of ore regeneration and thus crystal regeneration. Ulpian (A.D. 170–228) wrote about quarries in which rocks were renewed by growth, and Pliny the Elder (A.D. 23–79), in his *Natural History*, noted a

5

marvelous phenomenon of the Spanish mines, which, after being abandoned for some time, produced gold again. The classical mining technique involving reworking the tailings after they have been enriched by meteoric action—well described by the fifteenth-century French traveler Jean-Baptiste Tavernier in his accounts of his journeys—also supported these beliefs, which greatly influenced Roman legislation concerning mining. Later these ideas would be further distorted: for example, David Livingstone, the nineteenth-century explorer, reported that African tribes buried their gold to increase its value.

This concept of gem's self-generation is long-lived. In the Middle Ages, writers, following Pliny, distinguished between male and female crystals. Today our vocabulary still retains traces of this notion: mineralogists use the phrase "gem quality" to describe a clean, transparent crystal, but some European jewelers use the term "root" to describe a badly flawed, translucent crystal. A transparent crystal is often attached to its matrix by a less transparent, flawed section, reminiscent of the "bud" of our ancestors, developed from contorted roots.

The Definition of Gem

Strictly speaking, a gem is a transparent crystal whose color and sparkle can be enhanced by the lapidary, so that it can be used as adornment. The most valued gems —diamond, emerald, ruby, sapphire—are sometimes called "precious stones" while others are labeled "semiprecious" or "fine stones" (*fine* here meaning "noble," well rendered in *edelstein*, "noble stone," in German).

Although flawed and milky, a crystal can still be used if its color is attractive, and a jeweler might then speak of a "root" as well as an "ornamental stone." Amethyst roots and emerald roots are emeralds and amethysts turned opaque by their numerous flaws and inclusions, but because of the vividness of their color, they can be used as jewelry, even for objets d'art, and thus become "ornamental stones." Similarly, various rocks and translucent-to-opaque minerals, such as turquoise and jade, have a well-recognized commercial value and are used in jewelry, either alone or associated with transparent gems. These ornamental stones are naturally studied along with other gems. Various animal and plant concretions (pearls, ivory, amber) often used in jewelry are also a part of gemology.

In the broadest sense, the word *gem* describes any crystal, rock, or animal or plant secretion whose beauty enables it to contribute to the glamour and radiance of a piece of jewelry.

War Plunders and Treasures

The desire to accumulate riches has dominated the history of mankind, and war and looting have often resulted in the considerable accumulations of precious stones.

Gold, silver, and gems were part of war plunder. Under the Roman republic, the vic-

Aquamarine from Salinas, Minas Gerais, Brazil. Length: 9 cm. K. Proctor collection, United States.

Heliodor from Murzinka, U.S.S.R. Length: 5 cm. British Museum of Natural History.

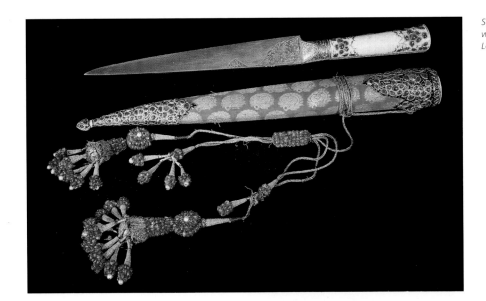

Seventeenth-century gold-inlaid steel dagger from Iran with an ivory haft, encrusted with gold and rubies. Length: 45 cm. Musée du Louvre.

torious general would offer part of his booty to the gods and dazzle the Roman citizens by displaying it during his "triumph," a ceremony honoring him. In 62 B.C. the third triumph of Pompey the Great, celebrating his victory over Mithradates VI, king of Pontus, was of incredible splendor and created in the Romans a taste for pearls and gemstones. A century later Pliny the Elder described it: "Nine shelves covered with vases made of gold and gems, thirty-three pearl tiaras, a quadrangular mass of gold with stags, lions, fruits of all sort wrapped in a vine, all in gold, a pearl mosaic with a sundial at its top, the portrait of Pompey himself in pearls, true excesses rather than triumph." Pompey also gave to the capitol Mithradates' famous collection of carvings, which included two thousand onyx bowls and various carved agates.

During the Fourth Crusade, the capture of Constantinople was completed on April 12, 1204, with its sacking; treasures gathered since the time of ancient Byzantium became a huge source of a plunder for Europe, making the churches of western Christendom much richer. In his *Conquête de Constantinople* ("Conquest of Constantinople"), one of the earliest extant historical works in French, Geoffroi de Villehardouin (1150–1213) wrote, "There was so much of it that it was without end or measure."

When Hernán Cortés and his allies overtook and sacked Tenochtitlán (today's Mexico City) in August 1521, it was a dreadful massacre. Immense treasures in gold, silver, and precious stones were sent to Spain, which apparently became the richest of the Old World's countries. In fact, these riches

Chest filled with natural pearls, part of the Iran treasury. Photo: Arnaud de Rosnay.

created significant monetary inflation and were eventually responsible for Spain's decline.

What remains today of all these plundered treasures, except for a few rare objects that are the pride of museums? The treasure of the national bank of Iran, which came mostly from the sacking of Delhi by Nāder Shāh in 1739 during his conquest of the Moghul empire, backed the Iranian currency under the imperial government of the shah. Among its most important pieces are the peacock Throne of Nāder Shāh (one of the seven Moghul thrones), covered with some large emeralds (225, 170, 130, and 125 carats) and numerous smaller ones, as well as spinels, rubies, diamonds, and a 75-pound golden globe graced by 52,000 gems, with emeralds covering the oceans, spinels, rubies, and sapphires the continents, and diamonds the Persian empire as well as the parallels and meridians. Innumerable pearls and unmounted stones, ornate weapons, crowns, gold plates and dishes set with gems complete this fabulous treasure. Two stones stand out as the elite of the collection. The first is the Darya-i-Nur ("sea of light"), a rectangular 185-carat diamond from Golconda, India, which probably came from the stone that Jean-Baptiste Tavernier described as the *Grande Table* ("great table"), and the second is the Nur-ul-Ain ("light of the eyes"), of 60 carats, the largest known pink diamond. The Koh-i-Noor ("mountain of light"), of 108.93 carats, which today belongs to the British crown, and the Shah, of 88.7 carats, which is in the Soviet treasury, were formerly part of this group. Many other, less celebrated stones have suffered from Persia's historical dramas since Nāder Shāh—what will become of these riches?

Dreams of Wealth: The Garimpeiro *of Brazil*

Today the extraction of gems is still often carried on as it was centuries ago, without any major changes in the methods used. Such methods are responsible for almost all Brazilian gem production since the Portuguese conquest.

When the Brazilian diamond deposits were discovered, the Portuguese authorities tried to prevent claims by individual operators. To escape the surveillance patrols, unauthorized prospectors would flee up the mountains; this is the probable origin of their name, *garimpeiros* (*grimpar* means "to climb").

Today the underground rights and mineral deposits belong to the state. Brazilian law allows any *garimpeiro* to start a *garimpo* ("digging place") outside preexisting mining claims, but he must pay the landowner a commission of 10 to 15 percent of the discovered gems' value.

Often from very modest backgrounds, *garimpeiros* live alone or in small groups, with their families. Poorly equipped, without even basic knowledge of geology, they travel the land in search of an imagined treasure. Sometimes big diamond or gold rushes, like those at the turn of the century, cause huge migrations. This recently occurred with the discovery of emeralds in the state of Goiás and gold in the Sierra Pelada.

A *garimpeiro* mines a small parcel of land, never undertaking large-scale operations. At most, he will dig a few shafts or, rarely, tunnels to reach the beryl or tourmaline crystals found in a pegmatite. Because this rock is often weathered, his work is easier and his quest for gems possible. His accommodations are extremely simple, sometimes only a tent or a shack made of branches. He may live in isolated, very difficult conditions but may also be found near large towns or in the vicinity of modern lines of communication. These unique conditions of gem prospecting in Brazil illustrate the willingness of men to endure extreme hardships in their search for a treasure.

The Heart of the Rocks: The Geology of Gems

Only a small number of rock types are most favorable to the formation and concentration of gems.

Deep-seated magmas, which are mixtures of liquids, crystals, and gases in various proportions, are the source of granites and the so-called volcanic rocks. As crystallization of large granitic masses nears completion, rocks called pegmatites begin to form deep below the earth's surface. The most common elements (such as silicon, potassium, aluminum, and calcium) crystallize first, to form the granite. The residual magma, rich in water and less common elements, crystallizes at around 500°C (930°F). The abundance of water in a supercritical vapor state and the presence of mineralizing elements (such as fluorine and boron) favor the formation of large crystals, of such minerals containing common elements, as quartz, feldspar, mica, as well as of those rich in rare elements, such as tourmaline, beryl, topaz, and spodumene.

Voids are not always completely filled during solidification; some pegmatites contain numerous geodes, in which crystals reach exceptional size. These are found in Brazil, Madagascar, California, Afghanistan, and Kashmir, for example.

Among the very deep magmatic rocks forming the upper mantle of the lithosphere are found kimberlites, which are peridotites characterized by their high potassium content, illustrated by the presence of phlogopite mica, in which pyrope garnet, diopside, and olivine are sometimes ac-

Garimpeiros of the Serra Pelada, Brazil. Photo: J. Cassedanne.

companied by diamond. Like all fluids, kimberlitic magmas can carry foreign bodies, such as eclogites or diamond crystals. These rocks form pipes, which in an explosive progression toward the surface perforate the African, Brazilian, Siberian, and Australian shields, from which they gather rock fragments along the way; their structure is therefore that of a breccia. Weathering by surface water turns the olivine they contain into serpentine, which forms the famous "blue ground" avidly sought by diamond prospectors.

Metamorphic rocks (from the Greek *metamorphosis,* "transformation," from *meta,* "after," and *morphe,* "shape") are the result of the transformation of preexisting solid rocks under various temperature and pressure conditions. Their texture and composition depends on their initial chemical composition. When subjected to conditions different from those of their original formation, certain minerals in these rocks can form, while others disappear. Various classifications attempt to account for the complexity of these phenomena, based on the rock's spatial relationship or chemical composition: contact metamorphism occurs around magmatic intrusions; regional metamorphism produces folded metamorphic

Topaz from the Ouro Prêto area of Minas Gerais, Brazil.

Fire opal from Mexico. 3 by 3 cm. Sorbonne collection.

Lazurite from Sar-e-Sang, Badakhscān, Afghanistan. 5 by 5 cm. Sorbonne collection.

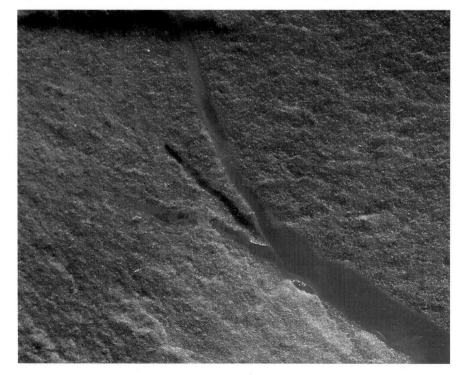

Opal from Australia. Length: 4 cm. Private collection.

rocks with no direct relationship to intrusions; impact metamorphism results from the impact of large meteorites; chemical groups such as silicate and alumino-silicate, calcic, and basic or ferromagnesian constitute other categories. Certain minerals appear to be valuable references in characterizing some convenient systems, apparently helping to explain these phenomena. Metamorphic rocks produce various gems, including ruby, sapphire, spinel, garnet, jade, and lapis lazuli, which are rarely mined in place.

Sedimentary rocks result from the precipitation of preexisting dissolved elements or from the sedimentation of rock fragments and isolated mineral grains. Gems rarely occur in them, except for those produced by oxydoreduction reactions or leaching. Such is the case, for example, with the malachite of the African Copper Belt, the producer of almost all the malachite used in the world. Also sedimentary in origin are the jaspers formed by finely grained quartz of various origins in siliceous sedimentary rocks, and the Australian opals, which slowly accumulate in cracks and veinlets of sandstones and conglomerates, fed by silica-rich solutions created by the breakdown of silicate minerals.

Some gems are found as by-products in the matrices of metal deposits. Such was the case of the amethyst from the Erzgebirge, mountains between Germany and Czechoslovakia, used before the discovery of the Rio Grande do Sul amethysts in Brazil (related to volcanic flows). This was also true for quartz worked since time immemorial in the Alps, of fluorite in Great Britain, and more recently, of rhodocrosite in Argentina.

Weathering phenomena, resulting from climate, affect all geological formations, which are attacked by erosion. Pegmatites are easily decomposed, especially in tropical climates, and some of their constituents are changed into clays, leaving the more resistant minerals, such as quartz, tourmaline, beryl, and topaz, loose in the soil. This makes gathering them easy, as in Brazil. The harder and tougher minerals, such as corundum and spinel, break off from metamorphic rocks and are found in alluvium, which is actually the only rock worked in Myanmar and Sri Lanka, two famous gem-producing countries. The same holds true for kimberlites, of which only a small number are mined in place. Some of the largest diamond deposits, for example, those of Namibia, are alluvial deposits.

From Deposit to Treasure: The Dealer's Adventure

As in all trades, experts are always on the lookout for remarkable discoveries and clues in large parcels of recently mined stones that will reveal the exceptional piece that will enrich a royal treasure or, better, will become the pride of a museum.

Jean-Baptiste Tavernier (1605—89) was one such expert. Son of an Antwerp map dealer who found refuge in France, his father's profession inspired his passion for travel. At the age of twenty-two, he already had explored most of Europe; in 1632 he set off for the Orient, joined a caravan, reached the Persian capitol of Ispahan, and started to buy fabrics and precious stones for resale in France. He married a jeweler's daughter and learned then how to appraise gems. He undertook numerous trips to Persia, India, Sumatra, and elsewhere and gathered an immense fortune. In 1668 he sold to Louis XIV several jewels for 900,000 pounds, among which was the famous French blue diamond. The king raised him to the peerage for his services, in particular to thank him for the information he had brought back from various parts of the world little known at that time. A number of circumstances forced him to leave France half-ruined. The elector of Brandenburg named him director of a commercial company in India; he accepted and returned to Asia. But he caught influenza while traveling down the Volga and died in 1689, at the age of eighty-four. His accounts of Persia under Shah Abbas I are still considered the best reference. Long considered simply a merchant, he left exceptional documents about regions of the globe then almost unknown to Europeans. He was one of the world's greatest gem experts.

Closer to our time, Harry Winston (1896—1978) was nicknamed the Tavernier of the twentieth century, although he contributed much less than Tavernier did to the knowledge of the world. Born in New York, he studied jewelry as a teenager in Los Angeles, where his father owned a jewelry shop. He founded a small company in New York, establishing excellent relations with bankers and managing to be adopted by the very exclusive New York society. He was the most important diamond dealer of his time and spent his life traveling the world, seeking to discover famous gems or rough diamonds.

He became a specialist in large stones and had some of the largest diamonds faceted, including the Jonker (125.65 carats), cut along with twelve other stones from a 726-carat rough, and the 75.52-carat Star of Independence (faceted from a 204.10-carat rough), named in 1975 in honor of the U.S. bicentennial and sold the day after it was cut for $4 million. In 1938 a 726.60-carat rough diamond was discovered in the state of Minas Gerais, Brazil, which he bought in 1939 after many vicissitudes for $600,000; from it twenty-nine stones were cut, including one of 48.26 carats. In 1953 he bought a 154.50-carat rough from South Africa, from which he obtained

Jean-Baptiste Tavernier (1605—89).

a 62.05-carat stone, the Winston, sold in 1981 in Geneva for $7.3 million. In 1972 he had one of the largest known rough diamonds cut, a 969.80-carat piece, found in the Dimico mine in Sierra Leone (the Star of Sierra Leone, which was part of this crystal, is only a 32.52-carat emerald cut). In 1974 he negotiated with Henry Oppenheimer, president of De Beers, for the sale of a $24 million parcel of rough diamonds, then the largest sale of rough in the history of the gem diamond trade. The negotiations were concluded in less than a minute. Harry Winston asked for something to sweeten the deal, a common practice; Henry Oppenheimer pulled from his pocket a 180.80-carat rough and rolled it across the table. Winston grabbed it, smiled and simply said "Thank you." Five diamonds were cut from this stone: the largest, weighing 45.31 carats, was named for the circumstances of its acquisition, the Deal Sweetener. Winston also bought historical diamonds, such as the

The Hope diamond. Smithsonian Institution, Washington, D.C. Photo: Dane Penland.

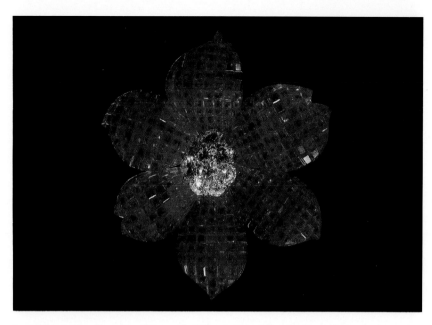

An invisible setting. The rubies slide on rails hidden in their girdles; the precise fitting requires a close collaboration between the cutter and the setter. Van Cleef and Arpels creation.

production, are heat-treated before faceting to improve their color. Sri Lankan sapphires are marketed less and less in the seaport of Colombo; they now usually go through Bangkok, where the lighter-color sapphires are heat-treated after faceting.

Numerous Brazilian and Colombian emeralds, as well as most Zambian emeralds, are sent to India (and now also Israel), where they are faceted or engraved; Jaipur and Bombay are two very active centers. Nevertheless, both Indian and Colombian dealers are tending more and more to travel directly to their customers in New York, Antwerp, London, and Paris to offer their goods. The small Sandawana production, from the Fort Victoria area in Zimbabwe, is sold through a system of "sights" similar to that used for diamonds.

Hong Kong, an important gem trade center, is seeing its influence decrease as it prepares to lose its status as a British colony and become part of China. It is possible that activity there will relocate to Singapore.

The largest trade center for gems other than diamonds, corundums, and emeralds is the entire state of Minas Gerais in Brazil, with activity somewhat stronger in its capital, Belo Horizonte. Rio de Janeiro in Brazil and Taipei, Taiwan, are also worldwide distribution centers.

The supply of jewelry is centered where its creators and its consumers are found. Because of the size of the American market, New York is very important but the activity is wide spread all over the United States, especially in Los Angeles, San Francisco, Houston, and Memphis.

In Europe Paris's position has been saved by the creativity of the *Haute Joaillerie de France*, designer jewelers who attract numerous foreigners; their specialty is the fitting of very small stones and fancy shapes (such as hearts) as well as engraved stones. The activity in London is now shifting to New York and Geneva because the large Christie's and Sotheby auctions take place there, The Po valley in Italy (Milan, Vicenza) maintains its traditional activity thanks to the production of 14-karat gold jewelry, set with colored stones generally imported from Idar-Oberstein, Germany.

Briolette des Indes (90.34 carats) and the famous Hope blue diamond, which he acquired in 1947 and donated to the Smithsonian Institution in Washington in 1958.

Distribution: From the Mine to the Public

The distribution of rough diamonds is centralized in London. The importance of Antwerp and Tel Aviv as cutting centers is diminishing in favor of the Bombay (Surat) area in India and New York.

Today's small ruby production is limited in effect to Thailand. The gems are faceted and sold in Bangkok. The rubies mined in Africa are sent directly to Thailand, Idar-Oberstein (Germany), or Paris. Bangkok is also the major distribution center for sapphires: it receives hundreds of pounds of sapphires extracted each year in Australia, which, like the local Thai and Cambodian

The Physical Properties of Gems

Wearability

To be used as jewelry or ornamentation, a mineral or rock must be resistant to corrosion, whether by liquids or solids. For example, despite its transparency and the vivid red and blue colors it sometimes exhibits, halite, the common salt, is certainly not a gem in the gemological sense of the term because it is soluble in water. A gem or ornamental material is a "noble" stone in the medieval sense of the word: it resists all common agents of wear, including fatty acids, domestic acids and alkalis, minor shocks, and scratches.

Hardness

Resistance to Scratching

The macroscopic hardness of a gem is measured by its ability to resist scratching. To compare the hardness of two gems, one simply rubs them against each other. If they scratch each other, they are of same hardness; otherwise, only the softer material is scratched. It is therefore possible to classify gems on a scale of hardness. Ten minerals were selected as references for comparison in the eighteenth century by the German mineralogist Friedrich Mohs and have since then been internationally adopted. These ten minerals, numbered from 1 (softest) to 10 (hardest), represent the qualitative scale of hardness, or Mohs scale: diamond (10), scràtched only by itself; corundum (9); topaz (8); quartz (7); orthoclase (6); apatite (5); fluorite (4); calcite (3); gypsum (2); and talc (1), which is scratched by all other minerals but scratches none of them.

The macrohardness of a mineral depends, of course, on its orientation during testing. A classic example is kyanite, whose hardness varies from 5 to 7 depending on whether the direction of testing is parallel or perpendicular to the crystal's length. The macrohardness of a rock can also vary widely. For example, Persian turquoise has a hardness of 6¼, whereas some quasipowdery turquoise from the United States possesses a hardness of only 1½ and therefore cannot be considered gem material.

The Mohs qualitative macrohardness, conventionally abbreviated H (for hardness), makes it possible to evaluate a solid's cohesion (bond strength in a monocrystalline mineral, cohesion of the components of an ornamental rock). Colored stones commonly used in jewelry, such as beryl, tourmaline, and zircon, have a hardness of 7½ (that is, they are scratched by topaz but scratch quartz), whereas ornamental stones, such as jade and jasper, most often have a hardness of 6½ (that is they are scratched by quartz but not by orthoclase).

Various quantitative measures of hardness have been attempted, especially through indentation techniques (microhardness). The results have been largely dependent on experimental conditions, so that lists of minerals sorted by increasing hardness may be slightly different, depending, for example, on the load applied. These quantitative measures are presently useful only in mineralogical research, but they clearly indicate that the steps of the qualitative Mohs scale are quantitatively very irregular—there is a much greater difference in hardness between topaz and corundum than between fluorite and apatite, for instance.

Resistance to Abrasion

In contrast with static hardness evaluations, dynamic hardness estimates are of particular interest to the gem cutter, for whom the stone's resistance to the lap's abrasion is an essential parameter. Quantitatively, the higher a gem's hardness, the slower it will abrade. Experiments conducted using the methods of the physicist Rosival have indicated that the sequence of minerals is almost identical to that obtained by the Mohs method. Using corundum's hardness, 1,000, as a reference, topaz is 175 and quartz 120, which is equivalent to say that topaz is 5.7 times less hard than corundum and 1.5 times harder than quartz. In this system diamond is estimated to be 100 to 150 times harder than corundum.

An experienced cutter will have to only "touch" his lap with a stone, making a mark barely visible with a loupe, to estimate the wear resistance and cohesion of a mineral or a rock (this "touch" will also help him determine whether the sample tested will "grease" the lap or not).

Modification of Cohesion

Pulverulent rocks, such as certain turquoises, cannot be used as is in jewelry. But certain techniques have been developed to reinforce gem materials through impregnation, in a way similar to the natural silicification that gives cohesion to amphibole fibers (hawk's-eye, tiger's-eye; see QUARTZ). The most commonly used technique is impregnation with a thermoplastic, used for American turquoises and opals, among others. Impregnation with silica gel is still experimental.

Kyanite from Minas Gerais, Brazil. Length: 3 cm. Sorbonne collection.

*Tanzanite from Arusha, Tanzania. Length: 3 cm.
G. Becker collection, Idar-Oberstein, Germany.*

*Amethyst from Las Vigas, Veracruz, Mexico. Length:
2 cm. S. Morehead collection, United States.*

Toughness

Resistance to Mechanical Shock

One could not possibly test gems using the methods developed to determine the resistance to shock of industrial materials. The results obtained in industrial laboratories can, nevertheless, be applied to gems; resistance to shock is, as a general rule, the inverse of hardness; and a shock too small to produce a rupture will induce it if repeated. Therefore, a rock crystal knocked against a diamond will often suffer less damage than the diamond will, and the facet junctions of a gem worn carelessly will become abraded. Heat treatments used to enhance the color of gems makes them more brittle by adulterating their internal structure; therefore, all heat-treated gems are also easily abraded—zircons, blue zoisite, and dark blue sapphires, for example. However, natural crystals differ from classic industrial materials in the possible presence of cleavage planes or parting planes (*spar* was the old term used by mineralogists: fluorspar, heavy spar, selenitic spar, satin spar, adamantine spar). A crystal having a perfect cleavage plane breaks easily along this plane under the shock of a blade or shear stress: topaz is particularly breakable in this regard. Diamond's perfect cleavage, used to preform the stone before faceting, can also be revealed with an unfortunate blow.

In addition, crystals often contain solid inclusions and fingerprints, which weaken their structure. The "gardens" of emeralds (see EMERALDS) make them more fragile than aquamarines, which are marketed only if they are almost completely clean.

Finally, just as a thin slab is easier to break than a thick block, a faceted stone will break more easily where it is the thinnest ("knife-edge" girdles, points of marquise and pear shapes).

Resistance to Thermal Shock

Only diamond will survive drastic temperature variations of one hundred degrees Celsius. Most gems are never subjected to such thermal shock, but such a mishap can occur, most often by accident, during the repair of a ring, if the torch's flame is applied for too long to a stone. Brutally returned to room temperature, such gems—which are generally poor conductors of heat—cannot withstand the internal stresses produced by these temperature variations and crack. This process may be intentionally induced to transform rock crystal into iris quartz. Good thermal conductors, such as diamond and corundum, are less subject to such accidents.

Color-producing centers are generally not stable over extended temperature ranges. Thus, certain gems may have their color modified irreversibly (amethyst becoming citrine) or almost irreversibly (such as rubies) when exposed to sufficient heat.

The pressure of carbon dioxide, which fills the negative crystals in numerous gems, rapidly and significantly increases when temperature rises; the crystal may not be able to withstand this internal stress and will crack. This may occur when cleaning a piece of jewelry in a "steamer" or in water boiling over a flame (if in contact with the bottom of the container, the gem may be at a much higher temperature than 100°C). This common accident is particularly frequent with Sri Lankan sapphires.

Resistance to Chemical Shock

By definition, a gem must resist most common household chemicals. This is not always the case: some organic gems such as pearls, phosphates such as turquoise, and still carbonates such as rhodocrosite and malachite are attacked by weak acids such as fatty acids (found in beauty creams, perfumes).

As a rule, when one of these gems is attacked by chemicals, it loses its brilliance and its "life" forever; so it is said that the stone is "dead." Strong acids can cause corrosion of such gems as peridot and lapis lazuli.

Diamond burns in air about 500°C (930°F); therefore it is superficially consumed if it falls into a wood fire. If a jeweler has to hold the flame close to a diamond during a jewelry repair, he will cover the stone with borax to isolate it from the atmosphere. It is not necessary to provide similar protection to oxides such as corundum; indeed, they may actually be attacked by the molten borax.

The Relative Abundance of Suitable Gem Materials

A gem must be more than "noble" to be used in jewelry. This artistic craft has to satisfy the demand for any particular piece. Therefore a gem will be commonly used only if it is abundant enough.

Overabundance of a gem, as is the case for rock crystal and almandite garnet, for example, may cause it to be little valued (during the conquest of the Americas, emerald was, for a short period, almost common). A rare gem, such as tanzanite or brazilianite, can only be a collector's stone, because it cannot be regularly provided to jewelry manufacturers. Some stones that once were rare and therefore costly, such as amethyst, became common after the discovery of important deposits (Brazil and Uruguay for the amethyst). The gems that are very often used, whose names are familiar to the public at large, are not rare (the annual production of faceted gem-quality diamonds is around 2 tons and sapphires are produced in Australia by the hundreds of pounds), but they are not that easy to come by either.

Color

To say that a ruby is red is to define the perception experienced when examining the stone in daylight, and what daylight means sometimes must be further defined. For example, alexandrite may be as green as an emerald in daylight at noon and as red as a ruby in candlelight. But what impression will a color-blind person have of the stone? There is no such thing as the "intrinsic" color of a stone. A gem modifies the light that strikes it, and the observer interprets as color the difference between the light modified by the gem and the surrounding light. Consequently, in red light (darkroom light or sodium lamps on a street), a ruby looks colorless and a sapphire, black.

Light

Visible light accounts only for a very small portion of the electromagnetic spectrum, the components of which are commonly defined by their wavelength in a vacuum (or their frequency). A beam of visible light consisting of only one wavelength is said to be monochromatic and is conventionally named, according to its wavelength, red, orange, yellow, green, blue, indigo or violet. Invisible ultraviolet rays, with wavelengths closest to those of the violet rays, are often called "black light" because they trigger an emission of visible light (luminescence) when shone on certain materials (nails, starched fabrics, insects, roots, some gems) in the dark.

The eye perceives as "white," that is colorless, a variety of polychromatic lights in the environment: typical white lights display a continuous spectrum that contains all the visible monochromatic rays. The intensities of the individual rays equal (as in direct sunlight at noon, the true white light), decrease from blue to red (as in light scattered by a clear north sky at noon, conventionally called "daylight"), or increase from blue to red (light at dusk, candlelight, the light of an incandescent bulb, conventionally called "evening light"). It is possible to produce a reference daylight by properly filtering the light of an incandescent bulb, but not with fluorescent bulbs, which have a discontinuous spectrum.

The Gem

A beam of white light striking a gem undergoes various modifications. The gem

Ruby and diamond necklace (detail). J. Vendôme creation, Paris.

Alexandrite from Zimbabwe under incandescent light. 2 by 2 cm. Private collection.

may cause equal or unequal absorption, dispersion, or scattering of the beam's monochromatic components.

Absorption

Physical Observations The absorption of a particular light ray by a gem is the weakening of its intensity along its path in the gem. The modification of the light caused by absorption in the gem increases with size. Therefore, a relatively large crystal with an attractive color may produce several smaller gems of a very pale color.

Equal absorption of all the monochromatic rays in a beam of light does not modify the composition of the light; this is the case for colorless gems and, more rarely, gray ones. But unequal absorption of the rays, called "selective absorption," does modify the composition of the light striking the gem. Such is the case for all colored stones; their color is that of the light that is not absorbed. This is why the appearance of colored stones may vary according to the composition of the incident light. A ruby absorbs almost all blue wavelengths and transmits most red wavelengths; thus the visible light emanating from a ruby is always very rich in red. The result is the blood-red color of some rubies, which shine much more in evening light, itself richer in red. An emerald absorbs most red wavelengths and transmits most blue and green-yellow wavelengths; therefore, the light from the stone is always rich in green, explaining the grass-green appearance of this

gem, especially noticeable in daylight. Alexandrite absorbs similar amounts of blue-green and red; therefore the light coming out is essentially green in daylight, which is rich in blue wavelengths, and mostly red in evening light, which is rich in red wavelengths.

Using Dyes to Intensify Absorption The color of a pale stone can be strengthened by artificially superimposing a substance that enables an additional absorption. For porous materials (such as jades, lapis lazuli, chalcedonies, and pearls) and gems with fractures that reach the surface (flawed rubies and emeralds), it is easy to make an appropriate dye penetrate deeply, following a technique used since antiquity. For uncracked monocrystalline gems, one simply paints the bottom of the pavilion with a colored varnish; this "painting" technique was especially used in the nineteenth century for pale emeralds to be bezel-set or set in a closed mounting. Painting the pavilion of a slightly yellowish diamond with a thin bluish film or putting some blue on the bruted girdle with a pencil is a similar classical artifice, used to make the stone appear momentarily colorless. Some gem materials are totally covered with colored paint. For example, carved marble may be painted with a blue paint containing golden flakes to make it look like lapis lazuli, and sometimes a blue layer one-tenth of a millimeter thick is created by diffusion in some colorless corundums.

Color-causing Centers All gems are composed of atoms of chemical elements, which are bonded together either by electric fields (ionic bond) or by exchanges of electrons (covalent bond). Each atom contains a nucleus surrounded by electrons, which are usually arranged in pairs. Those that are not part of a pair, called "unpaired electrons," may have an influence on light by capturing photons of a wavelength compatible with their energy (absorption) or by transforming ultraviolet light into visible light (luminescence). An unpaired electron may be attached to a transition element (as chromium and vanadium), a structural defect (as in fluorite), to a group of neighboring atoms in the gem (iron and titanium, or two adjacent sulfurs), or even to a large group of atoms (native metals, diamond). The absorption produced by an unpaired electron in the gem is the color-causing center.

A gem that contains color-causing centers in its own ideal crystallochemical structure is called *idiochromatic* and displays only one range of color: for example, peridot is always green and lazurite always blue. A gem that contains no color-causing center in its ideal crystallochemical structure is called *allochromatic*. Normally colorless, it owes its color to growth "accidents,"

Frogs carved in Australian chrysoprase. Commercial chrysoprase is usually dyed agate. Length: 4 cm. G. Becker design, Idar-Oberstein, Germany.

A tourmaline slab from Madagascar. 20 by 20 cm. G. Becker collection, Idar-Oberstein, Germany.

especially the partial substitution (up to 1 percent, sometimes much less) of non-color-causing elements, for example aluminum, with color-producing ones, such as chromium or iron (isomorphic substitution). It can then exhibit many colors. Therefore beryl can be red, yellow (heliodor), green (emerald), blue (aquamarine), or pink (morganite). Of course, the nature of growth accidents may vary during the gem's crystallization, so that numerous colors can appear, one after another. Such a gem is multicolored (for example, watermelon tourmaline). If the crystal field is not uniform over the gem (as in anisotropic crystals), the color-causing centers modify light differently in different directions. Rotated, the gem seems to change color; it is then called *polychroic,* or *pleochroic.* For example, cordierite appears yellow, blue, or violet according to the direction of observation. Pleochroism is more commonly called *dichroism* or *trichroism,* depending on the number of principal colors: three for biaxial gems such as kunzite (pale pink, violet, yellow), two for uniaxial gems such as ruby (purplish red, orangish red) or emerald (bluish green, yellowish green).

Modifications through Color-causing Centers A gem's color can be modified by producing color-causing centers, that is unpaired electrons. These centers can be created by an internal reorganization of impurities, which are forced to disperse in the crystal structure with thermal agitation. Such is the goal of heat treatment, practiced since prehistoric times for purification (a word from the Greek, *pur,* meaning "fire"). Heating helps to turn a green sapphire with rutile inclusions dark blue or a grayish-brown zircon light blue.

By exposing a gem to ionizing radiation (X rays, gamma rays), it is sometimes possible to force it to "trap" unpaired electrons in various defect structures. This technique turns colorless sapphires yellow and colorless topaz blue.

Finally, by damaging the gem's crystalline structure with appropriate particles (fast neutrons, for example), it is possible to produce unpaired electrons. Unattractive yellowish diamonds become bluish green after exposure in an atomic pile and then a bright daffodil yellow after stabilization by heat treatment of the irradiation damage caused by the neutron beam.

Dispersion and Fire

The speed of each monochromatic ray is a function of its energy (that is, its wavelength). Therefore, a ray of white light that penetrates a gem is broken up, or *dispersed,* into a fan of its spectral components, a rainbow with red and violet at the extreme borders. The greater the variations in the speeds of the extreme rays, the more "open" the fan and more discrete the colors composing the white light appear. In a faceted gem, light beams, which strike the facets at different angles, bounce back to the observer from all directions, dispersed into their monochromatic components. The eye reconstitutes the beam, but the bouncing light evokes the sparkle of a wood fire (if the optical path is long enough and the dispersion "fan" wide enough). This phenomenon is called *fire.* A crystal's potential fire can be estimated using the difference

Epidote from Pakistan. The particular angle at which this picture was taken makes it possible to see the strong green–reddish-brown dichroism. Length: 12 cm. Sorbonne collection.

Quartz from La Gardette, Isère, France, showing the dispersion of light. Length: 10 cm. Sorbonne collection.

between the speed of red light (at 686.7 nanometers) and blue light (at 430.8 nanometers) as references or, the difference in their indices of refraction.

A gem that exhibits only weak dispersion cannot display any fire after faceting; rock crystal is an example. A colorless material with too strong a dispersion, such as Fabulite, a diamond simulant, disperses colors in an unpleasant way.

A colored gem can display fire only if its color results from the combination of enough monochromatic rays. Thus blende shows fire, not benitoite.

Scattering

A particle located in the path of a light beam may scatter part of the incident light in many different directions, producing a variety of phenomena.

Sky Blue and the Myth of Blue-White
Particles of small dimension compared to the wavelengths of visible light scatter violet light ten times more efficiently than they do red light. This is why the north sky seems blue at noon (scattering by air molecules), white around the sun during the day (direct passage of light), and red at dusk (light from the sun then traverses a long stretch of atmosphere tangential to the earth and loses much blue).

For this reason a totally colorless stone should display a bit of bluishness when observed at 90 degrees to the incident light. But the volume of a gem is always too small for this to be discernible; therefore, the expression "blue-white" should be considered a misnomer. (Some misuse this term to describe slightly yellowish diamonds with a strong blue fluorescence due to ultraviolet rays in sunlight; for years a regrettable confusion resulted).

Diffraction Identical particles of a dimension slightly smaller than the wavelengths of visible light may form a regular lattice, with which the various monochromatic rays interfere. Depending on their wavelengths and the elementary dimensions of the lattice, each monochromatic ray will be *diffracted* in a particular direction.

Play-of-color (harlequin) opal is a notable example. It is made up of a juxtaposition of regular stackings of identical silica spheres: a mosaic of vivid patches of color, changing with the direction of observation, arises from the heart of the gem. Therefore, opal is cut in cabochons. These colors evoke the sparkle of a fire and may be called the fire of opal (not to be mistaken with the fire of diamonds, caused by dispersion, mentioned earlier).

These vivid colored lights are pure spectral colors, like those of the rainbow, the scarf of Iris, the gods' messenger; therefore, this phenomenon of pseudochromatism was called *iridescence* by early German authors. The perception of diffracted colors is weakened by the direct transmission of light. It is thus always preferable to wear an opal on a dark fabric, which enhances its appearance. It is also possible to accentuate diffraction by applying black varnish to the base of the cabochon. The precipitation of carbon black between the cells of a whitish opal with potential for play of color produces a substitute for Australian black opal, although it is somewhat too flashy.

Adularescence and Opalescence If particles smaller than the visible wavelengths are not regularly ordered, a slightly bluish sheen, not a pure spectral color, is produced. This phenomenon, called *adularescence,* is best seen in moonstone feldspar. When the disordered particles are larger, they scatter equally all wavelengths, without preferred direction, so that the gem appears cloudy and white, as in common opal. Consequently, this phenomenon is called *opalescence.* A light opalescence is only a *fog,* quite visible under a strong point light source such as the sun; a good example is girasol quartz. Intense opalescence makes the gem opaque, as in milky quartz. Minor opalescence caused by an exsolution texture, encountered in some Sri Lankan sapphires, can be eliminated with heat treatment, which dissolves the exsolution.

Play-of-color opal from Australia. 10 by 10 cm. German Precious Stones Museum, Idar-Oberstein, Germany.

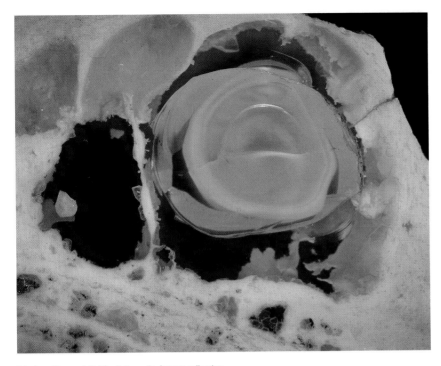

Mexican fire opal. 0.4 by 0.4 cm. Sorbonne collection.

105.53-carat cat's-eye tourmaline from Tanzania. F. A. Becker collection, Idar-Oberstein, Germany.

Chatoyancy Fibers scatter light mostly in a direction perpendicular to their elongation. When mineral fibers or needle-like growth tubes are all parallel in a stone, a cabochon cut produces a band of light, or ray, perpendicular to them, which evokes the eye of a feline. Of all the chatoyant gems (such as tourmaline, quartz, and beryl), only chrysoberyl can legally be called "cat's-eye" without further clarification. Considered to be amulets against the "evil eye," chatoyant gems are particularly valued in the Orient and the United States.

Asterism Elongated particles (acicular crystals, thin lamellae) that lie parallel to each other in two or more directions (exsolution textures) scatter light perpendicular to these directions. A cabochon cut will produce rays meeting at its summit, evoking a star. This phenomenon is called *asterism*. An asteriated gem may exhibit four rays (star diopside), six rays (star sapphire), or more rarely, twelve rays (rare star sapphires).

By exposing a gem that can develop an exsolution texture to the appropriate temperature for a sufficient length of time, it is possible to create an asterism. Developed to produce synthetic star sapphires, this technique is now also used on natural rubies and sapphires.

Adventurescence Platelets randomly oriented in a stone give it some scintillation, or sparkling flash. This irregular distribution, *a l'avventura* ("by chance") in Italian, gives it name to the phenomenon, seen in aventurine quartz, for example.

Iridescence

Iridescence has in today's English a different meaning from that given by the early German authors (see Diffraction). The reflection and refraction of light at both edges of a crack produce light interferences that cause generally rainbowlike colors. Contrary to the case of diffraction, the colors produced, called *interference colors,* are not pure spectral colors but a mixture of several wavelengths. This phenomenon is valued for stones only in iris quartz, where it is sometimes induced by heat shock. In pearls, however, it creates a soft silky surface appearance called *orient.*

Replacing the air in the crack with an oil that has an index of refraction similar to the gem's is enough to eliminate the iridescence. This is the purpose of "oiling" emeralds, a common practice today the world over.

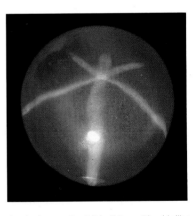

Synthetic star ruby. 1.5 by 1.5 cm. Djevahirdjian company, Switzerland.

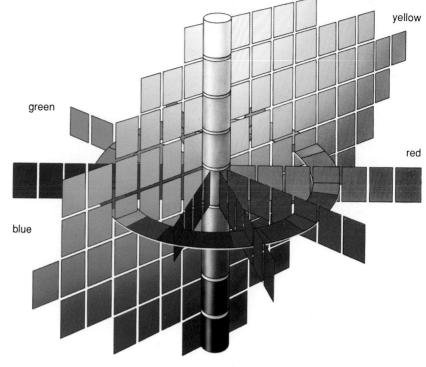

yellow

green

red

blue

The Munsell color space. The color of an object is compared to the color of these chips under a standardized white light. The difference in color between two adjacent samples is barely perceptible to a normal eye; therefore, this color space is physiologically homogeneous. Each chip is defined by three groups of numbers and letters, which characterize its hue (angular position in the plane perpendicular to the gray axis), saturation (distance from the gray axis), and tone (distance from the horizontal plane representing black).

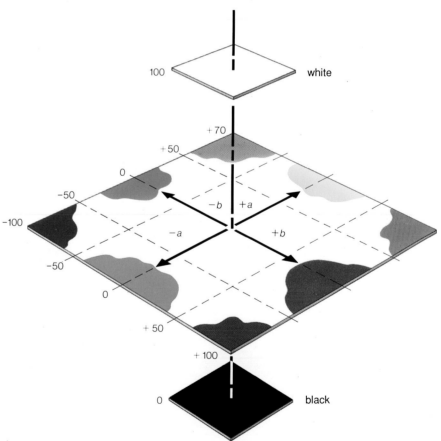

100   white

+70

+50

0

−50

−100

−50

$−b$ $+a$

$−a$ $+b$

0

+50

+100

0

black

Hunter's color space. The perpendicular axes emphasize the color opposites blue/yellow, green/red, and black/white. The impression of color perceived by a normal eye observing a body placed under a standardized white light, is defined at one spot, whose coordinates define the percentage of yellow (from 0 to 100 percent) on axis a, the percentage of red (from 0 to 100 percent) on axis b, the percentage of blue (from 0 to −100 percent), the percentage of green (from 0 to −100 percent), and the percentage of reflectance (0 percent for black, 100 percent for white) on the vertical axis. The horizontal surface area representing the possible color perceptions is reduced to one point for black and for white, and is maximum with an intermediate reflectance.

The Observer

Having the ability to perceive three color pairs—green/red, yellow/blue, and white/black—allows anyone to interpret all common color sensations. This is confirmed by the clinical observation of color perception anomalies, acquired either after an illness or hereditarily, transmitted by the sex chromosome (10 percent of men and 1 percent of women are affected). The mixing of blue and yellow light is perceived as colorless, although the mixture of a blue and a yellow pigment produces a green pigment. Most color sensations resulting from the perception of a polychromatic light are equivalent to those produced by the additive mixing of three reference lights—red, green, and blue—in appropriate proportions and intensity. A few sensations, however, cannot be reproduced in that way; these can be considered as an algebraic sum of these lights, since an equivalent sensation can be obtained only by mixing two of these lights with a mixture of the third and the observed light.

It thus seems possible to arrange all color sensations in a space constructed with orthogonal coordinates, representing the eye's response to these perceptions, respectively green/red, blue/yellow, and bright/dark. Such is the principle behind color spaces and color coordinates.

Nevertheless, the definition of consistent color spaces and the determination of color coordinates are riddled with theoretical and practical difficulties. The direct calculation of such coordinates supposes knowledge of the electromagnetic spectrum of the ambient light (generally obtained by comparison with a reference), a determination of a sample reflectance and transmittance for each monochromatic light (the results vary with the experimental techniques), the definition of sensitivity curves for the referent "average eye" (which may represent no actual eye), and then an integral calculation expressing the mutual interaction of these functions.

The visual comparison, under a normalized lighting, of an object under study with colored samples of known colored coordinates is another approach. The eye can indeed distinguish more than five million nuances of color if the surfaces to be compared are similar and placed next to each other, but their size, texture, and immediate environment can significantly affect this ability—and the number of nuances perceived can fall rapidly to less than five thousand.

Despite the absurdity of comparing a piece of colored cardboard with a transparent gem, some gemologists do not hesitate to use this procedure. The color coordinates, of course, cannot provide an acceptable description of a gem's color.

The "whiteness" of a diamond is determined under a normalized daylight illumination, against a white background, by comparison with a collection of master stones, selected during an international conference. A collection of master stones for colored stones cannot be assembled, because they may be pleochroic or display several colors.

The Importance of Color to a Gem's Value

Of all blue gems considered in their most attractive shade of color, sapphire offers the most attractive blue; the same holds true for ruby among red stones and emerald among green ones. Therefore, diamond, ruby, sapphire, and emerald are the best known, the only gems called *pierres précieuses* ("precious stones") in French.

The most vivid, the most saturated (with the least gray or brown) and the brightest possible shade is always sought for any stone. Whether through darkening, desaturation, or a variation of tone (such as a violet or green tinge to a blue stone), a gem's divergence from its "ideal" color curtails its attractiveness and hence its monetary value. A light blue and a dark blue sapphire have the same value; therefore, it is pointless to ask which is preferable. One should buy the stone to which one is most attracted.

Sapphire parure. The exceptional color of these sapphires suggests cabochon cut, because such a cut does not favor any orientation. The central stone in the necklace weighs 68.61 carats. Alexandre Reza creation, Paris.

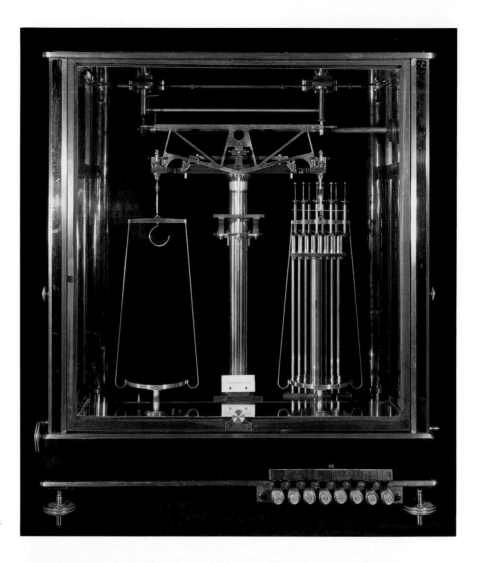

Precision scale from the end of the nineteenth century. Sorbonne collection.

Gem dealer's sccale from the beginning of the nine-teenth century. Sirakian collection, Paris.

Mass

Specific Gravity

Gems become rarer, and more expensive, with increasing volume. The volume of a given mineral species is proportional to its mass. This ratio, called *specific mass,* is an identifying characteristic of a mineral. However, in normal life, all objects are influenced by the earth's gravity; so for practical purposes the concept of mass is replaced with that of weight, the force with which a body is attracted toward earth, equal to the product of mass with the gravity field. Therefore, it is preferable to speak of *specific weight:* to measure the weight of a gem, one compares it to standard weights of known mass. It is interesting to compare the specific weights of two gems, especially if one must replace the other in a mounting. The ratio of a gem's specific weight to that of diamond is called the specific gravity of the gem compared to a diamond. Such calculation makes it possible to determine the weight of the gem intended to replace a given diamond. In everyday use, the term *specific gravity,* without further qualification, commonly abbreviated S.G., represents the density of an object compared to that of water. Specific gravity is a dimensionless number (that is, it is independent of the measurement units used) and an important characteristic in gem identification.

Units of Mass Used for Jewelry

The masses of gems were compared in past centuries to those of local seeds (from which comes the term *grain),* especially those of rice, wheat, and carob *(Ceratonia siliqua,* a Mediterranean tree). The weights of the different seeds, of course, varied greatly. Consequently, the *carat grain,* introduced to Europe by Arab merchants toward the middle of the sixteenth century, was quickly adopted as the gem trade developed. The term *carat* is probably derived from the Greek *keration,* meaning a small horn and, by extension, a carob bean. *Keration* also was used for a small coin showing horns of an ox; this coin was so small that the Greeks would put it on their tongues so as not to lose it.

Keraton became *qirāt* in Arabic, then *quilate* in old Portuguese, *quirate* in modern Portuguese and Spanish, *carot* and then *carat* in English, and *karat* and then *carat* in French. The seed taken as a definition of the carat produced references of different masses in different regions, sometimes different from one jeweler to the next in the same place. The most common values were close to 205 milligrams (197.20 milligrams in Florence, 215.99 milligrams in Livorno). The old carat was naturally divided into halves, quarters, eighths, sixteenths, thirty-seconds, and sixty-fourths. To end a confusion detrimental to the trade, the Weights and Measures Conference of 1907 adopted the suggestion made by the American mineralogist G. F. Kunz during the 1893 meeting to tie the carat to the metric system, defining the *metric carat* as one-fifth of a gram, or 200 milligrams. This unit, abbreviated m.c. or ct., was gradually made legal in all countries (in France by the law of June 22, 1909; for all Anglo-Saxon countries starting only in 1930) and is now an internationally recognized unit of measure. It is divided in hundredths, called *points.* The abandonment of the old carat was without difficulty, since it amounted to an increase by about 2.5 percent in the figures for mass. Gems' masses are always expressed in carats and hundredths of a carat rounded to the smallest point value up to seven for the third decimal (1.397 carats is rounded to 1.39 carats).

The metric carat, the unit of mass for gems, must not be mistaken for the karat, that measures the amount of alloy per twenty-four parts of a precious metal. The small Greek coin *keration* was worth ⅓ of an *obolus* (an obolus equals ⅙ of a drachma) or ¹⁄₂₄ of a *drachma,* both monetary units and units of mass. The drachma played a role as an international unit of currency only while Athens was a major power, in the fifth century B.C.; it was devalued (minting of a coin alloyed with base metals, around 413 B.C.) during the Peloponnesian Wars (460–404 B.C.). The drachma's international role was later held by the Macedonian gold *straterus* (Alexander the Great, 356–323 B.C.), then by the Roman *denarius.* In 87 B.C., Sylla, rebuilding Rome's finances, introduced the *aureus.* Despite numerous financial reforms (made especially by Caesar, Augustus, and Diocletian), the *aureus* lost its prestige. Returning to the ancient Greek sources, in 313 Constantine the Great created the *solidus,* a symbol of a strong, solid currency, from which is derived the French *sou.* The solidus originally weighed 24 gold carats. Unfortunately, in 367 inflation forced Constantine's successors to devalue the sou by 15 percent; it became an alloy, containing only 20.5 gold carats. This amount later dropped to 20 and then 18 carats. The present value of a karat, ¹⁄₂₄, is a reminder of the devaluations of the Byzantine gold *sou.* It served as an international currency for centuries, until Constantinople's fall, and was especially important from the Roman Empire until the thirteenth and fourteenth centuries.

The *grain,* defined in the seventeenth century as one-quarter carat, followed the evolution of the carat and became a *metric grain,* ¹⁄₂₀ gram, or 50 milligrams. This is an accepted unit of measure, used mostly in Western countries to weigh white to pinkish pearls, as well as by diamond dealers to describe the content of their lots of stone (a 2-grain diamond lot consists of diamonds weighing between 0.47 and 0.53 carats).

One should not mistake the grain with the English grain (0.0648 grams), which is the reference mass for English units. The troy ounce is 480 grains (31.1035 grams) and is particularly used as a reference mass for gold; it is different from the ounce avoirdupois of 437.5 grains (28.3495 grams), used for everyday measures.

Other units of mass are used locally. In Japan the 18.75-carat *mumme* (3.75 grams) is used for cultured pearls, and in Asia, the *rati* is approximately 0.91 carats, with multiples such as the *chevvu, chow* or *tank* of 24 *chevvu* in Sri Lanka, the *mesghal* of 40 *ratis* in Persia, the *tola* in India, and the *bali* in Myanmar (Burma) (both worth 58.18 carats) of 64 *ratis*.

The Influence of Mass on a Gem's Value

When all other factors are equal, the value of a gem is not proportional to its mass but to a power of its mass.

The proportionality rule, based on the square of the mass, first expressed by Nicolas Harlay de Sancy in the sixteenth century, seemed well established in the nineteenth century but survived World War I only for white and pink pearls. The pearl dealer offers "so many times the weight," that is, so many times the square of the mass in metric grains. This is why it is useful to compute the "once value" of a pearl necklace, that is, the sum of the squared mass of each pearl, to which will be attributed the value coefficient of the necklace. Being independent of mass, this value coefficient makes it possible to compare pearls of very different sizes. To add to an existing pearl necklace, one has to choose pearls with the same value coefficient as the necklace.

For precious stones, the practice is to offer so much per carat. Nevertheless, the price per carat increases significantly with mass, at least under normal circumstances, until a certain limit is reached, which depends on the mineral. Depending on the rate of this increase and the starting value, the pricing of good-quality stones may vary depending on the mass one considers. For example, rubies over a carat are far more expensive than diamonds of similar mass. One must also keep in mind that certain masses are psychologically more attractive, and therefore the price curve increases by steps, located at "remarkable masses": 1.00 carat, 1.50 carat, 2 carats, etc. Between a 0.99-carat stone and a 1.00-carat stone of similar quality, there may be a difference in price of 20 percent, sometimes more in a period of speculation (for example, diamonds of 1.00 and 1.50 carats were at one time so overpriced that their price per carat was equal or slightly higher than the price of 2-carat diamonds).

For ornamental stones, the mass is secondary to certain desirable dimensions. This is the case, for example, for recent lapis lazuli objects (for which the height of the carving is most important) and of tiger's-eye (for which the thickness of the carving is most particularly considered).

Clarity

Inclusions: Witnesses to a Gem's History

No compound or crystal can form isolated from the rest of the world; the environment both allows and limits its development. Animal and plant secretions

When the traditional premium value for mass is considered, a 1-carat modern round brilliant-cut diamond (diameter 6.5 mm) is four times more valuable than a 0.50-carat diamond (diameter 5.15 mm) of the same quality. Sirakian collection, Paris.

are exposed to the actions of the ecological environment; they may change with time, either cyclically with the seasons or accidentally because of disease. Rocks are the results of deposition or crystallization triggered by physicochemical action on preexisting materials, and variations in the environment (such as fluid circulation and temperature) can modify their formation and their composition.

Using materials from its surrounding medium, a crystal grows around a seed, which spontaneously formed when conditions were favorable. But a crystal's growth is generally not uniform over time, and it can even be interrupted, which will leave marks in the crystal structure (for example, quartz phantoms). Other crystals appear alongside at various times; these are described in geology by the term *paragenesis,* that is, they are "born around" the crystal. For each important gem, the reader will find a description of its mode of formation and paragenesis in part 2. The growing crystal can, of course, surround already formed minerals of its paragenesis, if they are in immediate contact: it traps them, as it can trap (in negative crystals) surrounding fluids (gaseous, liquid, or viscous materials). Certain constraining conditions may force it to twin. Sometimes mechanical strains induce a rupture: if the crystal is still in a growth phase, deposits form on each side of the crack, healing the accident, but numerous small negative crystals often mark its former position, a characteristic called a "healed fracture." If conditions for growth no longer prevail, then the crack remains as is, simply a fracture. A fracture can form where the gem grew (primary deposit) or where it was transported by erosion (secondary deposit) or even later because of tectonic movement or accidental shock during extraction, faceting, setting, or even normal wear.

The gemologist considers an *inclusion* to be anything visible inside a crystal (growth marks, twins and fossil faces, negative crystals, healed fractures, crystals, cracks), any foreign crystal in a monomineralic rock (pyrite in lapis lazuli, for example), and any accidental organic build-up coming from an animal or a plant in a gem (conchiolin accumulation in pearls, insects in amber).

When geological conditions change, the trapped materials may dissociate, forming a solid and a gas in negative crystals (some negative crystals contain a moving bubble). Similarly, some components of the crystal may reorganize separately in the crystal structure, oriented along certain crystallographic directions, forming an *exsolution texture.* An example is rutile that precipitates from a titanium-rich corundum. The inclusions tell the story of the gem. The observation of inclusions may help assess the gem's mode of crystallization and can sometimes indicate the type of deposit in which it was formed (hydrothermal emerald versus pegmatitic emerald). Inclusions also characterize synthetic crystals grown to imitate natural gems (synthetic rubies and emeralds).

Modifications of Inclusions

A gem may contain unattractive black metallic inclusions, which would be better eliminated. Removal is normally done dur-

A Brazilian amethyst with goethite crystals formed around a phantom quartz crystal covered by amethyst. Height: 2 cm. Compagnie Générale de Madagascar collection, Paris.

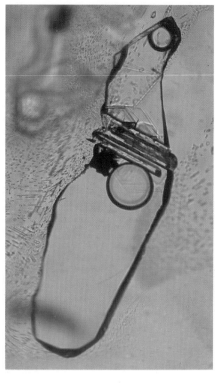

A negative crystal filled with crystallites and carbon dioxide in a Sri Lankan sapphire. Magnified 25 times. Photo: A. Jeanne-Michaud.

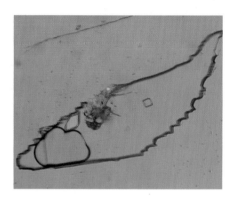

Negative crystals filled with a saline solution, a carbon dioxide bubble, and cubic crystals of a potassosodic salt in Brazilian topaz. Magnified 110 times. Photo: A. Jeanne-Michaud.

Rutile inclusions covered with negative quartz crystals in a Brazilian quartz. Height: 10 mm. Sorbonne collection.

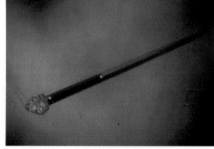

The trapping of a parasitic phenakite crystallite created an elongated inclusion filled with water and water vapor in this hydrothermal synthetic emerald. Magnified 130 times. Photo: A. Jeanne-Michaud.

Inclusions of dagger-shaped goethite crystals in an amethyst from the Dennys Mountains of Washington State. Height: 10 mm. Sorbonne collection.

ing faceting, but for some time miners and lapidaries have also used chemical or thermal treatments.

For example, a ruby or a sapphire with too dense an exsolution texture can be subjected to very high temperatures, to dissolve the titanium in the crystal structure and develop blue iron-titanium color-producing centers; a quick return to normal conditions (a sort of quenching) makes this state permanent. A corundum crystal can also be maintained at intermediate temperatures for a longer period, until the titanium creates an exsolution texture, which will produce an asterism after cutting. The rutile needles formed in this way are always much shorter than those created by natural phenomena, and the asterism does not always appear.

Another method, commonly used on diamonds, is to drill a hole through the gem surface to the inclusion using a laser; the included crystal is then dissolved with a chemical that does not attack the matrix (such as hydrofluoric acid for diamond). The dark or black inclusion, often metallic, is then replaced by a cavity, which is much less noticeable than the black spot, connected to the surface by a thin channel, 0.2 to 0.3 millimeters in diameter.

Beryl from Brazil containing large tubes filled with a saline solution and carbon dioxide. Diameter: 10.5 mm. Private collection.

A negative crystal filled with liquid and gaseous carbon dioxide in a Herkimer quartz from New York State. Magnified 50 times. Sorbonne collection.

Amber with an insect inclusion (Orthoptera blattes). Length: 2 cm. S. Hendrickson collection, United States.

An internal fracture filled with gaseous carbon dioxide and a saline solution in an amethyst from Las Vigas, Veracruz, Mexico. Magnified 10 times. B. Schupp collection, United States.

A pink ruby from Myanmar (Burma). The very thin rutile needles forming an exsolution texture give the stone a silky appearance; therefore the needles are called silk. Length: 4 mm. Private collection.

The Importance of Clarity to a Gem's Value

Inclusions in a gem scatter light and hinder the perception of its color and "life." Consequently, a clean gem is more valued than an "inhabited" one.

Inclusions are more visible when the gem has less color; thus, the obsession for clean crystals, especially in the case of diamonds. No crystal, however, is perfectly clean. Therefore it was decided to consider clean any diamond in which a well-trained eye could see no inclusion using a loupe of magnification 10 under appropriate lighting. Such stones have sometimes been the object of speculation. Any inclusions in a diamond that are visible with a 10× magnification are then classified, according to their importance, as "very very small" inclusions (VVS), "very small" inclusions (VS), "small inclusions" (SI), and inclusions noticeable with the unaided eye, making the gem "imperfect" (I). (This last category is also called piqué [P] in Europe.) The more included a diamond is, the less subject it is to speculation. The difference in value between a clean diamond and a VS stone before World War I was no more than 10 percent; now, it is more than 50 percent.

A lack of inclusions is never a priority in colored stones. Inclusions in colored stones scatter light, soften the color, and may impart a velvety look. One would be more attracted to a ruby or a sapphire with "silk" (rutile needlelike exsolutions), or an emerald with a "garden" (healed fractures), as long as these inclusions were not distracting. Even when heavily included, colored stones might still be cut because of their color; they are nevertheless less attractive and their price is lower.

Less valued gem species are cut and marketed only if they are clean or almost clean, with a few exceptions (red tourmaline, or rubellite, and red spinel, for example). When a particular optical effect is desired, such as asterism, black crystallites or irregularities in the fibers would then alter the value. For ornamental stones, although the amateur may not object to black inclusions in a green stone (jade, serpentine), he or she rarely accepts the presence of whitish veins. Sometimes certain inclusions are desirable, such as pyrite in lapis lazuli, evoking a sky studded with stars.

Gray-blue blemishes in pearls, resulting from a shallow conchiolin accumulation, are undesirable. Generally, a pearl will be drilled at this cumbersome peculiarity. Collectors value complete, well-isolated inclusions of insects and small animals in amber but not shapeless organic accumulations.

The influence of inclusion on the beauty, and so the commercial value, of a gem is mostly a question of common sense.

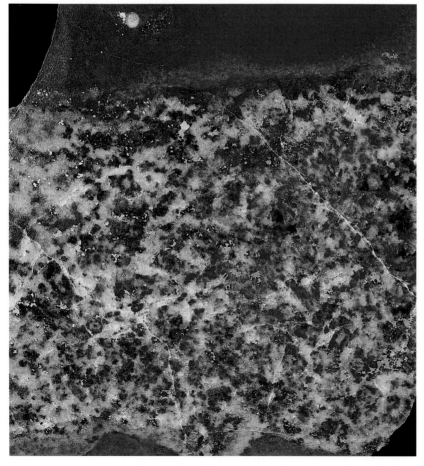

Lapis lazuli from Afghanistan containing pyrite inclusions. Length: 8 cm. Sorbonne collection.

Cutting Gems

Seals, Cylinders, Intaglios, and Cameos

The engraving or carving of hard stones, or glyptic, is little known today. The pieces produced since the end of the nineteenth century that are available for examination are generally mediocre and do not encourage the study of this "microsculpture." But artists have created true masterpieces since carving stone first became a means of expression. Glyptic arts were last fashionable from the early nineteenth century until the First World War. Since then, they have fallen into oblivion, though in recent years a revival has been seen, particularly in Germany and the United States.

Glyptic (from the Greek *gluptos, glyphein,* "to cut") was equivalent to writing when early man engraved in clay the first cuneiforms and hieroglyphs. It is the art of engraving, either into the surface, for seals, cylinders, and intaglios, or in relief, for cameos.

The first engravings were abraded or scraped shells, nacre, and soft stones, such as marble, made using points of silex, obsidian, or native copper embedded with fine sand. Later, small drill bits of various dimensions were used, covered with pitch and emery powder and spun between the fingers. The drill bit was then made to spin faster by winding it in a bowstring. The back-and-forth motion of this tool produced a fairly rapid rotation when the bit and the engraved object were lubricated with oil. Through the ages, the bow was replaced by a lathe with wheels and pedals. Depending on the material and the technique, the object to be engraved was either held against the secured drill bit or the bit was worked against the secured object. As technology improved, the choice of minerals to be engraved widened: from simple alabaster and steatite, artists moved to ivory and marble, then, starting around 3500 B.C., to serpentine, various agates, onyx, jasper, chalcedony, and carnelian, and finally to rock crystal and lapis lazuli, as well as hematite, widely used because of its abundance and ability to take a nice polish. When and how was such an art born?

The discovery of new primitive civilizations, first begun in the seventeenth century, has modified our judgment on the history of primitive arts. Today's archaeological research and discoveries, results of all kinds of undertakings (such as construction, irrigation, agriculture) as well as faster and more powerful equipment, continues to alter the knowledge already gathered on extinct civilizations, giving us a glimpse of the past. Prehistoric man began engraving the soft limestone of the caves in which they lived with silex splinters about fifty

thousand years ago. Using available raw materials such as bone and animal tusks, which themselves may have appropriate surfaces for engraving or polishing, he drew geometric designs, abstract at first and then figurative, especially hunting scenes. Then appeared anthropomorphic figures, symbolic and cultural. These early efforts in written communication probably were made in various regions of the world, particularly in Europe. But it was in the Middle East, around 5000 B.C., that glyptic, together with traditional sculpture, was born.

Indeed, the kinder climatic conditions, favorable to pastoral sedentary societies, provided an escape from the hazards of hunting and made it possible for the most gifted individuals to spend some time in artistic and religious activities. Man then displayed his power and his uniqueness through ornament, including seals.

Taking advantage of minerals found in Persia, Afghanistan, India, the Caucasus, Ethiopia, and the coast of the Red Sea, the Egyptian, Persian, Mesopotamian, and even Indian civilizations developed the art of carving seals between 6000 and 5000 B.C. Hemispherical, spindle-shaped, rectangular, square, or sometimes zoomorphic, these seals functioned as amulets, intended to exorcise evil forces and to win the favor of benevolent gods. Seals protected possessions and their owners and at the same time attested to the owner's authority as head of the family and identified his property. (The carved seal was pressed into clay or wax, marking one's possessions with a unique image.) They often represented familiar, important animals, in an effort to keep them abundant.

The first cylinders appeared between 4000 and 3000 B.C. Their use was identical to that of seals. Rolling them on wax or clay produced a series of the owner's unique mark, which proclaimed the permanence of the seal and forbade falsification of the

A green jasper cylinder from the Assyrian period (tenth century B.C.) Height: 17 mm. Private collection.

A milky quartz scarab bearing the seal of the Egyptian king Thutmose III (ruled 1504–1450 B.C.). Length: 6.76 mm; weight: 152.9 grams. Private collection.

document (or tablets). Worn as jewelry on a cord around the neck or around the wrist, cylinders, like seals, were used to guarantee the contents of earthenware jars filled with cereals, oil, or wine. As printed seals still do today, they ensured that the vessel they sealed was not opened by a third party.

Seals and cylinders helped authenticate clay tablets, whether the writing was in cuneiform characters or hieroglyphs. *Bullas,* round terra-cotta balls, were stamped with multiple seals to provide safe passage, just as our present passports are ornate with stamps from the consulates of the countries in which we can travel. Artists went through abstract and realist stages in more or less regular waves, as illustrated by the seals from Catal Höyük, Tell Halaf, Tell al-Ubayyid, from Erech, Djem-det-Nasr, Sumer, Mohenjo-Daro, Akkad, Ur, Babylon, and Nineveh. As in other human activities, periods of refinement followed periods of decadence, according to the fate of the civilization to which the art served as historical witness.

The main themes shown on cylinders were the exploits of venerated gods, the fertility goddess, and terrifying mythic animals, along with scenes of adoration.

Down through the centuries have come long frescoes of galloping deer, jumping ibex, schools of fish, hunting or hunted lions, bulls attacked or sacrificed, desert enemies, snakes, scorpions, tarantulas, even trees of life loaded with fruit as in Eden, horses dancing or pulling carts for hunting or war convey the image of life and death, proceeding as in a cartoon.

Artists in Parthia, Media, and the Achemenid kingdoms used similar themes; only costumes, cylinder shapes, and engraving styles make dating possible. The cylinder slowly disappeared, replaced by cones and intaglios, which in turn were replaced by the ball and ring seals of the Persian Sassanids.

The Egyptian civilization regulated the use of seals, principally the engraving of the scarab because it symbolized renewal and eternity. Worn as a pivoting ring, it was used by civilizations around the Mediterranean basin during the first millennium B.C. The scarab bore the name of the pharaoh or its owner in its cartouche. Certain cylinders also bore the name of the king or scribe using them.

Creto-Mycenaean intaglios were essentially lens-shaped, either round or elongated. The island fauna and flora and mythological scenes were the subjects favored by engravers during the second and first millennia B.C. The purity of the shapes, the modernity and freshness of the imagery are unexpected. Drilled through, they were worn on necklaces or were set in rings.

In the ancient Greek glyptic, the engraver found inspiration in the heroes of the *Iliad* and the gods of Olympus. The

A nineteenth-century gold ring with a brown jasper cameo veined with chalcedony, depicting a young man (perhaps Apollo). Private collection.

Greek masters from the middle of the first millennium are given credit for creating the first cameos, taking advantage of agate banding to highlight several subjects or characters against backgrounds of different colors, or one subject against the other in multilayer cameos. The Egyptians had, during the Ramesside period (1300–1100 B.C.), engraved scenes in relief but, having used uniformly colored rock, they did not achieve the same success as their northern imitators. Only during the reign of the Ptolemies (323–30 B.C.) did they engrave cameos like the Greeks. This same process, used for intaglios and employing two layers only, produced the *nicolos* of white and blue chalcedony or red-orange and white chalcedony. The engravers vied with each other to prove their skill, depicting mythological and historical scenes and portraits of heroes, philosophers, and scholars representing the gods with whom they identified themselves (such as Zeus, Heracles, Dionysus, Aphrodite, and Athena).

One of the most sumptuous periods for glyptic was that of Dexamenos of Chios, who was the first engraver to sign his exquisite creations, and of Pyrgotelos, whom Alexander the Great employed exclusively for his portrait.

Precious metal ingots were used since the third millennium to pay for commercial transactions, at the same time that tablets, authenticated by the imprint of a cylinder, were used. Only around the seventh century B.C. did the first coins appear, and their designs were often similar to those of cameos and intaglios. Engravers of coins, and later medallions, were also hard-stone engravers.

With the development of civilization and increasing wealth, collectors, kings, and princes pushed the artists to higher levels of achievement to satisfy their passion for jewelry, elaborate crockery and vessels, and the like. Mithradates owned several hundred agate vases. Ptolemy's Cup in the Cabinet of Medals at the Bibliothèque Nationale in Paris is a famous example of a precious cup, as is the Farnese Cup in the Museo Nazionale in Naples.

Long after the Hellenistic period, Greek artists went to work for Rome, bequeathing their knowledge to future generations of

Facing page top left: *A Cretan intaglio light brown jasper depicting a leaping bull. Length: 19 mm. Private collection.* Top right: *An eighteenth-century gold ring with a jasper cameo depicting Socrates. Height: 25 mm. Private collection.* Lower left: *A nineteenth-century gold ring with a jasper cameo depicting a lion bringing down a young stag. Probably Mogol. Height: 22 mm. Private collection.* Lower right: *A carnelian intaglio from the end of the classical Greek period (fourth century B.C.) depicting a wolf's head. Height: 6 mm. Private collection.* Bottom: *A Roman-period (first century A.D.) carnelian intaglio from Asia minor showing a wild boar. Height: 10 mm. Private collection.*

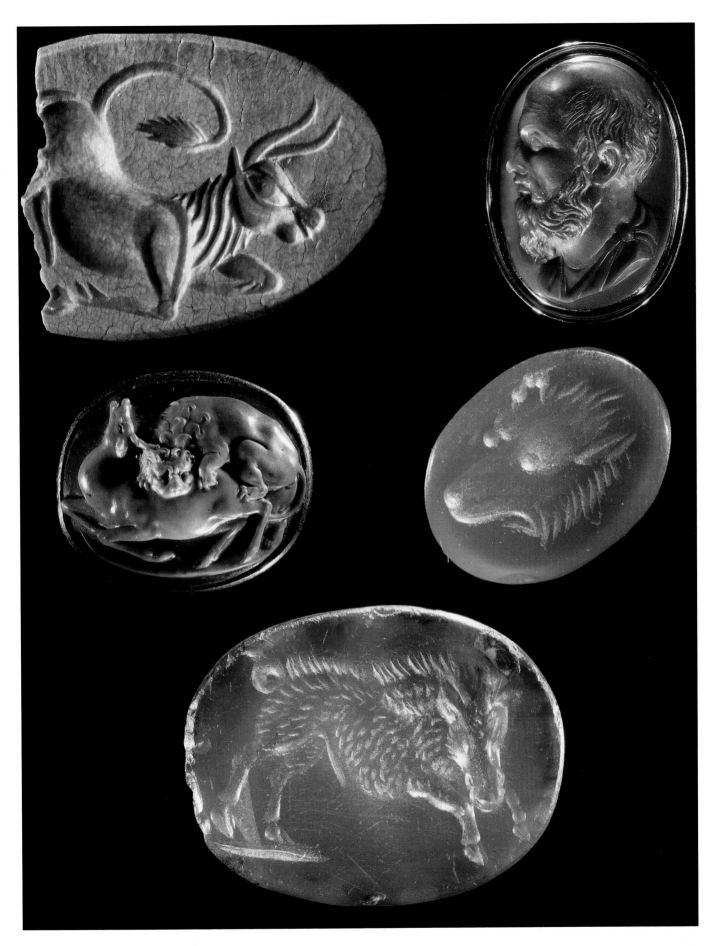

artists. Julius Caesar was a collector; Augustus had a famous private engraver, Dioskourides, although no portrait of this emperor by this artist exists. Nero, like nearly all the other emperors, was an amateur engraver and collector.

Two great cameos have survived from the Roman period. The Grand Camée de France (Great Cameo of France), or the Apotheosis of Augustus, actually represents Tiber as Jupiter and Livia as Ceres, accompanied by Germanicus, and probably dates to A.D. 19. The Gemma Augustea, in the Kunsthistorisches Museum in Vienna, is a bit smaller but quite perfect, a tribute to Augustus's glory. This achievement in glyptic was once part of the Saint-Sernin Basilica's treasure in Toulouse, France, during the Middle Ages. The portrait of Julia, Titus's daughter, signed by Evodos and kept in the Cabinet of Medals in Paris, is an example of a jewel in which the exceptional quality of the gem matches that of the engraving.

For three centuries intaglios and cameos worn in rings and necklaces or stitched onto clothing were immensely popular. Even modest folks had their own talismans, their good-luck charms; the poorest wore glass intaglios, engraved or molded copies of valuable stones. Comedians and politicians showed off with numerous rings: stones in their settings were even stitched to shoes. Ring settings were made of iron or bronze to keep the price down. As Roman decadence increased, the quality of

An oval green jasper intaglio from the end of the Hellenistic period (first century B.C.) depicting a gryllus composed of an eagle's head, an old man's head, and a wild boar's head. Height: 16 mm. Private collection.

the engraving was affected. The travels of the legions to England and all over Europe, including around the Black Sea, introduced new jewelry, worn by soldiers and officers.

Stones of Gnostic origin (second century B.C. to second century A.D.) were produced in the eastern part of the Mediterranean basin for prophylactic use, including the mysterious gryllus, animal bodies with human heads.

Since the Hellenistic period, the frequent use of various gems led ancient peoples to attribute curative and protective properties to them. Amethyst, for example, was supposed to prevent drunkenness, and red jasper was the stone of choice to evoke Dionysus or Bacchus.

The rise of Constantinople, which became the empire's eastern capital in 330, attracted attention to the engravers and stones of the Orient. These gems would enrich the treasures of Constantinople's churches, as cameos and intaglios depicting scenes of pagan mythology would be reinterpreted to fit the traditions of the Christian church. Christians would also develop their own symbolism, inspired mainly by the cross and the fish. This reinterpretation of pagan artworks continued in Europe when the Crusaders brought back to their respective homelands the treasures of the Byzantine Empire and adapted them to Christian ritual. Pagan cups became ciboria, scenes of Olympus became scenes from the Bible.

Despite the production of Arab and Sassinid artwork, the engraving of hollow glass temporarily replaced hard-stone engraving, which lapsed during the Middle Ages in Europe. Lotharingia (now Lorraine) became the home of this new style of work.

During the ninth century, the Frankish Empire rediscovered glyptic, producing numerous rock-crystal vases carved in Lotharingia, as well as intaglios representing Christ, the Virgin Mary, and the Apostles.

Glyptic was then used to decorate cult objects, reliquaries of saints and martyrs presented by kings or emperors to abbeys, convents, and cathedrals. Older engraved stones were used along with stones of the period, also engraved or cut in cabochons.

Shell engraving, which had preceded hard-stone engraving, began to flourish again at the end of the Middle Ages.

A true glyptic revival occurred in Europe during the fifteenth and sixteenth centuries, with great artists encouraged by patrons such as the Medicis, Francis I of France, the popes, the German emperors, and the kings of Bohemia. The beautiful agates found in the Alps and the Riesengebirge (Giant Mountains, between Poland and Czechoslovakia) and those imported from India and Madagascar, as well as the availability of extremely pure blocks of rock crystal, very likely helped to inspire carvers to attempt masterpieces requiring patience and virtuosity. Taking advantage of color

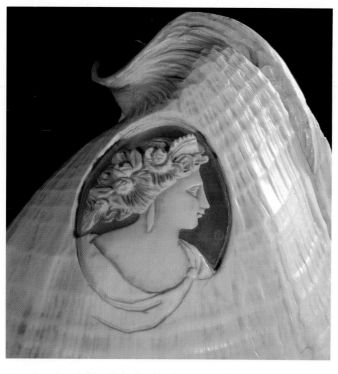

A Strombus gigas shell in which a head has been carved, from around 1920. Height: 14 cm.; cameo measures 5 by 4 cm. Private collection.

variations in gems, they often surpassed their ancient masters.

Italian workshops were thriving in European courts, where they drew the attention of the sovereigns. Donatello, Jacopo de Trezzo, the Masnagos, Domenico dei Cammei, Giovanni delle Corniole, Valerio Vincentini, the Miseronis, the Saracchis (who did a great deal of work for the Hapsburgs), and Matteo del Nassaro (who was brought to France by Francis I) were some of the innumerable artists. Their works are better known to us than those of Roman or Greek carvers, because they signed them and because they are closer to us in time. In an attempt to prove their superioriority to their predecessors, some carvers of the seventeenth and eighteenth centuries even signed their pieces with false Greek names to fool collectors. In France, after the death of Henri IV, the interest in glyptic revived only under Louis XV. In the eighteenth century, Europe saw outstanding artists such as Jacques Guay, the Pichlers, the Simons, Louis Siriès, Christian Friedrich Hecker, Lorenz Natter, Philippe Rega, the Brown brothers, and Philipp Christoph Becker. They generally gained fame by carving the portraits of various sovereigns in European courts and of famous contemporary men and women. Jacques Guay, who taught Madame de Pompadour engraving, carved some beautiful cameos of Louis XV.

At the beginning of the nineteenth century, these masters' students—the Simon family, Giovanni Santarelli, Antonio Berini, Giuseppe Girometti, Romain-Vincent Jeuffroy—also created beautiful cameos and intaglios. Some of these engravers are relatively unknown, however, because their works are held in private collections, making it difficult to appreciate their quality.

Despite the creation by Napoléon of a Grand Prix de Rome for hard-stone engraving, the interest in glyptic would fade in the nineteenth century. (The winner of this first Grand Prix in 1805 was N. P. Tiolier, later engraver general for the Paris Mint, like his father, Pierre Joseph.)

In the twentieth century, Lalique and Fabergé changed the art of jewelry by using carved glass and stones. The art of carving is still taught in France, Italy, and particularly in Germany. New technology has made the artists' work easier, reducing the time needed to produce a carving. It is easier to reproduce an engraving as a series, which brings the unit price down. However, true works of art are rare, since artists are no longer inspired to emulate ancient artists or encouraged by rich patrons. The jewelry is essentially made with faceted gems or cabochons. Only time will tell if this singular art still has a place in modern civilization, where the patience, dexterity, and talent it demands are now employed in other trades. This century of mass production cannot be one for the unique precious object.

Other Carvings

As long ago as the Aurignacian culture of 25,000 B.C., the carving of curved surfaces of soft materials (usually ivory and bone) with silex chisels had already been mastered. The meaning of the female figurines produced at that time, carved into an oval-shaped material, with the belly button in the center, is not known, but it seems logical to associate the figurines with a cult of fertility. Later these statuettes represented the divine presence in temples, and the donator himself was immortalized. Ritual and symbolic objects were also carved in ornamental stones for sacred ceremonies and to accompany a dignitary on his journey after death. But with the development of any culture comes an increase in luxury and an abandonment of former values, generally resulting in the culture's destruction and a plundering by invaders. With a few variations, this scenario repeated itself regularly; its first manifestation was the foundation by Sargon of an empire in Akkad (northern Mesopotamia, now Iraq), which extended from Sumer to the Mediterranean, around 2325 B.C. With its fall, some statuettes and sacred or symbolic objects became simple house decorations, and collectors prospered. They were princes, such as Mithradates, who owned a splendid collection of 2,000 delicately carved agate vases, or private persons, for example those whose traces have been found during Pompeii's excavation.

Cult and symbolic objects have been carved since prehistoric times by pre-Columbian Indians as well as the Chinese (essen-

A tourmaline bird and a rock-crystal flower. Length: 10 cm. G. Becker design, Idar-Oberstein, Germany.

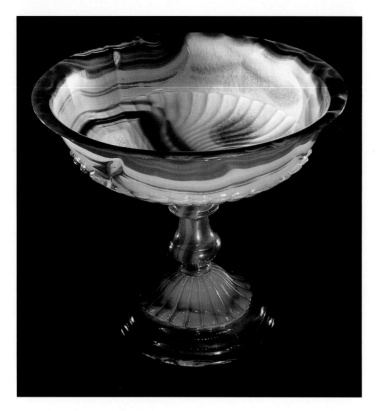

An agate bowl. Height: about 30 cm. German Precious Stones Museum, Idar-Oberstein, Germany.

A fish in Brazilian agate. Height: 5 cm. G. Becker creation.

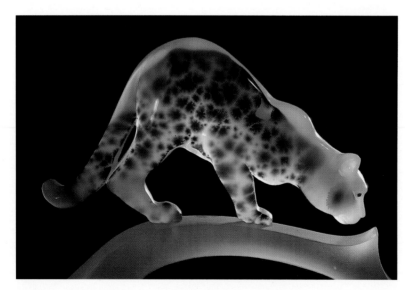

A panther carved in speckled agate. Height: 6 cm. G. Becker creation, Idar-Oberstein, Germany.

tially in jade). But utilitarian objects, such as snuff bottles, were also produced by Oriental artists. The collectors of the eighteenth and especially nineteenth centuries contributed to the establishment of a repetitive carving style for objects exported by the Chinese. Such objects for display are now produced everywhere in the Far East (Taiwan, Hong Kong, Japan) and even in Europe (by Asian immigrants) using various stones and ornamental materials, including ivory, coral, serpentine, jade, jaspers, tiger's-eye, turquoise, lapis, fluorite, amethyst, rock crystal, and amazonite.

In Europe, the most important center for hard-stone carving is Idar-Oberstein, Germany, where display pieces and objets d'art (animals, bowls), utilitarian objects (boxes), and faceted stones are produced. The artist uses the same tools used to engrave intaglios and cameos: various bits of bronze or steel that he machines himself on a lathe and sets on a rotating head, sometimes at the end of a flexible shaft. The two most common abrasives are diamond grit (diamond powder), carefully applied to the tool with a small hammer, and emery (alumina powder) thickened with a few drops of water. From time to time during the carving process, the object is flushed with water so that the artist can see the progress of his work.

Cabochons

The observation of pebbles polished by the action of streams, revealing the rocks' beauty, probably played an important part in the development of polishing techniques during the tenth millennium B.C. At that time polished ceremonial axes were produced in green rock, particularly jade. The preparation of the surface to be polished was probably done with sand on hard, approximately planar surfaces. (Quartz flagstones were still used at the end of the nineteenth century in the Ubangi basin to work rock crystal, and similar polishing slabs are still used by New Guinea natives to work jade.)

The discovery of vertical polishing slabs in Dordogne, France, has led to the conclusion that the final polish was achieved by simple rubbing, without abrasives. It is possible that the great technological discoveries of the fifth millennium (potter's wheel, in wood, propelled with the foot; use of the bow to spin the drill bits) helped in the fabrication of small objects. Today European gem cutters still use wooden wheels to polish corundum cabochons and still preform stones by hand, on a vertical wheel, holding them with their fingers to better "feel" them. It is difficult to say when this wheel, propelled by a bow and still used in India, was perfected.

Starting with the reign of Pericles (fifth century B.C.), equipment advanced significantly, thanks to the invention of pulleys and gears; they made the use of stream power at the beginning of the Christian era possible. Such a setup is still in use at the old mill in Idar-Oberstein: the lapidary lies on his belly in front of a huge sandstone wheel to shape agate.

The shaping of opaque to translucent crystals and rocks produces a semi-ovoid object reminiscent of a skull, called a *cabochon,* derived from the Old French *caboche* (from the Latin *caput,* "head"). Such a shape is very appropriate for highly included or opaque materials; it enables light to enter from all directions, to scatter off the inclusions, and to highlight the stone's color and enhance some directional optical effects (chatoyancy, asterism, iridescence). For transparent materials, it is imperative that light be reflected on the bottom surface of the cabochon, which is therefore also polished. Most antique cabochons are polished on both sides, which probably made it possible to take advantage of the magnifying properties of the most transparent ones.

Today only ornamental stones and highly included stones are cut in cabochons. Collector's stones (sometimes called rare stones) and those of a particularly attractive color are cut by hand, as in the past. However, common stones intended for jewelry that must be well calibrated (have identical

The polishing of a cabochon by a Parisian lapidary.

A small gem-cutting shop in India. A rope is coiled around the axis of a grinding wheel; the back-and-forth motion of the bow to which the rope is fixed drives the wheel. The cutter preforms or polishes with one hand and handles the bow with the other (foreground). Only the trimming saw requires electrical power (in the back). Photo: C. Charensol.

A nineteenth-century etching showing the grinding wheels used to work agate at the Idar-Oberstein mills.

Amethyst cabochons. F. A. Becker collection, Idar-Oberstein, Germany.

the bases; great care is taken to avoid affecting the other base, in order to retain the proper shape. (This preparation is increasingly done by machine.)

The preformed cabochon is then polished in a tumbler if it is tough enough. The tumbler is a plastic or metal cylinder, closed at both ends, that is, two-thirds full of plastic balls, preformed cabochons, and water mixed with abrasives. It rotates on its axis, so that polishing is achieved by rubbing (too fast a rotation may break materials to be polished; too slow a rotation does not produce any polish). Cabochons polished in this way have a slightly concave base (which may be later corrected by an additional polishing by hand). If the stone is not tough enough (if it has many fractures), the cabochon is polished by hand. Hand polishing can be recognized by the sharp edges between the curved and flat parts of the cabochon.

The tumbler, directly inspired by stream erosion, is also used to prepare polished stones of baroque shapes (especially siliceous stones); they are then drilled to be strung or are glued directly to silver mountings. To fashion spheres (for a necklace, for example), cubes are sawn with their edges slightly larger than the diameter of the sphere to be polished; the summits are cut in the same way. These roughly preformed balls are placed between two horizontal wheels turning in opposite directions. They are held in place by a plate drilled with as many holes as there are spheres. The final drilling is done by machine.

Balls of large diameter and large ovals are, of course, fashioned by hand. The rock-crystal balls used for divination are obtained, after preforming, by grinding and polishing with a conically shaped instrument that has an abrasive surface inside the cone.

dimensions) are cut mechanically, in series. Rectangular parallelepipeds are sawn from the stone to dimensions corresponding to the two principal diameters and the thickness desired for the cabochons and are then glued atop each other. The prism angles are rounded, and the stones attain a preliminary oval prism shape. Each oval slab then becomes a cabochon by abrasion of one of

Faceting

Origins

Lapidaries have known for ages how to produce a planar surface on a stone—one need only look at ancient intaglios engraved in a planar slab. However, the creation of regularly distributed planar facets on a crystal—thereby totally changing its aspect—does not seem to be much more than ten centuries old. Indeed, colored stones cut "en table" (into tablets) have been used in jewelry only since the thirteenth century, and they slightly predate diamond cutting. It was, perhaps, around the twelfth century that the necessary tools —horizontal metallic wheels, very planar, holding an abrasive—were developed, but they did not evolve significantly until the twentieth century.

A large planar facet makes a stone look more showy, because of the brilliant reflection of light on this mirror, or "table." It is nevertheless necessary to limit the size of this facet, with other inclined facets, to make it stand out, and that is the role of the four inclined "flats," which make the table a rectangle.

Of course, this faceting is complemented on the other side either by a large facet or by four inclined facets, just as on the visible side. It rapidly became clear that facets should be multiplied to increase a stone's brilliance, a concept that progressively led to an optical body reflecting back to the observer the maximum amount of incident light.

When it comes to diamond, the difficulty is that it can be abraded only by itself, and only in certain directions. Until the beginning of the sixteenth century, only rough diamond crystals were used in jewelry. Regular octahedrons, called "naive points," were particularly sought, and it is possible that the shape of some crystals was improved by cleavage.

These naive points, or "writing diamonds," were set in jewelry for a long time, as illustrated by the eleven diamond necklaces belonging to Francis I, who is credited with inscribing *"Toute femme varie"* ("All women vary") with diamond on a window of the castle at Chambord. Dodecahedrons and triangular slabs were also set in jewelry pieces. The improvement of horizontal wheels most certainly made it possible to wear out the points of octahedral crystals, which became "tables," and the octahedron edges or the dodecahedral faces, which became *diamants en losanges* ("lozenge diamonds"), *diamants taillés à facettes* ("diamonds cut with facets"), or *diamants taillés à pointe* ("diamonds cut in points"). These last often derived from a chipped octahedron repaired by obliquely polishing the octahedral face and were

Dutch painting from the nineteenth century depicting a diamond-cutting factory. Sirakian collection, Paris.

Rose-cut diamonds.

then called *poinctes faites* ("manufactured points").

Because faceting made the stone more brilliant, it became successful, and diamantaire guilds were organized in Venice, Paris, and Bruges. More than a hundred shapes were created.

It was in Bruges, in the second half of the fifteenth century, that Louis de Berquen was said to have lived. According to the Parisian jeweler Robert de Berquen (who, in 1668, claimed to be his descendant), his ancestor invented diamond cutting in 1476. However, no trace of this Lodewijk van Berckem has been found. It seems that he existed only in the imagination of his alleged descendant, who was anxious to increase his own prestige. In addition, diamond cutting predates this "invention" by at least 150 years.

A 16.66-carat briolette-cut diamond, a faceting style derived from Mazarin's double rose cut. Fred creation, Paris.

Diamond sawing. The position of the steel ball determines the pressure with which the diamond is pressed against the saw blade. Photo: De Beers.

At the end of the fifteenth or the beginning of the sixteenth century, diamond-cutting workshops perfected the rose cut, producing a shape reminiscent of a rosebud. Triangular facets in multiples of three, are cut symmetrically to produce a dome shape on a planar surface, originally a cleavage plane. Cardinal Mazarin (1602–61), who was credited with this invention, was essentially a collector who encouraged the art of faceting. He was probably the originator of the "double cut," as seen on the Florentin, a 139.5-carat yellow diamond (lost in 1918), which had triangular facets on both sides, based on a ninefold symmetry. Mazarin donated his eighteen diamonds, including the Sancy (55.23 carats, appraised at 600,000 pounds in 1691) to the French crown.

At the beginning of the eighteenth century, the geometrical pattern of facets that corresponds to the brilliant cut still in use was introduced. It was attributed during the nineteenth century to a Venetian by the name of Vincenzo Peruzzi, although his existence is historically questionable. It was, rather, the result of the evolution of the facet cut, which continued until the mid-twentieth century, with the perfect rounding of the stone and a change in thickness (and therefore proportions).

Diamond Cutting

Despite its extreme hardness—it can be scratched only by itself—diamond is easier to cut than a colored stone. Although a gem cutter can become a diamond cutter without any major difficulty, the reverse is not true. The diamond cutter determines the direction of the symmetry elements of the diamond to be cut and the position of the inclusions in the crystal. (To do so, he may have to "open" the stone on the wheel by polishing a couple of small "windows" on one or two of its sides.) Once he has defined the shape of the optical body(ies) he wants to cut, the diamond cutter preforms them by cleaving, sawing, and bruting, before actually faceting the stone.

Cleaving is the act of splitting the crystal along a plane perpendicular to the threefold axis (that is, parallel to the octahedral faces). After beginning the cleavage by making a deep groove with another diamond, the cleaver inserts a metal blade into the groove and gives a sharp blow with a wooden mallet. This very delicate operation is almost never done nowadays, and the profession of cleaver is in danger of extinction.

Sawing is cutting the diamond in two, by wearing it along a plane (to be the table of the future faceted diamond) perpendicular to a twofold-symmetry axis (that is, perpendicular to a cube or dodecahedron face). It is done with a thin circular blade of phosphorous copper, charged with diamond powder bound with olive oil. Diamond can be sawed only along the two directions indicated above. To avoid this constraint, a laser saw has recently been developed, but it is not commonly used. Despite all precautions, internal strain in diamond crystals, especially around inclusions, is such that about 1 percent of the stones burst during sawing. Consequently, stones that are almost colorless and extremely clean are rarely sawed but are generally worked directly by abrasion on a wheel (despite a lower final weight).

Bruting is the process of shaping the sawed diamond by rubbing it against another diamond. The diamond to be bruted is set at the end of a horizontal axle (driven by an electric engine); the bruting diamond is firmly secured, to shave off the parts protruding from the desired round outline. The bruting of an important stone or a fancy shape (heart, pear) is done on a wheel. There are now machines that automatically round the diamond by giving it a polished girdle.

Faceting itself is the act of grinding the diamond on a porous cast-iron wheel that has tiny grooves charged with diamond dust in olive oil. The diamond cutter's wheel, or *scaife,* has two zones: a cutting zone, where the diamond is "scraped" to remove material, and a polishing zone, where the facet just shaped is polished (with a finer grit) by removing the irregularities that result from cutting. Today driven electrically, the scaife was powered during the eighteenth century by the diamond cutter's wife. The diamond to be faceted or polished is held either by tin solder filling a small cup or by mechanical clamps. This *dop* (mechanical or with solder) is held on a *tang* (a piece of wood or metal) by strong copper wire; the tang rests on two points on the desk, in which the wheel is mounted, and the facet to be cut rests against the rotating wheel (3,000 rpm). All the famous "hands" in the world carefully adjust the angle of the stone to the wheel by bending the copper wire. However, an adjustable dop holder has been developed to allow work in series. The master cutter polishes the table and the first bezel facet, and the other cutters polish the other facets (enabling a faster cutting process, which is sometimes detrimental to the final result). Automated machines for cutting small stones ("mêlée") now produce acceptable results, if they are properly adjusted initially and are controlled during the cutting.

A facet can be ground or polished properly only in the direction along which elementary particles of diamond can be removed from the stone. For a repair, this direction, or grain of the stone, easy to find during the original cutting, must be recog-

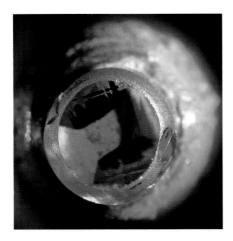

The first steps of a round brilliant. From left to right: bruted diamond, "four square," "eight square." The work shown is from the diamond-cutting section of the Private Technical School of Jewelry and Goldsmithery in Paris.

nized by the diamond cutter, who is helped by the polishing marks always visible in reflected light. There are three types of diamonds, named according to their orientation after bruting: the "four-point," with a table parallel to a cube face; the "two-point," with a table parallel to a dodecahedron face; and the "three-point," with the table very close to an octahedron face (it is difficult to grind and polish a true octahedron face, which has a tendency to wear out the wheel without being worn—it may stay for a month on the wheel without being significantly abraded).

To produce the faceted cut called a "brilliant cut," the diamond cutter, after cutting the table, cuts around it four "coins," which are the main crown facets, and then the corresponding "pavilion mains" on the pavilion. After obtaining this "four square," he puts bezel facets between the coins and other pavilion mains between the existing ones (coins are indistinguishable from bezels after cutting, and the term *bezel* is commonly used for both types of facets). When this "eight square" is produced (for diamonds smaller than 0.03 carat, it is left as is and called, therefore, 8/8), he may either grind the edges between the principal facets and obtain a 16/16 (for small stones up to 0.03 carat) or produce "star" facets on the crown side by polishing off the edges of the table and placing on the edges of the stone, on both sides, small triangles called upper and lower girdle facets by polishing the angles of the eight-square facets. He then obtains a solid with fifty-seven facets: on the crown side, the table, eight stars, eight bezels, and sixteen upper girdle facets; on the pavilion side, eight pavilion mains and sixteen lower girdle facets. The circular edge, which can be left bruted or can be faceted, is called the girdle; occasionally, the pavilion summit can be ground and transformed in a tiny fifty-eighth facet, called the culet, to avoid chipping. In addition to a round shape, the diamond cutter can obtain various fancy

shapes with the brilliant cut: the marquise, the pear, the heart, the oval, and the cushion, for example.

The faceting of a step cut, such as the emerald cut, which is derived from the old *en table* (tablet) cut, proceeds using a similar set of operations: polishing the table, then the four major steps on the crown and pavilion sides (which produces a rectangular *baguette*), then the four corners at each point, then the edges between the table or the pavilion and the edge (girdle) of the stone. The optical body created classically has fifty (or fifty-eight) facets, that is, the table and eight times three steps on the crown side, eight times three steps and a culet on the pavilion side (and eight girdle facets). Small side stones are also step-cut (in a lozenge, triangle, or baguette shape).

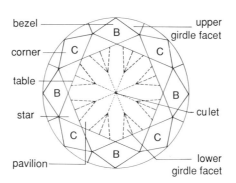

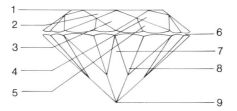

(1) Table; (2) Star; (3) Bezel; (4) "Corner" or bezel; (5) Upper girdle facet; (6) Girdle; (7) Pavilion main; (8) Lower girdle facets; (9) Culet.

A 2.07-carat "four-point" brilliant cut. The table (1) is surrounded by eight triangular star facets (2), four bezels and four "corners" (3 and 4), and sixteen upper girdle facets (5). The girdle (6) may be faceted or simply bruted. The eight pavilion mains on the pavilion side can be seen through the table.

Proportions Facet angles are chosen to concentrate the maximum amount of light in the stone and reflect it back to the observer. The older, thicker cuts have a large culet, which indeed plays the role of a facet for someone looking at the stone obliquely. These stones show a lot of fire, because light has a longer optical path, but, face up, the large culet looks like a black hole. The modern cuts, less thick and with a larger table, spread the light more than the old cuts but have less brilliance. Today's ideal proportions vary according to the desired final characteristics.

About 50 percent of the weight of a rough diamond is lost in faceting. A good diamond cutter always saves as much of the original crystal as possible and generally leaves the girdle next to the bezel, as a remnant of the original crystal. This leftover, called a "natural," often triangular, may show some surface features, such as etching pits or growth features (some cutters polish them).

The large diamond-cutting centers are presently Antwerp, New York, Tel Aviv (Ramat Gan), and Bombay (Surat). Smaller centers are in Brazil (Belo Horizonte, Rio de Janeiro), the Netherlands (Amsterdam), and the Soviet Union. Cutting shops are also found in South Africa, the Central African Republic, and Australia. In France and Germany, a minor activity takes place in, respectively, Saint-Claude (Jura) and Idar-Oberstein. In Paris some renowned craftsmen improve important stones by recutting them.

Colored Stones Faceting

As with diamond, the faceting of a colored stone starts with the study of the rough, in order to determine the crystallo-

A 35-carat cushion-cut diamond. Through the table, one can see the culet surrounded by eight pavilion mains. Chaumet creation, Paris.

graphic directions, the position of inclusions, and especially the color distribution. This last characteristic is most important in deciding the position of the future table, which is obtained by sawing with a diamond saw, a circular steel blade loaded with diamond dust (loading the saw with diamond, done in the past with a small hammer that drove the bort dust into the steel, is now most often done industrially. The shape of the stone is then preformed on a diamond-loaded copper or steel wheel rotating at 1,800 rpm for corundum; a Carborundum-loaded wheel is used for other colored stones.

In contrast to the operations performed on a diamond, the sawing and preforming of colored stones are done under a thin jet of water, which prevents heating and washes away the material ground from the stone to avoid its accumulation.

Faceting is done on a copper or brass wheel, called a *lap,* turning at 1,000 rpm. It is covered with diamond grit and kept wet by steadily dripping water. The stone is preformed by hand, without a dop. It is then glued to the end of a stick. This stick is held at a constant angle during the cut by fitting it into a ''jamb peg'' (a block, the shape of an inverted cone, with a series of holes, mounted on a vertical post next to the lap). Two technical improvements, made in the nineteenth century, may help the lapidary's work but are rarely used by the best cutters, since they require detailed adjustments perceived as a waste of time. The dop arm makes it possible to turn the stone exactly one eighth of a turn, and mechanical faceting heads hold the stone in an exact position on the lap. Today machines sold to amateurs have numerous gear systems with numbered dial controls to control the angle between the facet to be cut and the table (and therefore between the facet and the lap). However, the numerous adjustments required prevent the speed needed in the precise work for which French cutters from Paris and the Saint-Claude area are famous: adjusting stones on a mounting to produce an invisible setting.

The rest of the cutting process is similar to that for diamonds. After placing the table, the cutter puts eight bezel facets around it (principal facets of the crown); then he polishes eight stars by grinding the edges of the table down to a third of the bezels and then adds sixteen upper girdle facets (eight left and eight right) by grinding off the edges of the bezels. He thus obtains a crown similar to that of a diamond brilliant cut. For the pavilion, the lapidary generally uses a step cut, consisting of flats set all around the stone. For certain gems, such as emeralds, tourmalines, and spodumenes, the crown is preferably step-cut. Colorless crystals, often used as diamond

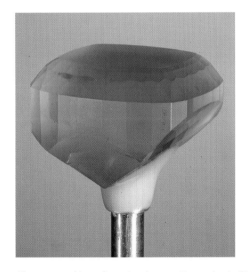 

The steps used in cutting colored stones: Top: *a chunk of Brazilian citrine;* Bottom left: *stone glued to the end of a dop;* Bottom right: *the finished stone.*

substitutes, are generally cut with facets on the pavilion, but the pavilion mains are recut. This is the case for zircons, especially, and for colorless topaz.

In addition to the classic shapes (such as cushion, oval, round, marquise, pear, square, ''emerald cut''), colored gems may be cut in an infinite variety of forms, depending on the intended use or desired special effects. Each gem must be considered individually by the lapidary. Also, although he uses an abrasive much harder than the stone he cuts, he must take cleavage planes into account, so that he does not split them during faceting (in which case the stone simply shatters). Topaz, fluorite, brazilianite, kunzite, and feldspars require considerable attention. Opal is worked on a lap covered with tripoli (silica powder).

A gem-cutting workshop in Paris.

Projects for a brooch, workshop designs. Right: *Cartier 1955;* Left: *Cartier 1960.*

maximum amount of light toward the observer, the light "loading" color as it traverses the gem. Thus, proportions depend on the crystal's index of refraction. For example, a gem with a low index of refraction must be cut thicker. A gem is considered well cut when, held on the fingers, it obscures the fingers completely (in other words, when one can see no "window" in the gem). This is possible only for crystals with a high index of refraction. For the others, such as quartz, the cutter must compromise, helped by the intensity of the light absorption by colored stones (such as amethyst). Like the diamond cutter, the lapidary often leaves a trace of the original crystal, a tiny "witness" called the "natural," often in the form of an irregular cavity on the stone's pavilion. Between 45 and 55 percent of the weight of a rough colored stone is commonly lost in cutting.

A great many colored-stone cutting centers are in Bangkok, where there are more than 200,000 lapidaries. Other centers are in Korea, Japan (at Kōfu, near Fujiyama), Taiwan, and Colombia; in Europe Idar-Oberstein is an important cutting center.

Cutting Synthetic Stones

Synthetic stones are worth only what it costs to grow them; so the mass yield is secondary, unlike natural stones. Here a yield of 5 to 10 percent is considered good (with the exception of "luxury" synthetics, often grown in flux). The crystals to be cut are sawed in cubes, cylinders, or parallelepipeds, then glued to the end of a mechanical dop on a long rod that may hold as many as sixty crystals. All dops are driven by this rod, so the sixty dops are turned together with a single turn. The results are reasonable, although the girdle is often too thick.

The Importance of Cut to a Gem's Value

A gem or ornamental stone has a higher value if it shows more life, if its shape is attractive. Artistry sets the prices of cameos, intaglios, statuettes, and other carvings.

For cabochons and faceted stones, the attractiveness of the shape and the life of the stone are taken into account. An asteriated gem drops in value if the star is not centered. A faceted stone has a higher value if it has more life, brilliance, and depth to it. A peculiar shape may be appreciated by only a small number of people. In all cases where the cut could be improved to give more life to the stone, the gem is considered both in its present state and as it would look after recutting.

As with diamonds, polishing a faceted colored stone may just involve polishing off the irregularities left after cutting until an optically smooth surface is obtained. Such irregularities may also result from a superficial melting of the gem, caused by rubbing against the wheel, which produces a microscopic glazed layer called a "Beilby layer" (such gems, for example, peridot, are very difficult to polish, since they tend to "grease" the wheel). This is why polishing is done at low speed (200 rpm) in a direction that closes the fractures. The lap is sometimes driven by the lapidary's left hand, so that he can better "feel" the progress made. Corundum (ruby and sapphire) is polished on a cast-iron lap charged with grit; spinel and chrysoberyl, on a brass lap with emery; topaz, on a tin lap with emery; quartz, on a lead lap with tin oxide; opal, on a wooden lap covered with a silk cloth soaked with tin or iron oxide. As with diamond, the optical body must transmit the

Evaluating a Gem or Ornamental Stone

For any given mineral species, the attractiveness and therefore the value of the stone can be evaluated by analyzing its color, carat weight, clarity, and cut. These value factors are abbreviated as the four Cs. However, these four variables are not independent, and the eye plays an important role as well. Of two gems that can be described in the same way, one always has a charm that makes it infinitely superior to the other. In addition, if one considers modifying a gem's appearance, it is clear that one value factor may be compromised for another. A recut obviously means a loss of mass, but it may enhance either the clarity, by elimination of a lateral inclusion (sometimes at the expense of life or symmetry), or the color (it is, however, quite rare for the first lapidary who cut the stone to have "placed" the color improperly; therefore, there is always a risk involved in recutting a colored stone). It may also affect the life of the stone (but again, one must be careful not to affect the way the color is "placed").

The value of a gem results from an optimal balance among these four factors, a subjective judgment that depends as much on the individual as on fashion trends by which he or she is influenced.

Synthetics and Simulants

Imitating nature, in an effort to understand and control it, is a characteristic trait of human behavior. The domestication of fire, over five hundred millennia ago, and especially, the ability to produce fire, learned about fifty millennia ago, allowed considerable progress in the imitation of gems. As early as the Solutrean epoch (twentieth to eighteenth millennia), a thermal treatment was performed on silex at about 575°F (300°C) to make it more homogeneous and give it a finer grain, in order to fabricate the famous blades called laurel leaves.

Ceramics, Enamels, and Glasses

One of the most ancient necklaces from the fifth millennium contains a superficially vitrified clay ball, probably intended to imitate obsidian. As early as the fourth millennium, steatite, vitrified in blue to imitate lapis lazuli, was used in the still-famous blue ornamental ceramics from Egypt and Mesopotamia. Soon ceramics were used on a quasi-industrial scale for the manufacture of various pottery and the production of amulets.

Enameling techniques progressed with the development of cloisonné, and, much later, in the tenth century A.D., of champlevé, a process intended to produce the

Tutankhamen mask in gold and blue enamel. Cairo Museum. Photo: Giraudon.

Glass mold from the first century A.D. of the print of the intaglio depicting Julia, daughter of the Roman emperor Titus. M. De Bry collection.

a solely decorative purpose were intended to imitate the Sumerian cylinder seals, glass pendants with alternating layers of light and dark glass imitated banded agate, earrings were made of massive colored glass. Glass manufacture served both decorative and utilitarian purposes, especially in Upper Mesopotamia and in the Levant countries. Glass is produced by melting a mixture of quartz, potash, and soda (with metallic oxides to give color), forming a paste, which has been molded since its inception (see, for example, the scarabs of the New Egyptian Empire). In Roman times molding techniques were used to duplicate cameos and intaglios, and Pliny the Elder already considered the identification of such imitations difficult. Most of the glass used in jewelry is molded from a paste, hence, they are often called *paste* in English.

In the Middle Ages, the *crystalliers* were involved in the manufacture of glass, and the Venetian glass became famous. Indeed, the Venetians created the *millefiori* ("thousand leaves") in the nineteenth century, a true mosaic of colors in which glass itself is a work of art. Most famous were the paperweight balls, erroneously called *sulfures*, collected by the French novelist Colette. Venetians also invented aventurine glass, glistening with copper platelets (see AVENTURESCENCE, earlier in part 1). During the classical period (around 1750), *strass* was developed by the Strasbourg chemist Georges Frédéric Stras (1700–73). Research to produce a closer resemblance between glass and the gems it imitated increased, which eventually led to the introduction of special glasses that were appropriate for multiple modern industrial uses. The glass used today in jewelry can be divided into "flint" or "crown," depending on the presence or absence of lead. In France, lead glass, with a higher index of refraction and dispersion, cannot be called crystal, to avoid confusion with quartz, also called rock crystal. (However, lead glass used for tableware —glasses, vases—is called *crystalline* if it contains 17 percent lead, *crystal* if it contains 17 to 24 percent lead, and *supercrystal* if it contains more than 24 percent lead.)

The proliferation of fakes has always worried governments, and many edicts and laws have been issued (in vain) to forbid their use. In 1355, a law in France prohibited the setting of glass in gold doublets for sale or wear. In 1636 the king of England tried to prevent court members from wearing fake gems, "which frequency is a shame to the real ones." In 1447, in Antwerp, "Nobody [could] buy, sell, pawn, or give any fake stone, or [he would] be fined twenty-five ducats, including a third for the sovereign, a third for the town, and a third for the informant." In the eighteenth century, Empress Maria Theresa of Austria tried in vain to make the manufacture of strass illegal.

appearance of inlays at a lower cost. Nevertheless, it was not until the middle of the second millennium that glass was manufactured as such. As early as the Eighteenth and Nineteenth Dynasties of Egypt (1400–1300 B.C.), glass was used in jewelry as a simulant as well as for its own virtues. Smooth blue glass cylinders set on a ring for

Stones Treated to Imitate Other Stones

The modification of gem materials with dyes or paints has been practiced since prehistoric times. The only goal of such treatments was apparently adornment. Most of the shells worn by prehistoric man were dyed, mostly red. During the third millennium, the jewelry manufacturers in Ur would locally discolor chunks of carnelian with an alkali and then heat treat the stones, so that they would resemble agate. Dyes also were commonly used to make certain stones displayed in the temples fluorescent, inspiring profound veneration by the faithful. In Rome the modification of materials became a true craze: tortoise shell was made to look like precious woods, and the treatment of agate was common. Today porous stones are impregnated with dyes to make them look like the more valued ornamental stones; examples are jasper dyed blue with potassium ferrocyanide to replace lapis, marble dyed red to resemble coral, and chalcedony dyed green to imitate chrysoprase. When immersed in a hot colored solution, rock crystal cracks, cracks fill with the dye, which was originally red, explaining the name *rubace* given to this gem material. Now the dye most commonly used is green, to imitate emerald.

Doublets and Triplets

The use of assembled stones is probably quite old; Pliny the Elder mentioned it. However, only when faceted gems became popular and the poor hardness of the imitations' facets became a problem did doublets and triplets become common. A quartz slab was glued to the imitation to protect its table, creating the first quartz-and-colored-glass doublet, sold in the middle of the fifteenth century. At that time, a forger by the name of Zocolino was already assembling two rock-crystal slabs with colored glue and selling his fabrications in closed gold settings. It was noticed that almandite garnet would bond to a drop of colored glass as the glass solidified, and manufacturers began producing garnet-and-glass doublets, in which a thin garnet slab was used for the table (because it was harder to scratch) and the bulk of the imitation was colored glass. Indeed, colorless garnet-and-glass doublets were produced in the nineteenth century to imitate diamond. Throughout the nineteenth century and well into the twentieth, garnet-and-glass doublets were very common in all colors. One need only reflect light on the crown facets of the older ones to see clearly the garnet-glass junction. In the more modern doublets, the crown has been cut very flat, so that the garnet slab reaches the girdle and the garnet-glass junction is hidden in the bruted part of the stone. If the doublet is intended to imitate sapphire or ruby, a garnet slab that shows rutile inclusions, reminiscent of "silk" in those corundums, is selected. Also during the nineteenth century, a nacre (mother-of-pearl) half-sphere was glued to another nacre half-sphere covered with nacre layers deposited by a pearl-bearing mollusk; these cultured-pearl ancestors were misleadingly sold as "Japanese pearls." Still produced today, these doublets are generally called *mabe* (the Japanese name for the mollusk most often used to create the nacre layer). Since the beginning of the nineteenth century, lapidary industry in the Jura, in eastern France, which has specialized since the eighteenth century in the fabrication of various imitations, has produced doublets using two colorless quartz slabs glued together with a green cement along the girdle plane: the slab chosen to be the crown was clean, while that selected to be the pavilion had a number of fingerprints, reminiscent of the "garden" of emeralds. The green cement gives the imitation its color. Such composites are still produced today, sometimes offered to tourists in Colombia under the name of "semiprecious emeralds." Doublets of a similar style were made with light aquamarine around 1930 and with colorless synthetic spinel around 1950, but they were not very convincing.

However, some triplets were rather convincing. Around 1965, light aquamarine–green cement–flawed tourmaline triplets were sold under the name *Smaryl;* in about 1968 some were made with nearly-

Siberian emerald–green enamel–Siberian emerald triplet.

Quartz–green enamel–quartz triplet. Top: *rough material;* Bottom: *faceted imitation.*

Garnet-and-glass doublet. Rough material on the right; faceted imitation on the left.

colorless Siberian emerald cut with a thick girdle, sawed, and reassembled with green enamel along the girdle plane. An assembled opal, prepared with a black cement, an opal cut in a flat cabochon, and a substrate of common opal, jasper, chalcedony, or glass, appeared in 1945 and was then quite popular. Since 1960 this imitation has been replaced by a quadruplet, made of a transparent quartz cabochon acting as a loupe, on top of a thin opal slab glued with an opaque black cement on a substrate of jasper, chalcedony, or glass. Some doublets imitating diamond were produced only in small quantities, such as, in about 1930, the assembly in a bezel setting of a slab and a "cone" of diamond, forming respectively the crown and pavilion of a "single" stone, to produce a larger gem (this method also allowed the use of flat rough diamonds). Around 1970 some assembled diamond-and-glass, diamond-and-YAG, diamond-and-Fabulite, and synthetic-corundum-and-Fabulite doublets had an ephemeral commercial career. (See DIAMOND, in part 2, for a discussion of the various imitations.) The reflections of the crown facets on the mirror formed by the assembly plane of these imitations made them easy to recognize, even in a bezel setting or a closed mounting.

Doublets comprising a crown of green sapphire exhibiting chevron-shaped inclusions or Siam ruby showing obvious twin planes and a pavilion of synthetic ruby or sapphire have been set in silver and sold since 1970 to naive tourists, especially in Bangkok.

Reconstructed Stones

Sometimes mineral powder or scraps are heated or mixed with a binding agent to produce a larger solid mass. Numerous reconstructed rocks, mimicking marble and granite, for example, have been produced

Plastic-impregnated American turquoise.

since the eighteenth century for statuary; such imitations were already known at the beginning of the Christian era (when sarcophagus in plaster was used to imitate true stone). Small amber chunks are commonly agglomerated through simple melting (using pressed amber and melted amber) or incorporated in a synthetic plastic resin. Fragments of turquoise are occasionally bound with plastic.

Plastics

In the past plastic materials were animal or plant materials (such as horn or amber) worked at low temperatures (212°F, or 100°C). In 1869 John Hyatt commercialized the process for making the first plastic, celluloid, in the United States; Alexander Parkes had already produced a form of celluloid by reacting camphor with cellulose nitrate in England in 1855. As early as 1900, Galalithe was obtained by mixing formaldehyde with milk casein. In 1906, Bakelite was born, produced by reaction of formaldehyde with phenol.

These plastics were used in the first half of the twentieth century to imitate organic materials and even stones (cameo imitations manufactured by molding). The plastics industry has grown enormously since 1925; it basically provides products for various industrial uses, but some of its products —polystyrenes, polyamides, polyesters— are also widely used in costume jewelry to imitate various stones. They are beginning to be used as gem materials proper in modern jewelry (plastic-wood-diamond assemblies, for example).

Synthetic Stones and Crystals

By the end of the eighteenth century, scientific methods had advanced far enough to permit the chemical analysis of a number of compounds; carbon was found in diamond, beryllium and chromium in beryl. The path was then clear for the first attempts at crystal growth, which began in the mid-nineteenth century: millimeter-size synthetic emerald crystals were produced by Ebelmen in 1848 and centimeter-size synthetic ruby crystals by Edmond Frémy in 1877.

Crystals can be grown either by random nucleation or by crystallization on a seed, using one of three types of fluids: (1) A simple melt resulting from the fusion of the material (if it does not decompose spontaneously, a condition that prevents its use in growing "incongruent" crystals such as beryl); (2) Concentration in an anhydrous solution or flux; (3) Concentration in an aqueous solution. The last technique is often closest to natural formation.

Crystallization from a Melt

The first synthetic crystals, sold in 1885, were red corundums fabricated from their melt in several stages. Alumina powder mixed with chromium oxide was melted on a refractory substrate by oxyhydrogen burners, forming a droplet at its top that crystallized during cooling. This solid was then turned upside down, to melt the lower part and obtain a globular monocrystal. To increase the crystal's size, alumina powder was then poured onto the globule via a platinum tube with two or three oxyhydrogen burners, set on each side of the tube to lower internal strain. Intended to mimic natural rubies, these crystals were sold, already faceted, under the name "Geneva rubies"; they fooled a few late-nineteenth-century jewelers.

August Verneuil, who had been the late Frémy's assistant, immediately understood the financial rewards of such a process and conceived the idea of adding the powder to the oxygen flow of the oxyhydrogen burners. The Verneuil process, developed in 1891, requires a "flame fusion" apparatus, still in use today: the powder melts in the torch's flame—reaching a temperature of 2,100°C (3,810°F)—and the melted droplet falls on the seed where it crystallizes. A refractory muffle surrounds the growing crystal to prevent thermal shocks. A peduncle or stalk forms and rapidly widens; crystallization ceases when the top part of the crystal becomes too hot to allow it to continue. Originally, in 1902, the refractory seed holder was fixed, so that the shape of each crystal was similar to that of preceding globules: it was thus commonly called a Verneuil *boule* ("ball"). Later the height of the "furnace" was increased and the *boule* was progressively lowered during crystal growth, so that the synthetic crystal took on an ever slimmer cylindrical shape, which, with the peduncle, resembled a bottle. Today Verneuil bottles can reach 3 feet in length and 4 inches in width. Verneuil synthetic corundums, first only red (colored with chromium), then also blue (colored with iron and titanium), were, from 1911, a great commercial success in jewelry as well as clock and watch making, where they were used as pivots in place of the natural rubies or flat rose-cut diamonds used in eighteenth-century watches. In 1913 Verneuil produced 2,000 kilograms (4,400 pounds) synthetic ruby and 1,200 kilograms (2,600 pounds) of synthetic sapphire annually. Soon other companies were formed to meet the growing demand, especially by the watch makers, who used the corundum to protect the movement in place of the "portrait-diamonds" (cut as flat parallel windows) sometimes used for this purpose in better eighteenth-century watches. Today 200 tons of flame-fusion synthetic

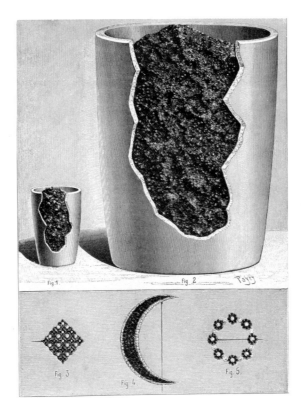

Original etching from Edmond Frémy's "La synthèse du rubis" (The synthesis of Rubies), Paris, 1891.

The crucible (30 by 30 cm) used by Frémy to grow synthetic ruby. Ruby forms on the walls of the crucible from an alumina and chromium oxide melt in the presence of lead oxide. National Higher School of Mines, Paris.

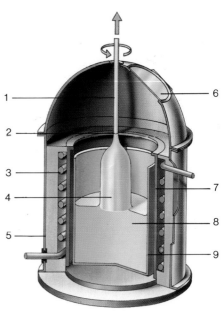

Czochralski pulling method: (1) rotating holder; (2) seed crystal; (3) electric resistance; (4) growing crystal; (5) thermal insulation; (6) window; (7) refractory crucible; (8) melted components of the crystal; (9) platinum crucible.

"Verneuil" or flame-fusion process. The crystallized and incandescent "boule," or "bottle," is seen through the aperture of the refractory muffle. Djevahirdjian company, Switzerland.

corundum are produced annually, primarily in the French and Swiss Alps. Synthetic spinels of various colors are commonly used for costume jewelry. Strontium titanate (Fabulite) and rutile (Titania) crystals, intended to imitate diamond, are also grown by this technique (over 300 kilograms [600 pounds] were produced in 1948).

In 1918 Czochralski developed a continuous crystallization technique that involved lowering a seed onto the surface of its melt, then raising it progressively during crystal growth. The crystal is thus "pulled" off its melt, hence, the name of the technique: "crystal pulling." This process enabled the growth of optically pure threadlike crystals or cylindrical crystals. When the technology for solid-state lasers developed, it became necessary to use crystals in which light would not encounter inclusions or excessive strain; the Czochralski process, more delicate and expensive than the Verneuil process, was adopted for the production of these industrial synthetic corundums. Many special fabrications adapted to the creation of various coherent lights were undertaken, such as YAG (yttrium aluminum garnet) and Linobat (lithium niobate). Jewelry is the ultimate outlet for excess production. However, only YAG is commercialized in large quantities as a diamond simulant because of its transparency, hardness, isotropy, stable lack of color, and fairly low cost. From 1968 to 1978, up to 8 tons were produced annually, sold under a variety of fancy names: Diemlite, Gemolyte, Burmalite. Crystals of GGG (gallium gadolinium garnet), which have a tendency to become yellowish in daylight, and KTN (potassium tantalo-niobate), which scratched easily (with a hardness of 6), had only limited commercial success.

A very clean synthetic crystal can be obtained via bulk crystallization of the melt, using a slow progression of crystallization conditions from the bottom of the crucible to the top of the melt. Only crystals for industry are grown by this Bridgman method, which is more expensive than the others. However, a modification, called "skull-melting," has been developed to produce cubic zirconium oxide, or cubic zirconia, first to meet the needs of the laser industry and then, since 1976, as diamond simulant. Zirconium oxide, monoclinic at room temperature, cubic above 2,000°C (3,630°F), melts at 2,750°C (4,980°F). When cold, it is an insulator; but when hot, it is a conductor, increasingly so as the temperature rises. Mixed with calcium or yttrium oxide (to stabilize the crystal in its cubic structure, as natural zirkelite), zirconium oxide powder is sintered at 1,800°C (3,270°F) in a cylindrical shape and then used as a secondary circuit in a transformer; the induced electric current melts the inside of the cylinder (by the Joule effect), whereas the outer surface acts as a crucible in which cubic zirconium oxide crystallizes. This material, one of the most convincing diamond simulants, is generally grown for that sole purpose, at the rate of 12 tons per year. It is sold under various names, including Blue River, Diemlite, Djevalite, C.Z., and Zirconia.

Flux Growth

Silicates are best dissolved with alkalis. It was therefore natural to think about growing them from such a solution, brought to saturation. This is how Ebelmen produced the first synthetic emeralds in 1848. Other laboratory experiments followed, without commercial application, however. The work begun by I. G. Farben in 1911 in Germany led in 1938 to the commercialization of a synthetic emerald called "Igmerald," but the process was abandoned in 1942. The true commercialization

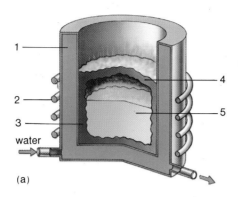

(a)

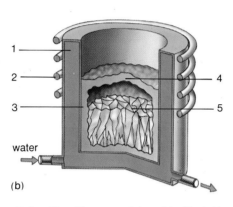

(b)

Skull melting: (1) water-cooled crucible; (2) electric resistance; (3) sintered self-crucible; (4) porous crust; (5) melted zirconium oxide (a) and cubic zirconia crystals (b).

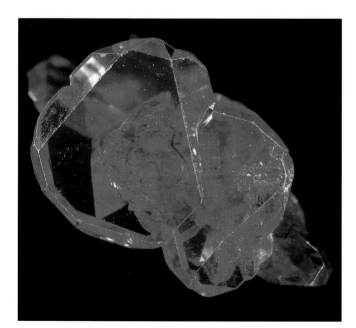

Synthetic ruby and emerald grown by the flux method. Length: 0.6 cm. Chatham Inc., San Francisco.

supply of crystalline components

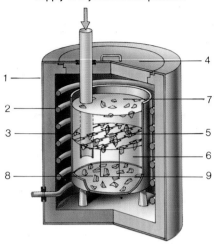

Hydrothermal growth: (1) thermal insulation; (2) electric resistance; (3) platinum crucible; (4) removable lid; (5) platinum holders; (6) solvent; (7) nondissolved crystalline components (less dense than the solvent); (8) nondissolved crystalline components (more dense than the solvent); (9) growing crystal.

of synthetic emerald started in the United States in 1946, where after fifteen years of experiments in San Francisco, Carroll Chatham developed a process to grow large, gem-quality monocrystals. These crystals were exclusively produced for the jewelry market, as were later all crystals grown by the flux method: synthetic emerald from Gilson (France) in 1964, Zerfass (Germany) in 1965, and Inamori (Japan) in 1977; synthetic ruby from Chatham in 1961 and Kashan (United States) in 1969; and synthetic alexandrite from Created Crystals (United States) in 1973. Indeed, such crystals, quite convincing to the jeweler, have no industrial use because they always contain growth accidents such as dislocations and flux material trapped in the fingerprints resulting from thermal shocks during growth. About 200 pounds of *flux* synthetic emerald made with the flux method are produced each year.

Microscopic diamond crystals are produced on an industrial scale under very high pressure (some thousands of atmospheres) from carbon dissolved in transition metals such as nickel and cobalt; they are widely used as abrasives, with an annual production of the order of 20 tons. In 1970 General Electric succeeded in growing a few gem-quality diamond crystals reaching 1 carat; the process, too expensive, was not further developed at the time. In 1985, however, Sumitomo Electric Industries, a Japanese company, marketed slabs of gem-quality yellow synthetic diamond grown by high-pressure technology, for electronic applications. In 1990 General Electric announced they were again producing transparent, near-colorless synthetic diamond macrocrystals for industrial purposes.

Hydrothermal Growth

Water is everywhere in the earth's crust, and crystals always form in its presence. The most beautiful ones are found in cavities created by water activity (in a broad sense): pneumatolytic emanations, pegmatites, hydrothermal veins, groundwater circulation, and the like. During the Second World War, a hydrothermal growth technique was developed to meet the demands of the telecommunications industry for perfect quartz monocrystals (700 tons are now produced each year). Thanks to a temperature gradient, a supercritical alkaline aqueous solution transports silica (present as powder or chunks) from the hot region of an autoclave to the cooler region, where a crystalline seed is "fed." The success of flux-grown synthetic emeralds prompted industrials familiar with hydrothermal growth to grow such gems too. In Austria Lechleitner produced faceted aquamarines covered by a thin layer of synthetic emerald in 1960. This product, called "Emerita," had an ephemeral commercial life. The Linde division of Union Carbide further developed this process and soon produced true synthetic crystals. Marketed beginning in 1965, these synthetic emeralds, too clean and therefore unconvincing, had only limited commercial distribution (the most important production was about 90 pounds in 1970). Union Carbide therefore decided to abandon synthetic crystals, selling its process and equipment in 1978 to a company that today produces and markets synthetic hydrothermal emeralds under the name "Regency."

Synthetic hydrothermal crystals intended as substitutes for natural stones, used by the jeweler only if they are limpid and clean, are also more convincing if their color-producing centers are identical to their natural counterparts. Such are synthetic amethysts and citrines grown in the Soviet Union since 1975. Their relatively high cost, however, makes it somewhat difficult to interest the public, since natural gems are only slightly more expensive.

At room temperature and pressure, an aqueous solution may be able to produce precipitates that, when sintered, can be substituted for the corresponding gem materials. Such is synthetic turquoise produced by Pierre Gilson since 1972. Similarly, a silica gel can allow identical microscopic silica spheres to form, which precipitate into compact regular structures; these have been sold as synthetic opal since 1974.

All crystals known to mineralogists have been synthesized in the laboratory, although sometimes only in microscopic sizes. Indeed, when a crystal grows by spontaneous nucleation, multiple nuclei create parasitic crystals, making it difficult to grow large cuttable monocrystals. Today the only mass-produced crystals are those needed for industrial applications (such as diamond and quartz) and those that can be substituted for valuable gems (rubies, emeralds, opals, for example).

Russian synthetic amethyst-citrine produced hydro thermally.

Chronology of the Major Jewelry Synthetics, Simulants, and Treatments

Date	Simulants and treatments	Synthetics
18,000 B.C.	Heat treatment of silex	
7000 B.C.	Ceramic	
6000 B.C.	Enamel	
5000 B.C.	Glass paste	
1500 B.C.	Glass	
Classical antiquity	Various dyes	
1300	Nacre buddhas	
1600	Imitation pearls (using *essence d'orient*); rubace	
1750	Quartz-glass doublets; strass	
1800	Doublets of half-cultured pearl and nacre: "mabe"	
1850	Colorless garnet-and-glass doublets	
1870	Celluloid	
1885		Burner-melted synthetic ruby ("Geneva ruby")
1900	Galalithe; quartz–green enamel–quartz triplets	
1902		Flame-fusion synthetic ruby (Verneuil)
1906	Bakelite	
1907		Flame-fusion cobalt synthetic sapphire (Verneuil)
1911		Flame-fusion iron-titanium synthetic sapphire (Verneuil)
1915		Cultured pearls with nacre nuclei
1920	Sintered phosphates imitating turquoise	Flame-fusion synthetic spinel (discovered in 1908—Verneuil)
1930	Beryl–green enamel–beryl triplets	
1935	Diamond–diamond doublets	
1938		"Igmerald" flux synthetic emerald
1945	Opal doublets	
1946	Irradiation	Chatham synthetic emerald
1947		Star synthetic corundums
1948		Synthetic rutile
1950	Synthetic spinel–enamel–synthetic spinel triplets	Tissue-nucleated cultured pearls
1953		Monocrystals of synthetic industrial diamond (Sweden)
1954	Sintered synthetic spinel, imitating lapis lazuli	
1955		Fabulite (strontium titanate)
1960	Quartz–opal–black cement–agate quadruplets; emerald overgrowth ("Symerald-Emerita")	
1964	"Neolite"-type sintered phosphates (turquoise and coral imitations)	Gilson synthetic emerald
1965	Tourmaline-beryl doublets ("Smaryl")	Synthetic hydrothermal emerald; flux synthetic ruby
1968	Emerald–green enamel–emerald triplets	YAG
1969	YAG-diamond doublets; Fabulite-diamond doublets	Soviet synthetic cobalt-blue quartz
1970	Sapphire–synthetic sapphire doublets; ruby–synthetic ruby doublets	1-carat synthetic diamond crystal (General Electric)
1971		Galliant (GGG)
1972	Laser drilling of diamond	Synthetic turquoise; synthetic alexandrite
1974	Plastic-impregnated turquoise	Synthetic opal
1975		Synthetic amethyst; synthetic citrine
1976	Iridescent glass "Slocum stone"; Gilson imitation coral	Synthetic cubic zirconia; synthetic lapis lazuli
1978	High-temperature heat treatment of corundums	
1980	Iridescent plastic; chatoyant glass "Catsteyte"	
1981	Diffusion-treated corundum; plastic imitation opal (Japan)	
1985		Macrocrystals of yellow synthetic diamond

Gem Identification

A refractometer with a glass hemisphere, from the end of the nineteenth century. Sorbonne collection.

To identify a gem, carved or faceted, involves determining, through its physical properties, and without destroying or damaging it, its mineral species, its composition, if it is a rock or of organic origin. Then one must demonstrate through the stone's unique crystallization features and other properties whether it is natural or synthetic and if it has been subjected to any kind of treatment. It is often possible to see with the naked eye if the stone has "life" and to compare to others to evaluate color, dichroism, and luster. However, one should not disdain the use of a few simple instruments:

- A *loupe* with a 10× magnification to identify composite stones (doublets, agglomerates), flame-fusion synthetics, some glasses, and certain products such as synthetic turquoise and opal, as well as to assess a gem's clarity.
- A *polariscope* to distinguish isotropic from anisotropic stones and, sometimes, to identify uniaxial stones among anisotropic stones.
- A *dichroscope* to observe pleocroic colors and to identify all colors in an anisotropic colored stone.
- A *refractometer* to determine the indices of refraction of a polished facet of a stone. By turning the stone's facet on the refractometer prism with monochromatic light shining through, the optical contact being provided by a drop of R.I. (refractive index) liquid, one can see one or two shadows moving up and down the scale, allowing the measurement of the gem's optical characteristics.
- A *palmer* to measure the stone's dimensions, in order to estimate the stone's mass with the help of standard tabulations in the case of diamond or to determine an approximate specific gravity by comparison with its actual mass for colored stones.
- A *portable balance* to measure the stone's mass.
- A longwave and, if possible, also a shortwave *ultraviolet lamp* (black light) to determine the luminescence produced under these radiations.
- A *hand-held spectroscope* to observe the absorption lines and bands in the visible range, often due to certain crystallochemical incidents (trace elements, dislocations, lattice vacancies).

All these instruments are often combined in a field kit, together with a stereoscopic microscope with at least 10× to 40× power, used to study inclusions, and with some S.G. (specific gravity) liquids, to measure specific gravity.

At home or in the lab, an accurate scale is useful for weighing gems. Most of the common gems can be identified with the instruments cited above, if properly used. If test results are inconclusive, it is necessary to call on a laboratory, where modern applied mineralogy techniques are available (radiography, X-ray diffraction, scanning electron microscope, infrared spectroscopy, and the like).

Classification

A 24.22-carat faceted aquamarine, the most common variety of beryl. F. A. Becker collection, Idar-Oberstein, Germany.

Minerals can be classified in a number of ways, depending on the user's interests. The classical crystallochemical classification is useful mostly to crystallographers and chemists. For petrologists and geologists, it is more logical to group silica, silicates, and aluminosilicates together. Often classifications are made on a geochemical basis, intended to show the links between mineralogy, petrology, and mineral deposits.

The jeweler is interested in gems' aesthetics but also in their abundance, which allows for a continuous commercial supply. European jewelers thus prefer aesthetic-commercial classifications—precious stones, fine stones, semiprecious stones, ornamental stones, rare or collector's stones—categories in which gems are subjectively grouped according to their attractiveness, and commercial value.

Here, an alphabetical arrangement is used, which provides the major advantage of partaking of no theory or prejudice but has the drawback of isolating each gem from its cousins and lookalikes. However, for each gem a list of minerals that could imitate it more or less convincingly is included.

Nomenclature

Using a name to designate an object helps to define that object. The obvious characteristics of an object initially help to name it: beauty, color, hardness, or a unique property characterizes some gems, and their primitive names derive from this characteristic—opal (precious stone), lapis lazuli (blue stone), emerald (green), hematite (blood red), ruby (red), pyrite (fire stone), amber (burning stone). But names are not derived only from such qualities. The locality of origin may be used as an interesting characteristic for a name as is the case for chalcedony (Chalcedon, now Kadikoy), jet (Gagas), and topaz (Topazos Island), to name a few examples. Sometimes a magical quality was used to name the crystal to which it was attributed, as for amethyst (not drunk). However, because it depends on subjective external characteristics, an old name may designate several gems, as emerald did; also, a gem with various aspects may have different names (as for the family of jaspers and agates). In addition, it is possible that the same name successively designated different stones (such a sapphire and topaz).

When observations became more plentiful, the study of gems became that of minerals in general, or mineralogy. Starting in the eighteenth century, mineralogists determined which mineral species corresponded to each denomination. This notion of species was often only a name for a natural chemical compound, ignoring, for example, polymorphism. This led to the creation of a vast number of mineral species that corresponded to only small chemical variations. Many personalities were honored in the process: kunzite, morganite, and the like. To avoid this confusion, a commission of the International Mineralogical Association was created, and a statute for new mineral names was adopted at its first meeting in Zurich in 1959.

Jewelers and gem enthusiasts adhere to this international statute. However, some color varieties kept their names because of widespread tradition. To emphasize a variety of particular interest for adornment, new names are sometimes put forward, such as tanzanite for blue zoisite. These appellations are checked by the Confédération Internationale de la Bijouterie

(CIBJO), whose nomenclature is used in this book. Thus, we distinguish among beryls—emerald, aquamarine, heliodore, morganite, goshenite, and red beryl.

Each entry provides the meaning of successive names through the ages (changes in the gem the name represents or change in the name for a gem). Sometimes there is still some confusion as to the right names, because jewelers and mineralogists often have conflicting information in their respective fields, and they accuse each other of ignorance: "The age and the ignorance of jewelers confused the names of precious stones so well that one can hardly establish something certain" (A. Boece de Boot, 1644); "It must have been that this mineralogist (Haüy) was informed by a total ignorant to state such a thing, which, by the way, is not surprising after all those foolish and ridiculous notions one can find in science books" (Th. Chriten, 1868). Pouget came to this disenchanted conclusion in 1762: "There are few books in which the subject is lied about more baldly than those about precious stones; I could write a book with all the mistakes and nonsense they contain."

A specimen of morganite, a collector's beryl, weighing 18.20 carats. F. A. Becker collection, Idar-Oberstein, Germany.

The most highly valued variety of beryl is emerald. This 12.93-carat stone is set in a ring. Van Cleef and Arpels creation.

Seventeenth-century Florentine hard-stone marquetry: carnelian, lapis lazuli, jade, and other materials. Height: 18 cm. National Higher School of Mines, Paris.

Note to the Reader

The fad for collecting gems that are solely intended for display in a showcase, strongly encouraged recently by some mineral shows, has led to the faceting of a number of minerals that cannot be considered true gems because of their rarity or fragility. For example, lepidolite mica (exfoliated by a simple touch) has been cut into ashtrays and cabochons, and halite, soluble in water or humid air, has been faceted. These exploits, often performed by amateur lapidaries, prove well enough that any transparent mineral can be faceted for the collector. Moreover, only a few dozen crystals of some gems, taafeite, for example, are known. Consequently, only the most common gems, ornamental stones, and organic gem materials will be dealt with in this volume. In addition, some arbitrary choices of collector's stones, taking into account the existence of faceted stones and their similarity in appearance to true gems, are included.

Part Two: The Gems

ACTINOLITE

Magnesian pole of the calcosodic amphibole family, principal component of nephrites (see JADE). Derived from the Greek *aktis, aktinos,* meaning "wheel spoke," alluding to the frequent radial distribution of its crystals. The substitution of iron for magnesium in actinolite can reach 50 percent, which produces a range of coloration from an almost colorless pale green to dark green with a strong pleochroism. Actinolite is a metamorphic mineral commonly found in carbonate rocks (dolomites).

Actinolites made of parallel fibers in which chatoyancy has been enhanced by a cabochon cut are sometimes incorrectly called "cat's-eye nephrites." Actinolites of gem quality are faceted for collectors. Hardness is 5.5; specific gravity is 3.05; principal indices of refraction, varying with iron content is approximately 1.620, 1.633, and 1.643; excellent cleavage. Afghanistan produces some beautiful crystals.

A "triangle" pendant, using Brazilian agate pseudomorphs after calcite. J. Vendôme creation.

AGATE

Chalcedony exhibiting layers of different colors; also chalcedony with remarkable inclusions (See also CHALCEDONY.)

Origin of the Name

Derived from the Semitic *aqiq* or *achit,* meaning "separation of a newborn's hair," the term was later applied to a valley close to Medina, in Saudi Arabia. The Greeks changed it to *achates,* a name also given to a river in Sicily (now called Drillo), where a deposit of various chalcedonies was mined; also *achates* in Latin, it became *agate* through progressive alteration. Agate has always been valued as a talisman and adornment; it was credited with the ability to quench thirst and to provide protection from fevers if it was held in the hand. Pliny the Elder reported that Persian magicians used agate to divert storms.

General Appearance and Varieties of Agate

Agate consists of successive layers of chalcedony of variable thickness, which may be planar or scalloped. Each of these layers exhibits a particular color and a more or less constant thickness. Each agate is the result of the filling of a cavity of variable dimensions in the host rock, up to several inches in diameter. The resulting nodule may consist entirely of agate layers following the external shape or have only an agate crust; all variations between these two situations are possible. The cavity may be covered by milky or transparent quartz, more rarely by opal, or it can be filled with residual water and gases.

The colors of agates are those of their component chalcedonies: white, bluish gray, gray-green, yellow-brown, brown, or reddish brown.

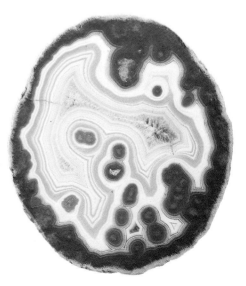

Agate from Idar-Oberstein, Germany. Width: 10 cm. G. Becker collection, Idar-Oberstein, Germany.

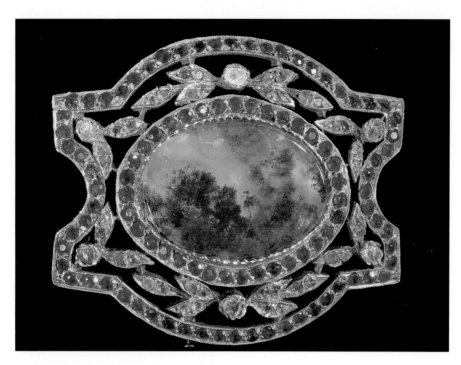

A nineteenth-century brooch with moss agate surrounded by diamonds, emeralds, and rubies. Garland
collection.

The shape and color of the layers is infinitely varied; their aspect is further modified or enhanced by cutting: a cabochon,
sphere, or slab each reveals particular characteristics, which may evoke eyes (concentric layers) or a rugged landscape (angular
layers), for example. Some of these shapes
have been given descriptive names, for example, ribbon agate, eye agate, and onicolo. Onyx describes an agate with thin,
regular layers and strongly contrasting colors. Agate is also the name of a chalcedony
with remarkable inclusions: manganese
dendrites, chunks of goethite, chlorite, and
the like; enhanced by clever cutting, these
natural designs may be reminiscent of
plants, animals, or mountains, for example.
Here again each may receive a specific denomination: moss agate, plume agate,
landscape agate. Pliny the Elder related
that Pyrrhus owned an agate in which the
veins and colored specks naturally seemed
to represent Apollo and the nine Muses.

When certain layers are opaque, the
agate is called a jasper-agate. Hundreds of
names have been given to agate; the Swedish mineralogist Wallerius wisely noted in
1747 that it was both impossible and useless
to list all the varieties. Pliny had already re-
marked in the first century that futility had

Mexican agate. Length: 12 cm. Compagnie Générale
de Madagascar, Paris.

pushed the Greeks to create innumerable names.

Occasionally chalcedony becomes pseudomorphic, replicating the cells and medullary channels of plants. It is then called petrified wood (see PETRIFIED WOOD). When agate shows an iridescence reminiscent of opal, it is called iris agate (see IRIS AGATE).

Color Enhancement

The chalcedony layers that make up agate are porous and can be dyed; the color remains more or less fast depending on porosity. The Sumerians applied acid to color light chalcedonies, to enhance the color contrast among layers and produce a more salable product. This practice is still common (see CHALCEDONY).

The Uses of Agate

In addition to its use in jewelry, (necklaces, cabochons, bola ties), agate is often used to carve bowls.

The collection of some two to four thousand bowls accumulated by Mithradates, king of Pontus, and transferred to the Capitoline Palace by Pompey the Great is still famous. Numerous Roman politicians also collected agate bowls.

This glyptic art was not limited to the Hellenistic period and the Roman empire: it was very popular with the Byzantine empire and under Muslim rule. After the sack of Cairo in 1062 and of Constantinople in 1204, western Europeans started to engrave agates and other stones. The art soared again during the Renaissance. Even today, the carving of agate bowls is one of the activities of cutting centers such as Idar-Oberstein, Germany. Large agate bowl collections were assembled by Europe's royal families, and most museums preserve magnificent examples. A superb ensemble is displayed in the Apollo Gallery in the Louvre in Paris.

Deposits

Agate forms at low temperatures, covering the walls of cavities in basaltic rocks or depositing in veinlets. It is found almost everywhere on earth. Historical deposits in Arabia, Egypt, Sicily, and the Nahe Valley in Germany (Idar-Oberstein) are now depleted, and the major commercial sources today are found in northern Uruguay and the Rio Grande do Sul region in Brazil.

Brazil's Paraná basin is a vast series of basaltic trapps covering approximately 1,200,000 square kilometers (460,000 square miles) with a height of more than 650 meters (2,100 feet). The agate region is formed by mounds of basalt flows of varying thickness, separated by breccias or silicified amygdaloid veins 1 to 3 meters (3 to 6 feet) thick. The most important mine is

Santo Ermirio, close to the town of Salto, on the Jacui River, where agate is found in abundance in a variety of nodules. The mining, underground and in open quarries, is done with modern equipment (bulldozers). During the dry season, the daily production is 5 to 12 tons.

Agates are also found in India, in the large basalt flows of the Deccan. Numerous other regions also produce agates: the Malagasy Republic, Bohemia (Czechoslovakia), Mexico, and the United States, where the so-called thunder eggs from the rhyolitic tuffs and lavas of Oregon are of particular interest because of their section, resembling a five-point star.

The Agate of Idar-Oberstein

As early as 1497, the area around the Nahe River, a Rhine tributary, near Birkenfeld, Germany, became an important cutting center because of the abundance of agates, chalcedonies, and amethysts. Using the energy provided by the numerous local streams to power hundreds of mills in which huge rotating sandstone wheels were used to polish gemstones, German artists built a worldwide reputation.

Toward the middle of the nineteenth century, the demand for artifacts was high: bowls, candelabra boxes, necklaces, knife handles, even amulets used by the hundreds of thousands in Africa. With the exhaustion of the local mines around Idar, production declined, until a native of Idar discovered the gigantic Brazilian agate deposits in the Rio Grande do Sul, which revived the cutting shops. Today this craft is flourishing, using only imported materials. Although working with agates is still the predominant activity, the faceting of colored stones, the manufacture of delicate objects, and the engraving of cameos and intaglios have come to symbolize the small towns and villages of this region. Since World War II, a museum dedicated to the

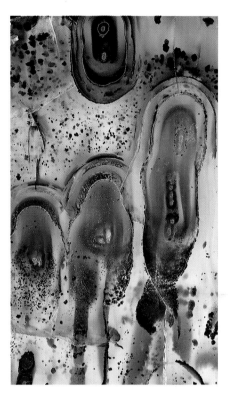

Montana agate. Length: 6 cm. G. Becker collection, Idar-Oberstein, Germany.

Eyelike agate (nicolo) from Mexico. Length: 7 cm. National Higher School of Mines, Paris.

Landscape agate from Brazil. Length: 2 cm. Compagnie Générale de Madagascar, Paris.

arts of engraving and faceting has allowed tourists to familiarize themselves with this craft.

IRIS AGATE

Agate in which the chalcedony layers are so thin (of the order of 1.5 micrometers) that they display rainbow colors and iridescence. This gem, originally found in India, is

A modern agate cameo. Height: 5 cm. G. Becker collection. Idar-Oberstein, Germany.

probably the opal of older civilizations, before the discovery and extraction of opals in Hungary by the Romans.

ALABASTER

Massive gypsum (hydrated calcium sulfate).

Origin of the Name

Alabaster comes from the Greek *alabastron,* itself derived from the privative *a* and *labe,* meaning "handle," that is, "without handle," because this material was used to carve perfume bottles without handles (glass *alabastrons* from the fifth century B.C. are on display in the Cabinet of Medals in Paris). A good collection of ancient Egyptian alabasters is displayed in the Musée de la Castre in Cannes, France.

Physical Properties

White and translucent when pure, alabaster is often associated with various oxides, especially iron, which give it various colors (yellow, brown, red, orange, pink), often distributed in bands.

Very porous, it can easily be dyed (as are the widely commercialized "eggs" of all colors). It is susceptible to fire (when dehydrated, it becomes plaster), it is light (S.G. about 2.3), fairly soft (H is 2; it is scratched by a nail), and not very refringent (R.I.

about 1.52). Although widely distributed throughout the world, it is extracted only from certain quarries, the most important ones being in Tuscany, Italy.

Uses of Alabaster

Its use in Italy dates back to the Etruscans. Once finished, alabaster objects are placed in cold water, slowly brought to boiling, then cooled. When dry, they closely resemble white marble.

Fibrous white gypsum is occasionally cut into cabochons and spheres; its low hardness is, however, a major handicap to its use in jewelry. The appearance of certain marbles is reminiscent of alabaster; thus "onyx marbles" are sometimes represented as alabaster in some countries.

ALEXANDRITE

A chromium-bearing chrysoberyl whose color varies depending on illumination: it is emerald green in daylight and ruby red in incandescent light or candlelight.

Origin of the Name

This mineral was named by Adolf E. Nordenskjöld in honor of Czar Alexander II of Russia (1818–81), because it was discovered on his birthday in 1831, in the famous Takowaja mines in the Urals (see EMERALD).

Because it also displays the colors symbolizing the holy Russia (red and green), alexandrite was immediately popular with the Russian aristocracy. It is still in high demand, especially in the United States (for gems of the same quality, alexandrite is as expensive, and sometimes more expensive, than diamond).

Physical Properties

The length of the chromium-oxygen bonds in chrysoberyl is between those of beryl and corundum and is responsible for the color of alexandrite (see part 1). Alexandrite is strongly trichoic, and the colors seen along the optic axes are purplish red, yellow-orange, and green. Absorption lines and bands due to chromium are easily visible; the band in the yellow extends more or less into this color, depending on orientation.

Deposits

Alexandrite is found with emerald and phenakite in some pegmatites (for example, Takowaja, the first known deposit and still the most famous for the size and quality of its stones). It has been encountered in recent years in a micaschist in Zimbabwe. But it is essentially an alluvial mineral, par-

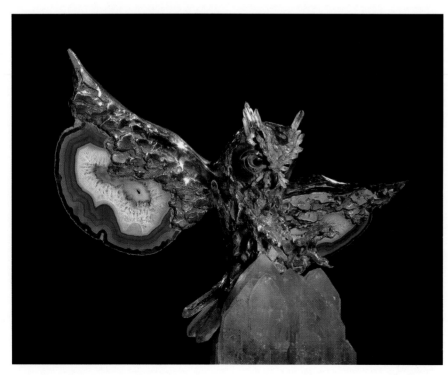

Owl in solid silver and agate, standing on a rock-crystal pedestal. Width: 42 cm. Mellerio (Meller) creation.

Alexandrite crystal from Takowaja, in the Ural Mountains of the U.S.S.R. Width: 5 cm. Private collection.

ticularly in Brazil, where it accompanies chrysoberyl in the region of Malacacheta, Corregu do Fogo, and Coimbras, north of Teófilo Otoni. Rough stones of over 18 grams (½ ounce) from Brazil resulted in faceted stones of over 5 carats, totally clean, showing a magnificent emerald green or a true ruby red depending on the lighting.

Alexandrite is also found in Sri Lanka's gem-bearing gravels in large but dark crystals, which are therefore less valuable.

A 65.7-carat alexandrite is displayed at the Smithsonian Institution, in Washington, D.C., and a 43-carat stone is at the British Museum; both are cut from Sri Lankan crystals.

Synthetics and Imitations

Alexandrite is sometimes imitated with glasses, even color-change doublets, but the most frequent imitators are flame-fusion synthetic spinels and especially corundums, which are blue-green in daylight and purple in candlelight (these comprise the majority of the "alexandrites" offered to tourists in the various towns named Alexandria, as well as in the Orient and South America).

Since 1973 a convincing synthetic alexandrite grown by the flux method has been sold in the United States. Its physical properties are like those of Russian alexandrite, but it contains inclusions characteristic of flux synthetics (flux inclusions and needle- or platelet-like parasitic black crystals especially). It is also produced in Japan.

ALMANDITE

An alumino-ferrous garnet, dark to violetish red.

Origin of the Name and History of Almandite

Known since antiquity, almandite was then confused with other red gems, all under the same *carbonculus,* "red coal." In Pliny's time, the town of Alabanda, situated about 50 kilometers (30 miles) east of Miletus and Ephesus in Asia Minor, was a trading and cutting center for these gems, so they were called *carbonculus alabandicus,* which eventually became almandite.

Later, Indian garnet was exported by the kingdom of Pegu (today's Myanmar, or Burma), and the port of Syriam became a trading and cutting center, where Louis XIV installed a trading post. The name "Syriam garnet" soon became "Syrian garnet" and "garnet of Syria."

Almandite was abundantly used in ornamentation. In the Louvre (Apollo Gallery) as well as the Paris Muséum National d'Histoire Naturelle (Natural History Museum), one can admire pairs of salt-and-pepper shakers, said to have been owned by Louis XIV, made in the seventeenth century of almandite garnet. In the Cabinet of Medals, the Chosroès bowl, a sixth-century Sassanian piece, includes engraved lamellar disks in almandite garnet, rock crystal, and green glass. A 174-carat star almandite is on display at the Smithsonian Institution.

Physical Properties

The iron in almandite is always partially replaced by magnesium, sometimes by manganese or calcium; so the R.I. varies from 1.77 to 1.83 and the S.G., from 4.0 to 4.3. There is a range of garnets, from the all-iron almandite to the all-magnesian pyrope; these gems, called pyraldite or pyrope-almandite, have specific gravities and indices of refraction between the two extremes (3.8 to 4.0 and 1.75 to 1.77, respectively). Although theoretically isotropic, because cubic, almandite often displays a small birefringence. It is the most resistant to scratches of all garnets (H is 7½).

The absorption spectrum, always distinct, indicates iron, with three bands in green, called "the almandite flag," sometimes accompanied by two other, less distinct bands, one orange and the other blue.

Deposits and Inclusions

Almandite is the most common of all garnets; it is commonly found in metamorphic rocks, especially in those resulting from

regional metamorphism of clay-containing sediments (gneiss, micaschists, amphibolites) as well as in rocks of the granulitic facies. It is seen also in potassic pegmatites and in aplites, associated with tourmaline. It is frequently found in igneous rocks such as dacite and andesite. It is found in leucogranites associated with andalusite. Its resistance to weathering agents makes it one of the most common alluvial minerals.

Gem-quality almandite comes primarily from alluvial deposits in Sri Lanka and micaschists in Jaipur, India, as well as from Brazil, Zambia, and Madagascar.

Almandite can trap several minerals during its growth, such as zircon or apatite, which may later be found at the center of the winglike fractures they induce. Titanium may also be included in the lattice and is expressed as rutile needles oriented along the crystallographic directions of the host crystal, especially the fourfold symmetry axes. Such crystals can become asteriated when cut into cabochons, if the rutile needles are numerous enough. Indian almandites are usually best for this type of cutting.

Cuts and Uses of Almandite

In the past, almandite garnets were cut into cabochons; darker stones were lightened by hollowing the base of the cabochon, to reduce the optical path in the gem. That is still the case today; the faceted cut is reserved for stones of a brighter red. Irregularly shaped low-quality almandites are simply polished in a tumbler, producing baroque beads that are either drilled to be strung or glued to silver jewelry. In France the creation of garnet jewelry using py-

A pair of nineteenth-century almandite garnet ear pendants. Garland collection.

Nineteenth-century brooch with almandite garnet and emerald from the Louis-Philippe period. Mellerio (Meller) collection.

ropes but especially almandites, is a specialty of the town of Perpignan.

Almandite garnet has been used as base material for garnet-and-glass doublets since at least the eighteenth century. Doublets intended to imitate ruby or sapphire are preferably made with almandites showing numerous rutile or hornblende inclusions to be more convincing.

ALUNITE

A hydrous aluminum sulfate, belonging to the rhombohedral system. Its name, derived from its composition, is a contraction of aluminilite.

Alunite is a hydrothermal indicator found in porphyry-type deposits. It accompanies turquoise and forms chalky-looking, dull masses of varying size, having some

cohesion, occasionally colored blue-green by copper compounds. It can be cut into cabochons and is then often mistaken for turquoise, especially in Iran (Neyshābūr and Kuh-e-Zar). It can always be identified by its low hardness. (See also TURQUOISE.)

AMAZONITE OR MICROLINE

A variety of potassium feldspar (see FELDSPAR).

The name amazonite was given to this green stone because of an Amazonian legend. According to early explorers, members of an all-female tribe in northern Brazil would give this stone to men of a neighboring tribe to rent their services in order to ensure their perpetuation. The region itself was called Amazonia.

The shapes of amazonite are those of orthoclase. It reaches impressive dimensions

in certain Minas Gerais pegmatites: a single crystal can weigh several tons. It forms enormous crystalline masses without distinct shapes but with perfect cleavage. Its pale green to blue-green color evokes turquoise or jade. When well crystallized, it may display a nacreous sheen due to its lamellar structure. It is usually traversed by thin white albite veinlets. Often limited to the periphery of the crystal, the green color, resulting from natural irradiation, disappears by heating over 300°C (570°F). Its specific gravity (2.56), hardness (6), and indices of refraction (around 1.52) are low.

Amazonite is used to make necklace beads, cabochons for costume jewelry, and small objects such as boxes and ashtrays. Its cleavage makes it difficult to carve. It enters into the composition of Berber necklaces from North Africa (it might come from the beryl pegmatites of Mauritania). It is a classical pegmatite mineral, found in Brazil, Madagascar, India, and the United States.

AMBER OR SUCCINITE

A tree-resin fossil at least a million years old. It should not be confused with ambergris, a secretion of the sperm whale used in the perfume industry as a fixative.

Origin of the Name

Amber was called *elektron,* ("resplendent thing") by the Greeks because of its color: the sun was poetically called *elektor.* The Latin term *electrum* is applied only to the natural resplendent gold-silver alloy, which the Greeks also called *elektron.* Today Greeks call amber *berenikis,* an allusion to the blond hair of the Egyptian queen Berenice II (who died in 221 B.C.), mother of Ptolemy IV Philopator. The Teutons named it *glesse* (luminous), from which comes the Latin *glessum* and the German word *glas,* which describes glass, and some amber varieties such as glessite.

The word *succinite,* used for amber during the last century, comes from the Latin *succinum,* itself stemming from *succus* ("sap"), referring to the origin of the material.

Amber owes its present name to its property of taking flame easily; an old root, *br (brulere, brucciare, brennen)* became in German *bernstein* ("burning stone"), through the Old German *börnsten,* and in Latin and Anglo-Saxon languages, *ambra, ambre, amber,* through the Old German *anbernen* ("to take flame"). These became *anbar* in Arabic (Arabs have recently played an important role in the amber trade). The Arabic *anbar,* initially used for perfumes to burn (incense, amber) could also be of Hellenistic descent, stemming from *ambrosia* ("drink and perfume of the gods"), from *ambrotos* ("immortal").

History, Virtues, and Healing Properties of Amber

Amber has been known since prehistoric times. Because of its luster, it was used to create ritual objects and amulets. It has been found in Bronze Age graves in the Baltic states (tumuli of Estes, in Lithuania) as well as in Italy (barrow of Ombres, in Montale). Associated with trade that enabled Mediterranean civilization to extend north for over fifteen centuries, it played a very important role in European prehistory. Rough amber was collected at the mouth of the Eridan (now Po) River according to Herodotus in the fifth century B.C.) and on the islands of the North Sea (Artistotle's "Electrid" islands, fourth century B.C.). Rough amber may have been traded for bronze, ivory, and carved amber. During the Etruscan civilization, from the fifteenth to the sixth century B.C., one of the amber trading routes went through the Alps, passed through Hallstatt, Austria, and followed the Oder and the Elbe; the small town of Bernstein, south of Vienna in Austria, certainly marked a stop along this route. An eastern route followed the Vistula and Dniester rivers to the Black Sea.

Phoenicians took delivery of amber at the Etruscan harbor of Adria (now in Italy) or the Greek harbor of Massilia (now Marseilles, France) and marketed it throughout the Mediterranean basin. Indirect exchanges probably were made, especially involving African ivory and northern amber (Etruscan artists created inlays of amber and ivory). Later, Arab pirates probably were intermediary agents.

Amber was appreciated for adornment. Homer told the story of a sailor presenting Eurymacas, Eumeus's nurse, with a gold and amber necklace in an attempt to seduce her. Wealthy Roman women mixed amber in their blond hair, already bleached with a preparation of quince and privet. Nero complimented his wife Poppaea Sabina by comparing her hair to amber.

Amber was also burned as incense, in honor of gods or ancestors or during banquets. During the Circus games, Nero burned thousands of pounds of amber that he had collected at great expense by organizing expeditions to the Baltic Sea. Copals, which are fossil resins of more recent origin than true amber but resemble amber, may also have been used for this purpose: Pliny mentioned *sacal,* used in Egypt as incense; in Solomon's era, copals were already being substituted for amber. Orientals and Arabs still appreciate amber as incense.

Amber was also considered an amulet, perhaps because of its electrical properties; hence its Lithuanian name, *gintaras* ("protector"). Modern medicine tends to find beneficial the electric field developed when wearing amber. It was thought to heal sore throats. In the Mediterranean countries, it

Amazonite and smoky quartz crystals from Lake George, Colorado. Height: 10 cm. Coil collection, United States.

A Baltic amber carving made during the first century A.D. *representing Eros and the lion. Such objects were favorites of Roman patricians. Length: 4.6 cm; weight 13.78 g. M. De Bry Collection.*

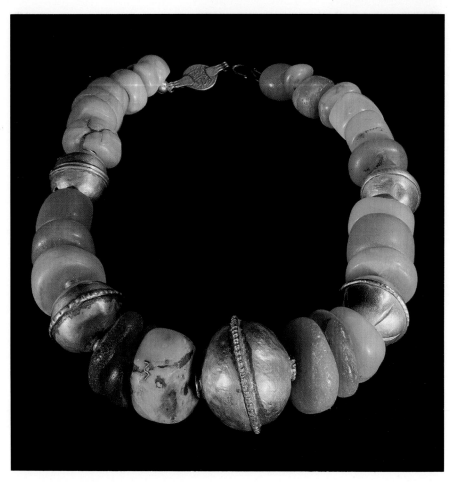

Berber necklace in amber and silver. Argana Boutique, Paris.

is still customary to adorn a baby with an amber necklace to prevent red blotches and skin irritations.

In the Middle Ages, the healing properties of amber were extended, and in the sixteenth century, Albert, duke of Prussia, is said to have sent a piece of amber to Martin Luther, who suffered from kidney stones, with the wish that the good stone chase the bad ones.

Famous Pieces of Amber

Amber with insect inclusions was considered desirable as early as the sixteenth century; in 1623 Pope Urban VII owned "a piece of amber containing three bees."

Amber pieces weighing more than a pound are rare; Pliny the Elder nevertheless reported a 13-pound block, and the Holy Roman Emperor Rudolf II is said to have received an 11-pound piece of amber in 1576. A 6-pound piece was found in 1848, and the Jutland may have produced pieces of 27 and 30 pounds.

The Natural History Museum in Berlin owns a block of almost 9.7 kilograms (20 pounds). The British Museum, in its natural history section, displays a Burmese amber block of 15.250 kilograms (33 pounds 10 ounces). A 34-pound block was discovered in Australia. The largest piece of brown amber, discovered in May 1979 in the Dominican Republic, weighs 18 pounds.

In the Middle Ages, amber was used to face portable altars. In the eighteenth century, the walls of one of the rooms of the Tsarskoye Selo palace, in Pushkin, Russia, was entirely covered with amber. In 1886 the treasury of France owned an amber bowl 35 centimeters high (15 inches) high and 17 centimeters (almost 7 inches) in diameter. In 1963 an amber museum opened in Palanga, Lithuania, that houses archaeological discoveries of amber along the Baltic coast as well as displays related to Baltic amber.

The Formation of Amber

That amber was so often found along the Baltic coast led to its Finnish name, *merikivi* ("sea stone") and inspired numerous myths. The ancient Balts told the story of the beautiful goddess of the mermaids, Jurate, who was engaged to the god of the waters, Patrimpas. She lived in an amber palace at the bottom of the sea. Seduced by the beauty and courage of Kastytis, a humble fisherman who cast his nets at the borders of her domain, Jurate forgot her engagement and kidnapped him, holding him in her palace. In a tantrum, Perkunas, master of the gods, threw his thunder, destroying Jurate's palace and killing Kastytis. Condemned to be chained to the ruins of her palace, Jurate, pounded by the waves, still moans in storms, crying liquid amber tears that the sea washes up onto the shore, amid seaweed and translucent amber stones from her palace.

The ancient Greeks also had a myth about the source of amber. Helios, god of the sun, agreed to the imprudent request of his son Phaeton to drive the solar carriage. But, inexperienced and clumsy, Phaeton soon lost control of his horses, and the carriage overturned, setting the crops on fire. The goddess Demeter protested harshly, seeing her wheat burn. Alerted, Zeus, master of the gods, struck Phaeton with lightning and hurled him into the Eridan River. His sisters, the Heliads, wept so much for him that the gods pitied them and turned them into poplars along the banks of the Eridan; but inconsolable, they still cried, and the tears of these trees became amber.

Tears are often associated with the formation of amber in mythology. Sophocles (494–406 B.C.) described amber as the solidified tears of the sisters of the hero Meleager, changed into birds; and not so long ago, Baltic fishermen would dive to collect "the tears of the sea birds." Theophrastus (372–287 B.C.) identified amber as the tears of the lynx, but it is possible that, by lynx, he meant the Ligurian people, who would have had Sicilian amber. To the Chinese, amber was the petrification of a dead tiger's soul; therefore they believed that it imparted strength and courage.

As early as Pliny, it was known that plants were the source of amber. Recent research, especially infrared spectrometry, has found that the resins that become amber come not only from gymnosperms (conifers), such as araucarias (*Araucaria agathis*) in Lebanon and araucarias, pines (especially *Pinus succinifera*), yews, and cypresses from the Baltic countries, but also from angiosperms (seed-bearing trees and plants), such as *Hymenoea courbaril* in the Dominican Republic and Mexico. The transformation of resin into amber is not systematic; the process, incompletely understood, involves heat, pressure, environment (such as contact with salt water) and time (several millions of years).

Geographical Distribution

With the exception of Africa and Antarctica, all continents produce amber, dating from as early as the Carboniferous period of the Paleozoic era. Some fossil cordaites and cycadophytes contain minute amounts of amberized resin, without insects, of course. Most amber sold today comes from either the Baltic, from the Oligocene and Miocene epochs (35 to 50 million years ago), or the Dominican Republic, from the Oligocene and Eocene epochs (25 to 35 million years ago). However, other sources may have some historical or geological interest.

Amber from Lebanon

Its color is light yellow to garnet red, even black. The oldest fossilized amber, dating from the Lower Cretaceous period (125 million years ago), it was probably known and marketed by the Phoenicians but was rediscovered only around 1830. The insects it contains, including varieties of mosquitoes and mite eggs, as well as bird wings, make it particularly interesting for its evidence of life on earth at the time the angiosperms appeared.

Amber from Eurasia

- Cretaceous amber (100 million years old) from the Parisian and Aquitanian basins in France.
- Austrian amber, millimetric, of the Cretaceous period, similar to Lebanese amber.
- Romanian amber from Valachia in the Buzau valley, along the eastern trade route of amber; known by the Romans, who established colonies to exploit it.
- Sicilian amber, from the Etna era, of the Miocene epoch (25 million years ago), with a yellow-green to red color. Probably known since antiquity, insects from six different orders have been found in it.
- Azerbaijani and northern Siberian amber (from the banks of Yenisei to the Kamchatka peninsula) of the Upper Cretaceous period (80 to 105 million years ago), known since the eighteenth century but only studied recently (1970). This amber is reddish or, rarely, yellow; sixty

groups of insects, distributed over fourteen different orders, have been recognized in it.
- Burmese amber, from the high valley of the Irrawaddy, of the Miocene epoch (30 million years ago). It was known and used by the Chinese as early as the Han dynasty (206 B.C. to A.D. 220). Its reddish to brownish color is reminiscent of Dominican amber. It contains some insects. This amber was extracted until World War II using primitive shafts 8 to 10 meters (25 to 30 feet) deep.
- Chinese amber, yellow in color, from Fushun in Manchuria; it has been little studied and is not well known.

American Amber

- Amber from Alaska and Canada, known since the nineteenth century in about fifty different places. It is most often from the Cretaceous period (70 to 95 million years ago), sometimes of Tertiary period, more rarely Devonian. The most

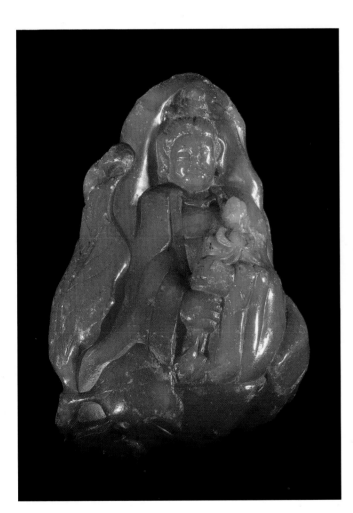 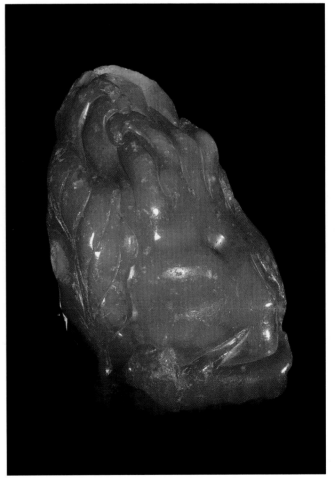

The two sides of a Chinese amulet, showing Buddha's hand in amber from Myanmar (Burma). Height: 8.2 cm; weight, 82 g. Private collection.

famous is that of Cedar Lake, in Manitoba, which is light to dark brown and rich in fossils (bear whiskers, crustaceans, arachnids, fifty-two insect families of twelve orders).

• New Jersey amber, from the Upper Cretaceous period (100 million years ago). Produced by sequoias, it contains the oldest ant fossils known.

• Mexican amber, or Chiapas amber, found in the region of San Cristóbal. It was used in jewelry and funerary decoration by pre-Columbian Indians. From the Miocene-Oligocene epochs (25 to 35 million years ago), it is light yellow to red-brown. It is produced by a leguminous plant, *Hymenaea courbaril*. One family of myriapods, sixteen of arachnids, and eighty-eight of insects distributed over nineteen orders have been recognized in it. The largest insect was a 20-millimeter-long cricket larva; the smallest, a 1-millimeter miniature wasp.

Mining and Commercialization of Amber

Baltic amber was the exclusive property of the Teutonic knights after their conquest in 1229–37, then became that of the duke of Prussia when the duchy was created in 1525 by Albert of Ansbach, and then finally that of the king of Prussia. The laws concerning amber were extremely harsh. Walk on the beaches was prohibited, and anybody who possessed rough amber was sentenced to death, by hanging for less than two pounds, by torture on the wheel for more than two pounds. In 1826 the town of Königsberg (today Kaliningrad) employed a full-time executioner to kill amber smugglers. The royal privilege to exploit and sell amber was granted to the company Koehn von Jaski of Danzig (today Gdańsk) from 1533 to 1642, was managed directly by the Prussian government from 1642 to 1811, and then was granted to the Douglas Consortium from 1811 to 1837. Made free in 1837, the amber trade was concentrated in 1854 in the hands of W. Stantien from Memel (today Klaipeda), before becoming the monopoly of the Stantien and Becker company in 1870, a monopoly bought back by the German state in 1899. Königsberg was then the main trading center.

Since then, 90 percent of the amber on the market has come from underground mines reaching 130 feet deep (especially the Anna shaft, drilled in 1875 and active until 1925). "Blue ground," a clay formation containing about 2 kilograms of amber per cubic meter, is extracted. Of the 500 tons gathered annually, only 20 percent is used for jewelry; 80 percent is melted for the chemical industry. Starting in 1922, mining in open quarries again became preva-

lent. Today it is the only technique used in Lithuania, where a working face can be 1200 meters (4,000 feet) long.

Domincan amber (from the Dominican Republic), mentioned by Christopher Columbus during his second trip to the West Indies, is found in clay formations in the northern mountains and in the El Seibo cordillera in the eastern part of the island, at altitudes of 1,000 to 3,300 feet. Steep slopes, abundant rains, and difficult access due to tropical vegetation make mining, still primitive in contrast to techniques used in the Baltic, quite arduous. Before 1979 rough Dominican amber was imported by dealers from Idar-Oberstein, the main center of the amber trade, who mixed it with Baltic amber. In 1979, it became illegal to export rough Dominican amber, and this variety has thus finally established a separate commercial identity.

In addition to jewelry (bracelets, earrings, necklaces, brooches), various objects are carved in amber (Buddhas, traditional Indian art, charms).

Fossiliferous Amber

In addition to having scientific interest, fossiliferous amber is also in demand commercially. All natural history museums have collections of such fossils. The most remark-

Mummified insect in French Guyana copal. Field: 1 cm. Dina Level collection.

Dominican amber with several inclusions of flying ants. Length of the insect: 3 mm. S. Hendrickson collection, United States.

able one was that of the Königsberg University, unfortunately dispersed during World War II. A group of 11,000 specimens was, however, saved by Dr. S. Ritzkowski of Göttingen, Germany. Interesting collections are maintained in the Amber Museum in Palanga (Lithuania), in the Warsaw Earth Science Museum (Poland), in the Geological Museum in Copenhagen (Denmark), and in the Stuttgart Earth Science Museum (Germany).

The animals—insects, arachnids, centipedes—that were trapped in the amber may have been attracted by its luminosity or its odor or may even have been accidentally ensnared in the sticky fresh resin. Often they fought to free themselves, occasionally managing to do so at the expense of a limb. In addition, the wind deposited leaves, pollen, feathers, and reptilian scales; mammals' hair may have become attached when the animals brushed against resin balls. The abundant production of resin would rapidly cover the trapped animal, although sometimes the process took long enough for fungi to develop. The victim occasionally emptied its alimentary canal while drowning in the amber, enabling the study of its parasites, such as the nematode threadworms of flies and mosquitoes. The resin is an excellent fossilizing agent, which often preserves only the external hard parts of the body; sometimes it did penetrate the entire animal and preserve its soft parts, mummifying it totally so it can be studied just as if it had recently died. Wood and mineral grains can also be found in amber.

Dominican amber generally contains more fossils than Baltic amber; the record seems to be one thousand to twelve hundred animals in one 4- by 3- by 2-centimeter piece. The largest known fossil is a dragonfly, 53 millimeters (over 2 inches) long with a 60-millimeter wingspan, discovered in the Dominican Republic; among the smallest fossils are miniature wasps about 0.5 millimeters long, 0.1-millimeter cockroach and arachnid larvae, fly eggs, and pollen grains 0.02 millimeter in size found in bee-leg receptacles. Pseudoscorpions, flowers, and a fully preserved frog have also been found in amber. After identifying the hundreds of animal and plant species found, scientists are now attempting to understand their symbiotic relationships, using the few fossil pieces in which they can be observed.

Physical Properties

Chemically, amber is a hydrocarbon chain that sometimes contains succinic acid, considered an oxidation product (but this is not a characteristic of amber). It dissolves with difficulty in organic solvents, such as sulfuric ether. Amber melts at between

Locust in Dominican amber. Length: 1 cm. S. Hendrickson collection, United States.

Ant in Baltic amber. Length: 0.1 cm. Private collection.

Ant in Dominican amber. Length: 1 cm. S. Hendrickson collection, United States.

250°and 300°C (475°and 575°F) and produces an aromatic odor when it burns.

Its color varies from light yellow to reddish brown ("amber" color). It can be totally transparent and homogeneous or be layered. A high concentration of tiny bubbles makes it cloudy, opaque, sometimes whitish (it is then less valuable). Slightly cloudy amber can be made more transparent by heating in rapeseed oil; however, this operation must be conducted with great caution so that the gem does not shatter because of internal pressure. Most amber that has been clarified in this way displays internal fractures, reminiscent of a golden lily pad. In black light, amber is brightly fluorescent, with a greenish white to bluish color. Ambers displaying a daylight luminescence (as a surface effect in reflected light) change color fairly rapidly. In daylight, amber darkens; it becomes garnet red after about ten years of such exposure. It is possible to lighten the color by immersing it in appropriate chemicals, such as pyridine, and it is, of course, possible to use a dye to make it reddish. When exposed to intense ultraviolet light for several weeks, amber decomposes into a whitish powder.

The specific gravity of amber is about 1.06 to 1.08, so it floats on water that contains some salt. When rubbed with a wool fabric, amber attracts dust and small pieces of straw, hence its Turkish name, *kehruba*

("straw thief"). Already known by the Greeks (Thales, seventh century B.C.), this property was described as "electric" in the eighteenth century, making use of the word *elektron,* the Greek name for amber.

Amber is soft (H is 2½) but takes a very good polish. As it ages, it tends to crack superficially because of oxidation and dryness. Its care mainly consists of avoiding oxidation, scratching (for example, by applying a natural wax), high heat, and strong light.

Pressed Amber and Melted Amber

Small amber pieces, scraps from cuttings or tiny natural pieces, can be agglomerated under pressure once they have been softened at 160°C (320°F). Developed in Prussia in 1880, this technique produces pressed, or reconstructed, amber, in which the original chunks, often darker than their outline, can still be easily seen, surrounded by masses of solidified melted amber. Amber dust and the very smallest pieces can be melted down and molded (especially into cigarette holders); this product is melted amber. Originally called "ambroids," these fabrications were considered imitations by the German authorities.

The current CIBJO nomenclature for these types of amber is confusing. "Natural amber" comes directly from deposits and is worked only for jewelry, whereas "melted amber" and "reconstructed amber" are often called "true amber" (and are exclusively so called, in Germany: *echter Bernstein*).

Copal: A Recent Resin

The only natural product similar to amber is copal, from the pre-Columbian Nahuatl word *copalli,* meaning "incense." It is secreted by various gum trees: *Agathis australis,* the gum arabic tree, from Africa; *Tetraclinis articulata,* the sandarac, from Australia, and *Hymenaea courbaril,* the algarroba, from South America. As they form, these natural resins can trap various animals and plant parts. However, the formation of amber from these plants is incomplete because of lack of time (1 million years or less). Therefore, copal is easily soluble in organic solvents such as sulfuric ether; its color is often yellower and cruder than that of amber, its hardness lower, its melting temperature lower, and it does not take as good a polish.

Recent (quaternary) copal is found in South America (Brazil, Colombia), New Zealand, central Africa (from Sierre Leone to Zanzibar), and Madagascar. Copal deposits are presently worked in Cotuí, in the Dominican Republic, between the two areas where Dominican amber is found.

Copal may have been used as amber in the past, especially to be burned (in Egypt, for example). In Solomon's time (tenth century B.C.), it was fraudulently represented as amber. Copal from Cotuí is often sold covered with plastic, making it more stable and less easy to scratch.

Imitations

In addition to straw-yellow glass, amber imitations are essentially plastics (artificial resins). With the exception of polystyrenes, which are fairly light (S.G. is 1.05) and easily soluble in organic solvents, all these artificial resins are distinctly denser than amber (most often 1.2 to 1.40). Red Bakelite has been used in the Far East, especially to imitate Myanmar amber.

During processing, various inclusions can be introduced into the plastics to make them more convincing: bubbles, dead insects (which did not fight to escape), even small pieces of amber or copal (Bernite). In the eighteenth century, insects were inserted into cavities carved in amber halves that were then reattached. Copal containing artificially introduced insects very convincingly imitates fossiliferous amber.

Necklaces of Dominican amber with baroque and faceted beads. S. Hendrickson collection, United States.

AMBLYGONITE

An aluminum and lithium phosphate belonging to the triclinic system. The name is applied to a range of stones, with those having a fully hydroxylated pole actually being montebrasite, whereas those with a fully fluorinated pole are true amblygonite.

Montebrasite was named for the French quarry Montebras, in Creuse, France, where it is found. Amblygonite is derived from the Greek *amblus* ("obtuse"), and *gonia* ("angle"), describing its crystal shape.

Its stocky crystals, set in quartz, are rare; however, limpid crystals with shiny faces, sometimes twinned, and showing a perfect cleavage have been found in Brazilian sodium-lithium pegmatites (Itinga and Boa Vista, Minas Gerais, and São Paulo).

Amblygonite's indices of refraction increase as the fluorine decreases (replaced with oxygen and hydrogen, for montebrasite): $n_p = 1.577$ to 1.610; $n_m = 1.595$ to 1.618; $n_g = 1.597$ to 1.636. Birefringence increases from 0.020 to 0.026, and the optic sign becomes positive when there is more than 70 percent montebrasite. In a similar manner, specific gravity decreases from 3.12 to 2.98.

The amblygonite currently on the market is actually a very light yellow montebrasite, weakly luminescent, with no distinct absorption spectrum. Its hardness is that of feldspar, which it resembles.

A yellow faceted 62.6-carat amblygonite is displayed at the Smithsonian Institution.

AMETHYST

Transparent to translucent purple quartz.

Origin of the Name

From the primitive Greek *a* and *methustes,* meaning "drunkard," that is "who is not drunk." Indeed, in a purple glass, water looks as if it is the color of wine, and one who drinks from such a glass can appear to be drinking wine while remaining sober.

The History of Amethyst

The virtue attributed to amethyst, the ability to protect from drunkenness, is recounted in the myth transposing the celebration of Dionesian mysteries in Eleusis to an orgiastic bacchanalia in Rome.

After numerous libations, Bacchus, god of wine, came across the beautiful nymph Amethyst, who was going to Diana's temple. He chased her and harrassed her so much that she feared she would not be able to escape Bacchus and implored Diana for help. Diana changed Amethyst into a pure, cold crystal in the arms of Bacchus. Furious, he poured his glass of wine onto the crystal, which took on a purple color. Then sober, Bacchus gave this crystal the power to protect those who wear it from drunkenness.

This myth also accounts for the common appearance of amethyst crystals, which generally are colored only in their pyramidal tips.

Combining the blue of the sky with the red of blood (from Christ or the martyrs), amethyst became an episcopal stone, and a symbol of humility, during the Renaissance; it adorned the Inquisition crosses.

Famous Amethysts

Amethyst was rare during antiquity, becoming common only after the discovery of important deposits in Brazil and Uruguay at the beginning of the twentieth century.

Amblygonite crystal from Itinga, Minas Gerais, Brazil. Length: 3 cm. Sorbonne collection.

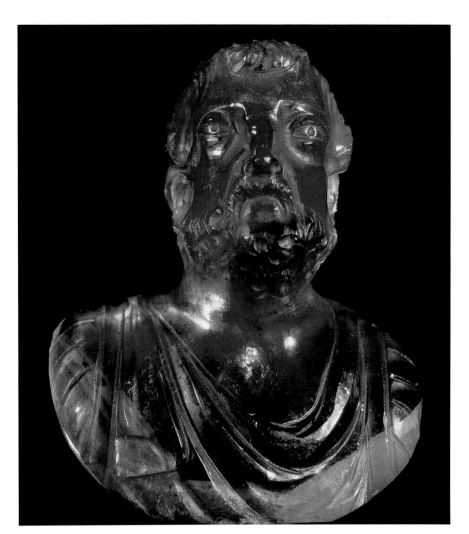

Amethyst bust representing Mithradates VI Eupator, king of Pontus (reigned 120–63 B.C.), probably from the first century B.C. Height: 3.1 cm. M. De Bry collection.

A fairly large amethyst carved in a globe shape adorns the royal scepter of England. The Smithsonian Institution displays a purple Brazilian amethyst weighing 1,362 carats; the British Museum has a 343-carat Brazilian amethyst and two Russian amethysts, a hexagonal one of 90 carats and a round one of 75 carats.

Large crystals weighing several kilograms have been found in Brazilian pegmatites; crystals reaching over 50 kilograms are known. Always translucent and included, with some milky portions, they are used for the carving of statuettes and are called amethystine quartz.

The Color of Amethyst

Amethyst ranges from a reddish violet to a bluish violet to truly purple tones. Of varying intensity, the color is often distributed in bands parallel to the termination faces of the crystal. Often only the pyramidal tip is colored, the rest of the crystal being colorless or smoky. The art of the lapidary resides in making the tint of the cut stone appear homogenous by "placing" the color appropriately.

The color distribution in a faceted stone can easily be seen by immersing the stone in water in a frosty container. This color seems to be related to the polysynthetic twinning observed in the mineral. It is attributed to the presence of iron (always detected at concentrations of a few ten-thousandths), involving an unpaired electron of a tetravalent iron ion that replaces the silicon in the quartz lattice (stable only at low temperatures in the quartz environment). Amethyst is commonly included, with "zebra stripes" due to twinning-related tensions, sometimes filled with carbon dioxide, or with goethite and hematite crystals in the form of irregular reddish fibers, blades, and the like.

Amethyst's color is stable only to 250°C (480°F). Most amethysts fade at higher temperatures. Fading may occur if the amethyst in a piece of jewelry is not protected from heat during repair or if the jewel falls into fire.

At around 500°C (930°F), faded amethyst becomes yellow citrine. If the temperature is increased, additional fading is observed, preceding, at around 600°C (1,100°F) the appearance of inframicroscopic water (an aggregate of the hydroxyl groups always present in quartz), which makes the quartz translucent (girasol), and then milky (this process has been used to produce moonstone imitations).

Amethyst is frequently heat treated to produce citrine. The reaction of amethyst to such treatment varies from one deposit to the next: amethyst from Madagascar fades but does not turn yellow, that from Montezuma (Brazil) becomes green; others turn yellow without first fading. All this implies that little-understood mechanisms, different from those mentioned above, come into play during light absorption.

Generally, citrines or faded amethysts can recover their original tint by irradiation, which regenerates tetravalent iron. However, when heated above 450°C (840°F), the amethyst color center is irreversibly destroyed.

Amethyst dichroism is often fairly distinct: the ordinary ray shows a violetish red and the extraordinary ray a bluish violet. The other physical properties are the same as those of quartz (see QUARTZ).

Deposits

The conditions for amethyst deposition vary greatly. Amethyst is widespread in geodes found in the basalts of Uruguay and Rio Grande do Sul, Brazil. It crystallizes late, at low temperatures, from 75° to 195°C (165° to 385°F), covering the cavities of silica-depleted igneous rocks with crystals. The main deposits are Irai Lageado, from which a very large portion of the Brazilian production originates, and Palmeiras.

Beautiful crystals are mined in various places in the state of Bahia, in particular the Grota do Coxo near Jacobina, 200 kilometers (about 125 miles) northwest of Salvador. The deposit is embedded in quartzites; it has been known for about fifty years and is still exploited. The geodes are almost always isolated and may reach over a meter in diameter. They consist of a thick layer of amethyst filling the cavities of an enormous quartzite chasm. Crystals can reach 30 centimeters in their longest dimension and vary from purple to dark violet in color. The gem parts may be big enough to cut 100-carat faceted stones.

In the region of Vitoria de Conquista, a number of deposits are found in gneisses or quartzites, in particular the mines of Fazenda Joanina, Coruia, Baixinha, and especially Montezuma, from which crystals, turned green by heat treatment at 650°C (1,200°F), are sold as "peridine"; these have not yet proven popular.

Amethyst necklace: the crystals are from Mexico, the slabs from Uruguay. J. Vendôme design.

Detail of an amethyst necklace with amethyst cabochons (160 carats total weight), emeralds, and diamonds (around 1960). Creation by Mellerio (Meller).

The large crystals from the alluvial deposit of Brejinho das Ametistas, near Caetité, can produce large faceted stones.

Because of its abundance, the Brazilian production caused amethyst prices to drop. Indeed, good-quality amethyst has become almost common since the end of the nineteenth century. Very recently, an enormous deposit was discovered in the Pará (Pau d'Arco) near Maraba; the color and quality are exceptional.

In the past, geodes from the Deccan basalts in India were the main sources of amethyst. Later, other deposits of minor importance became sources (Erzgebirge in Bohemia, Idar-Oberstein in Germany, Auvergne in France).

In the eighteenth century, most amethysts came from Russia (Murzinka, Ural), where they were extracted from veins in the granite. Their dark reddish violet color, becoming redder in candlelight, was particularly popular.

In France amethyst is found in Mont Blanc (glacier des Améthystes) and in the Vosges (lac des Corbeaux), but it has been sporadically extracted mainly from Auvergne since the eighteenth century, in Vernet-la-Varenne, Pégut, and other places south of the Puy-de-Dôme, from more or less amethystine quartz veins running through the granite. These veins, one to several feet thick and sometimes almost a mile long, consist of white quartz that became amethyst only in the thinner parts (approximately 10 centimeters [25 inches] wide). These deposits, exploited by J. Demarty at the turn of the century, employed about twenty workers; with the installation of a cutting factory in an old mill in the Tiretaine valley near Royat, the Taillerie de Royat, which popularized Auvergne amethysts, began. Its operation could not be sustained because of the competition from Brazilian amethyst.

Good amethysts are also found in Mexico (in the states of Guanajato, Veracruz, Guerrero, for. example), and in the United States, in Maine and North Carolina. Madagascar pegmatites have long produced beautiful gems, as have those in Zambia and Namibia.

Similar-looking Gems

Light purple amethyst can be mistaken for pinkish gems, such as kunzite and morganite. All purple gems may be mistaken for amethyst and probably were during antiquity: particularly noteworthy are purple sapphire, mauve spinel, almandite garnet, cordierite, and violet fluorite. Purple zircon and tourmaline have been used more recently. A little attention is all that is needed to distinguish these gems, using their very different optical properties.

Imitations

As early as the sixteenth century, quartz–purple glass–quartz triplets were fabricated to imitate amethyst and purple sapphire. Today amethyst imitations are primarily purple glass and synthetic purple corundums.

Synthetics

Synthetic hydrothermal amethysts have been grown in the Soviet Union since 1975 (see QUARTZ). Very clean and strongly dichroic, these amethysts are infrequently marketed because of their high cost. Their color is stable up to 500°C (930°F), in contrast with that of natural amethysts. They have a characteristic infrared absorption spectrum. The seed from which they were grown is often visible on the larger stones (1 centimeter long).

AMETRINE

Name given to a variety of quartz having the colors of both *amethyst* and *citrine*. It has also been called amethyst-citrine, citrine-amethyst, and trystine.

The rough and the faceted stones distinctly show the two colors, making this gem very unique. A 108.5-carat faceted stone is displayed at the Natural History Museum of Los Angeles County.

These stones appeared in 1980 in Brazil. Their origin, uncertain at first, is Bolivian. The coexistence of both purple and yellow colors can be obtained in natural amethysts by applying heat treatment. Synthetic ametrine has been produced in the Soviet Union.

ANDALUSITE

An aluminum silicate that crystallizes in the orthorhombic system. It is named for Andalusia, the region in Spain where it was originally discovered.

Iron can replace aluminum in the andalusite structure, up to 3.5 percent, which increases the indices of refraction (n_p = 1.629 to 1.638; n_m = 1.633 to 1.645; n_g = 1.639 to 1.648) but reduces the birefringence (from 0.011 to 0.007, biaxial negative). Traces of manganese may be present. The specific gravity of andalusite ranges from 3.12 to 3.18. Gem-quality crystals are brown or yellow with some green; their color is due to the presence of iron and manganese. Andalusite dichroism is usually strong, with the following associated colors: green-yellow, bright green, and brownish green. Pinkish brown andalusites are often encountered as well.

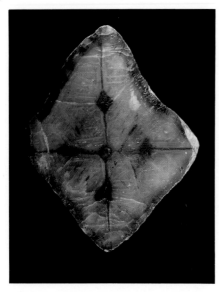

Andalusite (chiastolite variety) from the Dakotas. Width: 3 cm. Sorbonne collection.

In addition to a weak band in the blue-violet range, the absorption spectrum includes three to five fine lines in the yellow-green, especially strong for green andalusites from Brazil. No luminescence is observed under black light.

Negative crystals containing carbon dioxide or fine acicular crystals may be included in the gem. The crystals, often elongated, have an almost square section. There is a good cleavage parallel to the prism faces. The hardness is 7½. The physical properties and color of faceted andalusite, close to those of tourmaline, could fool a negligent observer. This gem is used mostly by Brazilian jewelers.

Andalusite is found associated with garnets in pegmatites and certain granites. It is, however, the typical mineral of contact metamorphism in clay sediments (at high pressure and temperature, it changes to kyanite and sillimanite).

The best gem andalusites come from the gem-bearing gravels of Sri Lanka and Brazil (San Tereza, in the state of Espírito Santo). A 28.3-carat faceted gem is displayed at the Smithsonian Institution, and another of 40 carats is in the Museum National d'Histoire Naturelle in Paris.

ANDRADITE

A ferrocalcic garnet, named for Andrada, a Brazilian mineralogist. See DEMANTOID; MELANITE; TOPAZOLITE.

APATITE

A series of fluorinated or chlorinated calcium phosphates, belonging to the hexagonal system. The extremes—or poles—of the series are fluorapatite, chlorapatite, and hydroxylapatite. Gem apatites are essentially fluorapatites.

Origin of the Name

Apatite comes from the Greek *apetein* ("to fool," "to deceive"). This name was given by the German mineralogist Abraham Werner in 1786, because the diversity of apatite's crystal shapes caused it to be easily mistaken for other gems, such as beryl.

Physical Properties

Numerous substitutions can occur in the chemical structure of apatite: calcium may be replaced by strontium, manganese, rare-earth elements (cerium, lanthanum, yttrium), alkalis (sodium, potassium, barium), and the like. In addition, a carbonate compound may partially replace the phosphate compound (especially in the massive

Apatite crystal from Durango, Mexico. Height: 5 cm. Sorbonne collection.

variety: see COLLOPHANE). Apatites are uniaxial negative, with a very weak birefringence; the values of the indices of refraction are 1.630 and 1.633 for fluorapatite, 1.646 and 1.651 for hydroxylapatite, and 1.667 and 1.668 for chlorapatite. The variations in the indices of refraction of gem apatites are usually from 1.630 to 1.640 and 1.633 to 1.645. Their specific gravity ranges from 3.17 to 3.23. Their luminescence is very weak.

The hexagonal crystals are rarely acicular, more often elongated or flat. They are terminated either by a simple basal face or by a pyramidal arrangement. Cleavage is normally indistinct but may be fair to good. Its low hardness (it defines 5 on the Mohs scale) makes it a collector's stone, difficult to use in jewelry.

Deposits

Apatite is widespread all over the world in sodium-lithium and potassic pegmatites, where purple and blue varieties are frequent. It forms beautiful crystals of all colors in deposits of tin and tungsten (Panasqueira, Portugal), in porphyry-type deposits, in alpine clefts, and in metamorphic rocks. It is usually extracted from secondary deposits, such as gem-bearing gravels.

Yellow apatite is the most common variety. Its absorption spectrum, attributed to rare earth elements, shows two groups of sharp lines, one in the yellow and the other in the green. Its luminescence is generally violetish. It comes primarily from contact iron deposits (pyrometasomatic) from Cerro Mercado in Mexico. Similar apatites are found on the Iranian island of Hormuz, in the Persian Gulf region.

Green apatite comes from the Murcia province in Spain (asparagus apatites) and from the Madras province in India (water-green apatites). It can be fairly dichroic, does not show a distinct absorption spectrum, and has a greenish luminescence.

Strongly dichroic blue apatite (with a blue extraordinary ray and a pale yellow ordinary ray) comes from the gem-bearing gravels of Mogok (Myanmar, now Burma) and from Sri Lanka. Its absorption spectrum shows lines in the blue and the green attributable to praseodymium, and it produces a violetish blue to sky blue luminescence.

Purple apatite is found in Saxony (Germany), Bohemia (Czechoslovakia), Ticino (Switzerland), Panasqueira (Portugal), and Maine (United States) It exhibits a yellow-green luminescence.

Cat's eye apatite has been found in the gem-bearing gravels of Sri Lanka.

Brazil (especially the state of Minas Gerais) produces apatites of all colors; pink in the gold mine of Morro-Velho, deep blue, green, chatoyant, and more, which generally come from various pegmatites (for example, Itatiaia, near the city of Governador Valadares).

The Smithsonian Institution displays two 29-carat apatites, a yellow one from Mexico and a yellow-green one from Mogok, as well as a 8.8-carat blue apatite from Sri Lanka; The Museum National d'Histoire Naturelle in Paris owns a 31.4-carat green apatite from Brazil.

AQUAMARINE

A light blue to greenish blue beryl, more valuable when it is a darker blue.

Origin of the Name and Folklore

The word comes from the Latin *aqua marina,* meaning "sea water," a term introduced in the literature in 1604 by Boece de Boot in translating a sixteenth-century Italian expression.

In India aquamarine was once considered an amulet, and in ancient Egypt it was carved into a talisman. Its occult properties were more extensively described during the Middle Ages. It guarantees a happy marriage and inspires mutual fidelity in both newlyweds. It protects sailors and those who travel by sea. It strengthens its owner, and it preserves and heals the eyes. All these alleged properties derive from its color and its usage as a magnifying lens.

Famous Aquamarines

Known in antiquity as beryl, aquamarine was most likely first found in Indian deposits (cited by Strabo at the beginning of this era) and from the gem-bearing gravels of Sri Lanka. A versified seventeenth-century translation of the *Liber Lapidum,* written in the eleventh century in Latin by Marbodus, future bishop of Rennes in France, indicates that this gem was then widely used: "The Elders valued that which light tone / Evokes the pure oil or the water of the sea."

Among the best-known antique aquamarines are Nero's loupe and numerous intaglios, including the portrait by Evodos (first century A.D.) of Julia (Titus's daughter), considered in the Middle Ages to be a portrait of the Virgin Mary (now displayed in the Paris Cabinet of Medals). During the sixteenth century, the Japanese carved netsukes in aquamarine. Among recent piece of jewelry, a parure presented by Brazil to Queen Elizabeth II is remarkable for its outstanding combination of dark blue aquamarines.

The discovery of large crystals made it possible to cut very large stones, used by museums, especially in the United States, to interest the public in gemology. The largest faceted aquamarine, a 2,594-ct (518.8-gram) step-cut is in the Los Angeles County Museum. A greenish 1,000-carat aquamarine (named Most Precious) and a bright blue 911-carat stone (from Três Barras, Brazil) are displayed at the Smithsonian Institution in Washington, D.C. In Europe the Kunsthistorisches Museum in Vienna owns a 492-carat stone, probably cut from a Russian crystal. Other beautiful aquamarines, of 331 carats and 293 carats are in the British Museum.

Aquamarine intaglio from the first century A.D. It was set in Carolingian times to be seen through the top side of the polished transparent stone. It depicts Julia, daughter of the Roman emperor Titus. Cabinet of Medals, Bibliothèque Nationale, Paris.

Mineralogy and Physical Properties

The color of aquamarine is due to the presence of ferrous iron in the channel of the beryl structure. The yellow component of greenish aquamarines may disappear after heat treatment. The vast majority of Brazilian aquamarines presently on the market is heated at the mine. This treatment accentuates the dichroism: blue along the extraordinary ray, and almost an absence of color among the ordinary ray. An absorption band in the violet is sometimes seen with the spectroscope, accompanied by a weak band in the blue. Aquamarine's specific gravity falls between 2.68 and 2.73; its indices of refraction, between 1.570 and 1.585 for the ordinary ray and 1.565 and 1.580 for the extraordinary ray, with a birefringence of 0.005 to 0.008.

Aquamarine from Virgem de Lapa, Minas Gerais, Brazil Height: 7 cm. K. Proctor collection, United States.

S ring with aquamarine and diamonds. J. Vendôme design.

Inclusions

Most aquamarines set in jewelry are flawless or almost so. Sometimes there are negative crystals with two-fluid phase inclusions, often seen as tubes running parallel to the sixfold axis; when they are numerous and thin, they are evoke a light rain in the stone. More rarely, platelike or needlelike ilmenite crystals are seen trapped in the basal plane, reminiscent of black chrysanthemum flowers.

Brazilian Aquamarines

The first Brazilian aquamarines were discovered during expeditions organized by the governor Duarte de Costa, between 1551 and 1554. It was an epic story of the *bandeirantes,* who, following the Jequitinhonha River, traversed part of the present state of Minas Gerais. Not until 1811 was the first large aquamarine found: a grass-green crystal weighing 7 kilograms, in the bed of the São Mateus River, close to Teófilo Otoni. Chunks of the rough stone were sent to Europe to be faceted. In 1850 numerous immigrants, in particular Germans from the Idar-Oberstein area, settled in the small town of Teófilo Otoni, which rapidly became Brazil's center for pegmatite mining. The new immigrants, with their knowledge of gems, realized the importance of this region, and close relations were quickly established between Brazil and Germany. The first *garimpeiros* settled about 75 kilometers (45 miles) north of Teófilo Otoni on the banks of the Marambaia River. Here, on March 28, 1910, two Syrians, the Tamouri brothers, found the most fabulous aquamarine crystal of this century. Biterminated, weighing 110.5 kilograms (48.5 by 38.4 centimeters), or 552,500 carats, it was a beautiful blue, so clean and transparent that a newspaper could easily be read through it. Its present value would be about $30 million. The American Museum of Natural History in New York owns a fragment of about 6 kilograms (29,000 carats), donated by the famous collector J. P. Morgan.

Sometime later, beautiful aquamarines were discovered in Santa Maria de Itabira, the name often used to refer to the best aquamarines, even those from other localities. This discovery was much publicized, and miners poured in, although this region of Minas Gerais was then covered by such a thick vegetation that it was accessible only by horse.

In 1954 a group of prospectors working an alteration zone on a hill slope in the Marambaia area exposed a 33.928-kilogram (173,000-carat) crystal, from which 57,200 carats of superb gems were cut. It became the famous Marta Rocha aquamarine,

Brazilian aquamarines (14, 24, and 41 carats). F. A. Becker collection, Idar-Oberstein, Germany.

named for Miss Brazil of 1954. This find triggered a rush of thousands of *garimpeiros,* who did enormous damage to this essentially agricultural area. The only crystal ever found at this site, despite the extensive mining that followed, was at a place called Pinheiros in 1964: a 22-kilogram aquamarine of the most delightful color ever seen, fractured in four segments.

In 1967 a 100 percent gem aquamarine was exposed by a bulldozer. A host of *garimpeiros* scattered throughout the area. One of the Três Barras mines produced over a ton of facet-grade beryl during its first days. Local farmers abandoned their farms to search for aquamarines.

In 1973, in an alteration zone situated close to the village of Coronel Murta, on the banks of the Jequitinhonha River north of Teófilo Otoni (Frade or Pedra do Frade deposit), remarkable aquamarines of an intense blue were discovered; they produced only small stones of 1 to 3 carats.

In northern Minas Gerais are thousands of small claims, from Governador Valadares to the south of Vitória da Conquista. Some localities became famous for the beauty of their stones, including Fortaleza, Medina, Pedra Azul, and Cercadinho. Outside of Minas Gerais, nice aquamarines have been found in the states of Espírito Santo, Goiás, and Rio Grande do Norte.

It is interesting to note that gem tourmaline is virtually absent from aquamarine deposits; only black tourmaline can form there.

Other Sources

After World War I, Madagascar became famous for the quality of the stones found there. The Tongafeno deposit, a pegmatite with coarse elements intruding in mica schist and rich in rose quartz, is famous for its magnificent blue aquamarines.

The Soviet Union was a source of remarkable and beautiful aquamarine crystals from the Ural Mountains, especially in the locality of Murzinsk, where beryl forms in perfect gem crystals in the cavities of granite, accompanied by smoky quartz, topaz, feldspar, and mica. A crystal group 27 centimeters high and 3 centimeters in diameter (about 10½ by 1⅛ inches) is displayed in the Leningrad (Saint Petersburg) School of Mines mineral collection. These deposits, known since the beginning of the nineteenth century, especially Alabashka, Sisikova, Yushakova, and Sarapulskaya, supplied the imperial cutting factories in Ekaterinburg (now Sverdlovsk). The Nerchinsk mining district in the Chita Oblast (formerly Transbaikalia) is also very important. Known since 1723, the Adun Chalon site is famous for the quality of the crystals found in the cavities of a pegmatitic rock intruding a granite. Beryls of various colors, including pale green, pale blue, yellow-green, and honey yellow, often associated with topaz, can reach large dimensions; a 30-centimeter-long (almost 12 inches) gem crystal, 5 centimeters (2 inches) across, is on display at the British Museum.

In Asia aquamarine is found in Afghanistan (the Kunar valley, Pech valley, and Laghmān valley in Nuristan) and in Pakistan (Gilgit area in Kashmir), where small (maximum 10 centimeter, or 4 inches long), perfect pale blue crystals associated with black tourmaline are reminiscent of those from Transbaikalia.

Aquamarine has also occasionally been found in other countries, in particular, Nigeria, Mozambique, and Namibia.

Maxixe Blue Beryl

A cobalt blue beryl was found in 1917 in the Maxixe mine, about 620 miles northwest of Teófilo Otoni, Brazil. This unusual beryl transmits its blue color, attributed to NO_3 color centers, by the extraordinary ray, whereas the ordinary ray is colorless, unlike that in aquamarine. Since that discovery, some light-colored Brazilian beryls, turned blue by gamma ray irradiation, have been marketed as "halbanite"; however, these beryls, which have a color close to that of the natural beryls from the Maxixe mine, often fade when exposed to daylight. Their color center, attributed to unstable CO_3^-, creates three absorption bands easily visible in the green, yellow, and orange parts of the visible spectrum.

Cut

Aquamarine is usually step-cut, with the table parallel to the crystal axis to favor the blue color (this also produces a higher yield). The Brazilian cut is characterized by a long culet, with pavilion facets on the narrow side forming a fairly small angle with the table.

Similar-looking Gems

Blue topaz, after being treated with radiation and then heat, closely resembles aquamarine. Other light blue look-alikes include zircon, sapphire, euclase, tourmaline, jeremejevite, and fluorite.

Imitations

Blue glass, garnet-and-glass doublets, and especially light blue synthetic spinel are used as imitations of aquamarine. All these products owe their color to cobalt. Thus, they display an absorption spectrum typical of this element and appear red when viewed through a Chelsea filter, unlike aquamarine, which appears more green.

AVENTURINE

A quartzite (or polycrystalline quartz) containing mica or hematite platelets.

Aventurine is probably the only gem to have a name derived from that of a manufactured product: a Murano glass from the region of Venice, Italy, containing randomly dispersed small copper platelets is called *a l'avventura*.

Nonoriented mica platelets give aventurine quartz its characteristic brilliance. The most valued aventurine is the green variety, which contains fuchsite inclusions. It comes from the vicinity of Madras and Mysore in India, as well as from Brazil.

In addition to its use in jewelry (as cabochons and spheres), it is carved to produce decorative objects, which can evoke jade quite convincingly. It occasionally displays scalloped growth banding reminiscent of malachite, for which it can be mistaken. However, the physical properties of aventurine (specific gravity of 2.64 to 2.69, hardness of 5, index of refraction of 1.55) make its identification easy.

The South Kensington Geological Museum in London displays a large aventurine vase from the Tomsk region of central Asia, donated by Czar Nicholas II, as well as a red-brown aventurine from Almería (Spain) and a blue aventurine from Jaipur (India).

Aventurine deposits are diverse. This gem material can form veinlets in schists and is also found in alluvial deposits. The Soviet Union has been the main source of aventurine (Zlatoust area in the Urals), but Bavaria (Germany) and France have also produced some (a brown variety was found near Nantes).

Aventurine glass, with triangular or hexagonal copper platelets has similar physical properties, but it can be easily separated from aventurine on the basis of its inclusions and its fake appearance. It is distributed worldwide.

AXINITE

A borosilicate containing aluminum, iron, manganese, and calcium, which crystallizes in a triclinic system. This cyclosilicate has a structure similar to that of tourmaline, which faceted axinites resemble.

The flat, sharp-edged crystals of axinite look like an axe, hence, its name, from the Greek *axine* ("axe"), given by R. J. Haüy in 1799. Its color varies from orangish-yellow (manganiferous variety) to "cinnamon" brown-violet, with much brilliance. Very dichroic (olive green–violetish blue–cinnamon brown), axinite generally shows three absorption bands of the blue and blue-green wavelengths; indices of refraction vary slightly with composition (n_p = 1.674 to 1.693; n_m = 1.681 to 1.701; n_g = 1.684 to 1.704, with a birefringence of 0.010 to 0.011), as does specific gravity (3.26 to 3.30). Its hardness of 7 and the absence of cleavage make its use in jewelry possible.

It is a mineral related to acidic pneumatolytic action, found especially in the alpine clefts of France and Switzerland. The

Aquamarine from Tongafeno, Madagascar. Mrs. B. Amster collection.

region of Bourg d'Oisans, France, was particularly famous for axinite in the nineteenth century. Today gem-quality axinites come from American and Mexican California, as well as from the state of Bahia, Brazil, where crystals over 20 centimeters long (almost 8 inches) have been found.

The Smithsonian Institution has a 23.6-carat faceted brown axinite from Baja California, Mexico.

AZURITE

A hydrous copper carbonate, crystallizing in the monoclinic system.

Its name comes from its azure blue color, opaque to translucent, which explains its use by painters (Armenian stone). Transparent in small chips or thin crystals, it is sometimes massive. It may form thick botrioïdal concretions or stalactites, just like malachite, with which it is often associated; their concentric blue and green zonations, very attractive, were called *verd azur* in the past. They were used as ornamental stones and even as cabochons, despite their low hardness, 3.4 to 4. Azurite's specific gravity is 3.77 and, like malachite, can be attacked by diluted acids, producing a strong effervescence.

In the past it was found in small amounts in the Chessy copper deposit, near Lyon, France, and later in Tsumeb, Namibia, where the most magnificent specimens were unearthed. Recently, spectacular crystals have been discovered in the Touissit deposit in Morocco, near Oujda. Deposits in Arizona (Morenci, Bisbee) sporadically provide beautiful specimens for ornamentation.

Azurite crystals from Conceptión del Oro, Mexico. Length: 0.4 cm. J. C. Boulliard collection.

b

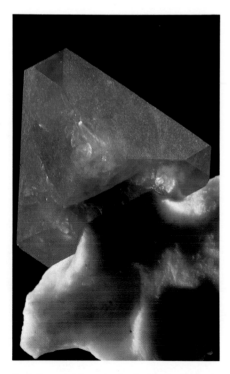

Benitoite crystal from San Benito County, California. Length: 0.8 cm. R. H. Gill collection.

BENITOITE

A barium and titanium silicate, crystallizing in the hexagonal crystal system (the only known example of triangular tetartohedry).

The History of Benitoite

Two prospectors, J. M. Couch and L. B. Hawkins, discovered this mineral in the fall of 1906 in San Benito County, California. They believed it was sapphire and presented it as such to a San Francisco lapidary, who submitted the samples to Professor G. D. Louderback. He identified them as a new mineral species, which he named benitoite because of its provenance.

The deposit is located in the western San Joaquin Valley, in the southern part of the Coast Ranges, a formation made of high-pressure metamorphic rock associated with serpentines. It is the only place in the world where benitoite has been found to date. Benitoite and other rare species are found here in natrolite-filled cavities in a folded amphibolite.

Exploited since 1907 with small shafts, the deposit was abandoned in 1912; it has been reworked since 1967 to produce mineral specimens for collectors.

Physical Properties

The sapphire blue color of benitoite, ranging from near colorless to deep blue, is attributed to titanium. It is generated only along the extraordinary ray; despite their tabular triangular shape, the crystals must be faceted in such a way that the table is parallel to the symmetry axis, which prevents a good yield. It is very dichroic, inert under black light but brightly luminescent (light blue) under short-wave ultraviolet. Benitoite is uniaxial positive, with indices of refraction of 1.757 for the ordinary ray and 1.804 for the extraordinary ray, with a birefringence of 0.047. However, the strong absorption of the extraordinary ray does not allow the clear observation of doubling. Fine natrolite needles are sometimes included in the crystals. A hasty observer may mistake benitoite for a Sri Lankan sapphire. However, the specific gravity is only 3.65, and the hardness is slightly less than that for quartz (6½ to 7). Despite the small size of its crystals and its rarity, benitoite is a good gem to set in jewelry because it is fairly tough.

Benitoite, however, remains a collector's gem: faceted stones over 2 carats are very rare. The largest known, at the Smithsonian Institution in Washington, D.C. weighs 7.66 carats. A complete parure was made with benitoites; the necklace, which included a 6.53-carat pendant, was stolen and then found, but the pendant is missing.

BERYL

A beryllium aluminosilicate, belonging to the hexagonal system. See also AQUAMARINE; EMERALD; GOSHENITE; HELIODOR; and MORGANITE.

Origin of the Name

Already familiar to the Greeks as *berullos,* akin to the Sanskrit *vaidurya* ("crystal"), beryl described at that time a colorless stone with some brilliance. Shortened to *brill,* this term engendered the Italian *brillare* and the French *briller;* English inherited *brilliance.*

Beryl was used to make loupes. The famous emerald loupe belonging to Nero was probably a light-colored beryl. Beryl thus became synonymous with *lens,* which in German became *brille* ("spectacles") and in French *bérique* and later *bésicles.* The name *beryl* has designated all varieties of this species only since the nineteenth century; it was formerly synonymous with aquamarine: "Beryl is a precious stone which bears the blue-green color of the sea" (Boece de Boot).

Structure and Physical Properties

This cyclosilicate consists of silica rings parallel to the base of the crystal, connected by aluminum and beryllium atoms. These rings form channels parallel to the prism axis, where a number of impurities are found (alkali metals such as potassium, rubidium, cesium, sodium, lithium, hydroxyl groups, and inert gases). In addition, part of the aluminum (about 2 percent) is often replaced by ions of similar size (isomorphic substitution), such as chromium, iron, titanium, vanadium, manganese, and magnesium.

Beryl almost always crystallizes well, showing hexagonal prisms with striations running parallel to the elongation; it is rarely smooth. Most often the prisms terminate at a basal face, sometimes accompanied by small pyramidal faces forming a crown; pyramidal terminations are rarer. Common beryls are elongated along the sixfold axis, although pink beryls are flat along this axis, as are some green Brazilian

Beryl crystals from Tres Barras, Minas Gerais, Brazil. Height: 5.5 cm. K. Proctor collection, United States.

beryls. A barrel habit also exists, terminating at a multitude of small, juxtaposed points (in aquamarine and morganite). An exceptional, imperfect basal cleavage may be enhanced by disc-shaped negative crystals parallel to the base (in Siberian emeralds). Crystals are often cracked along the sixfold axis and joined by quartz or feldspar. Beryls found in geodes have shiny faces and nicely formed terminations. Sometimes growing parallel, they may display an acicular or "bacillary" habit.

The fracture of beryl is conchoidal and uneven, with a glassy luster. Its hardness is 7½ to 8. It is tough, but the presence of numerous inclusions (especially healed fractures) may make it breakable.

The existence of structural channels containing various impurities accounts for the range in specific gravity (from 2.68 to 2.91), indices of refraction (ordinary ray: 1.568 to 1.602; extraordinary ray: 1.564 to 1.595), and birefringence (-0.004 to

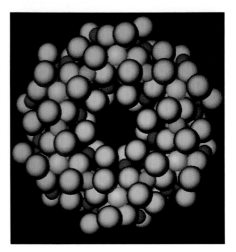

Computer-generated image of a beryl's structure: oxygen in yellow, aluminum in blue, beryllium in green, and silicon in red. Courtesy of the Mineralogy-Crystallography Laboratory at Pierre and Marie Curie University, Paris.

−0.009). The color is caused by elements that are foreign to the beryl structure. The dichroism is detectable, with the extraordinary ray always showing the bluer colors. Colored beryls used as gems have been given the following names: goshenite (colorless), aquamarine (pale blue to blue-green), emerald (green), heliodor (yellow), morganite (pink), red beryl, sometimes improperly called bixbyite (red). The term *vorobyevite*, used to designate a cesium-rich pink beryl, was coined by Vladimir Vernadsky in 1908 in honor of V. I. Vorobyev (1875–1906). Today it is used only by Soviet authors and is synonymous with morganite.

A dark brown beryl displaying asterism was found a few years ago in Brazil in the state of Minas Gerais; it contains fine ilmenite needles parallel to the prism faces.

Deposits

Beryl is found primarily in granitic pegmatites, where it is encountered with topaz and other beryllium minerals, which are often gems as well (such as euclase, chrysoberyl, phenakite, hambergite, and jeremejevite). Three types of beryl-containing pegmatites have been defined:

· Well-differentiated, zoned, granitic pegmatites, with abundant muscovite and microcline. They are often imbedded in metamorphic rocks in the neighborhood of granitic intrusions. The following succession can be observed from the outside to the core: a peripheral aplitic zone, a zone with microcline feldspar and quartz in a graphic structure, a zone with giant crystals of microcline and quartz. Beryl is localized at the edge of the quartz core and its environment,

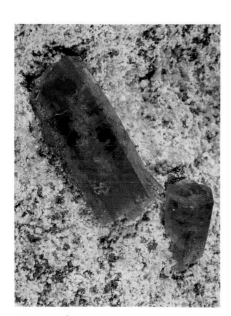

Red beryl from the Wah-Wah Mountains of Utah. Length: 3 cm. Sorbonne collection.

forming crystals a few centimeters to a few meters long. It is sometimes gathered in pockets of various sizes and distribution.

· Albitized pegmatites with muscovite. Beryl is related there to the albitization zone both at the border of the quartz core and at the proximity of the host rocks.

· Albitized pegmatites with spodumene and lepidolite, showing considerable albitization and zonal structure. Beryl is associated with spodumene (sometimes kunzite) and can reach 10 centimeters (4 inches). In lithium-rich zones, morganite is predominant.

Gem beryl is also found in pneumatolytic hydrothermal deposits, in particular greisens mined for tungsten, tin, and molybdenum. Red beryl has been encountered in Utah, in a region where sedimentary rocks are intruded by igneous rocks, in which red beryl crystals are found next to major faults.

RED BERYL

Red beryl was discovered in 1897 by Maynard Bixby in the topaz deposits of Utah, which has been mentioned since 1859 by H. Englemann. It has been found since in the Wah Wah Mountains and Thomas Range in Utah, as well as in New Mexico (Black Range and East Granite Ridge) and Mexico (San Luis Potosí).

Utah is home to the world's largest deposit of bertrandite—a rare beryllium silicate—impregnating a rhyolitic tuff. This abundance of beryllium explains the presence of red beryl (colored by manganese), which is associated with bixbyite (a manganese oxide) and spessartite (a manganese-rich garnet).

Red beryl crystals are small, at most 25 millimeters (1 inch) long with a 10- to 15-millimeter (½-inch) diameter, grouped in the geodes or fractures of the altered rock from which they are easily extracted. This gem nevertheless remains a collector's stone, an uncommon mineral rarely producing faceted stones of more than 1 or 2 carats.

BERYLLONITE

A sodic beryllium phosphate (hence its name) crystallizing in the monoclinic system, with a pseudoorthorhombic symmetry.

Beryllonite is a collector's stone. Colorless, sometimes yellowish with a glassy luster, it is biaxial negative ($n_p = 1.552$, $n_m = 1.558$, and $n_g = 1.562$). It is rather soft (H is 5), has a perfect cleavage, and is soluble in acids. Its specific gravity is 2.85.

Gem-quality crystals have been found in the Stoneham pegmatite in Maine, associated with beryl and phenakite, as well as in an altered pegmatite near Newry in the same region, associated with herderite, eosphorite, tourmaline, and albite.

A 5-carat faceted stone is on display at the Smithsonian Institution.

BEZOAR

A stone-like concretion formed in the digestive tracts of various animals, especially ruminants, reputed in the past to be of medical value.

Origin of the Name and History of Bezoar

The name refers to its occult virtues, from the Chaldean *bel* ("master") and *zaar* ("venom"); or from the Persian *bi* ("without") and *zarar* ("damage," "lesion").

The Oriental bezoar, from the vicinity of the town of Lar in Persia, was produced by the ibex when eating certain herbs. The concretion started on the herbal mass and grew in successive concentric layers. "Shah Abbas I (1571–1629) valued them so highly that he posted guards at Starbarum [near Lar] to control all bezoar stones exceeding a certain size," wrote Pierre de Rosnel in 1667. These "stones" can indeed reach the size of a goose egg and may cause the death of the animal. Generally, they are evacuated sooner by the ill creature. Other caprines also produce bezoars when their food makes it possible, especially in India (Coromandel coast) and in Peru ("Occidental bezoar").

A bezoar was said to be a cure for all kinds of poisons and infectious diseases, worms, epilepsy, and other ailments. Various animal concretions were considered equivalent to bezoar in the Middle Ages, including pig's stone, Malacca stone, lizard's stone, and "toad's stone."

Other materials have been identified with bezoar, such as whiskers or feather balls regurgitated by some predators, such as owls, and most ruminants, such as cows. At the turn of the century, when a farmer would find such a ball under his cows, he would attribute it to a spell and would have his herd exorcised.

Bezoar imitations were produced in the Middle Ages, when the identification of the stone as genuine was of utmost importance, as of course the imitations did not have any of the virtues of the natural ones, "which are said to be so accurately imitated by the Indians" (A. Boece de Boot, 1604).

BLENDE

See SPHALERITE.

BONAMITE

See SMITHSONITE.

BONE

A part of the skeleton of a vertebrate.

Bone has been used since prehistoric times to produce a variety of practical objects (such as needles), sometimes finely engraved. Bone can be carved after eliminating its fat constituents, that is, when it is left with its phosphate components only. Its structure is very porous, characterized by the presence of canals parallel to its elongation, known as the Haversian system; each of them consists of a central canal surrounded by oval laminae (filled normally by the bone cells). The overall texture is fairly coarse. Bone is white but yellows with time and is often dyed. It fluoresces vividly under black light. Its hardness is about 2½; its S.G., about 2. The bones used presently are fairly compact, such as the long bones of the ox and the mandibles of large whales. In addition to gambling chips, bone is used to manufacture small objects, such as rings and brooches. Camel bone has been often used in the Orient to make dagger and sword handles.

Antlers may resemble bone (see HORN). Bone is also a common ivory substitute.

BRAZILIANITE

A hydroxylated aluminosodic phosphate, crystallizing in the monoclinic system. It is named for its country of origin, Brazil.

While cleaning a wheat field located on top of the Corrego Frio pegmatite in Minas Gerais, Brazil, a farmer named Alfredo Severino da Silva picked up about 3 kilograms of transparent yellow crystals, which he thought were beryl or chrysoberyl. The small deposit was immediately exploited with a few partners, and about 40 kilograms of gems were collected. Local gem cutters were discouraged by the mineral's brittleness, its easy and perfect cleavage, and its low hardness (6½). Collecting came to a halt.

In 1944 a specimen was sent for examination to the Belo Horizonte Institute of Technology. Sometime later, two American mineralogists, F. H. Pough and E. P. Henderson, reported to the Brazilian Academy of Sciences on the existence of this new mineral from the Divino district near Conselheiro Pena, Minas Gerais. Mining started again, and numerous partial-gem crystals were uncovered, some very large—more than 20 centimeters (8 inches) long, weighing over 2 kilograms (4 pounds).

Golden to greenish yellow in color, brazilianite is weakly dichroic and does not luminesce. It has the luster of topaz and is

Brazilianite crystal from Corrego Frio, Minas Gerais, Brazil. Height: 2 cm. G. Becker collection, Idar-Oberstein, Germany.

biaxial positive ($n_p = 1.603$, $n_m = 1.612$, and $n_g = 1.623$). Its specific gravity is approximately 2.85. Because crystals may be large, there are large faceted stones (41.9 carats at the Smithsonian Institution, for example).

BRONZITE

See ENSTATITE.

C

CACHOLONG

A porcelainlike opal, so porous that it will adhere to the tongue. Its name, from the Kalmuck (Mongol), means "stone *(cholong)* from the Cach." The Kachgar is a tributary of the Yarkand in Chinese Turkistan (today Xinjiang), where Kalmuck tribes roamed until 1771.

CAIRNGORM

A dark yellowish brown to black quartz, named for the Scottish mountains in which it is found (*cairngorm* is an alteration of the Gaelic *carngorm*, "small mountain of blue stones"). See QUARTZ: SMOKY QUARTZ.

CALCITE

A calcium carbonate, crystallizing in the rhombohedral system. From the Latin *calx, calcis,* meaning "pebble" (numerous pebbles are calcareous). It is the main constituent of onyx marbles (see MARBLE).

Calcite is found in transparent crystals, which may be colored brown, yellow, or pink by trace elements. Despite its fragility (H is 3, perfect cleavage, soluble in diluted acids), it is sometimes cut into cabochons

Calcite crystal from Tsumeb, Namibia. Length: 5 cm. Sorbonne collection.

for collectors, because it spectacularly illustrates doubling. Calcite's indices of refraction are 1.658 for the ordinary ray and 1.486 for the extraordinary ray.

Its specific gravity of 2.71 makes it very helpful as a reference stone for heavy liquids used in separating natural from synthetic emeralds (see EMERALD).

The Smithsonian Institution in Washington displays a 75.8-carat yellow faceted calcite, and the Natural History Museum of Los Angeles County, a 15.14-carat orange calcite.

CAMEO

A carving executed in bas-relief, usually on banded agate, so that the subject appears in a light color against a dark background. Gem materials other than agate are sometimes used.

The terms *camahieu, gamahut, chamayeu,* and *camaeu* appeared in the thirteenth century after the sack of Constantinople on mid-April 1204. They all designated engraved gems, in relief or not, which were considered in the Orient to be jewels par excellence and were brought to Europe during the Fourth Crusade. *Camahieu* comes most certainly from the Greek *keimelion,* denoting a rare and precious object, jealously protected. The jewels, *keimelia,* were indeed guarded by "precious-object guards," *keimeiarkhes,* in the treasures, *keimeiarkhion,* of the palaces and temples ransacked by the Crusaders. To relate the word *cameo* to the Arabic *gama'il* ("flower bud") or to the Greek *kamatos* ("piece of work") seems more risky. *Camahieu* became on one hand *cameo* and on the other *camaïeu* in modern French. Synonymous in the sixteenth century with engraved sard or onyx, *cameo* now designates any kind of engraving in slight relief on an ornamental stone (especially hematite); when the engraving is done on a piece of bicolored nacre, it is called a shell cameo. Cameos have been simulated since antiquity with glasses, assembled colored chalcedonies, and recently, with assembled chalcedony and molded porcelain. (For further information, see the discussion of carved stones in part 1.)

CARBUNCLE

A term commonly used until the seventeenth century, which is now no longer used. It comes directly from the Latin *carbunculus,* meaning "glowing coal." Carbuncle initially comprised all red stones (ruby, pyrope, and others). The poetic metaphor was taken literally: carbuncles were supposed to light temples at night. Later the word seems to have been used only for red garnets (pyrope and almandite).

CARNELIAN

Red chalcedony. Its name, traditionally thought to be akin to *cornum* ("dogwood"), referring to the color of the pulp from this tree, is more likely a derivation from Cornum, a harbor in Sardinia (see SARD). First used as a synonym for sard, the term *cornaline* (*corneole* in Old French) was altered during the sixteenth century to *carneole,* which became *carnelian* in English. The description of sard by Pliny the Elder had convinced the scholars of the time that *cornaline* was derived from the Latin *caro, carnis,* meaning "flesh."

Actually, in the sixteenth century carnelian was believed to stop bleeding. It was also said to protect the wearer from the venom of spiders and scorpions; therefore, it was held sacred in Crete. In Persia it protected against the evil eye.

Cameo depicting Zeus in three agate layers (gray, milky, and amethystine chalcedony). Height: 2.2 cm. M. De Bry collection.

Engraved carnelian ring. Boutique Argana, Paris.

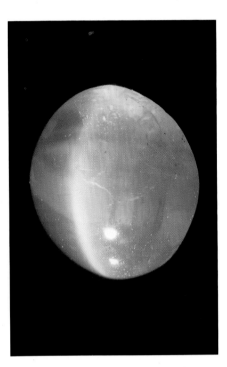

A 0.59-carat cat's-eye chrysoberyl cabochon from Brazil. Grospiron collection.

Detail of a nineteenth-century Turkoman breastplate from central Asia showing carnelian set in silver and gold. Private collection.

Carnelian is translucent and owes its red to brownish red color to iron oxides. Its color gradually becomes the brown of sard. Most carnelians on the market today are chalcedonies dyed with iron salts. A similar process was in use as early as the beginning of the Christian era.

Like sard, carnelian was used for carved seals and engraved intaglios. It has been imitated with engraved or molded glass. Toward the end of the eighteenth century, it became the only gem used on silver mountings by the Turkoman tribes of central Asia. Because of its abundance, it remains the favorite stone of Tibetan, Berber, and Kabyle craftsmen. The main sources of carnelian are the basaltic plateaus of the Deccan in India, Yemen, Rio Grande do Sul in Brazil, and Uruguay.

CAT'S-EYE

This name denotes chatoyant chrysoberyl exclusively. Chatoyancy, caused by numerous thin, tubular channels, is enhanced by a cabochon cut. It is always accompanied by some bluish opalescence characteristic of cymophane. The "iris" of the eye is often sharp and vivid, and this species, because of its hardness, luster, and appearance, overshadows all other chatoyant gems. These other gems (scapolite, prehnite, tourmaline, among others) owe their chatoyancy to the fibrous nature of their crystals or to included mineral needles (such as quartz), so the optical phenomenon seen in them is coarser.

Cat's-eye was highly valued in India during antiquity. Pliny the Elder called it *asterie:* "Asterie has a specific character of holding into it some kind of included light which moves with the inclination . . . it is difficult to cut." He seemed to distinguish among four types: asterie, astrios, astroite, and astrobole, according to the intensity of the phenomenon. He used the term "eye" only for orbicular agate, a gem bearing very different names, such as leucophtalmos, triophtalmos, lycophtalmos, or "Bel's eye," denoting a black center surrounded by white material, named for the Assyrian god Bel.

In the seventeenth century, the name *cat's-eye* was common to these two materials, however distinct. Boece de Boot wrote in 1644, "This precious stone differs from an opaque one which represents the image of a painted eye and that is also called cat's-eye or *oculus beli,* and *bell'ochio* in Italian, and is a variety of agate or onyx."

In Sri Lanka cat's-eye is supposed to protect the wearer from the evil eye. Boece de Boot reported that, in India, "they believe that the riches of one who owns this stone cannot decrease, but that they steadily increase. . . . [Cat's-eye] is so highly valued by the Indians that a stone that was estimated at only 90 crowns in Portugal sold for 600 in India." In Europe cat's-eye worn in a bracelet was supposed to improve sleep and "dissipate horrible dreams."

One of the world's best is the Maharan, a green 58.2-carat cat's-eye cut from a rough from Sri Lanka; it is currently on display at the Smithsonian Institution in Washington. The same museum also displays a gray-green 171.5-carat stone from the same country. The gem-bearing gravels of Sri Lanka seem always to have enjoyed a reputation as the best source for cat's-eyes ("The most noble [cat's-eyes] are found in Zeilan," wrote Boece de Boot). However, some have been found in northern India and in the state of Minas Gerais in Brazil. In 1979 several kilograms of cat's-eye were extracted from the alluvial deposits of Faisca Corrego do Barre (Minas Gerais) and Corrego Alegre (Espirito Santo).

An imitation made of fiberoptic bundles bound together is sold as "Catsite," "Catsteyte" or "Cathaystone."

CEYLONITE

A dark green, iron-rich spinel common on the island of Sri Lanka (formerly Ceylon, hence its name). Its index of refraction (1.77 to 1.80) and specific gravity (3.63 to 3.90) are higher than those for normal spinel.

CHALCEDONY

Cryptocrystalline quartz fibers that form solid, translucent fibrous concretions of uniform color.

Origin of the Name

This stone owes its name to *Karchedon*, the Greek name for Carthage, an important Phoenician port in North Africa, through which it was transported during antiquity. In the seventeenth century, the French terms *charcedoine* and *calcedoine* were equivalent. The derivation from Chalcedon (now Kadiköy), a port in the province of Bithynia (now Turkey) is no longer accepted.

According to Pliny the Elder, chalcedony made athletes invincible, which is why Milo of Crotona, a renowned Greek athlete of the sixth century B.C., always wore one to increase his natural strength before undertaking any match. Boece de Boot considered chalcedony a remedy for melancholy and hoarseness.

Physical Properties

The cryptocrystalline quartz fibers that constitute chalcedony are a few microns in diameter, several hundred microns long, and roughly parallel to each other. They frequently show torsion; therefore most chalcedonies do not show a total extinction of light in the polariscope under crossed polarizers.

Their index of refraction varies with their water content (absorbed through capillarity), from 1.525 to 1.545. Their hardness, 6½, is slightly less than that of quartz, as is their specific gravity (2.57 to 2.64), because of their porosity, due to their cryptocrystalline structure.

Their botryoidal appearance, with adjacent spherulites forming a mamillary layer, produces parallel "bands," sometimes visible in transmitted light.

Colors and Varieties of Chalcedony

When pure, chalcedony is milky and is only slightly porous. It can, however, contain iron or nickel and therefore display colors; such stones have been given particular names in the gem trade: whitish gray to pale milky yellow material is called *common*

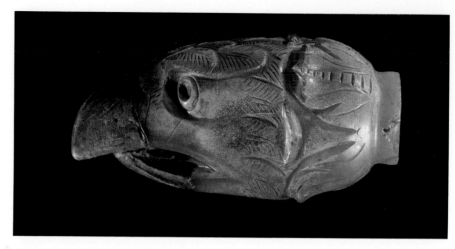

A chalcedony pommel on an imperial scepter, in the form of an eagle's head. Traces of gold can be seen on the beak of this carving, thought to be from the Flavian period of the Roman empire (first century A.D.). Length: 9 cm. Private collection.

chalcedony; light blue to bluish material is called *blue chalcedony;* green chalcedony colored by nickel has been named *chrysoprase;* and the green material colored by chromium, *green agate.* Red chalcedony is called *carnelian;* red-brown, *sard;* and black, *onyx.*

Color Enhancement

Since early antiquity, chalcedony's porosity has been noticed and used to advantage for dying. Most chalcedonies on the gem market today are dyed, a practice considered standard by the CIBJO, except in the case of chrysoprase; a common chalcedony dyed green must be called "green agate."

In Roman times chalcedony was given a dark color by soaking it for seven days and seven nights in a solution of honey and then carbonizing it with sulfuric acid. The main processes used today are similar:

- To produce a black color, chalcedony is carefully cleaned and impregnated with a concentrated sugar solution. It is then treated with sulfuric acid, which causes carbonization. Finally, it is heated to fix the carbonaceous deposits in the pores.
- To produce a dark brown color, chalcedony is impregnated with a diluted sugar solution and simply heated.
- To produce a blue color, chalcedony is impregnated with a potassium ferrocyanide solution and then treated with ferrous sulfate at a warm temperature, which produces a precipitation of Prussian blue in its pores.
- To produce a red color, chalcedony is impregnated with ferrous sulfate and heated.
- To produce a green color, chalcedony is impregnated with chromium salts.

Impregnating chalcedony completely with chemicals requires soaking for several weeks; too rapid a treatment will modify only the superficial layers. Organic dyes such as aniline are sometimes used, but they tend to fade with time.

Deposits

Chalcedony is found in the same places agate is. The two are almost always associated, especially in Brazil.

CHAROITE

A hydrated silicate of potassium, calcium, and sodium, crystallizing in the monoclinic system, closely related to the amphibole group. It was discovered in 1978 in the Murun Mountains in Yakutia (Soviet Union), near the Charo River, from which it received its name.

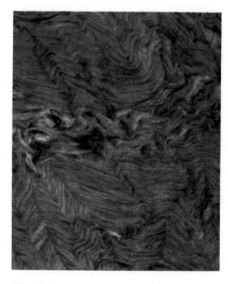

Charoite from Yakutia, U.S.S.R. Height: 5 cm. G. Becker collection, Idar-Oberstein, Germany.

Charoite is the main constituent of a rock made of intertwined fibrous masses. It has an attractive purple to violet color. Tough, with a hardness of 5 to 6, it takes a good polish. The index of refraction is approximately 1.55, and the specific gravity is 2.68. It is an ornamental stone that has been used to produce small carvings, vases, boxes, cabochons, and the like.

Charoite is found in contact with metamorphic calcareous rocks, in association with pyroxenes and feldspars.

CHIASTOLITE

An opaque, whitish andalusite containing carbonaceous inclusions along the diagonals of its almost square section, hence its name, from the Greek *khiastos* ("X-shaped"). It is also called "cross stone."

It was used in the coat of arms of the French noble family Rohan because of its design and its abundance in the castle's lands. Chiastolite slabs cut perpendicular to the prism have been considered amulets, especially in French Brittany and in the Basque country, at the border between France and Spain where the cross stone is found in areas of weak contact metamorphism.

CHLOROMELANITE

See JADE.

CHRYSOBERYL OR CYMOPHANE

A beryllium aluminate, crystallizing in the orthorhombic system. It was named at the end of the eighteenth century (it was then considered a variety of chrysolite) by allusion to its color (*khrusos*, meaning gold in Greek) and its brilliance (*berullos*, "beryl," that is, "stone with brilliance"). See also ALEXANDRITE and CAT'S-EYE.

Structure and Physical Properties

Chrysoberyl has an almost compact stacking of oxygen ions with octahedral vacancies between, half of them occupied by aluminum and an eighth by beryllium (for a description of this compact stacking, see CORUNDUM). The strength of its atomic bonding explains several of the properties of chrysoberyl: it has the highest hardness of all minerals after diamond and corundum (H is 8½), it is tough (cleavages are difficult; the fracture is conchoidal), its specific gravity is high (S.G. is 3.70 to 3.75), and it displays a high luster (indices of refraction are $n_p = 1.746$, $n_m = 1.748$, and $n_g = 1.756$,

with a birefringence of 0.008 to 0.009 and a biaxial positive character).

Aluminum and beryllium are almost always partly replaced by some iron (ferrous or ferric). This element is the cause of the coloration of common chrysoberyl, giving a greenish yellow to brownish color, accompanied by a very slight bluish component. When chromium substitutes for aluminum, the color becomes green or red, and the gem is called alexandrite (see ALEXANDRITE). Chrysoberyl is slightly dichroic, and an absorption band in the blue due to iron is sometimes seen in the blue region of the visible spectrum. The pseudohexagonal structure favors the formation of crystallographically oriented tubular channels. When they are numerous, they may impart some chatoyancy to the stone, which may be enhanced by cabochon cutting (see CAT'S-EYE). Even when nonchatoyant, chrysoberyl always displays a characteristic weak opalescence (see CYMOPHANE).

Crystals are often flattened and striated. They are also commonly twinned, three individuals simulating a hexagonal symmetry. Reentrant angles or, in their absence, striations allow easy identification of a twin, especially in thick crystals (from the Ural Mountains in the Soviet Union or from Brazil, for example). The cleavage is fairly distinct and produces wedge-shaped fragments, easy to recognize in the alluvium.

Gem chrysoberyl is rarely included. The most common inclusions are healed fractures containing two-phase inclusions or growth banding marking the limit between two growth sectors.

Deposits

Chrysoberyl deposits are very similar to those of beryl, with which it is commonly associated; its good toughness and high specific gravity make it a frequent component of alluvial deposits derived from granitic pegmatites. When it was still called "chrysolite," the gem-bearing gravels of Sri Lanka were the primary source of chrysoberyl; they still produce it today.

Chrysoberyl is fairly plentiful in Brazil in the state of Minas Gerais, particularly in the vicinity of Malacacheta and Córrego do Fogo (with sapphire), north of Teófilo Otoni, where it is found in the alluvial deposits of the rivers Córrego da Faisca and Americanas, near Padre Paraíso. The first pieces were found at the beginning of the nineteenth century, but they were not seriously examined until 1930. Mined exclusively in alluvial deposits, chrysoberyl is associated with beryl (aquamarine and heliodor), topaz, andalusite, garnet, zircon, and amethyst. It is mined in similar conditions in the states of Espirito Santo (Córrego Alegre) and Bahia (Teixeira de Freitas).

Tumbled crystals may reach spectacular dimensions, weighing from a few hundred

Chrysoberyl twin from the Lake Alaotra, Madagascar. Height: 5 cm. Sorbonne collection.

grams to several kilograms. This mineral maintains remarkably sharp crystal shapes in the alluvium. The decomposed pegmatite at Itaguaçu in the state of Espirito Santo produced magnificent chrysoberyl twins about fifty-five years ago, exceeding 8 centimeters (3 inches) in diameter, associated with beryl and quartz. Remarkably well formed, flattened crystals, up to 8 centimeters in diameter and often twinned, were found after World War II in the pegmatites of Lake Alaotra in Madagascar.

Famous Chrysoberyls

The Hope chrysoberyl is a very beautiful 45-carat round faceted stone with a peridot color, in the British Museum. Larger stones can be found at the Smithsonian Institution in Washington: a yellow-green 114.3-carat faceted cushion, a greenish 120.5-carat oval, cut in crystals from Sri Lanka, as well as a yellow-green 46.3-carat oval faceted from a Brazilian stone.

Gems and imitations of a green-yellow color, especially greenish yellow sapphire, may be mistaken for chrysoberyl (see PERIDOT). Only chromium-bearing synthetic chrysoberyl is marketed commercially.

CHRYSOCOLLA

A hydrous copper silicate, named for the Greek *khrusos* ("gold") and *colla* ("glue") because this mineral was used in antiquity to solder gold. It is, however, possible that this term was actually used for borax (from the Hebrew *borak*, "white"), a material the Greeks obtained from the salt lakes of India and Persia, which was also used in soldering.

Chrysocolla from Kambowe, Shaba, Zaire. Width: 14 cm. Sorbonne collection.

With its beautiful blue or green color, reminiscent of some turquoises, chrysocolla, an amorphous material, fills fractures or builds formations similar to stalactites by epigeny of other minerals. It is soft (H is 3) and light (S.G. is 2); some varieties even stick to the tongue. Sometimes silicification gives chrysocolla a better cohesion, making its use in jewelry possible (it is then properly a quartz with chrysocolla inclusions). It is a common mineral in the outcrops of copper deposits. Beautiful specimens come from the United States, Zaire, Chile, and elsewhere.

The Eilat stone, found in the ancient copper mines of King Solomon in the Sinai, is a mixture of chrysocolla, turquoise, pseudomalachite, and other copper minerals in variable proportions.

CHRYSOLITE

Gems with golden reflections, from the Greek *khrusos* ("gold").

Until the nineteenth century, many gems were called by this same name, especially those in which the golden reflections showed a hint of green, including some varieties of green sapphires, chrysoberyl, topaz, tourmaline, and peridot. Today chrysolite is synonymous with light-colored peridot.

The History of Chrysolite

It seems that the peridot deposit on Zebirget Island in the Red Sea was very strictly controlled by the Egyptians during ancient times; they used their slaves to extract the gems. Probably because the guards there were armed with whips that looked like snakes, the Greek historian Agatharchides wrote around 176 B.C. about a "snake island." This desolate island, called Topazos (see TOPAZ), where miners led very tough

lives, was also known as "death island." Alexander of Miletus, also known as Alexander the Erudite, mentioned an island "where gems have the color of virgin oil" at the beginning of the first century B.C. Diodorus of Sicily, a contemporary of Caesar and Augustus, related that "the Egyptians had this island heavily guarded and punished by death whoever tried to get close."

Hence, this gem was called *laiggourios* in Greek, that is, "guarded stone," from *laiggos,* meaning "small stone," and *oureo,* "to guard," an appellation confirmed by Epiphanes in the fifth century B.C. But this term allows a play on words: *oureo* also means "to urinate," and *lunx,* means "lynx"; some believed that this gem was the solidified urine of a lynx, because of its transparency and color. Around 320 B.C. Diocles attributed electromagnetic properties to this gem, which were soon confirmed by Theophrastus, who reported difficulties in polishing the "lynx stone." This corresponds to the electric properties of tourmaline and to the difficulties associated with polishing peridot. As Barbot wrote in 1858: "One should be suspicious of Ceylon peridots; the stones represented as such are often only tourmalines."

Ligure, French for *lyncurium* ("lynx stone") was, until the nineteenth century, also the term used to translate the Hebrew *lesham,* which designated the seventh stone in the priests' breastpiece (Exodus 28:17–20); *chrysolite* is the present translation, already used by Saint John in his Apocalypse at the end of the first century A.D. to designate the seventh stone of the foundation of the celestial Jerusalem (Apocalypse 21:19–20). The tenth stone, *tharschisch,* first called chrysolite and then beryl, was named chrysoprase by Saint John.

To Pliny the Elder, the gem from Topazos Island was, of course, a "topaz" (see TOPAZ).

In the Middle Ages, the Crusaders returned from the Orient with numerous peridots, then called "Crusaders' emeralds" or "evening emeralds," and used them to adorn the religious works of art. The descriptions of *ligure* and *chrysolite* were then quite similar, appropriate for all yellowish green gems. In 1669 Robert of Berquen, listing the various names used—topaz by the ancients, chrysolampe by Pliny, chrysoprase by Marbodus, and chrysopage by Albert the Great ("all these names, however, for one sole reason, that they shine and sparkle with a golden fire")—explained that they all indeed represented chrysolite, whose "true color is a green with some yellow in it."

But in 1868 the lapidary T. Chriten described chrysoberyl using the name chrysolite. Even so, at the beginning of the nineteenth century, the German chemist Martin Klaproth had defined chrysolite as

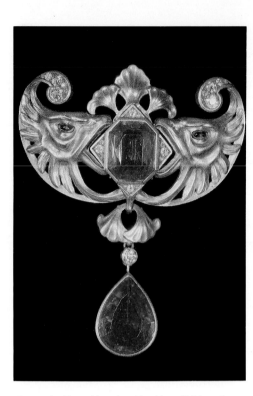

Engraved white-gold and peridot (chrysolite) brooch dating from around 1907. From a sketch by L. Hirtz, manufactured by Espinasse. Boucheron collection.

equivalent to Abraham Werner's olivine (see OLIVINE) and to peridot, then little used in jewelry. But habits are hard to break, so that while British mineralogists used the term *olivine* and the French *peridot,* Germans and Americans used *chrysolite.*

Today, *chrysolite* has fallen into disuse; all mineralogists use *olivine,* and most jewelers, *peridot.* "It is distressful to see a stone change names at any time and bear several names at the same time" (T. Chriten, 1868).

CHRYSOPRASE

A green nickeliferous chalcedony. Its name refers to its color, from the Greek *khrusos* ("gold") and *prasos* ("light green," the color of a leek, *prason*).

The term *chrysoprase* was used by both Pliny the Elder (A.D. 23–79) and Georgius Agricola (1494–1555) to describe various yellowish green minerals, such as some beryls.

Chrysoprase is translucent, light green to yellowish green, owing its color to very fine particles of a hydrous nickel silicate dispersed in its bulk. Its texture reveals irregular whitish clouds throughout, giving the stone depth and some life. It is cut mostly in cabochons.

Chrysoprase was found in veins in the serpentines near the town of Frankenstein, Silesia, (now Zabkowice, Poland) where it was discovered in 1740. It was actively mined under King Frederick William II of Prussia (1744–97), who was particularly attracted by the apple-green color of this stone. At Sans Souci, his castle in Potsdam, he assembled a collection of trays and snuffboxes carved in this gem; green parures in vogue in his court featured chrysoprase. Another deposit, near Visalia, in Tulare County, California, produced large quantities of high-quality chrysoprase from 1878 to 1911.

Both deposits are now abandoned. Chrysoprase comes from the state of Goias in Brazil and, more important, since 1965, from Maryborough in the Australian state of Queensland, where it is a very luminous green.

A green chromium-bearing chalcedony from the Great Dyke of Zimbabwe has been marketed for about fifteen years. According to CIBJO rules, it must be called green agate, which makes its promotion difficult, because this is also the correct name for chalcedony dyed with chromium salts, widely used as a chrysoprase imitation. This imitation has a uniform flat color and is almost opaque, in contrast with chrysoprase and Zimbabwe's green chalcedony. These three materials can be distinguished using their absorption spectra.

CITRINE

A yellow to brownish yellow or orange quartz. The name comes from *citron,* ("lemon" in French), because of the stone's yellow color.

Important Specimens

Citrine has become a common gem with the development of amethyst heat treatments that change amethyst to citrine (see AMETHYST). In addition, citrine became abundant after the discovery of Brazilian deposits. A 1,180-carat citrine from Brazil is on display at the Smithsonian Institution in Washington, D.C.

The Color of Citrine

The yellow color of natural citrine, sometimes also orangy or orange-brown, is attributed to the presence of microscopic colloidal particles of ferric iron hydroxides dispersed in the crystal. The iron hydroxide concentration may reach 0.0002. A slight yellow dichroism may be observed. The citrine color can be lightened with high temperatures; with more heat, the stone may become milky. When irradiated, citrine takes on a yellowish brown color.

Most citrines on the market today are heat-treated amethysts. First discolored at about 350°C (660°F), the amethysts are then brought to a temperature of about 550°C (1020°F), at which they turn yellow. The color intensity is related to that of the initial purple. Citrines produced from amethysts are not dichroic and often contain "zebra stripes" of fluid inclusions. They may become amethysts again if treated with radiation.

Other citrines on the market may come from treated colorless quartz. Rock crystals from certain deposits (especially in Japan) may be turned smoky by irradiation and become like citrine with subsequent heat treatment. These stones are then clearly dichroic and impossible to distinguish from their natural counterparts.

Deposits

Natural citrine is rare; it is usually found along with amethyst in Madagascar, the Ural Mountains, Salamanca (Spain), and Uruguay.

The most remarkable deposits are in Brazil, which is also the main producer. In this country, which is not part of CIBJO, treated amethyst is often sold fraudulently as "Rio Grande topaz" when it comes from Rio Grande do Sul amethysts and "Bahia topaz" when it comes from that state. Almost all citrines result from the treatment of amethyst or from that of a transparent, colorless to greenish gray quartz, locally called *lambreu,* sold under the name *citrine.*

The most important deposit, located in the Fazenda do Salto, northeast of Brasília and west of Vitória da Conquista, is a quartz breccia containing opaque to translucent crystals of a pale grayish green to amethyst purple color. The crystals are sometimes large (30 centimeters), contain

Nineteenth-century gold and citrine necklace (about 200 carats total weight) from the Charles X period. Creation by Mellerio (Meller).

A pair of ear pendants with 16.78 carats of citrine. Mauboussin creation.

Yellow-gold, diamond, and onyx necklace featuring a 102-carat citrine. Mauboussin creation.

healed fractures and growth zoning, and turn a nice yellow color with heat: colorless at 500°C (930°F), they take on color as they cool; but quartz fracturation allows for only a very small yield (about 1 percent). Amethysts from other areas (such as Rio Grande do Sul and Minas Gerais) are heat-treated in a similar way. Minas Gerais pegmatites occasionally produce rare but beautiful natural citrine crystals.

Similar-looking Gems

All yellow gems may be mistaken for citrine; the yellow orthoclase from Madagascar has similar properties and is fraudulently exported under the name *citrine*. A yellow topaz with a slight pink tinge and therefore a warmer color and higher luster has also deceptively given its name to citrines from Spain, Madeira, and Brazil (see TOPAZ).

Imitations and Synthetics

Yellow glass and yellow synthetic corundum are the most common imitators of citrine. A very clean synthetic citrine has been produced in the Soviet Union by hydrothermal growth since 1975 (see QUARTZ). This synthetic citrine can be distinguished from natural and heat-treated citrines using infrared spectroscopy.

COLLOPHANE

A massive apatite. It has a more or less finely granular appearance but may be sometimes botryoidal or mamillary, as is frequently observed in karsts. Occasionally it contains fossilized matter such as bones and teeth (see ODONTOLITE). Its name comes from the Greek *kolla* (''glue'') and *phainein* (''to appear'') because it looks like glue. This material was used in China to carve flasks and snuffboxes.

CORAL

A calcareous concentration, forming the mechanical support of a marine polyp colony. Its name comes from the Greek *korallion*.

The History and Virtues of Coral

Coral has been known and used since prehistoric times; coral inlays and ornaments have been found in Celtic graves from the La Tène period (recent Iron Age). During the Roman era, coral-working centers existed in Asia Minor at Smyrna (now Izmir, Turkey) and Magnesia (Greece). A number of magical virtues were then attributed to this gem, and their number grew

during the Middle Ages. For example, it was supposed to prevent murders and consequently to stop bleeding, protect from evil spirits and therefore appease hurricanes and thunderstorms, ward off panic and nightmares, and heal eye diseases and help teeth come out. Coral was worn as amulet to protect against the evil eye: in Italy men wore small coral horns on their chests, and women, small spheres. Coral parures were in fashion in Western countries from the Renaissance to the middle of the twentieth century; they are still much valued in the Orient and around the Mediterranean Sea, especially in Italy. The coral parure of Queen Margaret of Savoy, made of coral from Naples Bay, was quite famous, as were the display objects of the Japanese Matsuma collection. A coral museum has been built near Kōchi, at Tasashmizu, near the center of the Japanese coral industry.

Formation and Physical Properties

First considered by Theophrastus to be a petrified plant, coral was then thought to be a curious submarine bush from the time of Pliny until the eighteenth century. Its ''milky sap'' was observed by a gentleman from Lyon in 1613, and its ''flowers'' by the Italian naturalist Luigi Marsili in 1706. Jean André de Peysonnel first identified it as a marine animal related to the octopus in his

Coral "branch" with its "skin." Height: 20 cm. Compagnie Générale de Madagascar, Paris.

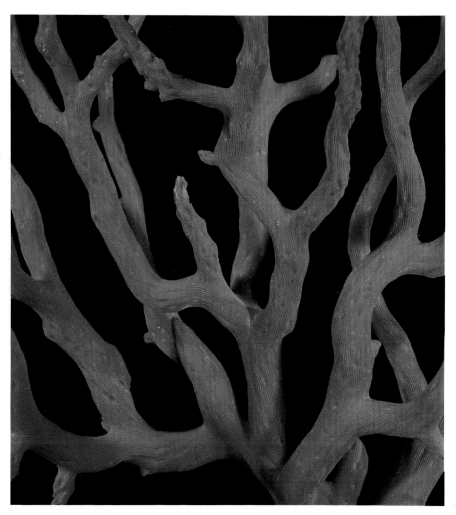

Coral "branch" from Corsica without its "skin." Height: 30 cm. Compagnie Générale de Madagascar, Paris.

1744 book. First vigorously fought by René-Antoine Réaumur and Bernard de Jussieu (who recognized their mistake as soon as they learned about Abraham Trembley's studies of the freshwater hydra), this hypothesis was proven by the studies of Lacaze-Duthier in 1863. The body of each coral polyp—about 2 millimeters long—is a sort of tubular sac with eight internal segments, with an aperture (mouth) at one end featuring eight finely fringed tentacles. This sac is surrounded by connective tissue into which the animal can retract completely, just like a sea anemone. All members of a colony are connected by a system of vessels running parallel to the axes of the "branches"; the vessels carry a white fluid (which can be seen by breaking a branch of living coral). The entire colony can retreat into the connective tissue when danger is perceived by only one of its members (this explains the 1706 interpretation of a "blooming of flowers," which occurred when the members of the colony reappeared after a threat had passed. The foot of the polyp and the base of the connective tissue secrete calcareous spicules, which eventually form an external skeleton for the colony. The colony then resembles a small tree without leaves, its petrified branches covered by a gelatinous bark (hence the interpretation by Pliny and his successors). The colony reproduces by a kind of budding of the connective tissue, at the ends of the "branches." The oldest members of the colony are closest to the anchoring point: reproduction may produce either a longer branch or a split branch. New branches are, of course, thinner than older ones, and cavities may appear at the split, which may be detrimental to future use of the branch (X rays help detect these cavities).

All members of a same colony are of the same sex; however, some "branches" of a "tree" may be of the sex opposite to the rest of the tree. Coral colonies can also grow and spread by sexual reproduction. Each egg reaches maturity at the end of a peduncle in the stomachic cavity of a female polyp, into which sperm, spread in the sea by the male polyps, come to fertilize the eggs; the result is a microscopic elongated larva. After floating freely in the sea, it becomes a small medusa and soon attaches itself to a rock; a "bud" forms, which becomes the first polyp of the new colony. The foot of this small animal begins secreting a calcareous anchor, while the connective tissue grows and a second bud appears, soon followed by a third. The calcareous structure turns into a colony representing the trunk of a new tree, from which several secondary "branches" will spread.

The formation of calcareous coral branches produces a radial texture marked by slightly different color nuances superimposed over concentric growth layers. This produces the typical appearance of rough and polished coral objects: alternating light and dark lines or alternating light and dark circles surrounding a small central cavity. Externally, the rough branches are grooved parallel to their elongation (this correspond to the primary vascular system of the living colony) and slightly depressed where each polyp lived.

Coral is almost exclusively calcium carbonate, with a bit of carotene fixed to it: the resulting color ranges from blood red to white. Some dead coral branches that fell to the marine floor become black because of organic putrefaction (this calcareous black coral should not be confused with organic black coral).

Nineteenth-century print showing coral fishermen.

Nineteenth-century Yemenite coral and silver necklace and ear pendants. Boutique Argana, Paris.

Because of its porosity, coral of a pale color can be dyed red. This age-old practice involves secret formulas specific to the manufacturer (sometimes turpentine can dissolve the organic dyes used).

Coral's macrohardness is 3½ and its specific gravity extends from 2.60 to 2.70. It is, of course, attacked by acids, with effervescence. Its ultraviolet luminescence is of variable intensity, often quite weak.

Coral Fisheries

Noble varieties of coral belong to related species: *Corallium rubrum,* found mostly in the Mediterranean, and *Corallium japonicum,* found in the seas between Japan and the Malaysian archipelago. Other species of the genus *Corallium* have also been distinguished: *C. elatius, C. secundum,* and *C. konojoi.*

Coral needs calm, clear, and temperate (13°–16°C or 55°–60°F) waters; extreme temperatures or excessive mud can kill colonies, which form true submarine forests at a depth as shallow as 3 meters (10 feet), rarely deeper than 300 meters (1,000 feet). The coral from Sciacca, Sicily, discovered in 1875, were so abundant that they triggered a drop in prices; however, they were dead corals, which actually disappeared completely after an undersea earthquake.

The most valuable coral once came

from off the North African coast; Linche and Didier, two fishermen from Marseilles, France, created the Compagnie du Bastion de France in 1561, named for the harbor built for this very purpose near Bône (now Annaba, Algeria). This trade was encouraged by the kings of France, who in 1719 created the Compagnie Royale, a very prosperous organization that employed eight hundred persons to fish coral between April and August. Dismantled by the French Revolution, these two companies abandoned their business to the Italians. Similarly, the working of coral moved from Marseilles to Italy. Today the principal centers—Torre del Greco (near Naples), Livorno, and Genoa—work coral from the Mediterranean or imported from Japan. Noble coral comes mainly from the Japanese Ryukyu Islands, between Okinawa and Miyako, and is found at a depth of 300 to 400 meters (1,000 to 1,300 feet).

In the past coral was harvested by divers, especially off the coast of the eastern Pyrenees in France, but since the nineteenth century, it has been collected by dredging across the beds from spring to fall.

The Working of Coral

A coral branch may reach 4 centimeters (1½ inches) in diameter and be 40 centimeters (15 inches) long; Japanese coral is often larger. A 26-kilogram branch and a small tree weighing 37 kilograms have been reported. In addition to its weight, rough coral is graded by its shape and color.

Bushy branches, such as those found off the French and Spanish coasts, are less valuable than the more massive ones. Indeed, thin branches can be only polished and drilled into small rods, used exclusively in necklaces. Likewise, branches with holes bored by marine creatures or with cavities have lesser value. The most valuable colors, in addition to fairly rare black and white varieties, are the distinctly pink (angel skin) or red (ox blood) varieties.

Coral is worked with steel tools and then polished. In Italy a variety of artifacts is produced, often in series, from balls, beads, brooches, and charms to small pieces of jewelry and cameos. In the Orient entire trees are carved into objets d'art, celebrating Buddhist themes or nature (birds, flowers).

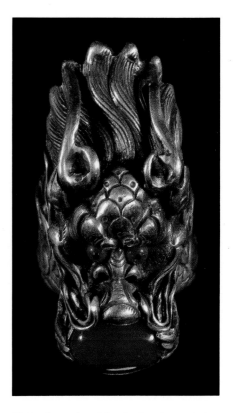

Tibetan silver and coral ring. Boutique Argana, Paris.

Contemporary Japanese carving in coral, depicting a bird. Height: 10 cm. Compagnie Générale de Madagascar, Paris.

The coral fashioned in Italy is generally exported to the Orient (India and China) and the Arab countries, where coral is often combined with turquoise in jewelry.

Because it can be damaged by chemicals, coral jewelry should be cleaned only with soapy water.

Imitations

Among the numerous coral imitations, the most convincing one is dyed corozo (also called by the misnomer vegetable ivory; see IVORY). In addition to glass, ceramics, and colored plastics, which are commonly used, various other materials have been altered to imitate coral: dyed limestones and marbles, dyed bone, and coral or marble powder dyed with cinnabar or minium and sintered with plastic. Even sealing wax has been fraudulently represented as coral! "Synthetic coral," recently available on the market, is only a synthetic calcite precipitate with a homogeneous texture. As coral is often combined with turquoise in jewelry, the same product with a different dye—a synthetic sintered phosphate called "neolite"—has been used to produce jewelry that seems to feature these two gems.

Coral Look-alikes

Pink coral beads may resemble pink pearls (see PEARL).

Other Corals

Biologists classify under the name *coral* a number of coelenterates (radially symmetric invertebrate animals with stinging tentacles) living in colonies, with calcareous or organic (essentially keratinous) exoskeletons. These are very different from *Corallium rubrum*, the only coral used in jewelry in the past, creating unfortunate confusion.

These corallines are classified as hydrocoralline, hexacoralline, and octocoralline, depending on the presence or absence of a "mouth" surrounded by a multiple of six or eight tentacles. Calcareous hexacoralline build coral reefs, such as those surrounding numerous atolls in the Pacific (such as Bikini) and those forming the Great Barrier Reef off the Australian coast. These stony corals, or madrepores, have formed entire geological strata, during the Mesozoic era, for example. They should not be mistaken for or assimilated with coral used in jewelry. However, they are sometimes cut (and dyed) for jewelry.

The corals used in jewelry are the branching colonies such as *Corallium rubrum;* their exoskeletons might be calcareous or horny, massive or porous. For example, the horny exoskeletons of the anthipatharians from the Red Sea and from the gorgonians of the Malaysian archipelago and Indian Ocean have been sold since the nineteenth century as black coral. Its formations may reach 10 feet in height and have the classic structure of coral colonies as described above, but its specific gravity is only 1.35 and its macrohardness 2½, the same as organic nail. Black coral is used mostly for bracelets and rings.

More recently, a calcareous blue coral has been gathered off the coast of Cameroon, and a golden horny coral, called "golden coral," off the coasts of French Polynesia. Horny corals are, of course, imitated with plastics, but also with dyed porous materials, such as dyed black serpentine.

Numerous other coralline colonies with calcareous exoskeletons are fished and commercialized nowadays, such as Allopora from the Cape of Good Hope (South Africa). But this coral, called South African star coral, is particularly porous and breakable, so it is always impregnated with some plastic and sometimes dyed, to be used in jewelry.

CORDIERITE OR IOLITE

A alumino-magnesian cyclosilicate, crystallizing in the orthorhombic crystal system. Its structure is close to that of beryl. A small percentage of aluminum and magnesium ions is always replaced by some iron ions.

Cordierite was named in honor of the French geologist Cordier (1777–1861). It is also called iolite, from the Greek words *ion*, meaning "violet" (the flower), and *lithos*, meaning "stone," because of its color. Cordierite is also known as dichroite or polychroite because of its strong pleochroism, but these names are rarely used.

Cordierite generally forms more or less transparent glassy chunks with a gray to blue color and an intense pleochroism, easily visible with the naked eye, exhibiting the following colors: blue, dark violet, and yellow. This quality may mean that cordierite was the "sunstone" that, according to Viking legend, enabled them to know the position of the sun when the sky was overcast.

Cordierite is faceted with the table perpendicular to the blue direction, which also corresponds to the pseudohexagonal axis of the crystal. Set in a piece of jewelry, one can see a characteristic yellow reflection through the side of the stone, between the prongs, which explains its old name, "water sapphire," now considered a misnomer. This gem is quite breakable: it has a good axial cleavage, separation planes that tend to develop because of alteration, and a hardness of 7. The luster is vitreous, with an index of refraction around 1.54. Cordierite is relatively light, with a specific gravity of 2.6.

Cordierite is found in both alkali and acidic rocks, such as granite and granitic pegmatites. It is also a classic component of clay-containing rocks that have undergone contact metamorphism, in association with andalusite and sometimes corundum and spinel. It is easily altered to muscovite and chlorite and then resembles jade (it was actually used as such by pre-Colombian civilizations).

Beautiful gems come from the gem-bearing gravels of Sri Lanka, and the best crystals are from Kragerö, Norway (where it was mined by the Vikings). Today cordierite comes mostly from Brazil, India, and Madagascar, where it is found in nice, limpid pieces of grayish blue. It has been used as a sapphire substitute and presented fraudulently in the past as "water sapphire." When rich in iron oxide inclusions, it takes a red aventurinescent aspect, reminiscent of blood, hence its name "bloodshot iolite" (Sri Lanka).

The Smithsonian Institution in Washington has a 15.6-carat faceted blue cordierite from Sri Lanka.

CORUNDUM

An aluminum oxide, crystallizing in the hexagonal system (rhombohedral hemiedry). See also RUBY and SAPPHIRE.

Origin of the Name

The Sanskrit *kuruvinda* became, in the Tamil (Dravidian) language, *kurund*, which was transcribed into *corindon* in the West. The French naturalist Romé de l'Isle (1736–90) applied this term to the present species corundum, defined by its specific gravity, hardness, and crystal shapes.

Because of its luster and often lamellar aspect, corundum was known in the past as *harmophane* (from the Greek *harmos*, meaning "joint," and *phanos*, "obvious") or *adamantine spar*. It is possible that common gray corundum may have been mistaken for diamond during antiquity (the *adamas siderites* of Pliny), especially in lapidary applications.

Structure and Physical Properties

Corundum's structure can be described as a compact stacking of oxygen ions (O^{2-}) held together by aluminum ions (Al^{3+}). A layer of oxygen "balls" touching each other in a hexagonal pattern is atop an analogous layer, so that each "ball" of the second layer falls into the "hollow" left between three adjacent balls of the underlying layer. All layers are superposed, two by two. Four adjacent oxygen "balls" leave between them a small tetrahedral space, while six neighboring oxygen "balls" (on two layers) leave between them a slightly larger octahedral space. The number of tetrahedral sites (or "vacancies") is double that of oxygen ions, which is equal to the number of octahedral sites.

Aluminum ions are too big to fit in the tetrahedral sites, but their diameter allows them into two-thrids of the octahedral sites. The electric field created by the aluminum ion is strong, and the aluminum-oxygen distance short; therefore, the "electrovalent" $Al^{3+} - O^{2-}$ bonds are very strong. This explains the high cohesion of corundum, the second hardest mineral after diamond (H is 9), its strength, high specific gravity (S.G. is 4), and its very high luster (indices of refraction: 1.77 for the ordinary ray and 1.76 for the extraordinary ray, with a small birefringence of 0.008, uniaxial negative). The distribution of ions also explains

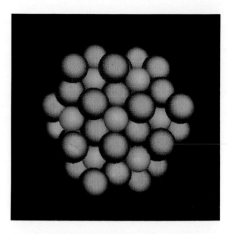

Computer-generated image of the structure of corundum. The oxygen atoms are in yellow and the aluminum atoms in blue. Courtesy of the Mineralogy-Crystallography Laboratory at Pierre and Marie Curie University, Paris.

the rhombohedral merohedry, due to the partial filling of the octahedral sites. There are no easy cleavages, but preferential "parting planes" correspond to the various oxygen surfaces that may "glide" over each other. This may happen along two families of planes. First, along the planes perpendicular to the threefold axis, this phenomenon produces the "lamellar" appearance of many common corundum crystals and allows easy breaking—with simple pincers—of numerous Kenyan rubies. Second, along the three rhombohedral planes, forming a quasi-cubic shape (faces at 93°56'), creating the "scaffold" appearance of the dislocations found at the intersection of mechanical twins in crystals having undergone tectonic strain (such as Thai and African rubies).

The sometimes enormous crystals (almost 70 kilograms for a 70-centimeter-long crystal from the Squtpansberg area in Transvaal) are often hexagonal prisms, sometimes associated with pyramidal or rhombohedral faces; the basal and prism faces are often striated because of the common lamellar twinning. Barrel shapes are often encountered, and crystals may also be flattened. They are found in granulated masses mixed with magnetite in very large deposits mined for abrasives (emery). Corundum is a good thermal conductor (one of the best after diamond); it melts at 2,050°C (3,722°F).

The Color of Corundum

Pure corundum is colorless. However, up to a few percent of some transition metal ions (such as chromium, titanium, iron, and vanadium) may substitute for aluminum, because they have a similar diameter and carry the same electrical charge.

Red corundum in zoisite from Longido, Tanzania. Length: 15 cm. Compagnie Générale de Madagascar, Paris.

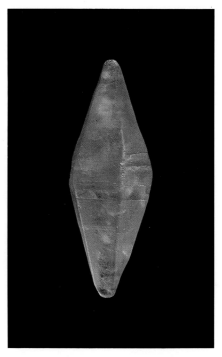

Corundum crystal from Sri Lanka. Length: 5 cm. Sorbonne collection.

This process introduces unpaired electrons, causing light absorption, and therefore colors the gem.

Oxygen O^{2-} may be replaced by the hydroxyl group OH^- of the same volume; this may contribute to an equilibrium of electric charges. Ions foreign to the ideal formula may enter either octahedral (chromium, titantium ferrous iron) or tetrahedral (silicon, ferric and ferrous iron) sites. Chromium induces a pink to red color. The iron-titanium association is responsible for a blue hue; iron alone can create green to yellow tinges (see the discussion of color in part 1). Different absorption properties due to various elements can overlap, producing the many color varieties of corundum: red corundum or ruby, blue corundum or sapphire, and pink, orange, padparadscha, yellow, green, and violet sapphires—that is, corundums of any color other than red or blue (*sapphire* is synonymous with *corundum* to the jeweler; its color must be specified if it is not blue).

"Silk" and Asterism

During the aluminous segregation resulting in the crystallization of corundum in nature, iron and titanium are always present; therefore, they are found scattered throughout the structure of corundum crystals. However, since the geometry of the oxygen atoms of corundum and rutile is compatible, it is not difficult for the titanium to be expressed as rutile needles elongated parallel to corundum's binary axis: taking advantage of thermal agitation, titanium just has to slide past the oxygen atoms, which are spread apart sufficiently at about 1,200 to 1,400°C (2,200° to 2,550°F) (in other words, titanium migrates through the crystal). The resulting exsolution texture consists of a series of coplanar needles, oriented at sixty degrees from one another. When present in small numbers, they give a sheen to the light transmitted by the corundum comparable to that produced by a light silky fabric; therefore, these needles have been called *silk*. When they are abundant, one can clearly perceive light scattering in particular directions, reminiscent of a star; such a corundum is cut as a cabochon, with the exsolution directions parallel to the base to "center" the star. The gem is then called a star sapphire; more rarely, a star ruby.

Deposits

Corundum may be found at the contact point between nepheline syenites and metamorphic rocks or in aluminum-rich sedimentary rocks. Also a product of high-pressure metamorphism, it may be associated with spinel in magnesian marbles such as those of Jegdalek, in Afghanistan. It may be the product of desilicification around acidic

Detail of a nacre, onyx, diamond, and yellow sapphire necklace. Mauboussin creation.

Pink sapphire brooch (12.78 carats total weight) with emeralds and diamonds, created in 1970. Creation by Mellerio (Meller).

pegmatites intruding in basic rocks such as limestones, amphibolites, or pyroxenites. It is also an element of the granulite facies, where it may be associated with green zoisite, as in Kenya, or with amphiboles as in Loire, in France.

Emery has been mined since antiquity in Naxos, Greece, as well as in Asia Minor, China, and India in an alluvial form. Gem corundums used in jewelry are mined in alluvial deposits, as in Sri Lanka.

Synthetics

Synthetic corundum has been available commercially since 1885 (see the discussion of synthetics and simulants in part 1).

CUPID'S DARTS

Rock crystal or light amethyst containing inclusions of long, thin, black crystals. Those inclusions are reminiscent of the darts thrown randomly by Cupid. They are highly valued in heart-shaped or oval cabochons and for decorative purposes. They come primarily from the pegmatites of Brazil and Madagascar.

CYMOPHANE

Synonymous with chrysoberyl, the name *cymophane* has fallen into disuse. It comes from the Greek *kuma* ("wave") and *phaneros* ("apparent") referring to the shimmering color of the mineral. See CHRYSOBERYL.

DANBURITE

A calcium borosilicate, crystallizing in the orthorhombic system. It is named for the locality where it was discovered: Danbury, Connecticut.

Crystals are common, elongated, and resemble those of topaz, although they have a poor cleavage. Generally colorless, danburite can be a brownish yellow, especially that from Madagascar.

Danburite shows a very weak absorption spectrum, similar to that of yellow apatite, and exhibits a sky blue luminescence under black light. Its hardness (H is 7) makes it interesting as an accessory gem. Its luster is that of topaz (indices of refraction: $n_p = 1.632$, $n_m = 1.634$, $n_g = 1.636$, with a birefringence of 0.006, biaxial positive or negative). Its specific gravity is 3. It is a pneumatolytic mineral, formed in limestones by the action of intrusive acidic rocks.

The beautiful colorless crystals from Siberia can reach large dimensions, up to several dozen centimeters. Gem danburites come from the gem-bearing gravels of Mogok in Myanmar, Bungo in Japan, and from the Charcas area near San Luis Potosí in Mexico.

Recently, superb golden crystals from Madagascar, over 50 centimeters long, have provided gem material yielding over 100 carats when faceted. The British Museum owns a 138.61-carat yellow-pink danburite from Mogok, step-cut, measuring 3.18 by 2.96 by 1.52 centimeters. The Ottawa Museum displays an 86.53-carat orange fancy cut from Madagascar.

Danburite crystals from Charcas, Mexico. Height: 5 cm. Sorbonne collection.

Diamond necklace with a 12.06-carat center stone and two pear-shape side stones of 5.89 and 5.28 carats. Van Cleef and Arpels creation.

DEMANTOID

A green andradite containing chromium.

Origin of the Name

Demantoid is derived from the Flemish *demant*, ("diamond"), from this stone's adamantine luster and fire.

Physical Properties

Demantoid is found only in small crystals, so faceted gems are small as well. The 10.4-carat stone displayed in the Smithsonian Institution in Washington is thus truly exceptional.

The color of demantoid ranges from a dark yellowish green in iron-rich stones to a bright emerald green in the stones with the most chromium. The classic chromium spectrum is easily observed. This gem is valued because of its high luster (index of refraction of 1.89) and strong dispersion (B to G interval of 0.057). Demantoid's specific gravity is relatively high, from 3.82 to 3.85. Unfortunately, its weak resistance to scratching (H is 6½) is at the low end of the acceptable limit for a stone to be set in jewelry.

Deposits and Inclusions

Demantoid is found exclusively in chromium-rich serpentines associated with as-bestos. It always contains fibrous inclusions of byssolite (a variety of actinolite); their fibro-radial distribution in a "horsetail" pattern is characteristic of this gem.

The most beautiful gems are found in the Ural Mountains, in an alluvial deposit near Bobrovka, south of Ekaterinenburg; other deposits are in Africa, Korea, and Italy (Valle Malenco and Valle d'Aosta in the Italian Alps). The Sferlun mine in Valle Malenco was worked for asbestos at the end of the last century and is now abandoned. Demantoid is found there, mostly as mineral specimens; however, some limpid crystal fragments have produced faceted stones of 1 to 2 carats. The chromium content of Sferlun's stones does not exceed 0.007 percent, which explains the weakness of their yellow-green color.

The Uses of Demantoid

Because of the small size of its faceted stones, demantoid has often been used as a side stone for rings and brooches, especially during the nineteenth century.

DIAMOND

Carbon, crystallized in the cubic system. It commonly contains traces of nitrogen and, rarely, traces of boron.

Origin of the Name

From *damazo*, which means "to tame" or "to train" (an animal), the ancient Greeks formed a word meaning unconquerable, from which was derived *adamastos;* this word meant "inflexible, that which cannot be moved" and described the state of mind every man should strive to attain. By extension, this word also was applied to the hardest of metals, of which Prometheus's chains and the weapons of the gods were made. The metal itself was naturally named *adamas*. During the fourth century B.C., Alexander led the Greeks to the Indus River. There they found diamond crystals, and, retaining the symbolism, used the term *adamas* to describe this very hard substance. Pliny the Elder used the same term

Diamond octahedron from Sierra Leone. 2 cm on an edge. Private collection.

during the first century A.D. The Western (*diamante, diamant, diamond*) and Russian (*almaz*) names for diamond are derived from that term, as is the adjective *adamantine,* which characterizes anything related to diamonds, but is mostly used to describe its luster.

The History of Diamond

Origins

Around the seventeenth century B.C., the fair-skinned Aryans invaded India from the northwest. They brought with them their highly hierarchical three-caste system (priests, warriors, and merchants). They founded Hinduism, which at that time had as its supreme god Indra, who was armed with lightning, or *vajra.* The Aryans conquered the Indus civilization, making the dark-skinned Dravidians a fourth caste, the pariahs or Sudras. The Dravidians probably already collected diamonds, because these stones looked so different from any others. In the sixth century A.D. reviving the ancient Hindu mythology, the Ratnapariska of Buddhabhatta and the Brihatsamhita of Varahamihira gave diamond great importance. It became the *vajra,* Indra's weapon, and, with the six points of its octahedron, symbolized true man resisting attacks from the north, the south, the east, and the west, from the evil powers of hell and from the heavenly powers. The man who wore a diamond was thus protected from fire, poison, theft, water, snakes, and evil spirits. The hardness of true diamond was well known.

However, all octahedral crystals were called "diamonds": the colorless specimens (true diamonds) were given to the priests, the Brahmans; the red ones (spinels), to the warriors, *kshatriya;* the yellow ones (perhaps diamonds) to the merchants, *vaicya;* and the black ones (magnetite), to the peasants, Sudras or pariahs. As early as the fourth century B.C., in the book *Artha-Castra* ("Teaching of Profit," written by his prime minister), Chandragupta Maurya (322–297 B.C.), the first emperor of India, established the laws regarding the mining and evaluation criteria (shape, clarity, specific gravity) of diamond, which clearly indicated the few mineral species involved at the time and the relevant taxes.

The symbolism attached to diamonds was transmitted with the stones to the Greeks and then the Romans. All the knowledge about diamonds acquired in the Orient was transcribed in the first century A.D. by Pliny the Elder, who considered diamond a very precious stone (but he listed several types of diamonds, including a black variety, easy to drill, probably magnetite).

Diamond was also used in the glyptic arts, which were in vogue during the Hellenistic and Roman periods. Engravers were always looking for diamond powder or chips. These "industrial" diamonds were exported by Rome to as far as China; the Chinese, who valued jade, had different beliefs and had not seen the beautiful crystals kept in India or sold in Rome. So they had an understandable tendency to consider the Romans somewhat crazy for wearing this rather unattractive utilitarian stone in a ring.

By repudiating the gods and symbolism of classical antiquity, Christianity triggered a collapse in the value of diamond crystals. The commercial routes that united Asia to Western Europe through the Middle East nevertheless survived the fall of the Roman empire. Industrial diamonds and high-quality crystals therefore still arrived regularly via the serene republic of Venice; its rulers (*dux* in Latin, transformed to *doge)* became independent of Constantinople as early as 912. During the Crusades Venice became the most important trading center for Europe and the Orient. The outlet in northern Europe was in Bruges (Belgium), therefore called the Venice of the north. The diamond trade developed along the roads between Venice and Bruges, and diamond centers formed in Paris and Frankfurt am Main, for example. Commercial transactions intensified with the Crusades; the first attempts at diamond faceting in Europe probably took place in Venice and then spread throughout Europe. The Flemish preeminence in diamond faceting in the seventeenth century was attested to by Robert of Berquen, a Parisian jeweler. He claimed to be the descendant of an old line of diamond cutters and said that his ances-

tor, Louis of Bruges, called Lodewijk van Berkem in Flemish, invented diamond cutting in 1476, receiving 3,000 ducats from the duke of Burgundy to facet three diamonds. This legend is based only on his claims, which are not supported by any archive in Burgundy or the Flanders. Moreover, diamond seems to have been faceted as early as 1300 and was cut in Paris in the fourteenth century.

Traditions and Lore

The properties of diamonds, presented in a very picturesque way during antiquity, were difficult to verify during the Middle Ages because of the scarcity of the gem. The ancient symbolism, so alien to tenth-century civilization, was revived with little change or incorporated and embroidered upon by medieval authors partial to the supernatural.

A number of diamond's virtues came about because it was confused with magnetite. Diamond was said to be magnetic and thus could reconcile spouses. Symbolic of heroism, it supposedly would resist the shock of a hammer blow, (this confusion between hardness and toughness damaged many stones). As a hero can be weakened by an unsettled life, so a diamond could be broken if immersed in goats' blood, a symbol of evil. Magical qualities were, of course, also attributed to the diamond: a high-quality crystal gave energy, strength, beauty, happiness, and long life; it kept evil spirits and catastrophes away.

Finally, diamond was given medicinal properties. Placed in the mouth, it cured the liar; placed on an ill part of the body, it helped to heal. In the twelfth century, Saint Hildegarde recommended crossing oneself while holding a diamond. At the beginning of the twentieth century, peasants still formed processions to borrow the dia-

Diamond twin. Across: 0.3 cm. E. Sirakian collection.

monds of local wealthy people, to help cure the sick.

In the sixteenth century, Pope Clement VII was prescribed a medicine made primarily of diamond powder; he died swallowing the fourteenth spoonful of this "medicine," which cost a total of over 40,000 ducats.

Around this time, diamond began to be considered poisonous. Diamond powder was one component of the famous "succession powders" of Catherine de Médicis (1519–89). It is possible that this legend was kept alive to discourage thieves from swallowing diamond crystals to hide them.

Development of the Diamond Industry —The Sixteenth and Seventeenth Centuries

The direct maritime route between Europe and India was opened in 1498 by Vasco da Gama and gradually benefited Lisbon, at the expense of Venice. At the same time, Bruges was declining, its harbor becoming the victim of silt, but Antwerp was growing and acquired a dominant position in the middle of the sixteenth century. However, the victorious fight of northern Netherlands for its independence and the conquest and looting of Antwerp in 1585 by Alessandro Farnese made it possible for Amsterdam to achieve dominance—even supplying Antwerp—and for Frankfurt-am-Main to develop.

The demand for diamonds was stimulated by the interest of royal courts in the stone. Cardinal Mazarin encouraged the French diamond cutters, so much so that he has been credited with the idea for the double rose cut. The eighteen stones that he left to the crown of France, later called the *Mazarins*, became an important part of the crown's diamond collection. To satisfy the European market, Indian princes began extensive mining of both recent and ancient diamond alluvial deposits. The older alluvial deposits were reworked after weathering allowed for more diamond crystals to be liberated from the rock, and it seems probable that this reworking was the source of the belief that diamonds "mate" (a concept based on the observation of twins) and are "born" in rivers.

The better-quality, less breakable crystals may be carried by rivers for longer distances without appreciable damage. The best stones were therefore associated with the stronger currents; in French they were called *diamants de belle eau* (literally, "diamonds of nice, or strong, water").

European dealers traveled to the mines to purchase stones. Jean-Baptiste Tavernier (1608–89) had style appreciated by both the Indian princes, who showed him their treasures and their mines, and the European sovereigns, who bought from him stones for their collections. Louis XIV of France raised him to the peerage; in 1669

Tavernier provided him with the "French Blue," part of which later became the Hope. His books about his six trips to India contributed to a genuine knowledge about diamonds.

The Brazilian Adventure

At the end of the seventeenth century, the demands of the Indian princes were such that the Dutch and the Portuguese stopped importing diamonds, leaving the market to their English competitors and thus enabling the London diamond trade to develop.

But, in 1725 Sebastiano Leme do Prado identified as diamonds the chips used in card games by gold prospectors in Rio do Marinhos, in what is today the state of Minas Gerais in Brazil. The region was actively prospected by many adventurers. This area, where the town of Tujido (today Diamantina) was built, was declared property of the Portuguese crown and put under military control. Other deposits were later discovered in Minas Gerais, as well as in the states of Bahia and Mato Grosso.

A slave working the mines would gain freedom if he or she found a rough stone weighing more than 17.5 carats. In 1853 a black slave won her freedom and a lifetime pension after finding the first large Brazilian diamond, the Star of the South (*Estrela do Sul*) in a tributary of the Paranaiba River. This 261.88-carat stone, colorless with a small hint of pink, was sold for the equivalent of $15,000 and faceted in a 128.80-carat oval. It was then displayed at the 1862 London Exhibition and sold to a maharajah for $400,000 in 1867.

Brazilian diamonds were initially suspect, so the Portuguese would transfer them to Goa before selling them in Lisbon, to give the impression that the stones came from India. But the large production from Brazil rapidly overwhelmed the production from India, where the mines were almost exhausted. Consequently, the price of rough diamonds fell by three-quarters from 1730 to 1735, recovering its earlier level only a century later. But this decline did not affect the price of faceted diamonds, which remained stable from 1670 to 1830. Despite the discovery of important deposits in the state of Bahia around 1844, intensive mining of the existing mines induced their exhaustion and a resulting shrinkage of production starting in 1850; the price of cut stones, however, was fueled by increased demand by the middle class and tripled from 1830 to 1869.

The Nineteenth-Century African Epic

The first African diamonds may have been found on the banks of the Vaal River in South Africa by natives who had been christianized by German priests. The journal

Diamond twin. Across: 1 cm. E. Sirakian collection.

recording their settlement at Pniel mentions the purchase of a 5-carat diamond, discovered in 1859 near Platberg. Nevertheless, it was only in 1866 that Schalk Van Niekerk, a trader, farmer, and collector of stone oddities, had his attention drawn to a stone with which the children of his tenant, Daniel Jacobs, were playing. Erasmus Stephanus Jacobs, then fifteen years old, had been sent to the bank of the Orange River with a Hottentot shepherd, Klondie, to cut a tree and make a cane. Klondie noticed a shiny stone, picked it up, and gave it to Erasmus, who in turn gave it to his youngest sister. When Van Niekerk examined the stone, he recalled reading about diamonds and thought that this rock might be one. He made a scratch test on a window (now displayed in the Colesberg Museum) and offered to purchase the stone from Mrs. Jacobs. She actually gave him the stone for his collection, because she did not want him to pay for a vulgar rock. Two German dealers, Gustav and Martin Lilienfeld, and a young Englishman, James Wykham, confirmed Van Niekerk's theory, so he asked John O'Reilly, a dealer in ivory, pelts, and ostrich feathers, to bring the stone to the assistant commissioner in Coleberg. The commissioner, Lorenzo Boges, showed it to a pharmacist, T. B. Kisch, who thought it was a topaz but sent it to a very competent amateur mineralogist in Grahamstown, Dr. Atherstone. He determined the specific gravity, made a scratch test on a window of the Catholic presbytery, and showed it to the town's jewelers, who tested it with their files. Then, convinced that it was a 21.25-carat diamond worth £800, he asked for permission to send it to the colonial secretary in Cape Town, Richard Southey. The stone was shown to the French consul, Héritte, considered to be a diamond expert, and then to a Dutch diamond dealer, Louis

The "Big Hole" in South Africa at the turn of the century. The ore is brought to the surface with large wheels turned by horses. Photo: De Beers.

Grease table used in South Africa in 1893 to separate diamond from other heavy minerals. Photo: De Beers.

Hond, before being sold for £500 (Schalk Van Niekerk received £350, which he shared with the Jacobses). Named Eureka, the rough stone was displayed at the 1867 Paris Exhibition, where it only aroused suspicions as to its true nature and provenance. It was later cut into a 10.73-carat oval, today the property of the South African parliament in Cape Town, to which it was given by De Beers in 1966.

In December 1868, back from an expedition subsidized by the London diamond cutter Harry Emmanuel, an English geologist named James R. Gregory wrote in *Geological Magazine:* "I have carefully and extensively examined the area where diamonds are said to be found, but I have found no indication at all that there are diamonds or diamond alluvial deposits anywhere. . . . The geological characteristics of this part of the country make it impossible . . . that a discovery really happened. . . . The discovery of diamond in South Africa is an imposture."

Indeed, despite Dr. Atherstone's insistence ("where this diamond was found, other diamonds are to be found"), Lorenzo Boges and T. B. Kisch searched for diamonds in vain at the confluence of the Vaal and Orange rivers. In March 1869, however, a Hottentot shepherd named Booi, who was looking for a job, found an 83.5-carat rough diamond on the Zandfontein farm and tried, without success, to trade it for a night's stay. He was finally sent to Van Niekerk, who immediately recognized the stone as a diamond and traded it for his horse, ten oxen, and five hundred sheep. James Wykham offered him £5,000, and the Lilienfeld brothers kept a sight privilege. Louis Hond, who happened to be traveling in the area, examined the stone and, after negotiating with the three partners separately, offered Van Niekerk £11,200 (approximately $56,000) in the name of the group. Van Niekerk accepted immediately, fearing the buyers might change their minds. The stone was sent to London, where Louis Hond sold it to the duchess of Dudley for the expected £25,000 (approximately $125,000). It was then presented to the Cape Town parliament, where the colonial secretary reportedly said: "This diamond, gentlemen, is the stone on which the future prosperity of South Africa will be built." The stone was cut into a 47.75-carat oval brilliant called the Star of South Africa; it sold for $552,000 at Christie's on May 2, 1974.

Reporting this discovery, a journalist at the *Coleberg Advertiser* wrote, "I wonder what our friend Gregory would say if he were around," and he mentioned the discovery of another diamond of 7.25 carats. The origin of the stones was no longer in question—this time Harry Emmanuel came in person. The rush was on!

From around the world came thousands of adventurers, who soon let their sideburns grow to protect their faces from the sun. They swarmed over the country, first far from the rivers, (since Booi found the Star of South Africa inland), then closer to the rivers. Farmers sold digging rights; carriers offered rapid transportation. Hopetown, so appropriately named, boomed. Fights broke out between prospectors and farmers. Sterile claims were salted with diamonds to be sold at a large profit. Everybody carried a weapon. A "Diggers Republic" was created in response to an authoritative appropriation of the diamond fields by the governments of Transvaal and Orange Free State; this republic kept matters relatively under control but eventually was dissolved in October 1871 when the region, Griqualand West, was annexed by the British.

Meanwhile, diamond prices had fallen by two-thirds, declining to eighteenth-century levels, because the Paris center had closed as a consequence of the war between France and Germany.

In July 1870 a wagon driver named Julius Bam found a diamond on the Koffiefontein farm; the friends he assembled to work the site were relatively discreet and worked without disturbance. It soon became apparent that this was the first diamond-bearing pipe, about 1,150 feet in diameter. The depth of the mine in 1874 was such that Julius Bam installed a pumping system powered by a horse. The rights to it were sold in 1891 to Alfred Mosely, who formed a mining company and found a 136-carat diamond the same year.

In August 1870 a foreman at Jagersfontein by the name of De Kerk, who had heard of Koffiefontein and visited the Vaal prospectors, decided to try his luck prospecting the riverbed that traversed his farm, which was dry during the summer. He found a 50-carat diamond. Few prospectors joined his effort, because Mrs. Visser rented her 10- x 10-meter (30- by 30-foot) claims at £2 a month, a fair amount of money at the time. In 1878 it appeared that Jagersfontein was also a volcanic pipe, 250 by 350 meters (82 by 1,150 feet). On June 30, 1893, a local worker drew the attention of one of the guards shortly before midnight; frightened, the miner brought the guard a 995.2-carat diamond (199.04 grams, 6.5 by 5 by 2.5 centimeters) that he had found. This high-quality diamond, then the largest ever found, and still the second-largest today, was called the Excelsior; its finder received £500, a horse and its trappings and the authorization to resign his contract. The Excelsior was cut in 1903 into twenty-one stones, including a 69.68-carat pear shape and seven stones over 20 carats, yielding a total of 348.61 carats, 35 percent of the original weight. A 310-meter (1,000-foot) shaft was drilled in 1910 to mine the pipe underground. Koffiefontein and Jagersfontein

The Kimberly mine in 1877. Each cable was used to haul the ore up from a claim. Photo: De Beers.

remained outside the territory covered by the 1871 claim law.

The Foundation of Kimberley and the Formation of De Beers

William Anderson arrived in South Africa in 1867 to prospect for gold, but hearing of the diamonds found far from rivers and bought by Van Niekerk, he caught diamond fever. He visited the workings of prospectors and went to Dortsfontein farm, the property of Adrien J. Van Wyk, who had bought it from Abraham Du Toit. In September 1870 he discovered rough diamonds in the walls of a shack built with mud from the pond; however, Van Wyk would not give him permission to dig. He also found diamonds in the pond of the neighboring Bultfontein farm, owned by Cornelius Du Plooy, who was more cooperative. Anderson planned to mine the two deposits, only about half a mile apart, with two friends. But his friends were indiscreet, and another rush was on!

All the vegetation was uprooted and the land could no longer be farmed. At the end of 1870, Van Wyk and Du Plooy had to sell their land, for £2,000 and £2,600 to . . . Martin Lilienfeld! But in 1871 a law passed by the Bloemfontein government concerning public claims and various taxes dissolved all Lilienfeld mining rights in these deposits, now known as Dutoitspan (the pond of Du Toit) and Bultfontein. At the same time, the De Beers brothers, who had bought the Voofuitzicht farm for £50 in 1860, gave per-

mission to a lone prospector, Corneilsa, to dig their pond in exchange for 25 percent of his finds. Corneilsa was naive enough to introduce Richard Jackson to the De Beers in May 1871. Jackson invited some prospector friends working in the Vaal to join him at this new deposit; but his friends' departure did not go unnoticed, and they arrived only a few hundred yards ahead of their pursuers to define their claims. Corneilsa, frightened, sold his claim for £110; Jackson chose claims outside of the kimberlitic pipe, and all he had left to show for his efforts was his pick and shovel. In October 1871 the De Beers brothers sold their farm for £6,300 to a syndicate of prospectors, claiming everywhere that they had been swindled. The syndicate in turn sold the land to the government for £100,000; the pond itself has since yielded over 600 million pounds of diamonds.

In July 1871 Fleetwood Rawstone, a miner working on the De Beers farm deposit, lost his claim gambling. He was camping 5,000 feet away and got into a fight with his drunken cook. Threatening to fire the cook, he sent him off to examine an abandoned area. On Saturday, July 15, 1871, the cook returned to visit Rawstone, who was playing cards, with three diamonds. They immediately took possession of the land and made an official statement on Sunday morning. A rush was on, and a government officer was distributing claims Monday morning. First called "New Rush," this mine was called Kimberley and finally Big Hole; indeed, the disorganized mining

Photograph taken around 1970 of the "Big Hole," abandoned in 1914, which is 465 m (1,522 ft) wide and 1,097 m (3,600 ft) deep. Photo: De Beers.

of 10-meter (30-foot) claims at the edge of the 200- by 300-meter (650- by 975-foot) wide pipe led, after many accidents and collapses, to the formation of a 400-meter (1,300-foot) deep hole. Around this time, incredible techniques were being invented to gain access to the claims: hundreds of cables set in motion by immense wooden wheels allowed miners to reach the workings and haul up the ore. Despite the digging of a 1500-meter (5,000-foot) deep lateral shaft, the mine was abandoned in 1914, as it was then very difficult to make a profit from it because of earlier diggings and a lower yield (1.15 carats per ton were found near the surface, but only 0.29 carat per ton at a depth of 1,000 meters (3,300 feet).

On June 5, 1873, these four mines and their camps officially became the town of Kimberley (in honor of the British administrator of the colonies, the count of Kimberley). This new town remained for many years a shantytown, where the cost of living was three times more expensive than elsewhere. The law allowed only two claims per owner, but this number was raised to ten in 1874, and finally repealed in 1876 because of the mining difficulties cited above.

Cecil Rhodes, a sickly young man, was sent at the age of seventeen to live with his brother Herbert, a farmer in the Natal. After a seventy-day trip from England, in 1871 he became a broker of gold-mine shares; soon he too caught diamond fever. Unsuccessful, he survived selling refreshments to the prospectors. With the help of two British partners, he bought a pump for £900, which he then rented to prospectors who had flooded claims. This allowed him to buy a claim at the De Beers farm in 1873 and then to become the co-owner of many others. After making numerous additional purchases, he founded the De Beers Mining Company Ltd. in 1880 and controlled the entire De Beers mine by 1887.

In 1873 eighteen-year-old Barney Barnato also joined his brother. He survived by selling just about anything and by organizing boxing matches. He thus became a diamond broker, in association with Louis Cohen. He listened to the geologists and, unlike many prospectors, believed them when they said that deposits continued vertically, deep below the blue ground. He bought the claims in the center of the mine of those who gave up after they failed to reach bedrock quickly, as expected in alluvial deposits. In 1880, with only six claims, he formed a company that became the Kimberley Central Mining Company. He owned more than seventy-five claims in 1883, when he decided to start digging a shaft.

In 1887 three groups shared control of the mines. De Beers Company Ltd., Kimberley Central Mining Company, and the Compagnie Française des Mines de Diamant du Cap de Bonne Espérance (literally, "French company of the diamond mines of the Cape of Good Hope"). Cecil Rhodes offered the French company £1,400,000; Barney Barnato, £1,750,000. They both reached an agreement, and Cecil Rhodes acquired 20 percent of Kimberley Central as well. The two men began to compete with each other to buy out the remaining claims soon afterward. Because of this competition, prices rose, though rough-diamond prices were down to 10 shillings a carat. Barney Barnato gave up in March 1888; the two companies merged, and Kimberley Central was liquidated on July 18, 1889, for the memorable £5,338,650 check signed by Cecil Rhodes. De Beers Consolidated Mines Ltd. stood alone; soon afterward it controlled the Wesselton mine discovered in December 1891, 3 kilometers (2 miles) from Dutoitspan, as well as Bultfontein, both annexed in 1899. De Beers was also the majority owner of the Griqualand West Company, which mined alluvial deposits, and therefore controlled 90 percent of the rough-diamond production at the time. The average carat price for rough diamonds went from 18 shillings 6 pence in 1889 to 32 shillings 6 pence in 1890.

Cecil Rhodes became prime minister of Cape Colony in 1890. He tried to subdue the Transvaal but had to step down when the Boer War started. He distinguished himself during the siege of Kimberley, which was defended with mining equipment. Rhodesia (now Zimbabwe) was named for him.

Building the World Market

After the 1892 crisis, the leading diamond buyers understood the necessity of uniting to negotiate with Cecil Rhodes and formed a syndicate in 1893. It was then generally agreed, after the discovery of several sterile kimberlite pipes, that no new diamond deposits would be found.

But in 1898, Thomas Cullinan, a mason who became rich through real-estate deals, noticed on a trip to Pretoria (400 kilometers [250 miles] away from Kimberley), a site that reminded him of Kimberley, the Elandsfontein farm. The elderly owner,

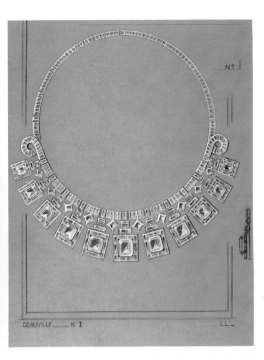

Workshop design diagram for a diamond and platinum necklace, made around 1950 for Cartier. Courtesy Cartier archives.

Diamond necklace with a 35-carat center stone. Chaumet creation.

Prinsloo, who had been forced to move once because of gold prospectors and another time because of diamond prospectors, refused to sell. Cullinan waited until his death; in 1902 (the year Cecil Rhodes died), he bought the farm from Prinsloo's daughter for £52,000. This became the famous Premier mine, so called because it was inaugurated by the premier in 1905. It is one of the largest-known kimberlite pipes (presently the fourth-largest worldwide), with an elliptical section of about 450 by 900 meters (1,475 by 2,950 feet; almost eight times the surface area of the Big Hole). It is the largest diamond mine in the world, and it produces eight to ten diamonds over 100 carats each year (one of the more recent was the Premier Rose, a 354-carat stone of exceptional quality found in 1978). This pipe contains fifteen different types of kimberlite. The average diamond concentration is 0.25 carat per ton, and about 2 to 5 million carats (about half a ton to a ton) are mined there each year. The pipe is intruded at a depth of 400 meters (1,300 feet) by an 80-meter (260-foot) thick gabbro vein, which caused distress for both geologists and miners from 1964 to 1968. Premier is the most heavily taxed mine in the world (87 percent of the profits go to the government) but also the only one to produce type IIa diamonds on a regular basis, called "electronic diamonds" in professional jargon because of their industrial applications (see further discussion later in this entry).

On January 26, 1905, a 3,106-carat (621.2-gram) diamond was discovered in the Premier mine. Suspected to be a cleft from a stone that was originally approximately 5,000 carats (1 kilogram), it was named Cullinan, in honor of Thomas Cullinan. This largest diamond in the world, measuring 10 by 6 by 5 centimeters, was bought for £150,000 (about $750,000) by the Transvaal government and presented to Edward VII of England on the occasion of his birthday on November 9, 1907, to seal peace after the Boer War. While the stone traveled anonymously by mail, spectacular security precautions were taken to transfer an empty box from Pretoria to London. A similar strategy was used to send the stone from London to the diamond-cutting factory of the Asscher brothers in Amsterdam. This time, the stone traveled incognito in Abraham Asscher's pocket by train and night boat. The study to prepare its faceting lasted one year, and cleavage began on February 10, 1908. Several stones were cut from this rough: first, the Great Star of Africa, or Cullinan I, a 530.20-carat pear shape, presently on the scepter of the British empire; then the Small Star of Africa, or Cullinan II, a 317.40-carat cushion now on the British crown; as well as seven other important stones (from 94.4 to 4.39 carats), Cullinan III to Cullinan IX, now part of the crown jewels, and ninety-six other stones of various sizes, for a total weight yield of about 35 percent.

The opening of the Premier mine was the first blow to Cecil Rhodes's monopoly. The second was the discovery in 1908 of a diamond by a railway worker near Lüderitz, in German South-West Africa (now Namibia). Immediately, a *Sperrgebiet* ("forbidden territory") was proclaimed, and Diamanten Regie controlled the six companies in charge of prospecting and mining the very rich alluvial deposits. The third blow was the European economic crisis of 1913, which caused a drop in demand and produced lower prices, threatening several dealers. In 1914 De Beers group controlled

The sorting of rough diamonds at the C.S.O. in London, Photo: De Beers.

The starting line of the race to stake claims in Lichtenburg, Transvaal, in 1926. Photo: De Beers.

only 40 percent of the world production. A conference among the main diamond producers was held in 1915 to help maintain prices by adapting production to demand. Quotas were fixed for each group according to its importance: De Beers, 48.5 percent; Diamanten Regie, 21 percent; Premier, 19.5 percent; Jagersfontein, 11 percent, and a common sales office was set up in London.

Despite new deposits discovered since, this quasi monopoly has been strengthened, to everybody's benefit, thanks to the Oppenheimer dynasty. Ernest Oppenheimer, of German origin but working in London, was sent to Kimberley in South Africa as a diamond buyer at the age of twenty-two. Broadening his interests, in 1917 he founded the Anglo-American Corporation of South Africa in conjunction with American engineers; their main interest was gold mines. He was thus able to buy the German mines when that country lost its rights to South-West Africa in 1919, and he founded the Consolidated Diamond Mines of South-West Africa (or CDM). He therefore attended the conference of diamond-producing countries in 1920, which extended the 1915 agreement.

In 1926 the rich alluvial deposits of Lichtenburg (Transvaal) inspired spectacular rushes. The claims were distributed as

the result of a race; the start was given as in a sporting event, and the fastest chose the claims reputed to be best. In three years these deposits yielded the same production as the major mines. And in 1926, the deposits along the embankments in Namaqualand, south of the Orange River, were discovered and put in production; in one year, they constituted an eighth of the world's production. Congo and Angola also became producers. To prevent being overwhelmed, the diamond syndicate in London bought anything it could; Ernest Oppenheimer convinced it to buy everything, in order to control sales. In 1930 the Diamond Corporation Ltd. united the four large African producers and soon grew into the Diamond Producers Association (DPA). At the same time, the Diamond Trading Company was organized to buy and sort all diamonds bought by the DPA and sell them through a central organization, the Central Selling Organization (CSO). This allowed the diamond producers and merchants to survive the depression of the 1930s and then to build reserves in anticipation of future crises. Ernest Oppenheimer and then his son Harry succeeded in negotiating agreements with new producers (Soviet Union, Australia) to maintain this mechanism, by which about 80 percent of the world's rough-diamond distribution is controlled.

The Distribution of Diamonds

Sorting

Diamonds arriving in London to be sold by the CSO are first sorted and cataloged by quality (more than five thousand categories exist, not taking provenance into account). Grading is based on the classic criteria:

- *Mass:* About fifteen groups are based on the diamonds' dimensions, determined with sieves. Another category groups important stones, weighing more than 14.8 carats.
- *Shape:* Each of the previous categories is divided into five major groups: (1) nicely formed octahedrons, called *stones* or *sawables* (good for sawing); (2) flattened monocrystals, resembling slabs, called *flats* or *makables,* to be cut as is; (3) monocrystals that have been cleft in nature during the deposition of the kimberlite, and the stones that will be cleft before cutting, called *cleavables;* (4) twins comprising two individuals, called *macles,* and (5) crystals inappropriate for faceting, such as those with multiple crossed twins, called *industrials.*
- *Color:* The nearly colorless stones are separated into nine main classes, from the perfectly colorless diamonds to the more yellow ones, called "Cape" (the name initially given to the diamonds coming from the area around the Cape of Good Hope, generally disdained because they were yellower than Indian or Brazilian diamonds; as was the case with the discovery of Brazilian diamonds, the first reaction of the jewelers was rejec-

A collection of colored diamonds. Collection and photo: De Beers.

Various shapes and colors of rough diamond. E. Sirakian collection.

tion). Fancy colors (for example, brown, yellow, and green) are separated into six additional categories.

Clarity: Eight groups are formed based on the potential clarity of the future cut stone, ranging from pure gems to crystals containing obvious inclusions.

The sights

Once the diamonds have been sorted, the CSO examines its buyers' requests and meets them based on the firm's honorability, financial standing, and technical ability. The CSO prepares a box for each of its buyers from the stones available. Each buyer is treated with the same care and concern for fairness, so that each is given the same chance with regard to its local clientele and its potential. When all the boxes have been prepared, the CSO invites all the buyers to examine what has been set aside for them; this is called a "sight." The main sight is in London, another is in Kimberley, and a third is held in Lucerne, for those stones yielding faceted diamonds under a carat.

"Sightholders" may discuss with the CSO's sales managers the reasons for the contents of their boxes and may offer remarks for future sights. But the box is to be bought as is (and paid for in cash, in dollars) or refused. Once the buyer agrees to purchase, he has four days to pay. It is extremely rare for a sightholder to refuse his box: he may be blacklisted from the group of approved buyers (indeed, by doing so, he breaks the moral contract by which the CSO provides him regularly with raw material according to his needs).

Once bought, the stones are shipped in a postal box, hence the name "box" given to the diamond parcels for each of the CSO's three hundred viewers, (95 percent diamond cutters and 5 percent rough-diamond wholesalers). The price for a box varies from $20,000 to several million dollars.

The preparation of a sight is a complex process, repeated every five weeks. There were twelve annual sights until 1964; this figure was reduced to eleven in 1965 and fell to ten after 1968. By creating cleverly managed stocks, this system helps avoid large price fluctuations for rough diamonds.

Cutting Centers

Today, the main European diamond-cutting center is Antwerp. After World War I, it attracted numerous Dutch diamond cutters. Antwerp specializes in high-quality diamonds.

Among the other European cutting centers are Amsterdam, where the memories of the early-twentieth-century splendors live on; Paris, where some craftsmen concentrate on recutting; Saint-Claude, France; and Idar-Oberstein, Germany. They maintain an old tradition and mostly faceted mêlée size stones.

New York developed as a cutting center with the arrival of Belgian diamond cutters during World War II. It is now an important center, where all kinds of stones are faceted, especially large ones.

The Ramat Gan cutting center near Tel Aviv developed along with the state of Israel. After concentrating on small stones, it moved on to cutting larger stones but is now going through a recession. The quality of the Israeli cut was fairly poor during the development of the diamond industry right after World War II, a result of the assembly-line approach that was adopted, in which one worker specialized in only one facet, so that a single experienced diamond cutter could supervise the entire workshop. Now the quality has improved and is comparable to Antwerp's.

The fourth major cutting center is in Surat, near Bombay, India. The stones are often small and rather poorly faceted, often by very young workers, sometimes children. Over the last few years, the quality of Indian diamond faceting has improved, and though some stones are still fairly mediocre, the mêlée produced is competitive.

Other cutting centers exist around the world, in Africa (Bangui, Kimberley), North America (Puerto Rico), South America (Belo Horizonte, Rio de Janeiro), and the Soviet Union. Their importance is minor compared to the four major centers. They may, however, develop in the near future, especially the Soviet Union, where the quality of the

A 2.07-carat diamond. E. Sirakian collection.

cutting has improved tremendously, and Australia, where the discovery of new deposits has triggered the formation of a diamond industry.

Diamond Bourses

Faceted diamonds are most often sold to world-traveling dealers who distribute them in turn to their country's diamantaires through bourses, or exchanges. Bourses are buildings that contain diamond dealers' offices, with meeting rooms offering appropriate lighting for diamond grading.

The main exchanges are, of course, found in the main diamond-cutting centers. They are accessible only to those who are properly introduced.

Bourses are federated worldwide in the WFDB (World Federation of Diamond Bourses). They often allow smaller buyers, those not big enough to be approved buyers by the CSO, to buy their rough diamonds from sightholders. "Outside" rough diamonds, that is, the rough which is not controlled by the CSO, are also often distributed through bourses. However, independent producers, such as Venezuela, commonly use a selling system very similar to that of the CSO.

Famous Diamonds

More than three thousand rough diamonds of over 100 carats, including about fifty over 400 carats, have been discovered since 1870. So, even if they have been given a name, these enormous stones tend to be forgotten after a while. Today there are more than fifty faceted diamonds weighing over 100 carats in existence, the largest being the Cullinan I. This increase in the number of large diamonds must be put in perspective, given the considerable increase in annual diamond production, which officially went from 50,000 carats (or 10 kilograms) at the beginning of the eighteenth century to 45 million carats (or 9 tons) in the last few years. Of course, these figures must be interpreted with caution; first, a good portion of the eighteenth-century production made its way through "parallel" routes, and second, the proportion of gem-quality stones, today about one-fourth, was certainly much higher previously, because there were no industrial applications of diamond at the time. However, even with these considerations, the production of gem-quality diamonds is about 250 times higher today than it was two hundred years ago. This is why some of the large historic diamonds, which were once coveted by princes or pledged to pay for entire armies, may appear to be poor relatives of the bigger newcomers.

■ One of the oldest diamonds appears to be the 90.34-carat Briolette of India. It was presumably bought in Asia Minor by Eleanor of Aquitaine, who accompanied her husband Louis VII of France during the Second Crusade (1147–49) and later gave the diamond to her son Richard I, the Lion-Hearted, of England. He reportedly wore it during the Third Crusade and presumably gave it as a ransom to Emperor Henry VI of Germany. The Briolette of India reappeared, worn by Diana of Poitiers, favorite of Henry II of France, from 1547 to 1559; it then disappeared again until 1950, when a maharajah sold the stone in New York.

Actually, the real Briolette of India was cut by Atanik Eknayan in Paris in 1908 and 1909. He used this style to take best advantage of the shape of the rough. The stone was sold in 1910 to Cartier.

■ One of the most famous diamonds is the Koh-i-Noor ("Mountain of Light"), a 108.93-carat oval on display in the Tower of London among the crown jewels. This magnificent diamond was the object of Indian legends and was supposed to give its owner the power to rule the world. It first appeared in 1304 in the jewels of the raja of Malva. After the battle of Panipat in 1526, it became the property of the Timurid prince Bābur, founder of the Mogul empire of India. It was then a 186-carat rose cut, "which could be safely worn only by a woman." Nāder Shāh, the last of the great Asian conquerors, was rather upset when he did not find the stone among the plunder after the pillage of Delhi in 1739. When he was told that the defeated Great Mogul was hiding the stone in his turban, he offered to seal the peace with him by exchanging headdresses, a traditional ritual. The Mogul complied, impassible. Nāder Shāh, anxious to check the accuracy of his information, retired to his tent to unroll the turban; bewildered at the sight of the stone, he exclaimed: "Oh, Koh-i-Noor" ("Oh, mountain of light"), the name by which the stone has been known since. Nāder Shāh was assassinated in 1747 by his companions; his successors withstood torture and poison rather than reveal the whereabouts of the famous diamond, which was finally found in 1793, hidden in the mud walls of a jail. The cruel Shuja el-Molk discovered it, but soon dethroned, he went into exile in Lahore. His host, Ranjit Singh, the "Lion of the Punjab," demanded the stone in exchange for his hospitality. In 1849 Great Britain conquered the Punjab and took possession of the Lahore treasure: the Koh-i-Noor was offered to Queen Victoria and was displayed in the Crystal Palace in London in 1851. But it did not impress visitors because its rose cut gave no life to the stone. So Queen Victoria had it recut by a Dutch diamantaire, Voorsanger, who gave it its present shape in thirty-eight days. Since then, traditionally only queens of England have worn the Koh-i-Noor.

■ A diamond that played a significant role in history was the Sancy, a 55.23-carat pear shape. Legend says that it was lost by Charles the Bold, duke of Burgundy, in front of Granson or Morat in 1476. Nicholas Harlay de Sancy, a royalist, mortgaged the diamond in 1586 to benefit the marquis d'O, a favorite of Henry III, redeemed it in 1594, and offered it in vain to Henry IV. He finally sold it to James I of England in 1604. Charles I inherited the Sancy, which was then worn by his wife, Henrietta of France, the daughter of Henry IV. She pawned the diamond again, through the duke of Epernon, to finance the fight against the English parliament. But Charles I was beheaded in 1649, and in 1657 Henrietta had to sell her jewelry. Cardinal Mazarin bought from her the Sancy and the Mirror of Portugal through the duke of Epernon and gave both stones to the crown of France in 1661. The Sancy was worn on a hat pin by Louis the XIV and was later set atop the crown used in the coronation of Louis XV in 1722. It was stolen on September 11 or 13, 1792, during the theft of the national Garde-Meuble, but found on March 21, 1794, in the house of a known criminal. Soon afterward, it was pawned again in Madrid, during the rule of the Directoire, to finance the campaign of Vendée in 1796. The consulate could not redeem it. The Sancy then passed from the Spanish to Russian, Indian, and English owners before being discretely returned to the Apollo Gallery in the Louvre in 1978.

■ One of the most feared diamonds is the Hope, a 45.52-carat cushion-shaped blue stone. In 1668 Jean-Baptiste Tavernier

The Largest Known Rough Diamonds

Name	Weight (carats)	Color	Location	Date	Cut Stones
Cullinan	3,106	near colorless	South Africa (Premier)	1905	Cullinan I (530 ct.) + 104 others
Excelsior	995.2	near colorless	South Africa (Jagersfontein)	1893	Excelsior I (69.68 ct.) + 20 others
Star of Sierra Leone	968.8	near colorless	Sierra Leone	1972	Rough
Incomparable ("Zale's")	890	brownish yellow	presumably Africa	Sold in 1984	Incomparable (407.48 ct.) + 14 others
Great Mogul	787.5	near colorless	India	1650	Great Mogul (280 ct.)— lost, or became the Orlov (189.62 ct.)
Woyie River	770	near colorless	Sierra Leone	1945	Woyie River (31.35 ct.) + 29 others
President Vargas	726.6	near colorless	Brazil	1938	Vargas (48.26 ct.) + 22 others
Jonker	726.6	near colorless	South Africa	1934	Jonker (125.65 ct.) + 11 others

The Two Largest Faceted Diamonds in Each Color

Nearly Colorless	Pink	Red	Brown	Yellow	Brownish Yellow	Green	Blue	Black
Cullinan I (530.20 ct.)	Darya-i-Nur[1] (185 ct., estimated)	Red Diamond (5.05 ct.)	Star of the Earth (111.59 ct.)	De Beers (234.50 ct.)	Incomparable (407.48 ct.)	Dresden Green (41 ct.)	Hope[2] (45.52 ct.)	Black Star of Africa (202 ct.)
Cullinan II (317.40 ct.)	Nepal Pink (72 ct.)	Halphen Red (1 ct.)	Cross of Asia (109.26 ct.)	Red Cross (205 ct.)	Moon (183 ct.)		Copenhagen Light Blue (45.52 ct.)	Black Orlov (67.50 ct.)

Some Famous Diamonds

Centenary (223 ct.)	Nur-al-Ain[1] (60 ct., estimated)		Kimberley (55.09 ct.)	Tiffany (128.51 ct.)	Iranian I (152.16 ct.)		Wittelsbach (35.32 ct.)	River Styx (28.50 ct.)
Orlov (189.62 ct.)	Princie (34.64 ct.)			Golden Sun (105.54 ct.)	Florentine (137.27 ct.)		Brunswick Blue (13.75 ct.)—lost	
Regent (140.50 ct.)	Hortensia (21.32 ct.)			Dresden Yellow (38 ct.)			Brunswick Blue II[2] (6.50 ct.)—lost	
Koh-i-Noor (108.93 ct.)	Paul I (13.35 ct.)						Blue of Marie Antoinette (5.45 ct.)	
Briolette of India (90.38 ct.)	Grand Condé (9.01 ct.)						Pirie[2] (1 ct.)—lost	
Shah (88.70 ct.)								
Sancy (55.23 ct.)								
Star of South Africa (47.75 ct.)								
Eureka (10.73 ct.)								
Star of Arkansas (8.27 ct.)								

1. These two diamonds are supposedly from the "Great Table" of Tavernier (about 250 carats), according to V. B. Meen (very controversial).
2. These three diamonds were cut from the French Blue diamond (67⅛ carats), according to E. W. Streeter.

The 45.52-carat Hope blue diamond. Smithsonian Institution, Washington, D.C. Photo: Dane Penland.

showed to Louis XIV several diamonds, including a "large blue diamond," cut in a fairly compact heart shape typical to India and weighing 112³⁄₁₆ carats. It became the *Diamant Bleu de la Couronne* (known in the United States as the French Blue) after it was bought for £220,000 in early 1669. It was recut in 1673 by the sieur Pitou into a 67⅛-old-carat heart shape and set in 1749 on the golden fleece designed by Jacquemin, later worn by Louis XV. It was appraised at £3 million in 1791. Stolen with the crown jewels, the stone ended up in the hands of Cadet Guillot, who fled to London, and the diamond disappeared. According to the gem dealer E. W. Streeter, the diamond was recut into three stones: a 44.5-old-carat cushion shape called the Hope, a 6.5-old-carat pear shape called the Brunswick Blue II (now lost), and a blue diamond "point" of about 1 carat called the Pirie (also lost). This report is controversial.

The blue cushion was probably worn by Maríe Luisa, queen of Spain, when she was painted by Goya in 1799. She was exiled to Compiègne by Napoléon in 1808. In 1812 the blue diamond surfaced in London at a dealer, Daniel Eliason, who sold it for 18,000 pounds sterling to Henry Philip Hope in 1830. Known then as the Hope, it was displayed in 1851 in the Crystal Palace along with the Koh-i-Noor, both symbols of triumphant England. Lord Henry Francis Hope, who adopted this name in order to inherit the stone, had to sell it in 1901 and subsequently divorced the American actress May Yohe in 1902. Perhaps it was at this point that the malefic legend started. Because it produces a blood-red luminescence when exposed to ultraviolet light, the Hope was said to cause the violent death of its owners. A terrifying legend dating back to Tavernier was invented to substantiate this belief, based on bits of history. Supposedly, Tavernier (who actually died at age eighty-four in Russia) was ruined and eaten by dogs in India; then Louis XIV (who in reality survived its purchase for forty-six years) died as soon as he wore the diamond; Madame du Barry, a favorite of Louis XV (who would never have allowed a favorite to wear a jewel belonging to the crown), supposedly wore it, which led to her execution, as did Queen Marie Antoinette and the princess of Lamballe, both of whom were killed during the French Revolution. Hope's wife (who actually died under normal circumstances) died ruined; a Russian prince (who never existed) killed his mistress on the night he offered her the cursed stone and later was stabbed; the Ottoman sultan Abdülhamid II imitated the Russian prince (which is incorrect) and died in a revolution (he actually died in 1918, nine years after being overthrown). The billionaire McLean perished in the wreck of the *Titanic* (this was immediately refuted), his son died in a car accident in New York, and his daughter overdosed on barbital (these last two statements are also wrong). Finally the Hope disappeared, causing the death of an actress (for good measure!).

The Hope was actually bought in 1901 by Simon Frankel, a New York jeweler. It was then sold in 1908 for $400,000 to a rich Spanish collector named Habib, living in Paris, who had to sell it in 1909. The dealer sold it immediately to Pierre Cartier, who sold it in 1912 to Mrs. McLean, who wore it until her death in 1947. She considered it a lucky charm, a symbol of hope, as its name suggested. The stone was sold in 1949 for $79,920 to the famous American jeweler Harry Winston. In 1958 Winston donated the stone to the Smithsonian Institution, where it is still one of the most popular displays.

■ One of the most beautiful historical diamonds is the Regent, a 140.5-carat cushion. According to nasty gossip, a slave discovered it in 1702 near Golconda (Andhra Pradesh) in India. He hid it in a bandage around his ankle and offered the diamond to a sailor in exchange for his freedom. The sailor killed the slave and took the 410-carat rough diamond. He sold it for £1,000 to the English governor of Madras, Thomas Pitt, later accused by his enemy of moral complicity with the murderer. It seems, however, that the diamond was actually

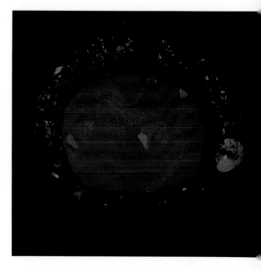

The Hope shows an orangey-red phosphorescence under short-wave ultraviolet radiation. Photo: J. Hatleberg.

Le Grand Condé, a 9.05-carat pink diamond. Musée Condé, Chantilly, France. Photo: Giraudon.

discovered in 1698, and Pitt negotiated with an Indian dealer to purchase it for £19,200 in 1700 and 1701. The dealer must have acquired the stone in an unusual way, since all stones over 10 carat belonged by right to the sovereign; the Hyderabad nizam would certainly have kept such a stone for himself. In 1702 Pitt then sent his son Robert to London, to have the stone faceted by the jeweler Harris, who took two years to complete the job. Robert Pitt then offered it to all the rulers of Europe, but they all turned down such a high-priced stone; even Louis XIV did not dare buy the stone in 1714. On the advice of the duke of Saint-Simon, Philippe d'Orleans, regent of France, purchased it in 1717 for 135,000 pounds sterling, that is, about 2,000,000 French pounds; with all the interest that accrued until the diamond was paid for, the total price came to a staggering 2,500,000 French pounds (about $5 million today). But the Regent, (now the name of the stone), was set on the coronation crown of Louis XV and was worn by Louis XVI during the first meeting of the Etats Généraux (the democratically elected parliament) on May 5, 1789. Transferred in 1791 to the national Garde-Meuble, the Regent was then estimated to be worth 12 million French pounds. Displayed to the masses, so everybody could touch it, it was stolen in September 1792 but was found hidden in a wooden beam on December 10, 1793. The diamond was then used as collateral to equip the French cavalry, first held by a German banker and then a Dutch banker. Redeemed on June 22, 1801, by the consulate, the Regent was considered by Napoléon to be a talisman; he had it set on the guard of his parade sword in 1803, then on his coronation sword in 1804, then on the imperial blade in 1812. The stone was taken as far as Blois by the deposed empress Marie-Louise in 1814 but was soon returned to Louis XVIII. The Regent was then successively set on the now-lost coronation crown of Charles X, on a Greek-style headband, and

on a hairpin belonging to the empress Eugénie. The Regent is presently displayed unset, as one of the treasures of the Apollo Gallery in the Louvre in Paris.

■ One of the most engraved diamonds is the Shah, a 88.70-carat square prism. Three of the prism faces show the names of its owners: "Bourkhan"—"Nizam Shah II, 1000" (A.D. 1590), "The son of Djahanguir," "Chahdjahan, 1501" (A.D. 1641), engraved by order of Shah Djahan, and "Kadjar Fath Ali Shah, 1240," (A.D. 1824). Shah Djahan was the Mogul sovereign of Delhi; Nāder Shāh took the diamond from his heirs during the plunder of Delhi in 1739 but did not dare engrave his own name on it. After Nāder Shāh's assassination in 1747, Persia experienced some troubled times: the sovereign Aghā Mohammad Khān was assassinated in 1797, but his nephew Fath 'Alī Shāh overthrew the usurper, Sadek-Khān. Fath promised that every drop of Sadek's blood would be spared if he would return the diamond (he actually kept his word, since he buried Sadek alive). In 1828 the Russian ambassador to Persia was assassinated during a riot, and the Shah was offered to Czar Nicholas I as compensation. It is now displayed in the Kremlin.

■ The only diamond that would have been voluntarily destroyed was the Pigott, or "broken diamond," a 49-carat oval, now lost. In 1763 it was given by an Indian prince to the English governor of Madras, Georges Pigott, and was sold when the man died in 1777. After a few peregrinations, the Pigott was purchased in 1818 for 150,000 pounds sterling by Ali, pacha of Ionnina (Albania). Ali, nicknamed the Lion of Janina (today's Ioànnina, Greece), was trying in vain to escape the authority of the sultan of Constantinople; as a consequence, the Turkish troops laid siege to the town. After two years of siege, Ali, fatally wounded, ordered his aide-de-camp, Captain D'Anglas, to destroy his two most precious possessions: his wife, Vassiliki, and his large diamond. It is said that he lived long enough to see his diamond being destroyed but died before it was his spouse's turn, so she was spared. Was the diamond really destroyed? The only thing known for certain is that neither Vassiliki nor D'Anglas had any financial problem afterwards.

The Crystallochemistry and Physical Properties of Diamond

In 1675 Isaac Newton thought that diamond must be combustible because of its adamantine luster; he was proved correct by two Italians, Averani and Targioni, in 1694. Lavoisier in 1772, followed by Smithson Tennant in 1796, proved that diamond was made up of carbon almost exclusively, and that it burns at 500°C (930°F) in an air

current. If it falls into a wood fire, a faceted diamond loses its polish because of superficial combustion (like anthracite does).

In a diamond crystal, each carbon atom shares four of its outer electrons with four neighboring carbon atoms. Breaking these covalent bonds requires much energy, which explains the high scratch resistance of the gem, the hardest of all known minerals, and its high index of refraction: 2.418 for conventional yellow light, 2.407 for red (at 687 nanometers), and 2.451 for blue (at 431 nanometers). This produces a dispersion of 0.044 (which causes the "fires" of the gem), weak when compared to electrovalent crystals such as sphalerite.

In the diamond crystal structure, each carbon atom is at the center of a regular tetrahedron formed by its four neighbors: the smallest repeatable element of this structure (the smallest unit cell) is a cube, with diagonals parallel to the carbon–carbon bonds. If each carbon atom is represented by a 1.54-angstrom-diameter sphere touching all its neighbors, the crystal has 66 percent void space. Nevertheless diamond has a high specific gravity (3.52), despite the weak atomic mass of carbon, because the diameter of the carbon "spheres" is almost twice as small as that of the oxygen ions that make up the much "tighter" structure of oxides and silicates such as corundum and topaz (the compact stacking of oxygen in corundum leaves only 25 percent void space). However, diamond's structure is metastable at normal pressure. If "restraints" were not present in its structure, diamond would immediately change into a graphite powder; this does happen when a diamond is held at 1,100°C (2,000°F) at normal pressure in a neutral atmosphere.

In graphite, each carbon atom shares an outer electron with three neighbors; the fourth one goes from bond to bond (this is why graphite is an electrical conductor). Graphite is a stacking of carbon "sheets" having a hexagonal structure; these sheets are weakly bonded to each other (residual bonding) and can therefore slide easily over each other (that is why graphite is used as a lubricant). The diamond–graphite transition results from the rupture of bonds parallel to a three-fold axis and the redistribution of the liberated electrons into a cloud, which renders the wavy sheet of carbon atoms planar and makes them move farther apart. The crystal decomposes, with a strong increase in volume (the specific gravity of graphite is 2.1 to 2.2).

The most common diamond crystal shapes are the octahedron (sometimes twins, as in spinel), the rhombododecahedron, the cube (sometimes twinned, as in fluorite), shapes derived from the cube such as the trisoctahedron and hexaoctahedron, and shapes resulting from the tetrahedral hemihedry (sometimes twinned with two or

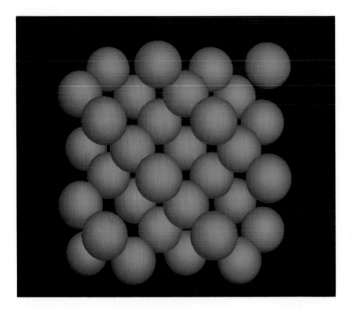

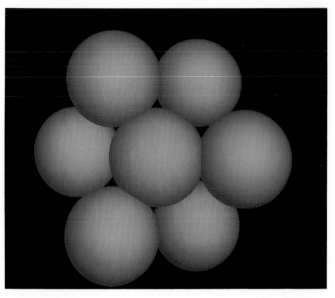

Computer-generated image showing the atomic structure of a diamond. Courtesy of the Mineralogy-Crystallography Laboratory at the Pierre and Marie Curie University, Paris.

Computer-generated image of graphite's atomic structure. Courtesy of the Mineralogy-Crystallography Laboratory at the Pierre and Marie Curie University, Paris.

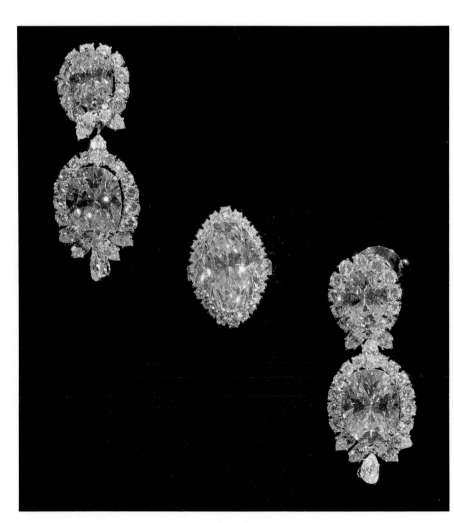

A 21.86-carat yellow diamond set in a ring. Van Cleef and Arpels creation.

more crystals). The twin plane of the hexagonal twin is very resistant to wear. Two crystals can be associated in a twin either by simple juxtaposition (the most common case, the "mating" of diamonds) or by interpenetration. Atoms of similar size and electronic structure, such as nitrogen and boron, may substitute for carbon in the diamond structure. Nitrogen makes 90 percent of diamonds opaque to short-wave ultraviolet; these diamonds are called Type I.

The five unpaired electrons of a nitrogen atom are usually arranged as a pair and three single electrons, each shared with a neighboring carbon atom. When nitrogen is abundant enough (from 0.1 to 0.2 percent), it forms flattened bodies called "platelets," laying parallel to the cube faces. When the nitrogen concentration is small (a few parts per million), nitrogen atoms are isolated in the diamond structure and create four bonds with their neighbors, like a normal carbon atom; the extra electron contributes to the absorption of violet light, which explains the yellow color of these rare (1 percent of Type I diamonds) and coveted Type Ib diamonds, also called *canary* diamonds. Diamonds containing no detectable amount of nitrogen are transparent to short-wave ultraviolet light and are called Type II. The purest, often perfectly colorless ones, such as the Cullinan, are called Type IIa and generally have irregular crystal shapes.

An electron vacancy is created whenever a boron atom, which has only three electrons, replaces a carbon atom. The unpaired electron from the fourth carbon neighbor absorbs energy from the red end of the visible spectrum; this explains both the electrical conductivity and blue color of these Type IIb diamonds.

Other colors, such as pink and orange, can be attributed to interstitial impurities and to local or extended defects in the diamond structure. The presence in a diamond of a certain defect related to nitrogen generally produces a blue luminescence of variable intensity. This fluorescence is the consequence of a characteristic absorption spectrum of slightly yellow diamonds, called Cape lines (with lines at 415 and 478 nanometers, for example). Some brown stones produce a greenish yellow luminescence due to a typical absorption feature called the 5040 pair (with lines at 496 and 504 nanometers), which has been attributed to a vacancy trapped at an aggregate of two nitrogen atoms.

Unlike most of its simulants, diamond is an excellent thermal conductor; it seems cold when touched to the skin. This property is used by small testers to help distinguish diamond from its various simulants.

Origin

Diamond crystallizes in the upper mantle of the earth, in a zone where exchanges with the deeper portions of the earth's crust can occur. It is stable at depths of 150 kilometers (1,100°C, 50 kilobar) to 200 kilometer (1,600°C, 60 kilobar). More diamonds form in the center of this zone, but they are small; larger crystals grow on either side, where they are not disturbed by abundant nucleation. Therefore, numerous small diamonds (up to 1 percent) are found in eclogites under the old continental shields (that is, the most stable parts of the earth's crust). Eclogites are granular rocks formed about 2.5 billion years ago, which contain little silica but, rather, consist of peridot, pyrope garnet, diopside, and enstatite. Chunks of various dimensions (up to 1 meter [3 feet] in diameter) of such extremely old rocks were brought to the surface about 92 million years ago, during the Cretaceous period. Such was the case for the so-called Jewel Box, the kimberlite eruption forming the Roberts Victor pipe in Orange Free State, South Africa.

Kimberlitic magmas also form in these deep zones. Their temperature is controlled by the heat produced by the earth's convection currents, radioactive materials (thorium, for example), and the endothermia of volatile compounds, such as methane and water. This makes the crystallization of small quantities of diamond possible (less than one part per million). The growing diamond crystal encloses residual minerals, resulting from the partial melting of the eclogites, especially garnet, olivine, and enstatite, as well as some sulfides, kyanite, pyroxenes, and chromite. The kimberlitic magma is lighter than its surrounding viscous environment; it therefore rises to the surface. This ascension increases in speed with decreasing depth, because of the kimberlite's gas content. The magma breaks off pieces of eclogite, peridotite and pyroxenite along the way, which more or less crumble. Consequently, some think that diamond does not crystallize in the kimberlite, which is only a means of transportation; for example, some diamonds from the Premier mine have been dated to 2.4 billion years ago, whereas the surrounding kimberlite is only 90 million years old. The kimberlitic mass then hits the earth's crust. If this happens in a zone of lower resistance, such as at the borders of the more stable cratons, the crust fractures and the kimberlite flows through at high speed, breaking

Yellow diamonds set in a ring (21.86 carats) and in ear pendants (the largest ones are 25.17 carats and the small ones are 12.06 carats). Van Cleef and Arpels creation.

Surface Areas of the Largest Known Diamond Pipes

Name (Country)	Dimensions in meters (feet)	Surface in hectares (acres)
Mwadui (Tanzania)	1650 x 1400 (5400 x 4600)	146 (361)
Orapa (Botswana)	1525 x 1000 (5000 x 3300)	106 (262)
Talala (Zaïre)	1100 x 900 (3600 x 2950)	95 (235)
Premier (South Africa)	850 x 450 (2790 x 1475)	32 (79)
Zarnitza (Siberia)	500 x 500 (1640 x 1640)	21.5 (53)
Finsch (South Africa)	500 x 475 (1640 x 1550)	18 (44)
Koffiefontein (South Africa)	500 x 300 (1640 x 985)	11 (27)
Jagersfontein (South Africa)	400 x 250 (1300 x 820)	10 (25)
Camatue (Angola)	475 x 300 (1550 x 985)	9.3 (23)
Mir (Siberia)	400 x 200 (1300 x 650)	6.9 (17)
De Beers (South Africa)	325 x 150 (1065 x 490)	4.8 (12)
Kimberley ("Big Hole") South Africa	300 x 200 (985 x 650)	3.6 (9)
Blaauwbosch (South Africa)	150 x 110 (490 x 360)	1.5 (4)

South African octahedral diamond crystal, 1 cm on an edge, in its kimberlite matrix. Sorbonne collection.

off granite and granodiorite chunks on its way up. It also produces enough friction to reduce the volume of the included rocks enough to break a diamond (the Cullinan is a good example). However, this high pressure also prevents the diamond from disappearing by reverting to graphite or oxidizing. At a distance of about 2.5 to 3 kilometers (1½ miles) of the surface, the kimberlitic mass explodes, creating results in a brutal drop in temperature that keeps diamonds from becoming graphite. The sedimentary rocks broken by the explosion fall into the kimberlite, which solidifies.

An amazing adventure brings diamond to us (if the kimberlite does not contain enough gases, it does not even reach the surface). The same crack in the earth's crust may be used several times by different kimberlite eruptions. The amount of diamond present and its quality varies from event to event: in the De Beers mine, the east end of the pipe is rich but the western part is barely worth mining. The record seems to be held by the Premier mine, where fifteen different kimberlites have been identified. Wide at the surface, with a diameter of 10 to 1,000 meters (30 to 3,200 feet), kimberlite pipes narrow as their depth increases. Kimberlite immediately becomes the victim of weathering: water infiltrates, oxidizing and decomposing the rock, which becomes yellow and powdery on the surface ("yellow ground"). Below the surface it remains a massive blue rock ("blue ground"). Diamond content diminishes with depth. A crumbly serpentine forms around the diamonds, even into the blue ground; this makes the separation of the crystals from their matrix easier.

Surface water carries away the yellow ground and the sedimentary host rocks, sometimes spreading them over consider-

able areas (60,000 kilometers^2 (23,000 square miles) in Zaire and Angola). Alluvial diamond deposits form along either ancient or modern waterways. These alluvial diamonds can even be transported to the shore and form embankments as in Namibia.

Old deposits consolidate over time and may produce a remarkable relief. The Witwatersrand (white-water cliffs), named by Dutch prospectors for the numerous waterfalls it contains, is famous not only for its gold, for which it was first mined, but also for its diamonds. Some of them are 2.5 billion years old, the oldest on earth.

As they are carried along the rivers, poorly crystallized and inclusion-rich diamonds tend to break and are eventually destroyed by the numerous shocks in the riverbeds. This creates a particular pattern in the distribution of diamonds, which has been used to locate kimberlite pipes.

Deposits

India

The Indian diamond deposits (already mentioned in the historical section), are located in five main areas, which cover most of the subcontinent. They were not discovered or mined simultaneously. Their production has remained small since the eighteenth century. Three deposits are in the south: the Cuddapah region, where the alluvial deposits of the Penner River were worked along a 60-mile stretch; the Nandyal region, on the plateaus located between the Penner and Krishna rivers; and the Golconda region. Diamond deposits are found in the east in the Sambalpur region, where the middle course of the Mahanadi River was especially rich, and in the north in the Panna region, located between the Ken and Son rivers in the central provinces, where alluvial deposits and kimberlitic pipes are still mined.

Borneo

Diamond was allegedly discovered on Borneo along the banks of the Landak River around the fifth century A.D. Song pottery reveals a Chinese presence in this area in the twelfth century or earlier. In the seventeenth century, Borneo paid a tribute in diamonds to the Celestial Empire. The diamonds are found in alluvium in the southern part of the island, still little known, called Kalimantan ("river of diamonds"). A large portion of this tropical area is a perpetual swamp drained by a few rivers. The alluvial deposits of the Kapuas River, in the center of the island, are worked with primitive equipment by small groups of four to twenty people, who dig shallow pits down to the bedrock. The ore is cleaned, sifted,

and sorted using bamboo baskets. The diamonds are often small.

If any diamonds that are found contain a gray or black phantom in the center, the pit is abandoned: an old Malay belief identifies these stones with the soul of the diamond, and of course, the mine will die if its soul is taken (however, Malaysians do wear these diamond "souls" as talismans). The small cutting center of Martapura serves the local market. A kimberlite pipe has recently been discovered about 40 kilometers (25 miles) north of the works.

South America

Diamond regions are located in the Brazilian and Venezuelan shields. Since the discovery of diamond in Brazil in 1725, other alluvial diamond deposits have been located in the states of Minas Gerais, Goiás, and Mato Grosso, and they are still worked today. Recently discovered sterile kimberlite may explain the origin of these deposits. The richest deposits, particularly famous at the end of the nineteenth century, are still mined at Morrou do Chapeu and Lençois in the state of Bahia, in a conglomerate of controversial origin.

North of the Amazon, diamonds have been found in all the rivers flowing from the Roraima Mountains, at the intersection of the borders of Brazil, Venezuela, and Guyana. Diamond was discovered in Venezuela in 1901 but was not seriously prospected until 1912. Access to the deposits is difficult, so the production of Venezuela, exclusively alluvial, is very irregular (from 600,000 to 1,250,000 carats a year) and difficult to control. Diamonds have also been found in the neighboring regions of Brazil and Guyana.

North America

Although they are not economically viable, the Murfreesboro kimberlites in Arkansas are famous. The first diamond was discovered there in 1906 in Prairie Creek by John Haddleston. He had noticed the resemblance between the rocks of this area and those of the South African kimberlites described thirty-six years earlier by Carwill Lewis. About a thousand small diamonds (with an average weight of less than 0.3 carat) are recovered every year by amateur prospectors. The Uncle Sam, a 40.23-carat rough diamond, was discovered there in 1924 and is the largest diamond from this locality. It was later faceted into a 12.42-carat emerald cut. Similar kimberlites are found in Kansas and on the eastern border of the Rocky Mountains (Colorado, Wyoming). In addition, small diamonds have been found in the gold alluvial deposits of northern California, in the glacier deposits of the Great Lakes (Ohio, Michigan), and in some valleys of the Appalachian Mountains (from Virginia to Tennessee).

In Canada a kimberlite pipe with some diamonds has been found on Somerset Island, in the Northwest Territories.

Europe

To date, no serious indications of diamond deposits have been found, although some diamonds were discovered in Bohemia and Scotland. The Czechoslovakian kimberlites are sterile.

Soviet Union

As early as 1830, gold prospectors had found diamonds in the Ural Mountains, especially at Krestovo and Dvichensk near Perm. After World War II, industrial demands led to the prospecting of relatively rich alluvial deposits north of Perm, on the Vychegda River. Diamonds were also recovered in 1893 by gold prospectors working the tributaries of the upper course of the Yenisei River, in western Siberia. These rivers drained part of the Siberian shield, an area seemingly favorable to the presence of kimberlites, according to the knowledge acquired in southern Africa. It was therefore decided to prospect central Siberia. In 1953, after eight years of efforts by hundreds of geologists, a placer was discovered in the basin of the Vilyui River, more than 1,000 kilometers (600 miles) north of the indications found at the end of the nineteenth century. In 1954 a group of kimberlite pipes was found, and discoveries then followed one after another. Despite the difficulties posed by the climate ($-30°$ to $-60°C$ [$-20°$ to $-75°F$] during half the year) and the remoteness of this area of Yakutia (the Trans-Siberian Railway passes more than 1,000 kilometers [600 miles] south), systematic mining was begun. The Soviet Union, which now extracts a quarter of the world diamond production, has thus become the second-largest producer of industrial diamonds (after Zaire) and the second-largest producer of gem-quality diamonds (after South Africa). The most famous kimberlites are Udatchnaya ("lucky one") and Mir ("peace").

China

Little is known about diamonds in China, where stones were allegedly found in the eighteenth century in alluvial deposits. Diamond prospectors walked over the deposits in shoes with straw soles, which were supposed to trap the diamonds. Diamonds have been found and mined along the lower course of the Huang Ho, in the provinces of Shandong and Henan. Some diamond-bearing kimberlites have been discovered in the Chinese shield.

An 80-carat total-weight diamond choker with a 30-carat clip. Van Cleef and Arpels creation.

Africa

Since the end of the nineteenth century, Africa has been the largest diamond producer by far, and the African continent is still the main producer. The rich deposits of southern Africa—kimberlites and alluvial deposits in South Africa, alluvial deposits in Namibia, kimberlites in Lesotho (producing since 1977), Botswana (Orapa was put into production in 1971), and Swaziland (found in 1973 and soon mined)—represent only a third of the world's production but are the most important sources of gem-quality diamonds. Diamonds have also been found in Zimbabwe but are not mined.

In southern Africa the huge diamond fields of Zaire, which extend into Angola, were discovered in 1907; they presently produce 40 percent of the world's diamonds, mostly industrial diamonds, of which Zaire is the primary producer. Alluvial diamond deposits are also worked in Congo and the Central African Republic, and kimberlites are mined in Angola and Gabon. In Tanzania the immense Mwadui kimberlite pipe, the world's largest, was discovered by John Williamson in 1935. It consists of 40 percent gem-quality diamonds, an exceptionally high proportion.

In western Africa, the alluvial diamond deposits of Ghana have been known since 1919 and those of the Côte d'Ivoire since 1929. Kimberlites have also been found in 1930 in Liberia and Sierra Leone, where both industrial and gem-quality diamonds (including the third-largest rough diamond, weighing 968.9 carats) are of high quality;

Triangular growth features on a rough diamond. Size: 0.1 cm. E. Sirakian collection.

Open-pit mining at the Finsch mine, South Africa, covering 3 hectares (almost 32 acres) Photo: De Beers.

other kimberlites were identified in 1936 in Guinea, in 1956 in Mali, in 1943 in Ghana, and in 1978 in Côte d'Ivoire.

Australia

The Australian shield, like the Brazilian shield, separated from the African continent during the breakup of the Gondwana continent and is therefore a favorable site for the discovery of diamond-bearing kimberlites.

Alluvial diamonds were indeed found in 1884 in New South Wales, a by-product of the mining of alluvial gold and tin. However the geological similarities between Australia and Africa suggested serious prospecting should be undertaken in the northwest, and indeed, diamond-bearing pipes were discovered there in 1980, in the appropriately named Kimberley Desert. The production of the Argyle and Ellendale mines has since been very promising, although the mines are poor in gem-quality diamonds (only 5 to 10 percent). In only a few years, Australia has become a major source of industrial diamonds. It also produces a large number of gem-quality diamonds of an intense pink. In years to come, this country may provide between one-third and one-half of the world's diamonds.

Mining

Extraction of the diamond-bearing ore on the surface can be achieved in a number of ways: with primitive techniques, as in India, or by digging open-pit mines and trenches, but most often, it is done on an industrial scale with heavy-duty equipment.

Powerful earth-moving equipment is used to extract alluvial diamond ore in central Africa. However, the largest mining operation in the world belongs to the Consolidated Diamond Mines and stretches over 100 kilometers (60 miles) of the Namibian coast. The diamond-bearing gravel is covered by 15 to 20 meters (50 to 65 feet) of sterile sand and lies below sea level. Huge 60-ton-capacity backhoes, helped by bulldozers, push the overburden toward the ocean, building a sea wall, that has to be constantly maintained. This structure is over 20 meters (65 feet) wide at its top, to withstand violent storms. Giant excavators remove 1,800 tons of sand per hour on a conveyor belt. The diamond-bearing layer is loaded into 35- to 50-ton-capacity trucks, and the irregularities of the underlying schist are carefully cleaned up with smaller machines, shovels, and brooms. There is a striking contrast between this delicate finish and the roar of about three hundred huge earth movers. About 60 million tons of sand are handled by the C.D.M. every year to extract 0.4 ton of diamond, a pro-

Prospecting for alluvial diamonds in Sierra Leone.
Photo: De Beers.

One of the largest mines in the world: the marine
deposits of Namaqualand. Photo: De Beers.

portion of 0.006 parts per million, a task
similar to isolating twenty-five people from
the world's population.

Large diamond pipes, such as Finsch
(about 500 by 400 meters [1,650 by 1,300
feet] in surface area, presently the sixth-
largest in the world) are first mined via an
open pit, with successive steps or benches
connected by inclines. The mine quickly resembles an inverted cone, with an average
slope of 45 degrees. At Finsch 3.5 million
tons of ore were mined in this way in
1977, producing 0.485 ton of diamond
(2,425,000 carats), a proportion of 0.4 parts
per million.

When the depth of the mine makes
open-pit mining economically impractical,
mining continues using shafts and tunnels.
The method of alternating "pillars and
chambers" along a tunnel, developed in
1890, was abandoned in 1977; it was a way
to remove the ore in blocks 5 meters (16
feet) wide and 12 meters (40 feet) high by
progressively collapsing a pillar of the
upper tunnel located above a chamber of
the lower level. This technique was replaced by the block-caving method developed in 1950: A two-meter (6½-foot-)high
cavity is dug into the kimberlite, causing
the ore to cave in under its own weight. The
crumpled rock falls into concrete reception
funnels, located about every 4 meters (12
feet) along a concrete-lined extraction tunnel below. It is then hauled out with a large
scraper, broken into smaller pieces, and
falls into mine cars. These cars run into a

Underground mining in South Africa. Photo: De Beers.

circular tunnel that surrounds the pipe and bring the ore to the main shaft, dug outside the kimberlite pipe.

The ore is then sieved, and the larger chunks are crushed to free the component minerals; diamond separates from the rock easily because of the serpentinization of the kimberlite, which makes it easier to break. The heavy minerals are separated using a technique based on density. They are then sent in a water stream to a grease table, to which diamond sticks (it is lipophilic) while other minerals slide away. Each evening the table is scraped, and diamond is recovered. More often X-ray luminescence is used: the concentrate passes through an X-ray beam, and luminescence triggers an air jet that blows the stone into a separate chute.

On average, 20 to 25 percent of the diamonds produced are of gem quality. The rest is used for industrial applications, such as abrasives (including those used to cut gem diamonds). The main producers of gem-quality diamonds are South Africa and the Soviet Union, Zaire is the largest producer of industrial diamonds, closely followed by the Soviet Union.

Physical Properties of Faceted Stones

Four main characteristics are evaluated in the grading of faceted diamonds.

The *color* of near-colorless diamonds is graded under standard light, defined as that of a clear sky, looking north at noon, at an average latitude. It can range from "exceptional white" to "tinted," as the yellow or brown underlying color increases. The Scandinavian countries and oldtimers still use a grading nomenclature referring to mines: "river," "top Wesselton," "Wesselton," "crystal," "top Cape," "Cape." The term "crystal" is confusing because, in some Anglo-Saxon countries, "crystal" refers to the top range of "river," that is, extremely rare. American gemologists follow the grading system devised by the Gemological Institute of America, using letters from D through Z to describe increasingly colored near-colorless stones. (The letters A, B and C are not used.) In evaluating color, one must make sure that the appearance of the diamond has not been altered by a bluish coating or deliberate abrading of the pavilion and that there is no trace of blue pencil on the girdle, which would make the stone appear "whiter" than it really is. The notion of "blue-white" must be abandoned (see the discussion of color in part 1). In fancy colored diamonds (such as yellow, orange, or brown), a greenish nuance may indicate treatment by irradiation followed by prolonged heating. High energy particles, such as neutrons or electrons, can indeed remove carbon atoms from their normal position in the diamond lattice and put them into structural voids, resulting in a green or blue color. Thermal treatment allows for a rearrangement of the atoms and the formation of more stable color centers. The resulting color is generally greenish yellow to brown, more rarely pink. The final result depends on the amount and type of impurities originally present in the stone and on the type of treatment used.

The *mass* of a diamond may be unnecessarily increased compared to its other dimensions by cutting a thick girdle.

The *clarity* is determined by the visibility of its inclusions. If no inclusion or defect is visible using a loupe with a magnification of 10, the stone is called flawless or "loupe clean." Otherwise, it may display "very, very small" inclusions (grade VVS), "very small" inclusions (grade VS), "small inclusions" (grade SI), or be classified as "imperfect" or "piqué" (grades I or P) if the inclusions are obvious. Colorless inclusions do not affect clarity as much as black inclusions do. Inclusions can be artificially modified: a very narrow hole is drilled with a laser beam from the surface to the inclusion, which is then dissolved with hydrofluoric acid. After treatment, only a small channel to the outside through the miniscule drill hole remains. Dust may, however accumulate in the cavity during normal wear, and the inclusion might become dark again.

The *cut* of a diamond is intended to give the stone maximum life. Therefore regardless of whether the stone is brilliant- or step-cut, the proportions of its various dimensions are most important.

Old cuts, sometimes irregular, with a high crown and a deep pavilion, a large culet and a small table, are often very fiery, but the large culet creates a "black hole" when the stone is viewed face up. The cuts made between the two World Wars are often very symmetrical, with an almost modern pavilion, but a high crown, a large culet, and a smallish table. They are therefore referred to as "half cuts," because one has to recut all of the crown but little of the pavilion to produce a modern brilliant cut.

A diamond whose color has been artificially modified. Private collection.

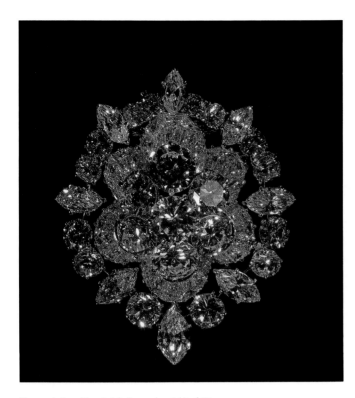

Diamond clip with a total diamond weight of 30 carats. Van Cleef and Arpels creation.

Cloud of inclusions trapped during the growth of this 1.99-carat diamond. Private collection.

Ring set with an engraved diamond representing a marquis's crest. Width: 1.2 cm. Boucheron collection.

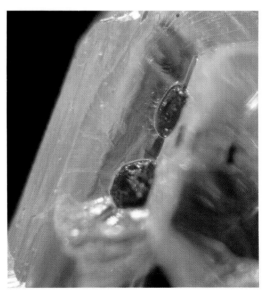

Pyrope garnet inclusions, 1 mm across, in a rough diamond crystal. E. Sirakian collection.

Modern cuts have a shallow crown (20 to 25 percent of the stone depth), a shallow pavilion (about 44 percent of the stone's diameter), and a relatively large table (55 to 60 percent of the stone's diameter). These stones have less fire and personality than old cuts—they tend to be "colder"—but they display their absence of color better. A modern cut with a relatively shallow crown and a large table appears to spread, whereas a chunkier stone looks smaller but warmer, more lively. Of course, proportions producing an excessively flat or deep diamond do not give the stone an attractive appearance, and such stones are nicknamed "fish eyes" or "nailheads," accordingly.

Gems of Similar Appearance

Theoretically, any colorless gem can replace a colorless diamond, but only common gems have actually served as substitutes. For example, rock crystal quartz accompanies diamond in its alluvial deposits, and in the rough may even look like diamond because of its crystal shape and frosty surface. It was called "young diamond" by old-time French lapidaries. When limpid, cut deep, and set in a closed mounting, it could fool the layperson, especially crystals from Herkimer, New York.

Colorless topaz, limpid and brilliant, has also been a diamond substitute. But the most common natural stone used to imitate diamond is probably zircon from Southeast Asia, made colorless through heat treatment (which also makes it more fragile), because of its high luster and despite its sometimes slightly turbid appearance. Among other substitutes, colorless sapphire from Sri Lanka is commonly used. The adamantine luster of numerous colored collector's stones recall fancy colored diamonds: sphalerite (blende), cassiterite, and titanite (sphene) are, however, too soft to be set in jewelry; they are safely displayed in collectors' showcases.

Finally, jewelry from the nineteenth century was often set with small rose-cut pyrite crystals (incorrectly called marcasites), used as side stones for watches or large gems to simulate the sparkle of diamond.

Simulants

Serious attempts to produce diamond simulants were made only after diamonds became popular, during the Renaissance. At that time, "crystalliers" produced and cut colorless glass (at the time, it was called "crystal"—implying that the stone was a fabrication—because of its resemblance to colorless quartz, always called "rock crystal"). In the eighteenth century, the recipe for glass paste was significantly improved, especially with the addition of lead salts, which increase the luster of the glass. This was discovered by the French chemist Georges Frédéric Stras (1700–1773) of Strasbourg, whose name, germanized in *strass*, now designates the lead-based glass used in cheap jewelry.

A new improvement came in the nineteenth century with the implementation of a reflector—a shiny coating or a small lead bead—fixed on the pavilion of faceted strass. They were called similidiamonds or simply similis, and could be very convincing in a closed setting.

Colorless garnet-and-glass doublets appeared toward the end of the nineteenth century and at the beginning of the twentieth century. The garnet slab, intended to provide a harder table, was so thin that its color could not be perceived face up.

Only in the 1930s were synthetic crystals used as diamond simulants in cheap jewelry, beginning with colorless synthetic corundum and spinel, grown by the Verneuil process and still in use today. These imitations are resistant to scratching but lack a true adamantine luster. Although it has a slightly lower hardness and luster, synthetic spinel is a little less "dead" than synthetic corundum, because of its isotropy and dispersion.

Synthetic rutile (Titania), commercialized in 1948, and strontium titanate (Fabulite), introduced in 1953, are both grown by the Verneuil process. They were quite successful at the time of their introduction, because their luster is close to that of diamond. However, they are soft (H is around 6), and their very high dispersion causes a total decomposition of the light instead of attractive fires.

Synthetic corundum and Fabulite and synthetic spinel and Fabulite doublets were thus fabricated and were more convincing than Fabulite alone.

During the 1960s developments in the laser industry led to the growth of artificial crystals with a garnet structure. Among these, a variety of yttrium aluminate, called YAG, was used doped with chromium or erbium; it is colorless when not doped. Resistant to scratches (H is 8), with a high luster (index of refraction is 1.83) for an average dispersion (0.026), it was rapidly adopted in jewelry, starting in 1969, especially to cut replicas of famous large diamonds, such as Elizabeth Taylor's 69.42-carat pear-shaped diamond. Until 1974 YAG was sold in large quantities under various trade names, despite the fact that its luster was still nowhere near that of diamond. It loses all its brilliance when placed in a glass of water, and its refringence is weak enough to allow an ink mark made on its table to be seen through its pavilion.

Several other synthetic crystals were produced in an attempt to compete with YAG, but none was really successful: GGG (gallium gadolinium garnet), with a higher index of refraction and hardness, turns yellow under the sun's ultraviolet light; Linobate (lithium niobate) and KTN (potassium niobotantalate) are too soft (H is 5½).

During the 1970s the industry succeeded in crystallizing cubic zirconium oxide (or zirconia), stabilized by small amounts of yttrium or calcium. This was achieved with the "skull melting" technique, in which sintered zirconium oxide is used as a crucible to hold the molten zirconium oxide to be crystallized at temperatures of about 2,300°C (4,175°F). With a luster close to that of diamond (index of refraction is 2.2), a high but not extreme dispersion (0.06), a good resistance to scratches (H is 8½) and a true absence of color, cubic zirconia, or CZ, is today the most convincing diamond imitation. It should really be called synthetic zirkelite, since natural zirkelite exists. CZ was introduced on the market in 1974 and rapidly replaced YAG. Tons of CZ are sold every year under various commercial names.

Synthetics

Controlled crystallization of diamond presupposes a prolonged period within the stability field of diamond, that is, pressures of 50,000 to 100,000 atmospheres (equal to the pressure exerted by the Eiffel Tower on a square centimeter) and to temperatures between 1,500° and 2,000°C (2,700° and 2,600°F.) Under these conditions, graphite is still metastable, so a catalyst is necessary to favor diamond crystallization: iron, nickel, cobalt, and even tantalum are the best elements for this purpose.

High pressures are obtained using a so-called belt apparatus. The effective volume of the sample chamber was originally only a few cubic centimeters; it is now about a liter (1,000 centimeters[3]; approximately a quart). The temperature is produced by an electrical current or a chemical reaction.

Once diamond has crystallized, it has to be cooled to room temperature before the pressure can be reduced; otherwise, it would turn into graphite. The crystals grown are generally numerous and small (a fraction of a millimeter), because growth is rapid (0.2 millimeter per hour). To grow large crystals, all parameters must be precisely controlled, and the slight decrease in pressure due to diamond crystallization must be avoided. Therefore, one has to start with grit; its component carbon atoms slowly migrate through the metal solvent catalyst onto the growing crystal. The production of optimum conditions, at just the limit of diamond's stability range, may be difficult to accomplish in practice. Instead of "feeding" the monocrystal, growing at a rate of about 40 microns per hour, the grit may turn to graphite.

Since the nineteenth century, many experimenters have tried to grow diamond; some truly believed they grew diamonds, but others abused the public trust. For example, in 1908 Henri Lemoine was convicted of fraud in his experiments because he "produced" Jagersfontein diamonds; he was condemned to six years in prison for deceitfully obtaining financing from Sir Julius Wernher, the South African banker and administrator of the De Beers Consolidated Mines.

The imagination and audacity of those who apparently succeeded is still puzzling. In 1880, Hannay, a British chemist, sealed steel tubes containing paraffin, bone oil, and lithium and heated them until red hot for several hours, in order to obtain a high internal pressure. Most of the tubes exploded, but three produced small crystals, today in the collection of the British Museum. Their true nature is still controversial—they could be diamond mixed with silica or silica alone.

Another Englishman, Parsons, crushed a gun's bullet in a closed cavity to produce high temperatures and pressures. Physicists have since determined that he reached 305,000 atmospheres and 17,000°C but not at the same time and for only a few nanoseconds (billionths of a second). Therefore, his experiments were not successful.

Henri Moissan, a Frenchman, used an electrical furnace to dissolve carbon in various metals, including pure iron. By cooling the metal abruptly, he obtained high pressures and grew some small, very hard crystals. They were later found to be silicon carbide, called moissanite in his honor.

It was only during the second half of the twentieth century that progress made in the production of high pressure and temperature simultaneously led to the growth of synthetic diamond. The Swedish company ASEA (Allmassa Svenska Elektriska Aktiebolaget) produced its first fourteen synthetic diamonds on November 15, 1953, using a pressure of 97,000 atmospheres and a temperature of 2,700°C (about 4,860°F). The following year, on December 16, 1954, General Electric, which was conducting similar research, also met with success and patented its process. In 1957 the company produced 100,000 carats of grit and began selling its product in 1958. This forced De Beers to start its own research program, which met with success in September 1958; In 1959 it installed a press to produce commercial synthetic grit in Johannesburg. In 1963 De Beers opened a synthetic-diamond factory in Shannon, Ireland, and reached several agreements with ASEA in 1967.

Initially twice as expensive as natural grit, synthetic grit became cheaper in 1965. Today, General Electric grows about half of the synthetic diamonds produced in the world. De Beers and ASEA together are the second-largest producer. The Netherlands, Czechoslovakia, Japan, China, and the Soviet Union also produce it.

In 1980 the world production reached

De Beers synthetic diamond grit. Average dimension: 0.1 cm.

about 100 million carats (20 tons), two and a half times the annual natural-diamond production (combining industrial and gem grades). In 1970 General Electric conducted a prestigious experiment: the growth of a dozen gem-quality diamonds weighing 1 carat. Some were faceted and produced round brilliants weighing from 0.26 to 0.46 carats, with good color (F to J) and a clarity reaching VS. Three faceted synthetic diamonds one-third of a carat each, respectively colorless, yellow, and blue, were donated to the Smithsonian Institution, together with a 1-carat rough crystal. In 1985 Sumitomo Electric Industries in Japan began to market slices of a vivid yellow synthetic diamond at a price equivalent to that of similar natural stones. De Beers also grows large, gem-quality, synthetic yellow diamonds, but only on an experimental basis.

DIASPORE

A hydroxylated aluminum oxide, crystallizing in the orthorhombic system. It decomposes when exposed to flame, hence its name, from the Greek *diaspora*, meaning "dispersion."

The aluminum may be replaced by iron, manganese, or even chromium. The color of diaspore varies from colorless to brown (with iron), even pinkish brown in incandescent light. The three bands in the blue region of its spectrum are reminiscent of blue sapphire. Its hardness is 6 to 7, but its perfect cleavage induces a lamellar structure that makes it hard to facet. Diaspore luster is high (indices of refraction: $n_p = 1.702$, $n_m = 1.722$, $n_g = 1.750$, with a birefringence of 0.048, biaxial negative). Its specific gravity is 3.4.

Diaspore is found in the metamorphic clay-rich limestones and bauxites, where it is associated with corundum. It may be found with kyanite in certain metamorphic schists. The best diaspore crystals to be faceted have been found fairly recently in Mugla, in western Anatolia, Turkey. These crystals are more than 20 centimeters long, yielding cut stones of over 10 carats.

DIOPSIDE

A monoclinic pyroxene, the magnesian pole (less than 20 percent iron) of the hedenbergite–diopside series of ferromagnesian silicates.

Opaque, black hedenbergite was named in honor of its discoverer, the Swede Ludwig Hedenberg. Diopside was named by the French mineralogist R. J. Haüy for its high birefringence, which causes a "doubling" of the images seen through its crystals (from *di,* "double," and *opsis,* "appearance").

Iron, always present, sometimes gives diopside a very pale green color (as in the stones from Piedmont, Italy), less "oily" than that of peridot, and a specific absorption spectrum—three bands in the blue range. This gem is far more valuable if a bit of chromium replaces some aluminum (up to about 2 percent Cr_2O_3 in chrome diopside). Chrome diopside has an attractive bright green color, and a typical chromium absorption spectrum (with a line in the red and bands in the yellow-green range) superimposed on the iron spectrum. However, chrome diopside is fragile because of its medium hardness (5½) and its excellent and shiny cleavages, probably due to twins. Its specific gravity is 3.3, slightly less than methylene iodide (diopside's is 3.25 and hedenbergite's, 3.62). Indices of refraction are about 1.67, 1.68, and 1.70 (diopside, 1.664, 1.671, 1.694; hedenbergite 1.725, 1.732, 1.755). Its birefringence is always 0.030 (biaxial positive), less than that of peridot.

There are also cat's-eye diopsides. Massive bluish violet diopside, called violane, is used in Italy for small ornamental objects and often shows a waxy luster.

A very dark green, almost black, star diopside, also slightly magnetic, is a common commercial variety of diopside. Its asterism, enhanced by the cabochon cut, is due to the presence of thin elongated lamellae of magnetoilmenite, forming an exsolution texture in two directions at 73 degrees from each other. The resulting star has four rays, with one sharp line cut obliquely by a more diffuse band. These stones have often been sold as "Indian black star sapphires" to tourists, who are surprised to learn their true identity back home.

Diopside can be produced from regional metamorphism and is a common component of true marbles, but it primarily results from contact metamorphism of acid rocks on limestones, especially dolomites. It is thus a frequent component of skarns, where it is found with calcium garnets and epidote. Diopside has also been found in the pegmatoids from Madagascar. Their origin is still an enigma; they probably were produced by an assimilation of magnesian host rocks by granitic intrusions; diopside is found there with spinel, phlogopite, and scapolite. Finally, diopside is always found in kimberlites.

The Smithsonian Institution in Washington displays some spectacularly cut diopsides: a 133-carat Indian star diopside, a 19.2-carat green diopside from Madagascar, a 6.8-carat yellow diopside from Italy, and a 1.6-carat Finnish chrome diopside.

DIOPTASE

A hydrous copper silicate, crystallizing in the hexagonal system.

Dioptase was discovered in 1780 by a Tatar, Achir Malmed, about 300 kilometers (185 miles) south of the Kariakovski military post, in the Semipalatinsk region of the Soviet Union, close to Chinese Turkistan. It was presented by General Bogdanof to the Saint Petersburg Academy of Sciences as "Kirghiz emerald." Some years later, a Cossack, Brigadier Bentham, persuaded Achir to lead him to the site of his discovery; with a small troop, he launched an expedition but had to abandon it after being chased by Kirghiz nomads.

In 1816 copper was finally detected in this mineral. A specimen was sent to the famous French mineralogist René-Just Haüy by the Russian mineralogist Vagner, who wrote: "This mineral substance was brought back from Chinese Bukharia by a trader named Achir Malmed, which confers it the name of achirite." Haüy called it dioptase, from the Greek *dia,* meaning "through," and *optos,* "to see," because cleavage planes can be seen by looking through the crystal. In 1821 Haüy wrote, "As a result one can see in a sense the nucleus of the dioptase through the crystals, and it is from this observation that I made the name of dioptase, referring to the structure of this substance, waiting for that which will indicate its composition." (R. J. Haüy, *Minéralogie,* 1821).

Diopside crystal from the Piedmont, Italy. Width: 1 cm. Sorbonne collection.

Dioptase crystals from Tsumeb, Namibia. Diameter: 3 cm. Sorbonne collection.

In 1820 a surveyor named Shangin found the original deposit in the Altin Tagh, mountains in Turkistan. This was a resounding discovery for Russia: indeed, no emerald had been found at this time in that country (the first emerald crystals would not be discovered until 1830 by Maxime Koshevnikov in the Ural Mountains).

Dioptase is easily broken, with a hardness of only 5, but it is a beautiful, vivid bluish green, often translucent, sometimes transparent. Its indices of refraction are 1.655 and 1.708 (it is uniaxial positive, with a birefringence of 0.053), and its specific gravity is 3.30.

The crystals are prismatic and generally terminate in rhombohedral faces. It is a rare mineral, found particularly in warm climates. The best-known specimens come from the copper deposits of the Niari Valley (Congo) and Tsumeb (Namibia).

Groups of small dioptase crystals have been set as brooches, even rings. It has been imitated for this purpose with small clusters of synthetic emerald crystals.

Dioptase is rarely faceted because of its poor toughness. The Ottawa Museum in Canada owns a 0.63-carat almost transparent faceted Namibian stone.

DUMORTIERITE

An aluminum and iron borosilicate, crystallizing in the orthorhombic system. This mineral was named for the French paleontologist M. Eugene Dumortier.

Dumortierite generally forms a multitude of needlelike inclusions in quartz, with a color ranging from light to dark violetish blue. This rock is sometimes called blue quartz or dumortierite quartz. Dumortierite is uncommon; it was discovered in Beaunan, near Lyon, in France, in a gneiss containing garnets, and is also found in Madagascar, the source of the best specimens.

In twelfth-century Iran, blue quartz was mistaken for lapis, which has a similar color. Beautiful specimens, used as decorative stones, are currently mined in Brazil.

ELEPHANT HAIR

Hairs from the elephant's tail are about 35 centimeters (13 inches) long and 1 millimeter thick. They are considered good-luck charms by African hunters, who wear them as bracelets. European hunters, for whom the hairs were merely trophies, also followed this tradition, soon imitated by fashionable European women.

The texture of elephant hair, like that of human hair, is reminiscent of tortoiseshell. Its coloration results from the concentration of a large number of microscopic brown disks (chromatophores) against a light background. Colored plastic thread has been used as an imitation.

EMERALD

A green beryl. According to the CIBJO ruling of November 29, 1968, it must contain chromium.

Origin of the Name

Various sources may have produced the Greek term *smaragdos*, which later became *emerald, émeraude, esmeralda, ismurud, smaragd, smeraldo,* and also *zomorod,* one of the old Arabic names.

In ancient Egypt the words *mefek-enma* or *mefik-ma* described all green stones (thus, turquoise from the Sinai was called *mafkat*). It allegedly produced the Sanskrit *marakat,* which, under the influence of the monster *esmarak,* reportedly became *smarakata,* which led to the Greek name.

The old Sanskrit term *acmagarbha* became *mahabharata* and allegedly became on one hand *marakata,* from which the Greek name comes, and on the other hand *barrakta,* from which the Hebrew *bareket* derives, as well as the other old Arabic name, *zabargad.* Rather than true emerald, *zabargad* probably designated peridot (also of green color) found on the Zebirget Island in the Red Sea (the "Crusaders' emeralds"

presented to the Catholic church during the Crusades were almost always peridots).

Finally, scholars of ancient Greek believe that the word *marmarysso,* which means "to shine," produced on one hand *marmaros,* which means "marble," indeed a shiny stone, and on the other hand *smaragdos,* meaning shiny green stone. *Smaragdos* actually superposes itself to *berullos,* a term transcribed directly from the Orient, where it also designated a shiny stone. This redundancy explains the belief that Theophrastus (372–287 B.C.) and Pliny the Elder (A.D. 23–79) knew that beryl and emerald were similar minerals. Actually, Pliny distinguished twelve varieties of emeralds. Three were of higher quality, from Scythia (now part of the Soviet Union), Bactria (in southwest Asia), and Egypt; they are believed to have been, respectively, dioptase, green sapphire, and flawed emerald from the mines of Upper Egypt. The nine other types were associated with copper deposits, from Cyprus, Ethiopia, Hermes, Persia, Thorica in

Attica (Greece), Media (now northwestern Iran), Chalcedonia, the Taygetus Mountains in Laconia (Greece), and Sicily: they represent malachite, chrysocolla, turquoise, green jasper, smithsonite, green marble, or other green stones. Pliny added tanos and chalcosmaragdos (turquoise and malachite scattered with copper sulfides) to the list, and set *beryllus* imported from India apart; it was the only crystal for which he reported a hexagonal shape.

Medieval authors followed Pliny's nomenclature; only in the sixteenth century was the identity of beryl and emerald suspected, when some emerald prisms were discovered in the New World. Not until 1797 was their identity established by the work of Louis-Nicolas Vauquelin. This famous French chemist discovered a new "earth," glucinia, in the two minerals, considered thus far to be calcium silicates. The word *beryllium,* introduced by the German chemist Link, has since replaced *glucinium.* The name *emerald* was then used to describe all members of the beryl family: "The gems relating to this species [emerald] are the so-called Peruvian emerald and the beryl or aquamarine" (René-Just Haüy, 1817).

The Symbolism of Emerald

Because *emerald* originally denoted any green stone, the symbolism and virtues attributed to the emerald are, in turn, actually associated with all green stones. Green, signaling new growth in the spring, is a symbol of hope in the semi-arid regions around the Mediterranean.

Therefore emerald was supposed to protect marriages, enhance fertility, ease childbirth, cure epilepsy and nervous breakdowns, fight poisons, maintain good health, protect travelers, lend eloquence to speakers, and bring money. To the Egyptians, emerald reinforced the immortality associated with the scarab (often carved in amazonite). A symbol of love, emerald was in Rome an attribute of Vesta and Venus.

Symbol of hope and eternal life, the green color was also chosen as an emblem by Islam. Emerald, of course, adorns the papal tiara. During the coronation of Napoléon in 1804, Pope Pius VII placed on the emperor's finger a large ring set with an emerald, ensuring a link between the emperor and the Catholic church.

Famous Emeralds

No famous emeralds were known prior to the sixteenth century, when the Europeans reached the New World. Most certainly the Holy Grail, for which King Arthur's knights searched, was supposed to have been carved from one large emerald. Presented by the Queen of Sheba to King

A 217.80-carat Colombian emerald (front and back), with an Islamic prayer engraved in the year 1107 of the Hegira. Mogul art of the seventeenth century. Height: 5.1 cm. Allan Caplan collection. Photos: Erica and Harold Van Pelt.

Solomon, the Grail was supposedly the chalice used by Jesus Christ during the Last Supper; it was eventually transferred to Genoa by the Crusaders, where twelve leading citizens kept it. It is still in the treasury of the Cattedrale di San Lorenzo in Genoa, but it was already considered to be an antique glass during the sixteenth century; this verdict was confirmed by experts when it was temporarily moved to Paris by Napoléon.

At the beginning of the ninth century, Charlemagne supposedly offered an enormous emerald to the Reichenau Benedictine abbey, near Constanz, Germany; it turned out to be a 12.9-kilogram green fluorite.

Leonardo da Vinci is credited with spreading the malicious rumor that Pope Alexander VI had set on his crook an emerald carved in the shape of Venus; he would press the carving against his lips every time he kissed his crook.

The Spaniards discovered emeralds in the New World. In 1519, Hernán Cortés received a block of limestone covered with emerald crystals several centimeters long as a gift from the Aztec emperor Montezuma. The Aztecs had saved this extraordinary

his sovereignty, and his vassals paid him tribute in emeralds. According to oral tradition, at the time of the conquest, the tribes from the Manta Valley in Peru worshipped "the queen of emeralds," a beautiful crystal "larger than an ostrich egg," to which they gave "its daughters," other smaller emeralds. However, the Inca priests hid everything before the arrival of the Spaniards, and the beautiful emerald was never found.

Always searching for gold and emeralds, conquistadores led by Gonzalo Jiménez de Quesada marched through what is now Colombia in 1537 to obtain 1,815 emeralds, a small, forgotten part of King Tanja's treasure, and from there continued in search of King Bogotá, El Dorado, the man of gold, described by, among others, Sebastián de Belalcázar, second in command to Pizarro. El Dorado supposedly reached power after reproducing the course of the sun. A five year novitiate in the shade of the temples was followed by a ceremonial outing where his body was completely covered by a layer of gold dust, followed by a symbolic navigation of Lake Titicaca. He was then immersed in the water, where he lost his golden covering, while emeralds were cast to him as offerings. Although this story was never shown to be more than a legend, and has been associated with customs of the Chibcha Indians, tales about it lived on after the arrival of the conquistadores, becoming the legend of a mythical land of wealth and plenty. Jiménez de Quesada did not find El Dorado, but he did defeat the Chibcha, whom he encountered in his search, and founded Santa Fé de Bogotá capital of New Granada, in 1538. His expedition marked the end of the Chibcha civilization, from which only poignant keepsakes in gold and emerald remain, housed in the Gold Museum in Bogotá, Colombia.

Spanish soldiers soon became *guaqueros,* that is, "grave diggers," (from the Quechua *huaca,* which became *guaca* in Creole, name of the cairn where offerings were placed, intended for the dead who were buried with their jewelry) in their quest for treasure. The violated graves yielded immense amounts of gold and emeralds, so this region, officially New Granada, was nicknamed "Golden Castilla." The Chivor site was discovered by Valenzuela in 1545; by 1555 the mines were being actively worked. The local work force was treated with such brutality that authorities in Spain had to intervene.

Emerald crystals were soon found in many European courts and were used for numerous sculptures. For example, in 1642 Denis Miseroni, member of a famous sixteenth- and seventeenth-century dynasty of Milanese engravers, carved a snuff bottle from a 26,800-carat, 10-centimeter-tall emerald crystal. This piece is now in the Kunsthistorisches Museum in Vienna.

piece in the rough because they were bewildered by its beauty. It became the property of Holy Roman Emperor Charles V and was donated in 1900 to the Kunsthistorisches Museum in Vienna by Emperor Francis Joseph I of Austria.

However, Cortés had saved for himself some other stones from the plunder of Tenochtitlán (now Mexico City) in July and August 1521, in particular five emeralds. He had them engraved by Aztec lapidaries, one in the shape of a rose, another in the shape of a horn, the third as a fish decorated with gold eyes, the fourth as a small bell with a black pearl clapper, and the fifth as a small bowl, with a gold stand and four small chains connected to a large pearl; the Latin motto engraved on it—"No greater man came from a woman"—may have referred to Jesus Christ.

When Cortés returned to Spain in 1527, these emeralds were coveted by Queen Isabel of Portugal, wife of Charles V. Nevertheless, Cortés saved them to use as an engagement present for his second wife, Juana de Zúñiga. In 1541, still carrying his precious emeralds he was shipwrecked on an expedition to Algiers, in northern Africa, and the stones were lost.

The Spaniards also pillaged temples. Francisco Pizarro conquered the Inca empire, killing Atahuallpa, the Inca king, on August 29, 1533, despite the fact that he had paid Pizarro ransom (a room 22 by 17 by 7 feet high filled with gold). During his reign the king wore an emerald as a sign of

The so-called "Montezuma emerald," from Chivor, Colombia (17 by 16 cm). Specimen and photo: Kunsthistorisches Museum, Vienna.

Oriental princes were immediately interested in Colombian emeralds. Exported to India via Turkey, a great number of them found their way into the treasures of the maharajas. Some princes turned emeralds into talismans; for example, the Mogul sovereign of Delhi owned a 78-carat emerald on which was engraved, "He who owns this talisman enjoys God's special protection."

Many emeralds were plundered in 1739 during the sack of Delhi by the Persian prince Nāder Shāh and are still part of the treasury of Iran; there, hundreds of emeralds weighing over 100 carats are set in jewelry, weapons, and various other objects. One of the most extraordinary is the giant globe, 45 centimeters (almost 18 inches) in diameter and 108 centimeters (42 inches) high with its stand; it is completely covered with precious stones, among which emeralds are used to represent oceans and rivers. In Istanbul, Turkey, the Topkapi Museum houses plunder mostly from Egypt, looted by Sultan Selim I in 1517; it is famous for its

emeralds, especially for the handle of a dagger set with three emerald cabochons, each 3 to 4 centimeters in diameter, which is the present logo of the museum, popularized by a movie. It was supposed to be presented to Nāder Shāh in 1747 by Sultan Mahmud I, but Nāder Shāh's assassination changed the plans, and the dagger was returned to Istanbul.

The czars of Russia also owned some beautiful emeralds, now in the Diamond Fund in Moscow.

The Liberty necklace is tied to the history of American independence. It was owned in 1777 by a charming Polish countess, friend of a Polish gentleman fighting under Lafayette with the American rebels. Upon learning of the capture of Philadelphia by the British general William Howe on September 26, 1777, on her way to a costumed dance, she became so worried about her friend that she went straight to Benjamin Franklin. Reassured as to his fate, she was so relieved that she took off her

emerald parure and presented it to Franklin, saying, "Here are thirteen square emeralds and thirteen pear-shaped emeralds, one for each of the colonies; I implore you to accept this present in the name of liberty." Placed with French bankers, the Liberty necklace reappeared in 1850 in a pawn shop, but nobody redeemed it; it is presently part of the Van Cleef and Arpels collection.

The emerald crystals in the Topkapi Museum, one weighing 3,260 grams and the other 1,310 grams, are allegedly the largest in the world. However, their identity is controversial; some believe that they are Venetian glass, manufactured during the Renaissance.

A number of exceptional emeralds are worthy of mention. The Devonshire emerald, a 6-centimeter high, 5-centimeter diameter prism weighing 1,384 carats, from the Muzo mine in Colombia, is in London's British Museum. The 660-carat Patricia emerald, named for Saint Patrick, patron of Ireland, the "emerald isle," measures 8 by 5.5 centimeters. Found in 1921 in Chivor, it is currently housed at the American Museum of Natural History in New York. The famous jeweler Harry Winston gave a remarkable 5-centimeters-diameter, 858-carat crystal from Gachala to the Smithsonian Institution in Washington, D.C. A dark green 2,800-carat crystal from the Ural Mountains is also at the American Museum of Natural History in New York. Finally, a crystal weighing approximately 6,000 carats was found in 1969 at the Tres Cruces mine; it is the largest crystal found in Colombia and is kept in the vaults of the Banco de la República in Bogotá.

The Color of Emerald

The vivid green color of emerald is attributed to a partial replacement (less than 1.5 percent) of aluminum ions by chromium ions in the structure of beryl. The element chromium was actually discovered in an emerald by the French chemist Vauquelin in 1797.

However, under the same conditions, the trivalent vanadium ion, identified by Goldschmidt in 1919, may also contribute to the color. Some Brazilian emeralds contain primarily vanadium, with only a few ten-thousandths of chromium. The presence of chromium has been chosen as the definitive criterion for emerald by CIBJO, to distinguish it clearly from greenish aquamarines, the color of which is due to an iron ion. As the absorption bands of chromium- and vanadium-bearing emeralds in the visible range are almost identical, and because chromium is a satellite of vanadium, there is no reason to change this definition.

The exact hue of emerald is influenced, of course, by other trace elements present in the crystal structure (irons and alkalis, for example); no emerald is identical to the next. The presence of chromium is revealed by absorption lines around 680 nanometers, visible with a hand-held spectroscope.

Iron, almost always present in emeralds, quenches their potential fluorescence: only rare, extremely pure stones from Colombia display a weak red luminescence. Conversely, synthetic emeralds often show a fairly strong red fluorescence in black light.

The color of emerald is often irregularly distributed in growth bands parallel to the elongation of the prism. Sometimes a nearly colorless core is surrounded by a colored rim. In this extreme case, the lapidary must use the rim as the pavilion of the faceted stone, the table being parallel to the optic axis.

Emerald shows a slight dichroism, with the ordinary ray a warm yellowish green and the extraordinary ray a cooler bluish green. Therefore, a faceted stone can appear "cooler" or "warmer," depending on the orientation of the table relative to the optic axis. A lapidary can choose the final color only if the dimensions of the rough make both options possible: he or she always looks for the best yield, so that an elongated prism is always cut in the "blue" direction and a short prism in the "yellow" direction.

Emerald dealers often describe a stone only by its color nuance, asking the customers if they prefer a yellow emerald or a blue emerald. Frequently, blue emeralds are step-cut (the classic "emerald cut") to accentuate their serene color, while yellow emeralds are often faceted as cushions or in similar styles, enhancing their warmer, livelier hue.

Physical Properties

The optical and mechanical properties of emerald are average for beryl: the index of refraction ranges from 1.571 to 1.590 for the ordinary ray and 1.566 to 1.597 for the extraordinary ray, with a birefringence of -0.005 to -0.007 (uniaxial negative). The specific gravity varies from 2.68 to 2.78, and the hardness from 7½ to 8. Its poor toughness is due largely to inclusions. Emerald's undistinguished physical properties indicate that color is primarily responsible for its value.

Deposits and Related Inclusions

Emerald is not a common mineral. It has been found in various parts of the world in biotite schists located in the vicinity of hyperacid intrusions, acting as a source of beryllium, and also close to ultrabasic rocks, especially serpentines, which provide the necessary source of chromium, without which the green color would not exist. Such deposits are found in Austria, Egypt, the Ural Mountains of the Soviet Union, Zimbabwe, the Transvaal, Brazil, and Australia.

Colombian emeralds, however, are found in a network of calcite veins, associated with a variety of minerals (dolomite, ankerite, fluorite, quartz, albite, pyrite, and parisite); these unique conditions have not been satisfactorily explained to date. In addition, the dense vegetation and steep topography of these regions do not facilitate observations in the field. Parisite, a rare-earth carbonate, is a good prospecting guide. The emerald-bearing veins cut through schists and black carbonaceous limestones rich in fossils; they are rarely more than a few centimeters (an inch or two) thick but can expand to over one hundred meters (300 feet). No hydrothermal alteration or regional metamorphism has been identified. Pegmatites are known in this area but do not seem to have any apparent connection with the emerald deposits. However, the emerald-parisite-fluorite-albite mineral association probably indicates a deep-seated source. The presence of granitic intrusions suggests that hydrothermal solutions played a role in mineralization. Lapidaries distinguish in an empirical but nevertheless judicious way between "mica emeralds" and "limestone emeralds," both characterized by their inclusions.

Like any other mineral, during its growth emerald traps small crystals that are forming around it (representing its paragenesis), as well as parts of its growth environment (in negative crystals). In addition, cracks suffered in situ can be repaired by crystallization between the two walls of the

The Liberty necklace, set with emeralds, is attributed to Falize. Van Cleef and Arpels collection.

Two emerald earrings (24.03 carat total weight). Van Cleef and Arpels creation.

Diamond necklace with a 4.50-carat emerald clip surrounded by 12 carats of pear-shape and marquise-shape diamonds. Gerard creation, Paris.

Emerald crystal from Muzo, Colombia. Height: 2 cm. Paris School of Mines.

fracture, forming a healed fracture or "fingerprint" inclusion. Mica emeralds contain, for example, mica, tremolite-actinolite (amphiboles), and niobiotantalates, and the fluids in their fingerprint inclusions are exclusively water and carbon dioxide. In contrast, limestone emeralds have inclusions of calcite, pyrite, and parisite, and their fingerprint inclusions contain carbon dioxide, a brine, and crystals of alkali salts.

Sometimes the healed fractures evoke the plants of a luxurious plantation and are therefore called gardens, especially in Europe. Emeralds so heavily included that they are translucent are often cut in cabochons to take the best advantage of their color.

Important Mica Emerald Deposits

Egypt

The long-abandoned deposits in Egypt are located about 60 miles east of the now-submerged Philae Island on the Nile, near the Red Sea, in the Djebel Zabara and Djebel Sikait. They were rediscovered in 1816 by the French explorer Frédéric Cailliaud. The emeralds were mediocre and attempts to reopen the mine around 1899 failed. The site may have been worked by the pharaohs but more likely by the Indians. Indeed, a legend tells how Sesha, the king of the snakes, who had swallowed the bile of the demon Vala, was frightened by an attack by the king of the birds Garura and spit this bile near the ocean, where emeralds have since been found.

Austria

As early as the Roman empire, expeditions to Austria were organized to discover Habachthal, the deposit the Celts called "the mountain of green jewels." Located at an elevation of 2,100 meters (6,900 feet), 70 kilometers (43 miles) southwest of Salzburg, the deposit, near the Legbach ravine, a tributary to the Habach, is difficult to reach. This deposit was virtually the only source of emeralds for the countries of Western Europe until the conquest of South America. It has been worked since the Middle Ages, especially under the authority of the archbishop of Salzburg, then under that

Rock-crystal bead necklace featuring a 31.70-carat heart-shaped emerald. Boucheron creation.

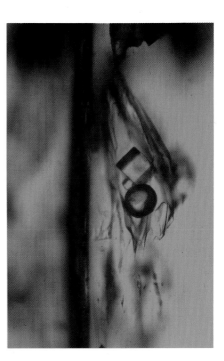

Complete emerald parure with cabochons and beads, for a total weight of 471.36 carats. Fred creation.

of the duke of Bavaria during the eighteenth century. In the nineteenth century, the claim was given to the Viennese jeweler Samuel Goldsmith and was practically abandoned at his death in 1871. Some mining activity took place from 1896 to 1913 and from 1932 to 1939. Today, the site is visited only by mineral collectors.

Soviet Union

Not until 1830 were emeralds discovered in the Ural Mountains of Russia, near Takovaja, 45 kilometers (28 miles) northeast of Ekaterinburg. Maxime Kochevnikov, a charcoal burner, reportedly found emeralds among the roots of a tree uprooted by a storm. Kokavine, the director of the imperial lapidary factories of Ekaterinburg, was alerted and started prospecting actively. By 1832, a 101.25-carat faceted emerald from this deposit had been presented to the czarina. In this same mine, the alexandrite variety of chrysoberyl was discovered on the day of czarevitch Alexander's majority. First mined in quarries and then underground, the Ural deposits have produced 16 tons of crystals, often of excellent quality.

The Russian emeralds mentioned by numerous early authors (for example, Haüy in 1817) may have been scattered crystals collected by chance, without further organized prospecting, just as Siberian diamonds were found before World War II.

India and Pakistan

No historical emerald deposits are known on the Indian subcontinent. However, emerald has been faceted by local lapidaries for a long time: roughs originally came from Egypt and then from Colombia. Turkey exported large quantities of Colombian emeralds to India and old Indian lapidaries still have a tendency to believe that they facet emeralds coming from deposits in Turkey.

The first indication of emeralds was discovered in 1943 in Kaliginan, in the Udaipur district in the state of Rajasthan; minor mining activity takes place at Bubani and Gamgurha, for example.

In Pakistan the Mingaora mine was discovered through crystals found in the bed of the Swat River and has been in operation since 1958. Other deposits have now been

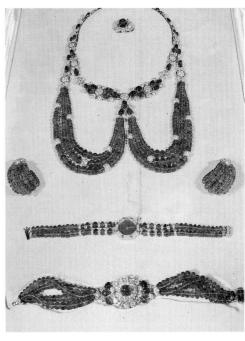

Three-phase inclusion in a Colombian emerald, characteristic of this deposit. Magnified 200 times. Photo: A. Jeanne-Michaud.

found in the Chitral area and near the Afghan border. The crystals are very clear, with an attractive color, but quite small.

In 1976 remarkable crystals were found in the Pandjir Valley, north of Kabul, Afghanistan. No accurate information is available because of the unstable political situation in these regions, especially since the Soviet invasion; it nevertheless appears that the Pandjir emerald mines are still worked by the Afghan resistance. It is only known that these deposits were not formerly uncovered; recent archaeological discoveries in northern Afghanistan uncovered numerous pieces of jewelry in lapis, carnelian, and beryl but not in emerald.

South Africa

The first African emeralds were discovered in 1927 in the Leysdorp area of northeast Transvaal, which was first worked only sporadically. Today the only producers are the mines of Gravelotte and Germania Hills, which produce medium-quality stones, distributed by the Gravelotte Emerald Company and the Cobra Emerald Company (from the name of one of the Germania Hills). The latter often contain golden and black inclusions of columbotantalite, which give them a very peculiar appearance.

Zimbabwe

The Sandawana deposit, discovered in 1956 120 kilometers (75 miles) southwest of Fort Victoria, is the most interesting of all emerald deposits in this country. Its production is fairly large, and the stones have a very vivid and warm color; however, they are fairly small, and cut stones rarely reach 3 carats. They are often rich in acicular tremolite inclusions, which may cause easy abrasion and difficulties in setting.

Tanzania

Since 1969 emerald has been found near Lake Manyara, south of the Moji Moto hot springs, associated with alexandrite. The geological and mineralogical similarities between this deposit and those in the Ural Mountains are remarkable.

Zambia

The Miku mine is located on the river of the same name, 48 kilometers (30 miles) west of Ndola. Discovered in 1931, it was studied in 1962 and 1973 and put in operation in 1978. Since then, it has produced clean, well-developed crystals, sometimes reaching 130 carats, exhibiting good color. Zambia has become one of the world's largest emerald producers.

Australia

Two small deposits were found while miners prospected for cassiterite and have been worked on a small scale: the Emmaville deposit in New South Wales was discovered in 1890, and the Poona deposit, in western Australia, in 1909. The emeralds they produced are mediocre.

Brazil

Since Brazil's conquest, Portuguese have spoken of emeralds from Brazil, but the stones were instead green tourmalines, which were long mistakenly associated with emerald. This has tended to depreciate true Brazilian emeralds, although Brazil is now the world's largest emerald producer, at least by weight.

In 1913 the first true emeralds were discovered in Piraja, near Bom Jesus das Meiras (today's Brumado), in the Serra das Eguas in the state of Bahia. This area, which contains one of the largest magnesite deposits in the world, has never been prospected for emeralds, and the few samples found are only collector's specimens. In 1962 the Salininha "emeralds" were mined in northern Bahia, on the banks of the Rio São Francisco. They were identified as emeralds, despite their very low chromium content (0.03 percent) compared to their much higher vanadium content (0.15 percent). The very poor quality of the crystal did not help matters, as only 0.3 percent of the crystals were facetable.

In the same state, the Carnaiba area, located 30 kilometers (about 18 miles) southwest of Campo Formoso, has produced some attractive crystals associated with molybdenite; their discovery in 1965 launched a true rush of *garimpeiros* in the

Serra de Jacobina, but the average quality of the stones produced is still mediocre.

In 1981 an important deposit was discovered by chance during embankment work in Santa Terezinha, in the state of Goiás, inspiring another rush for the "bambouro" ("treasure of precious stones," in Brazilian language). Indeed, the rumor spread that the local children loaded their slingshots with emerald crystals. The faceted stones that were found are small (2 to 3 carats), but their quality is good, despite abundant inclusions of talc, chromite, and especially pyrite.

Another indication led to a mine at Itabirito, near Belo Horizonte, and a deposit where emerald is associated with phenakite was recently discovered near Campo Formoso (Socoto), in the state of Bahia. Other emerald discoveries are likely in Brazil, where systematic prospecting has only just begun.

Other Countries

Emeralds were recently found in Madagascar. There are also a number of emerald indications, which are essentially mineralogical curiosities, such as the North Carolina deposits and the pegmatites near Nantes, France.

Important Limestone Emerald Deposits

Colombia

The richest and most famous emerald deposits in the world were mined well before the arrival of the Spaniards. Today they provide the world's most valuable production.

The emerald market in Santa Terezinha, Goiás, Brazil. Photo: J. Cassedanne.

Early in the Spanish conquest, emeralds found by the explorer Pedro Arias de Avila (1440–1531) were said to be coming from Peru. The exact location of the deposits was concealed from the invaders, who discovered them by chance or with force. Father Reginaldo de Pedraza, confusing hardness and toughness, prompted soldiers to test the authenticity of the emeralds with a hammer, which they were supposed to resist! The Spanish soldiers were encouraged in their destructive madness by local priests, who preferred that their sacred emeralds be destroyed rather than stolen by the invaders.

The Chivor mine was discovered in 1545 and intensively mined until 1672, when it was abandoned in favor of the Muzo mine, discovered by chance in 1594. Tropical vegetation soon covered all evidence of the works at Chivor. It was rediscovered in 1904 by Francisco Restrepo, and mining started again in 1911. During the war for independence (1819), the operation of the Muzo mines was directed by a friend of Simon Bolívar, José Ignacio Paris. The first samples of a rare-earth carbonate were found there in 1839, and the new mineral was named parisite in his honor. In 1849, after a short period of nationalization, the mines were given to private interests. In 1866 they were considered national property. In 1961 the Banco de la República founded a new company, Empressa de Esmeraldas, which controlled and mined all emerald deposits under the authority of the government. But significant illegal mining activity still goes on, and there is a general insecurity in these regions, controlled by private armies. Since 1975 mining has become even more intense; in Muzo twenty thousand miners and thirty bulldozers have worked since 1977 at an accelerated pace, which may eventually cause an early depletion of the deposit. The mining companies take advantage of a situation favorable to their interests, and do not plan for the future. They always fear a change in the political situation and therefore practice intensive mining. Around 1980 and 1981, the production of the Chivor mine was such that it became the world's largest but it has since significantly decreased. Heavy equipment and hydraulic jets carry many stones down to the valley of Rio Itoco: these tailings are still rich in emeralds and are washed by "emerald smugglers," or *guaqueros,* heirs to the grave violators. More than twenty thousand of them live in miserable conditions close to the river, searching very primitively for the stone that will, perhaps, make them rich. The mineral areas form a crescent northeast of Bogotá, from Gachala, 60 kilometers (37 miles) east, to Muzo and Coscuez, 100 kilometers (62 miles) north. This entire area is swarming with adventurers and is particularly dangerous: in 1973 more than 900 *guaqueros* were killed in money-

A bracelet and two emerald necklaces, one with a marquise-shape 8.5-carat emerald, the other with a 4.5-carat emerald clip. Gerard creation.

Washing emeralds in the garimpo of Baixo, Santa Terezinha, Goiás, Brazil. Photo: J. Cassedanne.

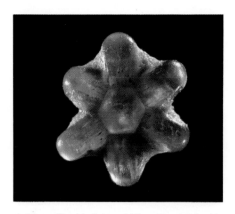

A 0.3-cm "trapiche" emerald from Muzo, Colombia. Sorbonne collection.

related conflicts, and the mines were temporarily closed.

The white calcite veinlets contrast with the bulk of the black limestone, helping to guide the miners. Some of the crystals found there rank among the best in the world, both in size and color. Of course, the quality of the crystal varies widely; a Colombian origin does not necessarily guarantee an emerald's quality.

Some crystals from the Muzo and Peña Blanca mines resemble the sugarcane or ore crusher called a *trapiche*, used in South America, and are thus called trapiche emeralds. These often cloudy stones consist of a central tapered hexagonal prism surrounded by six trapezoidal prisms, cemented together by carbonaceous inclusions and albite. This structure results from an unusual growth phenomenon. When cut into cabochons, these emeralds exhibit a six-ray star formed by the inclusions. However, many such crystals are faceted into seven smaller stones, weighing less than a carat and are used as side stones in jewelry.

Color Enhancement

Very pale emeralds may be varnished on their pavilion with a green substance to enhance their color. This technique was frequently used in nineteenth-century jewelry, especially in Russia.

Pale emeralds with fractures that reach the surface may be immersed in a green dye, which penetrates the fractures and reinforces the color. Careful observation helps in detecting this treatment, which may produce a peculiar absorption spectrum and a bright luminescence. Some emeralds contain very fine fractures making them iridescent under certain lighting conditions. Such stones are often immersed in a very clean oil (cedarwood oil) or resin having the same index of refraction as the emerald, making the cracks much less apparent. This is common practice in India

and Colombia. (In the past the so-called old-mine emeralds were held for several months in a water barrel before faceting; the lapidary could then seal these fractures during polishing, with the same outcome as today's oiling.)

Gems of Similar Appearance

Many green gems may be mistaken for emeralds. The most convincing look-alikes are: chrome tourmalines from Tanzania, green tourmalines as a group, green "chrome" fluorite, jade, chrysoprase, hiddenite, dioptase, peridot, tsavorite, green sapphire, zircon, and demantoid.

Simulants

Emerald has always been imitated, first with green glass. Democrites of Thracia was famous in the fifth century B.C. for his glass imitations of emerald. Numerous formulas for such glass were published throughout the sixteenth century, and this material is still often used in costume jewelry. Doublets combining natural and imitation stones seem to have been fabricated as early as the sixteenth century. Until the end of the nineteenth century, they were essentially quartz–green glass and garnet–green glass doublets. Around 1900 a triplet became quite common; it was made of a rock-crystal crown, attached with green cement to a rock-crystal pavilion, intentionally flawed to imitate the garden of an emerald. Then a multitude of similar assembled stones were fabricated: synthetic spinel–green cement–synthetic spinel triplets, beryl–green cement–beryl triplets, beryl–green cement–tourmaline (sold as "Smaryl"), triplets made with a very pale emerald sawed along the girdle plane and reassembled with a green cement. When dropped into a cold dye bath, hot quartz cracks, and the

fractures absorb the dye, so the stone looks like a pale emerald. Various green synthetic crystals, particularly YAG, have been used as emerald simulants with little success.

Synthetics

In 1848 J. J. Ebelmen, director of the Sévres Manufacturing Company, succeeded in growing a few small synthetic emerald crystals. Despite a succession of studies, especially by P. G. Hautefeuille and A. J. Perrey in 1888, who obtained crystals over 2 centimeters long, no commercial venture was begun for a century.

Some flux synthetic emeralds were sold in 1934 by the German company I. G. Farben, but World War II quickly put an end to this experiment. In San Francisco Carroll Chatham finished developing a method to grow emerald in a flux of molten alkaline salts. As early as 1949, he produced 50,000 carats a year, only a tenth of which were gem-quality. The synthetic emeralds, first sold on the American market, then on the European market, met with success and inspired rivals. In 1963, W. Zerfass in Germany and Pierre Gilson in France both started a commercial production based on the same principles. They were followed in 1971–75 by two Japanese industrialists, Y. Ariho and K. Kunitomi. The production of the Japanese company Inamori is presently fairly important. Other crystals are grown on a small scale in various places (the Lennix emeralds in Cannes, France, for example).

In 1960 the Lechleitner Company developed an overgrowth of hydrothermal synthetic chromium-rich beryl over prefaceted aquamarines and then a growth of hydrothermal synthetic emerald on parallel blades of beryl, attached together in that way. Sold as "Emerita" and "Symerald," these products had only limited success. The process was later studied by the American

The Itoco River guaqueros near Muzo, Colombia. Photo: P. Keller.

C. Chatham synthetic emerald. 3 cm across. Private collection.

corporation Union Carbide (Linde division), which specialized in the growth of synthetic quartz. Hydrothermal synthetic emerald appeared on the market in 1964. Linde stopped this activity in 1978 and sold its patent and equipment to the Regency Company, which still sells this product. An Australian company, Biron, and the Soviet Union currently produce and sell hydrothermal synthetic emeralds. Today both types of synthetic emeralds are on the market, but flux-grown ones are more abundant.

In addition to their fairly standard color, synthetic emeralds are generally less heavy (S.G. of 2.65–2.71) and have lower indices of refraction (ordinary ray from 1.562 to 1.586, extraordinary ray from 1.559 to 1.580, birefringence from 0.003 to 0.007) than natural emeralds. They also often exhibit a bright red luminescence under black light.

ENSTATITE

The magnesian pole (less than 5 percent iron) of the hypersthene-bronzite-enstatite series of ferromagnesian silicates, representing the orthorhombic pyroxenes group.

Enstatite's name refers to its resistance to fire (from the Greek *enstates,* "resisting"). Bronzite refers to the color of the mineral, and hypersthene (from the Greek *uper,* meaning "above, very," and *sthenios,* "power, strength"), to the hardness of this species, higher than that of the other pyroxenes.

An 11-carat brown enstatite from Sri Lanka is displayed at the Smithsonian Institution in Washington.

Orthorhombic pyroxenes rarely form nice crystals; most often they are massive, lamellar, or fibrous. The species at the magnesian end of the series show a light color—gray-green or light yellow. The iron-rich species are generally black, greenish, or brownish and attract little interest as gems.

Enstatite's dichroism is very weak. Its spectrum shows a distinct line in the blue-green frequency (around 505 nanometers). Its specific gravity of 3.2 to 3.3 increases with iron content, as do the indices of refraction (1.658 to 1.678; 1.659 to 1.687; 1.668 to 1.690). The optical character (biaxial negative) and the value of the birefringence help differentiate enstatite from kornerupine and bronzite (biaxial negative).

Enstatite comes from basic and ultrabasic rocks. The magnesian species are found in association with olivine and spinel in peridotite and are present in South African kimberlites.

The best gem enstatites come from southern Africa, the gem-bearing gravels of Mogok (Myanmar, formerly Burma), and Sri Lanka. The asterism of six-ray star enstatites from India is due to an exsolution of fine mineral needles.

EPIDOTE AND CLINOZOISITE

A hydroxylated iron and calcium aluminosilicate, crystallizing in the monoclinic system. The substitution of aluminum for iron creates a solid solution with clinozoisite, whereas the substitution of manganese for iron creates a solid solution with piemontite.

The name *epidote* was coined by the famous French crystallographer René-Just Haüy in 1801, from the Greek participate *epidotos,* meaning "increased," since one base of the crystal prism is double the other. Clinozoisite has the same structure as zoisite and was named for Baron von Zois.

Epidote often displays a pistachio-green color; hence, the name *pistachite* is sometimes used to describe this mineral when it is distinguished only by its color in some granites containing amphiboles transformed to epidote. Its color is very pleochroic (associated colors are green, yellowish brown, and dark red). It darkens with increasing iron content. A strong absorption band in the blue range is due to iron.

Epidote's moderate hardness of 6½ and its pefect longitudinal cleavage make this gem moderately tough. Its specific gravity and indices of refraction increase with iron content (clinozoisite: S.G. is 3.21; indices of refraction are 1.670, 1.674, and 1.690, with a birefringence of 0.020, biaxial

positive; epidote: S.G. is 3.49; indices of refraction are 1.751, 1.784, and 1.797, with a birefringence of 0.046, biaxial negative, with a modification of the optical character for about 15 percent epidote).

Common gem epidote shows an S.G. of 3.4 and R.I. of 1.730, 1.755, and 1.770. The chromium-rich grass-green variety is most valued because of its vivid color (tawmawite from Upper Myanmar). Crystals are often elongated, striated lengthwise, and terminated like a roof with two major faces. Stocky, flattened crystals are, however, found on Prince of Wales Island in Alaska. Most commonly, epidote forms aggregates of fibrous crystals, often having a radial structure. Epidote's toughness and its resistance to weathering enable it to survive erosion and other natural forces, so that it occurs in alluvial deposits, where it is found as a matte yellowish-green stone with elongated grains, reminiscent of frosty glass.

Epidote is found in a wide variety of deposits; they all correspond to the alpine variety of the green-schists facies of metamorphism (low temperature and low pressure).

Epidote crystals from the Oisans region in the French Alps are well known, but the best crystals come from the Knappenwand deposit, near Salzburg, Austria, which is world famous. Recently, beautiful gem-quality crystals were found in Kashmir. Epidote is known in many other countries, including Madagascar and Brazil.

Epidote crystal from Kashmir. Height: 10 cm. Sorbonne collection.

The epidote that is frequently found in granites that have experienced retrograde metamorphism may be used for jadelike ornamental stones (for example, saussurite from the Alps is a fine-grained rock containing epidote, albite, and chlorite). The association of green epidote with pink feldspars in a rock called unakite, found in the Unaka hills of North Carolina, produces an unusual-looking ornamental stone. Piemontite (from Piedmont, Italy) is a red manganoan epidote, with no great gemological significance.

An 11-carat faceted epidote from Madagascar is on display at the Museum of Natural History in Paris.

EUCLASE

A hydroxilated beryllium aluminosilicate, crystallizing in the monoclinic system.

The name refers to its easy cleavage (from the Greek *eu,* meaning "easily, truly," and *klasis,* meaning "to break,").

The blue to blue-green color of euclase is reminiscent of aquamarine and occasionally even of spodumene. Euclase's dichroism is weak. Because of its perfect and easy cleavage, this stone is too breakable to be worn as jewelry, despite its hardness of 7½. Its physical properties (S.G. is 3.10; indices of refraction are 1.650, 1.656, and 1.672, with a birefringence of 0.022, biaxial positive) are close to those of spodumene. Euclase can be separated from spodumene by its higher specific gravity and lower birefringence. Euclase is electrified when rubbed.

Its prismatic crystals are often elongated and flattened, with vertical striations. They terminate at more or less complex points.

Euclase is a pegmatite mineral and can be associated with beryl and topaz in the deposits from the Ouro Preto area of Minas Gerais, Brazil, especially the famous Capão da Lana deposit. Remarkable crystals of an attractive blue-green color, reaching 5 centimeters in length, have been found in the Gachala emerald mine in Colombia. In 1929 an almost 10-centimeter-long crystal was found in Lukangasi, in the Morogoro district of Tanzania. Beautiful intense blue euclases have been recently mined in Zimbabwe. Euclase is faceted only for collectors. A green 12.5-carat euclase from Brazil and an 8.9-carat yellow one are displayed in the Smithsonian Institution in Washington.

Euclase crystal from Ouro Preto, Brazil. Length: 5 cm. Private collection.

FELDSPAR

A group of alkali (potassium, sodium, calcium) aluminosilicates, petrographically the most important of all minerals forming the earth's crust. See also AMAZONITE; MOONSTONE; ORTHOCLASE; SPECTROLITE; SUNSTONE.

The name comes from an old German word, formed from *feld,* meaning "field," and *spath,* "lustrous, cleavable mineral." Together, the name translates literally as "spar of the fields," probably because of its abundance in the ground, due to rock weathering.

This mineral family has three extreme poles: potassium-rich orthoclase, sodium-rich albite, and calcium-rich anorthite. Feldspars are either monoclinic (sanidine, orthoclase, celsian, hyalophane) or triclinic (albite, microcline, labradorite, anorthite, oligoclase, andesite). They have analogous structures and similar physical properties: a perfect cleavage, a hardness of 6, a color varying from white to sometimes pinkish to gray. The often vivid iridescent colors, commonly said to be characteristic of labradorite, are not rare for only this mineral but can also exist in other feldspars, such as orthoclase, andesite, oligoclase, adularia, and anorthite.

Feldspars are used as gems mostly when they display a strong iridescence, in particular in the adularia variety of orthoclase (moonstone) and oligoclase (sunstone). The beautiful yellow color and transparency of the orthoclases from the Itrongahy pegmatite in Madagascar lend themselves to beautiful faceted stones. The somewhat nacreous, bluish green color of microcline (amazonite) makes it a common ornamental stone.

FIBROLITE

See SILLIMANITE.

FLUORITE

A calcium fluoride, crystallizing in the cubic system.

The word *fluorine* comes from the Latin *fluor, fluoris,* meaning "flow" (in Greek, *fluo* means "to flow abundantly"), referring to its good fusibility, which explains its use as a flux in metallurgy. In the sixteenth century, the German mineralogist Georgius Agricola described fluorite as "stones similar to gems, but less hard, and which melt with the heat of a fire."

When pure, fluorite is colorless; however, trace elements and structural defects often make it green, sometimes blue, light purple to dark violet, pink, or red. These colors are almost always distributed in bands parallel to the cube and the octahedron faces. This produces ribbonlike multi-color effects in veins, which can be preserved by slabbing plaques and tiles. Fluorite's low hardness and good cleavage make it difficult to use as a gem. Fluorite from Derbyshire, England, is highly valued for its banded colors. It is called Blue John, an alteration of the French *bleu-jaune* ("blue-yellow"), describing its color. In Roman times it was the raw material of the famous Murrhins vases. The Geological Museum in London displays a very beautiful Blue John vase. The Museum of Natural History in Paris has various Blue John fluorite objects, including a pair of 26-centimeter- (10-inch-) tall urns on Carrara marble stands. The pillars of the balustrade of the Paris Opera's central staircase are carved in fluorite from Voltennes, Saône-et-Loire, France.

Despite their brittleness, fluorite crystals have been faceted for collectors. The Smithsonian Institution in Washington displays, among others, a 354-carat yellow fluorite from Illinois, an 85-carat blue stone from the same area, and a 13-carat pink one from Switzerland.

With an index of refraction of 1.434, fluorite does not have much brilliance: "It gleams more than it sparkles," wrote Pliny the Elder. Immersed in water, a transparent fluorite "disappears," because its refringence compared to water is very slight.

Fluorite often displays healed fractures and negative crystals, with shapes derived from the cube (tetrahedron and orthogonal prisms, for example), containing a mixture of brine, salt, and gas. It can also trap other minerals, such as pyrite. When rubbed, fluorite produces an ozone smell, already appreciated in ancient times: "Another of its charms is its smell," wrote Pliny.

Its high specific gravity varies from 3 to 3.5 for the most compact varieties. Under black light, it often displays a violet luminescence, intense in the gem varieties, weak in the violet to black ones.

Fluorite is abundant in many geological settings. In hydrothermal veins with sphalerite, galena, and pyrite, it is often the matrix mineral, sometimes associated with baryte and quartz. In Cumberland the Blue John variety has been used for decorative purposes.

Massive ornamental amethyst may be mistaken for banded violet fluorite, but the

A fluorite crystal on galena from Illinois. Length: 6 cm. British Museum of Natural History.

difference in hardness enables proper identification. Similarly, green fluorite has often been used as a jade substitute to carve "Chinese goddesses" in series.

Transparent green fluorite from Otjiwarongo, Namibia, has an absorption spectrum close to that of emerald and has been used in jewelry as shallow cabochons. It has been incorrectly represented to tourists as "South African emerald." Synthetic fluorite has been faceted for collectors.

g

GAHNITE

A green spinel containing zinc, fairly rare as a gem. The name honors the Swedish chemist J. G. Gahn (1745–1818). Its specific gravity of 4.40 to 4.65 and index of refraction of 1.805 are higher than those for regular spinel. Gems from the gahnite-spinel series are called gahno-spinels.

GARNET

A group of silicates, crystallizing in the cubic system, defined by their specific crystal structure. *Garnet* alone refers to pyrope-almandite. The other members of the group are called either by their specific mineral name, sometimes followed by *garnet,* or by *garnet* preceded by a color description. See also ALMANDITE; DEMANTOID; GROSSULAR; PYROPE; SPESSARTINE.

Origin of the Name

The Sanskrit root *gar* ("to carry") became in Greek *geron* ("elderly") and in Latin *granum* ("seed"). From the Latin term came the adjective *granatus,* meaning "with several seeds," and the related name *granatum* was given to the pomegranate, which has numerous red seed-bearing capsules. By extension, *granum* also designates the insect cochineal, a plant louse used as a red dye.

The origin of *garnet* is best understood by comparing the color of common garnets (pyrope, almandite) with that of pomegranate seeds. In France the word *vermeille* was used from the twelfth to the nineteenth century to describe red garnets.

Crystallography and Varieties

The basic structure of garnets consists of silica tetrahedra (SiO_4) arranged around four-fold helicoïdal axes. The void spaces left in this three-dimensional structure are either octahedral sites (at the center of six oxygen atoms, located at each summit of an

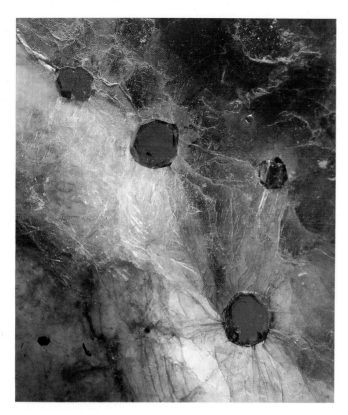

Garnet crystals (spessartite variety) in muscovite mica from Madagascar. Field of view: 3 cm. Sorbonne collection.

Nineteenth-century garnet scarab set in a pendant. Length: 3 cm. Boucheron collection.

octahedron) occupied by trivalent ions (such as aluminum, iron, chromium, and vanadium) or "distorted cubic sites" (at the center of eight oxygen atoms) occupied by bivalent ions (such as magnesium, iron, manganese, or calcium). Three bivalent ions and two trivalent ions are necessary to balance three SiO_4 tetrahedra.

Two main garnet groups are distinguished, based on the presence or absence of calcium. *Aluminum garnets,* sometimes called *pyralspites,* are the first: the bright red magnesian pyrope forms a series with the brick-red ferriferous almandite. The common intermediate terms are sometimes called pyrandine. They include the pink rhodolite. The manganese-bearing spessartite is generally reddish orange to violetish red. *Calcium garnets,* sometimes called *ugrandites,* are the second group: the chromium-bearing uvarovite is green; the aluminum-rich grossular is colorless, yellowish pink to orangy yellow (hessonite), or green (tsavorite); ferriferous andradite may be black (melanite), yellow (topazolite), or green (demantoid).

Complete isomorphous substitutions occur within each group. In addition, titanium may be found in andradite; yttrium, in spessartite. In grossular the SiO_4 tetrahedra may be replaced by H_4O_4 tetrahedra, forming a series toward hydrogrossular. Hydrogrossular often contains chromium or iron and may form a pink or green orna-

mental rock (sometimes including the crystallographically similar vesuvianite) found in Pakistan. Calcium garnets are often zoned.

The most common crystal shapes for garnets are the rhombododecahedron (ugrandites in particular) and the trigonotrisoctahedron (aluminum garnets and pyralspites). The cube is extremely rare (although it has been found in Washington state), as is the octahedron. The relatively high specific gravity and hardness of the various garnets explain their occurrence as alluvial minerals.

Synthetics

Synthetic silicate garnets have not been marketed yet. However, the laser industry has perfected some synthetic nonsilicate garnets, with a crystalline architecture similar to that of natural garnets. They are usually referred to by their initials: YAG (yttrium aluminum garnet) YIG (yttrium iron garnet), GAG (gadolinium aluminum garnet), and GGG (gadolinium gallium garnet). Colorless when pure, YAG has a high index of refraction (1.83) and has been successfully commercialized as a diamond simulant under various trade names (Diemlite and Burmalite, for example). Although it has a higher R.I. (1.95), pure GGG is difficult to grow and tends to become yellowish in daylight; it has met with little commer-

cial success. Colored YAG, doped with elements such as chromium or cobalt, has also been commercially unsuccessful.

GOSHENITE

A colorless beryl. Its name comes from the Goshen deposit in Massachusetts.

When irradiated with gamma rays, goshenite may turn yellow-orange or blue, or it may be unaffected; the reaction is related to the presence of trace elements. The colors obtained by this process are not always stable. Stones with a stable color resemble the blue beryl aquamarines and are called halbanite in Brazil. Their very characteristic spectra help to separate these two varieties of blue beryl.

Goshenite is rare; its morphology is similar to that of morganite, and like morganite, it is found in sodium-lithium pegmatites. Crystals reach about 10 centimeters, with a thickness of 2 to 3 centimeters. The most beautiful crystals come from the Criminosas mine, near Governador Valadares, in Minas Gerais, Brazil.

GROSSULAR

An aluminum-calcium garnet. The reddish orange gem variety is called hessonite.

Its name comes from the Latin *grossu-*

laria, meaning "gooseberry," because of its appearance.

A 64.2-carat hessonite is on display at the Smithsonian Institution in Washington.

Color and Physical Properties

Some of the aluminum in grossular's structure may be replaced by chromium or vanadium, producing a green color. Colorless (rare) to deep emerald-green gem grossular is called tsavorite, because it was originally found in Tsavo Park, Kenya. When the color is dark, the absorption spectrum characteristic of chromium and vanadium is distinct.

Some of the aluminum may also be replaced by ferrous iron, producing orange-yellow to brown crystals. Gem grossular with such a color is called hessonite. It may resemble any of the gems having a "hyacinth" color, including zircon, tourmaline, spinel, and padparadscha sapphire.

The aluminum is also sometimes replaced by iron and chromium; at the same time, hydroxyl groups may replace oxygen, with a resulting loss of silica. This produces hydrogrossular, a jadelike green rock (South Africa) or a pink stone (Mexico) similar to thulite.

Grossular has a high luster. Its index of refraction is about 1.72 for the massive varieties and 1.73 for the gem varieties. The specific gravity of massive grossular (3.4 for the pink variety and 3.45 to 3.55 for the green) is also lower than for gem grossular (3.57 to 3.67). Scratch hardness is quite good (7 to 7½).

Deposits and Inclusions

Grossular is a product of regional metamorphism of clay-rich limestones, especially when the metamorphism is triggered by granites. Grossular is also a mineral characteristic of skarns, where it is associated with epidote, scheelite, molybdenite, and chalcopyrite.

Gem grossular is abundant in the gem-bearing gravels of Sri Lanka and in the Tsavo National Park in Kenya. Hessonites from Sri Lanka have a peculiar texture; they have a granular appearance, caused by small crystals with a rounded outline, which look like they have been fused together; sometimes, small eroded zircons are included in the "grains." Generally, hessonite and tsavorite must be free of inclusions to be faceted.

Massive grossular used as ornamental stone comes from the Transvaal, east of Pretoria, South Africa (Turffontein, Buffelsfontein). This rock, produced by metamorphism, contains black chromite and magnetite inclusions. Various objects have been carved in this tough, homogeneous material, which has a waxy luster and a scaly fracture.

Green grossular may be embedded in vesuvianite, forming an ornamental rock used to carve small objects and cabochons. Some cabochons consist of vesuvianite at one end and grossular at the other, resulting in a very peculiar behavior in heavy liquids (since vesuvianite is slightly lighter than grossular). Such ornamental rocks are found in Pakistan (Quetta area), California, and near Xalostoc, Mexico (see also VESUVIANITE).

Imitations

Very pale grossular from Tsavo National Park has been used as the raw material for grossular–green cement–grossular triplets, intended to imitate tsavorite, which is avidly sought by collectors.

An 0.8-carat tsavorite (green grossular) from Tsavo National Park, Kenya. Private collection.

Grossular garnet crystals from Asbestos, Canada. Diameter: 2 cm. Sorbonne collection.

Goshenite crystal from the Criminosas mine, Minas Gerais, Brazil. Width: 5 cm. Sorbonne collection.

h

HALBANITE

The Brazilian trade name for a variety of beryl turned blue by gamma irradiation (the name was coined by the Halba company). The legal description of this material in France is "beryl with an artificially modified color." It is called "Maxixe-type" beryl in the U.S. See AQUAMARINE.

HAWK'S-EYE

A blue chatoyant quartz. See QUARTZ: CAT'S-EYE QUARTZ.

Detail of a 6-cm-long enamel and diamond dragonfly brooch. The eyes are of the hawk's eye variety of chatoyant quartz. Boucheron collection.

HELIODOR

A yellow beryl containing traces of iron. Its name comes from the Greek *helios* ("sun") and *doron* ("gift"). This name, "gift of the sun," was devised by the German colonial government of South-West Africa (now Namibia), which wanted to promote this gem.

The yellow color is generally attributed to a substitution of ferric iron for aluminum and, by some, to a slight radioactivity. When heat-treated for a few hours at temperatures between 280° and 600°C (535° and 1,110°F), heliodor becomes blue or colorless, but it will regain its yellow coloration when exposed to gamma rays.

The physical properties of heliodor are very close to those of aquamarine. Its indices of refraction are 1.567 to 1.582 for the ordinary ray and 1.563 to 1.576 for the extraordinary ray, with a birefringence of 0.004 to 0.007. Its specific gravity is 2.63 to 2.73.

Heliodor was discovered in 1910 in Rössing and Swakopmund, Namibia, in geodes of pegmatites, which have produced aquamarine and heliodor crystals of outstanding quality, accompanied by smoky quartz. Heliodor is also associated with topaz, aquamarine, and tourmaline in Transbaikalia (Adun Chilon) and in pegmatites from near Volhynia, Zhitomir, in the Ukraine, where crystals of excellent color, often corroded, can reach unusually large dimensions for this gem, up to 15 centimeters. Heliodor is also found in Madagascar and Brazil, particularly in the Marambaia and Medina areas. Beautiful crystals from Minas Novas and Sapucaia, also in the state of Minas Gerais. Recently, beautiful crystals were also found in Afghanistan (Kunar and Pech valleys, Nuristan) and in Kashmir (Gilgit area).

The largest faceted heliodor, a step-cut Brazilian crystal, weighs 2,054 carats. It is displayed in the Smithsonian Institution in Washington.

A heliodor crystal from Afghanistan. Size: 4 cm. Sorbonne collection.

HELIOTROPE

Chalcedony that has been "greened" by numerous inclusions of chlorite (also called plasma), with red iron oxide spots that evoke blood.

Heliotrope comes from the Greek *helios* ("sun") and *tropos* ("to turn around"), a reference to the use of this mineral, polished, to follow the movements of the sun in ancient times. The appearance of this green jasper, seemingly stained with blood, inspired its other names, bloodstone and martyr's stone.

This stone has often been used in Christian glyptic art for crucifixion and martyr scenes. Beautiful examples are kept in the Bibliothèque Nationale in Paris. Another famous specimen is the great nave, created by the Miseronis during the sixteenth century; it bears the coat of arms of the German emperor Rudolf II and is presently displayed in the Louvre. Today heliotrope is particularly popular for signet rings.

The best heliotropes come from the Kathiawar trapps in Deccan (India). This gem is also found in Brazil, Australia, and Oregon.

HEMATITE

A ferric iron oxide, crystallizing in the trigonal system.

The name of this stone comes from the Greek *haimatites,* because of the red traces, reminiscent of blood (*haimatos*), that it leaves on a streak plate (Theophrastus, fourth century B.C.).

As early as the third millennium, B.C., the Sumerians used hematite to engrave their cylinder seals; the stones probably came from the deposits around the Persian Gulf (Hormuz and Larak islands, for example).

The Egyptians, Greeks, and Romans made necklaces and amulets from hematite. Around 70 B.C., Zacharias of Babylon considered it a useful talisman, helping to obtain a favorable response to the petitions his owner submitted to kings. In the first century, Pliny the Elder claimed it was excellent in stopping bleeding. This belief was also found in North America, where Native Americans smeared their faces with red hematite before battle: it supposedly conferred invulnerability (also in the Mediterranean tradition). Although considered "vile," hematite was still used as a talisman during the sixteenth century. It was supposed to help win lawsuits, achieve grace, and combat venom and eye and liver diseases.

By the beginning of the nineteenth century, it was used only as a burnishing tool by the jeweler and a polishing paste by the lapidary.

This gem attracted new interest at the end of the nineteenth century, which continues today. It was used for seals and cameos, sometimes carved into a depression so the raised edge protected the carving. Today, it is also often used for jewelry, as beads, plaques, and in a variety of other shapes. Hematite appropriate for jewelry is massive and slightly fibrous, in the shape of convoluted "kidney ore" (as in Cumberland, England). Hematite from Santiago de Compostela (Spain) is more finely grained and was highly valued in the last century. Cumberland, England, produced much of

Hematite crystals from Casa da Pedra, Congonhas do Campo, Minas Gerais, Brazil. Height: 15 cm. Sorbonne collection.

the hematite used by lapidaries in Idar-Oberstein at the turn of the century, but these deposits have been exhausted.

Since 1980, large masses of slightly less compact hematite, with a moderately coarse fibrous structure, has come from the "itabirites" of Minas Gerais, Brazil. These rocks represent considerable reserves of iron ore, related to a high degree of metamorphism. This material is carved in Brazil and Taiwan into beads and other small objects. Because of tectonic stress over the entire region, magnetite is also present, irregularly distributed in the deposit; it may produce some magnetism in this hematite. The best specimens for lapidary work come from the Marian area, near Ouro Preto, and Itabira, close to Belo Horizonte.

Classic, fibrous hematite is nonmagnetic; its hardness is 6½. Because of its metallic luster (reflecting power: 17 percent), it was used as a mirror in ancient times. Its specific gravity is about 5 (from 4.95 to 5.15). Hematite is very common in sedimentary rocks, contact-metamorphism deposits, veins, and fumarole deposits.

During ancient times hematite was imitated with black schists; more recently, with psilomelane (a manganese oxide with a specific gravity of 4.35, a hardness of 6, and a black dust). However, its most frequent imitation is black glass and silicon. Between the two World Wars, small hematite beads were fraudulently sold as black pearls.

HESSONITE

A yellowish orange ferriferous grossular, so called because of its hardness, which is lower (in Greek *hesson* means "inferior") than that of other gems it may resemble

Green spodumene crystal (hiddenite variety) from Kulum, Laghman Valley, Afghanistan. Height: 10 cm. Sorbonne collection.

("hyacinth zircon," some tourmalines and spinels, padparadscha sapphire). See GROSSULAR.

HIDDENITE

An emerald-green, chromium-bearing gem spodumene. It was named for the mine superintendent W. E. Hidden (1853–1918), who discovered this mineral in North Carolina in 1879.

Crystals are extremely rare and often small: the largest known measures 9 by 4 centimeters. The historical Stony Point deposit has long been exhausted. A 2.4-carat faceted hiddenite is on display at the British Museum in London.

Hiddenite is trichroic, with associated colors of blue-green, emerald green, and yellowish green. It displays a typical chromium absorption spectrum, but luminesces only weakly under black light.

Some emerald-green kunzites irradiated with cobalt have been deceptively represented as hiddenite; their color is very unstable and fades after a few hours in daylight. There are, however, naturally green spodumenes with an unstable color (for example, in Afghanistan); they cannot be called hiddenites, since their color is not as vivid as true hiddenite.

Hiddenite was initially mistaken for green diopside, a mineral of similar appearance.

HORN

A dermic secretion covering two bumps on the skulls of some ruminant mammals, particularly buffalo, oxen, goats, and caribou.

Origin of the Name

The word *horn* comes from an old Indo-European root, from which were derived *cornu* in Latin, *corne* in French, and *horn* in English and German.

The Uses of Horn

In the past, horn was mostly used to make bowls and hunting horns, such as the oliphant of the medieval knights. The horn from the wild buffalo of southern Africa is the most desirable. However, the horns of a variety of ruminants, for example, chamois, have been used on a local basis.

Today in addition to its traditional use to produce various toilet accessories (shoehorns, for example), horn may be used to imitate tortoise shell.

Physical Properties

Horn is fairly light (S.G. is 1.35) and quite soft (H is 2), with a resinous luster. It is flexible and thermoplastic (it softens at about 100°C or 212°F). Burned horn has an unpleasant odor of burned flesh. Its surface contains microscopic chromatophores (pigment-bearing cells) on a background showing weak parallel striations, somewhat reminiscent of tortoise shell. The color of horn ranges from very light to very dark brown. Like all organic materials, it shows an intense fluorescence in black light.

Working Horn

Soaking for two weeks in cold water separates the horny shell from the bone. Horn can then be flattened using a press, after being softened with water or heat and impregnated with tallow or grease. It can then be worked by molding, just like tortoise shell. Horn can be dyed red, brown, or black with salts of gold, mercury, or silver.

Imitations

All horn imitations are plastics.

Other Kinds of Horns

Rhinoceros horn is generally considered a hair aggregate (of epidermic origin). It has a keratinous nature and shows a fibrous structure. Therefore, like regular horn, it has a resinous luster, a brownish yellow to black color, and can be dyed. It is not hard (H is 2), although it is tough and light (S.G. is 1.3). It is also thermoplastic and fluoresces under black light.

Valued by the Chinese for its fever-reducing properties, it is considered an aphrodisiac in the West. Rhinoceros horn can be easily carved into a variety of objects including bowls, fans, netsuke, and small display pieces. The Oriental Art Gallery of the Dublin Museum in Ireland displays a remarkable collection of such objects. Like tortoise shell, rhinoceros horn can be worked by molding or used in marquetry. Today its most important market is in Yemen, where it is used to carve the handles of the traditional daggers.

Antlers are fast-growing, decaying bony bumps. Their structure is similar to that of bone, but the Haversian canals are less distinct. Antlers are generally brown and are harder (H is 2½) and denser (S.G. is 1.70 to 1.85) than regular horn. They have been used as inlays for firearm stocks (especially in Germany during the sixteenth and seventeenth century) and for carving netsuke and other small display objects, as well as knife handles.

Similar Materials

Hornbill "ivory," actually a misnomer, is obtained from the beak of the hornbill bird, a large bird from Southeast Asia.

Hornbill "ivory" was worked early on by inhabitants of Sumatra and Borneo. It has been found in archaeological excavations of the Dayak culture, used for sword ornaments and earrings. It was introduced to China in the fifteenth century; the craftsmen of the Ming dynasty made ceremonial belt buckles and combs from it. Hornbill "ivory" then took the name *hoting*, literally "crane's crest," a translation of the Malay *gading* to Chinese. It was used for snuff bottles during the Qing dynasty. In Japan the craftsmen of the Tokugawa period made netsuke and *inrō* from it and called it *höden*. Hornbill "ivory" was introduced to Europe only during the nineteenth century. It is said to be worked today in Singapore and Hong Kong. This "ivory" is in fact a frontal horny mass of about 5 x 5 x 4 centimeters (2 by 2 by 1½ inches) with an outer red layer and an inner yellow layer firmly attached and having identical physical properties: they are translucent with a resinous luster, sectile, fairly soft (H is 3) and light (S.G. is 1.30). Its fibrous structure includes chromatophores similar to those found in horn and tortoise shell, which are more numerous in the red part than in the yellow part. Its thermoplastic properties allow it to be worked under pressure, just as horn and tortoise shell are.

Caribou hoof is worked by the Kivalina Eskimos in Alaska for jewelry. It takes an excellent polish.

HYACINTH

In 1604 Boece de Boot described four types of hyacinth based on color: fiery red, orange-red, saffron yellow, and colorless. In the mid-seventeenth century, the colorless variety was renamed *jargon*, whereas the orangy tones remained *hyacinth*: Oriental hyacinth (orange sapphire), hyacinth-the-beautiful (presently orange zircon and garnet, which have a similar hardness, also called Portuguese hyacinth and Bohemian hyacinth), Compostella hyacinth (now brownish citrine). By then, hyacinth was "much less in use and of lesser value than in the past," according to P. de Rosnel, jeweler to the king of France (1668).

Eighteenth-century Chinese drinking vessel carved from rhinoceros horn. Height: 15 cm. Private collection.

At the end of the eighteenth century, Romé de l'Isle defined hyacinth-the-beautiful as a mineral species with square prismatic crystals. It was later identified to be the same as jargon, and the name zircon, then preferred, was adopted by mineralogists.

However, during the nineteenth century, the name *hyacinth,* accompanied by an adjective, still designated not only (appropriately) today's zircon, but also hessonite, quartz, and even vesuvianite, because its crystal shape is similar to that of zircon.

In the twentieth century, *hyacinth* simply became synonymous with orange, and is used exclusively for zircon and garnet. *Hyacinth* alone, which has now fallen into disuse, should nevertheless be considered synonymous with orange zircon.

During the Renaissance, hyacinth was considered a talisman against plague and was worn in a ring or "hanging from the neck, like an amulet." Like all gems with a warm, sunny color, it was supposed to confer wisdom, care, and moral virtues, bring riches and honors, protect from lightning, and ensure a good night's sleep. See also ZIRCON.

HYDROPHANE

Transparent opal, (hence its name, from the Greek *hudor,* which means "water," and *phaneros,* "apparent"). Its play of color is apparent only when soaked in water.

HYPERSTHENE

See ENSTATITE.

i

IDOCRASE

See VESUVIANITE.

INTAGLIO

An engraving carved into an ornamental stone, often to produce a seal. Although in modern languages *intaglio* denotes that the design has to be cut away, this definition was obvious in ancient languages (in Greek, *glupho* means "I engrave"). Later it became necessary to distinguish intaglio from other glyptic art, such as cameos, which were carved in relief *(anaglupho)*. See the discussion of seals, cylinders, intaglios, and cameos in part 1 for more information.

IOLITE

See CORDIERITE.

IVORY

A phosphate secreted by elephants to form tusks. Ivory from other mammals (hippopotamus, walrus, narwhal, wild boar, sperm whale) or fossil mammoth tusks, should be appended with the name of the animal from which the ivory came. (In France such designations are legally decreed.)

Intaglio in carnelian depicting the head of Medusa, engraved by B. Arsène at the end of the nineteenth century. Height: 2.8 cm. Boucheron collection.

Patina ivory representing Tamo, the first Chinese patriarch. Carving from the Ming dynasty, at the end of the seventeenth century. Height: 10 cm. Private collection.

Origin of the Name

From the Latin *ebur, eboreus,* which is from the Egyptian *ab, abu.* In French the adjective *éburnéen,* means, "ivory colored."

The History of Ivory

Since prehistoric times, ivory has been used in carvings of both utilitarian objects, such as spears, and prestigious objets d'art, possibly religious, such as the Brassempouy Woman. Every civilization since has worked ivory. Ivory carving probably reached its peak in Europe in the thirteenth century, with the carving of extremely detailed traveling altars. The French school at Dieppe, then an important port of entry for ivory, was very creative from the fourteenth to the sixteenth century but suffered during the seventeenth and eighteenth centuries as the ivory trade declined in Western Europe. An interesting collection is kept in the museum in Dieppe.

Ivory carving began to develop in China around the fourteenth century. It reached true virtuosity in the seventeenth century, with the creation of pieces having three distinct layers. Starting in the nineteenth century, chinese carvings became stereotyped as a result of increased trade with Western countries.

The Japanese produced numerous netsuke, used to fasten items to the kimono sash and hold various objects, especially weapons. This type of carving has always been inspired by mythology, as well as by naturalistic designs (birds and flowers, for example).

Today ivory is used for necklaces, bangles, brooches, and other jewelry accessories, as well as small decorative objects. The largest trading center for rough ivory is Hong Kong, through which some 700 tons, half of the world's production, are transported every year (which translates into the slaughter of some 50,000 African elephants).

Chemical Composition and Texture

Ivory is a secretion of tooth pulp, found in the central cavity of all teeth. It is generally protected by a hard enamel on the outside and a cement at the root. Small nerve fibers protected by a gelatinous substance extend outward from the pulp cavity in a planar spiral pattern. Cross sections therefore show striae in various shades of cream, which look like an engine turning (called lines of Retzius); they are easily visible and characteristic of elephant ivory. Lighter lines running parallel to the tusk length can be seen in longitudinal section and represent growth marks. This "grain" is finer in hippopotamus ivory than elephant

Ivory plaque from eleventh-century Egypt, showing a drinker and a dancer. Islamic section, Musée du Louvre.

The carving of ivory. An eleventh-century Italian engraving, with Greek text. Marciana National Library, Venice. Photo: Giraudon.

considered most attractive because of its soft cream color and very fine grain. That from Ghana and Sierra Leone is least valuable.

Ivory is classified commercially as "hard ivory," which has a better luster but is more difficult to work, and "soft ivory," which is less sensitive to temperature fluctuations and less brittle. Only male Asian elephants (*Elephas maximus*) from the Indian subcontinent and Indochina peninsula bear tusks made of soft ivory, which turns yellow relatively easily. Most of the ivory represented as Indian seems to be African ivory imported via Zanzibar, in Tanzania (Sri Lankan elephants do not have tusks).

Frozen in polar ice, mammoth ivory (from *Elephas primigenius*) is found around the Lena River in Siberia, among other places. Generally, only small sections of these tusks are of an acceptable color for the fabrication of small objects.

Ivory from the African hippopotamus (*Hippopotamus amphibius*) comes from its incisors and canines, covered by enamel. These tusks may weigh 1 to 3 kilograms (2 to 6½ pounds.)

Ivory from the walrus (*Odobenus rosmarus*), an inhabitant of Arctic waters, comes from the upper canine teeth of the animal. The tusks may reach 1 meter (3 feet) in length.

Narwhal ivory comes from the male's left canine, which forms a spiraled pike up to 3 meters (10 feet) long. Medieval tales of the unicorn may have stemmed from this animal.

Ivory from the wild boar and the sperm whale comes from their curved, conical canines and can be used only to fashion small objects.

Physical Properties

Ivory has a cream color and fluoresces blue strongly under black light, like all organic materials. Its index of refraction is about 1.54. Its texture makes it fairly tough but extremely elastic (hence, its use in billiard balls). Ivory is not very resistant to scratching (H is 2). It is attacked by acids.

Because of its high proportion of organic matter, ivory is very sensitive to dehydration. When placed too close to a source of heat (a radiator, or even sunshine through a window), it may crack.

Ivory's specific gravity varies with its organic content. Elephant ivory ranges from 1.70 (soft ivory) to 1.90 (hard ivory); other ivories range from 1.90 (hippopotamus) to 1.95 (narwhal, walrus). It never reaches 2.

The Uses of Ivory

Ivory turns yellowish over time. Because old ivory is more valuable than recent pieces, it is tempting to try to age ivory artificially. For this purpose, the Chinese im-

ivory, coarse in walrus and narwhal ivory, and very coarse in boar and whale ivory. A fine peeling of ivory reveals fine, undulating fibrils under the microscope, crossed by darker lines, the sections of the fibrils (lines of Retzius) forming dots.

Chemically, elephant ivory consists of about 65 percent calcium phosphate that is close to hydroxylapatite, associated with about 35 percent of organic material (collagen with traces of elastin). These percentages may vary considerably in other ivories.

Sources of Ivory

Elephant ivory is produced by the animal's two upper incisors, which are not protected by enamel. These curved tusks have a central conical cavity extending one-third of their length. The majority of the ivory on the market comes from the African elephant (*Elephas africanus*). Its tusks weigh an average of 8 kilograms each, (17 pounds) and can reach almost 40 kilograms (90 pounds) for a 3 meter (10-foot) length. Two tusks weighing 47 kilograms (103 pounds) each and measuring 2.92 (9½ feet) and 2.82 meters (9¼ feet) are kept in the National Thai Museum. The heaviest pair of tusks is in the British Museum in London, with weights of 102.7 kilograms (225.9 pounds) and 107 kilograms (235.4 pounds) at a length of 3.28 meters (10¾ feet). The longest ones (3.77 meters [over 12⅓ feet] and 3.60 meters [11¾ feet] for a total weight of 132 kilograms [290 pounds]) are in the Smithsonian's National Museum of Natural History in Washington. Cameroon ivory is

Ivory and gold carving of a mother and her child. Height: 10 cm. Detail of Via vitae, *created by J.-B. Chaumet. Chaumet collection, Paris.*

Carvings in mammoth ivory by Alaskan Eskimos. Height: 8 cm. G. Griffith collection, United States.

merse it in tea (some say urine), which penetrates it and produces an old ivory color, or they brown the material with incense smoke.

Ivory is carved without any particular preparation, using wood-engraving techniques. It is polished on leather, either with tripoli (a silica powder) or pumice. A final polish with oil provides a certain patina. Ivory dust and scraps are used to produce "ivory black."

Ivory can be dyed with various metallic salts or organic materials, which easily penetrate its small tubes. This material has always been dyed with one or several colors, whether by the Phoenicians, the ancient Egyptians, the medieval ivory carvers, or the Chinese.

Care

Because of its porosity, ivory can easily absorb sweat, perfume, and beauty creams, which can irreparably damage it. Therefore, one should clean it often in soapy water and dry it slowly, away from heat. Ivory can also be tarnished by pollution or lose its polish during wear. It can be revived by cleaning it with alcohol diluted in water and powdered chalk. Cracks due to dehydration cannot be repaired; at most, one

can hope that they will close a bit over time, if the ivory is rehydrated inside a tight damp cloth.

Imitations

The most convincing imitation consists of alternate layers of opaque and translucent celluloid, properly charged (sometimes with ivory dust) and compressed together, to imitate the "grain" of ivory (however, only parallel lines are produced). This substance, called *ivoirine,* has been banned in France.

Various plastics are also used but are less convincing. Cream-colored plaster molds, covered with a product made of wax or stearine, have also been tried.

Look-alikes

Bones and antlers may look similar to ivory; see BONE and HORN for further information about these materials.

The corozo, or ivory nut, is another ivory look-alike. Formerly called vegetable ivory, it comes from a South American palm tree *(Phytelephas macrocarpa),* about 10 meters (30 feet) tall, called *pullipunta* or *homero* in Peru, *tagua* in Colombia, and *anti* on the Panamanian coasts. It produces

a fruit with six to nine nuts, which are the size of an egg. They contain a liquid that is potable while the fruit develops, but becomes milky, then white and solid at maturation. It is as hard as ivory and resembles it as well. This material is almost pure cellulose, has a typical vegetal structure with elongated cells, similar to wood, and a specific gravity slightly over 1.3. Ivory nut was used in the early twentieth century to manufacture small objects (such as beads, pendants, and buttons), sometimes produced by stamping. It has been dyed in various colors, including red. In addition to ivory, corozo can imitate nacre, and especially coral, depending on the color to which it is dyed.

Another palm tree, from north and central Africa, *Hyphaene thebaica,* or doom palm, is remarkable for its fan-shaped leaves and the nut in the center of its fruit, which tastes like gingerbread. This nut looks like the corozo nut but is slightly heavier (S.G. just under 1.4). Its cellular structure is very much like that of a leaf. It was used at the turn of the century to imitate ivory and, when dyed, nacre and coral.

Elephant molars, characterized by alternate layers of ivory and enamel, have also been used as imitations of ivory.

Hornbill "ivory" is another look-alike; see HORN.

j

JADE

A tough, hard ornamental stone, generally light green, with a fine or very fine grain. It can be an amphibolite, principally actinolite and tremolite (nephrite jade), or a jadeite pyroxenite (jadeite jade).

Origin of the Name

Despite numerous discoveries of polished jade objects in prehistoric sites and despite the existence of trade between China and Western Europe from the mid-twelfth to the mid-fourteenth century, jade apparently became known around the Mediterranean basin only at the beginning of the sixteenth century, after the Portuguese settlement in Canton, China, was established in 1517. Jade had been long used in China; it supposedly had medicinal virtues, such as preventing and healing diseases of the urinary tract. Portuguese traders imported small objects carved in jade which they called *pedre de ilharga,* literally "stone of the flank or loins." (Because of their resemblance to the Chinese objets d'art, the Aztec pieces brought home by the Spanish conquistadores were called *piedra de hijada.)*

In French this term became *siadre* or *éjade.* At the start of the seventeenth century, *éjade* was used by the educated society of the Hotel de Rambouillet: for example, V. Voiture thanked Angélique Paulet for the gift of an *éjade* bracelet, presented when he was suffering from kidney problems. The initial letter of *éjade* soon disappeared, and the name *jade* became international (although the Italian *giade* may derive directly from *siadre).* However, this new stone was called *lapis nephreticus* in scholarly books written in Latin, from the Greek *nephros,* meaning "kidney," and this phrase was translated as "nephritic stone," which became *nephrite.*

However, Damour demonstrated in 1863 that Chinese and Mexican jade were different. He introduced the term *jadeite*

Modern Chinese jade carving of a dragon. Height: 15 cm. German Precious Stones Museum, Idar-Oberstein, Germany.

for the sodic pyroxene from Burma, reserving *nephrite* for the amphibolitic rock from Chinese Turkistan.

The History of Jade

China

Chinese jades (nephrite jade) were rarely seen in Western Europe before the opening of five Chinese ports to the British following the 1842 Nanking treaty that put an end to the Opium War. Mexican Jades (jadeite jade) were also still little known, and New Zealand jades (nephrite jade) come from a region where civilization was still quite primitive. Therefore, the history of jade is closely associated with the Chinese and pre-Columbian civilizations.

China

To the Chinese, jade is a royal stone, *yu.* It has been represented since at least 2950 B.C. by the same Chinese character resembling a capital I with a narrow horizontal bar at the center. The top part of this character represents the heavens; the bottom part alone, the earth; and the central part alone, man. The king, intermediary between the heavens and the earth, is represented with almost the same character with just one additional line, an oblique slash appended to the baseline. He used jade as a ritual object during his prayers. This clearly

illustrates the great importance of jade in China, where the word *yu* is synonymous with "treasure," similar to *gold* in Western civilizations. Jade was used since prehistoric times to carve symbolic and ritual objects. In the nature cult, the six most important objects were the ritual jades: "To obtain the blessing of the sky, one needs a sky blue *pi,* a yellow *t'sung* on the ground, a green *kuei* toward east, a red *ch'ang* toward south, a white *hu* west, and a black *huang* north" *(Book of Rites* or *Liji).* These symbolic objects were also widely used for funerals.

The *pi* represented the sky and the color blue. It was a flat disk, pierced in its center (very similar to the character for the sun). First very simple, it was later adorned with symbolic animals: dragons, bats, and so on.

The *t'sung* symbolized the earth and the color yellow. It was a square prism pierced by a hole. The angles of the prism represented water, fire, wood, and metal.

The *kuei* was a kind of stylized blade. It symbolized both the East (guarded by the dragon), the spring, and power. It was also a kind of scepter given to generals. The green color symbolized wood.

The *ch'ang* was a tablet in the shape of a half *kuei,* symbolizing south and summer. The red color signified fire.

The *hu,* represented by a tiger (guardian of tombs), symbolized the West (where

the dragon, or demon is found) and the autumn. The white color symbolized metal.

The *huang* was a plaque shaped as a half *pi,* which symbolized north and winter. It was related to the hydra, the fish, and the water dragon. Black represented water.

Under the great emperor Yu, traditionally considered the founder of the Xia dynasty in about 2200 B.C., it was believed that jade could not prevent death but could prevent putrefaction of the body. The body would be placed with a *pi* beneath its back, a *t'sung* on its belly, a *huang* on the head, a *ch'ang* at its feet, a *kuei* to its left, and a *hu* to its right. Amulets would accompany the dead on their journey to the next world, along with all their earthly belongings: an emperor would be surrounded by his slaves, his wives, and his warriors (more than a thousand people were sacrificed during an emperor's funeral).

Elaborate jade carving under the Chang dynasty (sixteenth to eleventh century B.C.) attained true perfection; then the designs were simplified under the influence of Taoism and Confucianism. During the "Springs and Autumns" period (771–481 B.C.), jade became a symbol of love and signified human virtues. It also indicated the rank and prestige of the mandarins, by the number of "archer's" rings they wore.

Taoism developed a number of medicinal applications for jade, which also was used for both magic and romance. Jade was carved into musical instruments, first thin tinkling chimes and soon thereafter, during the Han dynasty (206 B.C. to A.D. 220), flutes, which supposedly pleased ancestors' souls. The Chinese emperors, concerned about securing the sources of jade, attempted to extend the empire westward as illustrated during the twelfth century B.C. by the journey of Wuwang, of the Zhou dynasty, to visit the jade queen. A thousand years later, the jade queen did fall in love with the emperor Wudi, of the Han dynasty, whom she received accompanied by five jade princesses.

With the growth of Buddhism, which assimilated aspects of earlier religions, naturalism developed, and the first jade figurines were carved. Buddha figurines were the most important carvings. The most famous is 1.50 meters tall (5 feet) and can be seen in the Mongol throne room in the Forbidden City in Beijing.

In addition to numerous naturalistic symbols, the eight Taoist immortals, Lao Tseu and the bodhisattvas, were also frequently carved. The most venerated figure was Kuan Yin, bodhisattva of mercy, also called "the jade goddess"; during the seventeenth century, the Jesuits tried to associate her with the Virgin Mary. The immortality mushroom of Taoism became the *Ju-I,* a curved ceremonial scepter carved in jade. After a troubled period, jade became a common material under Emperor

Jade disk (pi) *from the Later Han dynasty* (A.D. 24–220). *Photo: Lauros-Giraudon.*

Xuanzong of the Tang dynasty (A.D. 618–907). It was used for jewelry, ornamental objects, and tableware, and its use spread from the imperial court. All women followed the example of the concubine Yang Guifei, the "jade beauty" an imperial favorite, who lived in a world of jade. This period was the golden age of Chinese jade engraving.

During the thirteenth century, a trader traveling through China and Burma picked up a rock to balance the load on his donkey; this led to the discovery of jadeite jade in Burma. Some stones may have entered China under the Mongol emperor Kublai Khan. But the Chinese borders closed with the rise to power of the Ming dynasty in 1368. The renaissance in jade art, begun during the Song dynasty (960–1279), blossomed.

Trading with Western Europe began with the Portuguese, who settled in Macao in 1554. The export of jade was strictly forbidden, but a number of pieces were smuggled out. Snuff, popular in Europe, became fashionable in China, and numerous snuff bottles were carved from jade. Jade carving developed significantly during the Qing dynasty (1644–1912): Emperor Kangxi (1662–1722) opened imperial workshops, later developed by Emperor Qianlong (1736–1797). Under Qianlong the famous jade mountains were sculpted; the emperor himself worked on the grayish white carvings, including the 300-kilogram (660-pound) mountain on which are carved two of his poems, displayed at the Walker Art Center in Minneapolis, and the 7-ton carving sent in 1778 by the governor of Chinese Turkistan, which tells the story of the legendary Yu building canals on the floodplains.

In 1784 a peace treaty was signed between Burma and China, and Burmese jadeite began to be imported to China. Initially, the Chinese people did not consider jadeite to be jade; they called it *feits'ui* ("kingfisher," because the bird's bright feathers seem to resemble the luster of polished jadeite). This jadeite was used only for jewelry (cabochons and brooches) until 1880–90, when Burmese jadeite jade quarries opened.

There are many remarkable jade pieces, and a few are particularly worthy of note. The first is the imperial seal. According to legend, five centuries before Christ, a phoenix showed a jade boulder to the poor scholar Ho, who brought the block to his emperor; however the ruler did not recognize the jade's quality and punished the poor scholar by amputating his right foot. For the same reason, the next emperor ordered Ho's left foot amputated; but the third emperor did justice to Ho, accepting the jade. The cruel emperor Qin Shi Huangdi (who was the first to unify China, in 221 B.C.) had it carved into a seal, which replaced the *kuei* as an imperial symbol

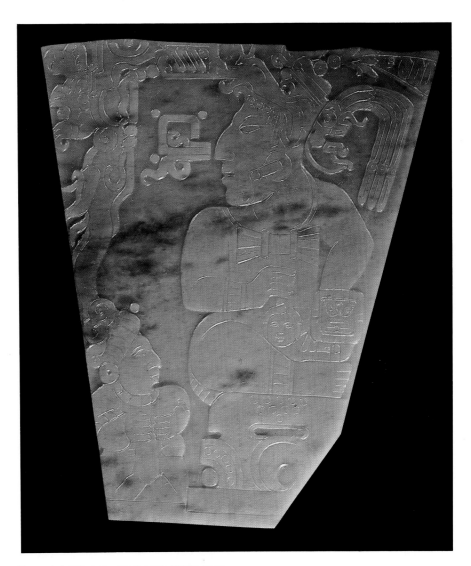

The symbol of life, in Guatemalan jade. Height: 12 cm. German Precious Stones Museum, Idar-Oberstein, Germany.

until modern times. In A.D. 9, it was chipped by Wang Mang, a rival who had usurped the throne of the Han dynasty. In 311 Emperor Xi Jin Huai Ti turned it over to his conquerors as a sign of submission (but was later executed). A lark appointed the seal to Genghis Khan three days before his coronation. Emperor Qianlong threw it in the Yangzi River as a sacrifice to stop the floods, but the jade fountain returned it the following year. In 1908, at only two years of age, Puyi was the last Chinese emperor to be made sacred with the imperial seal, under the name of Xuantong. The seal was displayed in 1926 in the Imperial Palace in Beijing, then in a museum. It was hidden in Shanghai in 1936 during the Japanese invasion and has not been seen since.

In the British Museum is a 0.5-meter (20-inch) jade turtle that symbolizes the world: its carapace is the sky and its belly, the earth.

The mausoleum of Turkish conqueror Tamerlane (1336–1405), the Gūr-e Amir in Samarkand, is covered with a nephrite block from Khotan weighing several hundred kilos.

Central America

Jadeite jade has been carved by the various Central American civilizations. The Olmecs produced their best art between the third and the first centuries B.C. The Mayans produced engraved masks in the fifth and sixth centuries, which are as famous as those from the Toltec civilization at Teotihuacán of the same period. The Toltecs sculpted jaguars and winged snakes in jade.

Starting in the fourteenth century, the Aztecs combined Toltec and Olmec design and added representations of skulls. They instituted a tax in jade, of which they were

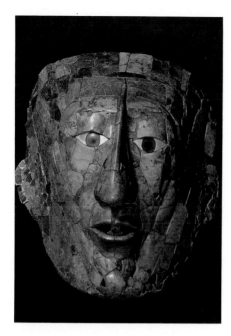

Mayan jade mask. Size: 6 by 8.6 cm. Photo: Bottin.

very fond, and the lack of raw material led to the "recycling" of older objects. Adding to the beautiful presents for Charles V, Montezuma said to Cortés: "And to those [presents] I add a few *chalchihuits* [green stones, jades] of such immense value that I would not give them to anyone but an emperor as powerful as yours, because each of these stones is worth twice its weight in gold."

Farther south, the Jivaros headshrinkers from the Amazon wore jade pendants as amulets.

New Zealand

The Maoris settled North Island, New Zealand, in the tenth century; they colonized South Island in the twelfth century and went hunting for jade. They call jade *pounama,* that is, "green treasure." They carved it into axes, ornate with human designs, talismans that are also used in the cult of the dead.

Physical Properties

Nephrite

Nephrite is a fibrous microcrystalline variety of tremolite, a calcomagnesian silicate, sometimes rich in iron. It is very compact and extremely tough. A high iron content produces a darker color. The extreme iron pole of the series is called actinolite.

The color of nephrite ranges from a grayish white "mutton fat" color to a deep green. Chinese called the green of Khotan nephrites and the color of nehprites with

graphite inclusions from the Baikal "cabbage" and "spinach."

The presence of iron may also produce rare blue colors or even red (in the unusual case of limonite inclusions). The absorption spectrum of ferrous iron may be observed.

Nephrite may contain black magnetite or hematite inclusions or white feldspar inclusions. Its hardness is 6. Its fracture is granular but may appear shiny along the fibers. Its specific gravity is about 3; its index of refraction, 1.61. Nephrite takes an excellent polish and has a characteristic greasy luster, praised by Confucius.

Jadeite

Jadeite jade consists of interlocking jadeite crystals. Jadeite is an aluminosodic silicate belonging to the pyroxene group, with an internal crystalline structure formed by chains of SiO_4 tetrahedra. The aluminum may be replaced in part by chromium or completely by iron (to produce acmite). The calcium and magnesium may also be replaced by sodium and aluminum, to produce diopside. Actually, jadeite jade is an intermediary between these two extremes, but its physical properties are only slightly affected by these replacements.

In a stone with a low iron concentration, the presence of chromium can create a very beautiful emerald-green color; the gem is then called emerald jade or imperial jade. A chromium absorption spectrum can then be observed.

If the iron concentration is high, the color of jadeite becomes dark green: it is then called chloromelanite (from the Greek *khloros,* "green," and *melas,* "black"). But it may display other colors: white (when it is pure), pink, lavender, yellow, and others, depending on which ions substitute for aluminum. Its hardness is 6½ to 7.

The fracture is granular; chloromelanite takes an excellent polish and its shiny

luster distinguishes it from nephrite. This is why Chi Yun said in 1800 that *feits'ui* jade had usurped the jade appellation; numerous jade enthusiasts today agree that jadeite is not jade.

The index of refraction is 1.66, higher for chloromelanite. Its specific gravity is 3.3, higher for chloromelanite, lower if the feldspar content is greater. (At Maw-Sit-Sit, on the Tawmaw Plateau of Myanmar (Burma), is found a bright green rock with a specific gravity of 2.9 that resembles jade. This rock, called maw-sit-sit, comprises a very fine-grained mineral assemblage in which a chromium-rich pyroxene, ueryite, is the coloring agent.)

Jadeite jade is more translucent and has a higher luster than nephrite jade, which has darker, duller colors and a greasier luster.

Deposits

Jades are characteristic of metamorphic rocks formed under high pressure at low temperatures (such as the Alpine jadeites, associated with glaucophane and albite). They also form lenses in serpentines. After weathering, these various-sized lenses always survive in the alluvium because they are so tough.

For years the only source for jade was the Jade Mountain, near Khotan, in the Xinjiang province of China. From this mountain flows the River of White Jade and the River of Black Jade. Jade was "fished" from the rivers by barefoot, young girls, who felt for jade with their feet among the pebbles. Ci Xi (Tz'uhsi), the last Chinese empress, had supposedly been trained to recognize the various qualities of jade by touch only.

Mining of the Jade Mountain, a twenty-day-walk from Khotan, started only in the thirteenth century, as the demand for jade grew. The procedure itself is iden-

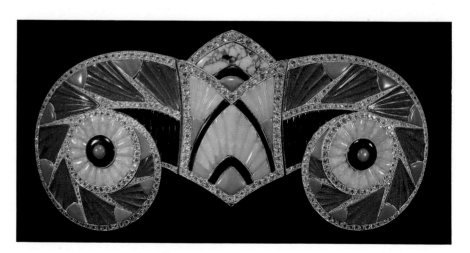

Art deco brooch with jade, lapis, turquoise, coral, onyx, and diamonds (1925). Boucheron collection.

tical to that originally used in the Afghan lapis mines: large fires were built against the rock, which was later cooled quickly with water, to produce fractures. Travelers reported that jade mined in this way was of lesser quality than that found in the rivers.

At the end of the nineteenth century, nephrite from the Baikal was mined and exported to China by Alibert, former barber of the czar. Originally from the Périgord region in France, Alibert always had an interest in the graphite and nephrite of Siberia, producing fabulous trophies with them for the Parisian mineralogical museums. This nephrite was used to carve the sarcophagus of Czar Alexander III in 1897.

Low-quality nephrite is mined today in Taiwan. Other deposits of varying importance exist in the United States and Canada.

In New Zealand, nephrite deposits are difficult to access, and mining is left to the Maoris, who trade only carved objects.

Jadeite is rarer than nephrite. Some isolated sites in the Andes and the Mexican plateaus must have provided raw materials to pre-Columbian civilizations. Today, jadeite is produced only in Myanmar (Burma), probably in alluvial deposits of the upper Irrawaddy Valley. Jadeite is also mined in

quarries on the Tawmaw plateau, 10 kilometers (6 miles) from Mogaung, but only during three months per year, because of the climate.

The Jade Market

The jade market is completely controlled by the Muslim Chinese of Hong Kong. It is extremely difficult to predict what a rough stone for sale will look like once carved. During the 1960s and the 1970s, a Chinese woman gained a reputation throughout the Far East for her ability to make such predictions.

The Working of Jade

Jade is only slightly softer than quartz, and it was worked in the past—with infinite patience—using quartz sand. It appears, however, that "red sand," rich in the more abrasive garnets, was also used, speeding the work. In the thirteenth century, the introduction of "black sand," rich in emery, saved additional time. Today carborundum has supplanted earlier abrasives, allowing the craftspeople to work so fast that quality has declined (it is more difficult

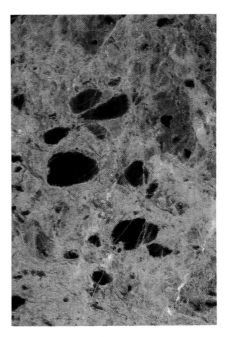

Maw-sit-sit from Myanmar. Length: 4 cm. Becker collection, Idar-Oberstein, Germany.

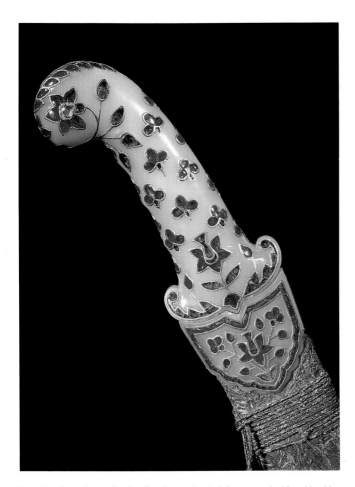

Seventeenth-century Indian kandjar dagger, in steel damascened with gold, with a light jade handle set with precious stones. Islamic section, Musée du Louvre.

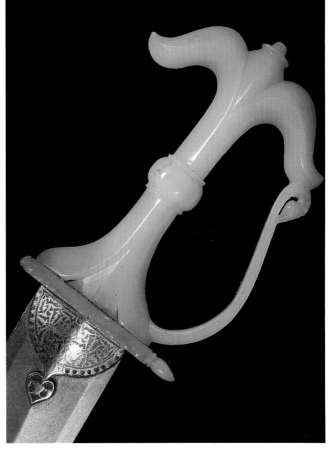

Eighteenth-century Indian dagger, in steel damascened with gold, with a jade handle. Islamic section, Musée du Louvre.

to repair a carving mistake when it is done so quickly).

The first jade plaques were cut with sandstone wheels. During the first millennium, the Chinese invented the *k'un wu,* a marvelous "knife" that was probably a corundum blade. The saw appeared later and became circular, made from steel, in the third century A.D.

Jade Treatments

Older jades preserved in humid graves have a tendency to be altered near the surface and develop a thick patina. Thermal treatment can actually transform the surface of recently carved pieces to give them a similar antique look. Because they are finely grained rocks, jades can absorb dyes easily. Lighter or yellowish jades are therefore often dyed. A hand-held spectroscope can help detect the presence of these dyes, which all tend to fade relatively quickly.

Gems of Similar Appearance

A great variety of green rocks and minerals can imitate green jade more or less convincingly. Those include massive grossular, massive vesuvianite, massive zoisite, saussurite with a high luster, smithsonite, prehnite with a waxy luster, massive apatite (collophane), flawed emerald, massive micas (verdite), steatite with a greasy luster, chalcedonies, aventurine quartz, green marbles, green antique porphyry, fluorite, serpentine, and so on.

These various materials can be distinguished from jade by their hardness, specific gravity, and indices of refraction. The most convincing look-alike is serpentine (which explains why, in China, *yu* also designates serpentine, as well as other green rocks).

Imitations

Glass has been sold as a jade simulant, sometimes molded, sometimes cut. Some ceramics can also imitate jade.

JADEITE

See JADE.

JASPER

A siliceous ornamental rock.

Origin of the Name

Jasper is a very old term, found in all languages: in Hebrew as *iapschpeh,* in Assyrian as *iashpu,* in Persian as *iashm* and *jashp,* in Greek as *iaspis,* transcribed into Latin as *iaspis, iaspe,* and then *jasper.*

Structure and Physical Properties

Jasper is a massive opaque rock with a fine grain, consisting of more than 80 percent microcrystallized quartz in association with other minerals, particularly iron oxides.

Its color is extremely variable, from almost homogeneous colors in red (long considered a remedy for menstrual cramps) or green (which was sometimes worn as a talisman to bring rain) to various color patterns in spots, clouds, scallops, with occasional small cavities filled with quartz. Because of such a variety in patterns, it has received innumerable descriptive names: picture jasper, orbicular jasper, jasp-agate, and ribbon jasper are but a few of them.

Jasper's cohesion is variable, as is its toughness. Its hardness of 6½ and index of refraction of about 1.54 are those of chalcedony. Its specific gravity varies with composition, from 2.6 to 2.9.

Sources and Uses of Jasper

Jasper is widespread, and only particularly attractive stones justify mining: such are the red and green jaspers from the southern Ural and the Altai ranges in the Soviet Union and some jaspers from India, Bohemia, Sicily, the United States, and Africa.

Jasper has been used for beads and cabochons for jewelry, as well as an ornamental material to produce bowls and other decorative objects. It adorns the interiors of such buildings as the Saint Wenceslas Chapel in Prague, which was so decorated by order of Charles IV, king of Bohemia and then German emperor.

JEREMEJEVITE

An aluminum and beryllium borate, crystallizing in the hexagonal system.

Jeremejevite was named for the Russian mineralogist Pavel Eremeyev. It is a very rare mineral, first found as small, colorless, hexagonal crystals in the altered pegmatite of Mount Soktuj (Nerchinsk district of eastern Siberia).

It was then encountered in Namibian pegmatites as crystals up to 6 centimeters long, associated with orthoclase. Jeremejevite was first mistaken for aquamarine. Jeremejevite first appeared as a gemstone in 1973 in a 1.5-carat emerald cut, faceted for a collec-

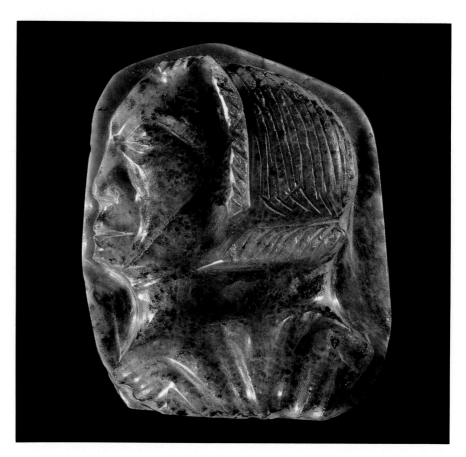

Cameo in jasper. Height: 4.2 cm. M. De Bry collection.

142

Jeremejevite crystal from Namibia. Height: 5 cm. Sorbonne collection.

tor. Some other blue jeremejevites have been cut since. Its hardness is 6½; its specific gravity, 3.28; and its indices of refraction vary from 1.640 to 1.653.

JET

A variety of lignite, produced by the carbonization of conifer remains.

Origin of the Name

The name comes from the Greek *gagates;* Gagas, or Gagates, was a town and a river in Lycia (Asia Minor), where a black rock was found, probably closer to bitumen than to jet. The word *gagates* was used by Pliny the Elder and produced *iaiet* and *jayet* in old French, *jais* in modern French. *Jayet* is still used in Switzerland. *Gagat* is the German word, and the English term is *jet*.

Until the last century, jet was occasionally improperly called black amber because it is found in amber deposits and has electrical properties somewhat similar to those of amber.

The History of Jet

Jet was known and mined on the northeast coast of England (Yorkshire) in the second millennium B.C. Jet beads, pendants, and amulets have been found in old burial grounds. The Romans exported English jet to Rome, where it was fashioned into jewelry; jet was also very highly valued during the Middle Ages. Jet amulets have been found in Native American villages in the southwestern United States. In the eighteenth century, the French *patenôtriers en jais* manufactured jet mourning jewelry, rosaries and crosses; this French craft was very active. At the end of the nineteenth century and the beginning of the twentieth century, several tons of jet were extracted annually (6.2 tons in French Indochina alone in 1895). This material was very popular during the Victorian era and became its symbol at the beginning of the twentieth century, but it is now much less popular. It has also been used to create liturgical ornaments such as bishop's crooks.

Formation and Physical Properties

Jet is produced by the carbonization of vegetal remains in a muddy, anaerobic environment, followed by compaction. It is found in bituminous schists and shales, in relatively small plaques (2 to 15 centimeters [1 to 6 inches] thick). It has a compact texture; the structure of the wood is obscured during lignification and is only rarely visible. Its fracture is conchoidal and quite shiny. Hardness falls between 2½ and 4. Its specific gravity is low, 1.30 to 1.35. Jet is tough and takes a good polish (R.I. around 1.65); it displays a nice velvety black luster. When rubbed briskly, jet may produce some static electricity; according to Pliny, it also emits a strong smell, but this might be due to a confusion with bitumen. Jet burns easily, as all carbonaceous rocks do.

Deposits

The most famous deposit is at Whitby, in Yorkshire, England, where jet is found in a black bituminous shale from the Upper Lias (about 135 million years old). The mining operations there are very old; at the end of the nineteenth century, mining was done via underground shafts about 15 meters (50 feet) deep, but the mines were soon exhausted. From 1 ton in 1888, production dropped to less than a hundred kilograms (200 pounds) in 1897.

French and Spanish deposits have produced excellent-quality jet from glauconious sands and blue clays of the Albian (about 100 million years old). Some chunks weigh as much as 7.5 kilograms. The main mines were in Asturias and Aragon, Spain, and in the Aude department of France. There, during the eighteenth century, 1,200 miners worked in the town of Sainte-Colombe, on the Hers River.

Numerous other deposits were mined at the turn of the century in the Ardennes and Ariège regions of France; in the Schwä-bischen Alpen of Germany, in the Czesto-chowa province of Poland; on Phuquoc Island in the Gulf of Siam, off the southern coast of Kampuchea; in the Irkutsk area of the Soviet Union, and in Colorado, Maryland, and Utah in the United States.

The Working of Jet

Until 1925 jet was worked primarily in Spain, to manufacture mourning jewelry. It is preformed with a steel knife, then on a leather wheel with tripoli and oil; finally, it is polished with the palm of the hand. During fashioning, jet has to be cooled often with water, to avoid cracking. Recently, plastic-impregnated jet made in the United States has been available on the market.

Carbonaceous Rocks Similar to Jet

Cannel coal is a spore lignite rich in volatile material. It burns with a luminous flame and is slightly denser than jet. It was extracted in Scotland as a jet imitation. It is, however, more brittle, less black, and more matte (R.I. of 1.4 to 1.5) than jet and does not polish as well. Cannel coal in large masses has been used to carve vases.

Pennsylvanian anthracite is a slightly metamorphosed coal. It is brittle but very shiny, with a resinous to semimetallic luster, and is relatively dense (1.5 to 1.7). It has been used in North America for carved objects such as vases and bowls, cameos, and mourning jewelry.

Albertite is a natural asphalt with a dark waxy luster. It is light (S.G. is 1.10), soft (H is 2½), and somewhat soluble in organic solvents. Cameos have been carved from it.

Gems Similar to Jet

All black gems may resemble jet, but obsidian and onyx (dyed black chalcedony) are the primary look-alikes. Black tourmaline (schorl) and black garnet (melanite) are more rarely used to imitate it.

Simulants

Jet has long been simulated with black glass, which in the past went under the deceptive name of Paris jet. At the beginning of the twentieth century, hard vulcanized rubber was used in place of jet, but it can be distinguished easily from jet by the large amounts of static electricity produced when the rubber is rubbed with a cloth.

Plastics are fairly convincing imitations, especially Galalithe at the end of the nineteenth century, and later celluloid, Bakelite, and polystyrene. They are easy to detect using a hot needle, which melts them.

k

KORNERUPINE

An aluminum and magnesium borosilicate, crystallizing in the orthorhombic system. Kornerupine was discovered in 1884 and named for A. N. Kornerup, a Danish mineralogist.

Kornerupine is a rare mineral. Its crystals are generally not well formed, but they may be large (23 centimeters in alkaline rocks from Greenland). It has a good cleavage, and its hardness is 6½. The specific gravity of gem material varies from 3.29 to 3.34. The principal indices of refraction range from 1.660 to 1.682; 1.673 to 1.696; and 1.674 to 1.699. The dark yellowish green color, with a distinct green–yellow–brownish red pleochroism, is attributed to iron, which always appears in abundance as a substitute for aluminum (absorption bands due to ferric iron can be seen in the violetish blue region of the transmission spectrum).

The first gem-quality kornerupines were discovered in a Madagascar pegmatite, but the gem-bearing gravels of Sri Lanka are the major source today. Kornerupine is also found in Mogok (Myanmar, formerly Burma), Kenya, Australia, and Greenland.

Faceted stones may reach 10 carats. The Museum of Natural History in Paris owns a 21.5-carat blue-green kornerupine from Madagascar, and the Smithsonian Institution has a 21.6-carat brown one from Sri Lanka.

KUNZITE

Gem spodumene displaying a lilac to pink color, sometimes quite dark. Charles Baskerville named this gem in honor of the American gemologist and mineralogist G. F. Kunz (1856–1932), who first identified this gem as spodumene and developed its use, in particular with Tiffany and Company.

Kunzite displays a very strong trichroism: the colors corresponding to n_p, n_m, and n_g are, respectively, violet, dark violet, and colorless to light yellow. To obtain the best color in a faceted stone, the table should be at an angle of about 25 degrees to the base of the prism. Faceting and polishing must be performed with great care to avoid breakage because of the easy cleavage of this mineral.

The largest faceted kunzite is an 880-carat triangle in the Smithsonian Institution. It is most likely from Itambacuri, in Minas Gerais, Brazil. The same museum displays two other Brazilian kunzites, weighing 336.2 and 296.8 carats. The British Museum owns a 61.7-carat stone.

The pinkish orange luminescence of kunzite is very strong under black light. When subjected to ionizing radiation (such as X rays and gamma rays), kunzite emits a very strong yellowish orange luminescence, followed by a strong phosphorescence. The stone becomes yellowish green with increasing doses of radiation; this color is reminiscent of hiddenite but is not stable in daylight, disappearing within a few days. If irradiation is repeated several times, the crystal no longer returns to its colorless state but retains a distinct green hue. These kunzite colorations have been the source of many disappointments after hasty bargains have been struck.

Historically, the first kunzite crystals were found in the Brancheville pegmatites in Connecticut, where remains of unaltered pink spodumene were spotted. But the first commercially significant deposit was discovered in 1902 at Chief Mountain, in the Pala area of California, where kunzite is associated with rubellite and amblygonite. The first Brazilian deposit was found in 1950 at Barra do Caite, near Conselheiro Pena, where gray spodumenes produce nice kunzites after heat treatment. However, the best kunzite crystals in the world were found in 1963 in an altered pegmatite near the small village of Itambacuri, north of Governador Valadares, in Minas Gerais, Brazil. Several tons of kunzite were uncovered near Fazenda Anglo (now Fazenda do Benedito) between the Rio Urucupa and Surubim rivers. Some crystals weighed 7 kilograms (15 pounds); they were associated with tourmaline and morganite. The two best crystals are in the Smithsonian Institution in Washington, D.C., and in the

Kunzite crystal from Fazenda Anglo, Itambacuri, Minas Gerais, Brazil. Height: 18 cm. K. Proctor collection, United States.

Inclusions and growth figures on the terminal face of an enormous kunzite crystal from Fazenda Anglo, Itambacuri, Minas Gerais, Brazil. Sorbonne collection.

Sorbonne collection of the University of Paris. More than one hundred *garimpeiros* worked this site, which was finally abandoned because of flooding.

Another pegmatite, found in 1968 at Corrego de Urucum, is famous for kunzite: more than 3,000 kilograms (6,600 pounds) of this mineral were extracted. Beautiful crystals of up to 1.7 kilograms (3.7 pounds) were obtained in 1970, when the production reached about 20 kilograms (44 pounds) a month. Kunzites were found in a gigantic cavity, several thousand cubic meters in volume, filled with all sorts of mineral fragments mixed with clay. To maintain prices, the owner took ten years to empty the deposit.

Kunzite has also been encountered in Madagascar, at Anjanabonoina. Important pegmatites, totally unsuspected until then, were discovered in 1970 in the upper Lagham Valley of Nuristan, Afghanistan. Spodumene is associated there with morganite and pink tourmaline and has been found in all its color varieties (from 2- to 3-meter-long rocky crystals to colorless, yellow, green, sometimes green-and-pink, and even pale to dark violet stones). The colored gem varieties vary in dimensions from a few centimeters to more than 60 centimeters for stones from the Mawi pegmatite in the Kolum Valley, a tributary of the Al-

ingar in the upper Laghman. The geodes there can be enormous, with the kunzites implanted on microline and quartz, sometimes accompanied by green or pink tourmaline. It is not unusual to find pieces over 1 kilogram (2 pounds) that are completely gem material. Access to the deposits is very difficult, and the present troubled political situation is not conducive to the development originally planned by the Afghan ministry of mines at the time of the discovery. Kunzite was also recently found in Kashmir pegmatites, in association with beryl and tourmaline.

All gems with a pink to lilac color may be mistaken for kunzite, in particular light amethyst, purple scapolite, morganite, tourmaline, topaz, spinel, and pink sapphire. However, kunzite's color and physical properties are very characteristic.

Kunzite has been imitated by synthetic pink corundum, often commercially described as being of a "kunzite color," as well as by synthetic pink spinel and even glass of the same color.

KYANITE

An aluminosilicate, crystallizing in the triclinic system, a polymorph with andalusite and sillimanite.

Called kyanite by Abraham Werner in 1789 because of its color (from the Greek *kuanos,* "blue"), this mineral was also named *disthène* by Renè-Just Haüy in 1801 because of its strong anisotropy in scratch hardness (from the Greek *dis,* "two," and *sthenos,* "solidity"). Indeed, the hardness within a single crystal changes from 5 to 7, depending on direction. Its cleavage is excellent, and it also has fracture planes due to multiple twinning, which make this mineral very difficult to facet. These fractures are seen as inclusions in all faceted kyanites.

Kyanite's typical color is light blue, with some darker blue, sometimes greenish areas. Its pleochroism is strong (violetish blue–colorless–dark blue). Indices of refraction are 1.713, 1.722, and 1.729. It is biaxial negative, with a birefringence of 0.017. The specific gravity of gem kyanite is 3.65. When cut into cabochons, the fibrous variety, hard to identify, becomes chatoyant and resembles sillimanite.

Kyanite is a common high-pressure mineral, produced by regional metamorphism of aluminous rocks, and is often associated with staurolite and garnet. Good specimens come from Sultan Hamib in Kenya; exceptional gem-quality crystals have been recently recovered in Brazil, where stones weighing as much as 10 to 25 carats have been faceted.

l

LABRADORITE

See FELDSPAR; SPECTROLITE.

LAPIS LAZULI

A dark blue rock of variable composition; its color is determined by the amount of its principal mineral constituent, lazurite (a sodium and calcium aluminosilicate rich in sulfur).

Origin of the Name

Lapis lazuli comes from the Latin *lapis,* meaning "stone," and the Arabic *azul,* which means "blue." The name of this rock

has changed often since ancient times. Theophrastus (372–287 B.C.), Pliny the Elder (A.D. 23–79) and Georgius Agricola (Georg Bauer, 1494–1555) called it sapphire; they described it as a star-filled sky or as a blue material punctuated by golden specks. Both descriptions fit lapis lazuli quite well, since it is rich in golden pyrite inclusions.

The word *lazurium* appeared during the sixth century A.D. as a derivation of the Persian *ladjevard,* which designated the color blue, became *lazul* in Arabic, and was distorted to *azur.*

In the fifth century A.D., lapis lazuli was introduced to Europe under the Latin name *ultramarinum.* Translated literally, this word means "beyond the sea," referring to its distant provenance. The derivation *ultramarine* now describes a family of silicate

minerals that includes nosean, sodalite, haüynite (haüyne), and lazurite.

The History and Uses of Lapis

There is no shortage of archaeological evidence for extensive lapis trade in early civilizations. The city-states of Sumer (in southern Mesopotamia, in the Middle East), including Erech, Ur, Lagash, and Eridu, were constantly at war with each other, fighting for hegemony. The outcome of these struggles significantly affected the lapis-lazuli trade, since its monopoly changed hands frequently. The city of Ur, which reached its zenith in the fourth millennium B.C., created some of the most ostentatious and interesting lapis artifacts, which were discovered in the tombs of the royal cemetery: cylinder

Dove in Afghan lapis lazuli from the end of the second millennium, found in Susa, Iran. Length: 15 cm. Musée du Louvre.

ous, as it still is today, both because of the incursions of the Kafirs, a predatory tribe from neighboring Nuristan, and because of the treacherous trail winding along very steep canyons. A local proverb warned: "If you do not want to die, avoid the Koran Valley" (the upper valley of the Kokcha River).

Today lapis lazuli is mostly worked in Western countries into small pieces for jewelry; it is commonly carved into figurines in the Orient. During the Renaissance and even more recently, lapis lazuli was abundantly used in inlays: numerous Florentine tables have lapis lazuli backgrounds. The palace in Tsarskoye Selo (now Pushkin, near Saint Petersburg) has lapis-lazuli paneling, and the columns of Saint Isaac's Cathedral in Saint Petersburg are lined with this gem.

In ancient times, lapis lazuli was apparently used mostly as the pigment ultramarine, a bright azure color used by painters, which was superseded only in 1826, when J. B. Guimet developed an inexpensive synthetic. The preparation of ultramarine pigment, detailed in several seventeenth-century formulas, was rather complex: it required several days and basically consisted of separating lazurite from its associated minerals. Steps included crushing, heating, cleaning with vinegar, drying on agate, and separating impurities with a paste made of resin, wax, or linseed oil, to finally extract the very pure pigment.

Like most gems, lapis lazuli has been credited with metaphysical properties. In Rome it was supposed to have a powerful aphrodisiac effect on its owner at the right moment. In the Middle Ages, it kept limbs healthy, made the body younger, freed the soul from error, envy, and fear, and interceded with God. As a powder, it prevented fevers and headaches and protected the eyes. But "only a pure heart [could] enjoy such benefits from the azur stone" (Marbodus, eleventh century).

Mineralogical and Petrographical Characteristics

Lazurite can be thought of as a sulfur-rich variety of haüyne; the large structural sites available in the very open cubic aluminosilicate structure are occupied by calcium, sodium, sulfate, and sulfur ions. Crystals are rare, always have a cubic dodecahedral shape, and may exceptionally reach 5 centimeters (2 inches) in diameter. They sometimes grow around phlogopite crystals. Their cleavage is excellent; the hardness of 5½ is somewhat low for a gem material. The index of refraction of lapis lazuli is about 1.5, and its specific gravity varies from 2.7 to 2.9, depending on the concentration of pyrite and other accessory minerals. Under long-wave ultraviolet light, scattered scapolite crystals produce an orange punctuation, more pronounced in

seals, balls, and carvings of various animals (ibex, stags, and birds, among others). The abundance of the blue stone was such that the surplus was exported to Egypt by sea (navigation with sailboats was known since the middle of the fifth millennium). The rich Mesopotamian cities controlled the distribution of lapis lazuli, which followed the great route of Khorāsān, marked by the major satellite cities of Susa, Giyān, Sialk, and Hissar. Gradually, these towns freed themselves from Mesopotamian sovereignty to become the first Persian kingdoms and took over the lapis-lazuli trade to their own advantage.

The lapis lazuli used in the palace of the Persian king Darius I (522–486 B.C.) during the Achaemenid period, always came from Sogdiana (presently Badakhshān, Afghanistan). Badakhshān was first mentioned in Chinese records from the sixth and eighth centuries and was then considered to be part of the Tukharistan. It became Muslim in 736, and the small town of Jurm,

150 kilometers (90 miles) north of the lapis mines, was the border town of Islam on the commercial road that led to Tibet through the Wakhan corridor. Arab geographers described Badakhshān as a region of rich pastures and farms that extended considerably westward and eastward. Marco Polo wrote: "There is also in this country a mountain where the finest azur in the world comes from. It is found in veins like silver."

At the beginning of the eighteenth century, mining methods were the same as those used many centuries earlier. Large fires were built against the rock, and when its temperature was high enough, it was sprayed with cold water. The sudden temperature change fractured the limestone, which was later chiseled away to extract the lapis lazuli. John Wood, a British officer in the East India Company's navy, visited these mines in December 1837 and was the first to accurately describe this part of Badakhshān.

The access to the deposits was danger-

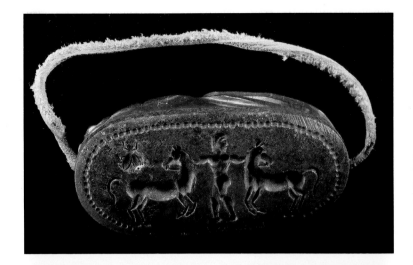

Etruscan scarab in lapis lazuli, dated to 600 B.C. Length: 4 cm. German Precious Stones Museum, Idar-Oberstein, Germany.

Mesopotamian cylinder seal in lapis lazuli. Height: 3 cm. Musée du Louvre.

Chilean lapis lazuli than in the Afghan material.

Most often, lapis lazuli is massive and microcrystalline, with a color varying from very light blue (lazurite associated with nepheline or calcite) to a resplendent violetish blue for the most valued varieties (almost pure lazurite). A number of minerals can be found as inclusions; pyrite is common and may even evoke gold, for which some have mistaken it. Actually, pyrite is more of a defect, because it eventually decomposes, leaving small cavities that alter the appearance of the polished rock. Such silicates as diopside, scapolite, forsterite, augite, and hornblende can influence the color of lapis lazuli if they are abundant enough.

Lapis lazuli is sensitive to chemicals: all acids attack its calcareous component, and hydrochloric acid decomposes lazurite to produce the odor of rotten eggs. Objects containing lapis lazuli should be cleaned with soapy water exclusively.

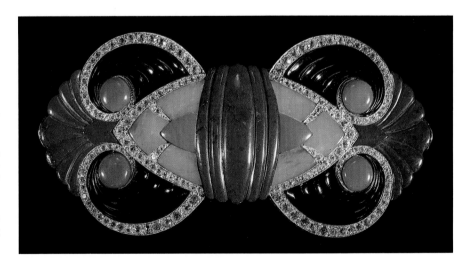

Brooch with lapis lazuli, jade, coral, and diamonds, crafted around 1931. Length: 10.7 cm. Boucheron collection.

Lapis-lazuli rhyton in the form of an ibex, an example of Achaemenid art from the fifth century B.C. Height: 48 cm. Photo: Held-Ziolo.

Deposits

In addition to the historic deposits still mined in Afghanistan, lapis lazuli has been found in Iran, in the Pamir Mountains, around Lake Baïkal, in Chile, in California, and in Myanmar (Burma).

In Iran lapis lazuli was reported in the Kachan area by numerous authors, particularly Hamud Allah Mostowfi (1316–55). It turned out to be dumortierite, whose blue to violet color resembles average-quality lapis lazuli.

In Siberia lapis lazuli was found in 1797 by an expedition sent by Empress Catherine the Great, who was intrigued by pebbles of this rock brought from the Lake Baikal area to Saint Petersburg in 1784. The primary deposit in the Sludyanka, Talaya, and Lazurnia valleys was not found until 1851. The production is minor and episodic, primarily because the host rock is a magnesium-rich marble quarried essentially to produce concrete.

In Soviet Pamir, lapis-lazuli deposits were discovered in 1930 by famed mineralogist A. I. Fersman (1883–1945), following the Ladjevard Dara ("Lapis-lazuli Valley"). They are located at an altitude of 5,000 meters (16,000 feet) and are said to be similar to the Afghan deposits.

In Chile lapis lazuli has been mined since the late nineteenth century in the Ovalle Cordillera, close to Antofagasta, near the springs of the Cazadores and Vias rivers, tributaries of the Rio Grande. As in other deposits, it is associated with marble but contains more white elements, which makes it less attractive than Afghan lapis lazuli. A dozen other Chilean deposits are also known, and the total production is significant.

Intense blue lapis lazuli, full of pyrite inclusions and with some calcite veins, has been sporadically extracted from the Italian Mountain in Colorado since 1939. It is, however, more of a mineralogical curiosity. In 1979 an important outcrop was discovered in the San Gabriel Mountains in the Angeles National Forest, at an altitude of 3,000 meters (almost 10,000 feet). Lapis lazuli forms parallel veinlets interstratified with pyrite-rich marbles. The mine, called Bighorn, produces stones of quality similar to the Afghan material; however, it is difficult to reach and is located in an area to which access has been restricted by the National Forest Service.

In Myanmar lapis lazuli has been found in the Dattaw Valley, close to the Mogok ruby mines.

The Historic Sar-e-Sang Deposit

The famous lapis-lazuli deposits of the Badakhshān province in northeastern Afghanistan are located at an altitude of 2,500 meters (over 8,000 feet) on the right bank of the Kokcha River, a tributary of the Amu Darya (known as the Oxus River in ancient times), 200 kilometers (125 miles) from Kabul as the crow flies.

Whatever the route, it takes at least four days to reach the mine from Kabul. One can follow the Pandjchir Valley for 160 kilometers (100 miles) with a four-wheel-drive vehicle and then go by foot or horse 135 kilometers (83 miles) over the Anjuman path. The other possibility is to drive to Kundūz on the magnificent road that follows the Salang path and continue on a difficult trail through the villages of Khanabad, Taliqan, Faizābād, and Jurm, which ends 3 or 4 kilometers (about 2 miles) from Hazrat-Saïd, covering in total 750 kilometers (465 miles) from Kabul. Then one has to ascend the 40 kilometers (25 miles)

Nineteenth-century lapis-lazuli talisman from Afghanistan, engraved with gold letters. Length: 3 cm. National Higher School of Mines, Paris.

Lapis-lazuli crystal from Sar-e-Sang, Badakhshān, Afghanistan. Diameter: 3 cm. Sorbonne collection.

The abandoned Darreh-Zu mine, near Sar-e-Sang, Badakhshān, Afghanistan. Note the traces of fire, used to fracture the rock. Photo: P. Bariand.

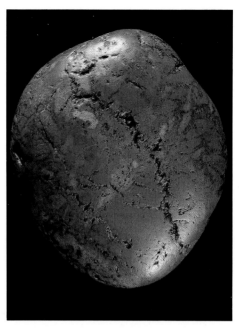

Lapis-lazuli pebble from the bed of the Kokcha River, Badakhshān, Afghanistan. Diameter: 8 cm. Private collection.

of narrow, rough track along the steep Kokcha Valley, in a high mountainous area cut by several narrow canyons. The vegetation is scarce, with only some tamarisk barely surviving at the bottom of the valley.

Climatic conditions are such that both routes are open only from June to November, and the Sar-e-Sang mine is worked for four months per year maximum. The base camp is located on the right bank of the Kokcha River, next to the confluence of the Kokcha torrent, at an altitude of 2,500 meters (8,000 feet).

This deposit consists of highly metamorphized rocks with gneisses, crystallized limestones (marbles), skarns, veins of white granite, and dykes of pyroxenites and hornblendites found in huge blocks in the river. Lapis lazuli forms beds or lenses varying in thickness from 1 to 4 meters (3 to 13 feet), with a lateral extension of 20 to 100 meters (65 to 328 feet), rarely reaching 400 meters (1,312 feet). The zones appropriate for mining are basically associations of dolomite and calcite, with forsterite, diopside, and scapolite often accompanied by phlogopite. The blue material is almost always associated with abundant fine-grained pyrite.

Lapis lazuli blocks are carried on the miners' backs to base camp, then with donkeys to Hazrat-Saïd. The yearly production is never very large; it was about 5 tons at the beginning of the nineteenth century and today is approximately 1 ton of excellent material. Two hundred kilos (about 400 pounds) go to Afghan lapidaries; the balance is exported. The ministry of mines sorts the pieces into five categories, ranging in value from 1 to 3. The first category, about 2 percent of the production, that is, about 20 kilograms (45 pounds), represents massive blocks of dark blue material, without inclusions or cracks, and the second category (14 percent of the production), essentially the same quality but with smaller blocks, less than 5 centimeters (2 inches) in size, are intended for jewelry. The other categories are used for carving ornamental objects; their color varies from light to dark blue, they show veins of calcite, and they contain varying amounts of pyrite.

Other Blue Ornamental Stones

Four blue ornamental stones resemble lapis lazuli well enough for two of them—lazulite and azurite—to have the same etymology as lazurite and for the other two —dumortierite and sodalite—to often be mistaken for lapis lazuli.

Imitations

Enamel and Glass

The azure blue color of lapis was very popular in the Middle East, generating the production of blue enamels intended to resemble the color of lapis lazuli. This was particularly true in Egypt, where apparently appearance was more important than authenticity. During the second millennium, Mycenaean jewelers used the champlevé technique. Cloisonné was used during the Egyptian Middle Kingdom (Thebes, early in the second millennium), and cloisonné enamel was already well developed by the

Ornamental Stones Like Lapis Lazuli

Material	Average S.G.	Hardness	Associated Minerals
Azurite	3.8	3½	Malachite
Lazulite	3.1	5½	
Lazurite	2.8	5½	Pyrite, calcite
Sodalite	2.3	5½	Feldspars, biotite
Dumortierite	3.3	7	Often included in quartz

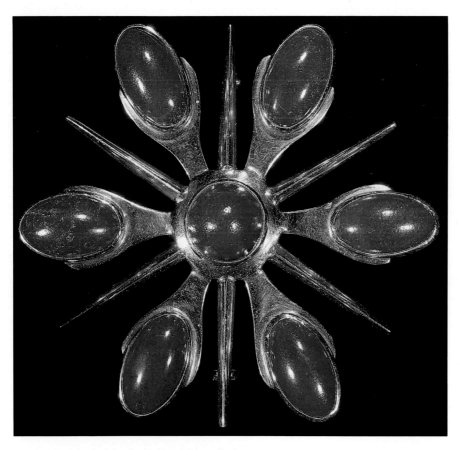

Brooch with Afghan lapis-lazuli cabochons. Private collection.

commonly used; they are easily dissolved with acetone (nail-polish remover) and sometimes by sweat (so that a dyed lapis necklace may "bleed" on its owner's neck). More resistant dyestuffs may be used. On occasion, overly white lapis lazuli is tinted with ultramarine powder mixed with the abrasive on the polishing lap, so that only the stone's surface is blue; the smallest scrape shows its true nature, essentially white calcite. More and more material from the lapis-lazuli mines are dyed; they *really* are actually no more than dyed marbles and are very common in India.

Synthetic Lapis Lazuli

The synthetic lapis lazuli produced since 1974 by the Gilson company is actually synthetic ultramarine powder sintered with or without small pyrite crystals. This dark blue material is porous and does not contain any resin. It is discolored on contact by hydrochloric acid, with a weak effervescence. Its mineralogical characteristics are closer to sodalite rather than lazurite, so the name "synthetic lapis lazuli" may be something of a misnomer.

LAZULITE

An alumino-ferro-magnesian phosphate, crystallizing in the monoclinic system. This blue mineral was formerly called klaprothite, in honor of the German mineralogist Martin Klaproth.

Lazulite forms mostly transparent, dark blue masses, which may resemble lapis lazuli despite their darker, more somber tone. It is associated with kyanite and rutile in the Graves Mountain quartzites of Georgia. It is also found in Madagascar and Brazil. In recent years, remarkable crystals associated with rare phosphates have been found in the Yukon Territories of Canada. Its specific gravity is 3.08, its hardness 5½, and its index of refraction about 1.62. It is considered a collector's stone.

LYDIAN STONE

A matte black jasper of very fine grain, formed by siliceous layers of radiolarians (marine plankton) cemented with a mixture of clay-, iron-, and carbon-rich compounds. Lydian stone is used by jewelers to test the gold content of an alloy by examining the color of the trace left on the stone by the metal (hence, the name touchstone is sometimes used for it).

Named for Lydia, a region of Asia Minor where it was first found, this stone was used for metals testing when precious metal coins were first manufactured, in the seventh century B.C. by King Ardys (657–617 B.C.).

time of the Assyrian epoch in the seventh century B.C. Enamel is still commonly used today, in particular for marble statuettes and vases, where it is intended to pass for lapis lazuli with pyrite inclusions.

In the third century B.C., large glass centers in Syria produced glass beads in series, particularly blue beads. Glass that is colored blue with traces of cobalt is still in use today, although it is much less common since the development of artificial lapis lazuli. Manufacturers try to avoid creating too homogeneous a color by creating wisps of various tints. To better imitate "star-studded" lapis, so much in vogue in Latin countries, they occasionally mixed aventurine glass (charged with small triangular or hexagonal platelets of copper) with the blue glass.

Dyed Jasper

Jasper dyed with Prussian blue (potassium ferrocyanide) is the most common lapis-lazuli imitation used in fashion jewelry. This product is fairly convincing, despite the absence of pyrite (or golden specks), which is actually little valued in Germany. The dye penetrates the porous jasper irregularly, leaving small white veins and quartz clusters reminiscent of calcite in-

clusions in lapis lazuli. This imitation was called by the deceptive name German lapis or Swiss lapis between the two World Wars.

Synthetic Spinel

In 1954 a German company introduced a synthetic cobalt-blue spinel sintered with some pyrite to re-create the polycrystalline appearance of lapis lazuli. It met with little success.

Aggregates and Resins

A fairly convincing imitation of lapis consists of crushed marble, dyed with copper sulfate, and sintered with a resin to crushed pyrite. These imitations, deceptively called reconstructed lapis, are fairly common. Their texture is always homogeneous but may be more or less coarse, depending on the grain size of the raw materials. A hot needle decomposes these products into a white powder.

Dyed Lapis Lazuli

Much of the Chilean and Afghan lapis lazuli has too many white inclusions to be truly attractive. The light blue color is thus reinforced with dyes, which penetrate among the grains. Organic dyes are most

m

MAGNETITE

An iron oxide, crystallizing in the cubic system.

According to Nicander (second century B.C.), as cited by Pliny the Elder, magnetite was named for the shepherd Magnes, who discovered it on Mount Ida, in Crete, when the nails of his shoes and the point of his crook stuck to the stone. However, it seems more likely that the name came from the famous antique deposits of Heraklion in Magnesia (now Thessaly, Greece); indeed, the Greeks called the stone *heraklia lithos,* literally "Heraklion stone," and later, *magnes lithos,* "Magnesia stone."

Magnetite is found in all intrusive rocks. Its hardness of 5½ to 6½ and high specific gravity of 5.18 make it a typical alluvial mineral. It was known in India as black diamond, symbolizing the Sudra caste. It probably is the source of the belief that diamond attracts iron and reconciles spouses. Magnetite has occasionally been cut for collectors.

It is frequently found as small octahedral crystals included in gem materials such as spinel and serpentine.

MALACHITE

A hydrous copper carbonate.

Origin of the Name

The word comes from the Greek *malakhe,* which means "mallow," a medicinal plant with variegated green leaves and pink to purple flowers; during the preparation of soothing infusions of it, mallow develops green bands and scallops reminiscent of those produced by malachite.

In the fourth century B.C., Theophrastus identified malachite with chrysocolla and turquoise, using the name *pseudes smaragdos,* literally "false emerald," which later became "bastard emerald" and "fake emerald." Although he described certain types as particular varieties of emerald, Pliny the Elder separately mentioned *molochite,*

which showed "a matter and darker green than emerald"; he said it served as an amulet to protect children. Scholars during the Middle Ages retained the Latin names and tradition in their works, but Boece de Boot wrote in 1604 about *"de malachite, vel molochite."* The French language of the Middle Ages included the terms *melochite* or *melocete,* and also *malaquite* in the dialect of Champagne, as early as the thirteenth century. German miners, as reported by Georgius Agricola in 1546, referred to *Berggrün,* "mountain green," just like they called azurite *Bergblau,* "mountain blue," which was translated in French at the time into *verd'azur* (literally "azure green"), referring to the azurite-malachite association.

The History of Malachite

In the seventeenth century, Pierre de Rosnel stated that malachite was common and that he paid little attention to it. However, it was highly valued in Russia, where it was used extensively during the nineteenth century to decorate palaces and churches. The walls of an entire room of the palace at Tsarskoye Selo are covered with malachite. Some pillars of Saint Isaac's Cathedral in Saint Petersburg are covered with malachite and lapis lazuli. The famous malachite columns of the ancient Artemis temple in Ephesus are now in the Saint Sophia Cathedral in Istanbul. Numerous palaces that are now museums (for example, the Hermitage Museum in Saint Petersburg and several royal and imperial residences in France, such as Trianon and Malmaison) own massive malachite tables, some with slabs as large as 90 by 65 by 5 centimeters (35 by 25 by 2 inches) and large nineteenth-century malachite vases.

Physical Properties

Malachite forms mamillary or stalactitic concretions with a concentric color banding. The alternating colors are a very dark green, a very light green, and a light green

Malachite earrings. Fred creation.

with dark emerald-green spots having a silky appearance, due to the presence of parallel acicular crystals. It often forms azurite pseudomorphs, with azurite remains in the center of the formation. All these colored variations are best enhanced by polishing. Despite its fragility (a hardness of 3½ to 4, susceptible to effervescence by weak acids), malachite is a very popular ornamental stone because of its vast array of green colors distributed in harmonious concentric patterns. Its specific gravity is about 4.

Malachite spheres and a 16-cm-tall malachite egg from Zaire. Chatta collection.

Polished slab of malachite from the Ural Mountains, in the U.S.S.R. Diameter: 10 cm. Sorbonne collection.

Deposits

Malachite is a common mineral found in the oxidation zone of copper deposits. Although it is widespread around the world, only few deposits produce high-quality material in quantity. The dimensions of malachite blocks are sometimes considerable; however, they can be used to carve large objects only if they are free of cavities and crumbly or less cohesive portions.

The most famous antique deposit in Cyprus was mentioned by all the authors of ancient times, the Middle Ages, and the Renaissance. The renowned deposits of the Urals, Nizhni Tagil and Bogolovsk in the north, and Gumeskevsk in the south, were discovered at the beginning of the nineteenth century, close to the cutting center of Ekaterinburg. They are formed in karstic limestones in which malachite fills the fractures, forming very large masses. Blocks of over 150 kilograms (300 pounds) have been extracted. The Saint Petersburg (Leningrad) Mining Museum keeps a block of malachite weighing over a ton and measuring 1 by 2 meters (3¼ by 6½ feet). The record seems to be a 30-ton mass, all cuttable, extracted at Gumeskevsk in 1835. These intensely mined deposits were soon exhausted, and only the Medro Rudiansk mine was still active at the end of the nineteenth century; it has now been exhausted as well.

So malachite, abundant during the nineteenth century, became sparse at the beginning of the twentieth century. But mines in the Belgian Congo (now Zaire) again made it popular, so that it is almost common again today. Malachite is abundant in the upper levels of the Shaba (formerly Katanga) copper mines. It forms thick crusts and stalactites in the numerous cavities of the local dolomitic layers. For example, a 3.5 by 2.6-meter (11½ by 8½-foot) plaque was found in the Luiswishi quarry, and stalactites 50 centimeters (20 inches) high and 20 centimeters (8 inches) in diameter are frequently found in the Sesa mine in Kakanda. Very active local craftspeople produce animals, ashtrays, spheres, even some very large (40-centimeter- [15-inch] high) eggs, a situation similar to that in the Urals in the last century.

MARBLE

A calcareous rock (made of calcium carbonate). Its name refers to its shiny luster, from the Greek *marmaros* ("shiny stone").

True Marble

True marble, as defined by geologists (a metamorphic rock formed essentially of calcite), is used extensively in statuary (such are the Paros and Carrara marbles) but rarely in jewelry.

However, green serpentine marbles, for example the green marble of Ha Tien in Vietnam, resembling jade, are carved in the Orient and sold to naive tourists as jade.

Travertine and Other Calcareous Concretions Called Onyx Marbles

Essentially made of calcite, calcareous concretions may form light-color rocks with scalloped motifs, which vary in hue from amber to orange to green. Their appearance is similar to that of alabaster. They were used in the past to make ointment boxes, so they were referred to by the adjective *onyx* (see also ALABASTER).

By calling them *alabastrites*, the Greeks differentiated them from alabaster, but the terms *marble, alabaster,* and *onyx* are often misunderstood and used improperly. Today most "true onyx" souvenirs bought by tourists (such as boxes, ashtrays, and lamps) are actually onyx marble, quite different from the onyx used in jewelry.

The physical properties of these scalloped limestones are significantly different from those of calcite: they have a low hardness (3), their specific gravity varies from 2.6 to 2.7, and their index of refraction is difficult to read with a refractometer (the ordinary ray of calcite often produces a shadow at about 1.5). They are porous and should not be exposed to acids, which cause them to effervesce and produce carbon dioxide. Travertines are widespread; historically, the Egyptian deposits of the Alabastron area near Thebes, mined in ancient times, provided the raw material for the carving of amphorae, vases, ointment boxes, and other objects. Today the production of "marble" for most ornamental objects comes from North Africa (Constantine, Oran, and the Algeria-Morocco border), Pakistan, Iran, Afghanistan, Mexico, and Argentina. In Gibraltar a calcareous material is sold to tourists, often as cabochons.

Assorted Sedimentary Limestones

Limestones are often used for statuary. They are sometimes dyed, as was the fine-grained limestone statue of Philippa de Gueldre in the Eglise des Cordeliers in Nancy, France, where the black color of the robe was produced by Ligier Richier using soot. They are also a primary material for various showcase objects. Encrinital limestone has been dyed red to imitate coral.

MARCASITE

The name by which jewelers refer to pyrite ("marcasites are angular pyrites," Chriten, 1868). Indeed, the words *pyrite* and *marcasite,* which have different origins, were synonymous until 1814, when René-Just Haüy differentiated the two species. The word *marcasite—marcassin* in Old French—may derive from the generic German word *Kiess,* which designates all metallic ores resembling stones. *Marmorkiess* may have been contracted into *Markiess:* "Some *marcassins,*" wrote Jean Bachou, translator of Boece de Boot, "shine like the metallic marble which grows with metals."

Marcasite is currently defined by mineralogists as an orthorhombic iron sulfide, easily altered. It may form radial spherulitic aggregates in sediments; in Champagne, France, these formations are locally called "thunder balls" and are often mistaken for meteorites.

MEERSCHAUM

See SEPIOLITE.

MELANITE

A black andradite, named for its color (from the Greek *melas,* "black"), used primarily in mourning jewelry.

Melanite has high specific gravity (3.7 to 3.9) and a high index of refraction (1.8 to 1.9), and it offers good resistance to scratches (H is 6½ to 7). It is a common metamorphic mineral, found, for example, in Monte Somma, Italy, and in California.

MICROCLINE

See AMAZONITE.

MOLDAVITE

A natural brownish green siliceous glass of meteoritic origin. It is found on the banks of the Vltava River in Czechoslovakia. This name, however, has also been used to designate glass-factory rejects, so any "stones" should be examined skeptically.

MOONSTONE

A variety of orthoclase microperthite (sodopotassic feldspar), also called adularia. Moonstone consists of alternating parallel planes of potassium-rich (orthoclase) and sodium-rich (albite) feldspars, forming an assemblage called a microperthite. The thinner component layers are smaller than visible wavelengths and scatter light, creating a nacreous or silvery appearance, with a bluish sheen called adularescence. This sheen is reminiscent of lunar light, especially when the stone is cut into a round cabochon, hence the name *moonstone.* Its luster is soft (index of refraction of about 1.52), and its specific gravity varies from 2.56 to 2.59, depending on the sodium content.

Most moonstones come from the gem-bearing gravels of Sri Lanka, but they are also found near Madras, in India; in Madagascar; and in the United States. Adularias from the Swiss alpine clefts produce very attractive stones after faceting.

Moonstone can resemble white chalcedony, as well as girasol quartz, which is sometimes produced by decolorizing citrine with a heat treatment, which explains its curious trade name, white citrine. Moonstone imitations in opalescent glass or synthetic spinel (with a girasol effect produced by annealing) have been encountered. Green moonstone is a slightly adularescent sodic feldspar (albite).

MORGANITE

A pink beryl with a slight tint of purple and little or no orange. This mineral was named by American mineralogist G. F. Kunz in honor of J. P. Morgan, the famous American banker and gem collector. The name *vorobyevite* was coined in 1908 by Vladimir Vernadsky for a pink beryl rich in cesium, in honor of V. I. Vorobyev (1875–1906), but this term is generally used only by Soviet authors.

The largest faceted morganite is in the British Museum, a 598.70-carat cushion shape cut from a crystal from Madagascar, measuring 51 by 38 millimeters (2 by 1.5 inches), with a very intense pink color. The Smithsonian Institution owns 235.5-carat and 250-carat step-cut Brazilian morganites, and the American Museum of Natural History in New York, a 235-carat stone.

Because it is rich in alkali elements, the gemological properties of morganite are higher than in other beryls: it has a specific gravity of 2.8 to 2.9 and indices of refraction of 1.577 to 1.662 for the ordinary ray and 1.512 to 1.595 for the extraordinary ray, with a birefringence of .007 to .009. Morganite can exhibit a very attractive pink color, which is attributed to a substitution of manganese and some alkali elements (lithium, rubidium, cesium) for aluminum. This gem is found in lithium-rich pegmatites, accompanied by other lithium minerals (lepidolite-mica, kunzite, pink tourmaline).

Morganite was first discovered in the Pala pegmatites in California. It was found as early as 1908 at Maharitra, Madagascar, often associated with pink tourmalines. There, it forms beautiful, perfectly transparent crystals reaching a maximum size of 20 centimeters with a violetish pink color, sometimes with a touch of orange or purple. Beautifully colored morganite is also reported in the Mount Bity area, at Anjanabonoina, south of Betafo, Madagascar.

153

Morganite crystal from Corrego do Urucum, Minas Gerais, Brazil. Width: 25 cm. Sorbonne collection.

These samples of outstanding quality contributed to the fame of this magnificent gem. It is, unfortunately, quite rare and has no equivalent in the world: high-quality morganite remains a collector's item.

Remarkable crystals have been discovered in recent years in the state of Minas Gerais, Brazil, where two deposits are particularly worthy of notice. In the Itambacuri

area (Fazenda Anglo), north of Governador Valadares, morganite is associated with kunzite. Superb crystals were found in 1968 in a geode nine meters (30 feet) tall by three meters (10 feet) in diameter in the famous Corrego do Urucum mine, near Galiléa, about 75 kilometers (45 miles) southwest of Governador Valadares. The walls of this cavity were lined with albite crystals and fine dark green tourmaline needles, on which were about two hundred morganite crystals. They display the habitual morphology of a flattened hexagonal prism. The largest, 20 centimeters (8 inches) in diameter, is now part of the Sorbonne collection in Paris. The geode was filled with all kinds of mineral debris, which had to be hauled out to collect the beryl crystals. These were certainly the best morganite crystals found to date. Morganites are also associated with tourmalines in the Sapucaia and Barra de Salinas pegmatites 50 kilometers (30 miles) northeast of Aracuai. Discovered at the turn of the century, they were seriously mined only after 1945; today the mines are abandoned. Since 1960 orange-to-salmon-color beryl from some Brazilian pegmatites has been heat-treated at the mine, using a glass tube over an alcohol flame. The stones

become pale pink, because the yellow component disappears from the original color. Such material represents the majority of the morganites on the market today.

Elsewhere, morganite is found in Mozambique (Muiane area), in Namibia, and in the Urals. In Afghanistan, in 1970, the Mawi mine in the upper Laghman Valley produced remarkable morganite crystals associated with pink tourmalines and kunzite. But no morganite from those localities can compare with the Madagascar morganites.

Morganite used for jewelry is generally flawless; occasionally, small albite crystals and fine rutile needles are found as inclusions. Kunzite, pale amethyst, and pink topaz may simulate morganite. Pink glass, and especially pink synthetic spinel and corundum, are used as imitations.

MORION

A dark brown to black quartz. The name comes from the Greek *morion* ("mandrake seed"). Pliny the Elder also called it *pramnion,* from the name of a hill on Ikaria Island, famous for its generous red wine. See QUARTZ: SMOKY QUARTZ.

n

Necklace illustrating the use of white and black nacre, with coral, emerald, and diamonds. Chaumet design.

NACRE

A calcareous concretion produced by the mantle in various mollusks, which lines their shells.

Origin of the Name

From both the Persian *nakar* and the Arabic *naqqara* ("drum"), this word first became *naccaro* and then *nacchera* in Italian. *Nacre* is the French variation, also used in English.

The History of Nacre

Shell jewelry has been crafted since prehistoric times, and Polynesian peoples sometimes used certain shells as currency. Nacre was used during ancient times for inlays, together with tortoise shell and ivory. During the Renaissance cabinets were often decorated with such nacre inlays.

Since the Renaissance, thick shells with nacre layers of two different colors have been used to carve shell cameos. This fashion was imported to France during wars with Italy, from which Francis I brought back famous engravers (such as Matteo dal Nassaro, who became Director of the Monnaie). Among the shell cameos from this period, Diane de Poitiers's bracelet and the buttons of Henry IV representing the twelve Caesars have achieved some notoriety. Shell cameos were popular in the

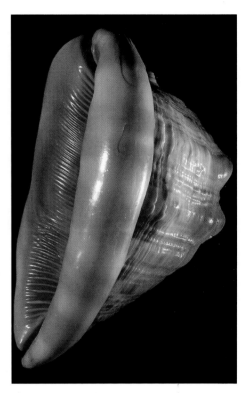

Nineteenth-century shell cameo depicting the nymph Arethusa, *engraved on Syracuse coins by Kinon, around 400 B.C. The presence of flying fishes around the face, rather than the classical dolphins, is reminiscent of another Sicilian coin, from Segesta. Height: 5.2 cm. M. De Bry collection.*

The shell of Cassis tuberosa, *from the Indian Ocean. Height: 21 cm. Private collection.*

eighteenth century, during the Belle Epoque, and are still manufactured in series today.

The outside portions of entire nautilus shells were turned into precious water jugs in the eighteenth century.

In the thirteenth century, the Chinese forced freshwater mollusks, such as *Dipsas plicatus,* to deposit nacre on small objects, such as Buddhas, which they sold to pilgrims. See PEARL.

Fisheries

The white nacres used in jewelry come mostly from the pearl oysters of Polynesia and the northeast coast of Australia; some

is from the Persian Gulf, as well as from Unio mussel shells from various lakes and rivers, such as the Mississippi River. Nacre used in shell cameos comes from warm-water marine gastropods, such as the helmet shell (*Cassis rufa*) and the queen conch (*Strombus gigas*).

Structure and Physical Properties

Nacre is formed in parallel layers of aragonite crystals in epitaxial orientation to each other, reinforced by a network of conchiolin (an organic material similar to keratin). These layers form characteristic microscopic ridges on the surface of rough

nacre, evoking the topography lines of a map: this growth banding resembles the fibrous texture of wood on carved or polished nacre. When nacre shows bands of different colors as in *Strombus gigas,* the parallel layers of each band are at right angles to each other. Chemically, nacre consists on average of 85 percent calcium carbonate, 12 percent organic material, and 3 percent water. It is soft (H is 3½) and not tough, despite an improved cohesion due to its conchiolin network. It should not be exposed to acids nor left in a dry area, where it could dehydrate and crack. Its specific gravity varies from 2.75 to 2.80. Nacre shows a soft iridescence perpendicular to its elementary layers; parallel to these layers,

A bird made from black and white nacre, diamonds, rubies, and rock crystal. Height: 11 cm. Mauboussin creation.

The hinges of some freshwater bivalve mollusks show protuberances called "teeth," which have been sawed off and used in jewelry, especially for hat pins, the "Unio tooth" being the most common. Nacre may resemble pearls or ivory when it is fashioned into beads or small geometrical shapes to be strung into necklaces. When cut into a cabochon shape to display chatoyancy, nacre may look like other stones showing a cat's-eye effect. The term *Chinese cat's-eye,* however, designates the multicolored operculum of *turbo petholatus,* which closes the shell of this univalve when it is retracted. This circular calcareous plaque, 12 to 25 millimeters (½ to 1 inch) in diameter, has a slightly bulging shape and resembles onicolo agate.

Shell cameos are carved in the white outer layer of the shell, with the red or pink layer forming the background of the picture. The resulting engraving is slightly convex. The characteristic texture of these nacres (pink "flames" against a lighter background) can be observed on the smooth, concave interior side. Shell cameos should not be confused with hard-stone cameos, which are carved in agates with two or three different color layers. See AGATE.

Organic Materials with a Similar Appearance

Buttons and small display objects were manufactured at the turn of the twentieth century from the fruit of the corozo, a Peruvian palm tree. The corozo nut, also called vegetable ivory, is very tough; it can be dyed, printed, and even stamped. See IVORY.

Imitations

Plastic with a nacreous luster is used today to imitate nacre.

NEPHRITE

See JADE.

it displays chatoyancy, which is enhanced by a cabochon or spherical cut. Its color varies, depending on the mollusk that produced it; it can be dyed.

The Uses of Nacre

At the turn of the century, nacre was primarily used to make buttons, sometimes after dyeing. A workshop with twenty-five skilled workers could produce about twenty thousand buttons per day. Nacre inlays are still popular today, and large numbers of small boxes with such inlays are manufactured today in such countries as Spain, Morocco, India, and the Philippines, for tourists. In Polynesia decorative shells, formerly used as currency, are strung into necklaces.

O

Obsidian

A silica-rich volcanic glass.

Origin of the Name

Obsidian comes from the Greek *opsianos,* itself derived from *opsis,* meaning "vision" or "show," because black obsidian, especially that from Ethiopia, was used to make mirrors. This term became *opsianus* in Latin, and then *opsidianus* and *obsidianus,* and its origin was forgotten; even Pliny the Elder suggested that a certain "Obsidius," invented for the purpose, was the origin of the word.

The History of Obsidian

Obsidian was already used in the Neolithic period to carve ritual objects and manufacture weapons such as arrowheads and dagger blades. The Aztecs called it *teotetl* ("divine stone") because of its many uses. One of the oldest pieces of obsidian jewelry is an obsidian bead necklace from the fifth millennium B.C., in the British Museum.

Aztec priests used an obsidian blade to skin and extract the hearts of men sacrificed to the sun god. Obsidian masks have also been found in abundance, such as that of the god Tezcatlipoca ("Shining mirror"). Like Mediterranean civilizations, pre-Columbian civilizations used obsidian mirrors for divining purposes; such a mirror is displayed in the Museum of Natural History in Paris.

Texture, Physical Properties, and Varieties

Because obsidian is a volcanic glass formed around gases dissolved at the time of the eruption, it is often rich in small gas bubbles. Its optical and mechanical properties vary with its chemical composition: its index of refraction is around 1.50, its specific gravity about 2.4, and its hardness 5½

Mexican carving in obsidian. Height: 9 cm. Private collection.

to 6. It breaks with a smooth, shiny, conchoidal fracture, which leaves extremely sharp edges.

Its color and appearance also depend on its composition. Common obsidian is very dark brown to black, but there are translucent to transparent varieties that are light brown with a nuance of yellow or green. In some deposits, the shapes of centimeter-size obsidian nodules is reminiscent of tears; such are the "Apache tears," which, according to a Native American legend, came from the eyes of the wives and sisters of a tribe's warriors after a murderous battle. Chatoyant obsidian is rich in lamellar crystallites parallel to the flow structure. A Californian variety in which white fibroradial crystals of feldspar or cristobalite develop against the black background is called "snowflake" or "flowering obsidian."

Deposits

Obsidian is widely distributed in all volcanic areas of the world. Today obsidian from North America (Glass Buttes in Oregon, Glass Mountain and Obsidian Butte in California) is used mostly by local Native American craftspeople.

Materials with a Similar Appearance

All natural siliceous glasses have similar properties and cannot be distinguished from obsidian when they are faceted. Among such materials, tektites (from the Greek *tektos*, "molten") found in 1787 on the banks of the Moldau (Vltava) River in Czechoslovakia (hence their local name, *moldavites*), later billitonites from Belitung Island in Indonesia, and australites from Australia are still little known, although they are said to be of meteoritic origin. They can be identified with certainty only by their appearance before faceting: more or less flattened drops with a pitted surface.

Other siliceous glasses, for example, those found in the Meteor Crater in Arizona, have been produced by the fusion of quartz during a meteoritic impact; others, called fulgurites, result from the fusion of quartz sand at the point of impact of lightning (in the Libyan part of the Sahara Desert), but this last variety, also called Lybian desert glass, is little used in jewelry.

Imitations

Glass is the only imitator of obsidian and other natural siliceous glasses. It can be identified by the higher values of its physical properties. Most faceted "moldavites" sold during the nineteenth century and at the beginning of the twentieth century are actually brownish green bottle glass.

ODONTOLITE

Fossilized mammoth ivory, composed mostly of phosphates. The name comes from the Greek *odous, odontos,* meaning "tooth," and *lithos,* which means "stone," that is, "tooth stone."

Odontolite has been found in significant amounts in the Gers department in France. It has the classical structure of ivory, but its chemical composition is closer to that of hydroxylapatite and collophanes (calcium phosphates), associated with small amounts of calcium carbonate (which cause effervescence with acids) and vivianite (an iron phosphate, responsible for the blue-green color). Its specific gravity is about 3, and its index of refraction around 1.6. The appearance of odontolite is reminiscent of turquoise. In the Middle Ages, it was used in cabochons in Europe.

By extension, all fossilized bones have been called odontolite. In China snuff bottles have been carved from this material. Odontolite can be imitated by recent ivory (specific gravity of 1.8), after calcination and dyeing with a copper sulfate solution (obtained in situ by the action of ferrous sulfate on an ammoniacal cupric solution, impregnating the tusk).

OLIVINE

A synonym for peridot. This name was coined by the German mineralogist Abraham Werner in 1790, in reference to the olive-green color of this mineral. This term is commonly used by mineralogists but rarely by jewelers. See CHRYSOLITE; PERIDOT.

ONICOLO

Onyx with black and white layers, resembling an eye when cut in cabochon. The name comes from an Italian alteration of the word *onyx.* See ONYX.

ONYX

A black chalcedony, or agate, with two planar layers, one black and the other white, or ribbon agate with layers of highly contrasting colors (such as white against dark brown, reddish brown, or black). *Onyx* is also used as an adjective for certain gem materials, such as onyx marble.

Origin of the Name and Lore

The name *onyx* comes from the Greek *onux,* which means "fingernail." According to myth, one day Cupid cut Venus's fingernails with an arrowhead while she was asleep. He left the pieces on the sand, and the Fates turned them into stone, so that no part of a celestial body would perish.

The term *onyx* denoted a number of chalcedony varieties before taking on its present restricted meaning during the late Roman empire. Perhaps because of the distinct separation of the light and dark layers, onyx was the only gem considered evil during the Middle Ages. It was supposed to provoke discord and separate lovers. Albert the Great said: "To generate sorrow, worries, or anxiety, you need only use onyx. Those who wear this stone soon become depressed, worried, and suffer from terrible dizzy spells at night."

According to a similar Arab tradition, onyx is called *el jaza,* or "sadness." This stone was supposedly so feared in China that only slaves would mine it, and it was immediately exported. Similarly, no inhabitant of North Africa in his right mind would wear onyx or place it among his treasures.

Pliny the Elder said that the name *onyx* was passed on from a stone of Carmania (now the Kermān province in southeastern Iran) to a gem. As Carmania stone, it was used to carve ointment jars, hence its name *onyx* (see ALABASTER). As a gem, its color was compared to that of a human fingernail, white with brownish yellow nuances, so the name fits a variety of agates.

The Texture and Color of Onyx

Today the term *onyx* designates a sard so dark that it appears black. However, most of the onyx on the market today is chalcedony dyed black by producing a carbonaceous precipitate (see CHALCEDONY). It is easy to distinguish among these gem materials using a bright light: natural onyx shows a weak translucent brownish tint, whereas dyed black chalcedony is opaque. However, the CIBJO does not differentiate these two materials, since this treatment has been used since ancient times; it has been used extensively in Idar-Oberstein since 1819.

Onyx may also denote an agate with black and white layers. Cut into a cabochon, such an agate shows an eye with a black center surrounded by a white rim, itself against a dark background. Such a material is generally called *onicolo,* an Italian variation of *onyx.* Agate spheres with one or several "eyes" have always been valued as talismans against the evil eye as well as protection from eye diseases. Their ancient names leave no doubt: *oculus beli, ophtalmos, leucophtalmos, triophtalmos,* and so on. More generally, *onyx* is applied to any agate with highly contrasting layers of colors other than brownish red, which can be carved into a cameo where the subject appears in a light color against a darker background. (See also AGATE.)

Pendant with a 2.07-carat opal and diamonds. Taillerie de Royat collection.

A 17.07-carat faceted Mexican fire opal. F. A. Becker collection, Idar-Oberstein, Germany.

All these varieties of onyx may be produced by dyeing the more porous layers of a regular chalcedony, a practice already known by the Sumerians.

Substitutes and Imitations

Black onyx can be imitated by all black gem materials. It has been used in place of jet. Black glass is a typical imitator.

Layered onyx can be imitated by two layers of molded glass. Most often, it is imitated by assembled stones (manufactured as early as the first century A.D.). Indeed, Pliny said, "Sardonyx is imitated by gluing together three very good stones, one black, the other white, and the third red, so that the artifice could not be detected." Most cameo imitations are carved in common chalcedony and glued to a base of black or red chalcedony. Sometimes the "carving" itself is just a white porcelain mold.

OPAL

A hydrous silica composed of a compact, more or less regular stacking of silica spheres, which are visible with an electron microscope.

Origin of the Name

Opal may derive from the Sanskrit *upala*, which means "precious stone." Play-of-color opal may already have been known during the Roman empire, though such stones may have had only some opalescent material showing a play of color. This may have been the source of the longtime confusion about the various concepts of opalescence (common opal, girasol quartz), play of color (harlequin opal), and iridescence (iris quartz).

Another possible source could be the name of the Roman goddess of fertility, Ops, the wife of Saturn. Her celebration was called the *Opalia*.

Opal was, and still is, considered a lucky charm in many countries. It is said to be sensitive to emotion; for example, it should become paler in the face of an enemy, redder in the company of a friend. It supposedly brings beauty, fortune, and happiness and is an excellent talisman for vision. To others opal would protect from the evil eye.

Opal was supposed to make people invisible, which explains its nickname *patronus furum,* or "patron of thieves," at the end of the Middle Ages. Since the nine-

teenth century, a specifically French superstition states that opal brings bad luck; various origins have been proposed, including *Anne of Geierstein,* a novel by Sir Walter Scott in which the enchanted princess Hermione wears an opal in her hair; or the accident that befell one of Napoléon's state coaches named "Opale"; or even Empress Eugénie's misfortunes. But the true source may be far more simple: nineteenth-century lapidaries and stone setters were penalized if they damaged the stones they were given to set. Frequent damage to this easily breakable gem created the perception that this stone brought bad luck. Today jewelers carry on this belief more or less consciously—some admit that by cracking any time there is a drop in temperature, opal brings bad luck, mostly to their wallets.

Opal is one of the few gems that reveals its beauty without the help of a lapidary. Its play of color has always been praised, and this gem has often been very highly valued.

Pliny the Elder reported that the senator Nonius was proscribed by Antonius (83–30 B.C.) for an opal estimated at 20,000 sesterces (seven years of income for an average family), which was the only belonging

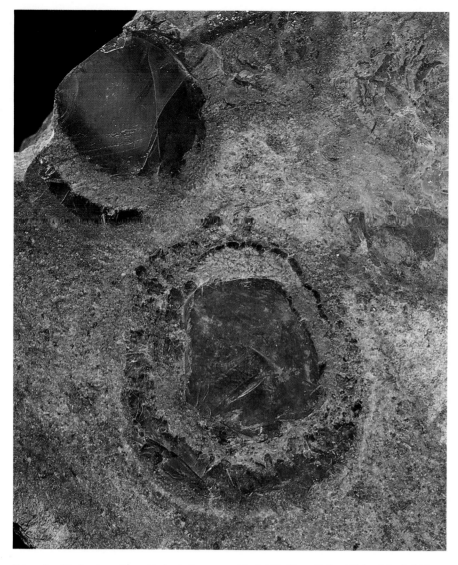

Fire opal and harlequin opal from Mexico in the same matrix. Height: 15 cm. National Higher School of Mines, Paris.

ently in a Vienna museum, and an 820-gram (1¾-pound) stone found in Queensland, Australia, in 1912. A 527.2-gram (1⅛-pound) opal is on display at the American Museum of Natural History in New York. Magnificent opals created by pseudomorphosis of fossils (belemnites, internal molds of gastropods, urchins, and even reptiles) come from Australia.

Structure and Physical Properties

The origin of the play of color in gem opal, absent in common (non-phenomenal) opal, was the object of many hypotheses until 1965, at which time German and Australian scientists elucidated the structure of opals using scanning electron microscopy. Opals consist of a stacking of silica spheres, 100 to 350 nanometers in diameter. The structure of hydrous silica inside the spheres is still uncertain.

When the spheres are not of the same diameter, the stacking is irregular, so that light is only scattered by the stone, producing the milky aspect of common, "potch" opal.

When all the spheres are of identical diameter, they may form a compact stack, producing a "pseudocrystal" (the overall texture is that of a mosaic; a play-of-color opal is made of several pseudocrystals). Light is diffracted by this lattice: the diffraction colors ("fires") produced depend, of course, on the angle of observation and the size of the spheres (at one extreme, reds are diffracted by 300-nanometer spheres, whereas at the other, violets are diffracted by 175 nanometer spheres; smaller spheres diffract only invisible ultraviolet light). Naturally, this diffraction occurs only if the spheres show a difference in index of refraction with their surrounding medium, that is the space between them (about 25 percent of the volume) is not filled with a silica gel having the same index of refraction as the spheres. The presence of various minerals (especially clays) in the space between spheres gives opal a dark background against which the play of color (all the colors produced by diffraction) is best seen.

Water contained in the amorphous silica seems to have a major impact on the appearance and longevity of opal. Opal's index of refraction (1.40 to 1.53) and its specific gravity (1.9 to 2.5) increase with water content in the same sample. The loss of water affects the quality of the play of color and induces cracks or even rupture ("crazing") in some samples; opal is thus a very sensitive gem material (especially during polishing). After it has been worked, opal should not be exposed to a dry climate (rough opal is often displayed immersed in water). Opal's hardness is about 6.

he kept with him in exile. Pliny was indignant: "What amazing cruelty and what an excess from Antonius, proscribing for a gem! But there is no greater obstination than that of Nonius, in love with the object of his proscription!" This anecdote was applied more than once: according to an eighteenth-century legend, the opal of Nonius was discovered among the ruins of Alexandria, sold in Constantinople for several thousand ducats, and a Frenchman named Lironcourt reportedly offered it in many countries for 40,000 thalers.

Joséphine de Beauharnais, Napoléon's first empress, owned an exceptional fire opal called *Incendie de Troie* (literally, "the burning of Troy"), now lost. The opal collection of Stéphanie of Belgium is famous; it is kept in the Hofburg treasury in Vienna. The Budapest Natural History Museum owns the largest collection of Hungarian opals. Queen Victoria of Great Britain (1819–

1901) helped promote Australian opals and fought the superstition surrounding them, unlike Empress Eugénie of France (1826–1920), who feared this gem.

Several opals are worthy of mention, including the 77-carat opal of Louis XVIII, kept in the National Museum of Natural History in Paris, and the 203-carat opal presented by the Australian government to Queen Elizabeth II of Great Britain in 1954. A 345-carat harlequin opal, a 143.2-carat Mexican fire opal, and a 58.8-carat Australian black opal are on display at the Smithsonian Institution. The largest block of opal, the Panther Opal, was found in Australia; it weighed 61.3 kilograms (almost 135 pounds) and was divided into three pieces of 36, 11.3, and 9 kilograms (79, 25, and 20 pounds). Previously found opals were much smaller: a 600-gram specimen, 12 by 5.7 centimeters (1.3 pounds, 4½ by 2¼ inches) was found in Hungary in 1775; it is pres-

Varieties of Opal

Various types of opal have been named according to the color of their background and the nature of their play of color.

- *Harlequin opal:* most common in jewelry, bright fires of all colors contrast against a translucent, whitish or milky background.
- *Black opal:* the fires are seen against a very dark background, dark violetish blue to green.
- *Fire opal:* generally green fires play against a reddish orange background. By silicification, fire opal becomes carnelian.
- *Hyalite opal:* glassy, without fires.
- *Cacholong:* white, with a porcelain appearance and no fire.
- *Hydrophane:* transparent, showing fires only if it is wet or immersed in water.
- *Common or potch opal:* whitish, lacking any fire. It may resemble prase, when mixed with small serpentine fragments, or moss agate if it displays ferromagnesian dendrites (it may also be called dendritic opal). Most commonly it shows smudges of colors and is found intimately associated with opaque chalcedonies and various opals without any particular organization, forming a material known as "jasp-opal."
- *Matrix opal:* opal associated with fragments of the rock in which it formed.

Deposits

Common opal is widespread throughout the world. It was deposited by silica-rich hot springs and geysers in zones of late volcanic activity (as in Iceland or Yellowstone Park). It may form during the low-temperature hydrothermal alteration of volcanic tuffs or effusive rocks, frequently in association with chalcedony.

Czechoslovakia

The only deposit of jewelry-quality opal known until the nineteenth century, this deposit was discovered at the time of the Roman empire in Slovakia. It is located in the Czerwenitsa andesites near Dubnika Na Vahu (formerly part of Hungary) and was mined until 1920. The production, known as "Hungarian opals," was never important. Hyalite and hydrophane sometimes accompany harlequin opal.

Mexico

The state of Querétaro is a major opal producer; opal is also found in the states of Chihuahua, San Luis Potosí, Guerrero, Hidalgo, Jalisco, and Michoacán. Fire opal was probably used by the Aztecs (A.D. 1325–1521) and was called *vitzitziltecpatl*, meaning "hummingbird stone," an analogy between its colors and those of the bird's wings. Chicago's Field Museum of Natural History owns one of the most famous opals in the world, the God of the Sun, from a sixteenth-century Mexican temple; it indicates the importance of this gem to pre-Columbian civilizations.

After the Spanish conquest, the Mexican opal deposits were forgotten. The Querétaro deposits were rediscovered in only 1855, by a servant at the Hacienda Esperanza: mining began at the Santa María Iris mine. Rhyolites there contain numerous cavities, originally gas bubbles, filled with excellent-quality opal, some of which even forms "floaters" the size of a hen's egg. Small quarries have been dug into the rock using primitive methods; modern workings do not differ much from the ancient ones. The potential of this area is high.

United States

A cowboy discovered an interesting opal deposit, Rainbow Ridge, in Nevada in 1905. Mrs. F. H. Lockheed assumed the mining claims and started mining. These beautiful opals, especially the black ones, have a tendency to crack when exposed to air because of their high water content (11 percent).

Australia

The most important opal deposits today are in Australia. Queensland opals were discovered in 1875, simultaneously in Yowah and Quilpie. They form veinlets and crusts in ferruginous sandstones covering hundreds of square miles. The farmers who found these opals could not sell them at the time because they lacked a market. But the owners thought that the stones were worth something; one of them, Herb Bond, offered them in vain in 1878 to London gem dealers, who thought that they were manufactured, because their fires were far more intense than those of Hungarian opals.

In 1889 Tully Wollaston managed to convince the Hasluck brothers, jewelers at Hatton Garden, the London jewelry market, to give these opals a chance. They were offered on the small Maiden Lane market in New York. When Wollaston returned to Australia, White Cliffs had just been discovered. A group of kangaroo hunters had found harlequin opal in the remains of a wounded animal: despite the lack of water in the area, this news soon attracted hundreds of prospectors to the "Kangaroo hunters' camp."

Opal sales finally met with success in London, allowing Ted Murphy to start production at White Cliffs in New South Wales, a site famous for its magnificent harlequin opals and its common fossil pseudomorphs in opal. The opal rush had begun.

In 1900 Isabel Gray opened a hotel and a general store in a small town called Eulo, between the opal fields of Queensland and New South Wales. The only woman to live in this desolate area, she was nicknamed the "Queen of Eulo" and became the toast of the region. Opal prospectors came from hundreds of miles around to take part in her dinner parties. She owned the best collection of opals in the world, but nobody

Opal quarry near Coober Pedy, Australia. Photo: D. McColl.

Opalized vertebra from the Coober Pedy opal fields, Australia. Photo: D. McColl.

knows the whereabouts of the stones since her mysterious disappearance. The annual Eulo festival has continued the reign of the legendary Isabel since 1968, and every year sees the election of a new Queen of Eulo.

Lightning Ridge was named by a shepherd who lost his three hundred sheep there, struck by lightning during a very violent storm. This is where the first black opals were discovered, in the drilling of a well for water. An unlucky prospector from White Cliffs, Charlie Nettleton, heard the news and dug a shaft on October 15, 1902, but extracted only common opal. Persistent, he worked for a prospecting company with capital of $125, and finally found some beautiful black opals. The Sydney dealers were not interested however, calling black opals worthless matrix opals. But because harlequin opal was also discovered at Lightning Ridge, a first rush took place in 1903, with some very serious clashes between farmers and miners. Nettleton decided to sell his black opals to Ted Murphy, the White Cliffs pioneer. Amazed, the latter called in Tully Wollaston, who decided to buy all existing black opals. Nevertheless, he had to mount a major marketing effort to establish them in the market, as he had done fifteen years before for harlequin opals. A second rush took place at Lightning Ridge in 1909, involving more than

fourteen hundred miners. Today Lightning Ridge is the only place in the world that yields the highly valued black opals. They are found in a clay layer about 1 meter (3 feet) thick, found at a depth of 5 to 7 meters (16 to 23 feet). Each vein is mined by two miners working together, who dig a series of small shafts next to one another. The outcome of their efforts is uncertain, as is often the case with gemstones. The most famous opals from this locality have received names: Light of the World, Red Emperor, Pride of Australia, Flame Queen, and so on.

Today the most productive opal fields are in southern Australia. Andamooka, discovered by chance by two horsemen in 1930, produces bright, clear opals (especially well suited for the manufacture of doublets and triplets). Coober Pedy (a variation of the aboriginal phrase *kupa piti,* meaning "men in holes") was discovered in 1915 by gold prospectors.

The living conditions in this isolated part of the world are quite harsh: there is no water, the temperature, a mere 45°C (110°F) from January to March, may reach 60°C (140°F); yet one thunderstorm is enough to cover the land with flowers. For these reasons, dwellings are dug deep into the ground, where the 25° to 30°C (75° to 85°F) temperature is easier to bear.

Opal from New South Wales, Australia, in the rough. Height: 30 cm. National Higher School of Mines, Paris.

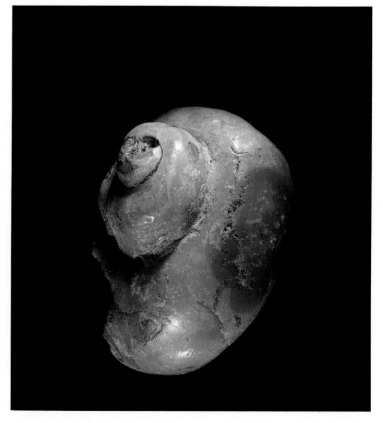

Opalized internal mold of a gastropod, found in Australia. Height: 3 cm. Private collection.

Brazil

Excellent harlequin opals were discovered in recent years in the northeast region of the state of Piauí, in northeastern Brazil. The mechanized mining operation there consists of a large open quarry at the foot of a sandstone cliff, at a place called Boi Morto ("dead ox"), which is west-southwest of Fortaleza. It produces about a ton of opal a year and places Brazil among the important opal producers.

Indications of opal have long been recognized in the geodes of the Rio Grande do Sul lavas. Others have been found since 1982 in the Conselheiro Lafaiete manganese mine and in the diamond-bearing gravels of Bagagem in Minas Gerais.

Green opal is found in the Fazenda Brejinho, northwest of Vitória da Conquista in the southern part of the state of Bahia. Opal is found accompanied by chalcedony, forming veinlets in a silica-poor asbestos rock. Opal blocks may reach 10 cubic centimeters (4 cubic inches) in size. Their color, similar to that of peridot, may be due to the presence of iron and possibly nickel.

The Marketing of Opal

The marketing of opal is dominated by Australian dealers. They even recently bought the rights to the Brazilian deposits, in order to control the market.

Each piece of opal is carefully examined after mining by an expert paid by the miners. It is generally bought and cut into cabochons at the mine. The manufacture of doublets and the treatment by precipitation of carbon in the lower-quality stones are also performed in the mining areas.

Modification of Color

Opal's play of color is best observed if not altered by transmitted light, that is, against a black background. Most translucent opals are therefore set against a black substrate, and opals are best worn on dark clothing.

By depositing black particles between the mosaic elements of a milky opal, in which the fires are obliterated by scattered white light, scattering is eliminated and the material becomes much more "flashy," with small, vividly colored patches contrasting against the black background.

This treatment is similar to that for onyx (involving sugar, then acid). It has been commonly used only since 1920 but had been known long before. John Mawe wrote in 1823 that "to improve the appearance of an opal, one should heat the stone, put it in oil or grease, which is burned afterwards."

Opal has been reinforced by impregnation with polymers, especially in the United States. This method is quite similar to that used for turquoise.

Natural Gems with a Similar Appearance

Only materials showing play of color can resemble harlequin or black opal: spectrolite and labradorite, as well as "korite."

Known since 1908, the "korite" deposit in Alberta, Canada, contains fossil ammonites (species *placenticeras*) with an aragonite shell that displays play of color. They are found in a brown slate. In some parts of the deposit, the material flakes off (such was the site farmers attempted to work in 1967), whereas in others it is more solid; these last have been mined commercially since 1977 for jewelry by a farmer named Kormos (hence the name *korite*). Only 5 percent of the material extracted can be used for jewelry, as a slate substrate with a thin, slightly silicified plaque of play-of-color aragonite, colored red or blue-green by ferruginous impregnations. Most of the material is too soft to withstand normal wear, so a colorless synthetic spinel cabochon is glued on top of the "korite" after polishing, to produce a synthetic spinel–korite doublet.

Simulants

The most common imitation of opal is opal-like glass, not very convincing, even if cracks have been induced to produce additional iridescence. A glassy nucleus covered with some kind of iridescent material and enclosed in a cabochon-shaped piece of transparent glass makes a believable imitation.

"Slocum stone" is a relatively recent and more convincing imitation. It is a kind of glass made from small glass beads, which produces iridescence.

Various opal-based assembled stones have been sold, including:
· Opal–black cement–substrate triplets, in which a very flat cabochon of gem-quality opal is attached with black cement to

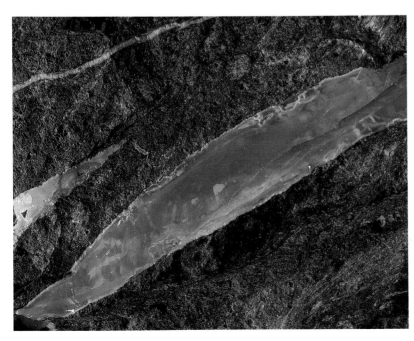

A 10-cm-long opal veinlet from the Conselheiro Lafaiete mine, in Minas Gerais, Brazil. Sorbonne collection.

Late-nineteenth-century ring with an opal center stone surrounded by emeralds. Garland collection.

a variety of possible substrates (matrix opal, chalcedony, or glass, for example).
- Rock crystal–opal–black cement–substrate quadruplets, in which a thin wafer of opal (maybe a fraction of a millimeter thick) is attached to some substrate (such as agate, chalcedony, onyx, or glass) with black cement and then covered with a rock-crystal cabochon (sometimes synthetic spinel is used instead of quartz).

To be convincing, these fabrications have to be seen face up. Assembled stones are often mounted in closed settings.

Since 1980 a Japanese company has produced a very convincing opal simulant, made of a regular stacking of styrene microspheres of an appropriate diameter, cemented together in a compact structure. This polymer simulant is less dense and less refringent than natural opal.

Synthetics

The process for producing 40-nanometer-diameter silica spheres in the laboratory based on silica gel is well known and relatively easy. However, it was only in 1972 that the growth of spheres to a diameter of 200 nanometers, a subsequent sedimentation in a compact structure, and nondestructive solidification were achieved to produce synthetic opals. Small amounts of organic polymers have been used at the time.

Starting in 1974, the Gilson company sold very convincing synthetic harlequin and black opals. Their microstructure is reminiscent of chicken wire when viewed from the top of the cabochon, resembling thin pillars perpendicular to the base when viewed from the side. There is never any matrix. The base of synthetic opal cabochons shows only one diffraction color, unlike natural specimens. Synthetic opal is now also produced in Japan and Australia.

ORTHOCLASE

A potassium feldspar. Its name refers to its two perpendicular cleavage planes (from the Greek *orthos,* "right, straight").

This collector's gem displays a light to golden yellow color, reminiscent of citrine, which is due to iron, as well as a slightly opalescent luster (S.G., 2.56; R.I., around 1.52; hardness, 6).

It has been found primarily in the pegmatites from the Itrongahy region in Madagascar, with crystals reaching up to 10 centimeters. Despite its attractive color, it remains a collector's stone.

Orthoclase crystals from Itrongahy, Madagascar, next to a 75-carat faceted stone of the same material. Stones courtesy Compagnie Générale de Madagascar, Paris.

PADPARADSCHA

A pinkish orange variety of corundum. Its name (*Padparadscha* means "lotus flower" in Sinhalese) derives from *padna,* "lotus," and *raga,* "color." In gemology, this term designates a natural corundum showing a yellowish orange to vivid orangy pink color, evoking a sunset or sunrise.

This rare and valued sapphire is found exclusively in the gem-bearing gravels of Sri Lanka. A 31-carat orange sapphire is displayed at the Smithsonian Institution, and another 100.18-carat stone is at the American Museum of Natural History in New York. A 1,126-carat orange sapphire was recently found in Sri Lanka.

Orange synthetic corundum, called synthetic padparadscha, imitates this gem. It is produced by flux or flame-fusion synthesis.

PEARL

A spherulitic calcareous concretion secreted by the mantle of some mollusks, especially saltwater Meleagrinas, also called Pinctadas, (or "pearl oysters") in the sea, and freshwater mussels, genus *Unio,* in lakes and rivers.

Origin of the Name

Daughters of the sea, pearls were called *morvarid* in Persian and *markarit* in Armenian. These generated the Greek common name *margarites,* or its poetic variant *margaron,* and later the Latin name *margarita.* (This is probably the origin of the feminine first names Margaret and Marguerite.) The Latin term has been used by biologists to name some species of pearl-bearing mollusks, such as *Pinctada margaritifera.* The Romans familiarly referred to pearls as *pirla,* a derivation from *pira,* which means "pear," referring to the elongated shape of pearls worn as ear pendants. This name became part of all modern Latin languages, influenced by the slang of the Roman legions.

History of the Pearl

Known since antiquity in the Orient and Far East, pearls were always highly valued; they also represented an important financial asset. In China they were used to pay taxes twenty-five hundred years before Christ. The Hebrews probably discovered pearls during their exile in Egypt, starting in the seventeenth century B.C. To them the pearl symbolized material wealth, which should be rejected by the just in favor of wisdom, as recommended by Solomon in the tenth century B.C. and written about in the eighth century B.C.: "Wisdom is better than pearls, and no gem can match it" (Prov. 8:11). The oldest pearl jewelry known was found in the grave of an Achaemenian queen in Susa (in present-day Iran); it is dated 520 B.C. and kept in the Louvre. Pearls were introduced in Greece only after the conquests of Alexander the Great and the plunders of the Egyptian and Persian treasures (around 330 B.C.). As a sign of distinction, Athenian men wore a pearl on the right ear; young women, on both ears.

The treasures of the Middle East were transferred to Rome after victories in the Orient during the second century B.C., after the triumphs of Lucullus and Pompey over Mithradates, king of the Pontus, in 66 B.C., and finally during the conquest of Egypt, in the first century B.C. During the triumph of Pompey, a pearl trophy was offered to Jupiter on the Capitol, and rich Roman women began spending fortunes to adorn themselves with pearls. Julius Caesar supposedly tried to regulate this trade, but he is also said to have presented Servilia, Brutus's mother, with a pearl costing 6 million sesterces (a considerable amount of money, if one considers that the average Pompeiian family spent about 2,500 sesterces a year). These extravagant expenses were sharply criticized by both Pliny and Seneca but did

not stop. During the imperial period, matrons from the upper classes wore ear pendants with two or three black pearls to differentiate themselves from prostitutes who wore only one large pearl in the ear. Because the pearls in such pieces of jewelry clinked together as the matrons walked these earrings were called "rattlers."

After falling into oblivion following the fall of the empire, the pearl returned to fashion during the Renaissance; the parures of the dukes of Burgundy Philip II and Charles the Bold dazzled their contemporaries. The importation of large quantities of pearls became possible with the discovery of new trade routes and new regions where pearls had long been cherished. From Peru to Mexico, the Spaniards plundered pearl parures and treasures, such as that of Montezuma II in Tenochtitlán (today, Mexico City). Spanish soldiers forced the local people to dive for pearls (in the Gulf of California, for example) so brutally that Jesuit missionaries had to step in and issue regulations. In Sri Lanka, the Portuguese demanded a tax in pearls as early as 1506. Pearls were often the subject of spoliations and speculations: Elizabeth I of England appropriated for herself the pearls Mary Stuart had received from Catherine de Médicis. A dealer name Georgibus of Calais was asked by Philip IV, king of Spain from 1621 to 1665, to whom he was offering a 126-carat black pearl called the Incomparable: "How could you have put all your fortune in such a small thing?" Georgibus

answered, "Sire, I knew there was in the world a king of Spain to buy it from me." And indeed Philip reportedly bought it for 80,000 ducats.

All royal treasures included some pearls. The pearl treasure of the French royal treasury was appraised at about 1 million germinal francs in 1791 and included, among others, a 27⁵⁄₁₆-carat pearl, the Queen of Pearls, estimated to be worth 200,000 francs.

During the nineteenth century, pearls were in vogue throughout the world, in the Russia of Czar Alexander II as well as in the England of Queen Victoria. At this time the Third Republic chose to sell the French crown jewels: the pearls were sold for 12,161,000 francs (gold francs), even after a number of pearls had already been sent to the United States.

The very high demand threatened to destroy the meleagrina banks, so far worked with moderation: from 1640 to 1768, the Dutch, who had succeeded the Portuguese in Sri Lanka, authorized pearl diving for only twenty days every three years (and incidentally took 50 percent of the harvest for taxes). But the British, succeeding the Dutch, fished the banks so extensively that there was no harvest in Sri Lanka from 1845 to 1862, and in 1863 the fisheries were limited to two hundred boats for twelve days. However, after the development of pearl culturing at the beginning of the twentieth century and the introduction of cultured pearls on the market in the

Diadem from the late nineteenth century set with baroque natural pearls. Chaumet creation.

1920s, the price of natural pearls plummeted: before World War I, a pearl necklace was worth the price of an eight-room house; now it merely represents one room of the same house. Natural pearls are still in demand, however, because of their remarkable size and orient.

The pearl market was established principally in Leipzig during the eighteenth century but moved to Paris and London at the end of the nineteenth century. There are still companies that specialize exclusively in natural pearls.

Today the great pearl collections are owned by the princely families of India and by the National Bank of Iran, which inherited them from the plunder of Delhi by Nāder Shah in the eighteenth century. The most magnificent pearls are collected in the United States.

Portrait of Gabrielle d'Estrées (1573–99) wearing pearls, painted by a member of the Fontainebleau school at the end of the sixteenth century. Courtesy of Laurin, Guilloux, Buffetaud, and Tailleur.

Famous Pearls

The most famous pearls are definitely those from Cleopatra's earrings. She bet Mark Antony that she could spend more than 10 million sesterces for a single meal and then swallowed one of her pearls after dissolving it in a glass of vinegar. Lucius Plaucus, judge of the bet, convinced her not to dissolve the second one, which was later cut in half to make two ear pendants for the Venus on the Parthenon. "Half a dinner became the parure of a goddess," concluded Pliny.

Remarkable pearls include:
- The necklace of Catherine de Médicis, which was also worn by Mary Stuart and Elizabeth I of England.
- The *Peregrina*, or Incomparable, a pear-shaped pearl purchased by Philip II of Spain, which became the property of Napoléon III. Repolished in 1912 and weighing 203.84 grains, it was later acquired by Elizabeth Taylor and damaged by her dog. Because of the Incomparable's notoriety, a pearl of the same size belonging to Charles II of Spain was named *Pellegrina*, and a pearl of 337 old grains acquired by Napoleon I was called *Pelegrina*; the last was later sold by the French republic to Prince Youssoupoff, as the Regent.
- The Queen of Pearls, weighing 109¼ old grains, was bought by Louis XIV in 1669 and disappeared in 1792 with the theft of the crown jewels.
- The Hope pearl is one of the largest pearls in existence at present; it is a baroque 5-centimeter (2-inch) long pearl weighing 450 carats (1,800 grains). It was named after its owner, Henry Philip Hope, the famous banker who also owned the celebrated blue diamond. Capped by a kind of crown, it forms a pendant.

Around the year A.D. 500, travelers to China told of a 7-centimeter (3-inch) pearl forming the trunk of a gold statuette representing the goddess Canon (Mercy). A 575-carat (2,300-grain) baroque pearl called Pearl of Asia is cited in many books.

Legends and Lore

The Hindu god Vishnu, guardian of the world, fished pearls in the ocean to adorn his daughter Pandaia; therefore Indian women wear pearls at their weddings, and pearls are particularly appreciated in India.

Pearls have often been associated with love and tears; they were dedicated to Aphrodite, the Greek goddess of love, and represented the solidified tears of Venus, the Roman goddess of love. They were thus said to prevent newlywed women from crying.

Pearls were favorites of the god of mercy, because they represented the tears of Adam and Eve, repenting their sin, and symbolized the tears cried by those in pain and misery. Muslims cherished them for that reason; Süleyman I, the Magnificent, Ottoman sultan from 1520 to 1566, always traveled with his pearl collection.

Pearls were said to make young girls candid and young women pure. Symbols of faith, purity, and religious fervor, in France they were commonly presented to young girls on the day of their first communion, often as a necklace of small pearls. As symbols of love and tenderness, they marked engagements. In 1635 the prince elector of Bavaria, Maximilian I, offered his fiancée a necklace with three hundred pearls as a pledge of love. In the nineteenth century, a ring set with one pearl was generally given to the fiancée on the day of her engagement.

Aragonite crystals from Sicily. Length: 12 cm. Sorbonne collection.

During the Renaissance, pearls were believed to be dew droplets solidified by mollusks which caught them in the small hours of the morning. Their beauty depended on the weather at the time of their conception, and thunder was responsible for blisters on the surface of the pearl.

Pearls have been credited with a number of therapeutic virtues when crushed in a beverage and ingested:

- In Rome they were a remedy for madness. During the classical period, it was considered a mark of esteem, even passion, to drink a cup of wine in which a pearl had been dissolved to the health of a friend.
- In China they were considered a medication for gastric difficulties.
- In seventeenth-century England, lemon juice with a dissolved pearl was recommended as a tonic.

The Formation of Pearls

The formation of pearls was investigated by the Swedish naturalist Carolus Linnaeus (1707–78). He discovered that a microscopic worm of the cestode group, a parasite of mollusks, inserts itself between the shell and the mantle of the mollusk. Irritated by the parasite, the mantle creates a cavity, which evolves into a sack, to isolate the parasite, by forming a calcareous concretion around it. The larger the concretion, the more the mantle is irritated and the more it secretes. So a pearl always grows, unless the mollusk ejects it with a brusk movement. Pearls are formed from their center out of concentric layers of thin aragonite crystals, parallel to each other in a lattice or net, formed by a chitinous organic material, called conchiolin. Any bivalve mollusk that does not move much and produces nacre can produce pearls; for fine pearls, the concretion must be solid enough to be suitable for jewelry.

Most pearls on the market come from relatively ancient stationary or burrowing bivalves: the *Meleagrina* genus of oysters in salt water and the *Unio* and *Naiad* genera of mussels in fresh water.

Meleagrina Oysters

Meleagrinas (or *Pinctadas*), the "pearl oysters," live on sandy, relatively shallow bottoms, 10 to 20 meters (30 to 60 feet) deep, in oxygen-rich warm waters; they avoid mud, in which they suffocate. The genus is divided into three species, based on the size of the shell. *Meleagrina martensi* is the smallest, with an adult size of about 7 centimeters (3 inches) in diameter; *Meleagrina vulgaris* has an adult size of about 10 centimeters (4 inches) and *Meleagrina maxima* and *Meleagrina margaritifera*, the largest, can reach 20 centimeters (8 inches) in diameter and may have a gray to black nacre. Beds of *M. vulgaris* and *M. maxima* form on the coasts of the Arabian peninsula (in the Red Sea and Persian Gulf) and in the Indian Ocean (Sri Lanka and Myanmar, formerly Burma); *Meleagrina martensi* is the only species on the Japanese coasts but coexists with *Meleagrina maxima* on the coasts of Madagascar. The Pacific coasts of Australia, the Philippines, New Caledonia, Tahiti, and Mexico are inhabited by beds of *Meleagrina maxima* only.

Natural Saltwater Pearl Fisheries

There were two great centers for pearl fisheries. One, in Bahrain, was controlled by Indian and Arab dealers, with whom traders had to negotiate. The other, in Sri Lanka, was controlled by the British, and the fishing season corresponded to a large gathering of native fishermen and European buyers in a temporary town difficult to reach. In the 1920s, three thousand boats were involved in pearl fishing in Bahrain and the Persian Gulf, but only one or two remain today to maintain the tradition. Depending on the location, a pearl-fishing boat was manned by two to twelve men. After reaching the fishing grounds, the divers held onto a rope attached to a heavy stone, the weight of which rapidly took them to the bottom. They plucked pearl oysters and put them in a net fixed around their waist or attached directly to the boat by a rope. The divers jerked the rope to signal to their colleagues on the surface that they were ready to ascend. Their stay underwater lasted for about sixty to ninety seconds. The divers wore clothes if they feared an encounter with stinging animals such as jellyfish. In Bahrain the oysters were opened and searched at the harbor. In Sri Lanka they were distributed in lots, to be sold closed. Thus, the buyer in Bahrain bought only the pearl, whereas the buyer in Sri Lanka bought the harvest of the diver.

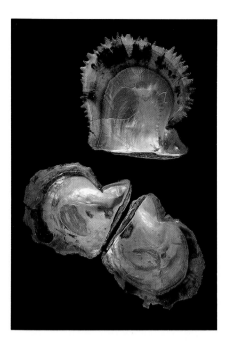

Meleagrina (or Pinctada) shells, more commonly known as pearl oysters, from Japan. Size: 9 cm.

In Japan, female pearl divers are called *amas*. They are clothed in white (to protect against sharks?) and swim free, linked to their buckets on the surface only by a rope tied around their ankles. The bucket serves three functions: it helps locate the *ama* in case she does not resurface after two minutes; it is a place for the *ama* to rest between dives; and it holds the oyster harvest. Pearl fishing with diving suits was attempted in 1914 in the Gulf of California.

Other fisheries were located off the coasts of Colombia, Venezuela, Panama, New Caledonia, Australia, and islands in the South Pacific.

Natural Freshwater Pearl Fisheries

Many rivers in Scotland, Bavaria, Sweden, and North America contain beds of pearl-producing mollusks. The Romans were familiar with pearls from England. In the Vosges, in eastern France, the pearls from the Neune River (called "Vologne pearls") were the property of the dukes of Lorraine. The pearl mussels were fished with a flat-bottom boat. The fisherman would first locate the beds of pearl mollusks with a sort of box with a transparent bottom and then grasp them with a split stick, acting as a forceps. The larvae of this mollusk go through a stage in which they are parasites in roaches. This gave rise to the idea of acclimating such mollusks to the great pools of the Malmaison Castle, an effort that did not succeed, to the great regret of Empress Joséphine, who was very fond of freshwater pearls.

Nineteenth-century print depicting pearl fishermen.

Japanese amas at work. Source: Jetro.

Physical Properties of Natural Pearls

Orient, Luster, and Color

The appearance of pearls in daylight is the result of their structure. Light reflected from the surface of the pearl gives it shine and luster. Light refracted inside the pearl and reflected from the successive layers of aragonite creates a soft iridescence known as *orient.* The orient is more distinct if the layers forming this lattice are thinner, that is, if their thickness approaches visible wavelengths. Therefore, pearls are harvested when the mollusk's metabolism is slower, in the spring or early summer. The pearls produced by the larger Meleagrinas have less orient, because their layers, proportional to the overall size of the shell, are much thicker. This prompted a tradition in the trade to separate carefully natural pearls from the Orient and the South Seas. This distinction still applies today to cultured pearls. The orient depends even more on the species producing the pearl: *Unio* pearls are much less vivid although they are still considered fine freshwater pearls.

The color of a pearl is that of the nacre of the secreting mollusk. Most often it is a slightly pinkish white (Oriental pearls), but the color can be yellowish or golden (pipi pearls from Tahiti) or even a more or less pronounced gray (like the pearl gray of the black pearls from Tahiti and Mexico). The color of a pearl results from the presence in the water of color-causing agents, which are ingested by and concentrated in the mollusk, depending on its species and alimentation. Freshwater pearls are most often a dull milky white.

When a pearl is not suited for the market because of its color, it may be dyed using silver salts. The pearl is immersed for several months in a solution (its exact composition varies from workshop to workshop), then it is exposed to light to reveal metallic silver, as in the photographic process.

Luminescence

Like all organic materials, pearls are luminescent in black light. White pearls fluoresce white, while black pearls fluoresce a weak reddish to brownish. Dyed pearls, of course, do not fluoresce.

Clarity

Occasionally, some cells from the growing pearl sack produce a substance with low calcium carbonate content. The layer formed includes a zone rich in organic material, which will eventually result in a black spot in the pearl. If such a spot is close to the surface, it adversely affects the value of

Cultured-pearl parure. Gérard creation.

the gem. If the pearl dealer believes that there might be a cleaner layer with good orient under the spotted superficial layer, he may attempt to peel the pearl, that is, carefully remove one layer and, with it, the spot.

When the center of a pearl is very rich in organic material, this mass shows more or less distinctly through the nacre layers, producing a bluish gray tint under the orient. Such pearls are called blue pearls.

Shape

Pearls can take on a variety of shapes, depending on their location in the mollusk. The most valued shapes are the perfect sphere and the pear, a sphere elongated on one side only. A button is a sphere flattened on one side, so named because Chinese mandarins indeed used them as buttons. A pearl of completely irregular shape is called baroque.

If a pearl forms because of the trapping of an organic mass that later decomposes, it may become hollow and very light. When a natural pearl comes out of the mollusk mantle accidentally but remains held between mantle and shell without being expelled, it may be at the origin of a "blister" on the shell, and it will be called a blister pearl. Once separated from the shell, such a pearl has nacre on one side, which distinguishes it from normal pearls. If such a pearl becomes deeply buried in the shell, it may be called a shell pearl. Once extracted, such a pearl can, by peeling, become either a blister pearl or a regular pearl. If a natural pearl wears into a barrel shape, it is possible to make it round again by peeling.

Specific Gravity

Because of the presence of organic matter, pearls are lighter than aragonite, and their specific gravity varies with the proportion of organic material. Blue and black pearls are lighter than regular white pearls (specific gravity: 2.65 to 2.75). There is an approximate relationship between the diameter of a pearl and its mass, so one can design "pearl gauges," which help to gain a good, quick approximation of the mass. The mass of a pearl is measured in grains (1 grain equals 0.05 gram). A 20-grain pearl is approximately 9 millimeters (⅓ inch) in diameter; an 8-grain pearl is about 6.5 millimeters (¼ inch) in diameter, the same diameter as a 1-carat round, brilliant-cut diamond.

Resistance to Various Agents

A pearl is easily scratched (the hardness of aragonite is 3½), but its structure, held together by the organic "net" of conchiolin, is relatively shock-resistant. Of course, a brutal blow may crack and split off

the outermost pearl layer, forming a "window" that can be removed by careful peeling (hopefully, the underlying layer shows good orient). Despite the tight fit of their layers, pearls are elastic, and the "dance of pearls," describing their trajectory as they fall from a broken necklace, is merely a poetic image. Because it is both calcareous and organic, a pearl is very sensitive to atmospheric agents; it truly "lives." If the weather becomes too hot, a pearl may crack and dehydrate. This often happens to pearls left in bank vaults; pearls really should adorn their wearers, which helps them rehydrate. Any agent that can attack limestone or organic matter will attack pearls as well, this is particularly true of fatty acids, perfume, and perspiration. An altered pearl is a dead pearl: its color turns greenish and its orient dulls, often irreversibly. Some people can wear pearls only over clothing. A pearl necklace should be put on only after all perfume has been applied. A pearl necklace must be cleaned on a regular basis with soapy water and dried without rubbing, to avoid scratches. It is preferable to restring pearls every six months, because silk and cotton threads conduct fatty acids and pollutants by capillarity into the heart of the pearl, and these damaging agents penetrate the pearl layers that were cut during drilling.

An incident that occurred between the two World Wars remains famous among pearl dealers. During an evening party, a guest's pearl necklace strung with knots, broke, and the central pearl fell. The family dog grabbed and swallowed it. Consternation! The little dog was immediately administered strong purgatives, and the pearl was

finally rejected from his body. However, the pearl had been partly dissolved in the dog's stomach and came out smaller. But, its orient and color had been considerably improved, and the pearl had doubled in value. The guest was delighted and thanked her host profusely. There are reports that the Sri Lankans force chickens to swallow dull pearls; a stay of about one minute in the bird's stomach is enough to give them a magnificent orient.

Drilling

To be used in jewelry, pearls are either half-drilled, generally with a rather large diameter hole, to allow to them to be screwed or glued to a 1-millimeter-diameter metal peg, or they are drilled through for stringing, to be used in necklaces and lace. Drilling was historically done in India with a bow drill; this instrument was made of a string attached to both extremities of a switch and coiled in its center around a metallic needle bit; the bit was covered with abrasives and rotated back and forth with the right hand holding the bow, while the left hand held the pearl firmly in place. This method is disappearing in favor of drilling done horizontally with an electric lathe. However, the basic approach remains the same: the pearl is drilled in two steps to prevent it from splitting, the main difficulty involving turning the pearl exactly 180 degrees once it has been half-drilled.

The drill hole is very thin. It was agreed in the 1920s that its diameter should never be smaller than 0.3 millimeter. If it is, the buyer is entitled to have the hole enlarged at the seller's expense.

Nineteenth-century print depicting the drilling of pearls with a bow-drill in Sri Lanka.

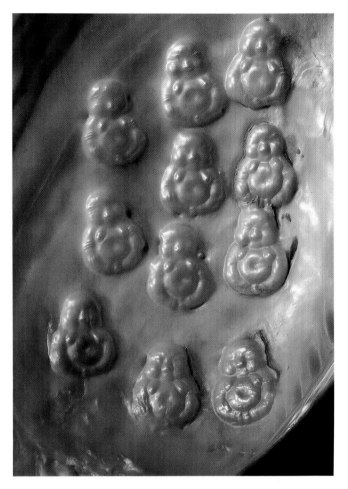

Nacre Buddhas on the shell of Dipsas plicatus. *Such objects were produced in China from the thirteenth to the nineteenth centuries. Private collection.*

Saltwater pearl farm in Ago Bay, Japan. Source: Jetro.

Other Natural Pearls

The edible mussel *Mytilus edulis,* the edible flat oyster *Ostrea edulis,* and the Portuguese oyster *Gryphea arcuata* also produce pearls; gourmets occasionally discover them when enjoying these shellfish. However, these pearls have the color, the orient, and the nacre of the rather unattractive shells. They rapidly peel, remain dull, and are of no use for jewelry—but they do make nice souvenirs!

Other, much rarer pearls are used in jewelry. The queen conch, *Strombus gigas,* secretes a pink pearl, which has the same color as the inside of its shell and can be recognized by its white flame structure against a pink background. These pink pearls, the color of pink coral, are eagerly sought by avid collectors. The giant clam *Tridacna gigas* produces similar pearls.

Pinna nobilis forms a brown pearl, which rapidly evolves into an easily cracked, fibroradial mass; it is mostly a collector's item.

Haliotis, the abalone shell, also forms

pearls. They are often greenish, with a strong iridescence, and generally not much appreciated. Attempts to culture pearls of this mollusk have failed because of their lack of popularity.

Cultured Pearls

Historical Perspective

The Chinese have long known that the mantles of mollusks secrete the nacre of their shells. Nacre Buddhas have been known since the twelfth century; they result from the deposition of nacre on a lead or tin model that has been inserted between the shell and the mantle of a freshwater mollusk and left in place for several years. In the nineteenth century, the Japanese used this technique to produce half pearls, formed from a half sphere of nacre fixed to the shell, under the mantle of the oyster pearl. The cultured half pearls were then glued to nacre, bezel-set into jewelry, and sold in Europe under the deceptive name Japanese pearls.

Linnaeus was the first to understand the formation of pearls and even managed to produce some cultured pearls, despite the poor antisepsis of the times. However, the true development of pearl culturing can be attributed to the Japanese. There was, for example, a research center at Lake Biwa, near Kyoto. The history of pearl culturing, however, is definitely that of the patience, will, and perseverance of a now famous self-made man, Kokichi Mikimoto (1858–1954). At the age of thirty-two, he decided to raise and graft pearl oysters to save the beds near Tobe from complete destruction by intensive fishing. He developed the technique of culturing in baskets attached to ropes in the waters around the island called the Pearl Island, now a cultured-pearl museum dedicated to Mikimoto. He also introduced a new method for grafting mantle tissue around the nacre nucleus to produce nacre layers. He persevered despite the high mortality rate of the oysters he manipulated and despite catastrophes that nearly destroyed all the oysters, such as typhoons and red tides (a rapid growth of algae that suffocates all marine creatures). At the end of his life, he oversaw a large cultured-pearl empire.

Saltwater Culturing Techniques

Japanese cultured pearls were introduced on the international market in 1920. The current technique that the Japanese use to culture pearls in saltwater starts with raising *Meleagrina martensi* from birth to the age of three, at which time a nacre nucleus is surgically inserted in the gonad next to a 0.5 centimeter-square piece of external palleal epithelium from a sacrificed one-year-old oyster. The gonad feeds this graft, which eventually forms a sack around the nucleus and covers it with layers of nacre. The cultured pearl grows for three to five years in the oyster, which is then killed (its meat is used in the food industry). The thickness of the nacre layer on the cultured pearl reaches 0.5 to 1 millimeter, depending on the health of the grafted oyster. One *Meleagrina martensi* can hold one or two grafts. Generally only one graft is introduced, and 30 percent of the oysters die after the insertion. Another third of the grafts do not cover the nacre nucleus properly. Thus, for an average-size nucleus (5 millimeters in diameter), only one-third of the oysters will produce cultured pearls. With a 9-millimeter-diameter nucleus, this proportion falls to 5 percent.

Japanese Saltwater Pearl Farms

Japanese pearl culturing farms occupy all the small creeks along the southern coast of Japan. Each farm consists of several

A freshwater pearl farm in Lake Biwa, Japan. Photo: J.-P. Poirot.

rafts formed by a wide-mesh (1-meter or 3-foot) net of bamboo, attached to floaters. Baskets holding the oysters are held with ropes under 5 to 6 meters (15 to 18 feet) of water. Each month the pearl oysters are brushed to protect them from parasites, such as algae or small mollusks. *Amas* dive to recover baskets that have fallen to the bottom during a typhoon or simply to inspect the rafts.

Cultured Pearls from Lake Biwa

Freshwater pearl culturing using the clam *Hieropsis schlegeli* has been developed since 1960 at Lake Biwa, near Kyoto, Japan. The mollusk sacrificed for the graft is either *Hieropsis schlegeli* itself or another mollusk. The graft is inserted, without a nacre nucleus, into the clam's mantle, and it produces oval to baroque cultured pearls with a broad, irregular center. Each clam can take up to twenty grafts in each valve, for a total of forty grafts, but in general only ten to fifteen grafts are set in each valve to avoid exhausting the animal. After growing for five years, the cultured pearls are carefully extracted from the mollusk, avoiding injury to the clam as much as possible, since it may produce one or two more generations of pearls. As a matter of fact, these Lake Biwa bivalves can live for as long as forty years, whereas a pearl oyster lives only seven to eight years. More rarely, cultured pearls with a nacre nucleus have been produced in Lake Biwa.

The pearl-culturing farms are marked by bamboos planted in the mud of the lake, to which horizontal bamboos are attached, supporting the baskets full of mollusks. The cultured pearls produced are generally baroque and are white or a pastel color.

Pearl-culturing Farms outside Japan

Non-Japanese saltwater pearl farms work with the larger *Pinctada* or *Meleagrina* oysters (*Meleagrina maxima* and *Meleagrina margaritifera*). The first attempts were made in Indonesia from 1922 to 1941. These were followed by developments throughout the South Pacific: in the Mergui Archipelago of Myanmar (Burma); in Australia since 1955 to 1959, both on the west coast near Broome and in the north at Cape York; in the Philippines since 1962; and in Tahiti since 1965. The Tahiti farms raise oysters and fish the young *Meleagrina margaritifera*, which produces black cultured pearls. However, the other pearl farms have difficulties finding oysters to graft, because the farming of *Meleagrina maxima* has still not been mastered. So pearl fishermen have become nacre fishermen, selling adult oysters to the farms. Since the end of the 1970s, freshwater pearl culturing has been developed in China following the model of Lake Biwa; Chinese cultured pearls are often marketed through Japanese dealers.

Appearance and Identification of Cultured Pearls

With the exception of black cultured pearls from Tahiti, cultured pearls are generally cleaned, bleached, and dyed in colors that sell well. Cultured pearls are graded according to their orient, clarity, shape, and size. A pearl with too thin a nacre layer is delicate; this layer may peel off the nacre nucleus after a sharp blow. It also reveals the chatoyant aspect of the nacre bead beneath, which becomes even more distinct when viewed in front of a very strong source of light. South Seas cultured pearls

The opening of a Meleagrina during pearl harvesting. Source: Jetro.

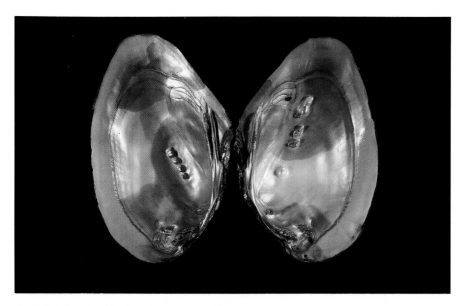

The shell of Hieropsis schlegeli, *with some cultured blister pearls. Private collection.*

have a thicker nacre layer, but their orient is not as marked; they may occasionally be peeled if the outer layer is of poor quality.

A classic cultured pearl with a nacre nucleus always seems somewhat too perfectly round to the eye. Freshwater cultured pearls, such as those from Lake Biwa, are always too baroque. In the laboratory, cultured pearls are easily distinguished from natural pearls, due to the presence of their nacre nucleus or organic center, easily seen using endoscopy, X-radiography or X-ray diffraction.

Other Types of Pearls

The Japanese and Australians have followed the ancient Chinese technique of inserting a nacre sphere or half sphere between the mantle and the shell of a mollusk. In the first case, a blister pearl is produced, which is cut from the shell and glued to a nacre slab; the assembled material is three-quarters cultured pearl. In the second case, after sawing off the shell, one gets a half sphere formed by the pearl layers detached from the nacre half sphere. This half sphere is filled with wax (to provide support) and glued to a nacre slab. The final product is called a mabe pearl, *mabe* being the Japanese name of the shell *Pteria* used to obtain the raw material. Mabe pearls are exported largely to Spain and other southern European countries.

Imitation Pearls

Around 1680 a French rosary maker by the name of Jasquin, living in Passy, on the outskirts of Paris, manufactured the first pearl imitations. Noticing that the scales of small fish could evoke the orient

of pearls, he produced a concentrate from them that he called *essence d'orient*. The imitation pearl was made from a hollow glass sphere obtained by blowing a thin glass tube, so that the sphere would be thin as well. The *essence d'orient* was introduced through one of the apertures and smeared on the internal surface of the sphere, which was then filled with white wax. Such imitations were fabricated until the early twentieth century; it was said that "a fake pearl breaks easily and slips under the tooth, in contrast with a natural pearl," referring to the imitations. This maxim is no longer true for the newer products made of opalescent glass beads covered with several layers of *essence d'orient,* fish-scale extract dissolved in an organic solvent. Today's imitation pearls do not break easily, but they flake; they do seem rough under the tooth, like natural or cultured pearls. The *essence d'orient* is sometimes replaced by chemicals, sometimes with lead compounds (as in Japan), sometimes by bismuth salts or even plastics. Nacre beads have been used to replace the glass beads. This product very much resembles a cultured pearl with a thin nacre layer and several years ago was at the center of a major scam in the Far East.

From the Mollusk to the Market

The world's stock of natural pearls is hardly renewed, since there have been no fishing campaigns for natural pearls since World War II. The trade essentially involves reselling old pearls, on a nevertheless strong market. Paris and London remain important trade centers. Some exceptional pearls are offered for sale by auction houses such as Sotheby's and Christie's, es-

pecially in Switzerland. Ear pendants that had belonged to Marie-Antoinette were sold some years back in this way. Most often, pearls from old European families are exported to the United States.

After harvest, cultured pearls are sold primarily in bunches—a number of strands with cultured pearls of similar diameter—in Kobe or Tokyo. Only Japanese buyers can buy cultured pearls from the farms. The quality of the pearls is closely checked by the government. These buyers also try to force foreign pearls, such as Chinese freshwater pearls and South Seas cultured pearls through Japan. However, they cannot control the development of local markets; for example, Papeete has become a market for the pearl production of French Polynesia. London and Paris have maintained their old pearl traditions and are the distribution centers for cultured pearls in Europe. However, the vast majority of cultured pearls with nacre nuclei are sold in the United States (through New York and Los Angeles); most mantle-nucleated cultured pearls are sold in the Middle East (Beirut).

Natural and cultured pearls can be half-drilled, for mounting with a metallic peg on rings, earrings, or brooches, or they can be drilled through to be strung in a necklace. A necklace in which the pearls decrease in diameter from the center to the ends is called a graduated necklace (a French style). If all the pearls are of the same diameter, it is called a choker. Pearl "fabrics" have been manufactured for scarves or ribbons, a style particularly popular among Indian royalty.

Japanese farms have been forced in recent years to readjust the price of cultured pearls to take into account increased labor costs and the consequences of worsening water pollution, resulting in a somewhat

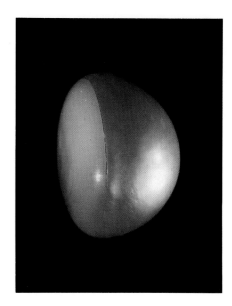

A mabe pearl: a ³/₄ cultured pearl–nacre doublet. Private collection.

The grading of cultured pearls in Japan. Source: Jetro.

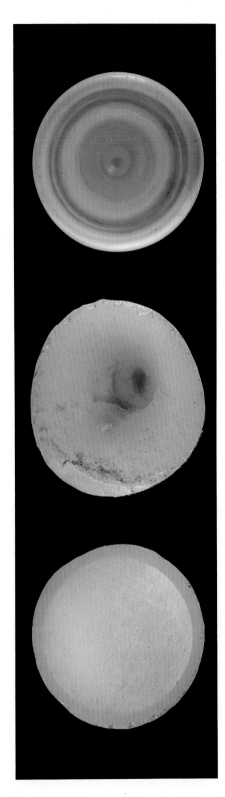

From top to bottom, cross sections of a natural pearl, a mantle-nucleated cultured pearl, and a cultured pearl with a nacre nucleus. Diameter: 0.5 cm.

stronger natural-pearls market. Both markets are rather strong at the moment (cultured pearls helped some French jewelry companies survive the diamond crash of the early 1980s).

To enable natural pearls of different sizes to be comparatively priced, the pricing of light-colored pearls (for example, pinkish or pale yellow) is done by squaring the mass in grain (called the "once the weight" price) by a value coefficient based solely on beauty, orient, cleanliness, and shape. A pearl is sold at so many times its base price (or "once the weight" value). This method applies to the global value of a graduated necklace, for example. Between 1915 and 1940, pearl dealers offered their customers pearl price lists, which were simply tables of squares helping them to compute more easily the "once the weight" value of their necklaces. Natural black pearls are sold by the carat, the price per carat taking mass into account.

Cultured pearls with a nacre nucleus can be sold by the "momme" (18.75 carats), carat, or diameter. The value coefficient depends on color, orient, cleanliness, thickness of the pearl layer, and size. Mantle-nucleated cultured pearls are sold by the carat. Their value is always less than that of cultured pearls of the same quality with a nacre nucleus. Just as a necklace of excellent imitation pearls may be worth as much as a cultured-pearl necklace of poor quality, a necklace of high-quality cultured pearls may cost as much as a mediocre natural-pearl necklace, for the same-size pearls.

Natural Materials that Resemble Pearls

Nacre beads, chatoyant in two diametrically opposed spots, are only mediocre pearl imitations. Some coral beads resemble conch pearls, despite their very different structure. Hematite beads show a metallic black luster but do not exhibit the orient of black pearls. Finally, the balas diamond has an adamantine luster and a gray translucence, which can evoke a light gray pearl.

PECTOLITE

A calcium and sodium silicate, related to the zeolite family.

Until the 1980s pectolite was known primarily as a gray gem material, found mostly near Paterson, New Jersey, and cut into cabochons for collectors. In the early 1980s, a major source of turquoise-blue material was discovered in the southwestern part of the Dominican Republic, near the town of Bahoruco, in an altered basalt. This material, also called larimar and presumably colored by copper, is very tough and is used mostly for cabochons and small carvings. Red dendrites of hematite are present in the "red plume" variety.

PERIDOT

An orthorhombic ferromagnesian silicate, forming a continuous series from the magnesian pole of forsterite to the ferrous pole of fayalite. Gem-quality peridot, also called *olivine* or *chrysolite*, contains about 15 percent fayalite.

Origin of the Name and History

The word *peridot* comes from the Old French *peritot*, which is of uncertain origin; it may derive from the Arabic *faridat*, meaning "precious stone." Forsterite was named in honor of the English mineralogist J. Forster, and fayalite refers to Faial Island in the Azores archipelago, where it was described for the first time.

Peridot was already known and valued during ancient times; it has been found in many archaeological digs. It came then from the Zebirget Island in the Red Sea (also formerly called Topazos; see TOPAZ; CHRYSOLITE). Berenice II (ca. 269–221 B.C.), mother of Ptolemy IV Philipator, is remembered in the name Berenice, the Egyptian port from which Zebirget can be reached.

Not until the Crusades was peridot introduced to Western Europe. It was often called "Crusader's emerald," and it adorns many reliquaries under this name: a good example is the chest of the Three Wise Men in Cologne Cathedral in Germany.

When the Spanish brought emeralds from America back to Europe, the public lost interest in peridot. In 1668 Pierre de Rosnel wrote that peridot was "a greenish stone like chrysolite, . . . in little usage" and repeated a saying about it, common among jewelers at the time: "He who has two has one too many."

Many writers have been impressed by the size and the abundance of peridot. To Pliny the Elder, it was the largest—*amplissima*—of gems. To Chriten in 1868, "It is the most common of all precious stones, and peridot is remarkable only by its size." Indeed the treasury of the Russian crown (now the Diamond Fund of the Soviet Union) has a 192.75-carat elongated step-cut peridot, measuring 5.2 by 3.5 by 1.05 centimeters (2 by 1.4 by 0.4 inches). It was formerly mounted, surrounded by thirty diamonds. The Geological Museum in London has a square step-cut 146.17-carat peridot. But the world's largest peridots are in the Smithsonian Institution in Washington: a 287-carat oval shape faceted in a Burmese crystal, and another 310-carat stone, the world's largest faceted peridot, cut from a Zebirget crystal.

Because of the yellowish green color of this gem, the symbolism and virtues of peridot are similar to those of topaz. However, some of its supposed powers are more specific, such as inhibiting sensuality and halting blood flow. It is said to heal fevers, including yellow fever, as well as intestinal and eye ailments.

Physical Properties

The crystalline structure of peridot is similar to that of chrysoberyl: silicon replaces the beryllium, and iron and magnesium replace the aluminum. Iron produces the olive green color, which may be quite dark, becoming black in fayalite. Peridot is idiochromatic and offers a very limited range of colors, with some minor variations due to the replacement of magnesium or iron by small amounts of manganese, calcium, nickel, and chromium. It does not display dichroism.

Gem-quality peridot is essentially magnesian and always shows an absorption spectrum typical of ferrous iron (three principal absorptions in the blue region of the spectrum). It does not luminesce in black light. Its indices of refraction are close to 1.65 (n_p), 1.67 (n_m), and 1.69 (n_g). The magnesian members of the series, which

Diamond and peridot necklace and ear pendants (the necklace centerpiece is 32.54 carats, and the pendants have a total weight of 42.13 carats). Fred creation.

are too pale and too rare (indices of forsterite, 1.635, 1.651, 1.670), and their ferriferous equivalents, which are too dark (indices of fayalite, 1.827, 1.869, 1.879), are not used in jewelry.

A doubling of the facet junctions on the side of the stone opposite the observer is visible because of peridot's high birefringence, 0.036. Gem-quality peridot is biaxial without sign (the optical axes are almost perpendicular).

The specific gravity of peridot, 3.35, is slightly higher than that of diiodomethane (3.21 for fayalite and 4.27 for forsterite). Peridot is slightly softer than quartz; its fracture is conchoidal, but its cleavage is not easy. It is barely appropriate for use in jewelry. It may be scratched when cleaned with a dry cloth (because of dust). In addition, it is attacked by acids, forming a silica deposit. One should never clean jewelry containing peridot in the acid-cleaning solutions commonly used for jewelry today. Peridot is difficult to polish; it "greases" the wheel. Chriten described his polishing method, still used today, as follows: "Peridot is simply faceted on a lead lap; it is not

always easy to work . . . . The slightest increase in temperature makes it crack although it is polished on a wheel mixed with tin and lead . . . . For safer results, one should use Venice tripoli [silica powder] and sulfuric acid, called by the old lapidaries 'drug' or 'sulphur oil.' "

Inclusions

Gem-quality peridot is usually inclusion free. Occasionally, very small crystals of minerals formed at high pressure and high temperature may be encountered as inclusions, such as chrome diopside, chrome spinel, and phlogopite. More frequently, "lily pad" inclusions are the result of a disclike fracture in a cleavage plane of small negative crystals filled with gases (carbon dioxide) or sometimes glass.

Mineralogy and Deposits

Peridot crystals are very rare and come almost exclusively from Zebirget. They are most commonly flattened and striated parallel to their length, with an orthorhombic

A 5-cm-tall peridot crystal from Zebirget Island, Egypt. National Higher School of Mines, Paris.

An 80-carat faceted peridot from Myanmar (Burma). German Precious Stones Museum, Idar-Oberstein, Germany.

pyramid at the top. Their size is generally between 1 and 2 centimeters (⅜ and ¾ inch), but in exceptional cases they can reach 10 centimeters (4 inches), as does one crystal in the British Museum.

Peridot originates deep in the earth, under high temperatures, characteristic of silica-poor rocks. Peridotites owe their name to this gem. It accompanies diamond in kimberlites and makes up dunites, rocks often rich in platinum. It may form important enclaves inside basalts. It is mined in alluvial deposits or in situ, if the host rock has been serpentinized by weathering.

The most important and most famous peridot deposit historically is Zebirget Island, (which is 2 by 3 kilometers or 1¼ by 1¾ miles), and is located in the Red Sea, about 80 kilometers (50 miles) southeast of Berenice, near Cape Banas. Its "treasure," probably mined as early as the first millennium B.C., was jealously guarded and kept secret from foreigners. Apparently it was overlooked even by the Crusaders, who dedicated the island to Saint John. Thus, the source of "chrysolite" remained a mystery until its discovery in the early twentieth century, when it was mined in 1906 by a French group working under the authority of the khedive, the Ottoman viceroy governing Egypt. Peridots were mined in large quantities (the equivalent of $2 million [1985 dollars] during the first four years) and were sent to France for faceting. In 1922, the mining rights were transferred to the Red Sea Mining Company. In 1958 the mines were nationalized and subsequently abandoned.

Zebirget Island is difficult to access because it is surrounded by coral reefs. It is mostly desert, with no fresh water. Its highest point is Peridot Hill (235 meters or 770 feet high), a mass of ultrabasic rocks surrounded by metamorphic rocks including serpentines, granulites, and slates. Peridot crystals are found in the open fractures of the rock, especially in the serpentinized areas, on the east flank of the hill. The crystals are often fractured by tectonic movements.

After World War II, the serpentines of the Kyaukpon Mountains in Upper Burma (Myanmar) became important sources of peridot. These mountains, with an altitude of 2,250 meters (7,300 feet) are near Pyanggaung, in the Bernardmyo Valley, about 35 kilometers (20 miles) north of Mogok. It is quite possible that the kingdom of Pegu provided some of the peridots so appreciated before the Renaissance, as well as a number of those used during the nineteenth century.

Today the world's largest producer of peridot is the San Carlos Apache reservation, near the Gila River in Arizona. In this very rich deposit, ants supposedly build their anthills (up to 1 meter or 3 feet high) with grains of peridot that they find in the ground. The deposit has long been known

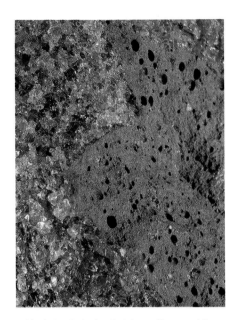

Peridot in San Carlos basalt, Arizona. Diameter: 15 cm. G. Becker collection.

by Native Americans, who use this gem for tribal ornament. Although it was intensely mined from 1904 to 1909, this deposit is now worked only sporadically. No production statistics are available. Peridot is found as small grains gathered in nodules, of 1 to 30 centimeters (⅜ to 12 inches). These nodules are found in a basalt flow—Peridot Mesa—covering a surface area of about 5.6 by 4.4 kilometers (3½ by 2¾ miles) with a thickness of 3 to 30 meters (10 to 100 feet). The nodules are often a yard or more apart, and the size of the peridot grains does not allow faceted stones larger than 3 carats. A remarkable exception is the 34.65-carat peridot from the collection of the American Gem Society, which was faceted in a triangular shape from an Arizona crystal.

Other localities also produce gem-quality peridot, including the sands of Hawaii, where small peridots contain traces of chromium, making their color more attractive; the Azores; Söndmöre, Norway; Aubigny County in Queensland, Australia, and recently, Tanzania.

Meteorites sometimes contain gem-quality peridot; for example, a meteorite that fell in 1749 in the Yenisei, in Siberia, believed by the Tatars to be a goddess from the heavens, provided a few rounded grains of peridot suitable for faceting in 1772.

Natural Gems with a Similar Appearance and Simulants

All yellowish green gems may resemble peridot, especially demantoid garnet, zircon, sapphire, chrysoberyl, sinhalite, tourmaline, topaz, beryl, obsidian (moldavite), and fluorite.

Synthetic peridot is not produced commercially, although it would be easy to manufacture forsterite in the laboratory.

The numerous peridot imitations are easy to identify: they include colored glasses, garnet-glass doublets, synthetic spinel—colored enamel—synthetic spinel triplets, and synthetic spinel and synthetic corundum in appropriate colors.

PEROVSKITE

A calcium titanate, crystallizing in the orthorhombic system. Perovskite is named for the Russian mineralogist L. A. Perovski.

This mineral, which accompanies diamond in kimberlites, has no gemological interest except that it was used as a model for the flame-fusion synthesis of strontium titanate. Strontium titanate is a cubic diamond simulant, popular in the 1960s, which has been sold since 1955 under the name Fabulite; it has no natural equivalent. Because it has the same index of refraction as diamond (n_d is 2.41), Fabulite represented a clear improvement over synthetic rutile. However, it is not hard (H is 5 to 6) or tough and is very sensitive to pressure (the point of a needle applied to its surface produces chipping). In addition, its dispersion is four times that of diamond, so it produces a strong decomposition of light instead of harmonious "fires."

Fabulite has been used as the pavilion for synthetic corundum—Fabulite doublets and even diamond—Fabulite doublets. The two materials are joined on the pavilion

side so that these fairly convincing imitations can be safely set and worn without damage from shocks.

PETALITE

A lithium aluminosilicate, crystallizing in the monoclinic system. This colorless to pale yellow mineral owes its name to its perfect cleavage, since it comes from the Greek *petalon*, which means "sheet" or "plaque" (D'Andrada, 1800).

Petalite is a rare mineral from the sodium-lithium pegmatites around Araçuai (Maxixe), in Minas Gerais, Brazil, and is faceted only for collectors. Petalite is not hard (H is 6), and it has a perfect cleavage. Its luster is vitreous (indices of refraction: n_p is 1.505, n_m is 1.512, n_g is 1.520), and its specific gravity is about 2.4.

It is a common inclusion of synthetic emeralds. A 55-carat petalite is displayed at the Smithsonian Institution in Washington, D.C.

PETRIFIED WOOD

Wood that has been fossilized through impregnation by silica (usually chalcedony, sometimes opal). It is also called xyloid agate, from the Greek *xylon*, meaning "wood."

The wood vessels and structure in the fossil are generally well preserved. Magnificent colors may result from the presence of various clays in the silica pseudomorph.

Phenakite crystals from San Miguel de Piracicaba, Minas Gerais, Brazil. Length: 4 cm. Sorbonne collection.

A slab of petrified wood from the United States. Width: 30 cm. Compagnie Générale de Madagascar, Paris.

True petrified forests include Red Deer Valley in Alberta, Canada, and, in the United States, Eden Valley in Wyoming and the Petrified Forest National Park in Arizona. Other examples are found on the Ahaggar plateau in North Africa, in Madagascar, and in Brazil. The silicified tree trunks are often sawed into polished slabs, used for ornamentation (tables, seats, abstract pictures, small objets d'art, bookends); cabochons are often cut from silicified fruits or silicified palm tree.

PHENAKITE

A beryllium silicate, crystallizing in the (hexagonal) rhombohedral system. Phenakite forms elongated and striated hexagonal prisms, terminating at a rhombohedron, a general shape that resembles that of quartz, hence, its name, from the Greek *phenax,* meaning "impostor" or "charlatan." Phenakite also forms flattened crystals with numerous faces, which are transparent and colorless.

Phenakite is a rare mineral, and its deposits are similar to those of beryl, with which it is often associated, as in the Tokovaja mica schists in the Urals. It was abundant in the San Miguel de Piracicaba pegmatite in Minas Gerais, Brazil, where several tons of this mineral were recovered about fifty years ago. It was recently discovered in similar crystal shapes in the same state, at Pica Pau, near Três Barras, as well as in the Socotó emerald deposit near Campo Formoso.

A 1,470-carat rough pebble was found in Sri Lanka, from which a 569-carat clear gem was cut.

Although it is colorless or pale colored, phenakite is hard enough to be used in jewelry (H is 7½ to 8, no cleavages) and displays the same sharp luster as topaz (indices of refraction of 1.654 for the ordinary ray and 1.670 for the extraordinary ray, with a birefringence of 0.016). It is nevertheless too rare to be more than a collector's item. Phenakite is also found as an inclusion in synthetic emeralds.

PLASMA

A green jasper consisting of chalcedony closely combined with various microcrystalline silicates, such as chlorite and amphibole. Its color ranges from a dark leek green to a dark apple green, and it often displays small white or yellow spots. Polished, it can be used as a mirror, hence, its name, from the Greek *plasma,* meaning "image." Plasma resembles green rocks such as jade and is found especially in India, China, and Oregon.

PLEONASTE

A black iron-rich spinel, common in the gem-bearing gravels of Sri Lanka, which has been little used in jewelry. It was named in allusion to its multiple crystal shapes, after the Greek *pleonasmos,* which means "superabundance." Its index of refraction, 1.77 to 1.80, and specific gravity, 3.63 to 3.90, are higher than those for regular gem spinel.

PRASE

A light green chalcedony colored by dispersed fibers of hornblende (chlorite may also be associated). Also, light green quartz colored by numerous fibrous actinolite inclusions. The name comes from the Greek *prasios,* meaning "light green," derived from *prasion,* that is, "leek" or "algae." Prase comes primarily from Vermont and Pennsylvania.

PRASIOLITE

A transparent light green quartz, named for its color, from the Greek *prasios,* which means "light green," and *lithos,* meaning "stone." This gem is very rare in nature. Since 1953 this term has been used to describe the amethysts from the Montezuma mine near Vitória de Conquista, in the state of Bahia, Brazil; these stones turn green when heated to 650°C (1,200°F), and have been marketed without much success. The same type of amethyst has been found in Arizona. The Smithsonian Institution displays a 22.3-carat "greened" amethyst crystal.

PREHNITE

An aluminocalcic silicate, crystallizing in the orthorhombic system. It was named for Colonel Hendrik von Prehn, who brought this new species back from the Cape of Good Hope, in South Africa.

Prehnite rarely forms well-defined crystals, although some have been found in Asbestos, in Quebec, Canada. More often, it produces pale green cryptocrystalline masses. Groups of helmet-shaped, flattened crystals have been found near Bourg d'Oisans, France. Sometimes it molds around zeolite crystals and takes on a stalactite shape.

Prehnite is transparent to translucent, with a somewhat greasy to nacreous luster (indices of refraction are 1.610, 1.625, 1.650). Its hardness is 6 to 6½, and its specific gravity 2.80. It was deceptively presented as "Cape emerald" in South Africa. Gem crystals of up to 5 carats have been faceted for collectors.

Prehnite is an alteration mineral accompanying zeolites in the cavities of igneous rocks, found, for example in the trapps of the Deccan (India), in New Jersey (USA), and in Australia. It is also found in alpine clefts with axinite and epidote.

PYRITE

A cubic iron sulfide with a brass-yellow color. Its composition may vary, as nickel or cobalt can replace the iron.

The name *pyrite* derives from *pur*, which means "fire," from the Greek *purites*. It is so named because this mineral has been known since the ancient times to produce sparks when struck, which can easily light dry twigs. "It is essential to military patrols, which, by hitting it with a nail or a stone, obtain sparks to light their fire," reported Pliny the Elder.

Calcinated or crushed, pyrite was also used in medicine to heal boils and scrofula. This practice was mentioned by Pliny the Elder and the Greek physicians Dioscorides and Galen and was still in use at the beginning of the seventeenth century; it was reported by Boece de Boot, doctor to the German Emperor Rudolf II of Hapsburg.

Also called Incan mirror because several pyrite mirrors were discovered in Peruvian graves during the Spanish conquest, pyrite was not used much before the seventeenth or eighteenth century.

Most often rose-cut, it decorated belt buckles, garters, or the frames of watches and pictures. According to T. Chriten, "It was forbidden in Switzerland to wear diamonds, so women wear nothing else but marcasite (pyrite) jewelry, for which they spend much money." After a decline in the use of pyrite, an important but temporary fad for pyrite ornament began in the middle of the nineteenth century. This sudden interest produced a flood of material from Switzerland and the French Jura, where pyrite was faceted and set, but this sudden abundance quenched public interest. Today pyrite is still used in small quantities in jewelry, in an attempt to imitate diamonds.

Pure and freshly polished, pyrite has a bright, light yellow metallic luster (reflecting power of 54 percent), but this mineral rapidly tarnishes to a grayish color. Relatively hard (H is 6½) but not tough, pyrite has a specific gravity of approximately 5.

Because of its golden color, pyrite is often mistaken for gold (it is also known as fool's gold), especially in the gems in which it is found frequently as an inclusion, such as lapis lazuli and emerald.

PYROPE

A red aluminomagnesian garnet. It is exceptionally colorless when pure.

Origin of the Name and Renowned Specimens

Pyrope comes from the late Greek *puropos,* derived from *pur,* meaning "fire," and *opos,* "appearance." It is very likely that this gem was known in ancient times and may have been confused by Pliny the Elder with other red gems under the name *carbonculus,* which means "burning amber."

The world's largest pyrope, the size of a hen's egg, comes from Bohemia (Czechoslovakia). It is now the centerpiece of a necklace kept in the Kunsthistorisches Museum in Vienna. Emperor Rudolf II of Hapsburg (1552–1612) reportedly paid 45,000 thalers for it (that is, about $30,000)). The Golden Fleece of the Great Elector of Saxony, displayed in the Grünes Gevölbe in Dresden, includes a 468-carat pyrope.

Physical Properties

Like ruby, pyrope owes its color to a slight substitution of chromium for aluminum. But iron always replaces part of the magnesium, preventing luminescence under black light. With a spectroscope one can see a small red transmission window with two sharp lines, due to chromium.

Prehnite crystals from the Combe de la Selle, near Bourg d'Oisans, Isère, France. Length: 4 cm. Sorbonne collection.

Pyrite crystal from Elba, Italy. Diameter: 10 cm. Sorbonne collection.

Light pyropes are called rhodolites. The index of refraction and specific gravity vary with the iron content, from 1.715 to 1.75 and 3.47 to 3.85 respectively. Pyrope's hardness is quite good, 7 to 7½.

Deposits and Inclusions

Pyrope is used in diamond prospecting because it is typically found in kimberlites, associated with peridot, diopside, and phlogopite. Some kimberlites do not carry diamonds; such are the kimberlites from Bohemia, where pyrope was mined near Trebenice, usually in alluvial deposits. These supplied a local lapidary and jewelry manufacturing industry, which disappeared at

the turn of the century. This activity is now concentrated in Idar-Oberstein, Germany. Pyrope is also found in eclogites.

South African kimberlites produce pyrope garnets, in particular in Kimberley. Pyrope is also found around Lake Baikal in the Soviet Union, in Arizona in the United States, in New South Wales and Queensland in Australia, in Brazil (in the "mine triangle" of Minas Gerais and Estrela do Sul, for example), in Tanzania, and in many other countries.

Uses for Pyrope

Rough crystals of pyrope are occasionally drilled to manufacture necklaces, rosaries, and other religious objects.

Gems with a Similar Appearance

Red spinel most resembles pyrope: its index of refraction is similar, but its specific gravity is lower, and its absorption spectrum and slight luminescence under black light help distinguish it from pyrope.

Rough pyrope and Bohemian garnet jewelry. Length of the brooch: 5.4 cm. Private collection.

QUARTZ

A silicon dioxide, crystallizing in the rhombohedral (hexagonal) system. See also AMETHYST; CITRINE; ROCK CRYSTAL.

Origin of the Name

Quartz is said to come from an old German mining term, *quaderz*, which meant "bad ore" or "matrix," as in the old invocation: "God, who creates the dull *(Kies),* the glistening *(Glanz),* and the matrix *(Quertz)* / Transform for us the last into ore." *Kies* is a metallic ore with the luster of brass, such as chalcopyrite *(Kupferkies,* "copper gravel"). *Glanz* is a metallic ore with a silvery luster, such as galena *(Bleiglanz,* "lead splendor") or hematite *(Eisenglanz,* "iron splendor"). German miners

were employed all over Europe and spread the use of this term. By the end of the eighteenth century, it was used only for massive, grainy, hard quartz, considered the "mother" of rock crystal. The entire quartz family was united under the term during the nineteenth century.

The word *quartz* may have been borrowed, in turn, by the Germans from the Slavs: the ancient Slavic *tvrudu,* meaning "hard," became *kwardy* in occidental Slav, *tvrdy* in Czech, and *twardy* in Polish, and could have evolved into *quard(erz)* in the mining community.

Another hypothesis links the Latin tradition that transformed *silex, silicis* ("stone") into *silica* and *calx, calcis* ("lime") into *calcite* with a parallel German tradition, which reportedly transformed *Crioz* ("gravel") into *Kies, Kiesel* ("silica"), *Greiss* (meaning "gravel" in modern German), and *quartz.*

Crystallography and Deposits

Quartz has many crystal shapes—more than a hundred have been identified. Most often it forms a hexagonal prism terminating at both ends by a hexagonal pyramid; prism faces are easy to recognize because of their striations perpendicular to their length. Sometimes certain prism faces are more developed than others, so that the prism section and the pyramid above appear triangular.

Quartz crystals have different general appearances, or facies, depending on their geological origin. Those from the alpine clefts show a chisellike termination because of the abnormal development of one of the faces (as in La Gardette, Isére, France); the often flattened prism gives the impression of a pseudoorthorhombic facies.

In low-temperature veins, quartz crystals show only the pyramid. In pegmatites

Cameo of a vestal virgin in rock crystal. Height: 1.9 cm. M. De Bry collection.

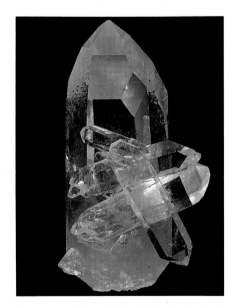

Quartz crystal from Corinto, Minas Gerais, Brazil. Height: 10 cm. Sorbonne collection.

crystals are often distorted. "Window quartz" shows facies on the surface forming negative steps, a result of dislocations of the crystalline lattice during growth. "Scepter quartz" is formed by a biterminated crystal perched, parallel, on a thinner prismatic one; it may have a variegated color.

Quartz twins are common and varied and can occur by contact or penetration. In

the first case, the crystals can be envisioned as separated by a plane, which is a common face, and are generally flattened (La Gardette or Japanese twins). In the second case, both crystals are so intimately entwined that they seem to be only one crystal; the repetition of rare trapezohedral faces allows their identification.

Some quartz crystals can weigh tens of tons and still be transparent, such as those from Minas Gerais in Brazil. In France, a crystal at Saint-Paul-la-Roche, in Dordogne, measures over two meters (6 feet) tall.

Free silica tends to express itself as quartz in all acidic rocks (granites, granodiorites, syenites, and others). Quartz may also be found in microcrystalline rocks and lavas, where it appears as small bipyramidal crystals, often of very nice quality.

Quartz is abundant in granitic pegmatites, in particular in the "block" zone (see BERYL). It may reach very large dimensions (several tons) in the quartz core of large pegmatitic bodies. Such a situation exists in Brazil, where quartz forms masses of several thousand tons.

It is a common matrix mineral in ore deposits. It can even produce some magnificent geodes, as in the tin-tungsten deposits of Panasqueira, Portugal. In alpine clefts, it marks the boundary between pneumatolytic and hydrothermal conditions. Quartz is also common in metamorphic rocks such as mica schist or gneiss but rarely forms nice crystals there. Finally, it is found as a minor component of sedimentary rocks. Its abundance (18 percent by volume) in the earth's continental crust, as deep as 18 kilometers (11 miles) below the surface, makes it a universally distributed mineral species. It is also a major component of dusts: gems that can be scratched by quartz are therefore difficult to use in jewelry, because they will likely be abraded by this omnipresent mineral.

Crystallochemistry and Physical Properties

Surrounded by four oxygen atoms, silicon forms SiO_4 tetrahedra, with an oxygen atom at each summit.

By sharing a corner, these tetrahedra build helicoidal chains with a sixfold symmetry (quartz β, a high-temperature variety formed above 573°C (1,060°F), or a threefold symmetry (quartz α, formed at low temperatures). Assembled at the tetrahedra corners that have remained free, these chains produce a crystalline edifice full of vacuums, consistent with the low values of the physical constants of this mineral (H is 7 by definition; S.G., 2.65; indices of refraction, extraordinary, 1.553 and ordinary, 1.544; uniaxial positive with a birefringence of 0.009).

Quartz has no good cleavage, and its

fracture is conchoidal. It exhibits a vitreous luster, sometimes even greasy. The helicoidal architecture also accounts for two peculiar properties of quartz: its rotary power, easily detected between crossed polarizers on pieces of quartz cut perpendicular to the optic axis, and its piezoelectricity, which is applied in watchmaking.

The Main Varieties of Quartz

Pure quartz—rock crystal—is colorless and transparent, but most quartz crystals are milky white and more or less translucent (quartz girasol, milky quartz). This mineral can also be brownish (smoky quartz, cairngorm), or even almost black (morion); this coloration is the result of natural irradiation, which induces structural accidents involving aluminum, which replaces silicon at some tetrahedral sites.

Exposure to a powerful source of radiation will turn colorless quartz black; this coloration can later be bleached by heating. Numerous colorless quartz groups from Arkansas have been treated in this way over the last ten years. The typical facies of natural smoky quartz enables experienced mineralogists to distinguish them from their treated counterparts.

Purple quartz is called *amethyst;* its color, due to iron, may be irregularly distributed within the crystal. When heated to about 250°C (980°F) amethyst becomes colorless; it turns yellow (to citrine) at around 500°C (930°F), or sometimes green (prasiolite). Rose quartz owes its color to titanium. Hematoid quartz owes its orange to red color to iron oxyhydroxides.

During its growth quartz may trap various minerals or defects that produce a peculiar appearance: Venus hair stone (quartz with golden yellow to red rutile needles); Thetis hair stone (quartz with green actinolite needles); Cupid's darts (quartz with black tourmaline needles); and iris quartz (with iridescent fractures).

Sometimes the abundance of inclusions makes quartz translucent or opaque; such an appearance may also be due to mineral precipitation inside the crystal due to exsolution of rutile, water, or other compounds. The main varieties are: *girasol quartz* (translucent), and *milky quartz* (opaque), filled with microscopic fluid inclusions; *rose quartz,* containing microscopic rutile needles; *hematoid quartz,* rich in limonite; *green quartz,* containing vermiculite, chlorite, or ripidolite; *prase,* quartz rich in actinolite; quartz can also contain cacoxenite, chrysocolla, dumortierite, riebeckite, and many others.

On occasion, the inclusions create specific optical phenomena. In *adventurine quartz,* aventurescence is produced by green mica or red hematite inclusions. In *cat's-eye quartz,* fibrous parallel actinolite

Necklace and ear clips with rock crystal and Thai rubies. Boucheron creation.

properties have inspired research into its synthesis, to produce pure, untwinned crystals, which are rare in nature. The outstanding early results of Spezia in 1905 were developed during World War II. Successful growth requires proper orientation of the seed, growth in an alkaline solution at a temperature between 200° and 500°C (390° and 930°F), under pressures as high as 1,800 atmospheres; the resulting growth rate is about 2 millimeters per 24 hours in the axial direction.

Synthesis takes place in an autoclave, into which a temperature gradient has been established to transport silica from the feed material to the seed. Today several thousand tons of quartz are produced annually using this hydrothermal method. The remaining difficulty is to obtain 30-centimeter- (12-inch-) wide high-quality seeds from pure, untwinned, natural quartz crystals. The high price of these synthetic crystals does not make them economical for use in jewelry.

The effects of various color treatments has also been studied. For example, cobalt-doped blue quartz has been marketed in the Soviet Union since 1969. The study of the origin of color in amethyst, citrine, and smoky quartz revealed the importance of iron, aluminum, and hydrogen. The Soviet mineralogist Balitsky later demonstrated the importance of the acidity and oxidation potential of solutions from which colored quartz is grown. He succeeded in 1976 in producing synthetic amethyst without a smoky or yellowish component, as well as synthetic citrine. To produce amethyst, a quartz containing only potential amethyst color centers (trivalent iron replacing silicon) is grown in a neutral solution at between 200° and 400°C (390° and 750°F), under a pressure of 150 to 1,000 atmospheres, and the amethyst color is revealed by irradiation. For citrine, the quartz is grown in an alkali solution with aluminum and alkali ion impurities. Synthetic amethyst from both the Soviet Union and Japan were abundant in the late 1980s, until tests based on twinning and on infrared spectroscopy made it possible to identify it positively.

CAT'S-EYE QUARTZ

A quartz with densely distributed, fine, fibrous inclusions, parallel to one another. Chatoyancy is obtained after polishing and is reinforced by a cabochon cut perpendicular to the fibers. When the fibers are grayish green hornblende crystals, the effect produced by the cutting is reminiscent of the eye of a cat. The linear "iris" is sharper and more distinct when the fibers are thinner. This sharpness can vary greatly from one sample to the next.

inclusions create the chatoyancy. In *hawk's-eye* the chatoyancy is due to blue riebeckite needles. In *tiger's-eye,* the riebeckite is oxidized to yellow.

Quartz also has fibrous microcrystalline varieties, the chalcedonies, as well as more or less pure polycrystalline varieties, such as jasper.

The chalcedony family has been given a variety of names, based on color. Chalcedony itself is gray-blue to white, *onyx* is black, *sard* is brownish, *carnelian* is orange to red, *chrysoprase* is green, and there are some varieties of *blue chalcedony.* When chalcedony contains attractive inclusions or concentric zones of different colors, it is called *agate:* there are many agates, including moss agate, plume agate, and petrified

wood. When agate has a bicolored structure in ribbons, it is called by the name of the corresponding chalcedony: *onyx* or *nicolo* for the black and white variety, and *sardonyx* for the brown and white one. When there is an irregular distribution of color, the material is called *jasper.* The most valuable varieties are green jasper, or *plasma,* and *heliotrope,* which is green with red spots.

Synthesis

Quartz is an important industrial material, especially in electronics, because of its electrical properties, its toughness and lack of cleavage, and to a certain extent, its transparency under ultraviolet light. These

Synthetic quartz crystals on the metallic support on which they grew. Photo: E. Diemer; courtesy Société Industrielle des Combustibles Nucléaires, France.

Spheres of quartz, amethyst, rose quartz, and agate. F. A. Becker collection, Idar-Oberstein, Germany.

The best cat's-eye quartz comes from the gem-bearing gravels of Sri Lanka, as well as from India. Less attractive stones have also been found in the Fichtelgebirge in Bavaria, Germany. In naming chatoyant quartz, it is strictly forbidden to use the phrase *cat's-eye* alone: that term is reserved for chatoyant chrysoberyl.

Hawk's-eye contains fibers of unaltered crocidolite (a term for well-ordered riebeckite, a blue amphibole). Such stones come from the Salzburg area in Austria and also from South Africa.

However, silicified crocidolite (also called crocidolite quartz), found in thin but wide layers in Griqualand (South Africa) has often been altered, producing yellow to brown tones. Sometimes hematite deposits form between the fibers.

Silky crocidolites are not always parallel; they may undulate, so that the chatoyancy effect seems to move when the surface of a polished sample is rocked. The less oxidized stones display delicate yellow to brownish yellow colors and are called *tiger's-eye.* The more oxidized show reddish limonite deposits, and although they have no name in English, they are called *oeil de taureau* in French, that is "bull's eye." When the hematite is abundant and forms shiny platelets among the chatoyant areas, the French call this material *oeil de fer,* that is, "iron eye."

After crocidolite fibers are cut open during the working of the stone, it is possible to modify the color of chatoyant quartz by allowing a dye to penetrate through the siliceous tubes that have been

Tiger's-eye necklace. Fred design, Paris.

Manganese dendrites in rose quartz from Minas Gerais, Brazil. Height: 6 cm. G. Becker collection, Idar-Oberstein, Germany.

Rose-quartz deposit at Alto Feio in Brazil. Photo: J. Cassedanne.

left partly empty by alteration (natural or induced with acid) of the crocidolite. A simple heat treatment is sometimes enough to enhance the red color of some of these stones.

Numerous other gems occasionally display chatoyancy, most often because of the presence of structural channels or parallel inclusions (as in beryl, tourmaline, scapolite, and other gems). Imitation cat's-eyes have been produced using bundles of glass optical fibers. This material is sold in the United States under the name Catsteyte. An older imitation is a glass that is stretched after introducing air bubbles into it.

IRIS QUARTZ

A rock crystal containing numerous air-filled cracks, in which iridescence is produced by interference. This iridescence is similar in appearance to a rainbow; indeed, iris quartz was named for the rainbow, which was the scarf of Iris, the god's messenger.

Iris quartz can be natural, but it can also be obtained by inducing thermal shock in regular quartz. The hot quartz is placed in cold water. If the water has dye in it, the dye will penetrate the cracks formed in the quartz on contact with the cold water, and remain. This technique has been known since ancient times. Pliny the Elder stated,

"There are treatises indicating how to dye crystal to imitate emerald, and no fraud is more profitable."

ROSE QUARTZ

A transparent to translucent quartz containing traces of titanium (less than 0.5 percent). Its pink color is attributed to titanium ions, which both substitute for silicon and are located in the gaps of the crystal structure. Titanium may also exist as very fine rutile exsolution needles (with a diameter of 0.01 to 0.2 micrometers, for a length of 0.5 to 10 millimeters), crystallographically oriented along the two-fold and six-fold axes of symmetry. This accounts for the often turbid aspect of rose quartz. A cabochon cut quite often reveals a six-ray star, sometimes a twelve-ray star. In contrast with the asterism that is easily seen in reflected light in corundums, the asterism of rose quartz is often more easily visible in transmitted light, because of the fineness of the rutile needles.

If the titanium content is more than a trace, the quartz turns a milky pale blue because of increased scattering of light, and it is no longer used in jewelry. Rutile needles are usually shorter, 1 to 500 micrometers long, and more numerous, up to 2 million per cubic centimeter.

Rose quartz is slightly dichroic, with the most intense rose seen along the optic axis. Its coloration does not affect its optical and mechanical properties. It loses its color when heated to 575°C (1,065°F).

The most valuable rose quartz comes from Brazil, where it is found only in the core of some pegmatites. Sources in Minas Gerais include the pegmatites from the Doce River Valley near Governador Valadares, Joainha in the Jequitinhonha Valley, Malacacheta, Peçanha, and Serro. In the state of Bahia, rose quartz is mined in Encruzilhada, and dark rose quartz is found in Campo Formoso, Castro Alves, and Jaguari. Other deposits exist in the states of Paraíba and Rio Grande do Norte. Rose quartz crystals from the Sapucaia pegmatites, from the Lavra da Ilha and Laranjeira in Minas Gerais, are particularly remarkable.

Rose quartz also comes from Madagascar (Tsileo and Amparikaolo), India (Warangal, near Hyderabad), and Japan (Gotō, in the Iwaki province). Other pegmatites containing this mineral are found in Bavaria, in the states of Maine and South Dakota, and in many other localities.

A 625-carat rose-quartz ball showing asterism is on display at the Smithsonian Institution.

Rose quartz can be found in enormous masses of over several hundred tons. Sometimes it is transparent enough to be faceted. Properly cut in cabochon, star rose quartz can be varnished on its base with a blue material to imitate blue star sapphire or a red material to imitate star ruby. A bit of attention is enough to detect this fraud, which is nevertheless more convincing than in most synthetic star corundums.

SMOKY QUARTZ

Light brown smoky quartz is particularly appreciated in Scotland, where it is called cairngorm and is used in the traditional Highlands costumes. Two large faceted specimens are displayed at the Smithsonian Institution in Washington: a 4,500-carat light brown stone from California and a 1,695-carat medium brown quartz from Brazil.

Smoky quartz may display all shades of brown, from light to dark, and even black. Its color is due to natural irradiation, produced by potassium, uranium or thorium in the pegmatites and silica-rich rocks in which smoky quartz is generally found. Such irradiation causes structural defects associated with aluminum impurities at the tetrahedral sites. Colorless quartz can be changed into smoky quartz by irradiation; it is discolored by heating.

The crystal shapes of smoky quartz are very characteristic: its generally stocky crystals are different from those of white or colorless quartz. Its distinctive crystal shape enables experienced mineralogists to easily distinguish natural smoky quartz from its irradiated counterpart, produced for the collectors' market.

Smoky quartz has been found with rock crystal in the granitic formations in Switzerland and the French Alps. Like rock crystal, it has been actively mined and sold to crystal-cutting factories in Germany, France, and Italy.

In September 1867 the Sulzers, a family of crystal hunters or "strahlers," discovered an important quartz vein on the Gletscherhorn (3,305 meters or 13,068 feet), near the Tiefen glacier, in the canton of Uri, Switzerland. During August of the next year, they finally managed to reach a small ledge about 30 meters (100 feet) above the glacier, which led them to small geodes. After overcoming major difficulties, they used explosives to reach an enormous cavity, 4 meters (13 feet) wide by 6 meters (20 feet) deep, which was filled with debris from a

Smoky quartz crystals from the Val Giuf Tavetsch, Graubünden, Switzerland. Height: 10 cm. Sorbonne collection.

ceiling that had collapsed long ago. The cleanup of this cavity yielded extraordinary crystals of black quartz, or morion, up to 150 kilograms (330 pounds) in weight. The news of the discovery spread fast, as 1 ton of crystals was quickly extracted, and the authorities threatened to stop the collecting. Therefore, on the next night, more than seventy people, friends and neighbors of the Sulzers, came to help finish the job, carrying more than 10 tons of crystals to the glacier! Only three crystal groups were left on the site, weighing about 300 kilograms (660 pounds), abandoned because of their weight. These included the splendid 135-kilogram Grandfather quartz, bought in 1881 by the Budapest Museum. Tired and resigned, the police officers in charge of watching the operation sold their property rights to those three pieces to the hotel owner at La Furka for 1,300 francs, and he sold them back to the Guttannen crystal hunters for 8,500 francs. The entire yield amounted to more than 14 tons of smoky-quartz crystals: over half had been somewhat damaged by the hasty mining and was sold to crystal-cutting factories in France and Germany. Thanks to the generosity of a sponsor, Gustav Revillion, the remaining stones were donated to Swiss museums in Bern and Geneva in 1890, where they remain today.

At the end of the nineteenth century,

remarkable crystals were found on Mont Blanc in France.

Some French pegmatites had occasionally yielded some outstanding smoky-quartz crystals but never enough to use for cutting. However, some remarkable crystals from the Pont-Percé pegmatites near Alençon were deceptively called "Alençon diamonds" at the time. Crystals weighing several dozen pounds were extracted from beryl pegmatites in the Limousin (quarries at Margnac and Chanteloube).

Presently, the largest producer of quartz is Brazil, where this mineral is found both in veins and pegmatites. Three states produce most of the smoky quartz: Minas Gerais (Soumidoro de Mariana, Diamantina, and Teófilo Otoni areas), Espirito Santo (Serra do Castelo), and Bahia (near Vitória da Conquista and Xique Xique).

Many countries have mined or still mine smoky quartz, and it would be pointless to list them all. The remarkable crystals associated with amazonite in the Pike's Peak pegmatites in Colorado, as well as those from the Cairngorm Mountains in Scotland, are, however, particularly noteworthy.

Because of a rising demand for smoky-quartz specimens, a number of colorless quartz crystal groups have been irradiated to produce a brown color. It is not possible to detect such treatment in cut stones.

r

RHODIZITE

A potassium aluminoborate, crystallizing in the cubic system. It was named for the pink color (from *rodizo*, "resembling a rose") of the masses it formed in the Urals of the Soviet Union, where it was discovered. When crushed into a powder, it imparts a pink color to the flame of a blowtorch.

Rhodizite forms dodecahedral crystals associated with tourmaline and lepidolite in Madagascar pegmatites ((Sahatany Valley). Its crystals are generally yellowish and small, although they can occasionally reach 4 to 5 centimeters in diameter. Its high hardness of 8, its resistance to shock, and its good luster (index of refraction is 1.69) would make it a good gemstone if it were not so rare. Its specific gravity is 3.4.

RHODOCHROSITE

A manganese carbonate, crystallizing in the orthorhombic system. It forms a continuous series with calcite (with a calcium content of up to 8 percent).

Its name comes from the Greek *rhodon,* meaning "rose," and *khrozo,* "to color." It is the "rose spath" of old German texts. It was also formerly called dialogite (from *dialoge,* "discussion") because its composition was often debated.

Rhodochrosite usually forms mamillary masses, sometimes stalactites. Attractive crystals also exist in polymetallic deposits as scalenohedra and rhombohedra, attaining lengths of up to 20 centimeters (8 inches) on an edge.

Despite its fragility (excellent cleavage, hardness of 3½, and solubility in weak acids with effervescence), zoned masses offering various tones of pink are valued for their color and appearance. Rhodochrosite is thus used to make small decorative objects (boxes, bowls, or small carvings) as well as for beads. The elementary crystals forming massive rhodochrosite are transparent and so birefringent (0.220) that it is possible to see doubling in them. This helps separate silicified polycrystalline rhodochrosite from rhodonites associated with limestones. Rhodochrosite may show inclusions of dark manganese-oxide veins.

It is a matrix mineral for polymetallic deposits (with copper, lead, and zinc) in the young cordilleras of the Americas; it is found in abundance from the Rocky Mountains to the Andes (in Montana, Colorado, Mexico, Peru, and Argentina).

Argentina is presently the main producer of rhodochrosite. In the Andalgalá mining district, at an altitude of 3,000 meters (almost 10,000 feet) in the province of Catamarca in northwestern Argentina, Capillitas rhodochrosite fills karstic formations. It forms crusts and stalactites that reach 60 centimeters (23 inches) in length and 20 to 30 centimeters (8 to 12 inches) in diameter. Probably known by pre-Columbian civilizations, these deposits were worked by the Indians, then by the Spanish, who were searching for precious metals. Around the middle of the nineteenth century, rhodochrosite, considered worthless because manganese had no commercial value, was discarded. The isolation of the mines did not favor mining, although manganese carbonate is now of interest to the metal industry.

Mining of rhodochrosite as a decorative or gem material began around 1930. It was then marketed as the "rose of the Incas" or "Inca rose."

An alteration product, rhodochrosite

Slice of a rhodochrosite stalactite from Capillitas, Argentina. Length: 15 cm. G. Becker collection, Idar-Oberstein, Germany.

Objet d'art in Argentine rhodochrosite. Height: 6 cm. G. Becker collection, Idar-Oberstein, Germany.

can form geodic crystals in stratiform manganese oxide deposits (such as those in Moanda, Gabon; and in Hotazel, on the southern border of the Kalahari Desert in South Africa). Perfect gem rhodochrosite crystals forming scalenohedra up to 7 centimeters (2¾ inches) in length have been found in the N'Chwaning mine and have been faceted for collectors: some of these pieces weigh over 60 carats (index of refraction for the ordinary ray, 1.597 to 1.605; for the extraordinary ray, 1.817 to 1.826).

RHODOLITE

Pyrope almandite garnet or pinkish pyrope, named for its color (from the Greek *rhodon,* meaning "rose," and *lithos,* meaning "stone"). See PYROPE.

RHODONITE

A manganese silicate, crystallizing in the triclinic system. Its name comes from the Greek *rhodon,* meaning "rose," referring to its color. Most often, rhodonite forms tough, fine polycrystalline masses (H is 5½ to 6½; specific gravity is 3.4 to 3.7). Their color is a pale to dark pink, with black veins of manganese oxide following fractures as a result of weathering.

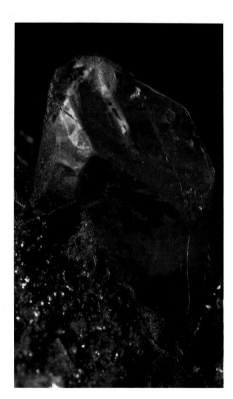

Rhodonite crystal from Broken Hill, Australia. Height: 2.5 cm. J. Saul collection.

Rhodonite has been an ornamental gem material since the nineteenth century, especially in Russia, the country with which it was associated by legend. This tradition is illustrated by Czar Alexander III's sarcophagus, made entirely of rhodonite. The Sedelnikova mines in the Urals, near Ekaterinburg, were then the main rhodonite producers. This gem has since been found in Madagascar and Brazil.

Attractive rhodonite crystals are rare; sometimes they are set in calcite, as in Franklin, New Jersey, or associated with sulfides (galena or sphalerite), as in Broken Hill, Australia. Some small gem-quality crystals from Broken Hill and from Conselheiro Lafaiete in Minas Gerais, Brazil, have been faceted for collectors. Their principal indices of refraction are close to 1.733, 1.739, and 1.744, with a specific gravity of 3.57. Like many silicates, rhodonite slowly forms a silica gel when exposed to hydrochloric acid.

Two types of glass are used to imitate rhodonite: a regular translucent pink glass; and a glass manufactured in Russia during the nineteenth century called *purpurine;* its opacity was obtained by developing dendritelike red crystallites (perhaps cristobalite). This glass has not been produced since the Russian revolution because the manufacturing process has been lost.

ROCK CRYSTAL

A colorless transparent quartz.

Origin of the Name

The word *crystal* comes from the Greek *krustallos,* "ice," derived from *kruos,* meaning "cold" or "frozen." In fact, during ancient times, rock crystal was believed to be the result of an extreme congelation, as Pliny the Elder clearly explained in his *Natural History.* Moritz Anton Cappeler (1685–1769) believed that it was infusible ice.

The History of Rock Crystal

The Greeks used rock crystal to carve seals and intaglios. The Romans hollowed it into bowls. After his fall, Nero broke two rock-crystal bowls on the floor in a final tantrum to "punish his century," so that no one could drink from them again.

The art of chiseling and carving bowls, baskets, and various objects in rock crystal has continued into the present, witnessing a succession of more or less ostentatious periods. The Muslim Fātimid dynasty (909–1171) was renowned for its bowls, which reached the German emperors as early as the eleventh century, who mounted them in the Byzantine fashion; such was the bowl of Henry II (973–1024), now in the Residence Museum in Munich. They also made pitchers; the best-preserved example can be seen at Saint Mark's Basilica in Venice. It was dedicated to al-'Azīz Bi'llāh (975–996), a great patron of the arts, who reigned from Maghrib to Syria.

The works of the great sixteenth- and seventeenth-century Italian engravers were particularly remarkable. Among their most famous masterpieces is the chest of Duke Albert V the Magnanimous, decorated with bas-reliefs, representing scenes from the Old Testament, which was carved by Fontana in around 1560 and is kept at the Residence Museum in Munich. Also noteworthy is the famous bowl (82 x 62 x 50 centimeters [32 x 24 x 20 inches]) carved by Saracchi, displayed in the Pitti Palace in Florence. In France, a remarkable collection is kept in the Apollo Gallery at the Louvre: cups, bowls, pitchers, and baskets, on which scenes from the Old Testament have been engraved, such as Noah's inebriation and Suzannah and the elders. Louis XIV's rock-crystal collection contained 532 pieces in 1723; it was one of the most important in Europe, comparable to those of the Medicis in Florence, the emperors in Vienna, and the dukes of Bavaria in Munich.

Crystal Balls

In Roman times crystal balls were used for medical purposes. Pliny the Elder explained that such balls concentrated sunlight to help cauterize wounds. One of the oldest ones to survive was found in the grave of the Frankish king Childeric I (436 481) and is kept in the Medals Cabinet in Paris. The world's largest ball, called the Warner Crystal Ball, weighs 48.5 kilograms (107 pounds) and has a diameter of 32.5 centimeters (12¾ inches). It is on display at the Smithsonian Institution in Washington, D.C.

Crystal balls were accessories for rituals in China and Japan. A crystal ball was often buried with Merovingian nobility and many kings of France after they died. Most were stolen during the French revolution: they are now supposedly in private collections. In the Middle Ages, crystal balls began to be used in Europe to predict the future, replacing the mirrors and beryl balls previously in use. Much was written about how to prepare the crystal sphere, which in particular had to spend three weeks in a grave. The crystal ball became an accessory of mediums who supposedly could see in them pictures of recent events; many sovereigns and public personalities were said to use their services. Even today, this type of clairvoyance is very popular. Japanese, German, and Brazilian lapidaries are very skilled at producing perfectly round spheres.

Feather necklace with rock crystal and diamonds. A. Boucheron creation.

Engraved rock-crystal bowl. Length: 20 cm. G. Becker designs, Idar-Oberstein, Germany.

Rock Crystal in Rituals

Yucatan sorcerers in Mexico and Apache medicine men used rough rock crystal to find lost objects or ponies. Aborigines in Australia and New Guinea believe that rock crystal can help bring rain, a belief that may also have been held by the ancient Greeks, as the term *hyalos,* which was applied to transparent quartz, seems to derive from *hyo,* which means "to rain."

Carved Rock Crystal outside the Mediterranean Basin

The carving of rock crystal was an art practiced by all cultures. The British Museum displays a 21-centimeter- (8-inch-) wide skull carved by Aztec lapidaries; another can be seen in the Apollo Gallery in the Louvre.

In the eighteenth century, Chinese lapidaries began carving rock crystal into snuff bottles and statuettes; even today, many Taoist and Buddhist figurines are produced in the Far East. Prestigious objects are also manufactured, such as the enormous briolette in the shape of an egg on display at the Smithsonian Institution in Washington; it weighs 7,000 carats (1,400 grams) and was faceted from a Brazilian rock crystal.

The beautiful quartz crystals from the Upper Ubangi in Congo have been cut, polished, and made into lip jewelry by the N'Bru tribes; these needles, up to 6 centimeters (2 inches) long, were implanted in the lower lips of the women.

Rock Crystal in Jewelry and Ornamentation

Faceted rock crystal cut in brilliant cut, cabochons, and beads, were widely used in popular jewelry, as illustrated by an eighteenth-century Italian parure in the Musée Massena in Nice, France. A number of miniature portraits, worn as jewelry, are protected by rock-crystal slabs. Today, delicately carved, it is back in fashion in designer jewelry.

Quartz was also used as a diamond substitute in popular jewelry; in 1604 Boece de Boot mentioned: "crystal, or pseudo-diamond." It was also the raw material for many quartz–colored cement–quartz triplets, manufactured to imitate various gems since at least the fifteenth century (and produced industrially since about 1900).

Irradiated, it takes on a smoky color or may be turned into citrines (especially in Japan). Before the introduction of manufactured "crystal" glass, quartz crystals from La Gardette in Isère, France, were often used in chandeliers, for example, in the ceiling lights of the Versailles and Fontainebleau castles in France.

Deposits

Rock crystal is widespread throughout the world and is found in many types of deposits; however, different regions have been famous at different periods. Extracted since time immemorial in the Alps, it was responsible for the trade of *cristallier* (literally "crystaller," actually crystal hunter) or *strahler* (from the German *strahlen,* meaning "to shine").

Rock crystal is abundant in the French and Swiss Alps; it is found in quartz veins and geodes, embedded in granitic bodies and gneisses. These cracks and cavities, sometimes enormous, look like the inside of an oven; so they are called *four,* or "oven," in French, *Kristallhölhe, Kristalloch, Kristallgewölbe,* or *Stralloch* in German, *fuorn* in Romansh, and *forno* in Italian. At the beginning of the eighteenth century, a group of strahlers headed by the Moor brothers were prospecting in the granitic Aar massif (in the region of Zinggenstock, Switzerland) in a quartz vein close to the Unteraar glacier, at an altitude of about 2,300 meters (7,500 feet). After lengthy preparatory work, in 1719 they reached an immense cavity, more than ten meters (30 feet) long, which produced more than 50 tons of crystals. The largest weighed more than 400 kilograms; (almost 900 pounds); it is easy to imagine the difficulties involved in transporting such giant crystals. Other spectacular examples include the giant quartz from Hegidorn, near Naters (Valais), discovered between 1770 and 1780, as well as the large colorless transparent crystal from Viesch (also in Valais), brought back by Napoléon and kept in the National Museum of Natural History in Paris.

Crystal hunters continue gathering rock crystal today, although now they are mostly interested in mineralogical specimens. In France, nice crystals are primarily found in the Mont Blanc massif and in the Isère department, especially in the La Gardette mine, near Bourg d'Oisans, which has produced some of the finest, clearest quartz crystals in the world. Mined by the local people for gold and quartz since the eighteenth century, this deposit was intermittently worked until around 1900; totally abandoned since, it is visited today only by mineral collectors.

Today most rock crystal comes from Brazil, in particular from Corinto in the Diamantina area in the state of Minas Gerais. It is found in a variety of deposits: in pegmatites, segregated in granitic rocks and lavas, in massive veins, and in eluvial or alluvial deposits.

Granitic pegmatites are rich in large crystals, especially at the periphery of the quartz core, where they may form spectacular geodes; rock crystal is often fractured and full of inclusions, particularly tourmaline. Basalts and andesites from the Paraná

Rock-crystal owls. Height: 20 cm. Carving by G. Becker, Idar-Oberstein, Germany.

Quartz crystals from La Gardette, Isère, France. Height: 12 cm. Sorbonne collection.

Quartz crystals from Minas Gerais, Brazil, Height: 15 cm. Sorbonne collection.

plateau in Brazil contain numerous geodes of milky quartz or amethyst (see AMETHYST) and agates (see AGATES). In the state of Minas Gerais, near Diamantina, beautiful quartz crystals are found in veins that can reach 50 meters (165 feet) in thickness and stretch for dozens of kilometers. In the state of Goiás, quartz can be found in lenses or stockwerks traversing the host rock in all directions. Enormous cavities filled with crystals have been encountered; one in the lavra do Roncador near Cristallina was 9 x 3 x 11 meters (30 by 10 by 36 feet) and produced more than 7 tons of quartz at one time.

Finally, alluvial deposits may produce transparent quartz pebbles weighing up to 5 kilograms (11 pounds). They are mined on a small scale in numerous areas, in particular in the state of Espirito Santo.

Since the discovery and mining of the large Brazilian deposits, quartz production in most other countries has almost ceased. Madagascar, Japan, and Australia were important sources at one time. Since the discovery of synthetic quartz, even the Brazilian deposits have been abandoned in part. They are presently mined mostly for the silica glass industry.

In New York State, the small crystals found in Herkimer are famous for their shape, perfect limpidity, and high luster; they have been erroneously called Herkimer diamonds. Such crystals are still offered

to naive tourists as diamonds, especially in the diamond-producing countries of Africa. On occasion, a rough diamond parcel is "mixed" with 10 to 15 percent quartz or hematite.

The Lead Glass called Crystal

In the eighteenth century, it became possible to produce perfectly transparent glass, and the carving of rock-crystal bowls declined. Proud of their achievement, glassmakers advertised their crystal-clear products, and the term *crystal* started to be applied to lead glass, while the term *quartz* no longer designated opaque vein quartz only and was applied to rock crystal as well. In France today, the term *crystal* can be applied only to lead glass (with more than 17 percent lead) used for tableware.

Lead glass containing less than 17 percent lead is called *crystalline,* and that containing more than 24 percent lead is called *supercrystal.* The terms *crystalline, crystal,* and *supercrystal* may not be used for jewelry. The index of refraction and specific gravity of a glass increases with its lead content; strain that develops in important pieces can be lessened by annealing, but some always remains (it can be seen with a polariscope), frequently causing spontaneous shattering.

The Synthesis of Rock Crystal

Synthetic colorless quartz or rock crystal is not used in jewelry. It is, however, an important product in clockmaking and watchmaking because of its piezoelectric properties.

RUBACE

Quartz that has been artificially cracked by thermal shock in a red- or green-dyed liquid. The dye penetrates the fractures, and the resulting stone is intended to imitate ruby or emerald. The spelling is sometimes *rubasse,* although some quartz naturally colored red by iron oxide also goes by this name.

RUBELLITE

Pink to red tourmaline. See TOURMALINE.

RUBICELLE

Red to orange spinel. This term is no longer commonly used.

RUBY

A natural red corundum.

Origin of the Name and History

The name *ruby* is relatively recent (thirteenth century) and stems from the Latin *ruber,* meaning "red." Ruby has always been held in high esteem. Indians called it *ratnaraj* in Sanskrit, which means "queen of gems," or *ratnanayaka,* "the premiere precious stone"; they believed that ruby had an inextinguishable internal fire. This reference to burning fire in rubies is found throughout the Mediterranean basin. Theophrastus, in the sixth century B.C., was probably referring to ruby in his discussion of *anthrax,* or "burning coal" (from *anthos,* meaning "flame"). It was also called *lychnites* (from *lychnos,* meaning "lamp" or "light," or *lyche,* which means "beginning dawn"); this was translated by Pliny the Elder as *lychnis.*

Pliny probably confused all bright red stones under the name *carbunculus,* a diminutive for *carbo,* meaning "burning coal," which evolved into carbuncle. In the eleventh century, Marbodus followed Pliny in distinguishing three-times-three species of carbuncle, which corresponds to the three kinds of ruby known at that time (rubies from Myanmar (Burma), Thailand, and Sri Lanka), the three types of red spinel (balas, ruby-spinel, and pleonaste), and the three varieties of red garnet (pyrope, almandite, hessonite).

In the fourteenth century, Jean de Mandeville, in an account of his trip to the Orient, reported that the Great Khan of Cathay (China) owned a carbuncle half a foot long. This stone, set on one of the pillars of his palace, shined so much at night that it illuminated the room as if it were day.

Because its color evokes blood and fire, ruby was naturally associated with courage. It was a royal insigna, worn on the crowns or helmets of kings. It protected knights from being wounded and kept them healthy. Siegfried's marvelous sword, Balmung, was set with a ruby on its handle. By extension, ruby was given the power to stop bleeding. Associated with passion, it was supposed to soothe anger and protect from seduction. Ruby was a symbol of victory, charity, and love.

Famous Rubies

Several ancient intaglios and cameos were carved in Burmese rubies. The most important ones were the portrait-seal of Alexander the Great (356–323 B.C.), which also served as a seal for Augustus (63 B.C. to A.D. 14) now lost, and the portrait-seal that Augustus had engraved, which was used by

Roman emperors until Vespasian. During the Middle Ages this ruby became the famous ruby of the kings of France (it weighs 15 carats) and later reappeared in a private collection. Other portraits are equally interesting, such as that of Livia, Augustus's wife, a 7.08-carat intaglio, and of Titus, set in a ring during the Renaissance. Closer to our time, an eighteenth-century ring contains a ruby cameo representing the marquise de Montespan; this piece is now in the British Museum.

The largest known gem-quality ruby is on the Saint Wenceslas crown, ordered in 1346 by Charles IV of Luxembourg (1316–78), king of Bohemia, to be put on the shrine containing the skull of Saint Wenceslas (duke of Bohemia, 921–29). In addition to this approximately 250-carat ruby, measuring 39.5 by 36.5 by 14 millimeters, the crown has nineteen sapphire cabochons, including six weighing 200 and 330 carats; a 100-carat spinel and forty-four other spinels; twenty-six emeralds; and twenty pearls. The cross atop this crown contains a thorn from Chirst's crown; this thorn was presented by John II, king of France, to Charles IV of Luxembourg, a prince educated in France, because Charles had fought alongside the French at Crecy, where Charles's father, John of Luxembourg, was killed. With a design inspired by the traditional French crown, the Saint Wenceslas crown was taken from the shrine only for the coronations of the kings of Bohemia. The last emperor to wear it was Ferdinand I of Austria in 1836. It is kept in the Saint Guy Cathedral in Prague and undoubtedly represents the most valuable jewel from the Middle Ages that is still intact.

In Iran large rubies from the sack of Delhi in 1739 are set in the great globe (50 and 75 carats), as well as in the throne of Nāder Shāh (35 carats). In his accounts of his trips to India, Jean-Baptiste Tavernier mentioned a 17.5-carat ruby bought in 1653 by the Bijapur maharaja. The Edwardes Ruby, a 167-carat translucent ruby crystal, named in honor of Sir Henry Benjamin Edwardes, a British administrator in India and pacifier of the Punjab, has been in the British Museum since 1887. Two important star rubies are on display in the United States: the Rosser Reeves ruby, a 138.7-carat Sri Lankan cabochon, is in the Smithsonian Institution in Washington, D.C., and the de Long star ruby, a 100-carat ruby cabochon from Myanmar (Burma) is in the American Museum of Natural History in New York.

Large gem-quality rubies have always been and still are rare, so their discovery is always an exceptional event. Gnaga Boh ("dragon lord"), a magnificent 44-carat rough ruby, cut into a 20-carat stone, was offered to the nineteenth-century Burmese king Tharrawaddy Min. In 1875 the sale of two rubies in Burma (now Myanmar), a 37–

A 6.17-carat ruby from Myanmar (Burma) set in a ring. Van Cleef and Arpels creation.

old carat cushion shape and a 47–old carat pear shape, required an armed escort. These stones were recut to 33.18 carats (32 5/16 old carats) and 39.60 carats (38 9/16 old carats) respectively and were sold for £10,000 and £20,000 (at the same time, the Star of South Africa, a rough diamond weighing 83.50 old carats, was sold for £25,000). In 1918 the last high-quality large ruby was discovered; it weighed 41 carats and was named the Peace Ruby. A 196.1-carat Burmese ruby is part of the mineral collection of the Natural History Museum of Los Angeles County. A remarkable 15.97-carat ruby, belonging to gemologist Allan Caplan, was recently displayed at the American Museum of Natural History in New York.

Deposits

Myanmar (Burma)

Rubies from the Mogok Valley in Upper Burma have been mined since ancient times, but their exact location was kept secret. A mysterious, totally inaccessible "valley of the rubies" was supposed to exist near the Chinese border. Pieces of raw meat were thrown into this valley, and the vultures brought back the rubies which were stuck to the meat. This legend is also associated with diamond and formed the basis of the tales of Sinbad the sailor. In the sixteenth century, a dealer of tamarin monkeys reportedly brought back a ruby from this region to the kingdom of Pegu (today's Myanmar). Seduced by the stone, the king peacefully appropriated the mine area for himself in 1597, by trading with the Chan state for another territory. Property of the

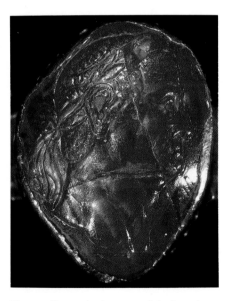

Myanmar (Burmese) ruby cameo of the Roman emperor Titus. Height: 1.25 cm. M. De Bry collection.

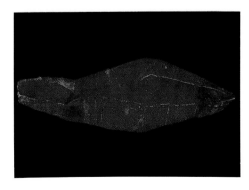

Ruby crystal from the Massai steppe in Kenya. Length: 1.5 cm. J. Saul collection.

Necklace with ruby cabochons, diamonds, and pearls. Chaumet creation.

Earrings set with two 20-carat ruby cabochons. Chaumet creation.

crown, the Mogok Valley was mined intensively; the lack of manpower led neighboring kings to agree exile their prisoners to this inhospitable region, covered with dense forest. Managed by greedy governors, the mines became a place of theft, revolt, and chaos starting in 1780.

In 1885, King Thibaw negotiated mining rights with the French Bouveillein and Company, but the London jeweler E. W. Streeter heard of the deal during a trip to Paris and asked the British Office in India to help him obtain the mining claims. Streeter obtained permission in July 1886 to send a military expedition to the mines, but torrential rains delayed its start until November. The British troops faced strong resistance, and Streeter's son was presented the freshly cut head of an "enemy" by a Gurkha auxiliary. Mogok fell on December 27, 1886, and Streeter discovered the Burmese system of mining rights, while Great Britain annexed Burma (now Myanmar). On February 22, 1889, Streeter obtained control of the mines from the British government for seven years after much difficulty and had to pay an annual rent of £26,666 and 16.66 percent of the profits. Thus was born Burma Ruby Mines Ltd., which had the right to mine mechanically any unoccupied stretch of land and also held the monopoly on buying rubies from any independent miners that remained in the area. All the best stones were smuggled out. Mean-

while, the company discovered that the town of Mogok was built on alluvial deposits, called *byon,* that were very rich in ruby. So the company bought the town, demolished it, and rebuilt it some distance away. It constructed an electric power plant at great expense (the equipment was transported with great difficulty at a speed of 1.5 kilometers [3 miles] per day over 100 kilometers), a road (unusable for seven months of the year), eight ore-processing plants, and other major facilities. The open-quarry mining technique consisted of removing all alluvial material down to the underlying rock and washing several thousand tons a day of this ore in large amounts of water (823,803 tons were washed during the 1897–98 season). Nevertheless, the company was profitable until 1908, when the price of rubies fell because of the introduction of synthetic ruby on the market and because of a recession in the United States. Despite all efforts, the company failed in 1931, and the old primitive mining techniques were again put into practice. *Byon* is mined in the valley during the dry season, when miners dig unsupported shafts 6 to 12 meters (20 to 40 feet) deep in the alluvial deposits. These shafts are extended into the underlying rock by tunnels slightly supported with bamboo for about 10 meters (30 feet); the entire edifice is intended to collapse after the *byon* is extracted. Water sometimes must be pumped

out, an operation performed with hollow bamboo, which are effective down to 5 or 6 meters (15 to 20 feet), making relays necessary at times. During the rainy season, alluvial steps are mined with artificial drains. Sometimes, karstic caves locally called *loos,* open there; they may represent a large network of cavities connected by natural galleries. Ruby-rich gravels have been deposited there by streams, so these caves are exploited despite the high risks involved, because the ruby content of the gravel can be as high as 25 percent.

Burma was a theater of military operations during World War II. In 1948 it became independent and then a socialist state. Since then, the borders have been closed to foreigners. In 1963 the mines were nationalized, and ruby production in Mogok dropped to almost nothing. The dense vegetation and numerous political problems made a geological study of this extremely complex deposit difficult. Metamorphic slates, gneiss, granites, pegmatites (with topaz, aquamarine, and tourmaline), and ultrabasic rocks with remarkable peridots are all present. Metamorphic marbles characterized by important karstic formations are found among the gneiss and are the source of both ruby and spinel. Mogok rubies are concentrated in the valley and the hill slopes; the gem-bearing gravels, or *byon,* contained all varieties of corundum, spinel, quartz, and tourmaline, as well as feldspar grains, altered pyrite, fragments of the surrounding rocks, and brown clays. This *byon* forms a layer 1 to 2 meters (3 to 6 feet) thick, 5 to 6 meters (15 to 20 feet) below the surface, with a lateral extension of up to 20 meters (65 feet).

Thailand and Kampuchea

Important fields of gem-bearing gravels are found on both sides of the Thailand-Kampuchea border; they result from the weathering of basalt flows. Since the cession of ruby mining in Myanmar, Pailin in Kampuchea (formerly Cambodia) and Chanthaburi in Thailand have become the world's most important sources of ruby. Described by numerous travelers and known since 1850 as the "Gem Hills," the Chanthaburi-Trat deposits are located in southeastern Thailand, about 330 kilometers (200 miles) southeast of Bangkok; they are an extension of the Pailin deposits, located 300 kilometers (about 200 miles) northwest of Phnom Penh in Kampuchea.

In 1893 the right to mine these fields was granted to a British company, The Sapphires and Rubies of Siam Ltd., a subsidiary of E. W. Streeter (who was then working in Mogok, Myanmar), with mediocre results. At the beginning of the twentieth century, 1,250 miners worked another gem field, opened by the Burmese at Bo Channa, about 50 kilometers (30 miles) northeast. Today, more than twenty thousand people are employed in these mines, which have become the property of the Thai government.

Weathering is intense in a tropical climate, and rapid erosion destroyed the basalt flows, concentrating corundum in alluvial deposits, along with magnetite, spinel, olivine, enstatite, zircon, garnet, and plagioclase feldspar. The gem-bearing gravel layer, or *rai*, is found at a depth of 3 to 8 meters (6 to 20 feet) ranging in thickness from 3 centimeters to 1 meter (1½ to 40 inches). Mining techniques are quite diverse; sometimes modern outfits with bulldozers or hydraulic jets are used to bring down the ore and concentrate it by specific gravity; but they can also be quite primitive, with the stones sold at the mine itself.

About 70 percent of the rubies on the market today are probably from Thailand. They are often of a darker red but exceptional stones have been found as well. They are sometimes heat-treated at the mine.

Sri Lanka

Alluvial deposits of light rubies and other gems are found at the southwestern end of the island, in the hilly area of Ratnapura (see SAPPHIRE).

Vietnam

In the late 1980s, important ruby deposits have been discovered in several areas of Vietnam. Some stones are comparable in quality to Burmese rubies.

Kenya and Tanzania

Large, heavily included opaque rubies found in green zoisite have recently been mined in the Matabatu Mountains in Tanzania. This rock is mostly used as an ornamental stone, but small pieces of transparent gem-quality ruby is also found (Lossogonoi mine). Translucent rubies from this area, commonly weighing several hundred carats, are carved into many shapes. In recent years, however, the Morogoro area has produced large quantities of high-quality rubies, some very similar to "Burmese" rubies. Tanzanian rubies are becoming an important component of the world's ruby market.

In Kenya, some very nice rubies are associated with ultrabasic igneous rocks.

Afghanistan

In Jagdalek, near Sarobi, ruby is associated with light red spinel in magnesian metamorphosed marbles. Nice gem crystals often measure over a centimeter.

Color and Inclusions

The substitution of a small amount of chromium for aluminum causes the red color of ruby, as well as its bright red luminescence under black light, which can be attenuated by iron, always present, as is titanium. The chromium absorption spectrum is always visible with a spectroscope.

Often a blue component is due to equal parts of iron and titanium. An excess of titanium forms rutile exsolution needles (see CORUNDUM), while an excess of iron destroys the fluorescence caused by chromium. When seen in daylight, which is rich in blue, rubies from Myanmar and Kenya, which contain little iron, add to their intrinsic color some red fluorescence, which makes them glow. Conversely, rubies from Thailand and Kampuchea, rich in iron, hardly fluoresce and have a distinctly darker color in daylight; this is why they are considered less valuable.

Rubies from Myanmar (Burma) contain calcite inclusions accompanied by colored growth disturbances, silks, and sometimes carbon dioxide fluid inclusions. They are fascinating because of their colors: purplish red down the optic axis, violetish red in the perpendicular direction. The best Myanmar rubies are called pigeon's-blood red. Kenyan rubies often have a less attractive orangy component. They also contain silk and calcite crystals but are often affected by polysynthetic twinning, revealed by separation lines at their intersections. Sri Lankan rubies are light red to raspberry red; their inclusions are similar to those of Myanmar rubies, but they display an exceptionally bright luster. Rubies from Thailand and Kampuchea are often dark, sometimes with a violetish or brownish component, reminiscent of spinels or red garnets. They are often pure but have been affected by significant stresses during their transport in lava, and mechanical twins, revealed by separation lines, are frequent; internal discoidal fractures surrounding a negative crystal are also not uncommon.

Ruby is preferably cut with the table perpendicular to the optic axis, in order to display the most attractive color. Opaque rubies, often having a somewhat nacreous appearance due the abundance of separation lamellae, are used for cabochons, small carvings, and even snuff bottles. Ruby's indices of refraction are always close to 1.770

The washing of alluvial gems in Bo Rai, Thailand. Photo: P. Keller.

Ruby and gold brooch manufactured around 1920. Height: 3 cm. Boucheron collection.

Carving of a bird in Tanzanian ruby. Height: 8 cm. G. Becker design, Idar-Oberstein, Germany.

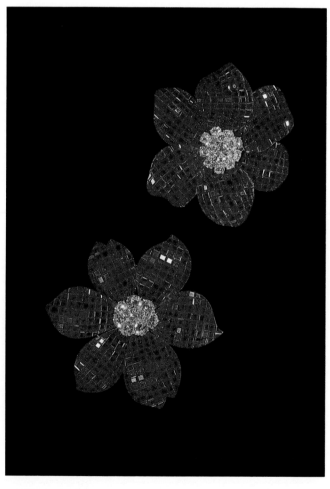

Detail of a necklace with ruby, nacre, and diamonds, including a 8.32-carat pink ruby. Mauboussin design.

Two flowers invisibly set with 430 rubies, for a total weight of 46 carats. Van Cleef and Arpels creation.

and 1.760, with a birefringence of 0.009 and a specific gravity of 4.

Ruby is occasionally heat-treated; for example, some have attempted to dissolve rutile silks when they are too abundant or, conversely, tried to create rutile exsolution to obtain a star ruby.

On occasion, the color of a highly included ruby may be artifically reinforced with a red dye.

Natural Gems Resembling Ruby

Some gems have a color close to that of ruby: pyrope and almandite garnets, red spinel, red tourmaline (rubellite), and red zircon. Pink topaz can resemble some pink rubies from Sri Lanka.

Simulants

Red glass, colored with traces of gold or selenium, sometimes with iron or copper, are the oldest imitations. In the thirteenth century, Thomas Aquinus noted that fake ruby was fabricated with the help of "iron crocus." The production of red garnet–glass doublets is relatively recent (eighteenth century). The garnet slabs selected for this process usually contained needle-like inclusions. The garnet-glass junction is normally located in the girdle in fabrications produced after the end of the nineteenth century. Two more recent types of doublet are offered to tourists in Bangkok: a green sapphire–synthetic ruby doublet and a Thai ruby–synthetic ruby doublet, the latter being particularly convincing.

Synthesis

Ruby is the only gem for which synthetics were introduced on the market before the twentieth century. Starting in 1885, a corundum powder mixed with chromium oxide was melted with an oxygen-hydrogen torch to form small ruby "boules." Faceted, this product was fraudulently sold as Geneva ruby.

At the beginning of the twentieth century, Verneuil perfected his flame-fusion process, resuting in a massive commercial distribution (200 kilograms, over 400 pounds, by 1908). As the process was improved, synthetic ruby production increased. To produce better imitations of natural rubies, synthetic rubies have been cracked and black material introduced in the breaks to imitate dendrites.

Flux synthetic rubies have been on the market since 1965. Their color is generally closer to that of Thai rubies, but their fluorescence is intense. Flux inclusions are often trapped during crystal growth. There is currently no hydrothermal synthetic ruby on the jewelry market.

These veil-like small solid inclusions are typical of flux synthetic ruby. Length: 0.2 cm. Manufactured by C. Chatham. San Francisco.

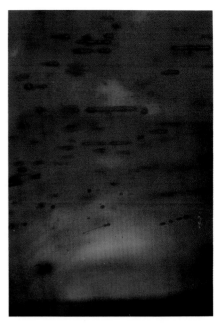

Telescoped air bubbles are trapped during growth, perpendicular to the growth curves of this synthetic ruby. Magnified 30 times. Photo: A. Jeanne-Michaud.

RUTILE

Titanium oxide, crystallizing in the tetragonal system.

Rutile comes from the Latin *rutilus,* which means "bright red," applied to hair, referring to the appearance of rutile needles in quartz.

Natural rutile is of interest to the gemologist only as fibrous inclusions (Venus hair stone) or exsolution needles ("silk" in rubies and sapphires).

Synthetic rutile is produced by the flame-fusion process, starting with very pure titanium oxide. It has been sold as a diamond imitation under the name titania since 1948, especially around 1950. Synthetic rutile comes out of the oven black and must be discolored by heat treatment in an oxygen flow. However, a slight yellowish tinge always remains, due to the absorption of violet light, up to 430 nanometers. Yellow and blue synthetic rutile have also been marketed.

Rutile is somewhat soft (H is 6), so faceted stones do not wear well. Its luster is adamantine, but its high birefringence causes a strong doubling effect (principal indices of refraction of 2.62 for the ordinary ray and 2.90 for the extraordinary ray).

Rutile's dispersion is six times that of diamond. Instead of harmonious fires, it therefore produces a true decomposition of light, which is unattractive. Its specific gravity is 4.25.

Rutile needles in quartz from Ibitiara, Bahia, Brazil. Height: 2 cm. G. Becker collection, Idar-Oberstein, Germany.

S

SAPPHIRE

Naturally colored corundum that is any color but red (for red corundum, see RUBY). (The discussion that follows concerns blue sapphire; sapphire of other colors is examined in a separate section at the end of this article.)

Detail of a sapphire necklace, including a 68-carat stone, for a total weight of 120 carats. Van Cleef and Arpels creation.

Origin of the Name and Virtues

Sauriratna and *sanipriya* in Sanskrit, *sampir* in Chaldean, and *sappir* in Hebrew led to the Greek *sappheiros,* which became *sapphirus* in Latin and *sapphire* in English.

This term was used to describe lapis lazuli until the thirteenth century.

Sapphire was known in ancient Greece as *hyakinthos;* this name was originally given to the blue iris flower and then by extension to a violetish blue gem, the sapphire from Sri Lanka. Pliny the Elder, as well as such later authors as Saint Epiphanius, Saint Isidore, and Marbodus, used the word *hyacinth* to describe all colors of corundum ("garnet, lemon or azur . . . , to polish this stone, one must use diamond powder").

When the meaning of the word shifted, virtues attributed to lapis lazuli were passed on to sapphire (in particular, its supposed power to heal eye diseases, probably reminiscent of the use of lapis lazuli as eye shadow in ancient Egypt). But the true sapphire, called hyacinth, was a talisman for travelers, protecting them against plague and wounds and ensuring an enjoyable resting place. It supposedly diverted lightning and conferred peace and wisdom on its owner.

Famous Sapphires

In past centuries, the color blue was considered sacred and was worn by priests to show their link with the heavens. In the Middle Ages, sapphire became the symbol of this union between the priest and the sky and was set in bishops' rings. For the same reason, the imperial Austrian crown made in 1602 by order of Rudolph II of Hapsburg is topped by a sapphire to symbolize the union between the sky and the emperor, considered sovereign pontiff.

The British imperial crown also has at its top a large stone, called Saint Edward's Sapphire, set in the center of a diamond cross. An interesting legend is attached to it. One day, Edward the Confessor, king of the Anglo-Saxons from 1042 to 1066, met a beggar; having no money with him, the king gave him his sapphire ring. This beggar was actually a messenger of God, and the ring was later returned by an angel to King Edward during his pilgrimage to Palestine. When Saint Edward's body was exhumed, the sapphire from his ring was put in the royal British treasury by the abbot of Westminster. The stone is still there, adorning the imperial crown ordered by Queen Victoria.

The British crown also holds the Stuart Sapphire, also called the *Charles II Sapphire,* on the center back of the headband. This sapphire measures 3.8 by 2.5 centimeters (1.5 by 1 inches). It was originally set in Charles II's state crown and was taken by his brother, James II, to France after his deposition in 1688; it then belonged to his sons and grandsons. The last of them, Henry Stuart, cardinal duke of York, died in 1807 and bequeathed the stone to George III of England. This sovereign had it set in the imperial crown under the spinel called the Black Prince Ruby, but this spot was later taken by the 317.4 carat diamond Cullinan II.

In addition to its large ruby, the Saint Wenceslas crown in Prague is set with a number of blue sapphires, six of them weighing more than 100 carats (see RUBY).

In France the National Museum of Nat-

ural History in Paris displays the Ruspoli Sapphire, a very peculiar stone weighing 132¹⁄₁₆ old carats (135.80 carats). It is cut in the shape of a rhombohedron (with no relation to its actual cyrstallographic orientation) and measures 2.9 by 3.8 centimeters (1.1 by 1.5 inches). This stone was found in Bengal, India, by a wooden-spoon dealer; it was bought by the Ruspoli company in Rome, later sold to a German prince, and then to a French jeweler before it became the property of the French crown.

Two noteworthy stones are among the largest blue sapphires. The Smithsonian Institution in Washington, D.C., houses the Logan Sapphire, a 423-carat cushion-cut stone from Sri Lanka. It is set in a brooch surrounded by diamonds. The second is the 258-carat bright blue sapphire from the Russian crown. It measures 3.9 by 3.4 by 2.2 centimeters (1.5 by 1.3 by 0.9 inches) and is presently in the Diamond Fund of the Soviet Union in Moscow.

Large star sapphires are on display in American museums. The 563-carat Star of India and the 116-carat dark blue Midnight

Star, both from Sri Lanka, are on display at the American Museum of Natural History in New York. The 330-carat Star of Asia from Myanmar (Burma) and the 316-carat Star of Artaban from Sri Lanka are at the Smithsonian Institution.

Translucent, highly included crystals can attain very large sizes, as in the three sapphires, weighing approximately 2,000 carats each, in which were carved the portraits of Lincoln, Washington, and Eisenhower. A 63,000-carat (about 12.5-kilogram) star sapphire was reportedly found in Myanmar in October 1966.

Deposits

Kashmir

The story of the Kashmir sapphires begins in 1881, when inhabitants of the Zaskar Mountains, a region at an altitude of 6,000 meters (approximately 20,000 feet) on the border of the Jammu and Kashmir state in India, started to trade sapphire for salt, weight for weight. Corundum had been long known to the inhabitants of this area; they used it to sharpen their tools. But the discovery of a pocket filled with blue crystals prompted them to take advantage of this unusual find. In 1882 these crystals appeared on the markets of Kulu and Simla, small towns situated farther south that were used as summer capitals. They were correctly identified, and in the winter of 1882, a jewelers' syndicate bought a parcel of nice crystals for $90,000. In 1883, the maharaja of Kashmir declared the mines his property, stopped all private sales, and sent the army to guard the deposits. Organized mining was begun in 1883, and crystals over 10 centimeters (4 inches) long were discovered in a glacial cirque near the village of Sumjam, on the southwestern slopes of the Zaskar Mountains, at an altitude of 4,650 meters (15,255 feet).

The first geological expeditions took place in 1887 with the arrival of the geologist La Touche. The examination of the alluvial deposits at the bottom of the mountain revealed some remarkable sapphires, including a 993-carat crystal. The next summer, more than 23,000 carats were extracted, but few of the gems had the quality of the original find. Private interests financed new studies in 1906, numerous efforts followed until 1979, when the mines were completely abandoned. A few soldiers remain to guard against clandestine mining.

The geology of this area is relatively simple: metamorphic marbles interstratified in biotite gneiss contain lenses rich in actinolite and tremolite, which coexist with pegmatite intrusions containing black tourmaline. Corundums are found in feldspars altered to kaolinite; classical pegmatite minerals (such as pink tourmaline, aquamarine, hambergite, and amblygonite)

A clip set with a 133.63-carat oval sapphire, surrounded by diamonds and other sapphires. A. Reza creation.

have been observed in the vicinity of these formations. It is unfortunate that this exceptional deposit did not enjoy the future that the original discovery (called the "old mine") seemed to promise.

Myanmar (Burma)

Blue sapphires in Myanmar are associated with the feldspars of intrusive rock above Mogok. The sapphire deposits mined in the valley are located next to the village of Kathe, about 10 kilometers (6 miles) from Mogok, and in Bernarmyo.

Sri Lanka

Sri Lanka is one of the most important gem-producing areas in the world. Its oldest description was provided by Nearchus, a Macedonian navigator who commanded the fleet of Alexander the Great: around 334 B.C., he mentioned an island, not far from Persia, where beautiful gems were discovered. In the sixteenth century, the Portuguese brought back precious stones from the area, followed by the Dutch a few dozen years later.

For centuries, hundreds of thousands of carats of various gems (such as sapphire, chrysoberyl, ruby, and spinel) have been mined from alluvial deposits of a still-unknown origin. The island is made up essentially of metamorphic pre-Cambrian rocks, such as gneiss and metamorphic marbles rich in spinel and forsterite, granulites and cordierite, and pegmatites rich in various gems. In addition to the gems, the alluvial deposits contain all the other components of the rocks from which they come.

Sapphire is the most important gem on the island, found between Kolonne and Ratnapura (the "city of gems" in Sinhalese). This region, located about 100 kilometers (60 miles) southeast of the capital, Colombo, is the main mining area for an alluvial layer of sands and gravels from the Kolonne pegmatites. Important concentrations of gems are also located in the central province of Elahera, in the Kaluganga Valley, about 90 kilometers (55 miles) northeast of Colombo. There gem minerals are uniformly distributed. The same situation exists near Amarawewa and Kochipadana in the southern province, about 175 kilometers (110 miles) southeast of Colombo. Mining is still very primitive: the gem-bearing alluvial material called *illam* is collected at the bottom of small shafts, which are a maximum of 15 meters (50 feet) deep. It is then washed, using wicker baskets as pans. After sorting, the washed gravel, called *dullam*, is examined by a foreman, generally the owner of the mine, who employs no more than two to eight people on average. Most stones are faceted at or near the mine with very rudimentary equipment, although machines with electric engines came into use during the last decade, especially for sawing.

It is difficult to estimate local production. The local geological survey reported about 61,000 carats in 1965–66 and 478,000 carats in 1973. But a significant part of the total production is probably smuggled or illicitly sold and cannot be accounted for.

Kampuchea and Thailand

Sapphire has been transported from the depths of the earth by volcanic eruptions on both sides of the Thai-Kampuchean border. The igneous rocks were quickly broken up in the tropical climate, and this material has been dispersed in alluvial deposits over wide areas. Mining is intense, accomplished with primitive techniques imported from Myanmar as well as modern mechanized equipment. Sapphires are mined in Pailin and Chamnop in Kampuchea and in Chanthaburi (Khao-Ploi-Waen and Bang-Kha-Cha) and Kanchanaburi in Thailand (ruby is found alongside sapphire at Pailin and Chanthaburi). These deposits, known long ago by local populations, were rediscovered in the nineteenth century. They yield (in mass) about one-third of the world's sapphires.

The heat treatment of sapphires from Thailand and Australia is done in Thailand. Thailand has become the largest world market for sapphires because it distributes large quantities of the gem to the international trade.

Australia

Huge sapphire-rich alluvial deposits were discovered in 1870 near Anakie in Queensland, Australia. They have the same origin as the Southeast Asian deposits.

Other equally large placer deposits

Sri Lankan sapphire crystal. Length: 2 cm. R. Titeux collection.

The washing of gem-bearing gravels near Ratnapura, Sri Lanka. Photo: Konrad Helbeig, ZAFA.

have been found in New South Wales, near Inverell. Sapphires are mined with powerful mechanized tools. The production reaches several hundred pounds annually. These sapphires represent, in mass, the majority of the sapphires that are sold in Thailand.

Other Sources

Various localities have produced sapphires on a sporadic basis, but their commercial significance is minor. In the United States, sapphire is mined in Montana, near Utica, on the banks of the Missouri River, and at Yogo Gulch, in a volcanic dyke on the Judith River. Recently a deposit was mined on the banks of Lake Nyaka in Malawi. Tanzanian alluvial deposits have produced some pastel stones. Nigeria also has had a significant level of sapphire production in recent years.

In France the Riou Pezouliou alluvial deposit near Espally-Saint-Marcel (Haute Loire) produced some blue sapphires associated with abundant red zircons. These stones were used in jewelry in the Middle Ages (referred to as sapphires of Le Puy). Other areas that have small sapphire deposits include Bohemia (Czechoslovakia), Angola, Madagascar, Norway, India, and Brazil (Rio Coxim in Mato Grosso and Corrego do Fogo in Minas Gerais).

Color and Inclusions

The color of blue sapphire is caused by substitution of both iron and titanium for small amounts of aluminum in the corundum lattice. Because these elements are more common than chromium that produces the red corundum ruby, sapphires are more common than rubies. However, too much iron creates a greenish cast that is not attractive. The absorption lines in the blue due to iron are often visible. The sapphires from the old Kashmir mines are renown for their deep, velvety cobalt-blue color, with a turquoise blue dichroism. However, mediocre Kashmir sapphires are more common, especially in the yields from later mining efforts. Of the 40 kilograms (90 pounds) of corundum mined in 1928, only a few pounds were of good quality.

Sapphires from Myanmar are famous for their intense blue color, which nevertheless has a tendency to become much darker in incandescent light, a phenomenon long recognized by the experts. As one wrote, "It is the strangest thing in the world to see a magnificent sapphire parure turn black in candlelight." Their blue–pale green dichroism is very distinctive.

Sri Lankan sapphires are known for their size and beautiful color. However, this same color is sometimes rather light and on occasion its distribution is uneven, so that a crystal may be partly colorless. Some stay blue in evening light, while others turn violetish. Their absorption spectrum then shows the combined presence of iron and chromium. The dichroism of Sri Lankan sapphires ranges from very distinct blue to colorless.

Sapphires from Thailand, Kampuchea, and Australia often have a slightly greenish blue color. While some stones are almost black, others display an attractive blue with almost no green. Their dichroism is typically blue to green. Sometimes an excess of titanium induces the presence of silk, which imparts a brownish component. Montana sapphires are often blue-green, but some display an acceptable blue with a blue-green dichroism.

All these sapphires have similar inclusions: colored growth banding, rutile needles, exsolution products, and fingerprints made of tiny fluid inclusions. The appearance of these inclusions can vary from one deposit to the next; sometimes the presence of other crystals as inclusions helps in identifying the source of the stones (tourmaline in Kashmir; apatite, mica, zircon, and calcite in Myanmar; apatite, mica, spinel, and pyrite in Sri Lanka; zircon, thorites, and niobotantalates in Australia, Kampuchea, and Thailand). Inclusions of carbon dioxide are more frequent in stones from Sri Lanka and Myanmar.

A sapphire is preferentially cut with the table perpendicular to the optic axis, to display the purest blue color. However, because the color is often irregularly distributed, the lapidary must carefully study the crystal in order to place the color on one side of the pavilion, so that the face-up appearance will be a uniform blue. Indian and Sri Lankan lapidaries are very skilled at this task. Star sapphires are cut in cabochons, so that the star is as well centered as possible.

Indices of refraction and specific gravity increase slightly with the iron content. They range from 1.76 and 1.77 to 1.77 to 1.78 (R.I.) and from 4.0 to 4.1 (S.G.). Most Thai and Australian sapphires are heat-treated at about 1,700° to 1,800°C (3,100° to 3,275°F) to bring out the blue color-causing center, to replace in part the green one already present. Most sapphires mined in Australia are exported to Thailand, where large furnaces have been built, so most of the world's rough blue sapphires are sold in Bangkok. The Thais also heat-treat many pale or milky Sri Lankan sapphires to give them a darker blue color. Most of these sapphires luminesce under ultraviolet light.

Detail of a diamond and sapphire cabochon necklace, with a 68.61-carat sapphire. A. Reza design.

Planar growth and color banding in a blue sapphire from Sri Lanka. Length: 0.5 cm. Sorbonne collection.

Detail of a necklace with a 143.15-carat yellow sapphire and pear- and marquise-shape diamonds. Fred creation.

Only inclusion-free sapphires can be heat-treated; inclusions, when heated, could cause such internal stress that the stone could eventually shatter. When microscopic inclusions have been heat-treated, the internal fractures around them help indicate that the stone was so treated.

Some very light corundums from Sri Lanka are treated with a superficial diffusion of iron and titanium (probably by surrounding them with a titanium-borax paste and heating them to 1,700°C (3,100°F). A very thin blue layer then forms on all facets of these "diffusion treated sapphires," penetrating only $\frac{1}{10}$ to $\frac{4}{10}$ of a millimeter deep. This treatment can be detected by a careful examination of the facet junctions, preferably in immersion (or by polishing).

Natural Gems Resembling Blue Sapphire

All blue gems may be mistaken for sapphire. Benitoite is the easiest to mistake, but this gem is rare, and faceted stones are small and comparatively more expensive than those of similarly colored sapphires.

Other similar blue gems include tanzanite, indicolite, cordierite, blue spinel, aquamarine, blue topaz, blue zircon, fibrolite, and kyanite.

Simulants

Blue glass colored with cobalt has been used since ancient times to simulate blue sapphire. Blue garnet-and-glass doublets were manufactued in large quantities during the eighteenth and nineteenth centuries for the same purpose. The garnet slabs that are used often contain needlelike inclusions. In more recent imitations, the garnet-glass joint is made at the girdle, as for ruby imitations. A green sapphire–synthetic corundum doublet set in white metal is marketed to tourists in Bangkok. Recently, blue synthetic quartz and blue cubic zirconia have also been used.

Synthesis

Synthetic sapphire grown by the flame-fusion (Verneuil) process has been marketed in large quantities since 1908. Fingerprintlike inclusions may be induced to better imitate natural sapphire. Flux-grown synthetic blue sapphire has often been produced experimentally, but it is not widely marketed because it is so expensive.

SAPPHIRES OF OTHER COLORS (FANCY COLORS)

Naturally colored corundum that is any color but red (see RUBY) or blue (see preceding discussion of blue sapphires).

Jean-Baptiste Tavernier reported that in the kingdom of Pegu (Myanmar), all colored gems were called "ruby" in the seventeenth century, and sapphire was therefore called "blue ruby." The present usage is just the reverse of this ancient practice: today a jeweler will call any corundum that is neither blue nor red a sapphire, and mention its color first. Most of these fancy-color sapphires are from Sri Lanka.

Fancy-color sapphires can be fairly large. The Smithsonian Institution displays a 92.6-carat yellow sapphire, a 42.2-carat purple stone, a 27.4-carat violet gem, and a 19.4-carat pink sapphire. The distinction between pink sapphire and ruby is mostly a question of opinion. Some bright, dark pink sapphires, close to a ruby color, are called pink rubies in France. Rare orange sapphires are called *padparadscha* only if they display a distinct pinkish tinge. Yellow sapphire is a favorite in jewelry because its bright color is attractive with diamonds. Some colorless sapphires can be turned yellow by irradiation; their color is not stable and fades significantly after a month in daylight. Other sapphires acquire a yellow color by heat treatment at 1,000° to 1,700°C (1,830° to 3,100°F) for twelve hours; the resulting color is stable. Most yellow sapphires on the market today are nearly colorless Sri Lankan sapphires that have been heat-treated in Thailand.

Green, violet, and nearly colorless sapphires are generally less in demand than yellow sapphires are. Some sapphires change color under different lighting conditions, just as alexandrite does, and are sought by collectors.

All fancy-color sapphires, especially yellow and pink ones, can be imitated by flame-fusion-grown synthetic sapphires.

SAPPHIRINE

A monoclinic magnesian aluminosilicate with a dark blue color. The rare flattened crystals show a distinct pseudohexagonal outline, with a vitreous luster.

Sapphirine is an indicator mineral of the granulite facies and is found in amphibolites associated with corundum. It is also, however, found in metamorphosed aluminous and magnesian rocks that are low in silica.

Small crystals from Madagascar have sometimes been cut for collectors (H is 7½; indices of refraction are about 1.71; S.G. varies from 3.40 to 3.58). Sapphirine has been found in South African and Sri Lanka and, more recently, in central Australia, in association with kornerupine.

The term *sapphirine,* because it is associated with a blue color, was initially synonymous with blue chalcedony. It was used in this way by René-Just Haüy in his 1817 *Treatise on Precious Stones.* Nose called by

the same name a blue feldspar from the Laach Valley in Alsace, France, a mineral then considered to be *latialite* (now called haüyne). In 1821, Giesecke gave this name to its present bearer, a mineral found in a Greenland deposit. The blue chalcedony–sapphirine confusion from the last century still occasionally occurs today.

SARD

A brown chalcedony.

Origin of the Name and Virtues

Sard probably derives from the Hebrew *sered,* which designated red stones. It became *sardion* in Greek; this term may have been used to name the ancient city of Sardis, capital of Lydia in Asia Minor, as well as the island of Sardinia, Italy, from which this mineral came. The Latin name *sardinus lapis,* "stone from Sardinia," was applied to the stone during the first century, becoming *sardine* in the lapidary books of the Middle Ages.

Sard supposedly protected wearers from witchcraft and brought happiness and victory. It also could neutralize the evil influence of onyx.

Color

Originally the term *sard* designated the brown and red varieties of translucent chalcedony. In the eighteenth century, this name was restricted to the reddish brown to dark brown varieties colored by iron oxides. Sard overlaps carnelian in its lighter tones and onyx in its darker ones. Most sard on the market today is actually chalcedony dyed with iron salts.

Uses and Imitations

Sard is valued for the carving of intaglios and seals. It is imitated with glass.

Bust of Diane de Poitiers (1499–1566) in sard; it was used as a tie pin around 1880. Height: 2.4 cm. Boucheron collection.

Deposits

Like carnelian, sard is found in India, especially around the Ratnapur mining center. The Broach and Cambay cutting centers are particularly famous for it. It is also found in Yemen, Saudi Arabia, Egypt, and in Rio Grande do Sul in Brazil. The historical deposit in the Nahe Valley of Germany has been long exhausted, and Idar-Oberstein cutting factories now use imported stones. Sard and carnelian indications are found all over the world, to the joy of collectors, especially in the United States (for example, in Yellowstone National Park).

SARDONYX

Agate with alternating reddish brown and white planar layers. The name comes from the Latin *sardonychis,* formed from *sarda,* meaning "sard," and *onychis,* meaning "onyx."

One of the most famous documented sardonyx pieces belonged to Polycrates, tyrant of Samos, who tried to present it to Fortune to prevent the goddess's fickleness. Sardonyx was highly valued in Rome, where the Roman general Publius Cornelius Scipio Africanus was the first to wear it. It was especially popular for seals, because "it did not tear off the wax while making the seal," perhaps because of its cryptoporosity.

In ancient Rome *sardonyx* apparently designated all varieties of zoned agates, which were imported from India, where they were worked into drilled beads. Most Murrhin vases, which Pliny exalted so much, were probably brown agate (probably stained), comparable to some kind of sardonyx. Such was also the case of the water

jug set in gilded silver from the collection of Louis XIV displayed in the Apollo Gallery in the Louvre. One of the most famous Roman cameos made of sardonyx can be seen in the French Bibliothèque Nationale: the Grand Camée de France which affirmed the adoption of Caligula by Tiberius, fully justifying his succession to the Augustan throne.

Like all chalcedonies, the color of sardonyx, due to iron oxides, can be obtained by dying a chalcedony that has layers of different porosity.

Sardonyx can be imitated with glass. The shells of some mollusks may also imitate sardonyx when they are carved into cameos (see NACRE).

SCAPOLITE

A family of minerals forming a solid-solution series between marialite (an aluminum and sodium chlorosilicate) and meionite (an aluminum and calcium silicocarbonate). Numerous intermediate forms exist, including scapolite and dipyre.

The name *scapolite* comes from the Greek *skapos,* meaning "rod" or "stick," referring to the shape of the crystals, and *lithos,* meaning "stone." The name *wernerite,* a variety of scapolite, was created in honor of the German mineralogist and geologist Abraham Werner (1750–1817).

Scapolite results from regional or contact metamorphism. However, beautiful crystals have been found in the Madagascar "pegmatoides" in association with diopside and phlogopite. Gem-quality crystals have been discovered in metamorphosed limestones as well. Sometimes the fibrous structure of this yellow to pink to pale violet

mineral (as the material from Mogok, Myanmar) can produce chatoyancy, which is enhanced by a cabochon cut. When very transparent and yellow, scapolite can imitate citrine; such stones are found in Brazil, Madagascar, Kenya, and Tanzania.

Scapolite is a very delicate gem because of its three easy cleavages and low hardness (H is 6). Its luster is vitreous (indices of refraction increase with the calcium content from 1.54 to 1.56 for n_e and 1.55 to 1.60 for n_o, as the birefringence ranges from 0.010 to 0.040, for a uniaxial negative character). Scapolite is fairly light (S.G. is 2.55 to 2.80). Its luminescence varies from orangy (pink scapolite) to mauve (yellow scapolite).

SEPIOLITE OR MEERSCHAUM

A massive hydrous magnesium silicate, crystallizing in the orthorhombic system.

The name *meerschaum,* meaning "sea foam," refers to the material's great lightness. Indeed, sepiolite was reportedly discovered originally as ivory-white chunks floating on the Black Sea. The name *sepiolite* comes from *sepia,* meaning "cuttlefish," and *lithos,* "stone." This "cuttlefish stone," or cuttlebone, also refers to the stone's ability to float on water. The term *magnesite,* originally used to describe this material, applies today only to magnesium carbonate.

Sepiolite never forms distinct crystals. Rather, it is encountered as white, kidneylike masses with a silky luster. It is scratched easily with fingernails, and it sticks to the tongue. This mineral is more or less compact and generally easy to crush. Sepiolite is found in basic rocks.

The main deposit mined today is at Eskisehir, west of Ankara, Turkey. The sepiolite there forms kidneylike masses at the base of a layer of smectic clays, used to extract grease from wool. Once cleaned of its clay crust and dried, sepiolite is transported to Izmir (Smyrna). Other deposits are found in Khorāsān, Iran; Moravia, Czechoslovakia; the Crimea, Soviet Union; Corinthia, Greece; Spain; and Morocco.

Sepiolite's hardness is low, about 2. Nevertheless, because of its thermal-insulation properties, it is used in the manufacture of smoking pipes, some of which are very elaborate. Sepiolite is very breakable and is also quite sensitive to even small shocks: its fracture is matte. Surgeons from Napoléon's armies, who operated without anesthesia, gave their patients a sepiolite pipe to squeeze between their teeth to help them bear pain. If the patient died during the operation, his pipe would fall and shatter on the floor. The French expression *casser sa pipe* (meaning "to break one's pipe") is a reminder of these grim but heroic times.

Sepiolite is imitated with plastics.

130-carat faceted yellow scapolite from Tanzania. G. Becker collection, Idar-Oberstein, Germany.

SERPENTINE

Various magnesian rock-forming phyllosilicates are grouped under this name.

Origin of the Name and History

The name comes originally from *ophis*, meaning "serpent" or "snake" in Greek, which was transcribed as *ophites* in Latin and translated as *serpentina* as early as the sixteenth century (Boece de Boot, 1609). This name supposedly refers to the snake-skinlike appearance of these mottled rocks.

Perhaps this resemblance also explains why serpentine was considered an amulet against snakebite from ancient times through the Middle Ages. Pliny the Elder (A.D. 23–79) also mentioned that it was effective against headaches. According to Galen (A.D. 131–201), crushed ophite drunk in white wine would destroy bladder stones. Boece de Boot reported that the Germans believed that serpentine bowls could reveal by their condensation whether the beverage they contained was poisoned or not. When applied hot to a sick body, serpentine stones supposedly could also cure lower back pain.

Serpentines were used to carve cylindrical seals in the third millennium B.C. They have since been used by all civilizations as raw material for small carvings and bowls. The National Museum of Natural History in Paris has a serpentine pot from Saxony, made in Germany in 1628.

Structure and Physical Properties

Serpentines comprise stacked layers that have the ability to slip over one another. This is due to the association, through shared oxygen atoms, of a silicate and a magnesian layer. However, the distances between oxygen atoms in these two layers are slightly different, producing stress. The result may be a limited development of the serpentine layer, or its coiling. This induces two different appearances: the compact *antigorite* facies and the fibrous *chrysotile* facies (chrysotile is a variety of asbestos).

Yellow to greenish antigorite from Cape Lizard in Cornwall, England, is called *lizardite*. It is translucent and soft (H is 2½) and is used to carve various souvenirs. Kashmir serpentine forms fairly tough masses, with a hardness of 4 to 5. It is called *bowenite* in honor of the mineralogist G. T. Bowen and is used in local crafts. Bowenite was used by Sumerians to carve cylinder seals. New Zealand's Maori tribes carved axes from it, while Penjab Indians made knife handles with it. Bowenite is called *yu-yen* in China and is sometimes offered to

Nineteenth-century engraved serpentine from China. Size: 18 by 16 cm. National Higher School of Mines, Paris.

tourists under the deceptive names of "Hunan jade," "Korean jade," or "new jade."

The color of serpentine varies from very pale green to an almost black dark green. It can be regularly distributed or form spots or veins. Serpentine has a vitreous luster (index of refraction is about 1.57) and is sometimes translucent but usually is opaque. It can be easily dyed because of its porosity. Its specific gravity is 2.6.

Deposits

Serpentines are formed by the autohydration of peridots, dunites, and peridotites; they are alteration products of magnesium-rich ultrabasic rocks. They are relatively resistant to atmospheric agents and do not support vegetation. Serpentines are widely distributed throughout the world.

Similar Rocks

Chlorites

Chlorites are formed by the alternate stacking of magnesian sheets with sheets made of two aluminosilicate layers on both sides of a magnesian layer. They form masses which have an appearance and physical properties similar to those of common serpentine. Therefore, they are called *pseudophite,* or false serpentine. Their hardness is 2, with an index of refraction of about 1.57 and a specific gravity of 2.7.

Bernstein Pseudophite

The pseudophite found in Bernstein, Austria (formerly a stop on the amber trade route) is carved for tourists. It is often sold under the deceptive name of "Styrian jade."

Fuchsite

Fuchsite is a chromian muscovite. Structurally, it can be considered a chlorite in which the magnesian layers have been replaced by alkali potassic ions that hold the two aluminosilicate layers together. It is found as an inclusion in quartz. (see AVENTU-RINE, erroneously called "Indian jade") and as compact masses called *verdite.* Verdite is slightly denser (S.G. of 2.8 to 3) and harder (H is 3) than common serpentine, and its index of refraction is about 1.58. The most famous verdite deposit was discovered in 1907 in the Transvaal (South Africa) on the north bank of the Nordkaap River, near Baberton. At the beginning of the century, this material was deceptively represented as "Transvaal jade" or "African jade." Other verdites come from Swaziland (South Africa), Vermont, and western Australia.

Others

Serpentine is imitated by various more or less altered igneous rocks that are used in ornamentation under the collective name of *green rocks.* These include ophiolites, antique green porphyry, and gabbros.

SIBERITE

A violetish blue tourmaline. The term is little used, as it can produce confusion, because the Soviets have used it for green diopside.

SILLIMANITE OR FIBROLITE

An aluminum silicate, crystallizing in the orthorhombic system. Sillimanite was named for American geologist Benjamin Silliman (1779–1864). Sillimanite crystals are rare; usually this mineral is found as undulating fibers with a perfect cleavage along their length (therefore, its alternate name, *fibrolite*). When impregnated with quartz, as it often is, sillimanite has such a remarkable toughness that it was used as raw material by Neolithic stone workers. It is often white, sometimes pinkish, and resembles jade when it is greenish to bluish. Very rare blue gem-quality sillimanite crystals have been faceted for collectors. They are reminiscent of cordierite. The Geological Museum in London displays a 19.84-carat stone. Sillimanite's hardness is 7½ (but only 6 to 7 for the massive varieties). Its specific gravity is 3.25, and the principal indices of refraction are 1.659, 1.660, and 1.680. Sillimanite's distinct dichroism (colorless–sapphire blue–pale yellow) makes it possible to distinguish it from euclase when it is faceted.

Sillimanite is a common mineral of clay-rich rocks that have undergone very strong metamorphism. It comes mostly from the gem-bearing gravels of Sri Lanka and Mogok in Myanmar (Burma).

SINHALITE

An iron-bearing aluminum magnesioborate, crystallizing in the orthorhombic system. It was named for the island of Sri Lanka, called *Sinhala* in Sanskrit.

This gem was identified in 1952 by the American mineralogist G. Switzer using X-ray diffraction; thereafter, B. Anderson and C. Payne observed a contradiction between the position of the medium index of refraction and the light color of a "faceted peridot." Indeed, only the position of the medium index of refraction (sinhalite is biaxial negative) and the presence of a fourth band in the blue range differentiate peridot from sinhalite, which was once considered to be a brown peridot.

Sinhalite is the second example (after taaffeite) of a new mineral discovered as a faceted gem, following meticulous observations, rather than as a crystal. Since its identification, minute sinhalite crystals have been found at the contact of a marble in New York State. In 1958 the only well-formed monocrystal was mined in the alluvial deposits of the Mogok Valley in Myanmar.

Gem sinhalites come from the gem-bearing gravels of Sri Lanka. Collector's items, they can attain large dimensions. A 109.8-carat stone is displayed at the Smithsonian Institution in Washington, D.C. Sinhalite resembles brown chrysoberyl or zircon.

SMITHSONITE OR BONAMITE

A zinc carbonate, crystallizing in the rhombohedral (hexagonal) system.

Smithsonite was named in honor of James Smithson, the English chemist who bequeathed the first funds for the Smithsonian Institution in Washington, D.C. Smithsonite was also called *bonamite* when it was sold by the Goodfriend brothers of New York City, who named it for the French equivalent of their last name.

The most common appearance of smithsonite is mammillary, in concretions or stalactites. This mineral can form masses full of cavities but also fills geodes of karstic origin. It is most commonly white, although various color nuances are produced by the replacement of zinc: green to blue results from copper; rose is due to cobalt; yellow, to cadmium; and brownish arises from iron.

Smithsonite is mechanically and chemically fragile (S.G. of 4.3, hardness of 5), but it has been cut for collectors. It may resemble turquoise when fashioned into a cabochon.

In regions where limestone is abundant, smithsonite sometimes forms enormous concentrations that have been mined as zinc ore. In the past, the nicest specimens

Smithsonite crystals from the Kelly mine in New Mexico. Length: 5 cm. Sorbonne collection.

came from the Laurium mine near Athens, Greece. Today, the Kelly mines in New Mexico produce beautiful bright bluish-green masses. Smithsonite is also found in various other deposits, for example, in Mexico, South Africa, and Namibia.

Calamine, a miners' term for a zinc silicate called hemimorphite, has a similar appearance. It also has been carved into small decorative objects.

SODALITE

The sodic term for the ultramarine or feldspathoid family. This family of minerals belongs to the tectosilicates, or framework silicates, formed by a three-dimensional framework of SiO_4 tetrahedra, bonded at all their summits. The open cavities of the structure are filled by cations such as sodium, potassium, and calcium.

Lazurite, the main component of lapis lazuli, and haüyne are other members of this family. Sodalite was named for its sodium content. It is almost always massive, although crystals have been found in the syenites from Mont-Saint-Hilaire in Quebec, Canada, and in the Sar-e-Sang lazurite deposit in Afghanistan. It forms enormous masses in nephelinic syenites, with veins of feldspar and biotite. Pyrite is always absent. It is decomposed by hydrochloric acid, forming a silica gel.

Sodalite is mined at Itaju da Colonia (Fazenda Hiassu) near Itabira, in southeastern Bahia, Brazil. It is used mostly as an ornamental stone, because its dark blue color is less "warm" than that of lapis lazuli, for which it is a common substitute. It is used to make boxes and small carved objects. Some crystals have been faceted for collectors. Its index of refraction is 1.48 and its hardness is 5½.

SPECTROLITE OR LABRADORITE

A variety of sodopotassic feldspar.

Its name comes from the Latin *spectrum,* meaning "spectrum," and from the Greek *lithos,* meaning "stone," because spectrolite displays all the colors of the visible spectrum.

The bright diffraction colors are caused by the stone's texture: alternating parallel lamellae of slightly different composition have thickness comparable to visible wavelengths. They therefore diffract these wavelengths when illuminated at an angle close to their normal. A cabochon cut enhances this optical phenomenon. The feldspar itself often has a bluish gray color; at an appropriate angle, the tone is reminiscent of the fires of a black opal, for which spectrolite is a substitute.

The mining of sodalite in Bahia, Brazil. Photo: J. Cassedanne.

Spectrolite's specific gravity is about 2.6, and its index of refraction, close to 1.52. It is the main constituent of Labrador granite (which is actually a syenite from Paul Island, Canada) used by monument masons. This material is used in architectural ornamentation and for façades as well as for funerary monuments.

In the past spectrolite was called labradorite, but this latter name is now used exclusively for a calcium-rich calcosodic feldspar.

SPESSARTITE

An orange to red manganoan garnet.

Origin of the Name

Spessartite was name for the Spessart, a mountain in Bavaria (Germany), whence the first described specimens came.

A red 109-carat Brazilian spessartite is displayed at the Smithsonian Institution, as is a 40.1-carat orange gem from Virginia.

It is likely that Sri Lankan spessartites were known during ancient times and were part of the group of stones known as *carbunculus* and *lychnes.*

Physical Properties

Spessartite always contains some iron, which replaces the aluminum as ferric iron and the manganese as ferrous iron. Spessartite's high index of refraction (1.79 to 1.81) and specific gravity (4.12 to 4.20) help distinguish it from hessonite, which has a similar color. Its absorption spectrum shows three weak bands in the blue and two char-

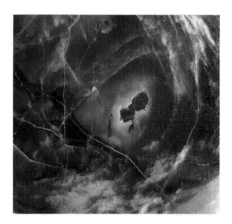

Polished slab of Brazilian sodalite. Length: 10 cm. G. Becker collection, Idar-Oberstein, Germany.

acteristic bands in the violet, due to manganese. Bands due to iron may be present as well. Spessartite's scratch hardness of 7 to 7½ is good.

Deposits and Inclusions

Spessartite may be formed as a metamorphic mineral with metasomatic input. This is the case in the Broken Hill skarns in Australia, the most important world deposit, where spessartite crystals of an attractive dark red color reach up to 5 centimeters in diameter.

Spessartite most typically is found, however, in potassic granitic pegmatites, where it is associated with beryl and tourmaline, as in Brazil and Virginia. It is also found in the gem-bearing gravels near Ratnapura, Sri Lanka, and Mogok, Myanmar (Burma).

205

A duck carved in labradorite (spectrolite variety). Length: 20 cm. G. Becker design, Idar-Oberstein, Germany.

A few spessartites, some of which have been faceted, were discovered in Manhattan, when foundations were dug on East 179th Street.

Few inclusions are found in this gem, except occasional fingerprints.

SPHALERITE OR BLENDE

A cubic zinc sulfide.

Disappointed by this ore, which does not contain lead, medieval German miners called it *blenden,* meaning "to deceive" in German. Americans named it in the same way, using the Greek adjective *sphaleros,* which means "deceitful."

It is the most important zinc ore, often found in association with galena. It is found in various kinds of deposits, including hydrothermal and pneumatolitic ones; gem sphalerite is most often found in sedimentary deposits, such as Picos de Europa in the Spanish region of Asturias (now Oviedo) and Tynagh in Ireland.

Sphalerite contains greater amounts of iron as its formation temperature increases, and this dictates its color. When pure, sphalerite is colorless, but a significant iron content gives it a black color (marmatite). Between these two extremes, all colors, from dark brown to light yellow, are possible. The amber to red sphalerites from Spain are gemologically the most interesting.

Sphalerite is a fragile mineral (H of 3½ to 4, perfect and easy cleavage, soluble in hydrochloric acid), making the faceted gem

A 30-carat faceted spessartite from Madagascar. Compagnie Générale de Madagascar.

A 23-carat faceted sphalerite from the Asturias, Spain. P. Fumey collection.

only a collector's item or a display object. It may look like a colored diamond because of its adamantine luster (n is 2.37); its intense fires and yellow color are attributed by some to cadmium and by others to iron (with three lines in the orangy red range, somewhat like zircon). Its specific gravity is 4.1.

Several faceted sphalerites are displayed in the Smithsonian Institution, including a 73.3-carat brownish yellow gem from Utah, a 48-carat yellow stone from Mexico, and a 45.9-carat yellow one from Spain.

Mammillary varieties, called *schalenblendes* (or "scaly blendes"), with a brown to light brownish yellow color, have sometimes been used for ornamentation (such as the sphalerites from the Vieille Montagne, near Liège, Belgium).

SPHENE

See TITANITE.

SPINEL

A magnesium aluminosilicate, crystallizing in the cubic system. Its red variety, called *rubicelle* in the past, is the most valued. Aluminum and magnesium are partially replaced by chromium and iron.

Origin of the Name

The word *spinel* appeared relatively late in history (seventeenth century) as an adjective for ruby. It derives most likely from the Latin *spina*, meaning "thorn," because the sharp points of its octahedral shape helped to differentiate its rough crystal from corundum, the "Oriental red": it was the "small red thorn." *Rubicelle* comes from the Latin *ruber*, which means "red."

Spinel has been known since ancient times in India, where it was called red diamond and was associated with the warriors' caste. It came from the diamond-bearing sands of the Penner River, west of Madras, in the Balaghat region (meaning "beyond the *ghat*," a mountain range in southeast India), which had been conquered in 1780 by Hyder Ali, after whom Hyderabad was later named. This province was most probably the Balascia mentioned in Marco Polo's tales at the end of the thirteenth century. The red stones from Balaghat were called *ballagius*, then *ballas* in German, *balais* in French, and *balas* in English. Here again, one can see the distinction between the two red stones, the balas (spinel) and the Oriental (ruby). Another possible source of the term *balas* is given in Pseudo-Plutarch's treatise on rivers, from about 225 B.C.: "There is on this mountain [Mount Ballenee] a stone called aster, which at the be-

Spinels from alluvial deposits in Myanmar (Burma). Diameter: 2 cm. Sorbonne collection.

ginning of spring, sparkles like fire during the night. In the local language, it is called *ballen*, which means 'king.' "

Historical Spinels

Almost all large historical red gems are spinels and are referred to as either spinel ruby or balas ruby.

The British Crown

In the middle of the fourteenth century, the king of Castile, Peter the Cruel, assassinated Abu Said, king of Granada, and seized his treasure, in particular the large red spinel he coveted. However, Peter was deposed by his half-brother, Henry II of Trastámara, in concert with the French, and had to request the help of the prince of Aquitaine, Edward the Black Prince, son of

Edward III of England. Peter was restored to the throne after winning the battle of Nájera in 1367 with Edward's help. To show his gratitude, he presented the Black Prince with his large spinel, known since as the Black Prince Ruby. The stone was inherited by Edward's son, Richard II, king of England, who was deposed in 1399 and died a prisoner of Henry IV in 1400. It was set on the helmet of Henry V at the time of the battle of Agincourt in 1415, where it played its alleged role of talisman against wounds by deflecting a blow from the duke of Alençon and saving Henry V's life. The Black Prince Ruby was mysteriously preserved during the Cromwell revolution (1640–58) and was later placed at the center of the Saint Edward's Crown, reconstituted in 1661 for Charles II. This spinel has an irregular, somewhat square shape, measures approximately 5 centimeters (2 inches) across, and is polished but not faceted.

Spinel and diamond brooch. Private collection.

necklace, displayed in the Indian Room of Buckingham Palace.

The British Museum displays a red 520-carat spinel in the shape of a polished pebble; it comes from Myanmar (Burma), where it was seized by British troops during the plunder of the summer palace of the emperor of China in September 1860. A 355-carat polished octahedral spinel also belongs to this museum.

The French Crown

Duchess Anne of Brittany put her jewels, as well as her duchy, into the hands of the royal family by marrying the king of France twice: Charles VIII in 1491, then Louis XII in 1499. Her daughter Claude gave the two large spinels she had inherited to her husband, Francis I: the Côte de Bretagne, weighing 206 old carats, mounted so that it could be worn as a brooch, and the Fève de Naples, a 121 old-carat stone, set on a A-shaped jewel, better known as the Roman A. Henry II added the Oeuf de Naples, a third spinel, weighing 241 old carats. Collectively known as the "three crown rubies," these stones would be successively pawned by Catherine de Médicis (to the duke of Florence), by Henry III (to the count of Vaudémont), the duke of Lorraine, and then a banker. In 1749, Jacques Guay masterfully carved the Côte de Bretagne, reducing it to 105 old carats, by order of Louis XV. The stone was then placed with the blue diamond on the Golden Fleece. In 1757 the Oeuf de Naples was sawed and carved into doves, mounted on the cross and plaque of the order of Saint-Esprit. After the theft of the national Garde Meuble in September 1792, the stones were lost and have never been found again. The Côte de Bretagne was kept in London by its thief, Cadet Guillot, until 1796. It was then given to an immigrant and presented to the future Louis XVIII, then a refugee at Blankerburg. It is presently displayed in the Apollo Gallery at the Louvre under the name Dragon.

The Russian Crown

Catherine II ordered for her coronation a crown topped by the 400-carat Lal spinel, a gift from the emperor of China. The crown, not ready in time, was used for the first time by her son, Paul I. It is now in the Armors Palace in Moscow.

The Treasury of Iran

The Iranian treasury contains the most beautiful spinels known, including several hundred stones of more than 20 carats and some weighing more than 100 carats. The largest stones weigh 500, 414, and 270 carats. The last is engraved with the name of

In 1838 Queen Victoria had it set at the center of the headband of the imperial crown, created for herself, which is now in the Tower of London.

The Tribute of the World spinel, or Kharaj-i-Alam, belonged to the Muslim sovereign of Delhi. The Turkic conqueror Timur Lenk (Tamerlane), also called Lord of the Favorable Conjunction (Venus-Jupiter), plundered Delhi in 1398 and took to his capital, Samarkand, the large 352-carat spinel, polished in an irregular shape. In 1502 the Safavids conquered the Timurids and became the owners of the Tribute of the World. To ensure good relations with his mighty neighbor, the Moghul emperor of India Jahāngīr, Shāh 'Abbās I offered him this talisman of power in 1612, thus acknowledging a symbolic vassalage. Jahāngīr had engraved on the stone the name of

his father, Akbar the Great; his own name; and the date 1021 (hegira). His successors also had their names engraved, until the plunder of Delhi in 1739 by Nāder Shāh, who had this long sentence carved: This is the ruby among the twenty-five thousand true gems of the king of kings, the sultan Lord of the Favorable Conjunction [Timur Lenk], who had these jewels transported from Hindustan to here [Esfahan] in 1153." From then on, the Tribute of the World shared the fate of the Koh-i-Noor diamond (see DIAMOND). After the annexation of the Punjab by Great Britain in 1849, the spinel was offered to Queen Victoria and displayed in 1851 in London along with the three other spinels with which it is set in a necklace. Only around 1910 was one of its early owners identified: it then became the Timur Ruby. It is found today on the same

Jahāngīr, Moghul emperor (1605–27) and a descendant of Tamerlane. When Jahāngīr decided to have his name engraved on this polished pebble, his favorite mistress opposed the idea, prompting the emperor to say that this stone would probably make him more famous than his ancestors' empire.

Crystallochemistry and Physical Properties

Spinels form a large family of minerals. Although only the aluminum-magnesium variety is of interest to gemologists, many other members of the spinel family have been faceted for collectors: these include hercynite (aluminum-iron), gahnite (aluminum-zinc), galaxite (aluminum-manganese), magnetite (iron-iron), chromite (chromium-iron), and other combinations of aluminum, iron, and chromium with zinc, manganese, magnesium, iron, and nickel, among others.

Strictly speaking, spinel (the aluminum-magnesium variety) is cubic. The oxygen atoms form a compact cubic stacking; the aluminum atoms occupy half of the octahedral cavities and the magnesium atoms an eighth of the tetrahedral sites. This explains this gem's high specific gravity (3.58 to 3.63), which allows it to survive the punishment of alluvial deposits, where it is often found. It has a good scratch hardness (H is 8) and its single index of refraction is high (1.715, ranging to 1.735).

The replacement of aluminum by chromium produces the highly valued red color. It also induces red fluorescence under long-wave ultraviolet light and an absorption spectrum typical of chromium.

The substitution of iron for aluminum or magnesium produces a blue coloration. There is no luminescence, and the absorption spectrum shows lines typical of both ferrous and ferric iron.

Twinned spinel crystals from Myanmar (Burma). Length: 1.5 cm. J. Saul collection.

Other substitutions are possible, some of which affect the appearance of this gem, which has a wide range of colors.

Bright, slightly orangy red spinels were formerly called spinel rubies; they correspond to the rubicelle, the most valued type of spinel, because their moderate chromium content produces a red luminescence at midday, which reinforces their red color (just like Myanmar, or Burmese, rubies). When paler, their color is pink. Slightly purplish red spinels were formerly called balas rubies; their color is reminiscent of almandite garnet. Dark green spinels are sometimes called ceylonite or chlorospinels, and the black variety pleonaste; they form a solid solution with hercynite. Blue spinels are usually not very bright (grayish blue or violetish blue) unless they contain traces of cobalt and belong to the gahnospinel family, of which zinc is a major component.

Spinel's crystal shapes are very predictable: they are essentially the octahedron, rarely modified by the rhombododecahedron, sometimes affected by a contact twin. Cleavage is poor, and fracture is greasy. Spinels are usually step-cut; they are found primarily in period jewelry.

Deposits and Associated Minerals

Spinel is one of the minerals produced by the reaction under high pressure of aluminum-rich intrusive rocks and their magnesian-rich host rocks, whether of metamorphic or sedimentary origin (such as dolomites). It is abundant in the Madagascar pegmatoides, where it is associated with diopside, calcite, scapolite, phlogopite, and uranium-rich minerals.

Sri Lankan spinels, associated with ruby and sapphire, are products of the metamorphism of limestones (like their Afghan counterparts from Jegdalek). They are mined in the alluvial deposits in the southwestern part of the island, where dark or black spinel (ceylonite) is associated with magnificent red, mauve, and violet spinels.

Recently the construction of a new road in the Karakoram Mountains of Pakistan to provide another means of access to the Hunza Valley triggered the discovery of beautiful rubies and spinels; they are in metamorphosed limestones associated with gneisses near the villages of Mutschual and Altiabad. The quality of the samples is similar to that of spinels from Myanmar, creating high hopes.

Spinel is very abundant in the metamorphosed limestones of the Mogok Valley in Myanmar, where it is associated with ruby. Its beautiful octahedral crystals, often twinned, display a variety of colors; they are locally called *anyan nat thwe*, that is, "cut by the spirits." In contrast, ruby crystals from the same locality are always retromorphosed and corroded. Large historical spinels probably came from Myanmar or Pakistan, although their origin is still uncertain.

Spinels have also been found in Chanthaburi, Thailand, with rubies and sapphires. They come from many other localities, such as Australia, Sweden, and India, with some beautiful discoveries in East Africa (Tanzania) in recent years. The

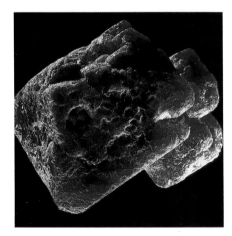

Octahedral spinel crystals. Length: 3 cm. National Higher School of Mines, Paris.

famous Badakhshān deposits in Afghanistan, located on the banks of the Amu-Darya (called the Oxus River in ancient times), have been cited by some authors as mines of rubies and spinels (J. Woods, 1843). Instead, they seem to be garnet deposits.

Gem-quality spinels are usually free of inclusions. Nevertheless, one can find in them octahedral negative crystals filled with carbon dioxide, alone or grouped in fingerprints. Spinel and apatite crystals may also be trapped, producing some internal cracks, generally in the shape of wings.

Synthesis

Flame-fusion synthetic spinel contains more magnesium than natural spinel, so its index of refraction is higher (1.72 to 1.73). To reduce internal stresses, the synthetic crystals are annealed; this blurs curved growth striae and distorts trapped bubbles, which take on angular shapes.

Synthetic spinels are intended to imitate gems of all colors but red (red is very difficult to obtain by the flame-fusion process). In jewelry colorless stones imitate diamond; pink ones, kunzite; yellow ones, topaz; and blue ones, aquamarine. Colorless synthetic spinel was also the raw material used in the fabrication of doublets intended to resemble emeralds and some other gems.

In 1990, flux-grown synthetic spinels in a variety of colors (blue, red, pink), made in the Soviet Union, appeared on the gem market. They cannot be separated from their natural counterparts by classical gemological testing.

Natural Gems with a Similar Appearance

Red spinel resembles ruby and red garnets. It can be distinguished from pyrope garnet by its lower specific gravity for the same index of refraction. Blue spinel looks like many blue gems.

SPODUMENE

A lithium aluminum silicate. Spodumene (a literal transliteration of the Greek participate *spodoumenos*, which means ''burned to ashes'') was named by Portuguese mineralogist D'Andrada in 1800 after finding some of its large rocky crystals, which look like burned wood covered with ashes.

Spodumene forms monoclinic crystals striated parallel to their elongation, with an almost rectangular section. They are often flattened, with oblique terminations, which may look frosty or dull. Spodumene crystals can reach gigantic dimensions: 90 tons for a single crystal in Connecticut, 12 meters (40 feet) long for some crystals from the Dakotas.

Before the discovery of Afghan deposits in 1970, this mineral was not believed to form attractive crystals. It is commonly twinned, and its color varies from colorless to grayish pink. Its gem varieties form smaller crystals, used in jewelry only since the turn of the century. The word *spodumene* describes colorless to yellow varieties; emerald-green gems are called *hiddenite,* and the sometimes very pale purplish to violetish pink variety, *kunzite* (see also HIDDENITE; KUNZITE). Color is caused by trace elements replacing aluminum, especially iron (yellow) and chromium (green).

Although rare, spodumene is a classic mineral of sodium-lithium pegmatites, where it is associated with rubellite, morganite, and lepidolite mica. It may be altered in pegmatites subjected to intense atmospheric weathering. Spodumene is as hard as quartz (H is 7) but is nevertheless very fragile because of two perfect, easy cleavages, almost perpendicular to each other, which run parallel to its length. Its specific gravity varies from 3.17 to 3.19.

Spodumene is biaxial positive, and its indices of refraction increase with the intensity of the coloration (n_p is 1.640 to 1.663; n_m is 1.665 to 1.669, n_g is 1.662 to 1.679, for a birefringence of 0.016). Trichroism is very distinct, and the most intense colors are observed along the directions of the small and intermediate indices, that is, the axis of symmetry, forming an angle of about 65 degrees with the edge of the prism. To obtain a faceted stone displaying good color, it is necessary to cut its table in these directions, almost perpendicular to the prism faces. Otherwise, the stone's color is ''diluted'' by the component with the weakest absorption. The absorption spectrum of yellow spodumene shows bands attributed to iron (around 435 nanometers in the blue). Long-wave ultraviolet light generally induces a weak yellowish orange luminescence. With heat treatment yellow spodumene may acquire a color close to that of kunzite.

Yellow spodumene is much less valuable than kunzite or, especially, hiddenite. Brazilian spodumenes often show tubular inclusions.

Euclase and fibrolite are natural gems with optical properties very similar to those of spodumene.

STAUROLITE

An aluminum and iron silicate, crystallizing in the monoclinic system. Its name comes from the Greek *stauros,* which described the cross on which criminals were crucified, referring to the appearance of twinned staurolite crystals (Delamétherie, 1792).

Nice prismatic staurolite crystals have an almost hexagonal or lozengelike section

Spodumene crystal on quartz and albite from Kulum, Laghman Valley, Afghanistan. Height: 3 cm. Private collection.

Twinned staurolite crystals from Minas Gerais, Brazil. Size: 8 cm. Sorbonne collection.

and often form penetration twins: the crystals may be associated at a 90- or 60-degree angle. Crystal faces can be shiny but are generally rough. Staurolite is brown to dark reddish brown. Some crystals exceptionally reach a length of 10 centimeters (4 inches).

Staurolite's hardness is 7½, and its specific gravity is 3.7 to 3.8. Its principle indices of refraction are 1.744, 1.749 and 1.756.

Staurolite is often associated with kyanite, quartz, and almandite garnets in mica schists produced by regional metamorphism of clay-rich sediments. It is extremely resistant to weathering and therefore is common in plowed fields. This is particularly true in Brittany, France, where abundant twinned crystals are sometimes used as crosses for rosaries. Gem staurolite is sometimes faceted for collectors.

STEATITE

Also called soapstone, saponite, agalmatolite, or pagodite.

A soft rock, principally made of magnesian aluminosilicates, the magnesian term being talc and the aluminous one pyrophyllite.

Origin of the Name

Steatite is derived from the Greek *stear, steatos,* meaning "tallow" or "fat," referring to the fact that this rock feels greasy or soapy to the touch. *Saponite* from the Latin *sapo, saponis,* meaning "soap" testifies to its use as a cleaning agent. *Agalmatolite,* from *agalma,* meaning "offering" or "statue of a god," and *lithos,* meaning "stone," is a reminder that the Chinese used this material to carve small Buddhas, miniature pagodas, and other objects; *pagodite* has the same meaning. *Talc* is a transliteration of the Arabic *talq,* which denotes all shiny sheet minerals (such as mica and gypsum). *Pyrophyllite* comes from *pur,* which means "fire," and *phullon,* which means "sheet," referring to this minerals's ability to exfoliate with fire.

As early as the third millennium, steatite that had been hardened in fire was carved into cylinder seals in Sumer and Akkad as well as scarab amulets in Egypt. Middle Eastern and Roman civilizations made molds from it from metallurgical applications. Steatite was also the earth from Cimolus (one of the Cyclades Islands in Greece), which was used to remove grease from garments during the time of Theophrastus; it was called Cimolean chalk by the Romans. Talc is still used for this purpose, retaining its erroneous designation *chalk.* Chalk used to write on blackboards is often white steatite. Locally, the name *soapstone* may apply to sepiolite, as in Morocco. The numerous objects (statues, ornamental bowls, and display objects) made in steatite near Ouro Prêto, Brazil, since the seventeenth century are called *pedra sabão.* In France the name *saponite* is used for a white clay, montmorillonite, which is very close in structure to pyrophyllite. The raw material for porcelains is another white clay, a variety of antigorite (a serpentine mineral), which does not contain magnesium; it is called kaolin, a variant of the Chinese *kaoling,* which means "high mountain," a reminder of is original deposit.

Physical Properties

When pure, talc is shiny white. It is, however, often colored by iron, which makes is green or sometimes brownish or yellowish. Both its greasy luster and greasy texture are characteristic. Its specific gravity varies from 2.75 to 2.9. Even when hardened in fire, it can be scratched with a fingernail (H is 1½ to 2). Pliny wrote that talc has this singularity that it is very soft by nature but blackens and darkens when heated in oil.

Deposits

Steatite is produced by hydrothermal alteration of ultrabasic rocks, especially peridotite and serpentine; it can also result from the metamorphism of dolomites in contact with hyperacid rocks (as in Brumado in Bahia, Brazil).

Steatite is mined mostly near Ouro Prêto, Brazil; near Lake Nyasa in southeastern Africa; and near Bombay in India.

The National Museum of Natural History in Paris has a collection of Oriental carvings in yellow and red pagodite from the seventeenth and eighteenth centuries; they represent legendary Chinese characters, including Lu Tong-p'ing, one of the eight Taoist immortals; Lieou Hai, a famous tenth-century minister; and the Buddhist goddess Louang-yin.

SUCCINITE

See AMBER.

Nineteenth-century Chinese carving in steatite. Height: 13 cm. Private collection.

Massive sugilite from South Africa. Width: 4 cm. J.-Y. Gauthier collection.

SUGILITE

A potassosodic and ferriferous lithium silicate, similar to sogdianite, crystallizing in the hexagonal system. It was discovered in 1977 on Iwagi Island in Japan, and its small crystals, associated with pectolite and albite in an alkaline syenite, were named for Professor Ken-ichi Sugi.

Sugilite forms vitreous masses with an attractive purple color attributed to manganese. It is not fluorescent. Its index of refraction is 1.605 to 1.610, its specific gravity 2.74, its hardness about 5.

Today gem sugilite comes mostly from the Wessels manganese deposit in the Kalahari, South Africa, where it is interstratified in braunite, occasionally forming fairly thick layers (more than 20 centimeters or 8 inches). It has been sold under the names of Royal Azel and Royal Lavulite. Purple sugilite is carved into cabochons and other shapes to be mounted in jewelry and is also used for small carvings.

SUNSTONE

A variety of calcosodic feldspar, also called *oligoclase.*

Numerous red to orange platelets of iron minerals, such as hematite or goethite, lie parallel to each other in the lamellar structure of the feldspar, against a very light yellow background. This produces directional reflections, which reportedly helped the Vikings find the position of the sun when sailing under an overcast sky. It appears that a careful reading of the Viking sagas indicates that the stone they used was actually cordierite and that the name *sunstone* has been incorrectly given to aventurinescent oligoclase. Its specific gravity is about 2.64, with an index of refraction of approximately 1.55.

Oligoclase is an accessory feldspar in granites and appears in syenites and monzonites as well. Nice specimens come from the southern coast of Norway (Arendal). Aventurinescent reddish glass containing triangular and hexagonal copper platelets has been used as a sunstone imitation, as in molded Buddhas from the Far East.

TAAFFEITE

A magnesium and beryllium aluminate, crystallizing in the hexagonal system.

Taaffeite was named for Count C. R. Taaffe; in October 1945 he bought a parcel of assorted faceted stones that had been unmounted from old jewelry by a Dublin jeweler. Among those stones, he noticed a birefringent purple "spinel," which he had analyzed; it was actually an unknown mineral. Taaffeite was therefore the first mineral to be discovered as a faceted stone. Since then, numerous spinel parcels have been examined, as well as all spinels from the gem-bearing gravels of Sri Lanka. Today taaffeites are becoming more common, and are mostly considered collector's items. The largest stone is purple and weighs 13.10 carats.

This research led to the premature announcement of the discovery of a new red mineral, taprobanite, named for Taprobane, "the garden of delights," the old Latin and Greek name for Sri Lanka; but taprobanite turned out to be a chromium-bearing taaffeite.

Taaffeite's optical and mechanical properties are very close to those of spinel (S.G. is 3.61; H is 8; n_o is 1.718, n_e is 1.723, for a birefringence of 0.005), which explains why this mineral was not recognized earlier. The color of taaffeite results from partial substitution of aluminum by chromium and vanadium (up to 0.5 percent), and of magnesium by iron, zinc, and manganese (up to 10 percent). Its hues are similar to those of spinel (blue, purple, and red), and a slight pleochroism can be detected with a dichroscope.

All gem-quality taaffeites found to date have come from the gem-bearing gravels of Sri Lanka, near the village of Niriella, in the Ratnapura area. In the rough these stones look like rounded pebbles without distinct crystal faces.

TANZANITE

A gem variety of violetish blue zoisite.

It was named by Henry Platt, vice-president of Tiffany, the jewelers in New York, for its country of origin. This appellation is accepted by mineralogists.

Around 1967 Manuel de Souza, a modest Portuguese craftsman originally from Goa, India, was a tailor in the town of Arusha, Tanzania. He also collected minerals, in particular a blue gem sold to him by the Massai under the name "blue sky" (a literal translation from Swahili). This stone was originally mistaken for dumortierite, then for cordierite because of its dichroism. It was simultaneously identified as zoisite by the Tanzanian Geological Survey and Heidelberg University in Germany. Manuel de Souza soon established himself a miner and started a small company, in competition with others. Tanzanite deposits are located about 40 kilometers (25 miles) southeast of Arusha. The mineral is found at the contact between gneiss and dolomitic marbles that have undergone intense metamorphism. The mineral is associated with grossular garnet, kyanite, diopside, and sometimes some yellow or green tourmaline, as well as some blue magnesioaxinite, which has been mistaken for tanzanite.

Crystals are prismatic, with a somewhat square section and pyramidal terminations with many faces. They may weigh several hundred grams, but the gem-quality material does not exceed 100 grams.

The first gems produced displayed a deep blue color. Later, rough material tended to be grayish blue and was heat-treated by local workers to produce an intense, slightly violetish sapphire-blue color, attributed to vanadium. This treatment also affects pleochroism. Heat makes the stone shock-sensitive and easily abradable. Tanzanite's hardness is 6½; its specific gravity, 3.35; and its principal indices of refraction, 1.685, 1.688, and 1.697.

Tanzanite has been extremely successful in the United States, where it was initially popular for its sapphire-blue color at

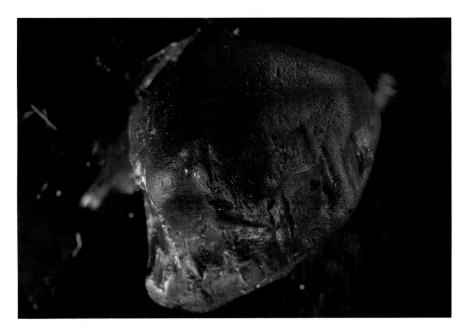

An 11.23-carat taaffeite crystal from Sri Lanka. Diameter: 1.5 cm. Private collection.

a time when good sapphires were scarce. After a steady decline, the mines began yielding large amounts of gemstones in the late 1980s. In 1990, a green zoisite, improperly called "green tanzanite," was discovered in small quantities.

The Smithsonian Institution displays a 122.7-carat faceted tanzanite, as well as a 18.2-carat chatoyant stone.

THETIS HAIR STONE

Rock crystal with inclusions of fine, undulated, actinolite crystals, reminiscent of green hair, such as the seaweed hair of Thetis, goddess of the sea. The best specimens are from Swiss alpine clefts and California.

THULITE

See ZOISITE.

TIGER'S-EYE

Yellow chatoyant quartz. See QUARTZ: CAT'S-EYE QUARTZ.

TITANITE OR SPHENE

A calcium and titanium silicate, crystallizing in the monoclinic system. Rare-earth elements may replace the calcium by up to 14 percent, and aluminum and iron may also be present.

The name *titanite* (Klaproth, 1795) ob-

Twinned titanite crystals on adularia from Kreuzlital, Tavetsch, Graubünden, Switzerland. Height: 4 cm. Sorbonne collection.

viously refers to the chemical composition of this gem, whereas *sphene* (Haüy, 1801) comes from *sphen*, which means "splitting wedge," referring to the crystal's shape.

Crystals are generally well formed, with various appearances: they are sometimes flattened, resembling a roof (a shape typical of intrusive and metamorphic rocks) or elongated, forming a penetration twin that looks like a groove (a shape typical of alpine clefts). In pegmatites large titanite crystals can weigh several pounds.

Tanzanite crystal from Arusha, Tanzania. Height: 3 cm. K. Proctor collection, United States.

The hardness of titanite is 5½ to 6; its specific gravity, 3.45 to 3.55. Its color is generally greenish yellow, with a weak pleochroism in the same colors, although it can also be brown or black.

Titanite's luster is adamantine and somewhat oily at the fractures (principal indices of refraction vary from 1.885 and 2.050, with a birefringence of 0.105 to 0.135, resulting in a strong doubling). Large gem crystals from which stones can be faceted come primarily from Madagascar. Alpine and Brazilian deposits (Capelinha in the state of Minas Gerais) yield only small crystals, from which large gemstones cannot be cut.

The Smithsonian Institution displays several faceted titanites (up to 9.3 carats) from Switzerland, New York State, and Mexico.

TOPAZ

An orthorhombic aluminum fluorosilicate.

Origin of the Name and History

The origin of the word *topaz* is uncertain and seems to be due to an error. It initially could have come from the Greek *topos,* meaning "land" or "country," and *azos,* a contraction of *aozos* (from the privative *a* and *odzos,* meaning "tree branch"). The compound would have meant "desertic land," which applies very well to the Zebirget Island in the Red Sea. Used to describe the local gem (our peridot), *topazion* was later related to the verb

topazo, the meaning of which has evolved from "to put in place" into "to search" or "to guess." This confusion was the source of two legends reported by Pliny the Elder, narrating the tales of Archelaus, of Cappadocia, and Juba II (52 B.C. to A.D. 24), king of Numidia and Mauretania (now Algeria and Morocco). According to the first, pirates were pushed by a storm onto Cytis Island, where, *looking for* something to eat, they discovered the mineral, which was therefore called topaz. According to the second, the mineral was found on the island of Topazos, so called because it was surrounded by fog (actually coral reefs) and sailors had to *search* a long time before being able to land there (access to Zebirget Island is still difficult today).

However, the topaz described by Pliny, between sard and callaïs (turquoise), was not the mineral we know as topaz. Pliny was rather lax in citing his sources but nevertheless indicated two varieties, the *prasoides* (from *prasoeides,* which means "leek green"), and the chrysoptere (from *khrusopteros,* meaning "with golden wings"). They both supposedly came from Alabastra, an Egyptian town renowned for its deposits of translucent marble, and Pliny reported that a 2 meter- (8-foot-) tall statue of Arsinoë II (316–270 B.C.), wife and sister of Ptolemy II Philadelphus, was carved in the "topaz" given by Philemon to their mother, Berenice I (340–275 B.C.).

But another report by Epiphanius (fifth century A.D.) only mentions "topaz" adorning the diadem of the queen of Thebes. The "topaz" of ancient times was probably some kind of serpentine or the mineral peridot, also called chrysolite, as is indicated by Boece de Boot: "The topaz of the elders, or chrysoprase, which is called chrysolite today" (*The Perfect Jeweler,* 1646).

The mineral we now call *topaz* was undoubtedly the *melichryse* of ancient times (*melichrusos,* from *meli,* "honey," and *chrusos,* "gold") or *xanthe* (*ksanthos,* "yellow" or "reddish"). Pliny the Elder indicated that melichryse belonged to the chrysolite family and noted, "India exports them; they are breakable despite their hardness."

During the Middle Ages and the Renaissance, *topaz* designated yellow gems. Boece de Boot mentioned "the chrysolite of the elders, as well as chrysolectre and melichryse or vulgar topaz," and indicated: "Presently topaz used in jewelry are gems of a golden yellow color . . . Oriental ones glow as very pure gold, and are harder than all precious stones except diamond . . . the European ones are as soft as crystal and are golden with more or less black." In 1669 Robert de Berquem noted, "For topaz, if it comes from Peru, it is not hard and its color is orangy."

Henckel, in 1737, and Romé de Lisle, in 1772, were the first to use the word *topaz* exclusively for this mineral in mineralogy.

Detail of a necklace of blue topaz, pearls, and diamonds. J. Vendôme design.

However, lapidaries and jewelers called various yellow gems *topaz* until the end of World War II, though in association with a qualifying word: yellow sapphire was Oriental topaz, royal topaz, or India topaz; yellow topaz was Brazilian topaz, Saxony topaz, West Indies topaz, imperial topaz, or noble topaz; citrine was Bohemia topaz, occidental topaz, or quartz topaz. Even today, a layperson may have some difficulty understanding these confusing distinctions, which are used in countries that are not members of the CIBJO.

Yellow topaz, "of the same nature as the sun by its golden color," was considered a stone of life and clarity. This is why, when "hanged from the collar and set in gold," it banished demons, protected from curses, and made "night frights" disappear. Topaz was believed to be the definitive cure for melancholia, to bring wisdom, and to keep its owner on a virtuous path.

Famous Faceted Topazes

The most famous faceted topaz is the very light yellow Bragance, a 1,600-carat stone belonging to the Portuguese crown. It was long believed to be a diamond. The slave who discovered it on the banks of the Malhoverde River in Brazil received his freedom in exchange, as well as a lifetime annuity for himself and his family. Other topazes were mistaken for diamond over the course of the nineteenth century, including the Pannar, an 800-carat stone that made headlines in 1858.

Since then, very large crystals have been faceted, and some museums exhibit cut topaz specimens of extraordinary size. For example, the Smithsonian Institution displays a 7,725-carat yellow topaz from Brazil, a colorless stone of 2,680 carats, and a pinkish orange gem of 129 carats, as well as a 34-carat dark pink stone and a 171-carat dark champagne-colored gem. Chicago's Field Museum of Natural History exhibits a 5,800-carat natural blue topaz from Brazil. National Museum of Natural History in Paris has a 377-carat blue topaz from the Urals in the Soviet Union.

Physical Properties

The aluminum in topaz may be replaced by small amounts (up to 1 percent) of iron, chromium, or other trace elements. When pure, topaz is perfectly colorless, hence; its nickname *pingo de água* ("water droplet") in Brazil. When faceted, the high luster of topaz is reminiscent of diamond, which also has a similar specific gravity (the first African diamonds were suspected to be topaz). Colorless topaz from Saxony and Brazil was used to replace diamond in inexpensive jewelry.

Yellow to brownish yellow topaz always has a warm color because it contains

A 41.86-carat faceted imperial topaz from Ouro Preto, Minas Gerais, Brazil. F. A. Becker collection, Idar-Oberstein, Germany.

an orangy component; it is also the best-known and most used variety. Citrine is its natural substitute. Blue topaz resembles aquamarine but is brighter and does not show a greenish "seawater" nuance. Today colorless topaz is commonly irradiated and heat-treated to produce a blue color. This permanent coloration occasionally is marred by a distinct metallic cast or residual radioactivity.

Pink topaz is the most valuable variety, especially if the color has some depth. Pink can be produced by heat-treating brownish yellow material at about 450° to 500°C (840°F to 930°F) in a sand bath (today magnesite is used). This process was discovered in 1750 by Dumelle, a Parisian jeweler. The dichroism of topaz is more distinct in heat-treated specimens than in natural ones. An absorption spectrum due to chromium can be seen only in heat-treated stones.

Hydroxyl groups may replace some fluorine, which has a nominal concentration of 20.7 percent at the pure fluorinated pole. This slightly affects specific gravity, which increases from 3.49 to 3.57, as well as the indices of refraction, which decrease with increasing fluorine concentration (n_p is 1.629 to 1.607; n_m is 1.631 to 1.610; n_g is 1.638 to 1.616; the birefringence is 0.009 to 0.008, with a biaxial positive character).

Ultraviolet (black-light) luminescence also varies to some degree with fluorine content; blue and colorless topaz, rich in hydroxyl groups, are generally weakly luminescent, whereas natural pink to orangy pink topaz, rich in fluorine, most often fluoresces an intense orangy yellow. Fluorinated topaz also has a tendency to fade in daylight.

Topaz is hard (H is 8) but fragile, because of its perfect basal cleavage, perpendicular to the length of the crystals. In addition, it often contains fluid inclusions rich in carbon dioxide and water (sometimes with salt), forming fingerprint inclusions. Sometimes topaz contains solid inclusions (rutile needles and "circles"), as well as colored growth features. When polished, topaz acquires a peculiar slippery texture that makes it almost possible to identify with closed eyes.

Deposits and Mineralogy

Topaz is common in Brazilian pegmatites, where it is associated with tourmaline, microcline (amazonite variety), and zircon. It also forms an abundant matrix for some tungsten and tin deposits. Finally, it appears in geodes in rhyolites from Utah, where it was formed by late pneumatolitic fluids.

Hard, heavy, and unalterable, topaz is a classic mineral of alluvial deposits. It is always well crystallized, with two predominant morphologies. The first is the losangic prism, which is often elongated with striations parallel to the elongation and commonly ends in a simple pyramid (imperial topaz from Ouro Prêto, Brazil; and Mardan, Pakistan), a pointed roof (Virgem da Lapa, Minas Gerais, Brazil), or a progressive series of pyramids (Utah). The second is the square prism, which may be associated with the basal face, with few modifications (blue topaz from the Murzinka pegmatites in the Ural Mountains of the Soviet Union. Rare, peculiar shapes include the yellowish bacillary aggregates or striated groups (picnite) resembling beryl in the Erzgebirge tin deposits in Germany.

Topaz crystals are sometimes enormous, as much as several dozen pounds in some Brazilian pegmatites.

Soviet Union

Topaz was particularly abundant in Russia in the nineteenth century, where it was found in association with aquamarine, smoky quartz, albite, muscovite, and lepidolite mica in the geodic cavities of a granite near the village of Alabaskha, close to Murzinka in the Urals. These blue crystals of exceptional quality were up to 10 centimeters (4 inches) long.

Beautiful gemmy colorless topaz crystals were found in a pegmatite rich in amazonite near Lake Ilmen, close to Miass in the Novgorod area of the Urals. In Transbaikalia, honey-colored gem-quality topaz with perfect crystal shapes, some 20 centimeters (8 inches) long, accompanied beryl in the Adun Chilon deposit (Nerchinsk area) and in the Borchtchovotchnyi Mountains near the Urulga River. Unfortunately, its color fades in sunlight. During the last decade, the same type of crystals was unearthed in the Volhynia pegmatites in the Ukraine.

Brazil

All shapes, sizes, and colors of topaz are very abundant in Brazil, mostly in the state of Minas Gerais, but also in the states of Espírito Santo, Goiás, and Bahia, for example.

"Water droplet" topaz was discovered as early as 1721 in the alluvial diamond deposits near Diamantina, where it is associated with beryl and chrysoberyl. Its origin, still uncertain, is probably potassic pegmatites that were deeply affected by atmospheric weathering and eventually released the crystals.

Topaz was discovered around 1768 in the Ouro Prêto area. This event was marked by numerous ceremonies at the royal court in Lisbon. In the eighteenth century, active but regulated prospecting of topaz took place, and the deposits were studied at the beginning of the nineteenth century. Imperial topaz is found only west of Ouro Prêto in a series of hills forming a belt about 20 kilometers (12 miles) long and 6 kilometers (4 miles) wide, oriented west-east. All the famous deposits in this area—Antônio Pereira, Olaria, Saramenha (Vermelhão), Capão da Lana, Dom Bosco—were formed by decomposed rock rich in altered potassic feldspar, quartz (sometimes

smoky), euclase, rutile, and hematite; the presence of phosphates (monazite and xenotime) suggests a pegmatitic origin. This hypothesis, first formulated by H. J. Gorceix in 1881, is much disputed today. Topaz forms "nests" in pockets filled with kaolinite, from which it is extracted manually by the *garimpeiros*. Crystals are generally small —2 to 5 centimeters (1 to 2 inches)—but they can reach impressive dimensions: 20 to 25 centimeters (8 to 10 inches) at Capão da Lana, 50 centimeters (20 inches) at Antônio Pereira.

At the beginning of the twentieth century, about fifty workers produced almost 2,000 pounds per year. The most productive mines were Boa Vista and Capão da Lana.

In recent years a method to separate topaz from its matrix using powerful water jets has been implemented at Capão da Lana. The ore is collected in a long drain, at the end of which it is concentrated, through gravity. The 900 tons treated daily are reduced to approximately 9 kilograms (20 pounds) of topaz (that is, a yield of 50 carats per ton), but only a small portion of that is of gem quality. Mining stops during the rainy season, from December to May.

In other areas mining is still practiced on a small scale. In Antônio Pereira, near Mariana, for example, the crystals are of far

Blue topaz crystal from Murzinka, U.S.S.R. Height: 5 cm. National Higher School of Mines, Paris.

Honey-colored topaz from Siberia, near the Urulga River in the U.S.S.R. Width: 10 cm. Sorbonne collection.

Small-scale topaz mining at Antonio Pereira, near Mariana, Minas Gerais, Brazil. Photo: P. Bariand.

Industrial-scale topaz mining at the Capao da Lana mine, near Ouro Preto, Minas Gerais, Brazil. Photo: P. Bariand.

better quality than those from Capão da Lana because they are not broken by water jets. Only the large reserves and significant amounts produced justify the barbaric technique used at Capão da Lana.

The color of hydroxylated crystals from Ouro Prêto varies from pale yellow to dark yellow with a hint of red but this tint is often the result of heat treatment or irradiation. In the Teófilo Otoni area, numerous pegmatites have produced superb crystals, generally colorless, in particular those near the town of Coronel Fabriciano.

In 1974 a *garimpeiro* discovered a pegmatite that is one of the world's richest sources of gem crystals. It is located 43 kilometers (about 27 miles) from Arçuai, near the small village of Virgem da Lapa, where industrial beryl had been prospected in 1939. Unaltered pegmatites in metamorphic rocks are mined in four different locations: in Limoero, for remarkable blue topaz and green tourmalines; in Xanda, for blue topaz, green beryl, and hydroxylherderite; and at Toca da Onca and Manoel Mutuca, for blue tourmaline. The abundance of the geodes is a result of small faults which control them structurally. Hundreds of *garimpeiros* working at Xanda in 1974 found so much blue topaz, a mineral unknown to them, that they threw it on the tailings with the matrix (although these were the finest specimens of this variety of topaz in the world).

Other Localities

Topaz is an abundant mineral, although it is not always of gem quality. It is found all over the world—in Japan, Australia, and California, for example.

In Europe the Saxony deposits are of only historical interest. In Africa topaz has been found in large quantities in the Nigerian tin deposits, in the remarkable pegmatites near Spitzkopje in Namibia, and as remarkable blue crystals in the Sainte-Anne pegmatite north of Zimbabwe and in the Madagascar pegmatites.

In the United States, the most remarkable specimens are from the Utah rhyolites. They are always well-formed, small crystals with a warm brownish orange color, but they are of interest only to the collector and fade rapidly in daylight. Similar crystals have been encountered in Mexico near San Luis Potosí in the same geological setting.

In recent years Pakistan has produced beautiful crystals, with a color similar to that of the Urulga River crystals in Transbaikalia. They can be as much as a few centimeters in size. They are associated with quartz in geodes found in pegmatites near the Afghan border. In Mardan, north of Peshawar, pink topaz has been known since ancient times. It is found at the juncture of pegmatites and amphibolites. The crystal shape of this pink topaz is similar to that of Ouro Prêto, and its color is reminiscent of the "peach blossom" morganite from Madagascar.

Topaz is also mined in alluvial deposits, as in Sri Lanka and Myanmar (Burma).

Rough crystal of imperial topaz from Ouro Preto, Brazil, and faceted stones of the same gem in a ring (8.34 carats) and a pendant (11.83 carats). Taillerie de Royat.

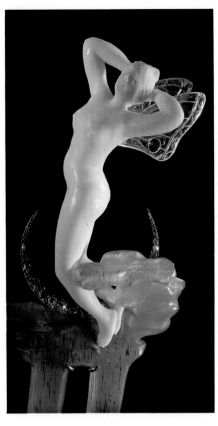

Hairpin with blond shell, ivory, and enamel, crafted around 1900. Height of the figurine: 4.6 cm. A. Boucheron collection.

Imitations

Synthetic yellow corundum imitates yellow topaz. The other stones that can imitate colorless, blue, and pink topaz are usually used as substitutes for other gems: diamond, aquamarine, ruby, or kunzite, for example.

TOPAZOLITE

A yellow andradite, more of a yellow demantoid. See DEMANTOID.

TORTOISE SHELL

A dermal keratinous secretion, forming the carapace of sea turtles.

The History of Tortoise Shell

Tortoise shell was well known to ancient civilizations and was used as veneer or lining. Caesar found such large amounts of it during his conquest of Egypt that he covered the triumphal arch erected for his entrance into Cleopatra's city with tortoise shell. First-century Romans used tortoise shell on colonnades and palace doors, and rich Romans followed the impetus of a certain Cuvillus Pollio and used it to simulate precious woods. Seneca was shocked: "I see the shells of the slowest and most deformed animal bought for enormous amounts of money, and the mottling of colors that makes them most attractive reduced, by a strange varnish, merely to imitate wood." Pliny the Elder noted, "One managed by a monstrous invention to deprive tortoise shell of its own appearance with dyes and to sell it a higher price by having it imitate wood; formerly, luxury was not satisfied with wood, now it turns tortoise shell into wood."

During the Renaissance, tortoise shell was highly prized, decorating many Italian cabinets; it was associated with nacre, ivory, and bronze. In France during the seventeenth and eighteenth centuries André-Charles Boulle, who was Louis XIV's cabinetmaker, used tortoise-shell inlays in his furniture. Later, objects made of this rare material were smaller: boxes, snuff bottles, and toiletry containers.

Turtles That Produce Tortoise Shell

Three types of tropical sea turtles have been hunted for their shells (as well as for their meat and grease): the *Testudo cephalo*, with a yellowish white shell, used mostly for small furniture; the *Testudo mydas* or green turtle, with a pale yellow shell with brown marks, used mostly for inlays; and finally, the hawksbill turtle, which has a translucent to transparent amber-colored shell, considered the most valuable. The hawksbill is found on the coast of India, in the Indian Ocean, in the Seychelles Islands, in the Sea of China, in the Philippines, in America, and in the West Indies. The turtles are generally captured when they come to a beach to lay their eggs; turned on their back, they cannot move.

The Various Plates

Thirteen main plates or blades, 9 to 12 millimeters thick, collectively known as the heart, form the dorsal carapace of the animal; these are surrounded by twenty-four square marginal plates. The most valued plates are those of a brighter color, usually amber yellow mottled with red or reddish brown. Each leg is covered by two blades, a large brown one used for molds and a smaller, lighter one, called blond shell. The beak and nails are also used for molds. The twelve blades of the plastron, the belly shield, which are opaque and whitish, are little valued. Tortoise-shell blades are separated from the animal using boiling water.

Physical Properties

Tortoise shell softens with heat, attaining the consistency of heavy paste in boiling water. Tortoise-shell objects must therefore be cleaned with soapy, tepid water and dried with a soft cloth. They must be kept away from high heat and high humidity. Unlike most organic materials, tortoise shell does not build up an electrostatic charge when rubbed. Like all organic materials, it

Nineteenth-century engraving depicting the hunting of sea turtles as they lay eggs.

is light (S.G. is 1.25 to 1.35) and has a low scratch resistance (H is 2½, like fingernails). Scratched tortoise-shell objects can be re-polished using a soft cloth with olive oil and fine hematite powder.

Under black light, it strongly fluoresces with a whitish tone. Under daylight, its color is amber yellow, translucent, mottled with brown spots.

Inclusions

The brown spots in tortoise shell are due to the concentration of many small brown discs, contrasting against a homogeneous light background. These discs are harder to see in blond shell.

Uses

To be usable, the blades are laminated with heat, 100°C (210°F), under pressure. They keep the shape of a mold after cooling, which allows the creation of a variety of objects. Chips resulting from shaping tortoise shell are molded together under heat to produce pressed shell; it is easy to distinguish this material from large shell blades by examining its texture under a microscope.

Simulants

Various tortoise-shell simulants are on the market:
- Horn chips and powder mixed and molded together with some tortoise-shell chips.
- Tortoise-shell veneer or lining over horn or plastic.
- Horn dyed with mercury, silver, or gold salts (this type of dyeing has been done since the eighteenth century).
- Mottled plastics (produced since 1863 in the United States; celluloid, the product of a reaction between camphor and cellulose, was introduced in Europe in 1876).

Careful examination of the texture of the mottled areas of the samples makes it easy to distinguish plastics, tortoise-shell imitations, and tortoise-shell veneer from tortoise-shell proper.

Organic Materials with a Similar Appearance

Amber, which is lighter and produces electricity when rubbed, may resemble blond shell. Horn also can look like tortoise shell but is often lighter in color and has a somewhat fibrous structure; the horny hoofs of the caribou also resemble it.

TOUCHSTONE

See LYDIAN STONE.

Multicolored tourmaline parakeets on a smoky-quartz branch. Height: 5 cm. G. Becker design. Idar-Oberstein, Germany.

TOURMALINE

A family of minerals, crystallizing in the rhombohedral (hexagonal) system, characterized by their alumino-boro-sodo-silicate crystal structure. The structure is maintained by ions substituting for each other in all proportions; these define the main tourmaline varieties: elbaite (named for the island of Elba in Italy) is rich in lithium; dravite (named for the Drava, a tributary of the Danube in Austria and Yugoslavia) is rich in magnesium; schorl (a generic German name), which is black, is rich in iron and is the most common tourmaline species. Calcium replaces sodium in uvite. The calcium-lithium tourmaline *liddicoatite* is named after the famous American gemologist R. T. Liddicoat, and produces some very attractive violet faceted stones and multicolored slabs. In addition, manganese, va-nadium, titanium, chromium, and other metallic elements can be present, producing considerable variations in light absorption, so that the tourmalines display all colors of the spectrum (and were therefore improperly called "the rainbow mineral"). This article concentrates on elbaite, since it is by far the most common gem variety of tourmaline.

Origin of the Name

Sri Lankan jewelers classified as *turamali* (meaning, perhaps, "locale") yellow zircons and yellow tourmalines of similar appearance found in the gem-bearing gravels of Sri Lanka. In 1703 a parcel of such material was sent to stone cutters in Amsterdam, who reportedly transcribed *turamali* as *tourmaline*. This mineral was first described by Garmann in 1707. It piqued the curiosity of the duke of Noya, a Neapolitan, who studied it and sent samples with comments in 1759 to Georges-Louis Buffon, the renowned French naturalist; since then, tourmaline has been well identified in France.

Tourmaline had already been used in jewelry but was probably mistaken for other gems. It was well known by Dutch sailors, who called it *aschentrekker* because they used its prismatic crystals, charged with static electricity, to clean their meerschaum pipes. In France it was called Ceylonese magnet for some time.

American jewelers have tried to promote this stone as the birthstone for the month of October. Some pretend that it acts as a muse for poets: ''It gives impulse to the artist's inspiration.''

Physical Properties and Varieties

Tourmaline forms hemimorphic crystals. It can be loaded with static electricity by rubbing or heating and then attracts dust. A tourmaline crystal thus cannot be cleaned of dust by vigorous rubbing but rather must be wiped with a soft, slightly damp cloth.

''Pure'' lithium tourmaline is colorless (it is then very rare, and called achroite). But numerous isomorphous replacements can occur, imparting a wide variety of colors. Barbot wrote in 1858: ''Tourmaline can represent all existing gemstones and yet retains some charm.''

Specific names have been given to the most attractive varieties: rubellite for the red to pink types, indicolite for blue ones, siberite for violetish blue stones, and verdelite for green gems. Heat treatment is sometimes used to enhance the pink in rubellites or to lighten the green or blue of darker varieties.

The color may vary from the bottom to the top of the crystal or from the core to the rim, highlighting a zoned growth pattern. For example, ''watermelon'' tourmalines have a pink core and a thin green rim, resembling watermelon slices. The dichroism is intense, as light is almost totally absorbed along the optic axis. Dark varieties, especially green ones, should be faceted with the table parallel to the prism faces, resulting in a lighter, more attractive stone. Light varieties, such as rubellite, should be cut with the table perpendicular to the prism faces, to intensify their color.

Some tourmalines, most of them green, are rich in tubular inclusions that run parallel to the optic axis and are cut into cabochons to reveal a pleasing chatoyancy.

With the exception of rubellites and chatoyant tourmalines, which are sometimes full of fingerprint inclusions, carbon dioxide–filled fluid inclusions, or hollow tubes, most tourmalines are cut only if they are inclusion free.

The indices of refraction of tourmaline are: n_e, 1.620 to 1.627 and n_o, 1.636 to 1.657, with a uniaxial negative character. They increase with the iron content, as does birefringence, which has a value of 0.015

for rubellites and 0.030 for dark green tourmalines, the average being about 0.020.

Tourmaline's specific gravity varies with iron content from 3.03 to 3.15. Its hardness is close to that of quartz (7 to 7½), and its stones are fairly tough (no easy cleavage), so this gem is easily used in jewelry.

Tourmalines are barely or not at all luminescent under black light. Their absorption spectrum is generally not characteristic.

Crystallography and Deposits

Tourmaline almost always crystallizes well. Its prismatic crystals are deeply striated along their length, and their section is a rounded triangle. They terminate at the top at a trigonal pyramid; the bottom shows pyramidal hemihedry. Iron- and lithium-bearing tourmalines form elongated prisms, whereas other varieties form short prisms, and may even look like garnets. Crystals are often fractured, held together by quartz.

Elbaite tourmaline is a typical mineral of sodium-lithium pegmatites, found in association with other lithium-containing minerals, such as lepidolite mica, kunzite, and sometimes morganite, as well as other silicates, including topaz, amazonite, and quartz. Gigantic tourmaline crystals have been discovered, some more than 1 meter (3 feet) long.

Faceted tourmalines of various colors. F. A. Becker collection, Idar-Oberstein, Germany.

Green tourmaline crystal in quartz. Height: 4 cm. G. Becker collection, Idar-Oberstein, Germany.

Soviet Union

At the end of the eighteenth century, tourmaline-bearing pegmatites were discovered in the Urals, near Ekaterinburg, where the cutting factories of imperial Russia were located. Tourmaline thus became very popular in Russia. It was used in jewelry, especially the red variety, rubellite, which was incorrectly presented as Siberian ruby. At the time this material came from Murzinka, an area already famous for aquamarine and topaz.

Brazil

In 1572, a few years after the beginning of the Portuguese conquest, green stones believed to be emeralds were discovered in alluvial deposits being prospected for gold, particularly near the Jequitinhonha River. They were sent to Portugal, faceted, and set in the crown of Nossa Senhora da Peña. Only much later were they identified as tourmalines; instead, green tourmaline from Brazil was called Brazilian emerald. This troublesome confusion persisted until the beginning of the twentieth century.

An emerald-prospecting expedition was launched around 1674 under the leadership of Fernão Dias Paes Leme; this group discovered the first Brazilian pegmatite in place. This "mountain of mica with green crystals" was located near Itabira, 70 kilometers (about 45 miles) from Governador Valadares, near the village of São José da

Safira (so called because of the presence of blue tourmaline, which had been mistaken for sapphire). Five hundred grams of various gems—aquamarine, topaz, and "emerald"—were sent to Lisbon, where the true nature of "Brazilian emeralds" was finally discovered.

Ironically, one of the most promising deposits of true emerald was recently discovered near Itabira; Paes Leme did not have much luck, but his son-in-law, Borba Gato, discovered the very rich gold placers near Ouro Prêto ("black gold"), then capital of the state of Minas Gerais, which made this town wealthy, under the name Vila Rica. Diamonds were discovered near Diamantina in 1712–15, and in 1811 the first large aquamarine—over 20 kilograms (44 pounds)—was extracted near Teófilo

Otoni. Brazil then definitely became part of the legend of the El Dorado.

Nevertheless, the commercial trade of tourmaline did not begin until the early twentieth century, with the development of mining activities directed toward beryl prospecting, which occasionally produced brightly colored elbaites. German dealers from the Idar-Oberstein area moved into the Teófilo Otoni region and in 1914 rediscovered the deposits mentioned in 1677 by Paes Leme in the Serra Resplandescente, north of Governador Valadares, near the famous mine of Cruzeiro. In 1920 a *garimpeiro* named Barbosa discovered a dozen multicolored tourmalines in the Lajão mine, on the slopes of the Itatiaia mountain. Nicknamed *papagaios* ("parrots"), these stones became very popular in Germany and Swit-

Bicolored tourmaline crystal, from Minas Gerais, Brazil. Height: 7 cm. R. Titeux collection.

Bicolored tourmaline crystals in quartz, from Coronel Murta, Minas Gerais, Brazil. Height: 11 cm. K. Proctor collection, United States.

221

Rubellite crystals from the Jonas mine, Itatiaia, Minas Gerais, Brazil. Height: 10 cm. R. Titeux collection.

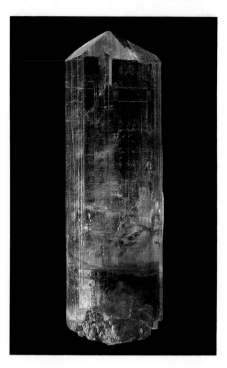

Green tourmaline from Anjanabonoina, Madagascar. Height: 9 cm. Sorbonne collection.

Madagascar

Tourmalines from Madagascar have been known since 1888, that is, since the French began colonizing the island. Remarkable crystals were faceted to encourage prospecting. The Mount Bity pegmatites were quickly discovered in the Antsirabe area, about 60 kilometers (35 miles) southwest of Antananarivo. This whole region contains important deposits, in particular the Sahatany Valley in the Andrianampy Mountains, Manitra, and Maharitra.

This region is particularly promising, as it is formed of quartzites and marbles (with tremolite and diopside), metamorphosed by granite, and injected with veins of pegmatite containing little mica but rich in black and multicolor tourmalines. Alkali feldspars and boron minerals (such as danburite, rhodizite, and hambergite) are also abundant, as are lithium minerals such as spodumene and lepidolite. Calcium-rich minerals, such as danburite and grossular garnet, appear in the vicinity of limestones.

Enormous geodes containing tourmaline crystals of an exquisite wine-red color were discovered in Antaboaka, near the village of Mandrarivo, together with amazonite, smoky quartz, and aquamarine. Beautiful rubellites associated with equally remarkable morganites were collected on several occasions near Vinankarena.

But the most interesting pegmatite is probably the one at Anjanabonoina, discovered in 1894 by Emile Gautier. He sent a gem crystal to the young Alfred Lacroix at the Natural History Museum in Paris (Lacroix would become one of France's foremost mineralogists and spend a good deal of his life studying minerals from the "Big Island"). Starting around 1911 this site produced about 15 kilograms (35 pounds) of rubellite and multicolor tourmaline in a ten-year period; almost 1,700 kilograms (3,750 pounds) were mined between 1920 and 1925. Abandoned in 1950, the deposit was reopened in 1970 by a woman named Liandrat, and in 1972 prospecting was supervised by the French geologist Heurtebize. In 1974 more than one hundred workers were at the site, which was again abandoned in 1976. Remarkable crystals of rubellite, morganite, and kunzite were extracted during this period. Madagascar also is famous for multicolored slabs and rare voilet-faceted gemstones of liddicoatite.

California

The rich pegmatites in the San Diego area were discovered at the beginning of the twentieth century. Tourmaline is associated here with quartz, feldspar, sometimes morganite, and especially kunzite, for which this locality was the first source

zerland and greatly contributed to the popularity of the gem. Later, at the beginning of World War II, mining of the colored stones increased as industry demanded piezoelectric quartz and mica at any price.

In the fifties more than a hundred small-scale operations were active in the state of Minas Gerais. The extraction of quartz, feldspar, and mica justified and supported the venture, while the occasional gemstones produced a profit. This was the golden age of the *garimpeiros*.

In thirty years, Brazil became the world's largest source of tourmalines. Although the origin of Brazilian tourmalines was previously vague, limited to the state of Minas Gerais, new pegmatites became famous and their names familiar: Santa Rosa, Cruzeiro, Golconda, Virgem da Lapa, Urubu, Jonas, and others. The increased interest in mineral collecting stimulated more prospecting and better preservation of mineral specimens.

The Cruzeiro mine was discovered in 1915, northeast of Governador Valadares, near the summit of Serra da Safira, at an altitude of 1,500 meters (5,000 feet). It consists of a series of parallel pinched pegmatite bodies and was mined for mica during World War II by about eight hundred miners. The discovery of rubellite in the central part of the pegmatite directed prospecting toward gems, which are found as beautiful crystals associated with cleavelandite (a variety of albite) in remarkable geodes. In 1970 this mine produced beautiful large

green crystals with black terminations. The best specimen is in the Natural History Museum of Los Angeles County.

Barra de Salinas is another locality famous for tourmaline. It is located northwest of Teófilo Otoni, near the small village of Rubilita. It is best known for the beauty of its multicolored tourmalines of all hues and its morganite crystals, which weigh several dozen pounds. In 1978 Barbosa's son discovered the most extraordinary tourmaline geode of all time in the Jonas mine, in the community of Itatiaia, near Conseilhero Peña. The cavity was 3 meters (10 feet) high and 2 meters (6½ feet) wide, covered entirely with gem rubellite crystals associated with cleavelandite, quartz, and lepidolite mica. Because the pocket was clean, the 4 tons of crystals that were finally extracted did not require cleaning with acid. Some crystals weighed several dozen pounds; the largest was 1.09 meters (3½ feet) long with a diameter of about 20 centimeters (8 inches). The best mineral specimen, with two shiny, gem-quality rubellite crystals with perfect terminations, was sold to a private collector for $1.3 million.

In the late 1980s, the small state of Paraíba, in northeastern Brazil, produced tourmaline in colors never seen before—turquoise, sapphire, and tanzanite blues and emerald green. These colors are due to a combination of copper and manganese. Some of these stones cost ten times more per carat than any tourmaline previously sold.

Polished sections of watermelon tourmaline from Minas Gerais, Brazil. Private collection.

A 28.30-carat faceted tourmaline from Maine. F. A. Becker collection, Idar-Oberstein, Germany.

known (see KUNZITE). The numerous rubellite crystals that were extracted were exported to China to be engraved or carved by Chinese craftsmen, as they were particularly appreciated by mandarins. But the fall of imperial China in 1912 and the ensuing civil war put an end to the Californian mining activity: faceted gem tourmalines were not yet popular.

The Tourmaline Queen mine has certainly been the largest gem tourmaline producer in the Pala area. It was reopened in 1972 to satisfy the demands of mineral collectors, producing remarkable crystals that have enriched public and private collections. One of the most magnificent specimens contains three crystals about 20 centimeters (8 inches) long, standing straight on the matrix, a few centimeters from each other; because of its most unusual appearance, this piece was nicknamed "candelabra" and is now displayed at the Smithsonian Institution in Washington, D.C.

The neighboring Tourmaline King mine has been dormant since the beginning of the century. In this area, the best tourmalines come from the Pala Chief mine, and the best specimen is displayed in the National Museum of Natural History in Paris (P. Morgan donation). In the Mesa Grande district, the Himalaya mine is the largest gem elbaite producer in North America (more than 90 tons since its discovery). Its biterminated green-and-pink crystals have been carved in fantasy cuts to bring out both colors of the mineral.

Watermelon Tourmaline from Maine

Pegmatites in Maine have been known for a long time, and the tourmalines are renowned for the quality of their color, such as pink or green (Mount Mica).

The relatively recent discovery of a large number of gem-quality crystals of remarkable color—"watermelon" tourmalines—in the Dunton mine near Newry has revived interest in these deposits, which remained nonproductive for many years. Their extremely bright mint green and pink tourmalines provide top-quality material for faceting. The largest geode (6 meters [19½ feet] long and 2 meters [6½ feet] high) has produced over 300 kilograms (600 pounds) of crystals in a single day. The largest crystal measures 27 by 10 centimeters (10 by 4 inches) and is presently in the American Museum of Natural History in New York. The mine is still active.

Afghanistan

Pegmatites have been long known in the lower Kunar Valley in Nuristan. These deposits were already being mined for industrial beryl and mica when tourmaline was found. Systematic prospecting led to the discovery in 1970 of very important gem-bearing pegmatites in the upper Laghman Valley in the east.

These pegmatites form veins almost 40 meters (130 feet) wide that can extend over several kilometers, cutting across acid rocks (diorites and gabbros) and metamorphosed marbles rich in calcic silicates. The present political situation in Afghanistan prevents further study of this deposit, which is also difficult to access. The mineral assemblage is typical of sodium-lithium pegmatites: quartz, albite, elbaite, morganite, aquamarine, spodumene, muscovite, lepidolite, spessartite, pollucite, and various phosphates. Only beryl, kunzite, and rubellite are mined. In these deposits the tourmaline attains an extraordinary degree of perfection in the quality of its transparency and in its colorless and colored varieties. Dark pink crystals can reach several pounds, but small, emerald-color gem-quality crystals are the main interest at the Kurgal deposit.

These tourmalines are mined secretly. Most of them are sent to Pakistan and then India, where they are faceted. Unfortunately, the final results do not match the quality of the rough stones, some of the best in existence today.

Other Deposits Worldwide

The historical deposits in the gem-bearing gravels of Sri Lanka today produce only some brown tourmalines. In Upper Burma (Myanmar), alluvial deposits are occasionally worked for tourmaline by Chinese prospectors.

In Africa emerald-green tourmaline has been discovered in Tanzania; it is particularly popular for jewelry. These "chrome tourmalines" are essentially colored by vanadium, although, like emeralds, they display a chromium spectrum and appear pink

Ring set with a faceted rubellite from Mozambique and diamonds. Private collection.

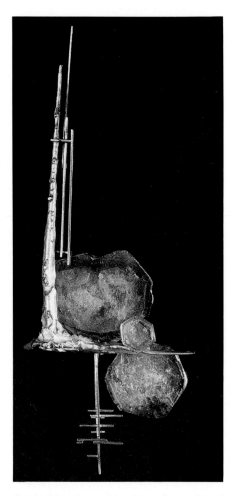

"Marine" brooch containing pieces of tourmaline of different origins. J. Vendôme design.

under the Chelsea filter. Some are chatoyant.

Numerous pegmatites have been discovered near Muiane, in the Alto Ligonha region of Mozambique, a country geologically similar to Madagascar. Large quantities of high-quality rubellite, morganite, and beryl were mined after World War II.

Tourmalines of an exceptional blue were found before World War I in Usakos, Namibia, in a small tin mine. They were sold in Idar-Oberstein many years after the mining company abandoned the site, because nobody recognized the interest in and commercial value of tourmaline at the time. Rubellites similar to the Madagascar crystals come from Otjimbingwe, Namibia.

Natural Gems with a Similar Appearance

Tourmaline resembles many gems. "It seems that nature wanted to prove to man that she could imitate to perfection her most perfect creations," wrote Barbot in 1858. Tourmaline's properties are distinctive enough that this species can be identified without difficulty.

Important Specimens

The most famous rubellite is no doubt the one King Gustav III of Sweden gave to Empress Catherine II of Russia in 1777; this stone, the size of a pigeon egg, weighs approximately 250 carats and is presently in the Diamond Fund of the Soviet Union.

A nice tourmaline collection is displayed at the Smithsonian Institution in Washington, D.C. Of particular interest are a 110.8-carat Manchurian rubellite, a 41.6-carat Sri Lankan brown tourmaline, a 172.7-carat champagne tourmaline from Mozambique, and a 41.7-carat yellow Brazilian tourmaline. There are also a 17.7-carat yellowish green stone from Elba, Italy; a 60-carat bluish green Brazilian tourmaline; a 25.5-carat Brazilian indicolite; a red-and-green tourmaline from California; and a dark green chatoyant Brazilian gem weighing 76 carats.

TSAVORITE

A vanadium- and chromium-bearing variety of green grossular garnet, found in Tsavo National Park in Kenya, after which it was named. See GROSSULAR.

TUGTUPITE

A beryllium aluminosilicate containing chlorine and sodium. It crystallizes in the tetragonal system (pseudocubic) and has a structure close to that of sodalite. Its name comes from Tugtup Cape (that is, Reindeer Cape) in Greenland. Tugtupite forms masses of an attractive variegated pink, used in Denmark as ornamental stone. Its hardness is 6 to 7, its refractive index about 1.5. Its luminescence is orange under long-wave ultraviolet and pinkish orange under short-wave ultraviolet. It fades after lengthy exposure to daylight.

Some rare cabochons have been cut, reaching 2 to 3 carats. Small gemmy fragments have been faceted for collectors.

TURQUOISE

A usually massive hydrous phosphate of copper and aluminum.

Origin of the Name and History

Turquoise was considered a gem as early as the fourth millennium B.C. The Egyptians mined it in the Sinai, calling it *mafkat*, a name engraved on pharaonic stelae located near the mines.

Because they concentrated only on color, ancient Greek and Latin authors grouped turquoise with lapis lazuli, some agates, and even some copper silicates such as chrysocolla. Theophrastus (312–287 B.C.) described fossil ivories colored green by copper, which had long been mistaken for turquoise and would later be assimilated

Turquoise serpent from Montezuma's treasure. British Museum.

with odontolite (fossils colored by vivianite, an iron phosphate).

In his *Natural History,* Pliny the Elder called a green stone that seems to match turquoise by the name *callais,* from the Greek *kallos,* meaning "beauty." At the beginning of the thirteenth century, Arnoldus Saxo wrote in his book *De Virtibus Lapidum:* "Turquoise is a blue stone, which owes its name to the fact that it comes from Turkey." This is the oldest known text in which the name *turquoise* appeared, and the name was associated with the mineral thereafter. Turkey did not actually produce turquoise but resold turquoise from Iran to the West. However, some prefer another explanation to this logical derivation: a deformation of the Persian *firouze* into *tourques* and then *turquoise.*

The first scientific description of turquoise was given by the Arab author Mohamed ibn Mansūr in 1300. He described its geographic origin, various qualities (including medicinal properties), and imitations of turquoise, as well as the most famous stones.

Turquoise was apparently introduced in China and India by Moghul invaders.

Occult Properties and Virtues

Like other gems with a range of colors that evoke both the blue of the sky and the color of water or plants, turquoise was a symbol of magical virtues in which some people still believe today. Indeed, blue always played an important symbolic role, synonymous with paradise to the Chinese,

the color of the gods Amon and Isis to the Egyptians, the color of the robes of the Hebrew priests, and a talisman to the Native Americans from the Southwest. Blue is a talisman against the evil eye in the Orient: draft animals, such as horses, camels, and donkeys, always wear blue ceramic pearls to protect them from exhaustion and accidents. The *Nozat Nameh Elahi,* a manuscript from the second century about precious stones written by Salem ad-Din, indicated that turquoise brought victory and good fortune. One century later, an Arab botanist named Ibn el-Beitar considered it an efficient remedy for scorpion bites, eye diseases, and stomach-aches. Persian, Indian, Afghan, and Arabic authors reported that turquoise had medicinal powers, informing its wearer on the state of his or her health by variations of its color. Numerous seals and rings were set with turquoise to promote prosperity.

In Europe turquoise was attributed with some occult virtues. Even today, rings set with turquoises, called "forget-menots," are given as presents. In his 1802 *Histoire naturelle (Natural history),* the French naturalist Georges-Louis Buffon considered such beliefs a sign of stupidity. In North America the Apache believed turquoise helped warriors and hunters aim accurately.

Turquoise was widely used in Tibet for the fabrication of ritual objects and jewelry, but it was rarely used by Europeans. Only a few Roman cameos were carved in turquoise. Numerous balls and cylinders were, however, discovered in Neolithic graves in France and Spain; a number of these were

actually variscite, often confused with turquoise under the name *callais.* The French mineralogist Damour was the first to make a distinction between two minerals in 1864.

During the Renaissance turquoise was used to make balls and cameos, under the influence of the Orient, which was the largest producer. Shakespeare's Shylock stated that he should not lose his turquoise ring. Thereafter, this stone was used with varied degrees of success, following the demands of fashion.

Mineralogical and Petrographical Characteristics

Turquoise crystallizes in the triclinic system. Copper atoms are surrounded by water molecules and hydroxyl groups. They occupy large sites in an oxygen framework held together by phosphorus atoms (surrounded by four oxygen atoms to form a phosphate group), as well as aluminum and also ferric iron ions (surrounded by six entities, oxygen, hydroxyl, or water). Aluminum, iron, and even zinc substitute for each other in all proportions, so all intermediate compositions exist, from the aluminum-rich pole (turquoise) to the ferric iron pole (chalcosiderite) to the green zinc pole (faustite). Turquoise crystals are extremely rare and have been encountered only at Lynch Station, Virginia. They are small flattened crystals showing a triclinic shape, up to 2 or 3 millimeters in size, disseminated in the fractures of a quartz veinlet. The index of refraction of turquoise is about 1.62. Its

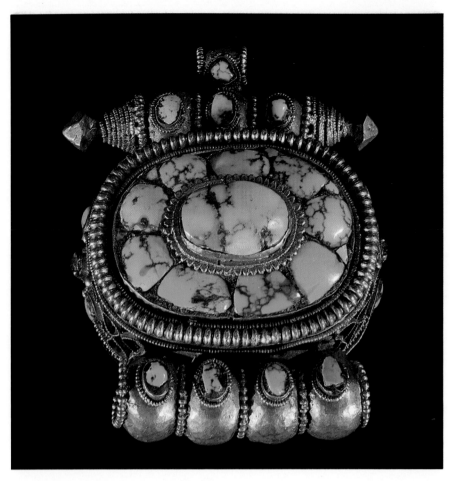

Tibetan reliquary of gold and turquoise. Length: 5 cm.
Boutique Argana, Paris.

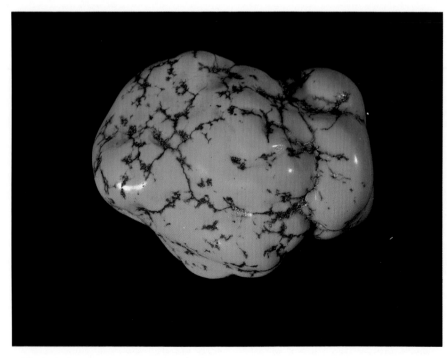

Polished Tibetan turquoise. Diameter: 5 cm. National
Higher School of Mines, Paris.

specific gravity, from 2.6 to 2.85, and hardness, from 4 to 6, vary as a function of porosity. Persian turquoise is the least porous and so, the densest and the hardest. A turquoise with weak cohesion and a hardness of less than 4 cannot be considered turquoise in gemology.

The color varies from pale blue to green and is caused by copper and iron; the most valued color is a sky blue. Gem-quality turquoise is massive, made from an assemblage of microcrystals along with other minerals such as limonite, quartz, pyrite, and sometimes chalcopyrite. Turquoise with dark veins is called matrix turquoise or spiderweb turquoise. Variations of color due to exposure to air and high heat suggest the presence of an unstable hydrous component. Persian turquoise has a reputation for its good stability, unlike the turquoise from the Sinai and the United States, which fades rapidly. This phenomenon is still not clearly understood and is believed to be due to a loss of water from the mineral. It is possible that this color instability is source of the various powers attributed to this gem in ancient times. To preserve the delicate blue of this stone, one should avoid dehydrating it or exposing it to heat, or acids and fatty compounds (cosmetics or perspiration, for example).

Turquoise is translucent in thin slivers, opaque when massive. It has a vitreous luster and a conchoidal fracture, and it takes a very nice polish. Turquoise is found in veinlets, more rarely in concretions filling the cavities of igneous rock, or is disseminated in grains or nuggets.

Deposits

The most important turquoise deposits are located in Iran, Central Asia (Tibet, China), and in the southwestern United States (Nevada, New Mexico, Arizona, Colorado, Utah). It has also been found in France, Germany, Ethiopia, Sinai (Egypt), Turkistan, Afghanistan, Saudi Arabia, Peru, Chile, Mexico, and Brazil, but it is not mined in those countries.

Turquoise is a mineral produced by a superficial alteration of copper deposits and is usually found in outcrops of important copper deposits of the "porphyry copper" type, which have been studied over the last twenty years all over the world (in the western United States, Chile, the Soviet Union, and Iran, for example). These deposits are formed by a dense network of quartz veinlets containing chalcopyrite, enargite, sometimes molybdenite, and gold, penetrating a monzonite or granodiorite, often porphyric in nature (therefore, it is not a porphyry in the traditional sense). Overall the copper concentration is low (0.5 to 1 percent copper), but the abundance of copper-rich veinlets justifies bulk mining of the rock, so these deposits are mined in open quarries. The development of such deposits has yielded sizable quantities of turquoise as a by-product and explains its ubiquitous presence on the market.

Turquoise also forms in igneous rocks rich in pyrite that have been altered by fumaroles. In France it has been found as an alteration product of amblygonite (a lithium phosphate) in the Montebras quarry, in the Creuse department.

Sinai

These deposits, the oldest known, located on the western coast of the Sinai Peninsula, at Wadi Maghareh and Serabit el Khadim, a six-day journey by camel from Suez. Systematically mined by the ancient Egyptians, they were forgotten for over three thousand years, although historically they represent an important era in mining activity. Ruins and inscriptions in honor of the goddess Hathor located near the mines were studied in detail by Sir Flinders Petrie in 1906; they attest to important mining activity at the time of the pharaohs. This region was formerly called Mafkat, or "land of the green minerals," but it is now called Cave Valley by the Bedouins because of the extensive remains of ancient workings. The oldest site, Wadi Maghareh, dates to the First Dynasty, as indicated by an inscription representing Semerkhet, seventh king of the dynasty (around 3200 B.C.).

During the Fourth Dynasty, around 2600 B.C., King Snefru produced many texts describing the mining activity, reporting in particular that turquoise production had been very good. Under Amenophis I (1557–30 B.C.) inscriptions recording a royal offering to Hathor, goddess of joy, love, and maternity, also mentioned mines in the Sinai. At this time, Harrurkhu's expedition was related on a stele: "Harrurkhu, having not succeeded in finding the turquoise he was asked to bring back, lost in the desert, the ground burning like an oven, his men threatening to abandon him, implored Hathor and discovered immediately a rich vein of this precious stone."

The turquoise mines were last active under Thutmose III (1504–1450 B.C.). The remains of this particular mining period were discovered in 1762 by the German explorer Carsten Niebuhr, sent by the king of Denmark to collect inscriptions, but it was not until 1817 that the precise content of his work became known. In 1845 a Major MacDonald decided to revive the ancient workings. Despite some success, he had to abandon his project because of the hostility of the Bedouins. He died, ruined, in Cairo in 1870 after an adventurous life, although he managed to save numerous inscriptions from destruction.

After unsuccessful attempts by French and British companies, the six mines have been intermittently mined by the Bedouins.

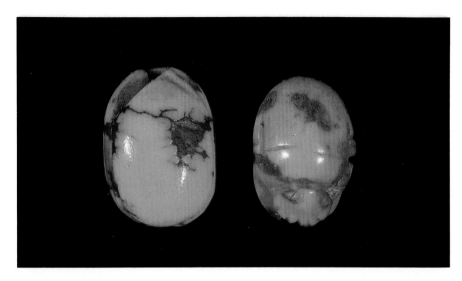

Egyptian scarabs carved in turquoise from the Sinai. Length: 0.8 cm. Musée du Louvre.

Engraved turquoise from Iran, Islamic art from the eighteenth century. Length: 7 cm. National Higher School of Mines, Paris.

Iran

Jean Chardin, a French traveler (1643–1713), wrote about those sites: "Turquoise mines are in Nichabour, in Corassan, and also between Hircania and Parthia, four days' travel from the Caspian Sea, in a mountain called Phirouscou, or Phiroux Mountain, named Caucasus by Pliny the Elder.... Discovered during the reign of Phiroux (Sassanid king Peroz, A.D. 459–84) and mined by orders of this prince, this mine was named for him, a usage that has been extended to its precious product. Indeed, the precious stone that is extracted there and that we call turquoise, because the country it comes from is the ancient and

true Turkey, is called *firouze* throughout the Orient.... One has discovered other mines of such stone, but it is neither as beautiful or as bright. These pieces are called 'new turquoises,' which is how we describe the new stones, to distinguish them from the others that we call 'old turquoises': the color of the former fades with time.... Everything coming from the old rock is kept for the king, who resells it or trades it, after keeping the best pieces. Miners and the superior officers assigned to oversee them smuggle as much as they can, and this is how one often has some fairly good opportunities to obtain some in the trade."

In the year 978, the Arab writer Ibn

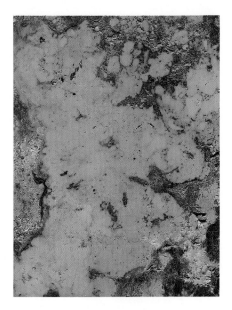

Polished turquoise from Neyshābūr, Iran. Length: 5 cm. British Museum of Natural History.

Haukal mentioned the famous deposits of the Iranian province of Khorāsān, which were described again by al-Bīrūnī (973–1048) and Al-Ta'alibi (961–1038). According to Mohamed ibn Mansūr, these mines had been worked by Isaac, the son of Abraham, who gave his name to one of the mines.

At the same time, Marco Polo mentioned turquoise deposits in the Kermān area of southeastern Iran. The most beautiful turquoises are in the treasury of Iran, in particular Nāder Shāh's amulet, carved in the shape of a heart and engraved with a verse from the Koran.

The world's most famous turquoise deposit is located about 40 kilometers (25 miles) northwest of the town of Nishapur, near the small mining village of Maadan (in Persian, "the mine"). It has been mined for centuries. The workings extend in altered igneous rock over about two square kilometers (about 500 acres). Turquoise forms small veinlets in the crushed zones of the deposit. Next to the turquoise, the rock takes on a typical reddish color, due to the presence of limonite. Blue alunite, jarosite, and pyrite are also present, although in small amounts. This deposit was actively mined under the authority of the Iranian general Houtoum Schindler (1881), governor of the Khorāsān at the end of the nineteenth century, a period during which extensive studies of Persia's mining resources were conducted. At that time the mines benefited from a management aimed not only at increasing production but also at improving working conditions. Unfortunately, greed led progressively to more disorganized workings and caused damage beyond repair. Today the deposit is run by a company from Mashhad.

Another turquoise deposit is in the copper-mineralized area located southwest of the city of Kermān and covers about 50,000 square kilometers (19,000 square miles). It is situated in Tertiary volcanic and sedimentary rock, reaching an altitude of 4,400 meters (14,500 feet). These copper mineralizations have been known and mined for a long time on a very irregular basis.

In 1967 the discovery of porphyry copper deposits led to the recognition of wide areas of copper mineralization. Through systematic study, many turquoise-bearing copper indications were identified: Kuh-e-Panj, Sar-Chechmeh, Iju, Meiduk, and others. These are probably the same deposits that had been mined historically.

North America

Juan de Grijalba, explorer of the Yucatan, was the first European to mention the presence of turquoise in the New World; in 1518 he obtained turquoise-inlay wooden masks from the local tribes.

Hernan Cortés brought back many turquoise objects from his expeditions: earrings, small animal carvings used in funeral rituals or mosaics; a good number of these are housed in various ethnographic museums throughout Western Europe. Quetzalcoatl, the god of wind and air in ancient Mexican mythology, introduced corn and the arts to the Toltec society, including the art of working gemstones. At celebrations in his honor, he was often represented symbolically covered with a turquoise mask symbolizing the serpent (*coatl*) wearing quetzal feathers (the quetzal is a bird from the forests of Guatemala). Each year, Montezuma's vassal tribes had to pay an expensive tribute of necklaces, golden diadems, and rough or cut turquoises. Because it was rare, turquoise was reserved for the gods; it could not be worn.

The deposits in the southwestern United States provided much turquoise to Mexico, since the stone is virtually absent from that country. Old pre-Hispanic workings discovered in Los Cerillos, New Mexico, testify to the intense turquoise-mining ac-

Turquoise and diamond necklace. Fred design, Paris.

tivity of local populations. An immense quarry remains 100 meters (325 feet) long and 60 meters (195 feet) deep. Pines that are now several hundred years old have grown over the tailings, which are even more impressive if one remembers that only stone hand tools were available for mining at the time.

Turquoise was exalted among local tribes. The Arizona Hopi represented the sky by the sun, the eagle, and the turquoise; the earth, by water, the rattlesnake, and the toad. The Apache believed a turquoise ball attached to the bow ensured a perfect shot. The Zuni, the first tribe to use turquoise in America, believed this gem protected them from demons (more than fifty thousand fashioned turquoises were discovered in one archaeological site at Pueblo Bonito, in Chaco Canyon). Some deposits known to the Indians are still being mined. However, today most turquoise comes from the porphyry copper of the southwestern United States. The most important mines are: Bisbee, Morenci, Courtland, Gleeson, and Copper Cities (including the Sleeping Beauty mine) in Arizona; Burro Mountains (including the Azur mine), Eureka, and Oro Grande in New Mexico; King, Creede, Villa Grove, Holy Cross, and Saint Kelvin in Colorado; and Bullion, Copper Basin (including Blue Gem mine), and Cortez (where an extraordinary turquoise mass weighing over 100 kilograms was found) in Nevada. In total, about forty mines are active.

Although it is often treated, turquoise is of great significance in the Southwest, where it forms the base (with jet, coral, and nacre) of the silver jewelry made by most Indian tribes: the Zuni are known for their inlays, the Hopi for their linings, and Navajo for their silver casts set with turquoise. However, so-called Indian jewelry is also manufactured by small commercial operations employing Indians or by companies that do not hesitate to use imitations, especially in Arizona.

Pre-Columbian knife handle in gold and turquoise. Size: 13.4 by 15.9 cm. Gold Museum, Lima, Peru. Photo: Vautier.

Similar-looking Blue-Green Gem Materials

Some gem materials resemble turquoise and may be mistaken for it, principally odontolite, which was in use primarily during the Middle Ages; alunite, which is primarily used in Iran; and variscite, relatively common in the United States. Silicified chrysocolla, lazulite, amazonite, faustite, ceruleite and smithsonite may resemble turquoise as well.

Treated Turquoise

Blue turquoise with good cohesion represents a very small percentage of the turquoise extracted from American copper mines. Sometimes turquoise is practically colorless and so weak that it crumbles between the fingers; these pulverulent varieties are sometimes called chalky turquoise.

The Indians had noticed that the color of low-quality turquoise could be improved by impregnation with bear grease but then soon turned green (this is why old Indian jewelry is often set with greenish "dead turquoise"). Also turquoise fades as it loses moisture. It has long been known that the color of some turquoise can be enhanced by dyeing with copper salts, but the resulting appearance is too flat and unattractive.

So the idea of enhancing the color of chalky turquoise by eliminating the parts that contain too much dust and soaking in water the remaining nodules came about. Once the color is restored, one must simply protect the mineral with an injection of plastic at moderate temperature, under pressure; this operation may last over a week. Initially the plastic used was colorless, but the demand for blue turquoise has inspired entrepreneurs to use colored plastics. Some turquoise samples are so porous before treatment that they contain about 30 percent plastic after being treated. This treatment can be easily detected with a hot needle.

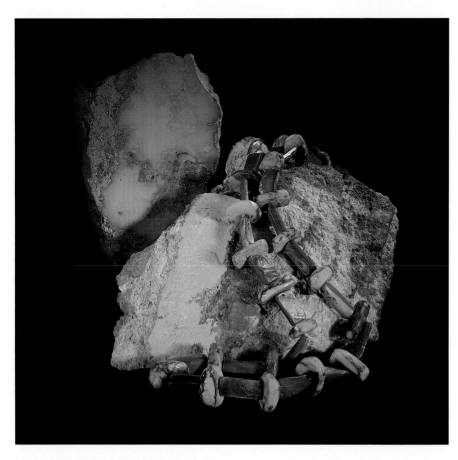

Rough turquoise, along with polished turquoise in a tribal necklace from Arizona. Sorbonne collection.

Tibetan reliquary of silver and turquoise. Length: 10 cm. Boutique Argana, Paris.

Residues from turquoise manufacturing can be collected, packed in a container, and sintered together with black plastic. This reconstructed turquoise looks like natural spiderweb turquoise. Sometimes turquoise powder is simply agglomerated with plastic: one should really call this product a turquoise-based imitation.

Imitations

As early as the third millennium B.C., the color of turquoise had become so popular in the Nile Valley that the first faience beads made by the Egyptians for adornment had a turquoise-color glaze. Egyptian faience was famous throughout the ancient world. Turquoise-color glasses appeared only during the sixteenth century B.C.; some examples were found in Tutankhamen's grave (fourteenth century B.C.). During the same period, enameling techniques were developed, and many turquoise-color enamels adorned jewelry and prestigious objects: for the Egyptians of this period, appearance, rather than authenticity, was sufficient. Enamel, glass, faience, and more rarely, porcelain, were the only turquoise imitations until the twentieth century. The development of the plastics industry resulted in colored-plastic imitations and, later, in simulants made of plastic charged with turquoise powder.

The first compressed and sintered phosphate imitations was manufactured in Germany by K. Hoffman in 1927. It was a mixture of malachite, aluminum hydroxide, and phosphoric acid compacted at 100°C (212°F). Veinlets of an amorphous black iron-containing material imitated the matrix. These materials were too matte and too greenish. Later, an aluminum phosphate colored by copper oleate was introduced under the deceptive name "Viennese turquoise": this product was blue, homogeneous, and matte. Since 1957 hydrargillite (synthetic gibbsite) has been the primary turquoise imitation, mixed with a copper phosphate and an aluminum phosphate. Sold as Neolite, it is now known as German block. Its composition may vary slightly from one manufacturer to the other. Its homogeneous color may be highlighted by black veinlets of amorphous iron-containing material intended to imitate the spiderweb matrix. This product is sometimes made cohesive by compaction or consolidated with plastics. It is also produced in a coral color.

Recently, powdered marble sintered with coloring have been introduced on the market. It is produced in turquoise, lapis-lazuli, and coral colors, so that jewelry manufacturers can use them easily. The homogeneous texture is reminiscent of rice pudding under the microscope. Of course, they effervesce with acid. All earlier imitations made from sintered powders turn a drop of hydrochloric acid yellow, unlike natural turquoise.

In addition to those imitations, a number of materials have been dyed to imitate turquoise, including chalcedony, howlite (a whitish calcium borosilicate), marl and earthenware, bone, and ivory (although these last two materials look more like odontolite).

Synthetics

Synthetic turquoise manufactured by Gilson has been marketed since 1970. It has the physical and mineralogical characteristics of turquoise. However, its texture reveals its synthetic nature: it is a fine-grained aggregate of more or less tubular elements parallel to each other.

Initially without a spiderweb matrix, this very homogeneous imitation of a light blue ("Farah") to dark blue ("Cleopatra") color reveals its typical "cream of wheat" texture under a magnification of 100× to 150×. The parallel sets of elementary cells may also be highlighted by fiberoptic illumination. A spiderweb matrix has been introduced in more recent products, in which the elements also no longer have a parallel orientation.

u · v · w

UVAROVITE

A chromium-bearing calcic garnet. It was named for Count S. S. Uvarov, former president of the Saint Petersburg Academy of Sciences. Its crystals are essentially mineralogical specimens. They come from serpentines and ultrabasic rocks, especially in Finland. Uvarovite's index of refraction is 1.87; its specific gravity, 3.77; and its hardness, 7½.

VARISCITE

A hydrous aluminum phosphate, crystallizing in the orthorhombic system. Its name comes from Variscia (now Voigtland in Germany), where this mineral was discovered.

Variscite generally forms cryptocrystalline masses or nodules of a pale green color (dark green at the fracture), which may take a very good polish. It can be mistaken for cuprous alunite and turquoise; however, pyrite and quartz are never found in association. Variscite is produced by a reaction of phosphate-rich surface waters with aluminous slates.

The best specimens come from the United States, in particular from Utah (it is therefore occasionally called utahite). A less attractive variscite, reminiscent of jade or turquoise, has been recently mined near Brisbane, in Queensland, Australia.

In France variscite was recently found in association with wavellite in the Pannecé quarries in Loire Atlantique. This may explain the numerous variscite objects found in the Celtic graves at Locmariaquer, Brittany, described in the past as *callais*.

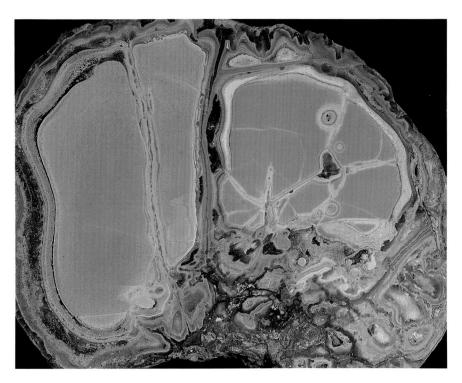

Polished variscite from Fairfield, Utah. Length: 12 cm. Sorbonne collection.

VENUS HAIR STONE

Rock crystal (quartz) with inclusions of fine, undulating rutile fibers, creating blond streaks reminiscent of the hair of Venus, the Roman goddess of love.

This ornamental gem was already popular in ancient Rome (as *veneris crines*). It was especially in vogue during the eighteenth century. Today the region of Ibitiara, approximately 400 kilometers (250 miles) west of Salvador (Bahia, Brazil), is the world's major source.

Remarkable inclusions of rutile and hematite may be found in smoky or colorless quartz from veins, sometimes forming very large crystals (dozens of pounds). Sometimes the rutile appears as fine golden inclusions, occasionally with a pinkish tinge;

Art deco necklace with rutilated quartz (Venus hair stone), lapis lazuli, and diamond. J. Vendôme design.

Vesuvianite or Idocrase

An aluminous silicate of calcium, magnesium, and iron, crystallizing in the tetragonal system. Calcium may be replaced in part by a variety of elements, such as lithium, sodium, potassium, manganese, iron, titanium, chromium, zinc, or copper, thereby producing various colors in this mineral.

Vesuvianite was named by Abraham Werner in 1795 because of its presence in the deposit at Mount Vesuvius. The term *idocrase,* still in use, was coined by René-Just Haüy in 1799 from *idos,* meaning "appearance," and *krasis,* meaning "mixed," because he believed its appearance was similar to that of other minerals, such as zircon.

The typical crystal shape of vesuvianite is a tetragonal prism topped by a truncated or acute pyramid. This gem is generally green with a weakly dichroic color, but it can also be yellow (xanthite, from the Greek *xanthos,* meaning yellow), brown, sometimes pink or bluish violet (cyprine, from *kupris,* another name for Venus, worshipped on Cyprus, which was famous for its copper deposits).

Vesuvianite's hardness is 6½. Its specific gravity varies with chemical composition from 3.35 to 3.45, as do the indices of refraction, (from 1.712 to 1.716 for the ordinary ray and 1.700 to 1.721 for the extraordinary ray, the optical character changing from uniaxial negative to uniaxial positive). Massive vesuvianite has also been called californite or has been deceptively presented as "California jade"; its index of refraction is 1.72.

Vesuvianite is produced by contact metamorphism and is associated with diopside and calcic garnet (hydrogrossular). Vesuvianite may also appear in basic rocks modified by endomorphism at contacts with dolomites. Such is the case in the Zhob Valley, in Pakistani Baluchistan, which is famous for its massive rock in which vesuvianite and grossular are intimately mixed, forming a complete series from pure massive vesuvianite to pure massive grossular. Xanthite comes from Amity, New York; cyprine from Telemark, Norway. Exceptional pinkish-purple and emerald-green gems have been faceted from crystals found at Jeffrey mine, Quebec, Canada in 1989.

Wernerite

See Scapolite.

Vesuvianite crystal from Asbestos, Quebec, Canada. Length: 0.3 cm. Sorbonne collection.

sometimes it is attached to the base of which it grew just like a plant. More rarely, it is set in an epitaxial relation with hematite crystals, creating a dramatic six-ray star.

The deposits are numerous and mined primitively; the most important are Remedios and Matinha, near Ibitiara. Beautiful specimens also come from Madagascar, the Alps, and other locations.

Verdelite

A green tourmaline. This term is little used.

Verdite

An ornamental rock consisting primarily of fuchsite mica. See Serpentine.

Vermeil

A term no longer commonly used after the nineteenth century. It comes from the Latin *vermicullus,* that is, "small worm," used for the cochineal from which a red dye was produced. Vermeil designated various orange red gems, such as hyacinth, orangy red sapphire, and red to orangy red garnets. This term should not be confused with the gilded or gold-plated silver known as vermeil.

$\mathcal{X} \cdot \mathcal{Z}$

XANTHITE

See VESUVIANITE.

ZIRCON

A zirconium silicate, crystallizing in the tetragonal system.

Origin of the Name and History

Hyacinthos originally designated a flower, probably the iris, in which an alpha and a iota (or an upsilon) seem to be intertwined (from the Greek verb *cyneo*, meaning "to kiss" or "to embrace," as the alpha seemed to embrace the iota). This name was later applied to a gem with the same color as the flower, light violet associated with yellow, probably a Sri Lankan sapphire. *Hyacinthe* became *yacut* in Arabic, designating corundums of any color. In Byzantium, *hyacinthe* became *jacynthe* in the eleventh century, then *jagonce* in the thirteenth century, and seems to have been applied to a variety of gems. Consequently, varieties of *jagonce* were specified, such as *jagonces grenas* or *jagonces balais;* these gems were characterized by their low hardness as compared to corundum and therefore were held in little esteem. *Jagonce* became *jargon* and, in the eighteenth century, *zircon*. This last term was adopted by mineralogists for *hyacinthe-la-belle* (or "hyacinth the beautiful") at the expense of the term *hyacinth*, which had been retained thus far but fell into disuse around the middle of the nineteenth century. The origin of *zircon* is sometimes attributed to the Arabic *zarkun*, meaning "red," or to the Persian *zargun*, meaning "golden."

Jargon, or nearly colorless zircon, was extensively used at the beginning of the nineteenth century. It was faceted in rose cuts and used as a diamond substitute or used as a side stone in watches and rings. It was cut in Switzerland with garnets. Its resemblance to diamond led to some fraud at the time. Today colorless zircon is not popular with jewelers, who tend to consider it a fake stone.

The Smithsonian Institution exhibits several large faceted zircons, including a 118.1-carat brown stone, a 97.6-carat brownish yellow stone, a 48.2-carat colorless stone, and a 23.5-carat green stone, all from Sri Lanka. This collection also contains a 103.2-carat blue zircon from Kampuchea, a 75.8-carat brownish red gem from Myanmar (Burma), and a 31.1-carat stone from Australia. The National Museum of Natural History in Paris has a 63-carat green zircon from Sri Lanka.

Physical Properties

Zirconium is a common element in small amounts; it may be replaced by hafnium, thorium, uranium, iron, and rare-earth elements. These various elements are responsible for the sometimes "hazy" (slightly opalescent) colors that zircon can display. Its absorption spectrum includes about fifteen sharp lines, distributed over the entire spectrum. The constant and most intense line is in the orange range. All lines are attributed to uranium, which is always present in zircons. Zircons containing a high concentration of radioactive elements have a very disorganized structure as a result of self-irradiation. These zircons are called *metamict* (from the Greek *meta*, meaning "after," and *mitos*, meaning "mixed") and are light green to brownish green. Their physical constants are then significantly lowered: their hardness drops from 7½ to 6; their specific gravity falls from 4.7 to 4; their indices of refraction, 1.93 (ordinary ray) and 1.99 (extraordinary ray), decline to

Two blue (11.67- and 21.25-carat) and a yellow (11.80-carat) faceted zircons. F. A. Becker collection, Idar-Oberstein, Germany.

Zircon crystal from Australia. Length: 1.5 cm. G. Becker collection, Idar-Oberstein, Germany.

A central peridot surrounded by small zircon side stones simulating diamond. Private collection.

Mineralogy and Deposits

Zircon generally forms tetragonal prisms with pyramidal terminations. Zircons with a high concentration of rare-earth elements often have a slightly flattened octahedral facies with curved faces, and these crystals are often polygenetic. Small zircons found in granites are generally transparent to translucent and colorless to milky, yellowish or greenish. Large crystals are exceptionally transparent, colorless to bluish (Australia), red ("hyacinths"), orange, or green (Madagascar). Most transparent crystals fluoresce an orangy yellow in black light.

Zircon is very common in granitoids, syenites, nephelinic syenites, pegmatites, and carbonatites. It is mined in alluvial deposits. Sri Lanka has the most important historical deposit, and its gem-bearing gravels produce zircons of all colors. Those imported in the past from the kingdom of Pegu came from Myanmar (Burmese) placers.

The high plateau located between Laos, Kampuchea, and Thailand is an important source of gem zircons, which are systematically heat-treated in Bangkok. Nice red zircons have been found in Madagascar, colorless ones in Mozambique and Australia.

In France the alluvial deposits of the Riou Pezouliou have been mined since ancient times near Espaly (Haute-Loire). They produce hyacinth red zircon crystals of a stocky habit, associated with magnetite and dark blue sapphire. They come from granitic enclaves trapped in altered igneous rocks.

A 13.77-carat faceted red zircon. F. A. Becker collection, Idar-Oberstein, Germany.

of heating brownish red zircons in an oxidizing atmosphere (about 1,000°C or 1,830°F, in air). The southern area of Sri Lanka (Matura area) may have produced some natural (non-heat-treated) colorless zircons in the past, which were incorrectly called Matura diamonds or Ceylon diamonds.

Heat-treating zircon in an oxidizing atmosphere can also produce a golden yellow color. When heat-treated in a reducing atmosphere (that is, with insufficient draft to produce complete combustion of the coals in the furnace), reddish brown zircons usually become blue. Several attempts may be necessary to produce a marketable blue; moreover, the color tends to revert to brown over the years. Heat treatment only reorganizes a structure that is intrinsically unstable. Long exposure to ultraviolet radiation can actually momentarily reverse the effect of the treatment.

Heat-treated zircons become very pleochroic, unlike natural zircons, which display little or no pleochroism. They are also more sensitive to shock; they are more easily abraded during normal wear, especially at facet junctions. So, despite their absence of cleavage, these stones should be considered fragile.

Metamict zircons that have been heat-treated at 1,450°C (2,640°F) can become either high zircons or an extreme type of low zircon, increasing in transparency and intensifying the green color. Zircons used in jewelry are generally inclusion free.

Natural Gems with a Similar Appearance

Zircon can potentially be mistaken for all gems, but its slightly opalescent appearance may make it recognizable with the naked eye. Colorless zircon was and still is largely used as a diamond substitute, although such use has declined with the development of modern synthetic diamond simulants.

Hyacinth zircon may resemble many gems: orange sapphire, spessartite, hessonite, spinel, and tourmaline are the more likely ones. Yellow zircon looks like yellow tourmaline; indeed, the two gems were not differentiated in Sri Lanka until recently. Green zircon can resemble demantoid; blue zircon, aquamarine and sometimes sapphire. Violet zircon can be mistaken for amethyst.

ZIRCONIA

See ZIRKELITE.

about 1.80, and the birefringence drops from 0.059 to a few thousandths. This is why gemologists call regular zircon "high zircon" and metamict zircon "low zircon." A complete series of intermediate types exists between those two extremes, referred to as "intermediate zircons."

Zircon has been heat-treated for many years. In 1821, C. P. Brard wrote: "the *jargons* are burned carefully and lose their yellowish tint and become white, completely colorless and with a luster much superior to the one they naturally had." Most colorless zircons on the market today are the result

ZIRKELITE

A titanium and zirconium oxide, also containing calcium and thorium, crystallizing in the monoclinic system with a pseudocubic symmetry. It has been encountered in Jacupiranga in São Paulo State, Brazil, and in Kamtchatka in the Soviet Union, but it is found mostly in Sri Lanka.

Synthetic zirkelite grown by the skull-melting technique (see part 1) has been sold since 1974 as a diamond simulant in two varieties. The first, grown in Europe, is a calcium-stabilized zirconium oxide, the second, grown in the United States, the Soviet Union, and many other countries is an yttrium-stabilized zirconium oxide, with a specific gravity of approximately 6. Various trade names have been given to this product. Its generic name on the international market is *CZ*, for cubic zirconia.

CZ's hardness is 8½; it is tough, with an adamantine luster (index of refraction of about 2.2). Its dispersion is higher than that of diamond. Zirconium oxide is currently the most convincing diamond imitation. However, its slightly hazy appearance is reminiscent of zircon, and it is colorless only if the raw materials from which it is produced are very pure. Some stones have a slightly brownish or yellowish tint. Yellow CZ has been sold as an imitation of fancy yellow diamond, and many other colors are now available as well.

CZ is a thermal insulator, unlike diamond. It generally exhibits a yellow luminescence under short-wave ultraviolet. Like most oxides, it is attacked by hot borax.

ZOISITE

A hydroxylated calcium aluminosilicate, crystallizing in the orthorhombic system. This mineral was named for Baron von Zois, an Austrian mineralogist. The replacement of silicon by aluminum or aluminum by iron is very limited, and manganese concentrations are low.

Crystals are rare: zoisite generally forms flattened fibers with a perfect cleavage or whitish to grayish mamillary groups. Masses of green zoisite associated with ruby in Longido, Kenya, are frequently carved into small objects. A finely grained pink variety, thulite, contains traces of manganese and rare-earth elements; it is associated with blue idocrase (cyprine) and carved to produce ornamental objects. Thulite, named for Thule, the ancient name for Norway, comes from Telemark, Norway.

Its hardness is 6, and its specific gravity ranges from 3.20 to 3.36. Its refractive indices are about 1.70.

Zoisite is produced by regional metamorphism of clay-rich limestones or by retromorphosis of the granulite facies in the eclogites from Saint-Philibert-de-Grandieu, in Loire-Atlantique, France.

A gem variety of blue zoisite is found in Tanzania. Recently, an emerald-green variety was also discovered, from which magnificent small gems can be faceted. See TANZANITE.

Appendix 1

Average Physical Constants and Chemical Composition of Gems

The table that follows is arranged according to the gems' indices of refraction. The most common gems are in **boldface** characters. Gem materials that require human intervention in their formation are in *italic* type.

Key to the Symbols

T = transparent
Th = hazy transparency
Tr = translucent
O = opaque
S.G. = specific gravity
H = hardness
Tough = toughness
Black square (■) = poor toughness
Open square (□) = moderately tough
Black pennant (▶) = tough
Greater-than symbol (>) = sensitive to chemicals
Bl = black
Br = brown
R = red
O = orange
Y = yellow
G = green
B = blue
P = purple
Pi = pink
Cl = colorless
Asterisk (*) = rare
× = frequent
+ = common
Open circle (○) = none
Black circle (●) = weak
Not-equal symbol (≠) = distinct
LWUV = long-wave ultraviolet
SWUV = short-wave ultraviolet
Open triangle (△) = weak
Black triangle (▲) = intense

An Oriental miniature dated 1582, representing the Valley of Diamonds, guarded by snakes. Eagles carry in their beaks pieces of meat in which diamonds are embedded, illustrating an Indian legend that appears in the tale of Sinbad the Sailor in the Thousand and One Arabian Nights. *Photo and document courtesy of the Bibliothèque Nationale, Paris.*

Transparency–Opacity	Indices of Refraction n_e/n_p	n_o/n_m	n_e/n_g	Mechanical Properties S.G.	H	Tough	Name	Color Bl	Br	R	O	Y	G	B	P	Pi	Cl	Pleochroism	Luminescence LWUV	SWUV	Crystallochemical Composition
T–O		1.434		3.18	4	■	**Fluorite**	*	*	*	*	×		×		*	×	○	○	○	CaF_2
T–O		1.45		2.1	6	□	**Opal**	*	*	*	*	×	+	×	+	*	×	—	○	○	Hydrous silica
O		1.45		2.1–2.6	6	□	Opal–black cement–X					*	*				+	—	▲	▲	Assembled stone with opal top
T–O		1.45		2.1	5–6	□	Synthetic opal										+	—	▲	▲	Amorphous silica
T–O		1.5–1.7		2.3–4.5	5	□	Glass (imitations)	+	+	×		+	+	×	+	+	+	○	▲	▲	Various amorphous silicates
T–O		1.50		2.45	5	□	**Obsidian**	+	+			×	×				+	○	△	△	Vitreous silicates
T–O		1.5		2.0–2.4	2–4	□	Chrysocolla						+		+		+	○	○	○	$CuSiO_3 \cdot 2H_2O$
T–O		1.482		2.3	5–6	□	**Sodalite**							+	+			○	△	△	$(Na_4Cl)Al_3Si_3O_{12}$ rock
O		1.50		2.43	5½	▲	Lazurite							+			+	○			$([Na,Ca]_{8-4}[SO_4,S,Cl]_{2-1})(Al_3Si_3O_{12})_2$
O		1.5		2.6–2.9	5½	■	**Lapis lazuli**							+			+	○	△		Lazurite-rich rock
O		1.5		2.5	5	▲	Synthetic lapis lazuli							+			*	○			$Na_8S_2(Al_3Si_3O_{12})_2$
O		1.5–1.65		2.7	3	▲	**Marble**			×			+	*		×	*	○	○	▲	Carbonate rock, $CaCO_3$
O		1.5–1.65		2.65	3	∧	**Coral**			+				*		×	*	○	○	▲	$CaCO_3$ plus organic matter
O		1.5		2.4	3–5	□	Turquoise imitations				+	+	+	+			+	○	○	△	Various sintered phosphates
O		1.50		2.4	6–7	▲	**Tugtupite**			+	+	+			+	×		○	▲	▲	$Na_4(BeAlSi_4O_{12})$ rock
T–O		1.50		1.3–1.8	2½	□	Celluloid (plastic)										+	○	△	△	Cellulose camphronitrate or camphroacetate
T–O	1.502	1.50	1.518	1.18	2	□	Perpex (plastic)								+	+	+	—	▲	▲	Polymethylmetacrylate
T		1.509		2.40	6	□	**Petalite**								+	+	+	○	△	△	$Li(AlSi_4O_{10})$
T	1.518	1.524	1.526	2.56	6	■	**Orthoclase**					+		+	+		+	●	○	○	$K(AlSi_3O_8)$
Th		1.52		2.56	6	■	Moonstone										+	○	○	○	$(K,Na)AlSi_3O_8$
O		1.52		2.56	6	□	Amazonite						+					○	○	○	$K(AlSi_3O_8)$
Th–O		1.52		2.64	6	□	Sunstone			+	+							○	—	—	$(Na_2,Ca)(Al_{1-2}Si_{3-2}O_8)$
O		1.53		2.3	2	■	**Alabaster**										+	—	—	—	Massive $CaSO_4 \cdot 2H_2O$
O		1.53		2.0	2	□	Meerschaum (sepiolite)										+	—	—	—	$Mg_2Si_3O_8 \cdot 2H_2O$
O		1.53–1.68		2.78	3½	∧	**Nacre**	×	×	×	×	+	×	×		+	+	—	▲	▲	$CaCO_3$ plus conchiolin
O		1.53–1.68		2.66–2.78	3½	▲	Natural pearl	×	×		×	+		*			+	○	▲	▲	$CaCO_3$ plus conchiolin
O		1.53–1.68		2.72–2.78	3½	▲	Cultured pearl	×				+				+	+		▲	▲	$CaCO_3$ plus conchiolin
O		1.53–1.68		2.72–2.78	3½	▲	Half-cultured-pearl (doublet)												▲	▲	Assembled cultured pearl and nacre
O		1.54		1.80	2½	▲	**Ivory**	+		×	×	+				×		○	▲	▲	Calcium phosphate and dentin
O		1.54		2.0	2½	▲	Bone	+									+		▲	▲	Calcium phosphate and organic matter
O		1.54		1.3	2½	▲	Corozo nut			+	×	+		*		×		○	▲	▲	Cellulose
T–Tr		1.54		1.08	2½	□	**Amber**		×	×	×	+					+	—	▲	▲	Hydrocarbon chain
T–Tr		1.54		1.1	2½	∧	Copal		×			+					+	—	▲	▲	Hydrocarbon chain
T–Tr		1.55		1.30	2½	∧	Tortoise shell		×	×	×	×					+	—	▲	▲	Keratin
T–Tr		1.55		1.30	2½	∧	Hornbill ivory		×		×	×					+	—	▲	▲	Keratin
T–Tr		1.56		1.80	2½	∧	Antler										+	—	▲	▲	Bony keratin
O		1.56		1.35	2½	∧	Black coral		×	+	+		+				+	—	▲	▲	Keratin
T–O		1.55		1.35	2¼	∧	Galalite (plastic)	+	×	+				+		×	+	—	▲	▲	Casein formaldehyde
Tr–O		1.54		2.6	6½		**Chalcedony** (Carnelian, Sard, Onyx, Chrysoprase, Green agate)		+	+			+				+	○	○	○	SiO_2
Tr–O		1.54		2.6–2.9	6½	▲	**Agates** (Jaspers, Heliotrope, Prase)	+	+	+	+	+	+	+	+	+	+				Siliceous rock
Tr–O		1.54		2.65	7	▲	Aventurine quartz	+	+	+	+	+	+	+	+	+	+	●	○	○	Quartz and micas
T–O		1.54		2.65	7	▲	Chatoyant quartz			+	+	+	+	+	+	+	+	●			Quartz and amphiboles
T–O		1.544	1.553	2.65	7	▲	**Quartz** (Rock crystal, Amethyst, Prasiolite, Citrine, Morion)	+		+	+	+	+	+	+	+	+	○	○	○	SiO_2
T		1.544	1.553	2.65	7	▲	Synthetic quartz			+	+	+	+	+	+	+	+	●	○	○	SiO_2
T		1.544	1.553	var.		□	Quartz-X doublet											—	—	—	Quartz-based assembled stone
O		1.55		var.		□	Quartz–opal–X triplet						diffracted colors					—	—	—	Assembled stone with quartz and opal

Transparency–Opacity	n_e/n_p	n_o/n_m	n_e/n_g	S.G.	H	Tough	Name	Bl	Br	R	O	Y	G	B	P	Pi	Cl	Pleochroism	LWUV	SWUV	Crystallochemical Composition
T	1.542–1.585	1.548–1.590	1.551–1.595	2.61	7½	□	Cordierite							+	✗	●		●	○	○	Mg₂Al₃(AlSi₅O₁₈)
T	1.54–1.56	1.55–1.60		2.55–2.80	6	■	Scapolite					+		+		×	+	●	△	△	(Na, Ca)₈₋₄(Cl₂, SO₄, CO₃)(AlSi₃O₈)₆
Tr–O	1.552	1.558	1.562	2.85	5½		Beryllonite										+	—	—	—	NaBe(PO₄)
Tr–O		1.56		2.7	6	■	Labradorite (spectrolite)							+				—	—	—	(Na, Ca)(Al₁₋₂Si₃₋₂O₈)₂
O		1.55		2.68	5½	□	Charoite											—	—	—	K(Na₂, Ca)₂[(OH, F][Si₄O₁₀]). H₂O
O		1.54–1.60		2.7–2.8	1½	▲	Pyrophyllite		+		*	+	+					—	—	—	Massive Al₂(OH)₂(Si₄O₁₀)
O		1.54–1.60		2.7–2.8	1½	□	Steatite		+		×	+	+					—	—	—	Massive Mg₃(OH)₂(Si₄O₁₀)
Tr–O		1.57		2.5–2.7	2–4	□	Serpentine					+	+					—	—	—	Massive Mg₆(OH)₈(Si₄O₁₀)
Tr–O		1.56–1.59		2.5	4–5	□	Variscite						+					—	—	—	Massive Al(PO₄), 2H₂O
O		1.58		2.7	3½	□	Alunite						+	+				—	—	—	Massive (K, Na)Al₃(SO₄)₂(OH)₆
T	1.560–1.572	1.563–1.578		2.65–2.70	7½	□	Synthetic emerald						+	+				●	▲	▲	Be₃Al₂(Si₆O₁₈)
T–Tr	1.565–1.590	1.570–1.600		2.68–2.85	7½	□	Beryl					+	+	+				● ●	△	△	Be₃Al₂(Si₆O₁₈)
						□	Goshenite										+	—	—	—	
						□	Morganite			*	×							—	—	—	
						■	Aquamarine							+				—	—	—	
						□	Emerald						+					—	—	—	
						□	Heliodor					+						—	—	—	
T	1.575	1.580		var.			Beryl-X doublet							+				—	—	—	Assembled stone with light aquamarine
T–O		1.59		1.05	2	□	Polystyrene (plastic)		×	×	×	*	×	×		×		○	▲	▲	Polymerized styrenes
Tr–O	1.59–1.63	1.605		2.62–2.90	4½–6	▲	Pectolite			×	×	+	×				×	—	△	△	NaCa₂Si₃O₈(OH)
O		1.62		2.74	6	▲	Sugilite								+	+		—	○	○	Massive (K, Na)Li₂Fe³⁺₂(Si₂O₅)₆
O		1.62		2.6–2.8	4–6	■	Turquoise					+	+	+				—	○	○	Massive CuAl₆(OH)₈(PO₄)₄, 4H₂O
O		1.62		2.7	5	□	Synthetic turquoise					+	+	+				—	○	○	Massive CuAl₆(OH)₈(PO₄)₄, 4H₂O
O		1.62		3.1	5	□	Odontolite							+				—	—	—	Fossilized ivory
Tr–O	1.62	1.61–1.66		3.0	6½	▲	Nephrite jade		*	*	×	+	+					—	▲	▲	Ca₂(Mg, Fe)₅[(OH, F][Si₄O₁₁]]₂
Tr–O		1.61–1.66		1.25–1.30	2½	■	Bakelite (plastic)		×	+	×	×	×					—	▲	▲	Phenolformaldehyde
Tr–O		1.55–1.62		1.50	2	□	Aminoplastics		×	+	×	×	+		+		×	—	▲	▲	Uroformaldehyde
T–O	1.615	1.630	1.640	3.1	5–6	□	Actinolite (sometimes chatoyant)		×				+				×	✗	—	—	Ca₂(Mg, Fe)₅[(OH, F][Si₄O₁₁]]₂
Tr–O	1.630	1.63	1.598–1.637	2.9	6½	▲	Prehnite						+				× ×	✗	▲	▲	Ca₂Al₂[(OH)₂ Si₃O₁₀]
T	1.603	1.612	1.623	3.08–3.00	6		Amblygonite/Montebrasite		×		×	+						✗	△	△	LiAl(F, OH)(PO₄)
T	1.606–1.629	1.609–1.631	1.616–1.638	2.95	5½	■	Brazilianite					+	+					●	—	—	NaAl₃(OH)₄(PO₄)₂
T	1.630	1.633	1.636	3.56–3.52	8	□	Topaz		+	*	×	+		+				✗	○	○	Al₂(F, OH)₂(SiO₄)
T						□	Fluorinated												△		Al₂(OH, F)₂(SiO₄)
T						□	Hydroxylated														
T	1.630	1.635	1.645	3.00	7	■	Danburite				×	+					+	✗	○	—	CaB₂(SiO₄)₂
T	1.615	1.630–1.646		3.1	5½	□	Lazulite					×	×	+				●	○		(Mg, Fe)Al₂(PO₄)₂(OH)
T	1.624–1.640	1.634–1.662	1.640–1.649	3.17	7½	□	Andalusite (chiastolite)		+	*	×	+	+					●			Al₂SiO₅
T	1.616–1.630	1.632–1.649		3.01–3.25	7½	■	Tourmaline	+	+	+	+	+	+	+	+	+	+	✗	○	○	(Na₂, Ca)Al₁₂(Fe, Mg, Li)₆ (OH, F)₈(BO₃)₆(Si₆O₁₈)₂
T	1.628–1.647	1.632–1.649		3.18	5	□	Apatite (Elbaite-Dravite)				×	+	+		+		+	✗	○△	○	Ca₅(F, Cl)(PO₄)₃
O	1.639	1.648		3.30	6½	□	Jeremejevite		×			×	+	+	×		×	✗	○△	○△	AlBO₃
O	1.66–1.68	1.66–1.68	1.670–1.696	3.3	6½	■	Jadeite jade		×	+		×	+		×	×	×	✗	○△	○△	NaAl(SiO₃)₂ rock
O	1.64–1.68	1.64–1.68		1.33	3	▲	Jet	+									+	—	—	—	Carbonaceous rock
Tr–O	1.654–1.680	1.654–1.680		2.95	7½	□	Phenakite		+	+		×					+	● ●	○	○	Be₂SiO₄
Tr–O	1.655	1.658	1.708	3.3	5	■	Dioptase						+					● ●	△	△	Cu₆(Si₆O₁₈), 6H₂O
T	1.486	1.658		2.70	3	■	Calcite	+				+	+			+	+	● ●	○	○	CaCO₃
T	1.654	1.658	1.673	3.10	7½	■	Euclase					+	+	+			+	● ●	△	△	AlBe(OH)SiO₄
T–O	1.658–1.678	1.659–1.679	1.668–1.688	3.25	5½	■	Enstatite		+				+					●	○	○	(Mg, Fe)₂(SiO₃)₂
T–O	1.659	1.660	1.680	3.25	7	■	Sillimanite					+	+					✗	△	△	Al₂SiO₅
T	1.660	1.666	1.676	3.18	7	■	Spodumene					+	+				+	●	▲	▲	LiAl(SiO₃)₂
T							Kunzite									✗					LiAl(SiO₃)₂
T							Hiddenite						+					●			
T	1.654	1.671	1.690	3.30–3.48	6½	□	Peridot (olivine)					+	+	+				●	△	△	(Mg, Fe)(SiO₄)
T	1.668	1.699	1.707	3.48	6½	□	Sinhalite		+									✗	▲	▲	MgAl(BO₄)
T–O	1.675–1.700	1.682–1.707	1.701–1.726	3.29	5½	■	Diopside (sometimes asteriated)	+					+				○	○	○	○	CaMg(SiO₃)₂

Gemstone identification chart (rotated table). Columns, left to right in original orientation: chemical formula, optical character, mineral/gem name, hardness (H), specific gravity (S.G.), and refractive index (R.I.) values.

Chemical formula	Gem name	H	S.G.	R.I.	R.I. (spot)
$(Al, Fe)_3O_3(BO_3)SiO_3$	Dumortierite	7	3.5	—	1.660–1.682
$Mg_2Al_3(Mg, Al)_6Si_2O_7$	Kornerupine	6½	3.27–3.45	1.674–1.699	1.673
$Ca_2(Fe·Mn)Al_2(OH)(BO_3)Si_4O_{12}$	Axinite	6½	3.29	1.688	1.685
$Na(Cs, K·Li_4Be_3B_{10}O_{11}Al_4O_{16})$	Rhodizite	8	3.40	1.690	
$Ca_2Al_3(OH)Si_4O_{12}$	Tanzanite	6	3.35–3.55	1.693–1.703	1.692–1.700
	Zoisite (thulite)	6½	3.1	1.700–1.706	1.70
$Mg·Fe_2Al_3(O)(OH)Si_4O_4Si_2O_7$	Sapphirine	7½	3.48	1.70	
$(MgFe·)_4Al_6O_6(SiO_4)$	Vesuvianite (massive)	6½	3.4	1.703–1.727	1.701–1.725
$·SiC_2·_5(Si_2O_7)_2$	Grossular (massive)	6½	3.35–3.55	1.705–1.732	1.72
$Ca_{10}Al_4(Mg, Fe)_2(SiO_4)_2$	Vesuvianite (idocrase)	6½	3.4	1.72	1.700
$AlOOH$	Diaspore	6½	3.40	1.721	1.702
$BeMg_3Al_8O_{16}$	Taaffeite	8	3.61	1.750	1.713
$MgAl_2O_4$	Spinel	8	3.58–3.61	1.722	
$MgAl_2O_4$	Synthetic spinel	8	3.65	1.723	
	Doublets/triplets of synthetic spinel	8	3.65–3.70	1.715–1.725	1.715
Al_2SiO_5	Kyanite	5–7	3.56–3.68	1.73	1.733
$MnSiO_3$	Rhodonite	6	3.7	1.731	
$Ca_3Al_2(SiO_4)_3$	Grossular	7	3.65	1.725	
	Tsavorite	7	3.7	1.738	1.734
	Hessonite	6½	3.4	1.74	1.734–1.741
$(Al, Fe)_2SiO_4(FeO)_2(AlOOH)$	Staurolite	7	3.8	1.756	1.73
$Ca_2(Al, Fe)Al_2(O)(OH)(SiO_4/Si_2O_7)$	Epidote	6½	3.73	1.733–1.780	1.73
$Cu_3(CO_3)_2(OH)_2$	Azurite	3½	3.73	1.838	1.74
$Mg_3Al_2(SiO_4)_3$	Pyrope	7½	3.65	1.756	1.74
$BeAl_2O_4$	Chrysoberyl	8½	3.73	1.748	1.74
	Alexandrite	8½	3.73	1.748	
	Cat's-eye	8½	3.73	1.748	
	Synthetic alexandrite	8½	3.73	1.748	
$BaTiSi_3O_9$	Benitoite	6½	3.65	1.757	1.75
$(Mg, Fe)_3Al_2(SiO_4)_3$	Rhodolite	7	3.8	1.76–1.78	1.75
Al_2O_3	Corundum	9	4.0	1.77	1.77
	Ruby	9	4.0	1.770–1.780	1.760–1.770
	Sapphire (sometimes asteriated)	9	4.0	1.768	
	Synthetic corundum (sometimes asteriated)	9	4.0	1.77	1.77
	Synthetic corundum doublets		4.0	1.77	1.77
	Garnet-glass doublet		var.	1.77	
$Fe_3Al_2(SiO_4)_3$	Almandite	7½	3.9–4.2	1.76–1.78	
$Mn_3Al_2(SiO_4)_3$	Spessartite	7	4.15	1.81	
$Zr(SiO_4)$	Zircon (metamict, or low)	6½	4.0	1.80–1.83	
$Y_3Al_2(AlO_4)_3$	YAG (synthetic crystal)	8	4.55	1.83	1.60
$MnCO_3$	Rhodocrosite (dialogite)	4	3.7	1.82	1.61
$ZnCO_3$	Smithsonite	5	4.3	1.85	1.615
$Cu_2(OH)_2CO_3$	Malachite	3½	3.9	1.875	
$Ca_3Fe_2(SiO_4)_3$	Demantoid	6½	3.85	1.88	1.900
$CaTi(O·SiO_4)$	Titanite (sphene)	5½	3.52	1.907	
$Zr(SiO_4)$	Zircon (high)	7½	4.7	1.96	
$(Ca, Y)O_2Zr_2O_7$	CZ (cubic zirconia)	8½	5.6–5.9	2.17–2.20	
ZnS	Sphalerite (blende)	4	4.1	2.37	
$SrTiO_3$	Strontium titanate (Fabulite; synthetic crystal)	6	5.13	2.41	
C	Diamond	10	3.52	2.42	
	Diamond-X doublet	6	var.	2.42	
TiO_2	Synthetic rutile	6	4.25	2.62	
Fe_3O_4	Magnetite	5½	5.2	R.P. = 17%	
Fe_2O_3	Hematite	6	5.3	R.P. = 18%	
FeS_2	Pyrite (marcasite)	6½	5.1	R.P. = 54–25%	

Appendix 2

Museums

Because precious stones have played important roles in all civilizations, many museums include gems in their collections. The following list comprises museums with noteworthy collections that can be viewed by the public.

Austria

Vienna

Hofburg Schatzkammer: The regalia of the Holy Roman empire and the Austro-Hungarian empire.

Kunsthistorisches Museum: The treasures of the dukes of Burgundy and of the Austrian emperors (goblet of Philip III the Good of Burgundy, emerald vase engraved by the Miseroni, Great Cameo of Vienna).

Naturhistorisches Museum: A nice mineral collection, including the Montezuma emerald offered to Charles V during the Spanish conquest of South America.

Canada

Toronto

Royal Ontario Museum: An important collection of faceted gems.

China

Beijing

Imperial Palace: Numerous objects in coral and jade, including a "jade mountain" weighing over 2 tons.

Colombia

Bogotá

Gold Museum: Some exceptional gem emerald crystals, including specimens of 1,759 and 1,020 carats.

Czechoslovakia

Prague

Saint-Guy Cathedral: The Saint Wenceslas crown (1346–71), the only piece of jewelry from the Middle Ages to survive intact. The Saint Wenceslas chapel is lined with amethyst, jaspers, and agates.

Loreta Convent: Treasure; gold monstrance set with 6,222 diamonds.

Denmark

Copenhagen

Rosenborg Slot (castle): The regalia of the Danish crown, much artwork, and engraved gems.

National Danish Museum: An interesting collection of rough amber containing insects, collected on Danish beaches.

Egypt

Cairo

Museum of Egyptian Antiques: A remarkable collection of pharaonic and Ptolemaic jewelry.

Ethiopia

Aksum

Sainte Marie de Zion: A collection of crowns from the "king of kings," a reminder of the past splendor of the ancient empire.

France

Paris

Musée du Louvre: In the Apollo Gallery the crown jewels, a remarkable collection of bowls, cups, and other objects carved in quartz, jasper, and lapis lazuli, the crown diamonds (the Regent, the Sancy, the Dragon spinel, formerly the Côte de Bretagne, and others), the regalia of the French crown, various examples of medieval jewelry set with gemstones, and two tables inlaid with stones. The various antique and furniture collections also contain very interesting jewels (for example, the Ramses breastpiece and ivory carvings).

Muséum d'Histoire Naturelle: Mineralogy Hall, Treasure Room. Collections from the former royal "curiosities cabinet," in addition to numerous faceted and carved gems (Ruspoli sapphire, garnet salt shaker of Louis XIV, Louis XVIII's opal, obsidian mirror, jade, quartz, pink beryl, kunzite, and others). Tables inlaid with gem materials.

Bibliothèque Nationale: Medals and Antiques Cabinet. Remarkable glyptic collection (cameos and intaglios) from classical antiquity to present (Grand Camée de France, Ptolemy's cup, and Chosroe's cup, for example), as well as ivories.

Musée de Cluny: Visigoth crowns and jewelry; medieval ivory.

Ecole Nationale Supérieure des Mines (National Higher School of Mines): Synthetic crystals by Edmond Frémy and recent synthetic crystals, as well as some natural gems, both in the rough and faceted (ruby, kunzite, emerald, morganite, and dioptase, among others).

Sorbonne Collection, Pierre and Marie Curie University: The world of gems in the rough.

Many churches throughout France own remarkable pieces of jewelry and carvings, for example, the large collection of religious jewelry in the Sainte-Foy Abbey in Conques, Charlemagne's talisman in Reims Cathedral, a Byzantine ivory diptych in Chambéry.

Germany

Aachen

Cathedral: Very nice collection of Rhenish religious goldsmithery (reliquary bust of Charlemagne and crown of Charles IV of Bohemia, for example).

Dresden

Grünes Gewölbe: The renowed jewelry collection of the prince electors of Saxony, including the famous 41-carat Dresden Green diamond.

Idar-Oberstein

Edelstein Museum: A systematic collection of faceted and carved gems, together with various objects made by local lapidaries, such as bowls and intaglios.
Ruppenthal Museum: A remarkable retrospective of the work in the Ruppenthal cutting factory since the last century (display objects and jewelry).

Munich

Residenz Museum-Schatzkammer: A remarkable collection of crowns and other jewelry from the Middle Ages, as well as numerous glyptic masterpieces from the Renaissance (treasury of Bavaria, assembled by Albert of Bavaria and Wittelsbach).

Stuttgart

Earth Sciences Museum: One of the best collections of fossil-bearing amber.

Great Britain

London

British Museum: In addition to the Mineral Gallery, which contains an exceptional collection of crystals and faceted gems, the museum also displays remarkable carved objects in the Oriental Antiquities department.
Geological Survey: A systematic collection of faceted stones.
Tower of London: Regalia from the British crown, including the Cullinan I diamond on the scepter, the Cullinan II diamond, and the Black Prince "ruby" on the imperial crown, the Koh-i-Noor on Queen Mary's crown, and many other gems.
Buckingham Palace: Indian Room. The Timur ruby, in the center of a necklace.
Victoria and Albert Museum: A remarkable collection of Indian jewelry, including engraved gems and jades inlaid with rubies.

Edinburgh

National Antiques Museum: Collection of objects from the Middle Ages.

Whitby

Jet Museum.

Greece

Athens

National Museum: The most important collection of Mycenaean jewelry (seventeenth century B.C.).
Benaki Museum: Religious gold jewelry set with gems.

Hungary

Budapest

Royal Palace: Regalia from the Hungarian crown, including Saint Stephen's crown, a symbol of Hungarian nationalism.
National Museum: Medieval jewelry.

India

Delhi

National Museum: Collection of Moghul jewelry assembled by the prime minister of Hyderabad at the beginning of the twentieth century.

Indonesia

Djakarta

National Museum: Weapons and objets d'art set with gems (massive gold throne set with diamonds of the Bandjarmasin sultans), jewelry and diamonds from Borneo.

Iran

Tehran

Markazi Bank: The Iran imperial treasure, remarkably well displayed, was, before the Iranian revolution, the most spectacular collection of jewelry, faceted stones, and jeweled artwork in the world (including Nāder Shāh's throne, a globe set with precious stones, Nāder Shāh's shield, regalia of the Iranian crown, famous diamonds such as the Darya-i-Nur, the Taj-i-Mah, and the Nur-ul-Ain, emeralds, red spinels, turquoises, pearls, and much more).

Iraq

Baghdad

Iraq Museum: A remarkable collection of jewelry and artwork from Mesopotamian civilizations (especially Ur).

Ireland

Dublin

National Museum: Jewelry from prehistoric times and the Middle Ages; nice collection of rhinoceros horn carvings.

Italy

Florence

Palazzo Pitti: Silver Museum. What is left of the famous collection of the Medici, gathered especially by Lorenzo the Magnificent, containing many examples of Roman glyptic art and Renaissance jewelry (with gems and ivory).
Museo Archeologico: Etruscan jewelry.

Monza

Basilica: Treasury; crown of the Lombard kings.

Naples

Museo Nazionale: A beautiful collection of Roman glyptic art, including the famous Farnese cup, found in the ruins of Herculaneum and Pompeii.

Rome

Villa Giulia: Etruscan jewelry.

Venice

Basilica San Marco (Saint Mark's Basilica): The remains of the richest European treasure in the eighteenth century, coming in part from the plunder of Constantinople in 1204. Contains in particular the famous *Pala d'Oro*, a retable decorated with almost 2,500 pearls and other gems.

Japan

Tasashmiza

Coral Museum: A display centered around coral fisheries and fashioning.

Tobe, Pearl Island

Mikimoto Museum: Displays on the history of cultured pearls.

Lithuania

Palanga

Amber Museum: Amber artifacts from ancient times to the present.

Mexico

Mexico City

National Museum: Pre-Columbian jades and cult objects set with turquoise, coral, and shell.

Oaxaca

Regional Museum: Mixtec Indian objects.

Netherlands

Amsterdam

Rijksmuseum: Engraved stones and objects from the Renaissance.

Poland

Warsaw

Earth Museum: Important amber collection.

Singapore

Singapore

Jade House: Important collection of jade and other hard stones.

Spain

León

San Isidoro Basilica: Treasure; bowls and chests in ivory and agate.

Madrid

Museo del Prado: Collection of vases and artwork from the Great Dauphin of France; table inlaid with gem materials.
El Escorial: Engraved stone tabernacle of the master altar.

Toledo

Toledo Cathedral: Treasure; objects made with gem materials brought back from South America during the Spanish conquest.

Sri Lanka

Colombo

National Museum: Regalia from the Kandy kings.
Temple of Buddha's Tooth: Ruby-studded reliquaries.

Sweden

Stockholm

Kungliga Slottet (Royal Palace): Regalia of the Swedish crown.
State Historical Museum: Gold jewelry from the Middle Ages set with precious gems.

Switzerland

Fribourg

Art and History Museum: Burgond jewelry.

Saint-Maurice

Abbey: Treasure; Roman glyptic art (sard vase).

Taiwan

Taipei

National Palace: The most valuable objects from the Beijing imperial treasure, evacuated to Taiwan by Chiang Kai-shek, among which are 5,000 jades of all Chinese periods.

Thailand

Bangkok

Royal Palace: Temple of the Emerald Buddha: famous jade Buddha.

Turkey

Ankara

National Museum: Hittite objects.

Istanbul

Archaeological Museum: Islamic jewelry.
Topkapi Museum: The remains of Constantinople's treasures after it was sacked, plus the treasure of Süleyman I the Magnificent, who transferred Islamic reliquaries from Cairo in the sixteenth century, plus various "gifts," including those of Nāder Shāh to the sultan after sacking Delhi in 1739. One of the greatest collections of gem-studded objects in the world, including one of the seven gold thrones of the Great Moghul, set with precious stones. Also contains a famous dagger ornate with emeralds, a violet diamond, peridots, and many other gems.

Union of Soviet Socialist Republics

Moscow

Diamond Fund of the U.S.S.R.: Treasure from the Armory Museum. Former treasures of the czars, including the regalia of the Russian empire (Lal spinel on the imperial crown, Orlov diamond on the scepter, numerous pieces of French jewelry decorated with gemstones). The treasure is complemented by many Siberian diamonds and some famous stones, such as the engraved Shah diamond.
Armory Museum of the Kremlin: Collection of Russian crowns and various prestigious objects set with gems (thrones, icons, even harnesses).
Academy of Sciences, Fersman Museum: Gem collection, as well as artwork in various gem materials.

Saint Petersburg

Hermitage Museum: Remarkable antique cameos and artwork. Moghul objects, table inlaid with gem materials, large objects carved during the nineteenth century in Siberian hard stones (jasper, rhodonite, lapis lazuli, and malachite).
Institute of Mines: Numerous gem objects.

Zagorsk

Monastery Museum: Religious jewelry set with precious gems (including a spectacular engraved emerald).

United States of America

Baltimore

Walters Art Gallery: Engraved gems.

Boston

Harvard University: The oldest mineral collection in America.

Elmhurst, Illinois

The Lizzadro Museum of Lapidary Art: An impressive collection of carved objects, some very large, primarily jade.

Los Angeles

Natural History Museum of Los Angeles County: Beautiful collection of rough and faceted gems.

Minneapolis

Minneapolis Institute of Arts: Important jade collection; the archaic jade collection is said to be the finest outside of mainland China.

New York

American Museum of Natural History: A remarkable collection of faceted gems, including large star rubies and sapphires, very well displayed.
Metropolitan Museum of Art: Egyptian jewelry, cameos and intaglios, other jewels, and various objets d'art.

San Francisco

Asian Art Museum of San Francisco: The Avery Brundage Collection comprises about twelve hundred pieces of carved jade and dozens of other gem materials.

Washington, D.C.

National Gallery of Art: Assorted artwork, including the chalice of Abbot Suger (from Saint Denis Abbey).

Smithsonian Institution: The world's largest collection of faceted stones and gem materials, displayed in three large rooms (including the blue Hope Diamond, star rubies, and sapphires).

Vatican City

Vatican Museum: Beautiful emerald crystals.

Glossary

amphibole: A family of silicate minerals rich in calcium, magnesium, and iron, which form certain types of rock (amphibolites) typical of regional metamorphism.

angstrom: Unit of length, equal to one ten-billionth of a meter—used especially for measuring atomic dimensions and mineral structures.

anisotropic: (optics): Describing a crystal in which the speed of light changes with direction (as opposed to isotropic).

aventurine glass: Glass in which numerous copper platelets, mostly triangular in shape, have been randomly dispersed.

basic attack: A chemical reaction produced using an alkali (such as sodium hydroxide).

bezel: A facet on the top of a brilliant-cut gem, extending from the table directly to the girdle.

bezel set: A setting technique in which metallic foil affixed to a piece of jewelry completely covers the girdle of a faceted gem.

breccia: Rock made of irregular fragments cemented together.

brilliant: A cutting or faceting style, as well as a round diamond faceted in this fashion.

Carborundum: Trademarked name for silicon carbide, a material used as an abrasive because of its high hardness.

champlevé: An enamel technique in which the enamel is poured into depressions carved in a metal.

chevron: In gemology, a V-shaped color zone.

CIBJO: Confédération internationale de la bijouterie, joaillerie, orfèvrerie, des pierres précieuses et fines, des perles fines et de culture et des activités qui s'y rattachent. The official English translation of the name of this organization is: International Confederation of Jewelry, Silverware, Diamonds, Pearls, and Stones. It's an organization that sets standards.

cleavage: The plane along which a crystal can be easily split.

cloisonné: An enamel technique in which the cavities into which the enamel is poured are formed by small metal strips soldered together. Such cavities may also be fitted with a faceted gemstone.

closed mount: A type of metal mount that does not allow light to penetrate the stone from beneath.

corner: The crown facet of a brilliant-cut diamond, which is perpendicular to the diagonal planes of the original octahedral crystal.

crown: Facets in the top half of a brilliant cut faceted gem that share an edge with the table. By extension, the top half of a faceted gem.

crystallite: Small crystal.

energy spectrum: The energies corresponding to the range of wavelengths in the visible spectrum.

exsolution texture: A physical arrangement of two minerals, separate at low temperature, that form one homogeneous crystal at high temperatures. The texture is generally characterized by alternating thin layers or crisscross streaks.

fingerprint (inclusion): An internal break in a crystal that has partially healed during crystal growth. It is characterized by a pattern of microscopic inclusions that may resemble a fingerprint.

geode: A natural cavity in a rock, either large or small, generally covered with crystals.

girdle: The edge of a faceted gemstone, located between the crown and the pavilion, defining the stone's outline.

grit: Diamond powder used as an abrasive.

hydrothermal: Describing a veinlike deposit produced by the growth of minerals in high-temperature solutions that originate far below the surface.

isotropic (optics): Describing a crystal in which the speed of light is the same in all directions (as opposed to anisotropic).

Kampuchea: A country in Southeast Asia, formerly known as Cambodia.

lithosphere: The solid part of the earth's crust.

Myanmar: A country in Southeast Asia, formerly known as Burma.

n_d: The index of refraction in standard yellow (sodium) light.

nanometer: One-billionth of a meter.

negative crystal: An empty space in a crystal, limited by true crystallographic faces.

parting: A preferential fracture plane, less easy to split than the cleavage plane, corresponding to a twin plane in corundum.

pavilion: Facets in the bottom half of a faceted gem. By extension, the bottom half of a faceted gem.

pegmatite: An igneous rock in which crystals can reach large dimensions; may concentrate rare-earth elements.

phlogopite: A mineral in the mica family.

pneumatolithic: Describing a process by which a crystal is grown from a gas or vapor under high pressure, such as supercritical water.

prongs: Slender projecting metal parts in jewelry with bent tips that secure a gem in the setting.

secondary: The electrical circuit in a transformer that serves the user (in contrast to the primary, which is powered by the energy source).

seed: A small crystal or crystal slab on which crystal growth takes place.

sinter: To transform a powder into a solid block using pressure and high temperature.

spectrum: Referring to the absorption spectrum of a gem in visible light: the pattern of dark or black lines and bands replacing some of the rainbow colors produced by the dispersion (through a spectroscope) of white light after transmission through a gem.

supercritical: Describing the physical state of a vapor that cannot be liquefied by simple compression (for water, above 374.3°C).

tailings: The waste rock from a mine.

trapping: The capture or enclosure of a crystallite or a foreign material by a growing crystal.

twin: A nonparallel, nonrandom association of two or more crystals of the same mineral species, based on the symmetry of the mineral species.

vacancy: In crystallography, the empty space normally occupied by an atom in the crystal structure of a mineral.

Bibliography

The additional reading suggested here was selected to help you further your knowledge of the marvelous world of gemstones. The historical works listed are first in chronological order and represent important steps in the development of gemological knowledge. More recent books, listed in alphabetical order by author, provide insight into various aspects of gemology. Monographs, categorized by subject, provide detailed information on particular gems. Periodicals are included for those who wish to stay current with the ever-changing field of gemology. Finally, because the gem enthusiast cannot be insensitive to the beauty of jewelry, two general jewelry books are listed.

Historical Works

Fourth century B.C. **Theophrastus** (372–287 B.C.). *Theophrastus on Stones.* Caley, E. R., and J. C. Richards. Columbus, Ohio: Ohio State University Press, 1956.
The first descriptive study of all stones and rocks.

First century A.D. **Pliny the Elder** (A.D. 23–79) *Historia Naturalis* (Pliny's natural history: An account by a Roman). Translated by L. Haberley. New York: Frederick Unger, 1957.
A compilation of knowledge and beliefs about gems in ancient Rome.

Eleventh century. **Marbodus.** *Liber Lapidum* (Book of stones), Hieronymus Victor, 1511, Vienna.
The most commonly used medieval book of lapidary: sixty poems in Latin verse describe the powers attributed to gemstones during the Middle Ages.

Seventeenth century. **Anselm Boece de Boot.** *Gemmarum et lapidum historia* (History of gems and stones), 1st ed., 1609. Translated into French by Jean Bochou: *Le parfait joaillier ou histoire des pierreries.* Jean-Antoine Hugetan, rue Mercière, Lyon, 1644.
The first technical book since the Middle Ages, one of the most important of the seventeenth century, despite the inclusion of many superstitions.

1817. **René-Just Haüy.** *Traité des caractères physiques des pierres précieuses pour servir à leur détermination lorsqu'elles ont été taillées* (Treatise on the physical characteristics of precious stones to assist in their determination when they are faceted). Mme. Veuve Courcier, rue du Jardinet, Paris.
The first practical gemology book, written by the father of modern crystallography.

1890. **George F. Kunz.** *Gems and Precious Stones of North America.* New York: Scientific Publishing.
A detailed work by the predominant American gemologist in the late nineteenth and early twentieth centuries.

1896. **Max Bauer.** *Precious Stones.* London: Charles Griffin and Company Ltd., 1904.
The epitome of gemological knowledge at the end of the nineteenth century, still used as a reference today.

1898. **Edwin W. Streeter.** *Precious Stones and Gems: Their History, Sources and Characteristics,* 6th ed. London: George Bell and Sons.
The opinions of a renowned London jeweler, well documenting diamond, ruby, emerald, blue sapphire, alexanderite, opal, and turquoise; fairly limited information on other gems.

1908. **George F. Kunz and C. H. Stevenson.** *The Book of the Pearl.* New York: The Century Company.
The definitive reference book on pearls, still in use today.

1913. **George F. Kunz.** *The Curious Lore of Precious Stones.* Philadelphia: J. B. Lippincott.
A description of the beliefs and symbolism associated with various gems throughout history.

Recent Works

Anderson, B. W., *Gem Testing,* 9th ed. London: Butterworth, 1980.
A handbook for the identification of gem materials based on the use of simple instruments. All the basics for the amateur gemologist.

Arem, Joel E. *Color Encyclopedia of Gemstones,* 2d ed. New York: Van Nostrand Reinhold, 1987.
A barren compilation of the properties of gem materials, most in list and tabular form, with abundant color photographs.

Bank, Hermann. *Aus der Welt der Edelsteine* (From the world of precious gems), 3d ed. Innsbruck: Pinguin Verlag, 1981.
An interesting book that first gives a brief description of the various gem materials used for jewelry and by collectors and then describes the use and fashioning of gems throughout history.

Cavenago Bignami Moneta, S. *Gemmologia* (Gemology), 4th ed. Milan: Ulrico Hoepli, 1980.
A complete description of all common gem materials, as well as some more unusual ones, such as barite.

Chudoba, Karl F., and E. J. Gübelin. *Edelsteinkündliches Handbuch* (Gemological handbook). Bonn: Wilhelm Stollfuss, 1974.
A gemological lexicon, followed by a listing of the physical characteristics of gems and descriptions of their most important inclusions.

Desautels, Paul. *The Gem Kingdom.* New York: Random House, 1970.
Describes most gems in an attractive format with good illustrations.

Eppler, W. F., *Praktische Gemmologie* (Practical gemology). Stuttgart: Rühle Diebener, 1973.
A descriptive gemological handbook, with many illustrations of inclusions.

Gübelin, E. J., *Edelsteine* (Gemstones). Zurich: Silva, 1969.
A poetic description of the main gem species and of their deposits by one of the leading experts.

———. *Innenwelt des Edelsteine* (Inner world of gemstones). Zurich: ABC Editions, 1973.
Descriptions of inclusions found in natural gems and their imitations, with 360 photographs.

Gübelin, E. J., and J. I. Koivula. *Photoatlas of Inclusions in Gemstones.* Zurich: ABC Editions, 1986.
The most comprehensive review of inclusions in gems, illustrated with over 1,400 color photographs.

Hurlbut, S. Cornelius, Jr., and Robert C. Kammerling. *Gemology,* 2d ed. New York: John Wiley and Sons, 1991.
One of the best gemology books presently available.

Keller, P. *Gemstones and Their Origins.* New York: Van Nostrand Reinhold, 1990.
A review of the most common type of gemstone occurrences.

Liddicoat, R. T., *Handbook of Gem Identification,* 12th ed., Los Angeles: Gemological Institute of America, 1987.
A very complete gemological handbook.

Nassau, K. *Gemstone Enhancement.* London: Butterworth, 1984.
The only existing reference on this important gemological subject.

Schlossmacher, K. *Edelsteine und Perlen* (Precious stones and pearls), 5th ed. Stuttgart: E. Schweizerbart, 1969.
A gemological handbook that includes descriptions and the physical properties of gems. Contains very complete discussions of the major gems, in a dense text, with few illustrations.

Schubnel, H. J. *Pierres précieuses, gemmes et pierres dures* (Precious stones, gems and hard stones). Paris: Grange Batelière, 1968.
A summary description of the main gems in a dozen pages, followed by about sixty pages of photographs.

———. *Pierres précieuses dans le monde* (Precious stones of the world). Paris: Horizons de France, 1972.
Preservation and museology of precious stones.

Smith, Herbert. *Gemstones,* 14th ed. London: Chapman and Hall, 1972.
A very complete gemological handbook.

Walton, J. *Physical Gemmology.* London: Isaac Pitman, 1952.
Thoughts on crystallography, mineralogy, and geology for the hobbyist.

Webster R., and B. W. Anderson. *Gems: Their Sources, Description and Identification,* 4th ed. London: Butterworth, 1983.
A reference book, the most complete gemological work, though somewhat dated.

Monographs

Amber

Patty, C. Rice. *Amber: The Golden Gem of the Ages.* New York: Van Nostrand Reinhold, 1980.
A well-documented book, describing the history of Baltic amber since prehistoric times as well as various aspects of amber.

Schlee, D., and W. Glöckner. *Bernstein* (Amber). Stuttgart: Stuttgarter Beiträge für Naturkunde, 1978.
Describes the properties of amber, its deposits and inclusions, suggests theory on its formation, and discusses associated fauna.

Stoppani, A. *L'Ambra* (The amber). Milan: Fratelli Dumorlard, 1886.
The history of Italian and Baltic amber.

Diamond

Le Diamant: Mythe, magie et réalité (Diamonds: Myth, magic and reality). Paris, Flammarion, 1979. Robert Maillard, Editor. English translation: Bonanza books, NY, 1984. *Diamonds: myth, magic and reality.*
Written by a team of seventeen experts, touching on the various subjects about which the public is curious: history, deposits, mining, faceting, use in jewelry, and industrial applications.

Balfour, I. *Famous Diamonds.* London: Collins, 1987.
A good reference book for famous diamonds.

Bardet, M. G. *Géologie du diamant* (Geology of diamond). Paris: Mémoire du B.R.G.M., no. 83, 1973–77.
Describes diamond deposits and geological theories about their formation. A technical book for readers who already have some basic geological knowledge.

Blakey, C. C. *The Diamond.* London: Paddington Press, 1977.
An easy-to-read book that examines various important aspects of the diamond: its history, mining, faceting, scams, synthesis, and specific industrial applications.

Bruton, E. *Diamonds.* London: NAG Press Ltd., 1970.
A very complete study of diamond, considered a reference despite its age.

Gaal, R. A. *The Diamond Dictionary.* Los Angeles: Gemological Institute of America, 1977.
A dictionary listing famous diamonds and terms related to diamond.

Lenzen, G. *Diamantenkunde, mit kritisher Darstellung der Diamantengraduierung* (Diamonds and diamond grading). Kirschweiler: Elizabeth Lenzen, 1979.
History of the diamond, followed by a discussion of the methods used in diamond grading (using color, mass, clarity, and weight).

Orlov, L. *The Mineralogy of the Diamond.* New York: John Wiley and Sons, 1977.
Describes the crystal forms, structure, physical properties, and genesis of diamond. A dense text, not for the layperson.

Tolansky, S., *The History and Use of Diamond.* London: Metheren, 1962.
The history of diamond cutting. Contains some discussion of deposits and describes some famous diamonds and the industrial use of diamonds.

Wilson, A. N. *Diamonds from Birth to Eternity.* Los Angeles: Gemological Institute of America, 1982.

Diamond geology for the layperson, with detailed descriptions of the world's diamond deposits.

Emerald

Kazmi, A. K., and L. W. Snee, *Emeralds of Pakistan: Geology, Gemology, and Genesis.* New York: Geological Survey of Pakistan and Van Nostrand Reinhold, 1989.
A collection of excellent scientific articles on Pakistani emeralds, covering most subjects of interest to the gemologist.

Mumme, I. A. *The Emerald.* Port Hacking, Australia: Mumme Publications, 1982.
Discusses deposits, history, geology and mining, physical properties, and simulants. A well-documented, dense text.

Sinkankas, J. *Emerald and Other Beryls.* Radnor, Pennsylvania: Chilton, 1981.
A compilation of everything written on the subject, an excellent, very detailed reference book.

Garnet

Rouse, J. D. *Garnet.* London: Butterworth, 1986.
A compilation of current knowledge about this gem family.

Ivory

Les Ivoires (Ivory). ABC Decor, Paris, 1972. G. J. Malgras, director.
A simple and clear account of ivory working since ancient times in Europe, China, and Japan, with many illustrations.

Van Lieu, Mai, and P. J. Schaeffer. *Ivoires de Chine* (Ivory of China). Brussels: Dereune, 1978.
The physical properties of ivory, fashioning in the Far East, and the present market, in a book accessible to the collector.

Jade

Bilitz, Luzzato O., *Antiche Giade* (Antique jade). Milan: Fratelli Fabbri, 1966.
A concise history of the mining, symbolism, and uses of jade in ancient China; includes a brief description of Mexican and New Zealand jades.

Gump R., *Jade: Stone of Heaven.* New York: Doubleday, 1962.
A complete discussion of the origin, symbolism, and uses of jade throughout Chinese history; also deals with jade from Myanmar (Burma) and the Americas.

Jet

Muller, H., *Jet Jewellery and Ornament.* Aylesbury: Shire Albums, 1980.
Jet in England during the Victorian period.

————. *Jet.* London: Butterworth, 1987.
An exhaustive volume on this now unusual gem material, abundantly illustrated.

Opal

Eyles, W. C. *The Book of Opals,* 7th ed., Rutland, Vermont: Charles E. Tuttle, 1976.
Describes deposits and present uses of opal.

O'Leary, B. *A Field Guide to Australian Opals.* Adelaide, Australia: Rigby Ltd., 1977.
Contains numerous photographs of the Australian opal rush at the end of the nineteenth century.

Perry, N., and R. Perry. *Australian Opals in Colour.* Sydney: A. H. and N. W. Reed, 1969.
Various aspects of the Australian opal, from deposits to uses in jewelry.

Pearl

Boutan, L. *La Perle* (The pearl). Paris: Doin, 1925.
A reference book on pearls and pearl-bearing mollusks.

Linthilhac, J.-P. *Black Pearls of Tahiti.* Papeete, Tahiti: Royal Tahitian Pearl Book, 1987.
A fairly detailed description of the culture and properties of this increasingly popular gem.

Strack, E. *Perlenfibel* (Pearl primer). Stuttgart: Rühle Diebener, 1983.
A detailed description of natural and cultured pearls, mabes, and imitations.

Streeter, E. W. *Pearls and Pearling Life.* London: George Bell and Sons, 1886.
Still an excellent reference for natural pearls.

Taburiaux, J. *La perle et ses secrets* (The pearl and its secrets). Paris: Hemmerle Petit & Cie, 1983.
Various aspects of pearl, especially pearl fisheries between the two World Wars.

————. *Pearls: Their Origin, Treatment and Identification.* Radnor, Pennsylvania: Chilton, 1985.
An examination of the modern science of pearls.

Quartz

Quartz, minéralogie, gemmologie, industrie (Quartz: mineralogy, gemology, and industry). Lyon: Association régionale de paléontologie, préhistoire et des amis du Museum de Lyon, 1979. M. Philippe, director.
An easy-to-read review of the various aspects and properties of quartz, its use since ancient times as a gem, its various industrial applications, and its synthesis.

Frondel, C. *Dana's System of Mineralogy.* Vol. 3: *Silica Minerals.* New York: John Wiley and Sons, 1962.
A descriptive mineralogical study of quartz and the other varieties of silica.

Ruby

Kessel, J. *La Vallée des rubis* (The valley of rubies). Paris: Gallimard, 1955.
An account of a trip to Mogok, taken with a French ruby dealer.

Schmetzer, K. *Natürliche und synthetische Rubine: Eigenschaften und Bestimmung* (Natural and synthetic rubies: Properties and identification). Stuttgart: E. Schwarzbart'sche Verlagsbuchhandlung (Nägele u. Obermiller), 1986.
A detailed description of the properties of natural and synthetic rubies, with numerous illustrations.

Sapphire

Berrangé, J., and E. A. Jobbins. *The Geology, Gemmology, Mining Methods and Economy Potential of the Pailin Ruby and Sapphire Gemfield, Khmer Republic.* London: Institute of Gemmological Sciences, Overseas Division, 1976.
A field report.

Mumme, I. A. *The World of Sapphires.* Port Hacking, Australia: Mumme Publications, 1988.
A useful reference book on this gem, in particular regarding mines and geological occurrence.

Turquoise

Pogue, J. *The Turquoise.* Rev. reprint ed. New York: 1973.
Memoirs of the National Academy of Sciences, vol. xii, Part II. Describes all aspects of turquoise; an excellent reference book.

Synthetic Gemstones

Elwell, D. *Man Made Gemstones.* Chichester, Great Britain: Ellis Horwood, 1979.
A clear and concise description of the various methods used to grow synthetic crystals used in jewelry, as well as synthetic diamonds.

Nassau, K. *Gems Made by Man.* Radnor, Pennsylvania: Chilton, 1980.
A clear description of glass, synthetic crystals and their fabrication, and the treatment of gem materials, followed by some theoretical notions.

Periodicals

The Australian Gemmologist. (The journal of the Gemological Association of Australia.) P.O. Box 35, South Yarra, Victoria 3141, Australia.

Boletin del Instituto gemologico español. Victor Hugo 1, 3, 28004 Madrid, Spain.

The Canadian Gemmologist. P. O. Box 1106 Station Q, Toronto, Ontario, M4T 2P2, Canada.

La Gemmologia. I.G.I. 20146 Milano, Piazza Gambara 7/8, Italy.

Gemologica. Asociación española de gemologia, Paseo de Gracia, 64, Barcelona 7, Spain.

Gems & Gemology. Gemological Institute of America, 1660 Stewart Street, Santa Monica, California, 90404-4088.

The Journal of Gemmology. Gemmological Association of Great Britain, Saint Dunstam's House, Carey Lane, London EC2V 8AB, Great Britain.

Revue de Gemmologie a.f.g. 14, rue Cadet, 75009 Paris, France.

Zeitschrift der Deutsches Gemmologisches Gesellschaft. Postfach 12 22 60, D. 6580 Idar-Oberstein, Germany.

Jewelry

Graham, Hughes, *The Art of Jewelry,* London: Rainbird G., 1972.
A history of jewelry since ancient times, followed by a brief description of the great jewelry collections displayed in museums.

Lenfant, J. *Bijouterie, joaillerie.* Paris: Dessain et Tolra, 1979.
An easy-to-read history of jewelry since ancient times, including original ideas on the various types of jewelry worn and a description of the main methods of jewelry manufacture.

ذكروذ ر آن جادو نا بكاز | كه آ راست زمـان به دو كار | د را ندىـشه كيف اف دشاه | ا كرا يه زى تنغ د راى كا و

A Persian miniature from 1810, depicting Fath 'Ali
Shāh Qājār seated on the Peacock Throne. Galerie Jean
Soustiel, Paris.